Things and Stuff

A classical viewpoint claims that reality consists of both *things* and *stuff*, and that we need a way to discuss these aspects of reality. This is achieved by using +count terms to talk about *things* while using +mass terms to talk about *stuff*. But as the cover photos show, this simplistic view is not accurate. The photo of red onions and garlic illustrates that essentially the same "reality" can be alternatively be identified with the count term 'onions' or a mass term 'garlic'. And languages differ in this, even though the "reality" is the same: the photo of a storm shows 'lightning' (English mass term) and 'Blitze' (German count plural term). Bringing together contributions from internationally renowned experts across interrelated disciplines, this book explores the relationship between mass and count nouns in a number of syntactic environments, and across a range of languages. It both explains how languages differ in their methods for describing these two fundamental categories of reality and shows the many ways that modern linguistics looks to describe them. It also explores how the notions of count and mass apply to 'abstract nouns', adding a new dimension to the countability discussion. With its pioneering approach to the fundamental questions surrounding count–mass distinction, this book will be essential reading for researchers in formal semantics and linguistic typology.

TIBOR KISS has been Professor of Theoretical and Computational Linguistics at Ruhr-Universität Bochum since 1999. He is also co-editor (with Artemis Alexiadou) of *Syntax: Theory and Analysis* (2015), and wrote various papers on problems of the syntax–semantics interface, dealing with quantification and word order, prepositions, non-finite complements and relative clauses.

FRANCIS JEFFRY PELLETIER has been a Joint Professor of Philosophy, Linguistics, and Computing Science, as well as a Canada Research Chair in Cognitive Science at the University of Alberta and Simon Fraser University. He is also a Fellow of the Royal Society (Canada). Notable publications include *Mass Terms: Some Philosophical Problems* (editor, 1979) and *The Generic Book* (co-edited with Gregory Carlson, 1995).

HALIMA HUSIĆ is a Postdoctoral Research Associate at the Linguistic Data Science Lab, Ruhr-Universität Bochum. Her work has focused on semantics, including event nominals, definiteness and the semantic effects of case alternation. In her recently completed dissertation, she discusses the countability of abstract nouns.

Things and Stuff
The Semantics of the Count–Mass Distinction

Edited by
Tibor Kiss
Ruhr-Universität Bochum, Germany

Francis Jeffry Pelletier
University of Alberta, Canada

Halima Husić
Ruhr-Universität Bochum, Germany

CAMBRIDGE
UNIVERSITY PRESS

Shaftesbury Road, Cambridge CB2 8EA, United Kingdom

One Liberty Plaza, 20th Floor, New York, NY 10006, USA

477 Williamstown Road, Port Melbourne, VIC 3207, Australia

314–321, 3rd Floor, Plot 3, Splendor Forum, Jasola District Centre, New Delhi – 110025, India

103 Penang Road, #05–06/07, Visioncrest Commercial, Singapore 238467

Cambridge University Press is part of Cambridge University Press & Assessment, a department of the University of Cambridge.

We share the University's mission to contribute to society through the pursuit of education, learning and research at the highest international levels of excellence.

www.cambridge.org
Information on this title: www.cambridge.org/9781108932820

DOI: 10.1017/9781108937979

© Cambridge University Press & Assessment 2021

This publication is in copyright. Subject to statutory exception and to the provisions of relevant collective licensing agreements, no reproduction of any part may take place without the written permission of Cambridge University Press & Assessment.

First published 2021
First paperback edition 2023

A catalogue record for this publication is available from the British Library

Library of Congress Cataloging-in-Publication data
Names: Mass-Count Distinction: A Linguistic Misunderstanding? (Conference) (2018 : Ruhr-Universität Bochum) | Kiss, Tibor, editor. | Pelletier, Francis Jeffry, 1944– editor. | Husić, Halima, editor.
Title: Things and stuff : the semantics of the count-mass distinction / edited by Tibor Kiss, Francis Jeffry Pelletier, Halima Husić.
Description: Cambridge, UK ; New York : Cambridge University Press, 2021. | Consists of revised papers, presented at a conference at the Ruhr-Universitäat Bochum, "The Mass-Count Distinction: A Linguistic Misunderstanding?", held in 2018. | Includes bibliographical references and index.
Identifiers: LCCN 2020055293 (print) | LCCN 2020055294 (ebook) | ISBN 9781108832106 (hardback) | ISBN 9781108932820 (paperback) | ISBN 9781108937979 (epub)
Subjects: LCSH: Grammar, Comparative and general–Mass nouns–Congresses. | Grammar, Comparative and general–Numerals–Congresses. | Grammar, Comparative and general–Quantifiers–Congresses. | Semantics–Congresses. | Language and languages–Philosophy.
Classification: LCC P271 .M257 2018 (print) | LCC P271 (ebook) | DDC 415–dc23
LC record available at https://lccn.loc.gov/2020055293
LC ebook record available at https://lccn.loc.gov/2020055294

ISBN 978-1-108-83210-6 Hardback
ISBN 978-1-108-93282-0 Paperback

Cambridge University Press & Assessment has no responsibility for the persistence or accuracy of URLs for external or third-party internet websites referred to in this publication and does not guarantee that any content on such websites is, or will remain, accurate or appropriate.

This book is dedicated to the memory of
Andrea Dauer
and
Susan Rothstein,
who in their individual ways made the world a better place.

Contents

List of Figures	*page* ix
List of Tables	xi
List of Contributors	xii
Preface	xv

1. Editorial Introduction: Background to the Count–Mass Distinction   1
   FRANCIS JEFFRY PELLETIER, TIBOR KISS, AND HALIMA HUSIĆ

Large-Scale Architectures for Count and Mass

2. Mass vs. Count: Where Do We Stand? Outline of a Theory of Semantic Variation   21
   GENNARO CHIERCHIA

3. Counting, Plurality, and Portions   55
   SUSAN ROTHSTEIN

4. Count–Mass Asymmetries: The Importance of Being Count   81
   JENNY DOETJES

5. Divide and Counter   115
   HAGIT BORER AND SARAH OUWAYDA

Implications from Individual Languages

6. Mass-to-Count Shifts in the Galilee Dialect of Palestinian Arabic   151
   CHRISTINE HNOUT, LIOR LAKS, AND SUSAN ROTHSTEIN

7. Object Mass Nouns as an Arbiter for the Count–Mass Category   167
   KURT ERBACH, PETER R. SUTTON, HANA FILIP, AND KATHRIN BYRDECK

8. Bare Nouns and the Count–Mass Distinction: A Pilot Study Across Languages   193
   KAYRON BEVILÁQUA AND ROBERTA PIRES DE OLIVEIRA

9. Counting (on) Bare Nouns: Revelations from American
   Sign Language   213
   HELEN KOULIDOBROVA

Compositional Analyses and Theoretical Issues

10. Ontology, Number Agreement, and the Count–Mass Distinction   237
    ALAN BALE

11. The Semantics of Distributed Number   261
    MYRIAM DALI AND ÉRIC MATHIEU

12. Container, Portion, and Measure Interpretations of Pseudo-
    Partitive Constructions   279
    PETER R. SUTTON AND HANA FILIP

13. Overlap and Countability in Exoskeletal Syntax:
    A Best-of-Both-Worlds Approach to the Count–Mass Distinction 305
    HANNA DE VRIES AND GEORGE TSOULAS

New Empirical Approaches to the Semantics of the Count–Mass Distinction

14. The Role of Context and Cognition in Countability:
    A Psycholinguistic Account of Lexical Distributions   321
    FRANCESCA FRANZON, GIORGIO ARCARA,
    AND CHIARA ZANINI

15. Plurality Without (Full) Countability: On Mass-Like Categories in
    Lexical Plurals   337
    PETER LAUWERS

16. Determining Countability Classes   357
    SCOTT GRIMM AND AESHAAN WAHLANG

17. Polysemy and the Count–Mass Distinction: What Can We
    Derive from a Lexicon of Count and Mass Senses?   377
    TIBOR KISS, FRANCIS JEFFRY PELLETIER,
    AND HALIMA HUSIĆ

References   398
Language Index   421
Subject Index   423

Figures

2.1: Relationships between sum-closed properties and related kinds	*page* 35
3.1: Link-style atomic semi-lattice of plurality	59
7.1: Quantity comparison in the style of Inagaki and Barner (2009)	172
7.2: Average judgment by conceptual class	177
7.3: Average judgments: nouns referring to discrete individuals	178
7.4: Average judgments: nouns referring to undifferentiated stuff	179
7.5: Average judgments: nouns referring to collections of discrete entities, Group 1	179
7.6: Average judgments: nouns referring to collections of discrete entities, Group 3	181
7.7: Average judgments: nouns referring to collections of discrete entities, Group 2	181
7.8: Average judgment: post-hoc classes	182
8.1: Example of Stimuli used for BS noun *bed* in English. Target sentence: "John has more bed than Mary."	200
8.2: Rating probabilities for NP and language at different experimental conditions	200
8.3: Example of stimuli used for the nouns *table* and *tables* for English. Target sentence: "John has more table than Mary."	203
8.4: Results of the picture-matching test	204
8.5: Example of Stimuli used for BS noun *stone* for English. Target sentence: "Who has more stone?"	206
8.6: Results of the quantity-judgment test	207
14.1: Subjective frequency scores for singular	327
14.2: Subjective frequency scores for plural	327
14.3: Frequency of occurrence in count and mass syntax of all experimental stimuli	329
14.4: Frequency of occurrence in mass and count syntax of the top 100 nouns that occur most frequently in a mass context	330

14.5: Frequency of occurrence in mass and count syntax of the top 100 nouns that occur most frequently in a count context 330
16.1: Distribution of nouns across Allan environments 364
16.2: Distribution of nouns across subtypes of Allan environments 367
16.3: Variable importance in classifying nouns as countable or uncountable across Allan (top) and subtype (bottom) environments with (right) and without (left) bare plural and bare singular included 370
16.4: Heatmap representing the clusters' distributional tendencies across countability environments 372

Tables

3.1:	Comparison of three groups of languages with respect to countability, plurality and portion readings	*page* 78
7.1:	Felicity with *nan-byaku to iu* ('hundreds of')	182
12.1:	A summary of terminologies	283
13.1:	Different classes of uninflected nouns across languages	314
14.1:	Subjective frequency scores for singular and plural	326
15.1:	Distributional behaviour of thirty lexical items (normalised between 0 and 1)	344
15.2:	Typology of lexical plurals	346
15.3:	Internal plurals	347
16.1:	Countability preferences of select nouns across the five environments (from Allan 1980: 562)	360
16.2:	Countability preferences of select nouns across the five environments as recognized in the database	364
16.3:	Correspondence between Allan environments and subtypes thereof	366
16.4:	Model accuracy results predicting countable and uncountable nouns	369
17.1:	Major classes in BECL	383

Contributors and their Affiliations

GIORGIO ARCARA. Senior Researcher, IRCCS San Camillo Hospital, Venice, Italy

ALAN BALE. Associate Professor, Linguistics Program, Concordia University, Montreal, Canada

KAYRON BEVILÁQUA. Instituto Federal de Santa Catarina, São José, Brazil

HAGIT BORER. Professor of Linguistics, Queen Mary University of London, England

KATHRIN BYRDECK. Institut für Sprache und Information, Heinrich-Heine-Universität, Düsseldorf, Germany

GENNARO CHIERCHIA. Haas Foundations, Professor of Linguistics, Cornell University, Ithaca (NY), USA

MYRIAM DALI. PhD student, University of Ottawa, Canada

JENNY DOETJES. Professor of Semantics and Language Variation, Centre for Linguistics, Universiteit Leiden, Netherlands

KURT ERBACH. Lecturer of English Linguistics, Reinische Friedrich-Wilhelms-Universität, Bonn

HANA FILIP. Professor of Semantics, Institut für Sprache und Information, Heinrich-Heine-Universität, Düsseldorf, Germany

FRANCESCA FRANZON. Professor, Scuola Internazionale Superiore di Studi Avanzati (SISSA), Trieste, Italy

SCOTT GRIMM. Associate Professor of Linguistics, University of Rochester, USA

CHRISTINE HNOUT. Department of English Literature and Linguistics, at Bar-Ilan University, Israel

HALIMA HUSIĆ. Postdoctoral Researcher, Linguistic Data Science Lab, Ruhr-Universität Bochum, Germany

TIBOR KISS. Director of Linguistic Data Science, Ruhr-Universität Bochum, Germany

HELEN KOULIDOBROVA. Associate Professor of English, Central Connecticut State University, USA

LIOR LAKS. Senior Lecturer, Department of English Literature and Linguistics, Bar-Ilan University, Israel

PETER LAUWERS. Professor of Linguistics, Ghent University, Belgium

ÉRIC MATHIEU. Professor of Linguistics, University of Ottawa, Canada

SARAH OUWAYDA. Independent Scholar, USA.

FRANCIS JEFFRY PELLETIER. Emeritus Professor of Philosophy, Computing Science, and Linguistics. Retired Canada Research Chair in Cognitive Science. University of Alberta, Simon Fraser University, Canada

ROBERTA PIRES DE OLIVEIRA. Full Professor, CNPq PQ-1 Researcher, Universidade Federal de Santa Catarina, Florianópolis, Santa Catarina, Brazil

SUSAN ROTHSTEIN† Professor of Semantics, Department of English Literature and Linguistics, Bar-Ilan University: Correspondence can be sent to Fred Landman at landman@tauex.tau.ac.il

PETER R. SUTTON. Postdoctoral Researcher, Institut für Sprache und Information, Heinrich-Heine-University, Düsseldorf, Germany

GEORGE TSOULAS. Professor of Linguistics, University of York, England

HANNA DE VRIES. Lecturer, Centre for Linguistics, Universiteit Leiden, Netherlands

AESHAAN WAHLANG. Researcher, Quantitative Semantics Lab, Department of Linguistics, University of Rochester, USA

CHIARA ZANINI. Postdoctoral Assistant of Italian Linguistics, Romanisches Seminar, University of Zurich, Switzerland

Preface

This volume contains papers, suitably revised, that originated in a 2018 conference at the Ruhr-Universität Bochum, "The Count–Mass Distinction: A Linguistic Misunderstanding?". The conference marked the end of a five-year project led by Jeff Pelletier and Tibor Kiss, and funded under an Anneliese-Maier Award by the Alexander-von-Humboldt-Foundation granted to Jeff Pelletier. We acknowledge the support of the AvH, without which the project, and of course the workshop and this volume, would not have been possible. The conference also featured papers which are not included in the present volume, but which did enrich the conference, and we are pleased to acknowledge their contributions. In particular, we are thankful to Brendan Gillon, Christopher Hicks, David Nicolas, Sandeep Prasada and Byeong-uk Yi for fruitful discussions. We would also like to thank Johanna Marie Poppek and Anneli von Könemann, who co-organized the workshop.

1 Editorial Introduction: Background to the Count–Mass Distinction

Francis Jeffry Pelletier, Tibor Kiss, and Halima Husić

The Count–Mass Distinction – henceforth, abbreviated as CMD – is a morphological and syntactic distinction that can be made for noun phrases ("determined phrases") in a language, and as such it varies from language to language. Indeed, it can be argued that there are some languages that do not manifest such a morpho-syntactic distinction. This distinction is also usually correlated with a conceptual or ontological distinction between "things" and "stuff".

In English (a language that does manifest such a distinction), it is common to categorize the underlined NPs in the following sentences as being count NPs:

Jeremy owns a car. Natasha likes three boys. Juan ate many apples. Sarah read each book on the list.

And on the other hand, the NPs in the following sentences are commonly categorized as mass NPs.

Hans drinks only cold beer. Sally used red chalk to emphasize her point. Chlorine gas is poisonous. The recipe calls for garlic.

Among the generalizations drawn from such examples are that count NPs use numerals, allow indefinite determiners, can be pluralized, and admit certain "individuating" quantifiers. Mass NPs do not do this. One very apparent difference between the two types of NP is that the count ones presuppose that there are separate, individual cars, boys, apples, books; the mass ones do not, but rather suggest some indeterminate amount of a given sort of matter. (Note that this preliminary description of the CMD has not taken into account "abstract nouns", where the notion of "matter" will have to be much different. This is touched upon by many of the contributions to this volume.) Some authors call this distinction between individuative NPs and non-individuative NPs a conceptual claim (that's how we think about whatever the NP describes); other authors think of it as an ontological claim (that's the way "reality" is organized). Either way seems to be a distinction between "things" and "stuff" (although there remains the issue of abstract nouns).

As we mentioned, this morpho-syntactic distinction is found within the class of NPs. But most writers also assign mass or count to the individual lexical items – words, for ease of reference – that are the head noun of the NP. This makes *car, boy, apple, book* and other words be classified as +count; *beer, chalk, gas, garlic* classified as +mass. And the individuation/non-individuation character of the NP is then also assigned to these words.

One class of puzzles in the area is this: although *cold beer* is a mass NP, and thus *beer* is a mass noun, it seems clear that there is nothing particularly strange or forced about the sentence *Hans drank three cold beers*. Given a presumption that the CMD is supposed to assign a unique one of +count or +mass to each noun, what shall be done with such apparent counterexamples? One strategy is to rule them "ungrammatical but interpretable", and this can be carried out in different ways. A popular way is to say that *beer* (for example) is "really" a mass noun, but that it can be "coerced" into having a count meaning by certain processes, such as being "portioned" (a can or bottle or glass of beer) or being "sorted" (*Hans drank three sorts of beer*). The other way around might see the "basic" meaning of *chicken* be +count ("the common domestic fowl *Gallus gallus*"), but that it gets coerced into a mass meaning in such sentences as *Louisa cooked chicken for supper*.

The issues surrounding these (and other) "coercions" form a large part of the argumentation of very many papers in this volume. Other issues that emerge concern so-called *furniture*-nouns and *bouquet*-nouns. Although (in English) *furniture* is a mass noun, we in fact count pieces of furniture, rather than weigh the total or take the total volume, when determining who has more furniture. In the other direction, words like *bouquet, thing, fence* are count nouns, even though placing two bouquets in a bride's hand does not make for a bride holding two bouquets but rather holding one large bouquet.

Another direction of research is in describing how different languages can differ in their versions of the CMD. Even in closely related languages, such as English and German, we find that direct translations will assign different count–mass statuses to the words. English *lightning* is called a mass noun; German *Blitz* is count. Is this a difference in conceptualization? It doesn't seem to be a difference in "reality". Further afield, there are "classifier languages" where, it is sometimes claimed, individual nouns are mass, and individuation takes place by means of classifiers applied to the noun. For an English example, *ice* is generally thought to be a mass noun, but *ice cube* (or *cube of ice*) uses *cube (of)* as a classifier. Some classifier languages, it is said, do this universally with all nouns.

All these topics are discussed in this volume, and the various surprising ways that they interact with one another are surveyed. A goal of this research area is to find some stable, comprehensive theory that finds a place for each type of word and an explanation for how different languages can diverge on the ways they differentially treat these topics. The reader will decide how well this is carried out. But we can say with certainty that the papers in this volume make important progress toward this goal.

1. The Beginnings of the CMD

Almost all the topics that are of current interest in research concerning the CMD were mentioned at the very beginning of study of the topic – although often mentioned as asides and without awareness of the intricacies involved in them. Since this is where it all began, we start by reciting the very earliest discussions of the distinction in English, because that will give the reader a chance to see how the different contemporary positions on the CMD have evolved due to attempts by writers over the decades to deal with one or another of the many subtopics. And we can sometimes see how some modern positions can sometimes seem to be awkward due to some ill-chosen initial starting point. (Of course, most of these intermediate moves came in the decades prior the present book, but one can see different modern emphases as reactions to one or another of the initial descriptions, sometimes at the expense of ignoring equally plausible alternative initial descriptions.)

Although Wikipedia[1] tells us that English grammar books appeared as early as 1586, and that by the mid-1800s there had been more than 1200 books and booklets that had been published on English grammar, Henry Sweet's two volume *A New English Grammar, Logical and Historical* (1892 and 1898)[2] stands out to us for its clear (although perhaps naive, simplistic, incomplete and just plain wrong) account of a distinction among nouns that includes a place for what we would call mass and count nouns. (Sweet himself called them "material nouns" and "class nouns", respectively, and he also had another group called "collective nouns", which he distinguished from the class nouns.) All of these were what Sweet called "concrete nouns", and in a later part of the book he discussed what he called "abstract nouns". The fact that he has separated the abstract from the concrete nouns has the consequence that the features he assigns to the concrete material and concrete class nouns – those nouns most closely akin to our (concrete) mass and count nouns – do not carry over to the abstract nouns, except in those cases where Sweet assigns them a status of "half-abstract, or intermediate between abstract and concrete". According to Sweet [§§150ff], a class noun is so-called "because it stands for a class or number of individual things having certain attributes in common". On the other side are such material nouns are as

---
[1] https://en.wikipedia.org/wiki/History of English grammars (last accessed 01 December 2019).
[2] The material relevant to the CMD is in vol. 2, that is, in Sweet (1898).

iron, glass, bread, water. They do not express any definite thing, as the class-words *tree* etc. do, but each of them includes the whole mass of matter possessing the attributes implied by the word ... Thus *iron* makes us think of hardness, weight, liability to rust, etc., associated together in a substance of indefinite form ... When a material noun is used to express an individual object of definite shape, it is no longer a material noun, but a class noun. Thus *iron* in the sense of "implement to smooth cloth with", or *glass* in the sense of "vessel to drink out of" are pure class-nouns.

We note that the examples provided are ones that are common in the literature of today. We further note Sweet's suggestion that these two types of words bring to mind different conceptions: individual things versus a "mass of matter" – a common comment in current psychologically oriented literature. Furthermore, the examples mentioned at the end should remind us of current theories of the "coercion" of mass to count (and conversely) that occur in very many of the modern works on mass and count nouns.

One of the few things missing from Sweet's account was provided by Otto Jespersen: the modern names for the distinction. Jespersen's opus magnum was a seven-part work that was published volume-by-volume between 1909 and 1949. Jespersen discussed what we call the CMD in Part 2 of this work, published in 1914, and subtitled *Syntax, First Volume* (Jespersen 1914).[3] Besides criticizing Sweet for not recognizing that concrete and abstract nouns both manifest a CMD, he gave a number of examples together with some explanations of the underlying semantic rationale for the distinction. His Section 5.2 (pp. 114ff), called "Mass Words", seems to be the first use of this term to describe these nouns[4] (as also is his use of "Countable Nouns" in the section just before). Here he says

[A] form which implied neither singular nor plural would be even more called for when we left the world of countables (such as *houses, horses; days, miles; sounds, words, crimes, plans, mistakes,* etc.) and got to the world of uncountables. There are a great many words which do not call up the idea of some definite thing with a certain shape or precise limits. I call these "mass words"; they may be either material, in which case they denote some substance in itself independent of form, such as *silver, quicksilver, water, butter, gas, air,* etc., or else immaterial, such as *leisure, music, traffic, success, tact, commonsense,* and especially many "nexus-substantives" like *satisfaction, admiration, refinement,* from verbs, or like *restlessness, justice, safety, constancy,* from adjectives.[5]

Jespersen goes on (a) to emphasize the relevance of the singular-plural number distinction to the count–mass difference, (b) to cite various differences between languages as to what is a countable term vs. a mass-word, (c) to

---

[3] Jespersen also repeated much of this discussion in his 1924 popular work, *The Philosophy of Grammar* (Jespersen 1924).
[4] Other than his earlier forward reference in Section 4.17 (pp. 72–3) to this section.
[5] Jespersen's nexus-substantives apparently means what is now more commonly called nominalizations from verbs and adjectives.

remark on cases "where the same word has to do duty now as a mass-word and now as a thing-word", (d) to remark on cases where a mass-word can "denote a mass" of something that is often designated by a thing-word (Jespersen cites *Oak and beech began to take the place of willow and elm*), and (e) of the tendency to use the same word for animals (countable) as for the food of that animal (mass) (Jespersen cites *fish*). Jespersen also remarks on (f) how "immaterial mass-words" can become countables when they come to stand for a single act or instance of the quality (*a stupidity* and *a beauty* are cited). This usage, he says, "is not so universal in English as in many other languages, and the best rendering of *eine unerhörte Unverschämtheit* is *a piece of monstrous impudence*". He also points to "the use of a mass word to denote one kind of the mass" (offering us *This tea is better than the one we had last week*; *Various sauces*; *The best Italian wines come from Tuscany*).

Finally, Jespersen is sensitive to the fact that (g) the CMD is drawn differently in different languages, although this is not made into a major topic. He remarks (p. 200) that "in English, but not in Danish, *tin* is used for a receptacle made of tin (for sardines, etc.). In English, *bread* is only a mass-word, but the corresponding word in many languages is used for what in English is called *a loaf*: *un peu de pain, un petit pain* = *a little bread, a small loaf*."

All of the topics in (a)–(g) form current strands of research within studies of the CMD, and each of them form a part of one or another of the papers in this volume. Although it is not explicitly mentioned by Jespersen, perhaps it is implicit in (b) and (g) that there is a possibility of languages not manifesting a CMD directly in the lexical nouns but instead by means of classifiers, or perhaps not even manifesting a CMD directly at all (examples of which are discussed in many of the papers of this volume).

2. Distinguishing Features of the CMD

There are different aspects of the CMD that are emphasized by different modern authors. All of them take a set of morpho-syntactic, also called grammatical, features as driving the division between count and mass nouns. The following list is usually assumed for English count and mass nouns, many of which are also present in other languages.

- singular/plural contrast
- direct combination with numerals
- constructions with classifier phrases
- restricted selection of determiners/quantity modifiers

Some of these characteristics are considered more relevant than others or even distinctive for countability. Chierchia (1998a, 2010; this volume, Chapter 2) thinks of the ability of some nouns to occur directly with cardinal numerals to be "the signature property" of count nouns, whereas non-count nouns (normally) require a "classifier phrase" in order to occur with cardinal numerals, as in *While John examined two blades of grass, Mary extracted two shovelfuls of mud.*

Besides these overt differences in the CMD, many theories rely heavily on certain referential properties of count and mass nouns, such as mass nouns having a homogeneous reference, i.e. being divisive and cumulative. These properties lead many authors to decide on an ultimate determinant which divides nouns into count and mass, such as (contextual) atomicity for count nouns (Rothstein 2010), overlap in the generator sets of mass nouns (Landman 2016) and the vagueness of mass atoms (Chierchia 2010) to name a few.

With regard to the morpho-syntactic features of the CMD and the referential properties of these nouns, we can observe many inconsistencies in English as well as cross-linguistically which have been discussed thoroughly. These inconsistencies can be divided in two groups: one consists of mismatches between the actual properties of the references, and the other is a matter of what we might call "variation" – nouns that exhibit properties of both mass and count nouns.

The first group comprises so-called fake mass nouns and homogeneous object nouns. Fake mass nouns (also called *furniture*-nouns, superordinates, object mass nouns, or aggregate nouns) are mass nouns according to the grammatical features, but have a reference similar to count nouns being individuated in units. **Five furnitures/silverwares* is ungrammatical since *furniture* and *silverware* require a classifier to enable counting pieces: *five pieces of furniture/silverware*. The difference between fake mass nouns and ordinary mass nouns (or object mass vs. substance mass) is the mode of measurement which in substance mass nouns is volume and in object mass nouns the number of individual entities. This difference was further supported by experiments conducted by Barner and Snedeker (2005) which employed quantity judgement tasks for identifying these classes of mass nouns. Since then, quantity judgement tasks have been used targeting the mode of counting in many languages besides English. Likewise, homogeneous objects nouns (also known as *fence*-nouns) are count nouns with a homogeneous reference, such as *wall, fence* or *sequence*. A wall can be divided vertically into several parts, each of which is still a wall. These two subclasses of nouns pose a challenge for formal theories that consider atomicity to be a distinctive property of count nouns and require adjustments to account for such nouns as well. Besides fake mass nouns and homogeneous object nouns, there is also an issue with nouns that have the same type of reference but different countability properties, such as *rice* vs. *lentils* or *onions* vs. *garlic*.

The other group of inconsistencies can be subsumed under the term *variation*. It regards nouns that cannot be classified straightforwardly as either count or mass, because they have features of both count and mass nouns. Such nouns have often been called dual-life nouns, flexible or elastic nouns. An example for such a noun is *cake*, which can be used as count and as mass, as illustrated below.

(1)   a. John ate five cakes.
       b. John ate five pieces of cake.
       c. John ate much cake over the last weekend.
       d. John ate many cakes over the last weekend.

Another phenomenon related to variation regards nouns that are classified as count nouns but permit also mass uses albeit with an implied difference in interpretation or meaning. Two such interpretations are commonly used in natural language and have been acknowledged in the literature on the CMD as a shift or coercion from mass into a count use: packaging (Bach 1986) as in (2) or sorting (Bunt 1985) as in (3).

(2)   a. We would like three waters.
       b. He put four milks in the fridge.

(3)   a. The restaurant that Kim suggested offers three wines.
       b. The hotel we visited last year provided pools with different waters.

In a similar way some nouns which are normally considered to be countable can – under certain circumstances – occur as mass although this shift is not as productive as the mass-to-count shifts in (2) and (3). Count-to-mass shifts can appear in advertising such as (4).

(4)   More car for less money.

Some researchers assume that almost every count noun is capable of turning into a mass noun by means of applying Pelletier's thought machine, the Universal Grinder (Pelletier 1975), which aims to grind the reference of a count noun, a hat or carrot for instance. The outcome of it should be referred to by a mass expression, as the following sentence with the bare use of *carrot* suggests.

(5)   There is carrot all over the floor.

When it comes to the semantics of count and mass nouns, we need to bear in mind that besides linguists, cognitive psychologists and philosophers also show interest in the CMD. However, the different fields that study the CMD have different conceptions of what the term "semantic" encompasses. On the whole, philosophers of language think of the term "semantics" as describing a relationship between language and the world. Cognitive psychologists on the other hand think of it as describing a relationship between language and mental concepts. And formal semanticists aim to offer model-theoretic interpretations of the nouns' references as a functioning input for a compositional analysis.

So, not surprisingly we get different viewpoints when it comes to explaining the semantics of count nouns and mass nouns. However, all our theorists seem to agree that there is a notion of individuation that plays a role such that only count nouns presuppose a principle of individuation while mass nouns do not. (Count nouns may inherit their principle from features of the context of utterance; mass nouns may in fact have such a principle but it is not activated in the context.) Depending on the area that a theorist calls home, the difference between *three chairs* and **three bloods* is:

a. chairs are individual objects; blood is a stuff and not an individual [philosopher];
b. one's conception of a chair is of some independent object, whereas blood is conceptualized as an undifferentiated puddle [psychologist];
c. chairs are a part of an atomic lattice whereas blood designates a non-atomic mereology [formal semanticist].

The articles of this book tackle many of the above-mentioned issues that regard the semantics of count and mass nouns across languages theoretically and/ or empirically.

3. The Articles in this Volume

This volume follows the organizational structure of the conference. It contains four longer, invited papers, followed by twelve shorter papers that touch upon or expand on or take issue with certain aspects of the invited papers and thus provide many independent observations and conclusions concerning the CMD. These twelve papers are grouped into three general areas of four papers each: Implications from Individual Languages; Compositional Analyses and Theoretical Issues; and New Empirical Approaches to the Semantics of the CMD.

We also include, at the end of the volume, language and subject indices, as well as a common-to-all-papers reference list. The language list is intended to provide locations where the CMD is discussed in languages other than English. English constructions are listed in this index only when they are being described as unique concerning a certain type of feature.

3.1. Invited Papers

The invited speakers at the conference offered us broad-scale accounts of what they took to be central issues in the study of the CMD – as, for instance, what is responsible for the distinction? Or how does it come to be differently realized in different languages? Or what is the role of plurality and its relation to the CMD? Or is there any relation or dependence between different inconsistencies which underlie the CMD?

Gennaro Chierchia's approach classifies all human languages into three groupings based on the way these languages manifest countability. This, of course, requires a criterion for what makes a noun be count, and Chierchia defends his choice by assuming a cognitive contrast between count and mass nouns motivated by the findings of Carey and Spelke (1996), according to which children in pre-linguistic age distinguish objects (as well defined units which retain their identity upon moving through space and entering in contact with each other) from substances (concepts like "water" or "sand" which do not have readily accessible minimal parts, and whose samples don't retain an identity when moving or congregating). Chierchia uses the term *cognitively count* for nouns which refer to "Spelke objects" and *cognitively mass* for nouns that denote "Spelke substances". He assumes that the CMD – as one dividing nouns into cognitively count and cognitively mass – is universal, but languages have different means to express this division. While Type I languages, such as English, have strong morpho-syntactic differences, Type II languages, such as Korean (also called classifier languages), do not present an overt difference in syntax or morphology since both (cognitively) count and mass nouns require classifier phrases. Count and mass nouns can, however, be identified by the choice of the classifier which is sensitive to (cognitively) count and mass nouns. Type III languages, such as Yudja, do not provide an overt difference between count and mass nouns either, since they all can combine directly with numerals, but the interpretation of numeral-noun combinations depends on the type of the noun. Cognitively count nouns have an interpretation that quantifies over individual items, while cognitively mass nouns imply a (hidden) classifier, or container for counting or measuring. Chierchia proposes a semantic mechanism that accounts for count vs. mass nouns and offers a compositional analysis for numeral noun constructions in Type I–III languages both for inclusive and exclusive plural readings. His logic can also account for the lexical variation and elasticity in the CMD which is present in every language in that certain modifications mirror coercion between count and mass references.

Susan Rothstein questions the relation between countability and pluralization. These features have been widely claimed to be necessarily interrelated: pluralization implies countability and countability is expressed by the ability to pluralize (cf. Chierchia 1998a, 2010; this volume, Chapter 2). She finds motivation for her concern in mass nouns which pluralize but do not refer to a multiplicity of kinds, but instead have an abundance interpretation, such as mass plurals in Greek, or the abundance reading of nouns such as *rain* or *fog* in English as well as the pluralization of events and abstract mass nouns. In addition to Greek and English, Rothstein provides further evidence for the non-relatedness of plurality and countability by means of a cross-linguistic study of several languages: Yudja, Dëne Sųłiné, Modern Hebrew, Wayaro, Panará, Sakurabiat, Ye'kwana and Taurepang, many of which are peculiar for their relation between countability and pluralization. For instance, Dëne Sųłiné provides a contrast between count and mass nouns but no plurality marking, and Taurepang is a language with a plural marker which attaches to every noun except for animate nouns that require a special plural -*damök*. Based on observation stemming from different languages, Rothstein concludes that the relation between plurality and countability allows for much more variation, and hence this relationship has to be inspected with more caution.

Jenny Doetjes re-evaluates the notions count and mass from different perspectives by elaborating on different meanings of nouns and different types of quantity expressions. She presents asymmetries that are evident throughout the CMD in the English language but also across languages. In particular, she discusses asymmetries in Mandarin, Dëne Sųłiné, French, Halkomelem, Blackfoot, Nez Perce, Hungarian, Cantonese, Yudja, Brazilian Portuguese and Indonesian. The asymmetries are expressed either in grammar or in meaning. With regard to these asymmetries, and motivated by the fact that count is (and mass is not) marked in the grammar of language, Doetjes argues that mass should be interpreted as the absence of count. Such a relational explanation of count and mass is further supported by a blocking principle in quantity expressions. She introduces a typology of quantity expressions according to which quantity expressions are divided in three groups: count quantity expressions; non-count quantity expressions; and anti-count quantity expressions. Crucial to this typology is the blocking principle according to which the existence of non-count expression is explained through the absence of count counterparts. Unlike this, anti-count quantity expressions, such as *much*, have a count counterpart, namely, *many*. Non-count quantity expressions, however, are those which combine with both mass and plural count nouns, such as *all*, and are not strictly reserved for mass nouns due to the lack of anti-count expressions.

It verges on the trivial to state that the CMD has semantic impact, and hence is addressed within semantics. But it should also be clear that any compositional semantic analysis must find its roots in syntax; this holds in particular if the CMD is severed from lexical categories, i.e., if the CMD itself becomes the result of the compositional combination of syntactic items. Following the general syntactic architecture developed in Borer (2005), Hagit Borer and Sarah Ouwayda deal with the syntactic structure of the nominal spine in Arabic, and in particular with the somewhat surprising co-occurrence of a classifier and plural realizations. Following T'sou's generalization, according to which classifiers and plural realization should not co-occur in the same syntactic structure, Borer and Ouwayda discuss the (Lebanese) Arabic

Editorial Introduction 11

feminine ending -*ah*, which can be added to nouns that are either mass or of indeterminate quantity, and act as a classifier in these constructions. Yet, plural marking is possible after -*ah* has been added as a supposed classifier. The construction, however, is not fully identical to a plural realization of a count noun. To solve this apparent paradox, Borer and Ouwayda propose a more fine-grained syntactic structure of the nominal projection, where cardinals are categorically distinguished from quantifiers. In a broader context, the paper suggests that the distinction between inclusive and exclusive plural readings should be addressed by assuming different syntactic structures for the different plural types (and hence, different compositional analyses). The apparent contradiction to T'sou's generalization is eventually resolved by assuming that the realization of the -*ah*-marker cannot be analysed as a classifier (divider), but instead as an agreement marker with a cardinality specifier. The obligatory presence of the specifier yields the pertinent interpretations.

3.2. Implications from Individual Languages

The invited papers have made claims that are to be applied to a wide swath of human languages – or even all – and which culminate in empirical remarks about how the languages of the world treat matters of count and mass – or alternatively, how the count–mass features would differentially appear in these languages. Papers in the next subsection of the book describe classes of apparent problems for some of these claims based on facts about certain languages, which in turn might thereby cast doubt on the universal applicability of some sweeping claims that were made.

The paper by Christine Hnout, Lior Laks and Susan Rothstein focuses attention on a mass-to-count shift that occurs in the Galilee dialect of Palestinian Arabic (PA). As in other Arabic dialects, a morphologically marked shift in gender (cf. also Borer and Ouwayda, this volume, Chapter 5) can result in contrasts between mass and count interpretations, so that masculine nouns are mass, while derived feminines are count. After discussing the peculiarities of the CMD in PA, the paper addresses constraints on the input to the mass to count operation, observing that nouns denoting solids and granular substances can be affected, while liquid- and powder-denoting nouns cannot. The input denotation of the operation is not only constrained, but it also determines the output (which sometimes can be idiosyncratic). A particularly relevant output condition governs the shift for *s*ˁ*enf* nouns, which are also analysed as mass nouns. The present analysis supports a distinction between natural and semantic atomicity in general. The analysis suggests in particular that count–mass shifts should not be thought of as the result of a contextually determined partition on the set denoted by a mass noun (as e.g. proposed in Chierchia 2010). Finally, the lexical coercion operation is contrasted with a highly constrained coercion, which involves the addition of a covert classifier in the syntax.

The contribution by Kurt Erbach, Peter Sutton, Hana Filip and Kathrin Byrdeck reminds us that object (or fake) mass nouns do not align with ordinary intuitions concerning the relationship between stuff and things. It is for this reason that they say that such nouns provide a good testing ground for theories of the CMD. As they remark, there are a number of theories in the literature to account for the peculiarities of object mass nouns. But, they also note, these theories have all been for those languages that overtly manifest a CMD: the type of languages that Chierchia (1998a, 2010; this volume, Chapter 2) calls Type I languages. They wonder whether other language types – particularly classifier languages such as Mandarin and Japanese – might also have object mass nouns. Here they argue first that it is at least in theory possible that such languages have object mass nouns, and to this end they proceed to test the determiner *nan-byaku to iu* ('hundreds of') with a number of nouns, using native speakers as subjects. The idea is that any noun that refers to collections of discrete objects, but which fails the countability test with *nan-byaku to iu* is a candidate for being an object mass noun. The authors provide a partial semantic analysis of how such nouns might fit into a grammar of Japanese (and presumably of other classifier languages, if they also had a determiner of the same nature as *nan-byaku to iu*). Although they are careful to say that their analysis is preliminary, nonetheless, if it does stand up it would raise serious objections to most theories of the cross-linguistic description of the CMD in all languages.

Kayron Beviláqua and Roberta Pires de Oliveira propose a novel methodology for testing how different languages differentially treat the various types of nouns that are in play when considering issues about the CMD. Using five types of nouns (Bare Singulars, Bare Plurals, Singular Flexible Nouns, Plural Flexible Nouns, and Mass Nouns), they propose testing how speakers of four different languages (English, Brazilian Portuguese, Rioplatense Spanish, and Cape Verdean) will judge the different types of pictorial representations of situations that compare amounts (size, number, and so on) of the five different types of nouns. (The tests are extensions of the ones made popular by Barner and Snedeker 2005.) Their pilot studies give some intriguing results, categorizing – in the terminology of Chierchia (1998a, 2010; and this volume, Chapter 2) – some of the investigated languages as number-marking, others as classifying, and, perhaps most surprisingly, another as neither. Although as they say, further more-detailed studies need to be performed, this methodology could open up a better way to test which of Chierchia's categories a language falls into than those methods currently employed.

Following upon Chierchia's (1998a, 2010; and this volume, Chapter 2) distinction in different count–mass language types, Helen Koulidobrova addresses the CMD in American Sign Language (ASL) and asks to which type ASL belongs. The structure of ASL initially suggests that ASL differs strongly from English and other Type I languages in Chierchia's proposal in that a CMD is not visible; thus it should be grouped together with Yudja and other Type III languages. Her investigations, however, show that such conclusions are not warranted and that ASL bear more resemblance to Type I than Type III languages, while clearly rejecting classification as a (Type II) generalized classifier language. Crucial empirical evidence for this conclusion is provided by the grammar of the quantifier-split in ASL. Koulidobrova shows that the quantifier-split in ASL is sensitive to the CMD after all.

3.3. Compositional Analyses and Theoretical Issues

While the CMD classifies nouns into (at least) two groups, one has to bear in mind that it has much wider implications beyond the individual representation of a word (a "lemma"). That count and mass nouns have different semantic representations is the initial point of a compositional structure. The fact that certain nouns can combine with numerals directly while others require a classifier phrase, tells us that numerals and classifier phrases need to have such a semantic and syntactic structure which is sensitive to the noun they are modifying. Likewise, the indefinite article and other quantity modifiers require an analysis which is compatible with the nouns they are accompanying. Compositionality is central in the papers of this section, which investigate the syntax and semantics of particular phenomena related to the CMD.

In his contribution, Alan Bale discusses the implications of interaction between three different theories of the semantics of the CMD with two theories of number marking. Link (1983) has proposed that count and mass expressions must be mapped to two different domains, while Rothstein (2010, this volume, Chapter 3) assumes a difference in type theory. Finally, proposals like Chierchia (1998a, this volume, Chapter 2) assume that the semantic difference is captured neither by a distinction of domain nor of type theory. Bale combines the predictions of these models with two theories of (morpho-)syntactic number marking, where number is either assigned low, i.e. within the NP, or – following Sauerland (2003) – high, i.e. as a sister node of a Determiner Phrase (DP). Various issues concerning coercion emerge in the different theories, including the topic of how single-domain-for-both-count-and-mass denotations can employ coercion, and as well, what it would mean for coercion to effect a change in domain for two-domain theories. Given the current state of affairs, Bale does not profess a favourite for any of the theories he describes, since advantages are counter-balanced by drawback. In conclusion, a "best overall theory" will involve a very intricate and detailed syntactic–semantic account that interweaves many different levels of explanation.

Following previous work (Acquaviva 2008; Alexiadou 2011; Butler 2012; Wiltschko 2012; Mathieu 2014) which proposed that morphemes corresponding to number can occupy several functional positions depending on the individual semantics of these morphemes, Myriam Dali and Éric Mathieu investigate some plural forms which require a yet-different syntactic position. They analyse bare nouns in Turkish and Western Armenian that possess a general (or transnumeral) number (cf. Corbett 2000) and argue that pluralization of such bare nouns is a two-step process which requires a renominalization effect as familiar from collective nouns in Tunesian Arabic (Dali and Mathieu 2016, 2021). The pluralization process requires two NumP projections, a lower one with the null exponent providing a singular form and a higher one which operates morpho-syntactically on the singular and returns a set of atoms. Such a procedure is known as a case of morphological compositionality where one number is built on another.

Starting with a discussion of different interpretations of pseudo-partitive constructions (PPC), Peter Sutton and Hana Filip propose analyses with respect to the individual interpretation of such PPCs. The main difference among these interpretations is the one between container+contents readings and ad hoc measure interpretations. The former makes both the container as well as the content anaphorically available while the latter blocks anaphoric reference to a container (+content) but licenses reference to the measured stuff. Sutton and Filip analyse PPCs in a dynamic, mereological framework which incorporates several ingredients that have previously been suggested to be relevant in a theory of the CMD, such as, for instance, Rothstein's contextual influence onto the counting units (Rothstein 2010) and Landman's counting bases (Landman 2016). Counting is permitted in case the context makes an individuation schema available which, applied to the counting base of singular count nouns, yields a quantized predicate as defined by Krifka (1989).

Assuming a pre-linguistic notion of countability inspired by Soja, Carey, and Spelke (1991), Gordon (1985) and Bloom (1990), Hanna de Vries and George Tsoulas discuss a set of asymmetries ranging over flexible nouns and various types of coercion. Comparing the processing costs of packaging, sorting and grinding with flexible nouns and elaborating on different proposals to this type of variation, both in terms of lexical reanalysis and covert classifier constructions, they consider a combination of two structurally different theories as the most suitable solution. Their paper presents an intriguing attempt to combine a constructionist approach with a lexicalist framework in order to account for asymmetries relating to countability across languages. This hybrid theory embodies Borer's exoskeletal syntax with Landman's Iceberg semantics in order to account for various relations of countability and number neutrality. The resulting theory correctly does not allow non-number-neutral noun phrases with uncountable nouns – a combination considered non-existent across languages. In this way, they offer a framework in which only [+countable] nouns can be [-number neutral] and "stuff reference" is not reduced to uncountable number neutrality.

3.4. New Empirical Approaches to the Semantics of the CMD

Empirical approaches to the study of language can come in many different guises. Corpus studies have been used to offer an objective state of the natural language use of many phenomena relevant in linguistic theories. The CMD has also been studied in this way. We furthermore observe a rise in experimental methods in the last twenty years in many different languages. In this subsection we include papers that exhibit some of the different strands of empirical approaches: psycholinguistic investigations by means of different kinds of experiments and significant corpus studies enriched with investigations of relevant lexical resources. Of course, other papers already introduced also can be seen as fitting under this description, but we see these four papers as especially relevant in this regard.

The paper by Francesca Franzon, Giorgio Arcara and Chiara Zanini remarks that one source of information that is weak or even missing from the discussion of countability in language is specific data on the actual occurrence of count vs. mass nouns in naturally produced cases of language, and they set out to discover this data as it occurs in Italian. Their review of the psychological literature on the question shows that there are unresolved differences in people's representation, processing and learning of count vs. mass nouns. And this paper suggests that a part of this inconsistency might be due to each study relying only on one speaker's intuitions as to what are relevant count and mass nouns. To help resolve this, they investigated the actual occurrence of mass and count nouns, by having subjects rate the subjective frequency of occurrence of 225 words (concrete nouns) in the singular and also in the plural. The results seem to show that there is a gradation here, not a binary distribution of "always singular" vs. "sometimes plural" – it seems there are "different levels of countability". To determine how many of the "always singular" turn out to be sometimes plural, the authors turned to the Italian itWaC corpus, to investigate the existence of a correlation between occurrences of a same noun in mass syntax and in count syntax. The results of this showed no significant inverse correlation between (allegedly) count and (allegedly) mass nouns. One of their overall conclusions is that their data is most easily explainable in a framework that does not make countability into a lexical feature.

The contribution by Peter Lauwers addresses the role of lexical plurals, a topic that has often been neglected in investigations of the CMD. Lauwers points out that although lexical plurals show plural morphology, the inherent number specification must be separated from counting. As lexical plurals do not pass ordinary countability tests, such as the combination with cardinals, they provide evidence for a dissociation between countability and plurality. Here, we note one of the common themes across the individual contributions, in this case relating Lauwers' paper to both Rothstein's and Borer and Ouwayda's papers. Lauwers not only argues that lexical plurals show a discrepancy between number marking and countability, but proposes that lexical plurals actually show more properties of mass than of count nouns. According to the ensuing analysis, lexical plurals are less count than other expressions, but neither are they entirely mass either. Lauwers thus takes up recent proposals (briefly mentioned in the contribution by Kiss et al. in Chapter 17 as well) that the CMD, although the name suggests otherwise, should not be seen as a binary opposition, but more like a continuum. Lauwers places his methodology in the perspective of the "empirical turn" on the CMD, and uses both corpus studies (which are focused in the present paper) and sentence rating tasks on thirty lexical plurals from French, which represent a broad variety of lexical fields.

Keith Allan (1980) was possibly the first to develop a categorization of nouns according to how many (and which ones) of the various tests for countability a given noun obeys. In turn this leads to a (sub-)classification of types of noun-countability. Scott Grimm and Aeshaan Wahlang largely extend Allan's database by using all nouns occurring in four of the five subcorpora of COCA (Corpus of Contemporary American English), filtered through their occurrence in CELEX, and determine whether Allan's classification can be maintained after such an extension. Using machine learning algorithms such as gradient boosting (random forest classification) and non-parametric clustering methods such as DBSCAN, they predict the actual occurrence patterns of the nouns. It turns out that the ability of a noun to occur bare (without determiners) in the singular or in the plural makes for the most accurate prediction. They conclude that there is a much more varied distribution of "types of countability" than any of the theoretical models would predict, which seems to be a common conclusion of all papers in this subsection. Of course, this conclusion provides severe challenges for many (small-scale) studies on the CMD.

Leaving syntactic proposals aside, many analyses assume that the CMD is a property of words. Tibor Kiss, Jeff Pelletier and Halima Husić question this conclusion from two directions: first they note that lexical items typically have more than one sense, yielding all kinds of ambiguities; secondly, they point out that the evidence presented for count or mass properties often rests on a very small set of nouns, which can lead to researchers missing the micro-variation within lexical classes. Using both BECL, a database of 11,000 noun–sense pairs with annotated countability status and also further corpus analyses, Kiss et al. distinguish four types of ambiguity, two of which are of particular relevance. They use these ambiguities as touchstones for proposals such as

Chierchia (1998a, 2010; and this volume, Chapter 2) and Rothstein (2010; this volume, Chapter 3). BECL allows a quantitative specification regarding count-to-mass and mass-to-count shifts, and a way to differentiate "dual life" nouns from cases of grinding. Following their typology of the CMD in particular, Kiss et al. argue that their findings are compliant with an analysis of the CMD where count expressions show more denotational structure than mass expressions.

The papers in this volume have "moved the yardstick" in our understanding of how the CMD should be understood. They have done this both by looking at very large-scale views of all natural languages and at detailed descriptions of specific topics within one language or comparisons between different languages. If some readers find some of the directions outlined by our authors to be less than completely convincing, these directions nevertheless will certainly challenge such readers to investigate alternative possible explanations.

Large-Scale Architectures for Count and Mass

2 Mass vs. Count: Where Do We Stand? Outline of a Theory of Semantic Variation

Gennaro Chierchia

1. Plan

A lot of the debate on the nature of the count–mass distinction centers on what the ultimate determinant of (un)countability is. Here are some of the current stances on this matter:

(1)   Mass nouns cannot combine directly with numerals because:
    a. They are not atomic, under some formally supplied notion of atomicity (Bunt 1979; Link 1983)
    b. Their generator sets have overlapping parts (Landman 2011, 2016)
    c. Count nouns have contextually supplied minimal parts; mass nouns don't (Rothstein 2010)
    d. The minimal parts of mass nouns are not 'maximally connected' (Grimm 2012b)
    e. Count nouns denote states with singular/atomic participants. Mass nouns denote states with non-singular/atomic participants (Schwarzschild 2011)
    f. The 'minimal components' of mass nouns are specified too vaguely to be used in counting (Chierchia 2010, 2015, 2017)

A primary problem that theories like those in (1) face is that of variation. I will illustrate and discuss the extent to which grammars may vary vis-à-vis the count–mass distinction with three main phenomena and use this as a springboard for outlining a theory of semantic variation, with a universal logical basis. The first form of variation concerns the most widespread empirical test associated with the count–mass distinction, namely how noun phrases (NPs) combine with numerals. The second is that of the so called 'fake' mass nouns (like *furniture*). The third concerns alternations between count vs. mass interpretations of nouns like *beer* or *chicken*.

From the point of view of *Numeral–Nouns* combination, three types of languages have been so far convincingly documented.

I am indebted to A.R. Deal, Jeff Pelletier, Roberta Pires, and Susan Rothstein for criticisms of versions of this paper. I miss terribly discussing and 'crossing sabers' with Susan, a wonderful scholar, long-time friend, and twin soul in many of our intellectual curiosities.

(2) a. Type I languages.
Numerals combine directly with some nouns, but not with others; for the latter a classifier or measure phrase needs to be interpolated
Example: *three chairs* vs. **three blood(s)* vs. *three ounces/drops of blood*
Most of the Indo-European languages belong to this type
  b. Type II languages.
Numerals cannot combine with *any* NP directly. A classifier/measure phrase is always needed, whether the noun is cognitively count or mass.
Example: i. san *(ge) ren
                    Three CL person   'three people'
              ii. san *(bang) yintao
                    three pound cherry   'three pounds of cherries'
Languages of this sort include Chinese (e.g., Cheng and Sybesma 1998, 1999), Japanese, Nuosu Yi (Jiang 2017), and Bangla (Dayal 2012).
  c. Type III languages.
Numerals freely combine with any type of noun. In combination with cognitively count nouns (e.g., *three cats*), numerals have the meaning they do in English. In combination with mass nouns they have a 'container' or a 'quantity of' reading (not necessarily *'standard' quantity of*).
Example: i. lepit cickan   Nez Perce (Deal 2017)
                    two blanket   'two blankets'
              ii. lepit kieke't
                    two blood   'two quantities (e.g. drops) of blood'
Languages of this sort include Indonesian (Dalrymple and Mofu 2012), Yudja (Lima 2014a), Nez Perce (Deal 2017)

This typology is meant to be descriptive: to arrive at the 'right' theoretical classification in terms of grammatical mechanisms is our main objective. In stating the typology above, I rely on the notion of *'cognitively* count vs. mass' noun/concept. The definition I have in mind here is the one stemming from the research of cognitive psychologists like Carey and Spelke (1996).[1] This rich line of work shows that children, *before* language, clearly distinguish concepts like 'teddy bear' or 'car' that have relatively well-defined units (which retain their identity upon moving through space and entering in contact with each other) from concepts like 'water' or 'sand' that do not have readily accessible minimal parts, and whose samples don't retain an identity when moving or congregating. Establishing precisely the nature of this dichotomy is part of the problem, but that the dichotomy exists is at this point well established. I use the label 'cognitive' in connection with the distinction just outlined to underscore the fact that it is present in the cognitive system of children before any manifestation of language, and, for that matter, it is also present in other non-human primates (cf., e.g. Hauser and Carey 2003).

---

[1] See also, e.g., Carey (1985), Soja, Carey, and Spelke (1991), Feigenson, Dehaene, and Spelke (2004).

A second form of variation concerns cases of 'misalignment' with respect to the cognitive contrast just characterized. In English, as in most Indo-European (IE) languages, there is a class of nouns that is cognitively count but patterns with the mass ones with respect to the tests prevailing in the language: *furniture, kitchenware, jewelry, luggage*, ... Half a table is no more a good instance of the table-concept, than it is of the furniture-concept. Furniture units are as well defined as table- and couch-units. And yet, *furniture* patterns with mass nouns with respect to pluralization, combination with numerals, use of the indefinite article, etc. I like to call nouns of this sort 'Fake Mass', not to downplay the phenomenon, but because Fake Mass nouns take on the grammatical behavior of mass nouns while being cognitively count, and patterning tendentially with count concepts in tasks that do not involve language.[2] Variation with respect to Fake Mass nouns manifests itself in three ways. First, there is variation that involves specific lexical entries across languages. For example, nouns like *luggage* or *jewelry* are Fake Mass in English but count in Italian (*bagagli* 'luggages', *gioielli* 'jewels'); *servitù* 'servants' is Fake Mass in Italian, count in English. Second, the phenomenon of Fake Mass seems to be absent from Type II and Type III languages; this claim requires some factual justification that will be provided shortly. And third, only a subset of Type I languages seems to have Fake Mass nouns. Greek is a Type I language that lacks them altogether (cf. Tsoulas 2009; also in p.c.).

The claim that Type II and Type III languages lack Fake Mass nouns rests on the following observations, which have to do with the way in which the count–mass distinction manifests itself in these languages. In Type II languages, also known as generalized classifier languages, the count–mass distinction manifests itself in the classifier system. Cheng and Sybesma (1998) a.o. have shown that languages like Mandarin or Cantonese have a grammatically identifiable system of count classifiers, which combine with cognitively count nouns, but not with mass ones; they include the 'sortally unspecific' classifiers, like *ge* in Mandarin, as well as some category specific ones like *ben* (the classifier for books, periodicals, journals, etc.). A Fake Mass noun in a language like Mandarin would, accordingly, be something that lexicalizes a cognitively count concept like *jiaju* 'furniture' but does *not* combine with count classifiers. As Cheng and Sybesma point out, such Ns do not exist: nouns like *furniture* naturally combine with unspecific count classifiers like *ge* and/or with category specific ones (like *jian jiaju*) with a

---

[2] Or tasks which involve language only marginally. See, e.g., Barner and Snedeker (2005); for recent developments of this experimental paradigm, cf. Scontras et al. (2017). Barner and Snedeker call 'Fake Mass' nouns 'object mass'. The terminology on them varies a lot. Doetjes (1997) calls them 'count mass'; Rothstein (2010) calls them 'superordinate mass'; Landman (2011) calls them 'neat mass'; Grimm (2012b) calls them 'functional aggregates'.

count interpretation ('whole piece' of furniture). And in so far as I know this holds across all Type II languages. In Type III languages, the issue takes a different form. In these languages, *Numeral–Noun* combinations behave as indicated in (2c): if the noun is cognitively count, *n* + *N* means the same as in English: n natural units of N; if the noun is mass, *n* + *N* means *n (natural) quantities of N* (e.g., *three bloods* = *three drops of blood* or *three puddles of blood*). So, a Fake Mass noun would be an N that is cognitively count, like, say, *canoe* or *table*, but that in combination with numerals freely allows for an interpretation parallel to that of mass nouns (i.e. *three canoes* = *three aggregates of canoes* or *three pieces of a canoe*), i.e. a cognitively count noun that gets 'counted' as a mass one. For the time being, I am not aware that this ever happens. If these observations withstand further empirical scrutiny, the conclusion that the phenomenon of Fake Mass nouns is attested only in (a subset of) Type I languages seems warranted, which cries out for an explanation.

The case of Fake Mass Ns is profoundly different, I think, from the case of *ambiguous* Ns like *rope* or *rock*, which give raise to a third form of variation. There are two equally natural senses of *rope*. One is that of a bounded, continuous string of some material suitable to tie things together. The other is any recognizable, not necessarily detached part of such a string. In this second sense, part of a rope still qualifies as *rope* (but not as *a rope*, unless it is cut off from the rest). Related to this is the ambiguity of Ns like *chicken*, that applies to whole animals in its count sense, and to animal parts (viewed mostly as food) in its mass sense. Or the ambiguity of words like *beer*, which is equally felicitous as a name of an alcoholic liquid and as referring to some *standardized* serving of the latter (a bottle or glass of beer). With Ns of this sort, some kind of reconceptualization seems to be going on in switching back and forth between its mass and count uses, conceptualization that crucially affects what counts as a minimal unit of the relevant concept: the minimal unit of the count sense of *beer* is a glass or a bottle of beer (half a bottle of beer doesn't qualify as a beer); the minimal units of the liquid are not really known, much less rigidly set by our lexicon, and any recognizable small amount of the liquid may be a candidate; but they differ from the minimal units of *beers*. With nouns like *furniture*, instead, what counts as a minimal unit does not seem to change significantly with respect to the categories (*tables, chairs, couches*) of which it is a superordinate.

Potentially ambiguous Ns are subject to variation both within and across languages. For example, arguably the word *hair* is predominantly mass in English: one says things like *my hair is white* not *my hairs are white*. The latter is, however, how a literal translation of the functionally equivalent Italian phrase *i miei capelli sono bianchi* would sound. At the same time, English does admit things like *I found three blond hairs on your jacket*, showing that it tolerates count uses of *hair*, in specific contexts. This type of variation/elasticity is pervasive: I think we will find manifestations of it in any language. It being so widespread suggests that the variation across potentially ambiguous Ns is more socially and culturally determined than grammatically determined. We all can have fun in imagining a society of vampires in which one could walk in a bar and order a blood on the rocks; or a society of wood worms where one does not digest *shelf*, but *table* is fine. Even this cartoon-like imagery has its limits, however: geometrical shapes like circles or triangles, and other shape-based concepts like that of *hole* are notoriously hard to massify (see Gathercole 1986, for an early discussion of these matters).

My goal in this paper is to sketch a theory of these three forms of variation, which are summarized in (3):

(3) Three forms of variations in the count–mass phenomenology
 a. Macrovariation in how numerals combine with count vs. mass nouns (i.e. the typology in (2))
 b. Variation affecting Fake Mass nouns, that appears to blur the cognitive basis of the count–mass distinction
 c. Variation in potentially ambiguous nouns and (re)conceptualization

It should be underscored that one can easily conceive more options than those in (2). For example, a priori there might be a Type II language with clear cases of Fake Mass nouns. Or one could expect there to be mixed systems: e.g. a system which is basically like English, with two types of Ns, but where a subset of the cognitively mass nouns behaves like in Yudja, i.e. they allow for direct combination with numerals, under the interpretation *quantity of* without standardization. So far, systems of this sort are unattested. In working out a proposal, it is worth keeping in mind that it has proven useful to work with frameworks that err in the direction of restrictiveness as opposed to frameworks that allow us to describe attested and unattested patterns with equal ease.

One can talk of the forms of variations in (3) in radically different ways. At one extreme, one might be tempted to say that while Type I languages divide their lexica in a count and a mass region, Type II and Type III languages don't: in Type II languages every noun is mass, while in Type III languages every noun is count. At the opposite end, one can try to maintain that the count–mass distinction is universal, modulo fairly minor socially driven variations in the way potentially ambiguous concepts are lexicalized. And intermediate positions are also conceivable. I have already given some reasons (if tentatively, pending further empirical inquiry) for following the second perspective. I will explore the thesis that the only 'substantive' form of variation is the one that involves (re)conceptualization of potentially ambiguous nouns. If this is so, where do the striking grammatical differences between Type I–III languages come from? The thesis to be developed is that they come from two sources: type theory and covert uses of certain general classifiers (which are grammatical formatives in their own right). Let me draw a couple of analogies to give some sense of where I am headed. Certain concepts can be intensionally coded in very different ways, even though they are extensionally equivalent. For example, relations can be viewed as a set of ordered pairs, or as a 'Curried' function-valued function. Sets of ordered pairs vs. Curried functions differ only intensionally. By the same token, a given concept, say *piece(s) of furniture*, can be coded in different ways, which in turn may affect the way in which it undergoes operations like pluralization and counting, while 'referring' to one and the same thing, etc. I think that the difference between Type I and Type II languages and the phenomenon of Fake Mass nouns are to be thought of along these very lines: languages exploit differently certain semantic types/categories that are extensionally equivalent from a mathematical standpoint. Another familiar way in which languages vary is in whether they exploit grammatical resources like pronouns only overtly or also covertly, a prime example of the latter being pro-drop phenomena. I think that at the basis of Type III languages is the covert use of a classifier-like function analogous to *(natural) quantity of*.

Whether or not one is able to articulate this still quite tentative thesis cogently, or even just coherently, the count–mass distinction keeps being a very useful testing ground for theories of meaning because we are constantly finding out more empirical aspects of the problem and they are game-changing as they bring to light prima facie stunning forms of variation. And how can we have a universal theory of meaning, counting, etc., in light of that much variation? At the same time, as our grasp of semantics grows, our theoretical options may be getting a little clearer. In working out a framework for understanding the variations in (3), I will try to abstract away from what is the ultimate determinant of the count–mass distinction in the sense of the approaches in (1), to the extent that it is possible. But I won't be able to hide my belief that some of the approaches in (1) appear to be better suited than others in understanding the nature of the generalizations in (3).

2. A Base-Line Framework

In the present section, we review how approaches to the count–mass distinction grow out of theories of plurality. All modern theories of plurals employ a domain U of individuals ordered by a relation '$\leq$' and closed under a plural sum operation '+', a practice we will follow as well. The assumptions about plurals we will make for the purposes of this paper are meant to be uncontentious, to the extent that anything is.[3] Theories of plurals based on structures $<U, \leq >$ rely for counting on a notion of ('structural') atomicity. (Absolute)

---

[3] In particular, we adopt a lattice-theoretic terminology, a la Link (1983). But a set theoretic one (cf. Landman 1989; Schwarzschild 1996) would work equally well for our purposes.

atoms are the members AT of U that are minimal with respect to the ordering
$\leq$ (i.e., AT(x) $=_{df}$ $\forall$y [y $\leq$ x $\rightarrow$ x = y]).[4] Properties are modelled in the usual
way, as functions from worlds to (characteristic functions of) subsets of
U. The introduction of properties affords us a useful notion of 'relative'
atomicity: an individual x is an atom relative to P (a P-atom) in w iff no other
individual of which P is true in w is a proper part of x. Generally, when we
combine numerals with a property P, we count P-atoms (e.g. *three bears*
means three individual/atomic things of which the property *bears* is true).
A standard assumption is that the singular property *bear* is true of individual
bears, i.e. bear-atoms. The plural property *bears*, instead, is true of any sum of
bears, i.e. it is closed with respect to '+' or, equivalently, it is a *cumulative*
property. The singular property *bear* can be viewed as the generator set of its
plural counterpart *bears*. We will also say that a singular property P is
'quantized', because all of the things of which it is true have the same size
with respect to how P-atoms are counted: each thing of which *bear* is true in
any w counts as *one* bear. Its plural counterpart *bears* is not quantized, because
it applies to sums of varying numbers of bear-atoms. These considerations take
us to the following morphisms between properties, often used in counting:

(4)   a. AT(P) 'extracts' from P the P-atoms:
AT(P) = λw λx P$_w$(x) $\wedge$ $\forall$y[P$_w$(y) $\wedge$ y $\leq$ x $\rightarrow$ x = y] Type: <<s,et>,<s,et>>
       b. *P closes P under sum:
*P = λwλx $\exists$Y[Y $\subseteq$ P$_w$ $\wedge$ x = +Y]   Type: <<s,et>,<s,et>>
where Y is of type <e,t> and +Y is the sum of the extension of Y
       c. Numerals (first approximation)
          i. 3(bears) = λw λx $\exists$Y [Y $\subseteq$ AT(bears)$_w$ $\wedge$ |Y| = 3 $\wedge$ x = +Y]
          ii. 3 = λPλw λx $\exists$Y [Y $\subseteq$ AT(P)$_w$ $\wedge$ |Y| = 3 $\wedge$ x = +Y]
       d. Numerals (presuppositional version)
          i. 3 = λP: *(AT(P)) = P. λw λx $\exists$Y [Y $\subseteq$ P$_w$ $\wedge$ |Y| = 3 $\wedge$ x = +Y]
(Plural agreement languages; e.g. IE languages)
          ii. 3 = λP: AT(P) = P. λw λx $\exists$Y [Y $\subseteq$ P$_w$ $\wedge$ |Y| = 3 $\wedge$ x = +Y]
(Singular agreement languages, e.g. Ugro-Finnish, and Type II–III languages)

The world argument is notated as a subscript on a property P. Whenever the
world argument is either understood or irrelevant, we will ignore it. AT(P)
pulls out the P-atoms (which may or may not be atoms in the absolute sense).
For singular properties like *bear*, it holds that *AT(bear) = bear*. The characterization of numerals in (4c) is a first approximation that needs comment. For
one thing, we are assuming that *numeral + N* combinations have a basic
predicative meaning of type <s,et> and a predictable generalized quantifier

---

[4] We will assume here that U and $\leq$ are pragmatically set; once pragmatically set, they remain
constant across worlds (i.e. in modal reasoning). This is different from Chierchia (2010) where
both U and $\leq$ are taken to be relativized to worlds. The present approach is meant as a slight (?)
simplification of the view developed there.

variant obtained via ∃-closure.[5] Second, the number marking on NPs in *numeral + N* combination varies across language type: in IE languages, NPs (other than in combination with the first numeral) are plural marked; in Urgo-Finnic and Turkic languages NPs are always marked in the singular, in combination with any numeral. This variation can be modulated, e.g. by adding suitable domain restrictions in the definition of numerals, as illustrated in (4d). Third, the definition of numerals should be made compatible with how complex numerals like *thirty-three* are compositionally built up. An important reference in this connection is Ionin and Matushansky (2018). The definition in (4c) is designed to be implementable within their approach, but to do so here would take us too far afield. And fourth, we are ignoring here the event-argument; taking it into account should not change dramatically the architecture of the present proposal.

The sketch just given reflects a widespread view on the nature of counting, which relies on a notion of (*relative*) atomicity. When mass nouns enter the scene, a notion of 'non-atomic' property needs to be determined, and this is where theories diverge widely, as sketchily indicated in (1). The general idea is that non-atomic properties are not good companions to numbers because they somehow don't allow access to units that can be readily counted. Non-atomic properties like *water, blood*, etc. apply to samples that can be measured. But the measure has to be 'external' to the property, unlike what happens with atomic properties. In other words, water samples cannot be counted because they lack an atomic structure (in some sense to be specified), but their size can be measured using some general measure suitable for liquids. The problem is how to spell out this very rough intuition about (un)countability, and the theories in (1), or rather the slogans through which they are summarized, are different attempts to do so.

2.1. Atomic vs. Non-Atomic Properties

I will now outline, briefly and informally, the view on (non)atomicity I favor, just to give some intuitive content to it. But as I said, much of what is proposed on variation would go through on other approaches. On Chierchia's (2010, 2017) proposal, lack of atomicity has to do with vagueness: while the nature of the units associated with count properties are clear enough to be counted, those associated with mass properties aren't. To spell this out, worlds are taken to be ordered with respect to the *standards of precision* prevailing in them; $w \propto w'$

---

[5] Here is one way of doing so:

(a) $3(\text{bears})_{GQ} = \lambda P \lambda w \, \exists y \, [3(\text{bears})_w(y) \wedge P_w(y)]$
   $= \lambda P \lambda w \exists y \exists Y [\, Y \subseteq AT(\text{men})_w \wedge |Y| = 3 \wedge y = +Y \wedge P_w(y)]$

(It is also possible to assume that the GQ version of *numeral + N* combinations is the basic one and extract the predicative variant out of it).

is to be understood as conveying that the standards of precisions in w′ are at least as sharp (and possibly sharper) than those in w.[6] Properties in general tend to be partial: any (non-empty) P in any w has a positive extension (the things of which P is true in w), a negative extension (the things of which P is false in w), and typically also a vagueness band (things for which P is undefined in w). Precisifications of w (i.e. {w′: w ∝ w′}) are worlds in which the vagueness of each property P is resolved (partially or totally), by sharpening the criteria for having P: i.e., some things for which P is undefined in w get to be assigned to the positive or negative extension of P in w′. Precisifications affect vagueness in a monotonic fashion with respect to the ordering ∝: if u is in the positive (or negative) extension of P in w and w ∝ w′, then u has to stay in the positive (or negative) extension P in w′. 'Base'-worlds are those that are '∝-minimal.'[7] Intuitively, they are the worlds where standards of precisions are set (typically through implicit conventions) by a community of speakers so as to ensure reliable and successful communication. Thus Base-worlds are historically and socio-pragmatically determined.

Here is how this frame is meant to help us understand vagueness in general and 'massiness' in particular. A property like *table* in any base world w will be true, say, of your dining table; it will be false of your chairs; it will also be false of the left half of your dining table. However, it can be undefined for the old table with three legs missing sitting in your garage. You need not take a stand as to whether that is (still) a table or not. This means that for certain purposes (e.g. if you intend to prop it up somehow and use it for emergencies) it may still count as a table; while for other purposes (e.g., if you plan to use it as firewood) it may not count as a table. Contrast this with the water you just spilled that now forms a puddle on the floor. It is definitely water, while, e.g., the floor it sits on is not water, but wood. Half of that puddle is also definitely water. But as you consider smaller samples, you become uncertain. There rapidly come parts of the puddle that are too small to be identified/recognized/ perceived and one doesn't know whether the property *water* applies to them in w. In any run-of-the-mill Base-world, there are pretty small (e.g. droplet-sized) water amounts to which *water* applies; but we know that there are precisifications of the water-property in which parts of those water droplets may also turn out to be water, or not, as the case may be. This knowledge (or lack thereof) is what blocks combining numerals directly with *water*. *Three water(s)* doesn't work, in languages like English, because *three* looks for reliable/stable/lexically determined water-atoms. But we know that all perceivable water samples

---

[6] As usual, '∝' is taken to be reflexive, transitive, and antisymmetric. The basic idea for this formalization of vagueness is based on supervaluations (e.g. Fine 1975) and from 'data-semantics' (Veltman 1985; see also Landman 1991).
[7] More explicitly, w is a Base-world iff for any w′, w′ ∝ w → w = w.

may turn out to be aggregates, sets of smaller water samples, once sharper criteria are applied. What about a single H_2O molecule? Does that count as *water*? Honestly, I am not sure it does. Possibly, in some precisifications of the epistemic state (i.e. set of Base-worlds) common to my fellow speakers, it does. But in actual communication, the issue just doesn't arise. We live happily by leaving the matter unsettled: in Base-worlds we assume that *water* is undefined for water molecules.

So here is a formal candidate for a useful notion atomicity, relevant for counting. A property P is count iff there are (possible) Base-worlds w, in which $AT(P)_w$ is non-empty and, for any precisification w' of any base world w, $AT(P)_w \subseteq AT(P)_{w'}$. A property is mass iff it is not count. Being not count entails that what may qualify as a smallest P-sample in some base world w turns out to be an aggregate (i.e. a sum of smaller P-samples) in some precisification thereof. Any non-empty property P has a non-empty generator set AT(P) in some base world w; only count properties have *stable* generator sets, for which I will use the boldface **AT**(P), which grow monotonically across precisifications:

(5) a. $AT(P) = \lambda w \lambda x\ P_w(x) \land \forall y[P_w(y) \land y \leq x \to x = y]$ P-atoms
     b. $\mathbf{AT}(P) = \lambda w \lambda x\ P_w(x) \land \forall y \forall w'[w \propto w' \land P_{w'}(y) \land$ Stable P-atoms
        $y \leq x \to x = y]$
     c. Modified definition of numerals
        i. $3 = \lambda P: *(\mathbf{AT}(P)) = P.\ \lambda w \lambda x\ \exists Y\ [\ Y \subseteq P_w \land |Y| = 3 \land x = +Y]$
           (Plural agreeing languages; e.g. IE languages)
        ii. $3 = \lambda P: \mathbf{AT}(P) = P.\ \lambda w \lambda x\ \exists Y\ [\ Y \subseteq P_w \land |Y| = 3 \land x = +Y]$
            (Singular agreeing languages, e.g. Ugro-Finnish, and
            Type II–III languages)

AT(table) (or *AT(heap)*)[8] by hypothesis/definition is non empty, in at least some possible Base-worlds; *AT(water)* by hypothesis/definition is empty in any Base-world. Numerals need stable atomicity to work in construction with a property, as seems plausible enough and spelled out in (5c). Accordingly, *three (bears)* is a well-defined, contingent property, but *three(water)* is going to be the logically empty property.[9]

Base-worlds for *water* are worlds in which *water* is true of vaguely specified (e.g. droplet-sized or perhaps even larger) amounts of water. This entails that minimal water amounts are going to overlap, a feature the present approach shares with, e.g., Landman's (2011, 2016) take. However, natural Base-worlds for *rice* or *sand* include some in which we regard whole grains as minimal rice

---

[8] I refer to Chierchia (2010, 2017) for a discussion of the conceptual and formal differences between mass nouns with vague atoms and inherently vague concepts like *heap* or *cloud* with context-dependent but stable atoms).
[9] See Gajewski (2002, 2009) and Chierchia (2013, ch. 1) a.o. for how logical falsehood may systematically give rise to ungrammaticality.

amounts, and we leave, e.g., half grains in the vagueness band. In such worlds, minimal rice amounts are *not* going to have material overlaps. I regard this as a plausible consequence of the view just sketched, and as a (small) advantage over Landman's theory that links massiness to overlap.[10] Be that as it may, readers are welcome to replace, for the purposes of the following discussion, the present notion of stable atomicity with their preferred one and explore the extent to which the goal of achieving a restrictive theory of cross-linguistic variation may be reached.

2.2. Ambiguous Concepts and Reconceptualization

Armed with *some* formally explicit notion of count vs. mass property, we can tackle the issue of ambiguous nouns like *rope, beer,* or *chicken*. The basic idea is that the relevant concepts come in related pairs. On the one hand, *rope* is associated with a sharp enough notion of minimal unit: any continuous, undetached string of material suitable for tying occurring in nature. On the other hand, it also comes with a more vaguely specified notion of amount of rope, possibly undetached from a larger rope portion, in principle sufficient to tie up something. By the same token, *chicken* on the one hand can be used to talk about whole animals, and on the other hand to talk about chicken parts, viewed primarily as food. Similarly for *beer,* etc. Much work on the count–mass distinction (e.g., Pelletier and Schubert 1989/2003; Landman 1991; Krifka 1994) provides us with a natural way of thinking of this phenomenon in terms of (partial) functions that link a mass or count property P to its natural counterpart:

(6) a. Packaging: For any property mass property P_M, $\Sigma(P_M)$, if defined, is the count property corresponding to P_M
b. Grinding: For any count property P_C, $G(P_C)$, if defined, is the mass property corresponding to P_C
c. 'Axioms' on Σ/G: i. $\Sigma(G(P_C)) = P_C$ ii. $G(\Sigma(P_M)) = P_M$
E.g.: $\Sigma(G(beer_C)) = beer_C$; $G(\Sigma(beer_M)) = beer_M$

An important condition on packaging is that $\Sigma(P)$, when defined, is generally true of *conventional* or *standardized* units of P-amounts, not just of any natural quantity of P occurring in nature. For example, if $beer_M$ is mass, $\Sigma(beer_M)$ is true of glasses or bottles of beer, not of drops or puddles thereof.[11] In the same

---

[10] Moreover, all group-level nouns like *group, bunch, set, quantity,* ... are going to allow for overlaps in their parts while being perfectly count, which forces a theory like Landman's to distinguish 'bad for counting' overlaps from 'good for counting' ones.
[11] Another standard packager often used is based on the notion of *kind* or *type of P,* exemplified in sentences like:

(a) There are only three wines I like, pinot, chardonnay, and malbec.

Adding it to the present framework presents no particular problem.

spirit, if $chicken_C$ is count, $G(chicken_C)$ is true of chicken parts that qualify as food (e.g., it wouldn't apply to, say, chicken blood, or to chicken DNA).

The way in which one can imagine these morphisms to be used is that each community of speakers adopts slightly different variants $\Sigma, \Sigma', \Sigma'', \ldots G, G', G'', \ldots$ of packaging and grinding functions, defined for different properties, perhaps in slightly different ways. For example, standard Italian uses systematically a count version of the noun for *hair*, namely $hair_C = \Sigma(hair_M)$; it doesn't really use $hair_M = G(hair_C)$; so we could say $G_{ITALIAN}(hair_C)$ is undefined. And one can imagine a society of vampires where $\Sigma_{vampire}(blood_M)$ is defined. Intralinguistically, it looks like use of grinding and packaging may be tied in sometimes idiosyncratic ways to specific constructions. So, as we mentioned, English uses $hair_M$ predominantly, but in it allows *I found three blond hairs* (= $*\Sigma_{ENGLISH}(hair_M)$) *on your jacket*. And so on.

It seems reasonable to speculate that an approach based on packaging and grinding provides us with a good way of accounting for concept ambiguity and reconceptualization. Further formalization of these phenomena, which appear to occur to some extent in every language, may eventually be worked out, but it would be perhaps premature within the horizon of our current concerns. What is important to underscore is that functions like Σ and G, that link variants of closely related properties, bring about a change in the basic units to which properties apply: $\Sigma(beer_M)$ has an extension distinct from that of $beer_M$, in any world. To the extent that Fake Mass nouns like *furniture* apply to *whole* pieces of furniture and sums thereof, and its extension coincides in any world with that of the Italian count concept $MOBILE_C$ '(whole) piece(s) of furniture', treating them via extensions of packaging and grinding would appear to be unwarranted.

2.3. Quantized Properties vs. Sum-Closed Ones; Count Kinds vs. Mass Kinds

In Sections 2.1–2.2 we discussed how count properties like $bear_C$ are taken to be true of individual members of U that retain an atomic status in any world. Quantized count properties like $bear_C$ generate via the star-operator their sum-closed counterpart $*bear_C$. I will stick to the graphic convention using small characters for quantized properties like $bear_C$ and caps for their closure under sum $BEAR_C = *bear_C$. The distinction between generator sets and sum-closed properties has a reflex in the domain of mass properties, at least for some theories. Usually, a mass property is taken to be sum-closed, e.g. $BLOOD_M$. On some approaches,[12] sum-closed mass properties will have a generator $blood_M$ true in any world only for the minimal blood samples in that world, whatever they may be. It is controversial whether generators of mass properties are used in the languages of the world. I will argue below that they are – following

---

[12] In, e.g., all of those in (1) except Bunt (1979) and Link (1983).

Renans et al. (2018) – in languages like Modern Greek that allow for systematic pluralization of mass nouns, with an 'abundance' meaning;[13] such languages are typologically not so infrequent.

NPs in English are property-denoting when used predicatively (e.g., *that is blood*) or to restrict quantifiers (e.g., *I found some gold*), but in some argumental positions they have been argued to refer to kinds:

(7) a. Gold is in short supply
     b. Bears are widespread

No single bear or single piece of gold can be in short supply or widespread per se: these properties have to do with the distribution of instances of kinds across space and time. Considerations of this sort have led to the conclusion that sum-closed properties stand in one–one correspondence to kinds. Kinds can be taken as primitives; but it is also natural to regard them as functions from worlds into the total sum of the instances of that kind. Following this second option, Chierchia (1998a) proposes a way of linking sum-closed properties and kinds:

(8) a. $^\cap P = \lambda w.\ \iota x P_w(x)$ defined only if P is a sum-closed property
        $x \leq k_w$, if k_w is defined
     b. $^\cup k = \lambda w \lambda x.$
        $\emptyset$, otherwise
     c. Examples:
        i. $^\cap BEAR_C = \lambda w.\ \iota x BEAR_{C,w}(x)$
        ii. $^{\cup\cap} BEAR_C = {}^\cup\lambda w.\ \iota x BEAR_{C,w}(x) = \lambda w \lambda x.\ x \leq \iota x BEAR_{C,w}(x) = BEAR_C$
        iii. in short supply$_w$($^\cap GOLD_M$)
        iv. widespread$_w$($^\cap BEAR_C$)

Notice that the $^\cap$-operator is undefined for quantized properties like *three bears* or the singular *bear$_C$*. Sentences like (7a–b) have the logical form in (8c.iii–iv).[14] Kinds on this view are technically individual concepts of type $<s,e>$, but I am often going to abbreviate the type of kinds as e_k. The functions defined in (8a–b)

---

[13] Here is an example, from Renans et al (2018):

(a) Trehun   ner-a   apo   to   tavani
     Drip-3PL water-PL from the   ceiling   'a lot of water is dripping from the ceiling'

[14] The one in (7) constitutes the simplest (and least controversial) form of kind predication, that involves kind level predicates. There are also cases where bare NPs occur as the argument of object-level predicates:

(a) Bears hibernate in winter
(b) Bears were just sighted in this area

On one analysis, the bare nominals in (a)–(b) are still kind-denoting, but they give rise to a quantificational interpretation, determined, essentially, by the aspectual properties of the relevant sentences. Generic sentences like (a) are understood as saying something about all bears; episodic sentences like (b) seem to involve some instances of the bear-kind. See Chierchia (1998a), Dayal (2004) a.o. for analyses along these lines. For comparisons with other approaches, cf., e.g., Dayal (2011).

make explicit an isomorphism between the notion of sum-closed property and that of kind. While a sum-closed property is a function of type <s,et> that in any world maps any sample/instance of the property into truth, a kind is of type <s,e> and in any world directly picks out the maximal sum of what the corresponding property is true of. In a sense, sum-closed properties and kinds constitute different ways of coding the same information.[15] Their types (and hence their logico-linguistic roles) are different; but there is a clear isomorphism between them, which the pair of operations in (8) seeks to capture. This will play an important role in theories of variation. And just as there are count and mass properties, so there will be count and mass kinds, a straightforward consequence of there being two kinds of properties, and an isomorphism between any sum-closed properties and a (certain notion) of kind. This set up can be visualized in the diagram of Figure 2.1.

Most of this apparatus is meant to be weakly theory bound. Every theory countenances count vs. mass properties and some ways of packaging and grinding them; and every theory should have room for some systematic correspondence between sum-closed properties and kinds. A point of controversy is the existence of generator sets for mass properties, which some theories (e.g. Link or Bunt) do not countenance. But the greater controversy concerns how to use an apparatus of this sort in understanding variation across languages (and, I think, also diachronic change). In what follows I am going to refer to structures like those in (9) as 'Base-line (count–mass) structures/theories.'

3. What Varies and What Doesn't

A preliminary general issue should be addressed before getting into specifics. I think most authors would regard Base-line structures like (9) as a 'logic' in

---

[15] The only difference is that in a world w with, e.g., no bears, $BEAR_{C,w}$ is the empty characteristic function, while $^\cap BEAR_C(w)$ is undefined. That's the reason for the disjunctive characterization of the $^\cup$-operator in (8b).

It should also be borne in mind that there are different notions of kind. In particular, Dayal (2004) argues that singular definite generics (like *the dinosaur* in *the dinosaur is extinct*) denote *taxonomic* kinds that have a group-level denotation, distinct from that of regular kinds. Moreover, Carlson (1977a), who has spearheaded the relevance of the notion of kind for semantics, thought that NPs like *people in the next room* are not kind-denoting, on grounds that sentences like (a) are deviant:

(a) ?? People in the next room are rare
(b) People like those in the next room are rare

However, things are more complex than that, as (b) illustrates. In fact, Dayal (2013) suggests that there are reasons for considering NPs like those in (a)–(b) kind-denoting as well, and dubs them 'indexical kinds'. I am going to follow Dayal here and assume that the correlate of *any* sum-closed property is a kind. Predicates like *rare* or *extinct* are sometimes marginal with indexical kinds, because they select for something like 'well-established' or 'regular' kinds, i.e. kinds for which some sort of regular behavior can be contextually identified. This hypothesis enables us to maintain a full-blown isomorphism between sum-closed properties and kinds.

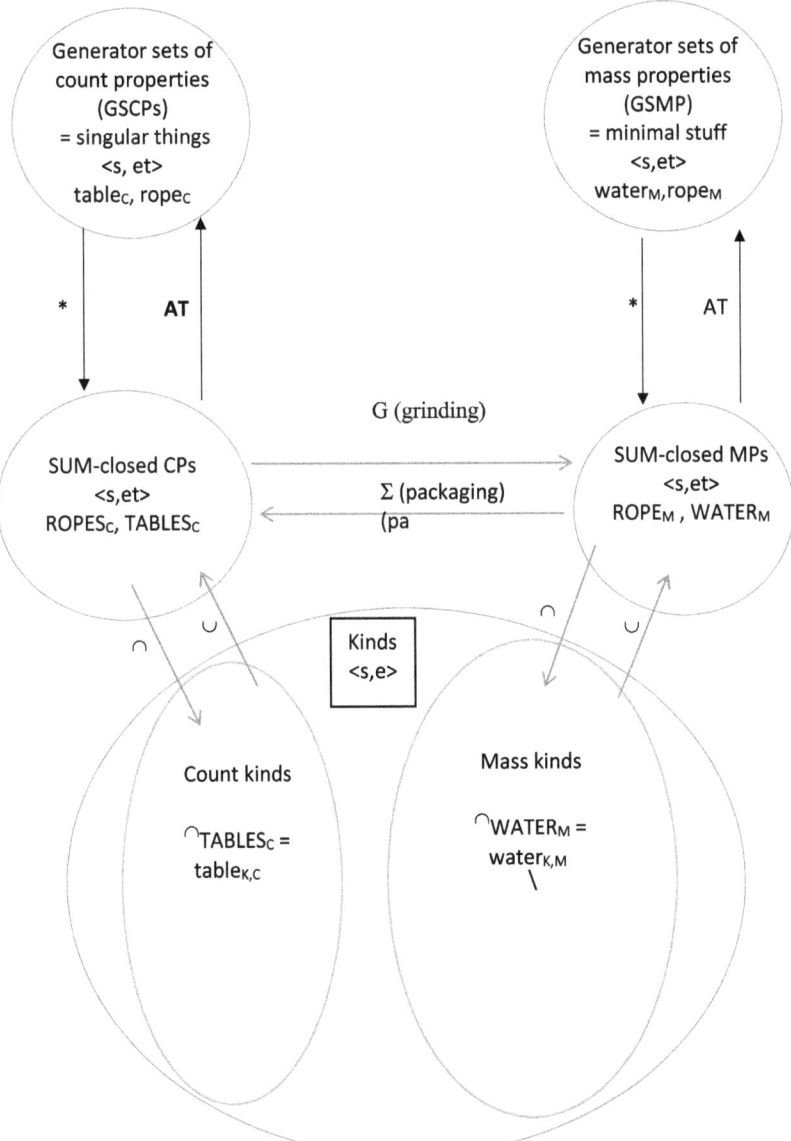

Fig. 2.1: Relationships between sum-closed properties and related kinds

the same sense as, say, Link's classical work: it constitutes a set of categories, with specific relations and operations on them that precipitate a notion of logical consequence, once a mapping onto language is provided. Where this logic comes from remains a matter of speculation for now (certainly within the limits of the present paper). My inclination is to regard Base-line theories as a 'schematism' that supervenes on our natural computational capacities (i.e., something like 'merge' and 'copy-merge' or the untyped λ-calculus) under the pressure of a preexisting conceptual space of 'substances' and 'objects.' To put it somewhat coarsely, our computational endowment enables us to readily cast and generalize the preexisting 'natural' divide between objects and substances. In particular, my notion of atomicity, which is linked to vagueness in a formally explicit way, maps directly onto the notions of 'Spelke object' vs. 'Spelke substance': a Spelke object is something whose identity conditions are clear enough to allow tracking across space, and to enable operations like summation without loss of individuality; a Spelke substance is made up of entities that are not so finely identified (because of vaguer identity criteria). Accordingly, on my approach, a Spelke substance *has* to be coded as mass, a Spelke object *has* to be coded, at some level, as count. In this sense, my theory is arguably more restrictive than its competitors, and any apparent mismatch with the cognitive count–mass contrast is a prima facie problem for it. We will deal with some such apparent mismatches in Sections 3.1–3.2. On any other theory in (1), it seems to me that that the link between the logico-linguistic characterization of atomicity and the cognitive one is way more flexible, and ultimately arbitrary. But the latter is not a picture supported by the available linguistic evidence, insofar as I can tell, and what follows is an attempt to substantiate this claim.

3.1. Classifier Languages

It is useful to start exploring variation through the lenses of Type II languages. Besides being by now fairly well studied, these languages will give us the opportunity to discuss some of the different notions of classifier and classifier phrase that play a role in the count–mass distinction. In Section 2, we gave an analysis of numerals as property modifiers of type $<<s,et>, <s,et>>$, in line with Ionin and Matushansky (2018) and many others. Suppose this is so universally. Suppose, furthermore, that Ns in classifier languages are kind-denoting. It follows that Ns in these languages can never directly combine with numerals because of a type mismatch. One needs to interpolate some operation that affects the type of NPs, turning them into properties to allow for numerals to modify them. And one might expect such type-changing operations to be typically overtly morphologically realized. This arguably provides us with a natural function for classifiers. One very simple way of turning kinds into properties is by extracting their instances via the **AT**-function along the following lines:

(10) a. $ge = \lambda x_k.\ \mathbf{AT}(^\cup x_k)$ Type: $<e_k, <s,et>>$
 b. $ge(ren_{K,C}) = \mathbf{AT}(^\cup ren_{K,C}) = person_C$
   where $ren_{K,C}$ is the (count) person-kind

Classifiers of this sort make Ns capable of combining with numerals, as *classifier+N* combinations like (10b) wind up (i) with the right semantic type to be arguments of numerals and (ii) with (stable) atoms as their extensions (and hence capable of satisfying the atomicity presupposition typical of numerals). Classifiers like *ge* will be undefined for mass nouns, as the latter lack (stable) atoms. Hence the function in (10) constitutes a strong, wholly general candidate for what Cheng and Sybesma call count-classifiers (and are also sometimes called 'individual' classifiers).

There are various lines that can be taken on what Cheng and Sybesma call 'massifiers', by which they mean classifiers that are not inherently restricted to count nouns. With respect to the latter, I will pretty much follow here the line developed by Jiang (2018, 2020). In illustrating it, I will limit myself to a few basic observations and also stick to English as a metalanguage, for ease of illustration. I am going to consider just two main kinds of classifier-functions: measure phrases and container phrases. The former can be exemplified as in (11a), the latter as in (11b):

(11) a. pound: $\lambda x_k \lambda n \lambda w \lambda y.\ ^{\cup}x_{k,w}(y) \wedge \mu_{PD,w}(y) = n$ Type:$<e_k,<n, <s\ et>>>$
Where 'n' is the type of numbers and $\mu_{PD,w}$ is a measure function that maps individuals in a world into their weigh in pounds.

b. $\lambda y.^{\cup}meat_{k,w}(y) \wedge \mu_{PD,w}(y) = 3$

san bang rou
three pound. meat

c. i. yibei = $\lambda y \lambda w \lambda x.\ ^{\cup}cup_{k,w}(x) \wedge fill_w(x)(y)$ Type $<e_k,<s\ et>>$
There were three cups of coffee (on the table) ⇒
$\exists y\ 3(\lambda w'\lambda x.\ ^{\cup}cup_{k,w'}(x) \wedge fill_{w'}(x)(coffee_{k,w'}))_w(y)$
$= \exists y \exists X\ [\ X \subseteq AT(\lambda x.\ ^{\cup}cup_{k,w}(x) \wedge fill_w(x)(coffee_{k,w})) \wedge y = +X\ ]$

ii. yibei = $\lambda x_k \lambda n \lambda w \lambda y.\ ^{\cup}x_{k,w}(y) \wedge \mu_{CUP,w}(y) = n$ Type:$<e_k,<n, <s\ et>>>$
John drank three cups of tea ⇒
$\exists y[^{\cup}tea_{k,w}(y) \wedge \mu_{CUP,w}(y) = 3 \wedge drank_w(y)(john)]$

A measure phrase combines with a kind k and a numeral n and returns a property true of individuals or sums of kind k that measure n, by some specific measure, in this case a weight-based one. To say that an individual (or a sum) x weighs n pounds is to say that it can be partitioned into n one-pound-sized parts.[16] As can be seen by the types in (11), the inputs and outputs of measure

---

[16] I.e., given that n = $<<s\ et>, <s\ et>>$, we define $\mu_{PD,w}(x) = n$ as follows

(a) $\mu_{PD,w}(x) = n =_{df} n(\lambda w'\lambda y\ \exists\ \Pi_{PD}\ [\ \Pi_{PD,w'}(x)(y)])(w)(x)$

where Π_{PD} is a function that maps an individual (or sum) x in a world w into a set of non-overlapping and jointly exhaustive parts of x each weighing one pound.

phrase classifiers are the same as those of count-classifiers, but the former have a number as an additional argument. The function in (11a.i) naturally goes with the constituency in (11a.ii), which appears to be well motivated for languages like Mandarin, but will require some local modification for other languages. Container-phrase classifiers are very varied and have several readings (see Rothstein (2016), Jiang (2020), and references therein), which we will not consider in detail; typically they involve relational nouns (like *slice*, *part*, *quantity*, *head*, ...) or nouns associated with a 'content' (like *cup*, *basket*, *bucket*, but also *drop*, *puddle*, ...). Two recurrent construals of this type of classifier are illustrated in (11b). The first interpretation is in a sense analogous to that of count classifiers, the second to that of measure phrases. The important thing for our purposes is that classifiers employ atomizing relational nouns or measure functions (i.e. functions from individuals into numbers) whereby a numerical value may be attached to entities; consequently, classifier phrases denote quantized properties.[17]

There are three main points of these cursory remarks. The first is that the obligatory interpolation of quantizing functions in Type II languages upon combining numbers with nouns can be understood/explained in simple type theoretic terms: Ns in such languages are kind-denoting, and something is needed to map them into quantizable properties. **AT** is one such function; measure functions are others; container phrases can be used either way (as **AT** forming and as measures). The second point is that one expects, under this type-driven view, that the count–mass distinction will be reflected in the classifier system; in particular, since not all kinds are atomic, the **AT** function will be partial, and classifiers based on **AT** will be ungrammatical with mass kinds. And third, one would not expect there to be Fake Mass nouns, for that would involve making **AT** undefined for some count kind (so that, e.g., *ge* would not apply to them). Thus, the main typological features of generalized classifier languages fall into place, while sticking to the horizon of a strictly universal Base-line theory of the count–mass distinction.

There may well be other ways of deriving the existence of Type II languages from Base-line structures. One that often finds credit[18] is to assume that in these languages Ns are not differentiated between count vs. mass, and classifiers are needed to introduce differentiations that make them useful in counting. On this view, Ns must denote properties P that are 'disjunctive' in that they are true of both P-atoms (stable units) and P-amounts (unstable units). I have two main arguments against this line of approach, one more conceptual, the other empirical. The conceptual

---

[17] Also like *numeral+N* construction, measure phrases will have generalized quantifier variants, to be obtained via existential closure.

[18] See, e.g., de Vries and Tsoulas in the present volume and references therein.

argument is that properties appear to be universally differentiated in mass vs. count, modulo a few potentially ambiguous cases. People, teddy bears, and artifacts come organized in natural units to the pre-linguistic child; sand, water, etc. do not. Does it make sense that upon learning her language the child would obliterate such a robust distinction in favor of a genuinely count–mass neutral notion of *person* or *cat*? The thesis that any property can be count–mass 'neutral' is strongly reminiscent of Quine's (1960) 'ontological relativism' thesis, which Spelke and collaborators have proven wrong. On the present account, the presence of generalized classifiers is type driven and does not affect the cognitive dimension of nouns.

The more empirical argument against the 'undifferentiated property' view is that properties are not of an argumental type: their main logico-linguistic role is that of being predicated of something, or perhaps that of restricting a quantifier. Thus, if the category N is mapped onto properties, one should expect there to be languages in which bare Ns, or at least some subclasses thereof, display a non-argumental behavior, e.g. by being disallowed in all or some argumental positions. We will see shortly that Type I languages are indeed languages where these distributional restrictions on bare nouns occur extensively. But in contrast with this, not a single Type II language has been found that disallows bare NPs, *any* bare NP, from occurring in any argumental position. This is true even of Indo-European languages like Bangla that have developed a generalized classifier system (Dayal 2012). It is even true of those typologically rare Type II, generalized classifier languages that have developed something like a definite article, such as Nuosu Yi, as documented in Jiang (2018). On an approach where the presence of an obligatory classifier is systematically tied to the fact that Ns are kind-denoting, the argumental behavior of Ns is wholly expected and predicted.

3.2. Basic Indo-European: English and Other Type I Languages

IE languages typically have a clear distinction between mass and count NP, where the latter can directly combine with numerals (without classifier phrases), while the former cannot. IE languages also have very extensive singular–plural (and sometimes dual, etc.) morphologies. A natural and widely agreed upon way of interpreting IE-like number morphemes is as regulators of the denotation of the Ns of type $<<s,et>, <s\ et>>$. In what follows I will sketch how a system of this sort fits the Base-line theory, focusing first on count nouns.

3.2.1. Count NPs in IE The following is a fairly standard implementation of the idea that number morphology 'regulates' NP denotations (cf. e.g. Sauerland 2003; Sudo 2014):

(12) a. i.

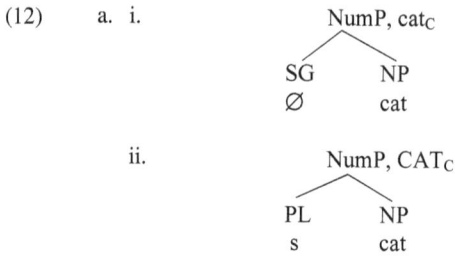

ii.   NumP, CAT$_C$
                    PL   NP
                      s   cat

b. i. SG = $\lambda P: \mathbf{AT}(P) = P.P$
    ii. PL = $\lambda P: {*}\mathbf{AT}(P) = P.P$

The trees in (12a) specify the syntax of number phrases (NumPs). The (functional) head of the phrase is the number morpheme, into which the (lexical) head of NP incorporates, via head-raising. The SG morpheme is interpreted only once,[19] but can be 'exposed' in multiple morphemes scattered throughout the DP (as is overtly visible in, e.g., Romance languages), and triggers agreement phenomena on the VP. The semantics of number morphemes is that of restricted identity maps: they introduce presuppositions. The presupposition of singular NPs is that they are true of P-atoms (where P is the basic denotation of the N-head); the presupposition of plural NPs is that they are sum-closed.[20] The *-operator applies freely in the semantic composition, but the semantics of number features guarantees that the outcome is the correct one, so that, e.g., the singular NP *cat* winds up denoting the atomic property cat_C and the plural NP *cats* the sum-closed property CAT_C, as annotated on the trees in (12a).

This hypothesis on the interpretation of number features is predicated on the assumption that, unlike what happens in generalized classifier languages, Ns in IE are property-denoting (and not kind-denoting). An immediate consequence of this assumption is that (bare) NPs in IE cannot occur in argument position, without their denotation being further compositionally modified. This is a welcome result. Some IE languages, like French, virtually disallow bare arguments in any position. Others, like English, disallow bare singular count NPs, but allow bare plurals. The latter circumstance is probably due to the covert use of argument forming operators, as in the following example:

---

[19] We make this assumption for simplicity. See Sudo (2014) for the view that each occurrence of *number* is meaningful.
[20] The actual semantics of plurality and singularity in full-blown sentences is much richer than what we can get into here. It requires among other things resorting to implicatures. See e.g. Spector (2007), and references therein.

(13) a. Cats are common
b.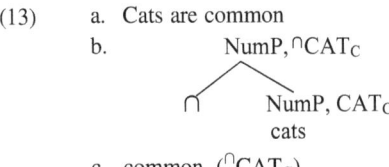
   NumP, ∩CAT_C
   ∩   NumP, CAT_C
       cats

c. common_w(∩CAT_C)

The covert availability of the argument forming operator '∩' is clearly a language particular option. It is immaterial for the present purposes whether this option is realized via a phonologically null determiner D, or by simply adjoining a null operator to NumP (as in (13b)). Notice that since '∩' is restricted to sum-closed properties, this immediately predicts that bare singulars are disallowed in English.

The details of how argument formation takes place across various IE languages (including those that lack articles altogether and allow generalized bare arguments, like Hindi or Russian) are too rich (and controversial) to be dealt with here.[21] What is important to note is that in (most) IE languages, NumPs are of the right type for combining with numerals; moreover, the presupposition embedded in numerals – that the Ns be (stably) atomic – is appropriately enforced by number morphology, as illustrated in (14):

(14) a. *three cats* ⇒ 3(λP:***AT**(P) = P.P (CAT_C)) = 3(CAT_C)
b. three bloods ⇒ 3(λP:***AT**(P) = P.P (BLOOD_M)) = UNDEFINED

The *numeral+N* combination in (14a) yields a well-defined, quantized property, while the one in (14b) turns out to be deviant. This is a good start. But it rules out too much. Mass nouns have singular morphology. This is visible in English mostly through agreement, because in English the singular morpheme is null. But in many languages (e.g. in all the Romance languages) singular morphemes are overt, and clearly visible throughout within the DP. Number morphemes, on the present hypothesis, are linked to (stable) atomicity, a property that mass nouns lack, and it is not obvious how to modify this assumption without creating havoc with count nouns.

A standard move in this connection is to assume that singular morphology is ambiguous. There is a 'meaningful' one, which combines with count Ns, and a 'meaningless' one, which combines with mass nouns. Now, positing ambiguities is certainly necessary sometimes (and we will see an instance of it in connection with Nez Perce), but it is hardly ever, per se, a source of insight. Moreover, it is very unclear under this view how one would account for the phenomenon of Fake Mass nouns, which, on the present approach, are as atomic as it gets. What could force them to take on the behavior of mass nouns?

---

[21] See Dayal (2011) and references therein.

42 Gennaro Chierchia

3.2.2. Mass Nouns in IE Clearly something in the grammar of number marking needs to be modified for English and (most) other IE languages. One possibility that comes to mind is to weaken the meaning associated with number morphology, say, along the following lines:

(15)   a. i. SG = λP:**AT**(P) = P.P   Original setting (stable atomicity gets checked)
           ii. PL = λP:***AT**(P) = P.P
       b. i. SG = λP:AT(P) = P.P   New (proposed) setting (lack of +closure gets
           ii. PL = λP:*AT(P) = P.P   checked)

On the new proposed setting, SG extracts the generator set from a property, without caring whether a property is (stably) atomic or not. (This will only work for approaches to atomicity in which mass properties do have generator sets.) Similarly, pluralization checks whether a property is closed under sum, regardless of (stable) atomicity. In a language with this setting, we would expect any kind of noun, whether count or mass, to take on both plural and singular morphology. However, numbers have independently built into them a (stable) atomicity presupposition (cf. 5c above). Hence one would still expect mass nouns to be unable to combine with numerals. These seem to be features of Greek, where indeed mass nouns do *not* combine with numerals, but do pluralize freely, with an abundance interpretation. The latter should arise as an implicature, much like the *more than one* implicature comes about for plural count nouns (cf. Renans et al. 2018). So maybe the settings in (15b) do characterize some languages. But not English, nor the majority of IE languages.

For the latter, I am going to adopt an idea due to Giorgio Magri.[22] The idea is to turn mass properties into properties that are (stably) atomic but in a sort of trivial manner, through a type theoretic trick which makes them retain their mass behavior with respect to pluralization and counting. That way, the singular morpheme can retain its original setting. Magri's idea is that mass properties P can be coded as singleton properties P_{SGL}, i.e. functions of type <s,et> that at each world are true of just the maximal entity of which P is true (if there is one, else P is empty). One can define a 'singulative' function along the following lines:

(16)   a. SGL(P) = λP:P∈MASS λwλx. P_w ≠ ∅ ∧ x = $+P_w$
       b. Suppose that the extension of P_w is the set {a, b, c, a+b, b+c, a+b+c}; then: the extension of SGL(P)$_w$ will be the singleton set {a+b+c}

Singleton properties are atomic, in that, when non-empty, they are true of just one thing.[23] Note the similarity between Magri's notion of singleton property and our notion of kind: they only differ from each other in a trivial way. In fact, this

---

[22] Magri developed this idea in his undergraduate honors thesis in philosophy at the University of Milan.
[23] Moreover, singleton properties are stably atomic in our sense: since precisifications grow monotonically, AT(P_{SGL})$_w$ has to be included in AT(P_{SGL})$_{w'}$, whenever w′ is a precisification of w.

similarity predicts that our kind-forming operator '∩' should be able to apply to singleton properties generated via SGL, for they are necessarily sum-closed, and therefore different from the regular singular count properties, like cat_C, etc., which will be singletons in some worlds, but not in others. Hence, we expect mass nouns to undergo kind-formation as freely as their count plural cousins, which allow them to occur bare, without determiners, in argument position in spite of being morphologically singular. The general idea is that the SGL function applies freely (like the *-operator). Singular morphology makes sure that SGL applies to mass properties, so that they can pass through the number-marking gate. At the same time, turning mass properties into singletons, while being just a type theoretic maneuver, will have consequences on semantic composition. I will now sketch the main ones, if only in informal terms. Since singleton properties are trivially closed under sum, it makes sense that the *-operator (i.e. pluralization) should not apply to them, on the ground that languages dislike trivial applications of morpho-semantic operators. Moreover, the cardinality of singleton properties P_{SGL} is clearly logically determined: whenever non-empty, they necessarily contain one P_{SGL}-atom. This seems to constitute a plausible enough reason why they should be unable to combine with numerals. The numeral *one* is logically true of them, and any other numeral is logically false. These consequences of resorting to SGL (lack of pluralization, impossibility of combining with numerals) give us the basic behavior of mass nouns.[24]

A further bonus of treating mass properties as singletons is that it creates a very natural niche for Fake Mass nouns: they too can be treated as singleton properties. This readily explains why they pattern with mass nouns with respect to pluralization, combination with numerals, quantification, etc., while retaining their atomic structure vis-à-vis less linguistically driven mental operations. In a sense, the existence of Fake Mass nouns can be viewed as a copy-cat effect, a type-theoretic re-dressing of cognitively count properties: the SGL function, which is independently available for mass nouns, is idiosyncratically extended to some sum-closed atomic properties.[25] The functional effect of this move is to de-emphasize their inherent atomicity: once a

---

[24] Treating mass properties as singletons also requires some adjustments in how modification and quantification gets implemented. For example, the DP *some clean water* must have a denotation along the following lines:

(a)   Some clean water ⇒ $\lambda P \exists y \exists x [water_w(x) \wedge y \leq x \wedge clean_w(y) \wedge P_w(y)]$

Arguably, these adjustments are independently needed for partitives (some of the water/apples).

[25] It is straightforward to extend the SGL so as to include some count, sum-closed properties:

(a) $SGL^+(P) = \lambda P:P \in MASS \cup D. \lambda w \lambda x. P_w \neq \emptyset \wedge x = +P_w$
      Where D is a subset of the set of sum-closed count properties such that $FURNITURE_C$, $JEWEL_C, \ldots \in D$

Which count properties are coded as fake-mass has to be learned by the child on a case-by-case, language-particular basis, which seems to be correct.

sum-closed property is turned into a singleton one like *furniture*, the definite description *the furniture* will have to refer to the totality of furniture around; it won't be able to carry the uniqueness presupposition associated with true singulars like *the table*. That is, we won't be able to use *furniture* to readily pick out singularities. This makes Fake Mass nouns particularly suitable for superordinate nouns, which collapse together more basic categories (like *table*, *chair*, etc.). An approach based on a type-theoretical re-dressing like the present one also makes sense of the fact that there doesn't appear to be any truth-conditional/referential difference whatsoever when a noun is coded in its canonical singular/plural count way (like Italian *mobile/i*) and when it is coded as Fake Mass (*furniture*). Everything appears to kind of fall into place, and we have a plausible account of a phenomenon of an apparent grammar–cognition mismatch.

The present take also has interesting cross-linguistic consequences. The phenomenon of Fake Mass nouns ought to be a side effect of the existence of a meaningful, strong singular morphology, and should therefore happen only in languages that do have the relevant morphosyntactic settings, which are not found in, e.g., Type II languages, where pluralization works very differently.[26] Moreover, they should not be found in languages where the singular/plural contrast, while pervasive, has the weak setting in (15b). Since singularity in these languages is not based on stable atomicity, but on lack of sum-closure, there is no pressure to resort to the SGL-function. Languages that allow pluralization mass nouns, therefore, ought to lack the Fake Mass noun phenomenon, and this is indeed the situation reported for Greek.

It may be useful to make a quick comparison with approaches to Fake Mass nouns which have been or could be developed within some of the other theoretical lines in (1). Consider, for example, approaches like Link's or Bunt's. It is really hard to imagine how nouns like *furniture* or *footwear* could be viewed as being non-atomic in the sense developed there: a piece of furniture, say a table, ought to be made up of other pieces of furniture, all the way down. One could say that the sense in which something is non-atomic is conceptual and shouldn't be narrowly linked to our cognitive system. But if furniture can be conceptualized as non-atomic in Link's sense, then surely any (other) Spelke object also could, equally well. And we basically lose the connection between the grammatical count–mass contrast and the parallel one that seems to hold in pre-linguistic cognition, not to mention the fact that one would expect the phenomenon of Fake Mass to occur randomly across any language. But it seems, instead, that it is tied to rather specific grammatical settings. Similar considerations apply, it would seem, to overlap based

---

[26] See, e.g., Jiang (2017) for the syntax and semantics of plurals in Mandarin.

approaches, like Landman's. Furniture or kitchenware do not overlap more for English than for Italian speakers. But Italian has both a literal Fake Mass counterpart to *furniture* (namely, *mobilia*) next to a perfectly count near synonym (*mobile/i*), and lacks altogether a Fake Mass counterpart to *kitchenware, footwear*, etc. Now, in spite of this, one might try to develop a line where closely related concepts lexicalize different components of some natural class of objects: *mobile* goes for single, whole pieces of furniture, *mobilia* goes for sets of pieces of furniture that allow for overlap, somehow. Again, if this is so, Fake Mass nouns should be possible in any language, regardless of whether a language has a strong singular/plural morphology. The evidence we have so far does not support this expectation.

We have illustrated in broad strokes an approach to IE languages that at its core is fairly uncontroversial: Ns are property-denoting; number features operate on properties and trigger presuppositions of singularity/atomicity vs. plurality. In these languages Ns clearly fall into two distinct categories, which we accounted for with the simple idea that numbers are property-modifiers with an atomicity presupposition built in. A problem that comes up in this connection is the role of singular morphology: it imposes atomicity requirements on count nouns (e.g., *the table* has a uniqueness presupposition that must be determined by its being singular), but no such requirement, it seems, on mass nouns. The standard move in this connection is to hypothesize that singular morphology is ambiguous between a meaningful version and a meaningless one, a move we have considered above. We have departed from this line, and considered what it would take to preserve the hypothesis that singular morphology is always meaningful. How could we modify the notion of atomicity in such a way that mass properties could count as atomic? We have come up with two hypotheses. The first is that for a property to be atomic is simply for it to be not closed under sum. The other is a type theoretic trick that rides on the partially ordered structure of the domain, namely to code a sum-closed property as a singleton property. We have seen that the first hypothesis matches up pretty well with Greek, where mass nouns pluralize but do not combine with numerals; the second hypothesis matches pretty well with English and the majority of IE languages. On this second hypothesis, we have an explanation for the phenomenon of Fake Mass nouns, i.e. an apparent mismatch between grammar and cognition/perception. For *any* sum-closed property, count as well as mass can be coded as a singleton property in an information-preserving manner. So, some count properties can be thus represented in the lexicon and thereby take on the behavior of mass nouns. Clearly, it is in the logic of the proposed system that the inherent differences between mass vs. count properties are never going to be obliterated: mass properties *have to* be realized as singleton ones, to get around singularity checking; count properties can readily pass singularity checking without the extra coding. So, count nouns will choose the SGL option more rarely, perhaps as a device to de-emphasize individuals with respect to their aggregates.

In summary, while the departure from the traditional view that singular morphology can be meaningless leads to a representation of 'massiness' admittedly more complicated than usual, the overall outcome is arguably a more explanatory account, which provides a theory of variation fully in line with the Base-line take on the count–mass contrast.

3.3. Languages with Generalized Numerals: Type III

The main characteristic of Type III languages is that they allow numerals to combine freely and directly with any kind of noun. The languages of this type documented thus far share some other features, besides the behavior of numerals: they lack determiners and allow bare NPs in any argumental position. The patterns of pluralization across Type III languages seems to vary more. From the limited data reported in Lima (2014a), it looks like pluralization in Yudja could bear similarities to that of Mandarin; as for Nez Pearce, there is a fairly detailed analysis of pluralization by Deal (2017), which reveals patterns more similar to those found in IE. All known Type III languages, however, are uniform in the way *numeral+N* combinations are interpreted. If the N is count, no significant difference in interpretation emerges with respect to IE languages: numerals count the 'natural units' identified by N. In combination with mass nouns, contextually relevant quantities or parts or units are counted, which may turn out to be bags, drops, piles, ... This naturally leads one to hypothesize that the generalized numeral option is somehow linked to the covert use of some very general classifier-like element similar to *quantity*. To see what is involved, it might be useful to start with a quick look at how context-dependent classifiers like *quantity* work in English and, on that basis, subsequently turn to Yudja and Nez Perce.

3.3.1. Quantity In English, context-dependent classifiers like *quantity* combine with bare NPs (both count and mass – (17a)), in what are known as 'pseudopartitive' constructions. Use in partitives (17b) is also possible.[27] They also allow for an amount/measure construal, such as the one illustrated in (17c), which we will ignore here (see Scontras 2017 for an interesting take on them, consistent with the present approach):

---

[27] Traditionally, the term *pesudopartitive* is reserved to structures of the form *classifier of NP*, where the NP is bare, while partitive is for structures of the form *classifier of DP*, with a full, definite DP.

(17) a. There were two quantities of water/apples on the floor
      b. One quantity of John's blood was used for a transfusion for his brother
      c. I consumed the same quantity of food you did

In all their uses, quantity-phrases create count DPs, which justifies regarding them as context-dependent classifiers. In terms of our approach to atomicity, this entails that the DPs created via context-dependent classifiers of this sort identify stable atoms, suitable for counting. A possible approach, outlined in Chierchia (2010), is via context-dependent functions quantity$_1$, quantity$_2$, ..., unit$_1$, unit$_2$, ..., etc., which partition their complements into countable parts. A function quantity$_{n,w}$ applies to an argument x, which can be a kind, in pseudopartitives, or an individual or a sum of individuals, in partitives; *quantity $_{n,w}$ (x)* is of type <et> and *quantity$_{n,w}$ (x)(y)* holds iff y is a part of x disjoint from any other part z in the same partition *quantity$_{n,w}$ (x)*, and such that the total sum of the members of the partition +*quantity $_{n,w}(x)$* is the same as x.[28] Here is an example of the denotation of the underlined portion of the DPs in (17a–b):

(18) a. In a world w with four apples, a, b, c, d, where a+b are in a basket, and c+d just sitting on the floor:
         quantity$_{3,w}$($^\cap$APPLE$_C$) =   {a+b, c+d}
      b. In a world w where a is the part of John's blood used in a transfusion and b is the rest of John's blood:
         quantity$_{7,w}$(j's blood) =   {a, b}
      c. One quantity of people in that room is very upset
      d. Two quantities of salt in that box were mixed with some other powder

Going via the kind in (18a) in giving the semantics for *quantity* is a simple way to ensure that the property associated with the NPs *apples* or *water* in pseudopartitives are sum-closed, for '$^\cap$' is undefined for quantized properties.[29] The cells in a partition *quantity$_n$* are typically 'maximally connected' sub-units

---

[28] The formal definition, within the approach to atomicity we are pursuing, might go as follows:

(a)   quantity$_n$ = λxλwλz :∃Y∀w'(w∝ w'→ Π$_{n,w'}$(x) =X). Π$_{n,w}$(x)(z)   Type: <e, <s,et>>

The presupposition in (a) ensures rigidity across precisifications. For any x, Π$_{n,w}$(x) is of type <e,t> and partitions x into a set of individuals that jointly make x up. If x is a kind, then the partition divides up its instances; if x sum, it divides it up into its components. If it is a plain individual (as in *a quantity of that apple*) it breaks it down into some of its mereological parts.

[29] In plain terms, I am assuming that the bare NP underlined in a pseudopartitive like (a) is kind-denoting:

(a)   Two kilos/baskets of rice/apples

Nothing of any substance changes if it turns out that it is better to regard it as a sum-closed property, instead.

Recall also that we are using here a notion of kind broader than the one usually found in the literature that includes also indexical kinds. See fn. 14.

of the relevant totality (like baskets, puddles, piles, ...), but sometimes can be more loosely identified (as in, e.g., (18d)).

One feature of quantity-phrases in English is that when they apply to a *count* noun P_C it yields a partition that does *not* coincide with the one in P-atoms. Something like *there are three quantities of apples on the table* virtually never means *there are three apples on the table*. This is very natural: if we want to talk about apple-atoms, the basic noun suffices, and so quantity-phrases are used to get at a different quantization of apple aggregates. Bear this detail in mind as we consider Yudja or Nez Perce.

There are many imaginable variants of the analysis just sketched that might work for our purposes. All we have tried to provide here is an approach to context-dependent classifiers which is compatible with the (English) data and explicit enough to test the claim that they have covert counterparts in generalized number languages, to which we now turn.

3.3.2. Yudja In Chierchia (2015), I have begun to explore a rather simple-minded approach to Yudja, which is, however, consistent with data presented in Lima (2014a), insofar as I can tell. The basic idea is that Yudja is a kind-oriented language like Mandarin (and therefore, ultimately, a Type II language), which has only one very general classifier that recruits a null counterpart to something like $quantity_n$. This classifier goes unexpressed precisely because it is so general. Consider:

(19) Txabïu   ali   eta   awawa
      three   child sand get
      'Children got three sand(s)'
      (The) children got three containers with sand

For the present purposes, and in line with Lima (2014a), we assume that the numeral *txabïu* 'three' and the N *eta* 'sand' in (19) form underlyingly a constituent as in (20), a constituent which is then split up by movement (presumably, leftward float of the numeral):

(20)   a.   ClP (= Classifier Phrase)
               /   \
           NumeralP   ClP
              | /   \
           txabïu   Δ_n   NP
                             |
                         eta 'sand'

b. $\Delta_n(k) = \begin{cases} AT(^\cup k), \text{ if defined} \\ quantity_n(k), \text{ otherwise} \end{cases}$

The null classifier notated as Δ_n in (20a) is interpreted as in (20b). If the null classifier Δ_n combines with a count noun, as in, say, *txabïu ali* 'three + child', it respects its natural atomicity, so that *three + child* never means 'three aggregates of children' or 'three parts of a child'; it just means 'three children.' If, on the other hand, Δ_n combines with a mass noun, like *eta* 'sand', it will acquire the meaning of some contextually salient, natural partition of the (relevant) sand. The null quantifier differs from its overt counterparts, like *quantity of* in English in that the latter typically overrides the atomicity of its argument, and re-calibrates it into something else, as we saw in Section 3.3.1, while the null classifier Δ_n doesn't seem to allow that. The hypothesis of a null atomizing function constitutes a way of understanding why all nouns in Yudja freely combine with numerals, and also why they are interpreted the way they are. It is also readily consistent with the possibility of having generalized bare arguments (because every N is kind-denoting, and hence argumental) and the extreme scantiness of plural marking. Further work is of course needed to verify/falsify this hypothesis.

3.3.3. Nez Perce One of the ways in which Nez Perce differs from Yudja is in having apparently a richer system of number marking, which we will now summarily describe (referring for details to Deal's 2017 work, from which all examples are taken).

(21)   The number marking system in Nez Perce.
    a. Plural is overtly marked on:
       i. Animate Ns:
          'aayat   ha-'aayat
          woman-SG woman-PL
      ii. Some adjectives:
          ki-kuckuc taam'am
          small-PL   egg
    b. The quantifier-system of Nez Perce is constituted by the following Qs:
       'oykala   la'am   'ileni   miil'ac   tato's
       all$_1$ all$_2$ a lot   a few/little some of (partitive)
    c. With count nouns, Qs in Nez Perce requires syntactically plural forms:
      i. 'oykal-o   ha-'aayat/   *'aayat
        all-HUM   woman-PL/   *woman-SG
      ii. 'oykala   *kuu'pnin/ k'i-uupnon'   tiim'en'es
        all   *broken-SG/ broken-PL pencil   'all broken pencils'
      With mass nouns, we get two forms with different meanings:
      iii. a'ilexeni   cimuuxcimux   samq'ayn
         a lot   black-SG   fabric   'a lot of black fabric'
      iv. a'ilexeni   cicmuuxcicmux samq'ayn
         a lot   black-PL   fabric   'a lot of pieces of black fabric'

There are three main ways in which the singular/plural contrast manifests itself. First, it is overtly marked on some human Ns. Second, it is marked on some adjectives; note that adjectives in the plural form, in combination with mass nouns, induce an atomic interpretation (just like numerals do) – cf. (20c.iv). And third, the Nez Perce Q-system selects for sum-closed NPs: this requirement is evident from the fact that with count nouns, quantifiers select for Ns in plural forms, while with mass nouns, quantifiers go either with the (atomized) plural or with the singular form interpreted cumulatively, similarly to what happens in English with partitives and pseudopartitives. The atomization of mass nouns (when they pluralize) does not involve a count reconceptualization of the latter (i.e. 'standardized' packaging), but some contextually salient partitioning.

In what follows, I will sketch a slight(?) modification of Deal's analysis. First the presence of a fairly articulated number marking system suggests that Nez Perce is a property-oriented language, i.e., in essence, a Type I language, with generalized bare argument formation (like Russian or Hindi). This is so because, as we saw, number marking is generally associated with property-oriented, presupposition-inducing operators like SG and PL. Second, and this is the substantive parameter, number marking in Nez Perce recruits the same atomizing function Nez Perce uses as a generalized classifier. We hypothesize that the interpretation of SG and PL in Nez Perce is as in (22a), with a simple illustration provided in (22b):

(22) a. i. $SG = \begin{cases} \lambda P. \Delta_n(P), \text{ if defined}^{30} \\ \lambda P. P, \text{ otherwise} \end{cases}$

ii. $PL = \lambda P : *SG(P) = P. P$

b.   NumP
     /   \
    SG   NP
          samq'ayn   'fabric'
          tiim'en'es 'pencil'

SG morphology employs Δ_n; in combination with a count noun like *pencil*, $\Delta_n(PENCIL_C)$ is defined and picks the $PENCIL_C$-atoms (i.e., the atomic property *pencil$_C$*) with individual pencils in its extension. Hence, counts nouns are expected to behave pretty much like in English. The quantifiers of Nez Perce require sum-closed properties, so *pencil$_C$* will have to be pluralized to combine with any Q; pluralization will be visible only on animate NPs and on adjectives – cf. (21c.i–ii). In combination with a mass noun like *fabric*, i.e. Δ_n

---

[30] I assume that Δn is polymorphic:

(a)   if α is of type e_k, then $\Delta_n(\alpha) = AT(^\cup\alpha)$, if defined, and quantity$_n(\alpha)$, otherwise

(b)   if α is of type $<s,et>$, then $\Delta_n(\alpha) = AT(\alpha)$, if defined, and quantity$_n(^\cap\alpha)$, otherwise

(FABRIC$_M$) there are two options: either some partition (in terms of, say, pieces of fabric) is contextually salient, and then Δ_n(FABRIC$_M$) = piece ($^\cap$FABRIC$_M$), or no such partition is contextually salient, and then SG lets through just FABRIC$_M$ (i.e. the sum-closed, non (stably) atomic property itself). To satisfy the presupposition of a numeral or of plural marking, however, some salient partition *must* be available. This analysis of SG yields the two options observed with quantifiers when they combine with mass nouns: either the SG marked mass noun has to be the basic sum-closed property, e.g. FABRIC$_M$, or it has to be the sum-closed, atomized (i.e. plural) *Δ_n(FABRIC$_M$). This seems to deliver the observed paradigm.

(23) a. Count Ns with quantifiers
   i. *   'oykala   kuu'pnin   tiim'en'es
            all   broken-SG   pencil
       ⇒ all(SG (broken(pencil)) = all ((broken ∩ pencil$_C$)) = undefined
   ii. 'oykala   k'i-uupnon'   tiim'en'es
            all   broken-PL   pencil
       ⇒ all(PL(broken(pencil)) = all(*(broken ∩ pencil$_C$)) =
       λP. *(broken ∩ pencil$_C$) ⊆ P
  b. Mass Ns with quantifiers
   i. 'oykala   cimuuxcimux   samq'ayn
            all   black-SG   fabric
       ⇒ all(SG (black(fabric)) = all(black ∩ FABRIC$_M$) =
       λP. (black ∩ FABRIC$_M$) ⊆ P
   ii. 'oykala   cicmuuxcicmux   samq'ayn
            all   black-PL   fabric
       ⇒ all(PL(black(fabric)) = all(*Δ_n (black ∩ FABRIC$_M$)) =
       λP. *quantity$_n$(broken ∩ FABRIC$_M$) ⊆ P

Deal convincingly points out that the limited character of the overt evidence available to the learner in Nez Perce provides a strong poverty of stimulus argument in favor of the universality of the count–mass distinction.

Summing up, what we have called Type III languages are characterized by the use of a context-dependent atomizing function that resembles closely classifiers like *quantity$_n$*. Such an atomizing function is essentially identical to *quantity$_n$* for mass nouns, while for count nouns it retains the inherent atomicity of the noun. The atomizing function Δ_n is employed in two ways. If the language is kind oriented, it is employed as a null classifier; if the language is property oriented, it is employed in the definition of number marking. What determines the kind vs. property orientation of the language are the same factors that do so for languages that lack Δ_n, namely the pattern of pluralization (whether it is more similar to IE languages or to generalized classifier languages). The unavailability in languages like English of Δ_n may be a blocking effect in the spirit of Chierchia (1998a), due to the overt presence in English of a rich inventory of overt context-dependent classifiers like *quantity, unit, amount, aggregate*, etc. Whether this last speculation has a real basis is for further research to determine.

4. Summary and Concluding Remarks

The approach to variation in Section 3 is meant to provide more of an existence proof than a conclusive theory, if there ever could be such a thing. The starting point is a Base-line theory in which nouns are interpreted 'naturalistically', i.e. each noun has a natural atomicity or inherently lacks it (or else, it is inherently ambiguous between a mass vs. count variant viz. G/Σ), with rather minimal, culturally driven variations (like, e.g., *bear* is predominantly count in English, but might be ambiguous in a bear-eating society). Grammatical variation comes from two sources: type theory and covert use of grammatical resources. Their respective roles can be summarized as in the following scheme:

(24) **Property-oriented**   **Kind-oriented languages**   **Availability**
      languages   **of Δ_n**
      Most IE languages (Type I)   Classifier Languages (Type II)   NO
      Nez-Perce   Yudja   YES, Type III

In this analysis, Type III languages cut across Type I and Type II languages.

Property-oriented languages are subject to further variation in the way number is interpreted. Here is what we found:

(25) Variation number marking
      a. English (and most IE languages)
         i. SG = λP:**AT**(P) = P.P
         ii. PL = λP:*SG(P) = P.P
            - No numerals with mass nouns
            - No pluralization of mass nouns
            - Presence of Fake Mass Ns (SGL function is active)
      b. Greek
         i. SG = λP:AT(P) = P.P
         ii. PL = λP:*SG(P) = P.P
            - No numeral with mass nouns
            - Pluralization (of 'abundance') of mass nouns
            - No Fake Mass Ns (SGL inactive)
      c. Nez Perce
         i. SG = λP. Δ_n(P), if defined; λP. P, otherwise
         ii. PL = λP:*SG(P) =P.P
            - Numerals with any kind of Ns
            - Pluralization of mass noun (with a quantity of interpretation)
            - No Fake Mass Ns (SGL inactive)

Note that each characterization of singularity has its plausibility. English has the strongest one: a property P is true of some individual u only if that individual can be regarded as *one* P-atom. The SGL-function is activated by

Mass vs. Count 53

the strictures of this characterization. Greek opts for the notion of not being sum-closed (anti-cumulativity). This allows mass nouns to pluralize, while still banning combination with numerals. Nez Perce uses atomization in the form of the covert classifier Δ_n, which retains the atomic character of count nouns but introduces context-dependent atomizations of mass nouns; when no atomization is pragmatically available, mass nouns are let through in their more natural forms, as sum-closed, non-atomic properties – this is the 'ambiguous singular morphology' option. And there are surely other plausible microvariations in what makes a noun singular/atomic. The notion of *plural*, on the other hand, remains constant, as is the sum-closure of the singular, and hence a function of the latter.

There are various ways of implementing the kind- vs. property-orientation of languages. The one we will suggest here is to assume that the interpretation of the noun root, e.g. $\sqrt{}$ *woman* in English or its counterpart $\sqrt{}$ *nürén* in Mandarin, is unspecific among its natural semantic interpretations, which include the set of woman-atoms, the sum-closure of the latter and the corresponding kind (cf. (26a)). A nominal root is then merged with little n, a merger that drives the rest of the syntactic derivation as in (26b), as proposed within the 'Distributed Morphology' approach – see Lima (2014a), Deal (2017). The semantic role of little n is similar to the role of functional heads: it introduces a (language specific) presupposition. This presupposition determines the type of the noun denotation that the part takes along into any further semantic compositions higher up in the syntactic derivation, such as a property or a kind.

(26) Noun interpretation and Distributed Morphology
  a. ‖$\sqrt{}$woman‖ = ‖ $\sqrt{}$nürén ‖={woman$_C$, *woman$_C$ (= WOMAN$_C$), woman$_{k,C}$ (= $^\cap$WOMAN$_C$)}
  b. kind orientation

  $$n, \lambda x_k.x_k(\|\sqrt{}\text{nürén}\|) = {}^\cap\text{WOMAN}_C{}^{31}$$

  n, $\lambda x_k.x_k$ $\sqrt{}$nürén, ‖ $\sqrt{}$nürén ‖

  c. $n, \lambda P_{<s,et>}.P_{<s,et>}(\|\sqrt{}\text{woman}\|) = \{\text{woman}_C, \text{WOMAN}_C\}$

  n, $\lambda P_{<s,et>}.P_{<s,et>}$ $\sqrt{}$woman, ‖ $\sqrt{}$woman ‖

  d. i. Kind oriented languages: n $\Rightarrow$ $\lambda x_k.x_k$
     ii. Property-oriented languages: n $\Rightarrow$ $\lambda P_{<s,et>}.P_{<s,et>}$

---

[31] The formula $\lambda x_k.x_k(\|\sqrt{}\text{nürén}\|)$ constitutes a slight abuse of notation. It is to be understood in terms of 'pointwise' function application:

(a) $\lambda x_k.x_k(\|\sqrt{}\text{nürén}\|) = \{a: \lambda x_k.x_k \text{ (a) is defined and } a \in \|\sqrt{}\text{nürén}\|\}$

In Mandarin, little n triggers a presupposition that the interpretation of its sister is kind level. Hence a classifier will be needed to combine with numerals. In English, little n triggers a presupposition that Ns are properties. Which property (atomic or plural) will be further determined by number marking. The setting of this parameter is learned in the way any parameter is learned: through its morphosyntactic manifestations. For example, upon finding out that her language allows direct *numeral+N* combinations and/or that plural is overtly marked and multiply exposed (e.g., through verb agreement), the child will determine that the interpretation of little n is as in (26c).

A fairly simple Base-line theory, which determines a formal notion of atomicity, strongly linked to the pre-linguistic distinction, but more general than it,[32] appears to account for a rather dazzling set of macro- and microdifferences across languages. This happens with no variation at all in the underlying logic of mass vs. count properties and some variation in the *types* a language chooses to exploit (which is a matter of labelling/categorization) together with some variation in which functors may be used covertly. No deep differences in 'mode of thinking' emerge. But some 'zooming in/out' effect in how natural units are put in focus does emerge. One might hope that all forms of semantic variation could be understood along similar lines.

---

[32] For example, the count–mass contrast extends to eventuality-denoting nouns: *knowledge* is mass but *belief* is count. And to abstract nouns: *beauty* is mass, *quality* is count. See Husić (2020) for a very intriguing attempt of extending a vagueness-based approach to the count–mass contrast in the realm of abstract nouns.

3 Counting, Plurality, and Portions

Susan Rothstein

1. Introduction

The goal of this paper is to explore the relation between plurality, discreteness and countability. It is often taken for granted that the singular–plural distinction is relevant only for count nouns, since mass nouns do not have natural plural readings where they denote pluralities of individuals, as illustrated for English in (1):

(1)   a. Cats are lying on the floor.
       b. #Muds are lying on the floor.

(1a) is felicitous with a natural existential reading where the plural gives information about quantity. The sentence is true if at least one and possibly more individuals which are cats are lying on the floor. (1b) does not have this

[Editorial note (all editorial notes by Fred Landman)] This paper is an edited version of the last version that Susan wrote, a manuscript finished a month before she was first taken into the hospital, and three months before she died. The file was called "provisional final version". She had told me that she thought very little needed to be done still, but since we were both extremely busy at the time, she didn't go into details (except for some points noted in footnotes below). Normally, she would have made those changes, given it to me for editing and a final round of comments, and then sent it off. As it is, this time I had to do the editing one stage earlier and not long after she died. I have edited all Susan's papers and books in this way since 1992 (she hated proof reading, and was happy with me suggesting little bits of formal cleaning up that she didn't have the patience for), and I can say that the paper I worked on was actually finished. I didn't have to do more than I would usually do anyway; in fact, less, because in other papers I might even at this stage have substantial comments to make which would have led to changes, but I did not have such comments for this paper, which I think is a lovely, mature Rothstein paper. As usual, editing Susan's papers is hearing her voice coming up from the page and entering into a dialogue, which at this stage was moving in its own way.

    [Editorial note] Susan did not write acknowledgements for this paper. She would have thanked the audiences where she presented this material, the students and colleagues in the weekly meetings of her research group at Bar-Ilan; she would have thanked me in a witty way; but her greatest thanks would have been for the researchers that took the questionnaire that she and Suzi Lima designed to the communities in the Amazon region where they did their fieldwork, who joined them at the conference where the results were discussed, and who wrote papers for Lima and Rothstein (2020). And among them, she would have had no higher praise than for Suzi Lima. This paper owes a lot to Suzi's work, their collaboration, and the many conversions they had, and to Suzi herself, who very soon after our first meeting became a dear friend of both of us.

interpretation. To the degree that it is felicitous, it can only be interpreted as meaning that instances of different kinds of mud are lying on the floor: the plurality gives information about the multiplicity of kinds and not instantiations.[1] This reading is not a quantity reading, since "I collected few muds/a lot of muds" tells you nothing about the quantity of mud collected, while "few muds" can be exemplified by a lot of mud, and "many/a lot of muds" can be exemplified by what amounts to very little mud. These readings raise a set of independent issues, and since I will focus on quantity interpretations of noun denotations and the contribution of plurality to these quantity interpretations, I will ignore kind readings in this paper.

The contrast in (1) correlates with the fact that count nouns can be modified by numerals while mass nouns cannot. In English, count nouns modified by *one* are in the singular form while count nouns modified by *two* and above are in the plural. In (2a), the numeral gives information about the quantity of cats on the sofa. (2b) is infelicitous without heavy contextual support indicating why it is plausible to talk about types of mud, and the numeral does not give any information about the quantity of mud on the sofa, only about the number of types of mud. A mass noun can be combined with a numeral only when a classifier or expression indicating a measure unit is used. In the counting expressions in (2c), *puddle* and *item* characterise the individual portions of mud and furniture which are being counted.[2]

(2)   a. There is one/a cat on the sofa.   There are two/three/many cats on the sofa.
       b. #There is one/a mud on the sofa.   #There are two/three/many muds on the sofa.
       c. There is one puddle of mud.   There are two items of furniture in the room.

There are cases like (3), where a mass noun does pluralize and can be modified by a numeral.

(3)   We ordered here two coffees, three beers and one water.

---

[1] [Editorial note] This is a paragraph that Susan wanted to reformulate in the light of our discussions concerning attested examples like (i), from my then-forthcoming book (Landman 2020), where the available reading of "mud" does not involve different *kinds* of mud, but different *samples* of mud:

(i)   Edzwald and O'Melia's analyses of *three muds* from the Pamlico estuary (N.C.) indicate the stability of *the natural muds* (...) is lowest in the upstream, fresh water part of the estuary.

[2] Rothstein (2009, 2011, 2016, 2017) argues that individual classifiers such as those in (2c) and mensural classifiers such as *kilo, liter* etc. are of different types and interact with numerals in different ways.

These are considered to be standardized portion readings. The noun seems to have shifted from a mass noun to a count noun because of the specific "restaurant context".

It is often assumed (e.g. Chierchia 1998a, 2010) that plurality and countability are necessarily related. One way of expressing this might be as follows. Counting the number of cats involves determining how many individual cats there are. "There are four cats on the sofa" is true if the plural individual on the sofa is made up of four discrete, non-overlapping single individual cats. It is thus natural that the set of individual cats is grammatically salient and marked in contrast to the plural set. Since we do not count mud, and mud does not come in inherently individuable stable units, there is no set denoting single units of mud and the singular–plural contrast is not relevant. In (3), the plural marker indicates that the noun has shifted to a count interpretation. Theories differ as to why *mud* is mass and why, unlike *coffee* or *water*, it cannot shift to a count interpretation, but the assumption that the lack of countability and the lack of pluralization are related is pretty widely assumed, as we will see below.

The goal of this paper is to explore the relation between countability and plurality, especially in examples like (3). There are two possible analyses of these examples. One is that the noun has shifted to a count noun, and therefore pluralizes, and the second is that pluralization has in some sense coerced the mass noun into a count noun reading. As we will see, these two analyses are not equivalent, since the second requires a plurality operation to presuppose a set of discrete individuals on which it can operate. We shall show that plurality in English is not presuppositional in this way, but suggest that in other languages it might well be. We shall further show that plurality and countability are not necessarily dependent on each other: countable nouns are not necessarily marked plural and plural nouns are not necessarily countable.

The structure of the paper is as follows. We begin with reviewing basic properties of the count–mass distinction (Section 2) and of the semantics of plurality (Section 3). The next section of the paper reviews cases of pluralization of mass nouns in two count–mass languages, and proposes a semantic analysis of the data. We then turn to data from a recent fieldwork project on indigenous languages of Brazil which suggests that the semantic properties of pluralization may vary from language to language. These data together suggest that an account of the relation between plurality, discreteness and countability must be much more nuanced and allow for more variation than has previously been assumed.

2. The Count–Mass Distinction

As is well known, the count–mass distinction is a distinction between nouns which can and nouns which cannot be directly modified by numerals, as in (4), and "count–mass languages" is a term used to describe languages which have a count–mass distinction among numerals, for example, English.

(4) a. three cats b. #three sands; #three muds; #three furnitures

A count–mass distinction is usually associated with other grammatical properties. For example, in English, count nouns usually display a singular–plural contrast, independent of the presence of numerals; as indicated in (5), count nouns are modified by *many* and *few*, while mass nouns are modified by *much* and *little*, and count nouns can be the complement of *every*, while mass nouns cannot:

(5) a. many cats, #much cat(s)   b. #many muds, much mud
                                      #many furnitures, much furniture
     c. every cat   d. #every mud; #every furniture

Cross-linguistic variation with respect to the count–mass contrast occurs along at least three different parameters. First, languages with a count–mass distinction may differ as to which nouns are mass and which are count. For example, *furniture* is a mass noun in English, while in Modern Hebrew, the corresponding nominal has both a mass form *rihut*, which translates as "furniture", and a count form *rehit*$_{sg}$/*rehit-im*$_{pl}$, which best translates as 'item/items of furniture'. Second, count–mass languages may differ as to the grammatical properties which characterize mass and count nouns. For example, while in English one asks "How many Ns?" when N is count and "How much N?" when N is mass, Modern Hebrew uses *kama* in both cases. Thirdly, not all languages have a count–mass distinction. For example, in Mandarin no noun can be directly modified by a numeral. All nouns, including those which are typically "count", require a classifier when combining with a numeral, parallel to the English mass nouns in (2c):

(6) a. sān   *(zhī)   gǒu   b. sān   *(píng)   jiǔ
        three Cl$_{small\ animal}$ dog   three   Cl$_{bottle}$ wine
        "three dogs"   "three bottles of wine"

At the other extreme, Lima (2014a) shows that there are languages, *in casu* Yudja, in which all nouns can be directly modified by a numeral, as shown in (7). In (7a) individual pacas (a small rodent) are counted, while in (7b) portions of flour, in context most plausibly bags of flour, are counted:

(7) a. Txabïu ba'ï wãnã   b. Txabïu asa   he   wï   he
        three paca ran   three   flour in   port in
        "three pacas ran"   "there are three (bags of/quantities of)
                                   flour in the port."

3. Plurality

The by-now classical theory of plurality, which I will adopt here, is based on Link (1983). Singular count nouns denote sets of individuals, and plural count nouns denote Boolean (semi-)lattices, i.e. the denotations of the corresponding singular nouns closed under sum.[3] Plural count nouns are thus cumulative in the sense of Krifka (1989).

(8)   Pluralization
      *P= {x ∈ D: ∃Z ⊆ P: x = ⊔Z}
      i.e. the plural operator applied to the set X yields the closure of X under sum.

(9)   PL({a, b, c}) = *{a,b,c} = {a, b, c, a⊔b, a⊔c, b⊔c, a⊔b⊔c}

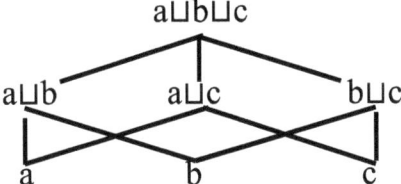

Fig. 3.1: Link-style atomic semi-lattice of plurality

In English, and in many other languages, singular individuals are part of the plural denotation, thus accounting for examples like (10a) as well as "at least one" readings as in (10b):[4]

(10) a. Do you have grandchildren? Yes, one grandson.
      b. I have had students who did not matriculate in maths. At least one.

The plural morpheme marks the operation in (8).

(11) BOY = {a,b,c}; *BOY = {a, b, c, a⊔b, a⊔c, b⊔c, a⊔b⊔c}

In English-type languages, then, the singular–plural distinction marks the contrast between sets of entities with a cardinality of "1" and sets of entities of non-determined cardinality. In mass noun denotations, no such distinction is made. Mass noun denotations are assumed to be closed under sum, i.e. to be inherently plural, or inherently cumulative, and thus plural marking, indicating closure under sum, is irrelevant and/or redundant (Chierchia 1998a). The

---

[3] Link (1983) treats plural count nouns as denoting semi-lattices. Landman (2010) argues convincingly that they denote complete lattices. For our purposes here, this distinction does not matter. While the operation given is the complete lattice operation that adds the minimum 0 to the closure under sum, I will ignore 0 in this paper.
[4] There is no reason why all languages should behave like this, and in fact Bale and Khanjian (2014) argue that in Western Armenian, the unmarked form of the noun denotes the set of individuals closed under sum, while the plural marked noun denotes the set of plural individuals minus the atomic elements.

association between count nouns and plurality is thus assumed to be fundamental. As Chierchia (2010: 108) writes:

the mass/count contrast in number marking languages is typically centred on the distribution of singular versus plural morphology ... in number marking languages the distinction affects the distributions of plural versus singular morphemes.

There is, however, a lot of cross-linguistic variation in the expression of plurality. For example, in Dëne Sųłiné, a Northern Athabaskan language spoken in northwest Canada, there is a count–mass distinction, but no marking of plurality (Wilhelm 2008).

(12) a. *sôlághe dzóä*   b. **sôlághe thay*
         Five   ball   five   sand
         'five balls'

Thus, the grammatical expression of a count–mass distinction does not necessarily require a morphological contrast between singular and plural count nouns.

In the next section, we will examine examples of the converse situation, i.e. languages which have a count–mass distinction where the singular–plural distinction shows up on many mass nouns as well as on count nouns. The examples will be taken mainly from English, with some reference to Modern Hebrew.

4. Pluralization of Mass Nouns in a Count–Mass Language

Cases of pluralization of mass nouns can be divided into two kinds: (i) cases where the mass noun has shifted to a count noun, and has acquired the ability to pluralize along with all the other properties of count nouns, and (ii) cases where the mass noun can pluralize but has not shifted to a count interpretation. We will look at each in turn.[5]

4.1. Plural Mass Nouns which Shift to Count

English has a range of nouns which are flexible and can appear in both mass and count constructions, such as *stone* and *brick* in *not much stone* vs. *many stones, a lot of brick* vs. *three bricks*. The shift from mass to count is apparently free, in the sense that there is no contextual restriction. The count

---

[5] Two other cases which we will not discuss here are: (i) *pluralia tantum* such as *scissors, trousers, alms* (English) and *mayim* "water", *šamayim* "heavens", *ofanayim* "bicycle" in Hebrew, though note that these have formally dual endings rather than plural; (ii) plurals of kinds such as *my three favourite Scotch whiskies*. As discussed above, these are not quantity readings.

noun denotes a concrete portion of the substance denoted by the mass noun. In some cases, such as *stone*, there are no restrictions on what the portions are. In other cases, what counts as a portion in the denotation of the count noun is highly restricted. While stones may be just pieces of stone, bricks are chunks of brick of a standardized shape and size. There is a well-defined subgroup of these nouns where the mass noun denotes a substance which is eaten or drunk, and the count noun denotes a standardized portion of this substance, as in *a lot of coffee* vs. *three coffees*. Bare plural readings and definite expressions are also available with an existential interpretation.

(13) a. The waiter handed out beers and coca colas to all the guests.
b. He handed out the coffees and the beers to the people who had ordered them.

While these nouns are flexible, they can only be used in restaurant contexts, and we refer to them as *horeca* nouns (following the Dutch mass noun *horeca* standing for *ho*tels–*re*staurants–*ca*fés).

Note that flexible nouns, such as those in (13), have all the other properties associated with count nouns, in particular they occur with numerals, with *each* and *every*, and with reciprocals.

(14) a. Three coffees, two waters; three porridges
b. Every beer you drink will cost you five Euros.
c. Each coffee is brewed separately.
d. I see that our coffees are standing next to each other on the bar getting cold.

There are two possible explanations for examples like (13). One possibility is that the mass noun N shifts to a singular count noun interpretation, where it denotes a set of discrete standardized portions of N, and then, as a count noun, pluralization applies in the normal way. The other possibility is to analyse (13) as the result of coercion.

Pluralization is an operation which applies to singular count noun denotations and gives the closure of a set of discrete entities under sum. It can thus be taken to presuppose a set of contextually discrete atoms as an input. When applied to a mass noun, the presuppositions of the plural operator are accommodated, and the mass noun is coerced into an interpretation in which it denotes a set of contextually discrete entities, in this case standardized portions, closed under sum. A similar explanation of coercion would account for (14).

However, the existence of a large range of examples where mass nouns pluralize but the resulting nouns do not denote sets of discrete entities closed under sum and do not have all the properties of count nouns suggests that plurality is not presuppositional in the way just outlined. We look at these examples in the next sub-section.

4.2. Plural Mass Nouns which Clearly Haven't Shifted to Count

There are at least three kinds of mass nouns which pluralize but show (almost) none of the other properties of count nouns.

First, plurals of mass nouns may denote **multiplicities of events**. As Moltmann (1997) notes, plural nouns such as *rains* can be modified by adjectives expressing multiplicities, as in *frequent rains*, although in other respects *rain* behaves like a mass noun, as is shown by the infelicity of (15):

(15) How many rains were there this winter?[6]

While weather mass nouns naturally occur in the plural with eventive readings, the phenomenon occurs with other nouns too, as in (16):

(16) a. He has *depressions* very often.
      b. #He has had *three depressions* this year.
      c. He has had *three events/periods of depression* this year.

Epstein-Naveh (2015) explores the phenomenon in Hebrew, showing that *gešem* "rain" can occur in the plural and be modified by a frequency adjective. The example in (17) shows clearly that the plural *gšamim* "rains" denotes events of rain and is not to be interpreted as an abundance plural of the type we will discuss shortly.

(17) me'at   miška-im   še-megi'im   be-cura   bilti   sdira
      little   precipitation-PL   that-come-PL   in-form   not   regular
      šel   gšam-im   nedir-im   ve-šitfon-ot ...
      of   rains.PL   rare-PL   and-flood-PL ...
      "the little precipitation that come irregularly in the form of infrequent rains and floods"

As (17) shows, these plural nouns can be modified by frequency adjectives which must agree in plurality with the noun. However, unlike the examples in (13) and (14), these nouns show no other properties of count nouns. For instance, numeral modification is impossible.

(18) a. #šlosa   gešam-im   yardu   etmol   /ha-xoref
         three   rain.PL   fell.PL   yesterday/this   winter
         Intended: "there were three events of rain yesterday/this winter"
      b. #gešem   exad   yarad   etmol
         rain.SG   one   fell.SG   yesterday
         Intended: "One rain fell yesterday/It rained yesterday"

---

[6] I found one example on the web of *rains* used as true count noun, namely in a scientific article entitled "Distinguishing in a puddle the water from two rains; a crucial methodological issue", www.ncbi.nlm.nih.gov/pubmed/21300567.

Again, the phenomenon is not restricted to weather nouns and Epstein-Naveh identifies a number of other pluralized mass nouns that may have eventive interpretations. As well as other weather nouns such as *šeleg* "snow" vs. *šelagim* "events of snow occurring", these included *nezeq* "damage" vs. *nezaqim* "events of damage occurring" and *laxac* "pressure" vs. *lexacim* "events of pressure being exerted".[7] Ghaniabadi (2012) mentions similar cases in Persian.

Next we have **"abundance" plurals**. Plurals of mass nouns have been identified in uses which express excess or large quantities, as in (19) (Corbett 2000, using the phrase in Cowell 1964; see also Acquaviva 2008).

(19) a. "Snow looks gorgeous on your fountain – mine is just full of water and fallen leaves as *the rains are heavy today and the winds gusting to 30 mph.*" (http://willows95988.typepad.com/tongue_cheek/2009/01/snowing-in-provence-.html)

b. "Elgar's life was the time when crowds would wait on the white cliffs of Dover to cheer home a line of ships, with names like HMS Formidable, their hulls pulverising the waters, as they advanced *through the fogs of the English Channel*" (www.bmj.com/content/341/bmj.c6965/rr/686305)

Note that the temporal adverb *today* in (19a) and the episodic verb in (19b) mean that *rains* and *fogs* cannot be taken as denoting a plurality of events. Instead, these nouns seem to denote pluralities of concrete instantiations or portions, but, crucially, these concrete portions are not discrete and are certainly not countable.[8] Abundance plurals are widespread: Alexiadou (2011) and Tsoulas (2009) report on abundance plurals in Greek, Ghaniabadi (2012) documents them in Persian, and Doron and Müller (2014) in Modern Hebrew.[9]

---

[7] Acquaviva (2008: 110) quotes an example from Lucretius (*De Rerum Natura* 5.25) suggesting a similar usage with the plural of the Latin count noun *solibus* 'suns', given below in (i). He suggests that the plural noun refers to "sun stages as ever-returning sun-events". Note also a similar usage in Rupert Brooke's poem *The Soldier* in (ii):

(i) Pars terrain nonnulla, perusta **solibus** adsiduis
"a large part of the earth, scorched by continuous suns"
(ii) "Washed by the rivers, blest by suns of home."

[8] Note that *miška-im* in example (16), which appears with the quantity expression "a little" is an example of *pluralia tantum*.

[9] [Editorial note] One of the most beautiful examples of a plural of abundance is *veel waters – a lot of waters*, as it occurs in the translation of Numbers 20.11 in the Dutch Statenvertaling of 1637, when compared with the same paragraph in the English Geneva Bible of 1560:

(i) Toen hief Mozes zijn hand op, en hij sloeg de steenrots tweemaal met zijn staf; *en er kwam veel waters uit*, zodat de vergadering dronk, en haar beesten.

(ii) Then Moses lift up his hande, and with his rod he smote the rock twise, *and the water came out abundantly*; so the Congregation and their beastes dranke.

I include this example here, because Susan would have loved to do so.

Thirdly, we have **plurals of abstract mass nouns whose denotation denotes multiplicity of instances** (Acquaviva 2008; Grimm 2016). Abstract nouns are often pluralized to denote a multiplicity of instances, but like eventive and abundance plurals, these do not have the other properties of count nouns, as shown in (20). Although some cases of these nouns may be found with numerals, speakers intuitions are that they are infelicitous or highly marked:

(20)   a. "The *affections* are more reticent than the passions, and their expression more subtle." (EM Forster: Howard's End)
        b. #My *three affections* are...

Similarly, *harms* occurs frequently in the plural, but *two harms* is marked.

Our generalizations, at this stage, are as follows. In general, mass nouns can pluralize without acquiring all the properties of count nouns, most specifically without being directly modifiable by numerals. In these plural uses, they do not denote sets of sums of necessarily discrete individuals or entities, although they may make reference to pluralities of possibly overlapping quantities or instantiations. There is a specific subset of mass nouns which pluralize and which do occur with numerals. These are the highly restricted portion readings which occur in *horeca* contexts, such as *three beers, two coffees*. Here it seems that the pluralized mass nouns have acquired all the properties of count nouns. Notably, in English and in Hebrew, three properties co-occur: if a pluralized mass noun can freely occur with numerals, then it also has a singular indefinite reading and its denotation involves discreteness. The singular noun occurring in a count context denotes a set of discrete entities, while the plural denotes this set closed under sum.

Let us assume, then, that when a pluralized mass noun has acquired all count properties, it has in fact shifted to count. Pluralization then indicates the application of the standard plural operator in (8) above. The question is, what is the semantic effect of pluralization in the cases where shift-to-count has *not* taken place? We will turn to this in the next section.

5.   A Semantics for Plurals and Count–Mass

We assume the account of the count–mass distinction in which count nouns are derived from mass nouns (Krifka 1989; Chierchia 1998a; Rothstein 2010). In Rothstein (2010), count noun denotations are relativized to contexts. The domain of type e is the mass domain, a join semi-lattice, and root nouns are interpreted at type $<e,t>$ as sets closed under sum. The interpretation of mass nouns is identified with that of root nouns. Count nouns are derived from root nouns via an operation $COUNT_k$, where context k is a subset of the domain of type e, and $COUNT_k$ applies to a root noun at type $<e,t>$ and results in an expression $N_k = COUNT_k(N_{root})$ of type $<e \times k, t>$, denoting the set of k-indexed entities which count as atoms in context k. These atoms are contextually determined discrete non-overlapping entities each of which counts as "one" instance of N in context k. (See also related discussion of overlap in Landman 2011, 2016). Examples are given in (21):

(21)   ⟦stone$_{mass}$⟧ = MASS(STONE$_{root}$) = STONE$_{root}$
⟦stone$_{count}$⟧ = COUNT$_k$(STONE$_{root}$) = {$<e,k>$: e $\in$ STONE$_{root}$ $\cap$ k}

stone$_{mass}$ denotes a set of quantities of stone; while *stone*$_k$ denotes a set of type $<e \times k, t>$, namely:

{$<e,k>$: e $\in$ STONE$_{root}$ $\cap$ k}, i.e. the set of indexed entities which count as one in context k.

While I shall assume this account in what follows, the details are not crucial.

The plural operator, given in (8) and repeated here, when applied to N_k gives *N_k, plural count nouns, the closure of N_k under sum.[10]

(22)   Pluralization
*P= {x $\in$ D$_{e \times k}$: $\exists$Z $\subseteq$ P: x = $\sqcup_{e \times k}$Z}
i.e. the plural operator applied to the set X yields the closure of X under sum.

When pluralization applies to N_k, the semantic effect is straightforward. The question is: what is the semantic effect of the pluralization operation when it applies to mass nouns? We have identified two different situations in the previous section: cases like *the coffees* where the plural noun has all the properties of a count noun, and the remaining cases, such as *rains, affections*, where the noun does not.

Examples like *the coffees* have been analysed as the result of coercion (see e.g. Pelletier 1975; Sutton and Filip 2016b; and many others). The details of how this coercion would work are rarely spelled out explicitly, but a possible analysis would go as follows. *Coffee* is a mass noun. Pluralization applies to count nouns; in other words, it presupposes a count noun input. As a result, *coffee* shifts to a count denotation in which it denotes a set of contextually determined discrete *portions* of coffee. This is the presuppositional account outlined above, and, as mentioned there, I think it is problematic. The problem is that this analysis predicts that *all* occurrences of pluralized mass should be able to shift to a count reading: just make discrete portions available in context, and there is no reason for the shift *not* to take place. As we have seen, this is not the case.

The alternative account that I favour is to assume that in cases like *the coffees*, the COUNT$_k$ operation has applied implicitly and derives a count

---

[10] Where the lattice structure and operations are lifted to $<e \times k, t>$ in the obvious way.

noun denoting a set of contextually determined portions, as proposed in Khrizman et al. (2015). Thus instead of assuming that these cases involve a mass noun with a reading shifted to count, I propose that these cases involve a noun that has shifted to a true count noun. On this analysis, *coffee* in this context is a flexible count noun, just like *stone* or *brick*, but more like *brick* than *stone* since the portions in the count noun denotation are standardized.

In contrast to *the coffees*, where pluralization has been applied to a count noun, I would assume that *rains* and *affections* are derived by pluralization applying to a mass noun. This non-presuppositional account of pluralization allows us to explain the contrast between *(three) coffees*, where the N is a count noun homonymous with a mass noun, and *affections* or *rains* where the pluralized noun remains mass. Of course, what is missing still is an account of the semantic effect of pluralizing a mass noun like *rain* and *affection*.

On the surface, pluralizing a mass noun should have no semantic effect at all. Since mass nouns are inherently closed under sum, pluralization applied to a mass noun is the identity function. However, the discussion in the previous section suggests that there *are* semantic effects to pluralization in the mass domain. The question then is whether pluralization is the same in the mass and the count domain, or different, and how the semantic effects are derived. We examine some possibilities.

The first option is to assume there is a single pluralization operation, as in (8) and (21), expressed by the plural morpheme. The operation applies to a singular count noun denotation and gives the closure of that set under sum. Since the plural morpheme can only apply to a morphologically singular noun, it does not apply to plural count nouns.[11]

The same operation applies to the denotations of morphologically singular mass nouns. Since the input set is closed under sum already, the output is the same as the input, but there are two effects. First, as has been argued in Carlson (1977b) and Chierchia (1998a), mass nouns are ambiguous between a kind interpretation and a reading in which they denote sets of instantiations of the kind. Thus, *mud* can denote either the kind mud or the set of instantiations of mud. Since kinds are individuals and pluralization applies to sets, the pluralized mass noun can only be interpreted as denoting a set of instantiations. The first effect of pluralization is thus disambiguation. This effect is noted in Pelletier and Schubert (1989) and Acquaviva (2008). Pelletier and Schubert suggest that mass plurals refer to "a kind viewed as a concrete sum extended in space and/or time and large enough to be a feature of the environment", while Acquaviva observes that pluralizations such as *fogs, rains, sands* and *snows* "filter out the reading as an abstract kind". He supports this with the following

---

[11] We can see this from the fact that plural nouns denoting sets of single items such as *scissors, trousers*, don't have a morphologically double-plural form.

example, where a concrete instantiation of water can be referred to by either the bare singular or the mass plural, as in (23a), while the kind reading can only be expressed by the bare singular, as in (23b):

(23) a. The river discharges its water/waters into the lake.
b. The formula of water/*waters is H_2O. (Acquaviva 2008: 109)

The second effect is to focus attention on sums of instantiations. Mass nouns are non-atomic, and thus will normally contain contextually determined, but overlapping portions in their denotations. Closure under sum means that sums of these portions are also in their denotations. While such sums are not countable, they are nonetheless contextually distinguishable as sums. Pluralization draws attention to these sums, giving rise to either an abundance implication or to a plurality of instances or event instantiations. This can be thought of as following from Grice's Maxim of Manner. Since a bare singular mass noun is the simplest form of the noun, there must be a reason for using the plural form, especially in situations in which a kind reading is not plausible. Since pluralization is closure under sum, marking the mass noun as plural would draw attention to sums in the denotation of the noun N, i.e. instantiations of N which are either large (= the abundance reading) or multiplicities of instantiations (= sums of events or instances). Thus by choosing *waters* in (23a) we are drawing attention either to the large sum of water discharged into the lake or, possibly, to the fact that the water discharged into the lake is the sum of water from a number of different sources.

A second option is to try and derive the same effects semantically, rather than pragmatically. Fred Landman (p.c.) has suggested that pluralization in the mass domain might be seen as an operation which is related, but not identical, to the operation in (8) and (21). Suppose that pluralization in the mass domain is the operation which Bale, Gagnon, and Khanjian (2011) have suggested as the interpretation of the plural morpheme in Western Armenian.[12] Bale et al. argue that singular morphology in Western Armenian is associated with a number neutral interpretation of a noun N, which is an interpretation such that $N = *N$, i.e. an interpretation that includes singular elements and pluralities, and that plurality forms PL(N), where PL is the operation that maps neutral interpretation N onto $N - N_{ATOM}$, which is the same as $*N - N_{ATOM}$, the plural set minus the atomic elements. As we saw above, this is not the interpretation I assume for plural nouns in the count domain in English. But, plausibly, it is the effect of pluralizing a number neutral, i.e. inherently plural, set. In this case, plurals of mass nouns would denote the denotation of the N minus its minimal elements. The effect would be the same as the effect

---

[12] The operation itself is already in Link (1983), and there is a large literature on its semantic (dis) advantages.

described above: it would force a non-kind interpretation of the mass noun and would force the N in context to be witnessed by *sums* of instantiations or portions, rather than by single portions, thus giving the abundance or the multiplicity of instances interpretation. On this approach, the effect would be derived semantically via the operation *N $-$ N$_{ATOM}$, and not pragmatically.

We will not choose between these two explanations here since both converge on the same main conclusion: plurality is not presuppositional and does not entail either discreteness or countability.

We now turn our attention to the final question to be discussed in this paper: is there cross-linguistic variation in the relation between plurality, discreteness and countability, and is pluralization always non-presuppositional?

6. Cross-linguistic Variation in the Relation between Plurality and Countability

6.1. Variation

In the previous section we saw that pluralization in English is the operation of closure under sum, but does not presuppose discreteness of minimal parts. Discreteness of minimal parts is guaranteed by the count operation. Singular count nouns denote sets of contextually determined discrete minimal elements, while plural count nouns denote such sets closed under sum. Thus, while pluralization of N in the mass domain makes salient sets of sums of instantiations of N, it does not entail that the minimal parts of these sums are discrete. In English (and Hebrew) countable nouns are a subset of pluralizable nouns, and there is no presupposition of discreteness associated with pluralization.

An obvious question is whether this relation between plurality and countability is the same cross-linguistically? In this section, I shall show that the answer is no.

We have already seen that there are languages which have a count–mass distinction but no marking of plurality. The examples are repeated here for convenience (Wilhelm 2008).

(24) a. sôlághe dzóå b. *sôlághe thay (Dëne Sųłiné)
    Five ball   five   sand
    "five balls"

There are also languages where all nouns behave like *coffee* in English, and mass nouns can pluralize and denote sets of pluralities of discrete entities. An example is Ojibwe (Mathieu 2012b):

(25) a. niizh baagan-a b. niizh azhashki-n
    two   nut-PL   two   mud-PL
    "two nuts"   "two chunks of mud"

Counting, Plurality, and Portions 69

But we will focus here on two sets of cases which are very different. One is languages where pluralizable nouns are a subset of countable nouns. The second is languages where pluralizable nouns *do* denote sets of discrete entities or portions, but these nouns are not countable. Together this suggests variability in the relation between countability and plurality.

6.2.   Languages Where Pluralizable Nouns Are a Subset of Count Nouns[13]

We begin with data from Yudja. The Yudja language (family Juruna, Tupi stock) is spoken by a growing community of around 800 people,[14] most of whom live in the Xingu Indigenous Territory in the Amazonian basin in Brazil.

In Yujda all nouns can appear bare, with a singular/plural and indefinite/ definite interpretation:

(26)   Senahï kota   ixu   (Lima 2014a (03a))
       man   snake eat
       "A/the/some man/men eat(s)/ate a/the/some snake(s)"
       literally: "an undefined number of men eat(s)/ate an unspecified number of snakes"

Lima (2014a) reports that all nouns are countable, as shown in (27) and (28). Note that in neither case is there plural marking on the noun:

(27)   txabïu ali
       three   child
       "three children"

(28)   a. txabïu yukïdï
           three   salt
           "three portions of salt"   (Lima 2014a)
       b. Txabïu apeta   pe~pe~pe
           three   blood   drip~RED
           "Three (portions of) blood dripped (in different events)"

---

[13] The data from Yudja are drawn from Lima (2014a, 2016), and Rothstein and Lima (2018) and were collected through a variety of methods including elicited judgements, in depth interviews and psycholinguistic experiments carried out in the framework of language documentation projects in a series of fieldwork trips by Suzi Lima between 2009 and 2016. All data not directly referenced as appearing in published works were collected by Lima on fieldtrips. Most of the speakers who are reported on come from Tuba Tuba village. The data from the other Brazilian languages cited here is drawn from research by a variety of means between 2015 and 2017 in the framework of the project "A Typology of Count, Mass and Number in Brazilian Languages", coordinated by Suzi Lima and Susan Rothstein, the results of which appear in Lima and Rothstein (2020).
[14] Siasi/Sesai, 2014 *apud* Enciplopédia Povos Indígenas no Brasil, https://pib.socioambiental.org/pt/povo/yudja.

As Lima (2014a) shows, examples like (28) are very different from English examples such as *three coffees*, which we discussed above. As discussed above, in English the counting of what appear to be mass nouns is only possible in restricted contexts, namely *horeca* contexts, and only when the portions counted are standardized portions relative to that context. If someone spills a big bottle of beer, a drop of beer and a test-tube of beer in three different places on the kitchen floor, we cannot describe this by saying "there are three beers on the floor to wipe up". In Yujda, this is not the case. Any individuable portion of a substance can be counted directly, and a big heap of salt, a grain of salt and a quantity which would fill a teaspoon together can be referred to using (28a). Similarly, if an injured person moves along a path dripping a drop of blood, a small puddle of blood and a big puddle of blood, this can be referred to as in (28b), using *txabïu apeta* "three bloods". Thus all nouns can be taken to denote pluralities of countable individuals. The individuals need not be stable through space and time, but can be individuable portions which are salient in a given context. Note that while in (28b) the portions of blood are dripped in different events, the numeral must count portions of blood and not the events. The reduplication indicating event repetition is not obligatory in (28b), and furthermore, the numeral has a special suffix when it is used to count events.

There is a plural marker, but it is restricted to [+human] nouns and it is optional. As well as occurring on bare nouns, as in (29), it can also occur on nouns modified by numerals.

(29) Senahï-**I**   kota   ixu
      man-**PL**   eat   snake
      "(The) men eat/ate a/the/some snake(s)"
      Lit.: a plural set of men eat/ate an unspecified number of snakes

In (29), *senahï-i* must denote a true plurality (i.e. singular interpretations are ruled out). Crucially, the plural marker cannot occur on *ixu* "snake". Lima shows that this is a lexical restriction, and is not connected to the grammatical role of the noun. In relevant contexts, [+human] nouns in direct object position can be marked plural, while [−human] nouns are never marked plural, even when they are subjects.

Lima (2014a) suggests that count nouns denote maximal self-connected countable portions. Stable individuals, or natural atoms, denoted by nouns such as *senahï* "men", *ixu* "snake" are "privileged portions", and the noun does not usually denote parts of these privileged portions. But, it seems, the expression for "three bananas" *can* be used to denote three pieces of banana, three bunches of bananas, three individual bananas. The last is the preferred option, which is predicted if natural atoms have a privileged place in the ontology. Crucially, plurality does not mark countability, but seems to indicate a non-singular reading on [+human] nouns.

Yudja is not the only language in which pluralization can apply only to a subset of countable nouns. Bardagil-Mas (2020) makes the same case for Panará. The Panará data are particularly interesting since they raise the question of the presuppositions associated with pluralization.

Panará is a Jê language spoken by about 450 speakers in Mato Grosso. All nouns can occur with numerals. Pluralization, marked by the suffix *mẽra* can occur only with individual denoting nouns, while some speakers prefer to restrict plurals only to [+animate] nouns, as in (30) and (31):

(30) rê-   s-   anpun joopy-mẽra
     1.SG.ERG 3.SG.ABS- saw   jaguar-PL
     "I saw jaguars"

(31) #rê-   s-   anpun pakwa-mẽra
     1.SG.ERG 3.SG.ABS- saw   banana-PL
     "I saw bananas"

Examples like (31) can be repaired by the addition of a numeral:

(32) rê-   s-   anpun nõpjó   pakwa-mẽra
     1.SG.ERG 3.SG.ABS- saw   a few/three banana-PL
     "I saw three/a few bananas"

Despite the fact that mass nouns may occur with numerals as in (33a), they do not usually pluralize as shown by (33b):[15]

(33) a. rê-   s-   anpun **nõpjó**   mõsy
        1.SG.ERG 3.SG.ABS- saw   a few/three   corn.
        "I saw three/a few cobs of corn/portions of corn."
     b. *rê-   s-   anpun (**nõpjó**)   mõsy-**mẽra**
        1.SG.ERG 3.SG.ABS- saw   a few/three   corn-PL
        "I saw three/a few cobs of corn/portions of corn."

In some cases, the addition of the numeral may "repair" the sentence and license the plural:

(34) a. *rê-   s-   anpun kjorinpe-mẽra
        1.SG.ERG 3.SG.ABS- saw   rice-PL
        Intended: "I saw rices."
     b. rê-   s-   anpun nõpjõ kjorinpe-mẽra
        1.SG.ERG 3.SGABS-   saw   three rice-PL
        "I saw three plates/sacks of rice."

---

[15] Bardagil-Mas (2020) claims that all nouns can appear with numerals, although the data presented do not include examples of nouns denoting liquids appearing with numerals.

Crucially, there is a possibility of pluralizing liquid-denoting nouns, but with a very specific interpretation: the plural morpheme coerces an interpretation in which the noun does not denote (portions of) the substance denoted by N, but animate individuals connected with the substance, as in (35):

(35) a. rê-   s-   anpun   nãnpju-mẽra.
          1.SG.ERG   3.SG.ABS-   saw   blood –PL
          "I saw a few girls who were doing the menstruation ceremony."
          Impossible: "I saw (portions of) bloods."
      b. rê-   s-   anpun   nõpjõ   nanpju-mẽra
          1.SG.ERG   3.SG.ABS-   saw   three   blood-PL
          "I saw three girls who were doing the menstruation ceremony"
          Impossible: "I saw three portions of blood."

(36)   rê-   s-   anpun   inta-ra.
          1.SG.ERG   3.SG.ABS-   saw   rain–DUAL
          "I saw two rain-men/men who came with the rain."

In the context of the generalization that for many speakers pluralization only applies to animate nouns, this strongly suggests that the plural operator presupposes that the noun it applies to is [+animate] and coerces an animate interpretation of the nouns in (35) and (36).[16] Crucially, as the examples in (33) and (34) show, numerals can modify mass nouns, in which case the mass noun denotes a plurality of countable portions, but pluralization itself does not induce a discrete portion reading.

As in Yudja, plural markers are restricted to animate nouns and, for some speakers, nouns denoting salient individuals. Note that in (32), the numeral may contribute to making individuals in the denotation of N salient and thus licensing the plural marker. It seems that portions per se are not salient enough individuals to meet the presuppositions of the plural operator.

6.3. Languages in Which Plurality Entails Discreteness (Portion Readings) but not Countability

We have seen so far that plurality does not presuppose discreteness. In English and Hebrew, we saw that both count and mass nouns can be pluralized, but that only (plural) count nouns necessarily denoted sums of sets of discrete entities. Count nouns are thus a subset of pluralizable nouns. In Yudja and Panará, in contrast, plurality presupposes animacy (or possibly a high degree of individuation), and a subset of countable nouns are pluralizable. In this section, we

---

[16] Fred Landman (p.c.) drew my attention to some similarities between the coercion illustrated in (35) and (36) and the coercion to "associated animates" evidenced in plurals such as "The two ham-sandwiches haven't got their orders yet."

examine a third group of languages where not all pluralizable nouns are countable, but where pluralization does entail discreteness.

Sakurabiat (Mekens) is a Tuparian language spoken by fewer than 100 people in the Rio Mequens Indigenous territory. It is endangered, with only fourteen fluent speakers. The data in this section come from Galucio and Costa (2020). Numerals in Sakurabiat modify nouns and do not require plural marking.

(37)   a. kie sakurap   b. turu sakurap
           one spider monkey   two spider monkeys

With relatively solid substances, counting portions is possible:

(38)   a. kie tometome   b. turu tometome
           a puddle of mud   two puddles of mud

(39)   a. kie yẽra   b. turu yẽra
           one meat   two meat
           "one piece of meat"   "two pieces of meat"

With granulated and powdered substances, an explicit container is required:

(40)   a. *kie pereyã   b. kie pereyã aap
           one manioc flour   one manioc flour pot
           "one pot of manioc flour"

(41)   a. *kie kuut   b. kie kuut tek
           one salt   one salt measure/container
           "one measure/recipient of salt"

With liquids, the norm is to use an explicit container phrase. If the numeral occurs directly with a noun denoting a liquid, then a contextually determined container is understood, implying a null container phrase. Free portion readings are not available.

(42)   tuero "chicha;fermented.beverage"
        a. *kie tuero   b. kie kwãe tuero (piro)
           one chicha   one pan chicha (have)
           "(there is) one pan of chicha"

(43)   tuero obaat ese-i-a-t o-kupi
        chicha three/many SOC-come-THV-PST FOC 1SG-sister
        "My sister brought three pans of chicha"

With "water" the container is obligatory, and a numeral modifying the noun is interpreted as denoting "river".

(44)   uku 'water; river'
        a. kie kwãe uku piro   b. turu uku so-a-r-õt
           one pan water have   two water see-THV-PST-I
           "there is one pan of water"   ONLY: "I saw two rivers"
                                              (Not: I saw two pans of water)

The only example of a liquid that occurs without any classifier in the corpus was "blood". Galucio and Costa note that it is also the only liquid marked with a possessive.

(45)   turu   s-au
       two   3- blood
       "two pools of someone's blood"

Sakurabiat has a plural marker -*yat* which has two uses: it can be used as a plural (46) or to contrast a plural with a singular meaning, as in (47). It is optional in the presence of a numeral.

(46)   Aramira   woman
       aramira-yat   women, a group of women

(47)   pedro-yat   Pedro's family

The plural attaches to all nouns (except those denoting animals). Crucially it can attach to liquids and (in context) granulated substances with a portion reading. However, these nouns cannot be directly counted.

(48)   uku-yat   so-at-õt
       water-PL   see-PST-I
       "I saw a lot of puddles of water" (not necessarily a lot of water)

(49)   a. kuut   so-a-r-õt   etu-pi   sayẽ
          salt   see-THV-PST-I   basket-inessive   AUX.distributed
          "I saw salt in the basket"
       b. kuut-iat   so-a-r-õt   etu-pi   sayẽ
          salt-PL   see-THV-PST-I   basket-inessive   AUX.distributed
          "I saw salt (in packages) in the basket"

The portion reading is obligatory, and the plural morpheme in (48) and (49) cannot be interpreted as an abundance reading.

Similar facts are reported for two Karib languages, Ye'kwana and Taurepang. Ye'kwana is spoken in northeast Brazil and Venezuela by around 6000 speakers, while Taurepang is spoken in roughly similar areas by around 670 speakers (Coutinho 2020a, 2020b).

Ye'kwana allows bare nouns (50) and has a plural marker -*komo/-chomo*, which attaches to all nouns except for nouns denoting animals (51):

(50)   yanwa   faduudu   n-ame-i   (Ye'kwana)
       man   banana   3-eat-PRP
       "the/a/some man/men ate a/the/some banana(s)."

(51)   yanwa-komo   faduudu-komo   n-ame-i-cho
       man-PL   banana-PL   3-eat-PRP-PL
       "The/Some men ate the/some bananas."

Pluralization of substance denoting nouns results in a free portion reading of mass nouns.

(52) Marcelo   n-enö-I   **yadaachi-chomo**
      Marcelo   3-drink-PRP   caxiri-PL
      "Marcelo drank portions of caxiri."

(53) **munu-komo**   nonoojo   nato
      blood-PL   floor   3.cop
      "There are many portions of blood on the floor."

Numeral expressions combine with nouns denoting sets of individuals. When the noun occurs with a numeral, it does not pluralize (54):

(54) Marcelo   **äddwawä**   faduudu   n-ame-i
      Marcelo   three   banana   3-eat-PRP
      "Marcelo ate three bananas."

However, despite the fact that bare substance nouns can pluralize and denote sets of portions, they cannot occur with numerals without the intervention of a classifier:

(55) a. Isabella   tuna-komo   neneanä
         Isabella   water-PL   saw
         "Isabella saw portions of water."
      b. *Isabella ädwawa   tuna   neneanä
         Isabella   three   water   Saw
      c. Isabella   ädwawa   chäwötö   tuna   neneanä
         Isabella   three   bowl   water   saw
         "Isabella saw three bowls of water."

Taurepang shows a similar pattern with respect to the relation between plurality and counting. Nouns can occur bare, and the plural -*ton* attaches to all nouns except for nouns denoting animals. These are pluralized using a special plural -*damök*.

(56) a. kurai-ton   ere'ma-'pö-da   b. öynö-ton   ere'ma-'pö-da
         man-PL   see-PAST-ERG   pan-PL   see-PAST-ERG
         "I saw the men."   "I saw the pans."

(57) a. kachiri-ton   ere'ma-'pö-da   b. aro-ton   ere'ma-'pö-da
         caxiri-PL see- PAST-ERG   rice-PL see- PAST-ERG
         "I saw (the) portions of caxiri." "I saw the portions of rice."

Coutinho clarifies that the plural gives a multiple of portions reading and is not an abundance plural. Unlike in Ye'kwana, numerals combine with nouns which are marked plural. (58) and (59) give examples of numerals occurring with plural human-denoting and artefact-denoting nouns:

(58) Seuröwöne kurai-ton etopök wo'nan se'na
Three man-PL went hunting
"Three men went hunting."

(59) Sakörörö canau-ton komemasa'da iwentamato peda
Four canoe-PL built sell POS
"I built four canoes to sell."

However, as in Ye'kwana, numerals cannot be combined with substance denoting nouns, either in the bare or pluralized form (60–61). These constructions require container classifiers:

(60) *U'wi ainapö'ya seröwarö sakörörö
Manioc_flour toast today four

(61) *Sakörörö u'wi-ton ainapö'ya seröwarö
Four manioc_flour.PL toast today

(62) U'wi ainapö'ya seröwarö sakörörö enpakapö'ya
manioc_flour toast today four bowl
"Today I toasted four bowls of manioc flour."

What these data clearly show, then, is that plurality in these two Karib languages and in Sakurabiat induce portion readings, which from the context in which they were used are clearly discrete, but the data shows that this is not enough to allow counting. Thus, the pluralization operation applied to mass nouns results in a set of contextually salient discrete portions closed under sum, but this set is not countable. Plausibly, then, pluralization in these languages presupposes a contextually salient set of discrete portions, but this operation is distinct from the mass-to-count shift, which is either lexical or, as I assume, expressed via an implicit classifier, and which results in a set of discrete *and* countable nouns.

We see then in these languages that pluralization is independent of countability and of the count–mass distinction.

7. Discussion and Conclusions[17]

We began this paper by making reference to widely held assumptions that the singular–plural distinction and the count–mass distinction are closely related. The availability of plural morphology was taken to be a "signature property" of count–mass languages (Chierchia 1998a), and though the existence of languages such as Dëne Sųłiné (see example 24) showed that the

---

[17] [Editorial comment] Susan did tell me that the main thing that had to be done was to rewrite the concluding section, get rid of redundancies, sharpen the conclusion, etc. I have done a bit of that, but not beyond what was really there in the text.

count–mass distinction need not be associated with a singular–plural distinction in mass nouns, Chierchia (2010) maintained both that plural morphology is not expected in languages without a count–mass distinction and that in count–mass languages the singular–plural distinction will target count nouns (although abundance readings of pluralized mass nouns may be available).

Chierchia (1998a) gives the rationale behind the relation between count nouns and pluralization as follows. Mass nouns are lexical plurals, i.e. they denote sets closed under sum. Mass-to-count shift, when it occurs, picks out a set of discrete atomic entities relevant for counting, and pluralization closes this set under sum.

The underlying idea, expressed in terms of atoms, seems highly plausible. Counting requires access to a set of discrete minimal elements, atoms, as expressed in a standard interpretation of a cardinality predicate such as "three", given in (63), in which the cardinality of x is 3 iff the set of atomic parts of x has a cardinality of 3.

(63) *three:* $\lambda x.|\{y: y \sqsubseteq_{ATOM} x\}| = 3$

It is natural therefore (though not necessary) to have a morphological mechanism which distinguishes between the set of atomic instances of N, derived via the count-to-mass operation, which must be accessed in the case of counting, and the set of sums of these entities derived via pluralization. Since mass nouns are not countable and their denotations do not allow a subset of discrete atomic instances to be determined, this contrast between singular and plural is irrelevant for mass nouns. Plural mass nouns, if they occur, either have an abundance interpretation or will receive count noun interpretations by coercion.

Our explorations in this paper have suggested that the contrast between sets of sums and sets of discrete minimal entities is orthogonal to the count–mass distinction, both in English and Hebrew and also in more underrepresented languages.

We have examined three groups of languages, and found that while in all of them plausibly a pluralized noun denotes a set closed under sum, the relation between pluralization and count nouns is different in each group. Our results are summarized in Table 3.1.

We see that in English and Hebrew, count nouns are a subset of nouns which can pluralize, but only pluralized *count* noun denotations are generated by a set of discrete elements. Pluralized mass nouns denote sums, with possibly an abundance interpretation, but these sums are not necessarily sums of discrete entities. Discreteness, including event context-dependent discreteness, is entailed only by countability.

In Yudja and Panará, pluralization applies to a subset of count nouns: in Yudja this is the set of [+human] nouns, while in Panará for some speakers this

Table 3.1. *Comparison of three groups of languages with respect to countability, plurality and portion readings*

	Count–mass?	Plural mass nouns?	Portion readings for substance nouns?
English, Hebrew	Count–mass distinction: only some nouns occur with numerals.	General plural marker. Pluralized mass nouns (i.e. plural but not countable) do not presuppose discreteness.	Countable portion interpretations available through a restricted mass-to-count shift and through classifiers.
Yudja, Panará	All nouns occur with numerals.	No general plural marker. Plural marker occurs with [+human] (Yujda) and [+ animate] (Panará) nouns.	Countable portion readings available for all mass nouns with numerals and *many/big*. Portions readings, overriding individual entity readings, may be available for notional count nouns.
Sakurabiat, Ye'kwana, Taurepang	Count–mass distinction: only some nouns occur with numerals.	Plural markers available. Plural mass nouns presupposing discreteness are possible, but these are not countable.	Portion readings available by pluralizing mass nouns, but these are not countable.

is the set of [+animate] nouns, and for other speakers the set contains nouns denoting stable and salient individuals. In these languages, it seems that countability requires highly context-dependent discreteness, with portions of substances being countable, while pluralization is used to mark pluralities of highly stable individuals, who maintain their discreteness across contexts.

The third group includes Sakurabiat, Ye'kwana and Taurepang. These are the languages in which count nouns are a subset of the pluralizable nouns, but where pluralizations of nouns must denote sets of discrete minimal elements closed under sum. Crucially, although these minimal elements are discrete, they are not countable, and the plural noun cannot be combined with a numeral. Thus, in these languages the plural operator does presuppose a set of discrete minimal elements (which can be individuals or portions), where coercion induces a portion reading on substance denoting nouns, but unlike in English these portion readings are not countable. So, while (at least at first sight) all the conditions that would make nouns countable in English seem to be there, this is not enough in these languages to make the interpretations count.

In Ye'kwana, where numerals modify non-pluralized nouns, it would be possible to argue that this is because numerals do not have the same presuppositions as pluralization, and thus do not coerce a discrete reading on substance nouns, but in Sakurabiat (a Tupian language) and Taurepang (a Karib language), numerals may occur with plural nouns. This is shown in (58) and (59) above for Taurepang, and in (64) for Sakurabiat (from Galucio and Costa 2020):

(64)   turu te   aramira=yat   se-suruka   taose puuk kwak-so-ab=ese
       two FOC woman=COL;PL 3C-run.PL.THV peccary   sound-see-NMLZ=LOC
       "Two women ran when they heard the pig."

Again, despite the fact that numerals in general can modify pluralized nouns in these languages, there are pluralized substance nouns with discrete portion interpretations which are not countable. This suggests that context-dependent discreteness is not sufficient to license countability; instead what is required for countability is probably something more like stable discreteness across contexts.

These data suggest that pluralization, i.e. the closure of an N denotation under sum, and countability (which requires discreteness) are conceptually distinct. Pluralization may, but need not, be presuppositional. In English and Hebrew it does not presuppose discreteness. In Sakurabiat, Ye'kwana and Taurepang it does presuppose discreteness, and in Yudja and Panará it presupposes a human or animate denoting noun. Coercion effects support this claim. However, as Sakurabiat, Ye'kwana and Taurepang show, satisfying a discreteness presupposition need not be sufficient to make a noun countable.

This shows that the derivation of count nouns is independent from pluralization, and that countability is a grammatical property, not an effect that is derived presuppositionally. Furthermore, it suggests that the role of context in deriving count nouns may differ from language to language. All in all, the present paper supports the claim that pluralization and countability are conceptually distinct and that the precise way in which they are connected varies across languages.

4 Count–Mass Asymmetries: The Importance of Being Count

Jenny Doetjes

1. Introduction

The term count–mass distinction (or mass–count distinction), despite its success as a name for a domain of research, suggests a symmetry between count and mass that is not supported by cross-linguistic data. In different domains of grammar, data point towards the idea that 'count' plays an important role in linguistic systems while 'mass' is better characterized as 'not count'.

A first asymmetry is related to the grammatical encoding of count vs. mass. Whereas grammatical markers that are associated with count meaning are common (e.g. number markers, sortal numeral classifiers), grammatical markers that are restricted to mass meaning are at best rare (see for instance Doetjes 1997; Borer 2005; Pelletier 2012).

A second asymmetry between count and mass is related to the sensitivity of quantity expressions to count and mass meaning and count morphology. As in the case of sortal and mensural classifiers, quantity expressions can be divided in two classes, depending on whether they only combine with expressions that have a count denotation or not. Numerals are examples of quantity expressions that are sensitive to count meaning, and so are distributive universal quantifiers and expressions such as *several*. Degree related quantity expressions, such as expressions denoting a large quantity, are examples of quantity expressions that are often insensitive to the count–mass distinction; cf. English *a lot of water/books*. Mass-only expressions (such as *a bit, much*) share most of their properties with quantity expressions that are insensitive to the count vs. mass meaning of nouns, and I will argue below that these should not be considered

---

I would like to thank the organizers and the audience of 'The Count–Mass Distinction: A Linguistic Misunderstanding?' (Bochum 2018) as well as the students of the course I taught at the 2019 LOT Summer School in Utrecht. Many thanks also to Jeff Pelletier for his comments on a previous draft of this paper and to all those who helped me with data from their native languages. Finally, I would like to express my gratitude for the inspiration and the many encouragements I received from Susan Rothstein, whose stimulating and critical presence I will miss at future conferences on the count–mass distinction.

to be direct counterparts of count-only quantity expressions such as *several* and the numerals.

A third asymmetry concerns possible meanings of nouns. Whereas there is strong evidence that an opposition between count and mass meanings plays an important role in the lexicon even of languages that seem at first mass-only, there do seem to exist count-only languages (see in particular Lima's work on Yudja; Lima 2014a, 2016; Lima and Rothstein 2020). Deal's (2017) recent arguments against this claim (and in favor of the universality of the count–mass distinction) will be argued to be inconclusive. The linguistic importance of count meaning both for nouns and for selectional properties of grammatical expressions will be argued to reflect the cognitive salience of countable units (objects, agents) and counted quantities (number) in core knowledge systems (see also Doetjes 2017a; for an overview of core knowledge systems, see Spelke and Kinzler 2007).

The second part of the paper will consider count meanings across languages. What types of meanings are count? What are reliable diagnostics for count meaning? Are there differences in this respect between obligatory number marking languages (also commonly called 'count–mass languages') and languages that do not have obligatory number? It turns out that the types of nouns that can be used in count contexts (e.g. in combination with numerals) are strikingly similar across languages.

The data discussed in the paper offer evidence that something like 'natural atomicity' or 'natural countability' exists, but this property is broader than 'atomicity' in a strict sense. The difference between languages with and without inflectional number marking does not seem to be related to fundamental differences in available count meanings, but rather to the presence vs. absence of a grammatical system of number marking and the use a language can make of such a system in order to express what Grimm (2012b) calls 'degrees of individuation'. Despite clear tendencies, whether a noun can or cannot have a count or mass meaning depends often on arbitrary choices.

The organization of this paper is as follows. Section 2 gives a brief overview of the ways in which the terms count and mass have been used in the literature and makes clear how these terms will be used in the current paper. Section 3 focusses on count–mass asymmetries, while Section 4 examines nominal countability and the notion of 'natural atomicity'. Section 5 gives an overview of the main conclusions.

2. Background: What Do Linguists Mean by Count and Mass?

The difference between nouns that can be pluralized and ones that cannot because of the type of meaning they have goes back to early grammatical descriptions, as illustrated by the following description of the meaning of nouns that name metals in *The Port-Royal Grammar*, written in the seventeenth century by Antoine Arnauld and Claude Lancelot:

la ressemblance si grande qui est entre les parties des metaux, fait que l'on considere d'ordinaire chaque espece de metail, non comme une espece qui ait sous soy plusieurs individus ; mais comme un tout qui a seulement plusieurs parties. (Arnauld and Lancelot 1660: 38)

the great resemblance which obtains between the parts of metals results in our considering each species of metal, not as a species which has under it several individuals, but only as a whole which has several parts (Translation: Rieux and Rollin 1975: 75)

The grammar mentions on the same page that certain nouns do not have a plural 'par le simple usage'; in other words, they are simply not used as plurals even though there is no clear reason why.

Tracing the history of the terms 'mass' and 'count', Lasersohn (2011) attributes the first use of the term 'mass', or rather 'mass-word', to Jespersen (1914), who used the term 'thing-word' for (at least some types of) count nouns. The term 'count' was introduced later, around the 1950s. Gleason (1955: 224) explicitly divides English nouns into count nouns and mass nouns: 'English nouns fall in two major classes with regard to the semantic value of number. They may be referred to as count nouns and mass nouns.' Even though mass nouns typically refer to some quantity of substance, Gleason insists on the fact that the classification is in many cases arbitrary: while *rice* is mass, *beans* is count, and *molasses* is mass or count plural, depending on the dialect. Normally, plurals of mass nouns will result in a type reading, e.g. the plural *metals* is used for types of metal. But he also notes that this is not necessarily the case: in *the beauties of poetry* the word *beauties* is plural but does not seem to denote a plurality. The difference that is made between count and mass is thus based on grammatical properties of nouns that are typically found in English. Gleason also acknowledged the general possibility of using typical count nouns with a mass interpretation, as illustrated by his famous example of a mother termite complaining about her son Johnny in (1) (Gleason 1965: 136–7). He concludes that given the right context, all nouns may well have mass and count uses.

(1)   Johnny is very choosey about his food. He will eat book, but he won't touch shelf.

Within the philosophical literature, Quine (1960) focuses on semantic properties of 'count terms' and 'mass terms.' Quine observes that mass terms are characterized by the referential property of cumulative reference, as illustrated in (2):

(2)   Any sum of parts which are water is water. (Quine 1960: 91)

The type of reference that characterizes count terms such as *apple* is called divided reference. The noun *apple* gives information of 'how much counts as an apple' (Quine 1960: 91); in other words, it contains information on what the units of counting are. Divided reference is reserved for count terms. Mass terms do not divide their reference, and this is considered to be a property of the term rather than of the stuff they name: *shoe, pair of shoes,* and *footwear* 'range over exactly the same scattered stuff, and differ from one another solely in that two of them divide their reference differently and the third not at all' (Quine 1960: 91).

Plurals also have divided reference (that is, *shoes* differs in this respect from *footwear*). In the first stages of acquiring plural forms, however, children may well not be aware of this, because they may treat plurals as if they were mass terms, which lack divided reference (Quine 1960: 93). The parallels between plural and mass expressions can be illustrated by the validity of the inference in (3), which shows that plurals are characterized by the property of cumulative reference illustrated in (2) for mass nouns as well (see Cartwright 1979 for further parallels and differences between plurals and mass nouns).

(3)   If the animals in this camp are horses, and the animals in that camp are horses, then the animals in both camps are horses. (Link 1983: 303)

C.-Y. Cheng (1973) formalizes the absence of divided reference observed for mass expressions in terms of distributive reference. In addition to cumulative reference, mass nouns are claimed to also have distributive reference, resulting in the validity of the following inference:

(4)   a. If A is water, then a subpart of A is water as well.
        b. 'Any part of the whole of a mass object which is w is w.' (C.-Y. Cheng 1973: 287)

Distributive reference distinguishes mass nouns from plurals, as illustrated by the invalidity of the inference in (5):

(5)   If A is apples, then a subpart of A is apples as well.

The combination of distributive and cumulative reference is called homogeneous reference. The concept of distributive reference has widely been acknowledged to be problematic: even for nouns such as *water* it is clear that at some point it will not be possible to divide a quantity of water into two subparts that are water as well (see for instance Quine 1960; Bunt 1979; Hoepelman and Rohrer 1981; Landman 2000). For nouns such as *furniture* or *footwear* the question is even more serious, as the inference in (6) is similar to the inference in (5).

(6)   If A is furniture, then a subpart of A is furniture as well.

Whereas for the noun *water* one can maintain that it cannot be determined what counts as a minimal part, it is very clear what a minimal part of furniture is. A subpart of a piece of furniture is not a piece of furniture (McCawley 1975), despite the fact that the noun has the distribution of a mass noun (see Bunt 1985; Lønning 1987; Nicolas 2002b for discussion on how to interpret distributive reference in such a way that it applies to these nouns as well).

Link (1983) also makes a distinction between mass and count terms, but focuses mainly on the difference between objects and substances, claiming that there is a difference between a count domain and a mass domain, both of which are subsets of the domain of individuals, which is formalized as a Boolean algebra. The distinction between the two domains makes it possible to distinguish between an object and the material this object is made of, which explains the so-called ring paradox: a ring can be new, while the gold the ring is made of is old. The same physical object can thus be old and new depending on whether we consider it as a special type of object (a ring) or a piece of material (gold). As in the case of C.-Y. Cheng (1973), the focus is on material denoting mass terms, and the distinction between object denoting mass nouns and substance denoting mass nouns is not explicitly made.

While count terms denote sums of atoms (and can be pluralized), the mass domain is ordered by the relation $\leq_m$, a relation between portions of matter and their material parts. The distinction between material parts vs. atomic individuals is particularly well suited to showing the relation between mass and count uses of the same noun, e.g. *shelf* and *book*, which may get substance readings. However, it is not clear what status predicates such as *furniture* should have in this type of system: the noun *furniture* does not denote a substance, but rather collections of objects, that themselves have material parts (see also Bale forthcoming). Even though Link's system accounts for the ring paradox, the proposed distinction between two domains does not account for similar properties of nouns such as *furniture*. Wooden furniture can be made of old wood, resulting in exactly the same paradox that Link describes for the noun *ring*: the furniture could be new while the wood would be old. Since Link, it is commonly accepted that the domain of individuals corresponds to a Boolean lattice (or, depending on whether the null element is included or not, a complete join semi-lattice), even though the way the terms mass and count are used varies depending on the author.

Chierchia (1998a, 1998b) emphasizes the fact that real distributive reference does not exist, as even in the case of typical, substance denoting mass nouns such as *water*, there are minimal parts: at some point, if we divide a quantity of stuff which is *water*, the subparts will not be *water* anymore. He concludes that all nominal predicates are atomic in the sense that they have minimal parts. Nouns such as *water*, for which it is not so clear what the minimal parts are, are claimed to have 'vague minimal parts.' Distributive reference and atomicity do not play a role in defining the count–mass distinction, which is based on a difference in the way a noun enters syntax: mass nouns denote individuals (kinds) while count nouns denote singular predicates (sets of atoms).

This basic difference accounts for a number of properties of the two types of nouns. A count noun, that is, a noun that enters syntax as a singular predicate, can be pluralized, and as only plurals can be transformed into kinds, kind-denoting count nouns must be plurals. A mass noun comes into the syntax as a kind-denoting expression, which can be turned into a number neutral predicate. The minimal parts of mass nouns are not salient enough for numerals, resulting in the insertion of measure words or classifiers. Moreover, mass nouns typically do not denote singular predicates or undergo pluralization, and can be used as bare nouns with kind-denoting predicates.

Obligatory classifier languages such as Mandarin are analyzed as languages with only mass nouns. Nouns cannot combine with numerals unless a classifier is inserted:[1]

(7)   a.   sān   běn   shū   [Mandarin]
             three CL^{volume} book
             'three books'
       b.   liǎng   jīn   mǐ
             two $CL^{1/2\ kilo}$ rice
             'two half-kilos of rice'

Chierchia assumes that all nouns in numeral classifier languages enter the syntax as kind-denoting expressions. On the other hand, a language with obligatory number marking such as English has both mass nouns and count nouns: nouns with a singular–plural opposition are count and enter the syntax as singular predicates that can undergo pluralization, while nouns that are incompatible with numerals are mass and enter the syntax as kinds.

The proposed parametrization does not take into account languages that lack both number marking and numeral classifiers, as illustrated by the Northern Athapaskan language Dëne Sųłiné, a language which lacks nominal number marking and classifiers (as documented in Wilhelm 2008):

(8)   a.   sǫlághe   k'ásba
             five   chicken
             'five chickens'
       b.   #sǫlághe   ʔejëretth'úé/   bër
             five   milk/   meat
       c.   ??náke   tł'ólátúé
             two   beer
             'two beers' (acceptable in the sense of two servings, as in English)

---

[1] The following abbreviations are used in the glosses: CL classifier; COP copula; IMPERF imperfective aspect; PL plural; PRES present tense; SG singular; PRT particle.

d. sǫlághe   nedádhi   bër
   five   pound   meat
   'five pounds of meat'   (Dëne Sųłiné; Wilhelm 2008: 46, 47)

These data also illustrate the fact that a difference between count and mass meaning can play a role in languages that lack the type of morphologically marked count–mass distinction that is found in languages such as English, which are commonly called 'count–mass languages'.

In the absence of inflectional number, effects such as the ones illustrated in (8) are often seen as an ontological rather than linguistic phenomenon. According to Wiltschko (2005, 2012), for instance, roots in languages without inflectional number marking may have ontological properties that make them incompatible with, e.g. numerals, while Rothstein (2010) uses the term 'natural atomicity' for inherently individuable meanings, which exist cross-linguistically, independently of whether a language is a grammatical 'count–mass language' or not.

Rothstein (2010) distinguishes three types of atomicity that play a role in natural languages. The first type of atomicity is atomicity in the sense of Chierchia (1998a): all nominal predicates are atomic, including mass predicates. Atoms are in some cases well defined (e.g. in the case of *furniture*), but can also be vague (e.g. in the case of *water*).

The second type of atomicity is natural atomicity. The meaning of a naturally atomic noun is inherently individuable, as in the case of mass nouns such as *furniture* and most count nouns.

Natural atomicity is neither a sufficient nor a necessary condition for the meaning of count nouns in a grammatical count–mass language such as English: count nouns are characterized by a third type of atomicity, which is semantic atomicity. Root nouns are subsets of the mass domain M and denote Boolean lattices, which can be either naturally atomic or not. A root noun can be turned into a semantically atomic predicate and thus become a count noun by the operation $COUNT_k$, which turns a nominal root into a set of ordered pairs of an individual and a context. This introduces a context dependency, which makes it possible to define atomicity for those nouns in which atoms may vary depending on the context. Nouns such as *fence* and *bouquet* are problematic for the claim that count nouns have atomic reference: fences can be made up of several smaller fences, and a big bouquet can be divided into several smaller ones. Therefore, these nouns are not naturally atomic: depending on the context a different unit can be selected as a unit for counting (see in particular Rothstein 2010).

Semantic atomicity is to a certain extent an arbitrary property: a noun can be count in one language and mass in another. Inflectional plural forms are only possible for count nouns, which restricts count nouns to languages with inflectional plurals such as English. If a language lacks semantic atomicity, natural atomicity may still play a role. The patterns in Dëne Sųłiné above can thus be attributed to natural atomicity, as the language does not have the type of grammatical count–mass distinction that is present in English.

It is clear that in languages such as English, the count–mass distinction has an important morphological component. Nouns such as *furniture*, which lack a singular–plural opposition, fail to combine with expressions such as *several* and numerals, despite their atomic meaning. Morover, number marking plays an important role in triggering meaning shifts as in (1). On the other hand, the examples of Dëne Sųłiné show that there is also a distinction between nouns based on the availability of count vs. mass meanings in languages that lack a morphologically marked count–mass distinction (Wilhelm 2008). It is this non-morphological distinction that will be at the center of the discussion in this paper.

In what follows, I will make a difference between count vs. mass grammar on the one hand, and count vs. mass meanings on the other. In Section 3, I will argue on the basis of count–mass asymmetries that mass should be interpreted as the absence of count. Count grammar presupposes the availability of units that can be counted, and as such it is only compatible with predicates that have count meanings in the sense that they provide such units, which, for the time being, one may think of as non-vague atoms. Non-count grammar is indifferent with respect to the presence vs. absence of count meaning, while non-count meaning fails to provide information about countable units. I will be abstracting away from more complex cases of count meaning, as illustrated by *fences* and *bouquets*. In Section 4, I will include these types of count meanings as well, and turn to the question of which types of count meanings are found cross-linguistically, and how these meanings relate to (natural) atomicity.

3. Count–Mass Asymmetries

As indicated above, asymmetries between count and mass can be found at the level of syntactic environments in which nouns are used on the one hand, and at the level of noun meanings on the other. In what follows, I will discuss three types of asymmetries between count and mass, focusing first on grammatical expressions (grammatical markers in Section 3.1 and quantity expressions in Section 3.2) and then on the meanings of nouns that are used in count environments (Section 3.3). Each of these sections will include discussion on cognitive aspects of countability.

3.1. Grammatical Markers

Grammatical markers that are known to interfere with the count–mass distinction are number marking on the one hand and classifiers on the other.

Number markers are normally found on nouns that have a count interpretation, and come in many different forms (see among many others Corbett 2000; Dryer 2005; Cabredo Hofherr forthcoming). In Tagalog, for instance, the number marker *mga* is optionally added to noun phrases that have plural reference, even though it is incompatible with numerals. According to Schachter and Otanes (1972: 112): 'Tagalog makes a distinction between pluralizable and unpluralizable nouns that is like a distinction made in English. [...] In general, Tagalog count nouns correspond to English count nouns and refer to items that are perceived as distinct units: e.g., *bahay* "house", *baro* "dress", *bata* "child".' On the other hand, Wiltschko (2012) claims that non-inflectional plural markers can be combined with all nouns, based on evidence from Halkomelem (Central Salish) and Blackfoot (Algonquian), and takes this to be evidence for the absence of a count–mass distinction in these languages. Note however that the examples she gives do not always make clear whether a plural interpretation is present; Mathieu (2012b) treats the plural in Halkomelem as a so-called 'plural of abundance', which is exceptional in the sense that it expresses abundance rather than plurality (for mass plurals in Greek, see also Tsoulas 2009; Alexiadou 2011):

(9)   a.   th'exet   th'exeth'éxet
              gravel   gravel.PL
      b.   speháls   spelháls
              wind   wind.PL   (Halkomelem; Wiltschko 2012: 153)

On the other hand, some of the Blackfoot data presented in the article (cited from Frantz and Russell 1995) clearly indicates a plural interpretation for the noun in the context of the plural marker, suggesting that the use of the plural marker triggers a count interpretation:

(10)   aiksinoosak   aiksinoosakiksi
          'bacon'   'bacon' (slabs or slices of)   (Blackfoot; Wiltschko 2012: 153)

Similarly, the Sahaptian language Nez Perce (Deal 2017) allows easily for plural markers in the context of nouns such as *maayx* 'sand', triggering a type of meaning that is excluded for the corresponding count plural in English:

(11)   Yiyoosyiyoos   maayx   wewluq-se-∅.
          PL.blue   sand   want-IMPERF-PRES
          'I want quantities of blue sand.'   (Nez Perce; Deal 2017: 144)

As already indicated above, the distribution of inflectional number markers in a language such as English is quite complex: it is by no means the case that all nouns that have a count interpretation also have a singular–plural opposition and can be classified as 'count nouns' (cf. *furniture*, *scissors*, etc.). On the other hand, the presence of a singular–plural opposition normally forces a count interpretation.

Numeral classifiers come in two types, depending on whether they are similar to measure words in a language such as English (mensural classifiers) or not. The two types are illustrated in the example in (7), repeated in (12):

(12) a. sān   běn   shū   (Mandarin)
        three CL^{volume} book
        'three books'
     b. liǎng jīn
        two   CL$^{1/2\ kilo}$ rice
                            mǐ
        'two half-kilos of rice'

The classifier *běn* is a sortal classifier, which Grinevald (2005: 1020) defines as follows: 'Sortal classifiers [...] specify units (not quantity) in terms of which the referent of the head noun may be counted [...]. They often appear to be semantically redundant, expressing one of the inherent semantic characteristics of the head noun.' Numeral classifier languages usually have a closed set of sortal classifiers. There is often one so-called general classifier, which does not provide any information about the form or shape of the referent. This general classifier is not very different from a number marker in the sense that it does not provide information about the units that are counted; this information must come from the noun (Doetjes 1997).

According to Chao (1968: 508), the general classifier can replace almost any sortal classifier, while it is incompatible with nouns that have a mass interpretation, such as *shuǐ* 'water'. It seems, however, that the possibility of using nouns such as *shuǐ* 'water' with the general classifier, resulting in a count interpretation, is subject to variation. Among the speakers I consulted, most rejected forms such as *yī/sān ge shuǐ* 'one/three CL^{general} water'.[2] One of them specified that *shuǐ* could be used with the general classifier when it refers to the character for the noun *shuǐ* (水) but not to refer to quantities of water. On the other hand, several speakers indicated that in colloquial, informal speech *yī/sān ge shuǐ* could be used to refer to standard portions of water (or other liquids), provided an appropriate context. The use of *shuǐ* with a general classifier typically occurs in informal situations when ordering standard bottles of water in a shop or in a restaurant (for count interpretations in restaurant contexts in various languages, see, among others, Borer 2005). One of the speakers added that it would be very odd to use these forms to ask for a drink when visiting a friend. Among the speakers who at first rejected the use of the general classifier with *shuǐ* 'water', some mentioned that they could use it more easily with other nouns that denote drinkable liquids, such as *píjiǔ* 'beer', and one of them noted that this is easier if the numeral is left out (for bare

---

[2] I would like to thank Hang Cheng, Han Hu, Chou Mo, Jianan Liu, Jing Sun, and Yang Yang for their judgments and examples.

classifier–noun structures, see, among others, Cheng and Sybesma 2005). These preliminary data indicate that some kind of mass-to-count shifting processes may occur in the context of the general classifier *ge* in colloquial Mandarin, but they also show that these shifts are heavily context dependent and subject to speaker variation and lexical variation.

Whereas sortal classifiers are sensitive to count meaning, mensural classifiers are indifferent to the presence vs. the absence of count meaning, as illustrated in the examples in (13):

(13) a. liǎng jīn   mǐ/   píngguǒ
        two   CL$^{half\_kilo}$ rice/ apple
        'two half-kilos of rice/apples'
     b. liǎng píng   (de)   mì/   gǎnlǎn
        two   CL^{pot} (DE)   honey/ olive
        'two pots of honey/olives'   (Mandarin; Doetjes 2021)

In this respect they are similar to measure words in English, as illustrated by the English translations. More generally, while number marking and sortal classifiers are both commonly found across languages, grammatical markers that depend on the presence of mass meaning are at best rare. In other words, grammatical markers typically signal count meaning, rather than mass.

The observation that grammar marks count as opposed to mass plays an important role in the work of Borer (2005). Borer hypothesizes that count meaning is syntactically introduced in the grammatical structure of noun phrases by a Classifier Phrase, which hosts grammatical expressions with the abstract feature *div*. This expression can be a number marker, a classifier, or an indefinite article. The feature *div* is responsible for making nouns compatible with numerals and other count quantity expressions. Mass is in this respect default: no grammatical marking is required, while count meaning requires grammatical marking.

For Pelletier (2012), the lexicon is blind to the count–mass distinction: a noun such as *chocolate* has a denotation that comprises both chocolates and portions of chocolate-stuff. The combination of count syntax and a noun activates a semantic rule that deletes the 'mass part' of the meaning of the noun, while mass-syntax deletes the 'count part' of the meaning of the noun.

In both approaches, the count grammar is necessary to trigger or extract a count meaning for a noun, suggesting that mass is in a sense the default that can be left unmarked, while count needs to be marked. Another way of looking at this is in terms of cognitive salience. The reason why grammatical markers typically signal count as opposed to mass could be the importance of countability from a cognitive point of view.

Recent approaches to human cognition argue for a small number of innate core knowledge systems, which center 'on a set of principles that serves to individuate the entities in [their] domain[s]' (Spelke and Kinzler 2007: 89). Core knowledge systems are innate, basic systems of knowledge representation within the brains of humans as well as animals, and include systems of object representation, agent representation, and number representation. Object representation is based on cohesion (the fact that objects form integrated wholes that remain the same in space and time), continuity (objects do not disappear and reappear), and contact (objects influence each other in direct contact, not at a distance). Moreover, object representation is assumed to be limited to about three objects at a time (Feigenson, Dehaene, and Spelke 2004). The core system of agent representation sets agents apart from other countable entities. For instance, agents may interact without contact, even when they are goal oriented, and act in reciprocal ways Spelke and Kinzler (2007). For number representation, a distinction is made between the approximate representation of numerical magnitude, which is characterized by a ratio limit, and precise representations of distinct individuals, which are absolute number representations limited to about three entities. These systems underscore the importance of counting and countability for human cognition. According to the 'Whole Object Assumption', object representation also plays a role in language acquisition. Children expect nouns to refer to whole objects when acquiring the meaning of count nouns (Macnamara 1972; Carey 1978; Markman 1991). Experiments by Shipley and Shepperson (1990) and Brooks, Pogue, and Barner (2011) confirm this assumption.

The importance of countability and individuation for cognition can be seen as the source of the asymmetry between count and mass in languages: the prevalent presence of grammatical markers that signal or presuppose count meaning across languages does not imply that mass is default in the sense that nouns are mass unless they are grammatically marked as count, but rather results from the fact that count is cognitively salient.

3.2. Quantity Expressions

As the following examples show, quantity expressions can be subdivided into three types depending on their sensitivity to count and mass properties of nouns. They can be limited to count nouns, they can be indifferent to the count–mass properties of the nouns they combine with, or they can be limited to mass nouns. The first pattern is found for cardinal numerals and other cardinal quantity expressions (e.g. *several*) as well as for distributive universal quantifiers (e.g. *every*), and I will refer to this class as COUNT QUANTITY EXPRESSIONS. As illustrated in the examples below, these expressions require the presence of either a singular or a plural count noun in English:

(14) a. one/a single/every house
b. #one/a single/every water/furniture
c. two/several/few/many house*(s)
d. #two/several/few/many waters/furnitures

The second pattern is found for many degree expressions and for the non-distributive universal quantifier *all*. I will refer to this class as NON-COUNT QUANTITY EXPRESSIONS. In English the noun that follows is normally a count plural noun or a mass noun. In the case of *all* the complement can be a definite DP.

(15) a. more/a lot of houses/water/furniture
b. all of the houses/water/furniture

When used with degree related quantity expressions such as *a lot* or *more*, singular count nouns may be used, resulting in a particular type of interpretation:

(16) Buy more house for less money!

In this example, *more* indicates the amount of space a house defines and not a number of houses (see for instance Beviláqua and Pires de Oliveira 2014 and their chapter in this volume, Chapter 8 for recent discussion on this type of reading). This could be seen as a type of mass use (*house* is not interpreted as a type of object but as an amount of space that one can live in), but one could also assume that *more* defines a measure on a singular object. In English as well as many other languages, non-distributive universal quantifiers can also be used with singular nouns, in which case they quantify over subparts of the object denoted by its complement (cf. *all of the house*). Languages may vary in this respect, as illustrated by the fact that Dutch *alle* 'all' is incompatible with count singular nouns.

The third type of quantity expression typically combines with mass nouns. Again, these expressions are often degree related expressions, and often indicate small quantities. I will refer to this type of quantity expression as ANTI-COUNT QUANTITY EXPRESSIONS. In English, these nouns typically combine with mass nouns:

(17) a bit of furniture/water/#house

At first sight, the properties of quantity expressions seem symmetrical: they can be sensitive to count or to mass, or otherwise they are indifferent with respect to the count–mass properties of their complements. Below I will first argue the symmetry between count and anti-count is apparent and that anti-count quantity expressions should be seen as a subtype of non-count quantity expressions rather than as a type of its own. Then I will show that count and non-count quantity expressions can be found across languages and do not depend on the presence of inflectional number, and I will argue that these two types are related to two different ways of representing quantities.

3.3. Anti-Count Quantity Expressions and Blocking

Quantity expressions that indicate a relative degree can fall in all three classes of quantity expressions, as illustrated by the triple *many, a lot, much*. If these expressions are not restricted to count contexts, they often have a life outside of the nominal domain, as illustrated by the examples in (18), which show that *lot* and *much* can modify eventive and gradable verbs, while the count quantity expressions *many* and *few* cannot be used to modify verbs:

(18)   a. He works a lot/more/too little/too much/*(too) many/*(too) few.
        b. *She jumped many/few.
        c. much/a lot/*many appreciated

The set of count quantity expressions contains many members that do not have an anti-count homologue. This is by definition the case for the numerals, but also vague quantity expressions such as *various, different, several* do not have an anti-count equivalent. The set of anti-count quantity expressions is much smaller, and they typically form pairs with count quantity expressions with a similar meaning that are restricted to count nouns: *many* and *much, little* and *few*, and *less* and *fewer*. This makes it possible to account for the distribution of these expressions in terms of blocking or the Elsewhere Condition (see Di Sciullo and Williams 1987 for the difference between *many* and *much*). This means that anti-count expressions are not inherently incompatible with count nouns; rather, the existence of a count alternative that is restricted to nouns with a count meaning will block the use of anti-count expressions in these contexts.

It is important to realize that this type of approach implies that there are specific pairings of quantity expressions that trigger the elsewhere effect. Whereas the distribution of *much* is blocked by *many* in the context of plural nouns, *a lot*, which has a similar interpretation, is not blocked and can be found with count nouns. Even though this may seem a reason not to assume blocking at first, there are strong arguments to assume that this type of pairing exists in the domain of quantity expressions. This can be illustrated on the basis of French. French degree expressions usually combine with nouns, verbs, and adjectives. However, certain degree expressions are only used with nouns and verbs, while a special form is used in the context of adjectives (the data are actually slightly more complicated; see Gaatone 1981). The two patterns are illustrated for *tellement* 'so, so much/many' and for the pair *si* 'so' and *tant* 'so much/many':

(19) a. si/tellement/*tant beau   (French)
       'so beautiful'
    b. tant/tellement/*si de livres
       'so many books'
    c. tant/tellement/*si dormir
       'to sleep so much'

Data with pronominalization strongly suggest that the more limited distribution of *tant* is due to blocking by *si* in '*much*-support' contexts (Corver 1997). *Much*-support is illustrated in (20). Even though the adjective *fond* can normally be modified by the degree expression *as*, *much* needs to be inserted when *fond* is replaced by the pronominal form *so* (see Corver 1997: 127).

(20) a. John is as fond of Mary as Bill.
    b. John is fond of Mary. Maybe he is as much so as Bill/*as so as Bill.

Similar data can be found for the French pair *si* 'so' and *tant* 'so much/many.' Whereas *si* is used as the modifier of an adjective, *tant* needs to be used as the modifier of the corresponding pronominal form. This pattern suggests a blocking analysis of the distribution of *tant*: the form is equivalent to *si*, but in those contexts where *si* can be used, the more specific form is used. The example in (21a), taken from an article by Yaël Eckert in *La Croix*, illustrates the use of *tant* in the context of a pronominalized adjective. As shown in (21b,c), *si* must be used when no pronominalization takes place and cannot be used when the adjective is replaced by a pronoun. The last example shows that *tellement* is not affected and can replace both *si* and *tant*.

(21) a. Philosophe, Mafalda [...] l'est tant que ses interrogations nous   (French)
       parlent encore, cinquante ans plus tard [...][3]
       'Malfalda is philosophical; she is even so much so that her
       interrogations still talk to us, fifty years later'
    b. Elle   est   si/*tant   Philosophe   que ...
       she   is   so   philosophical   that ...
    c. Philosophe,   elle   l'est   si   que ...
       philosophical   she   it is   so   that
    d. Elle l'est tellement/ est tellement philosophe que ...
       she it is so much/is so philosophical that ...

---

[3] The article by Yaël Eckert from which this example has been taken was published on 19 March 2014 in *La Croix* at the occasion of the fiftieth birthday of Quino's Mafalda comic strips: www.la-croix.com/Culture/Livres-Idees/Livres/La-petite-Mafalda-a-50-ans-2014-03-19-1122702 (last consulted in July 2019).

The fact that *tellement* unlike *tant* is not replaced by *si* in the context of an adjective, despite their very similar meanings, shows that blocking is not an automatic, necessary process, but applies to specific pairs.

A further argument in favor of the idea that blocking requires some sort of a lexical pairing of two expressions is the distribution of English *less*. According to prescriptive grammar, *less* can only be used with mass nouns, and has to be replaced by *fewer* when combined with count nouns. On the one hand, the Oxford English Dictionary notes that, despite this rule, *less* with count plurals is frequently attested, even though it is 'generally regarded as incorrect' (see also Kperogi 2015: 104–5). On the other hand, *fewer* and *less* coexisted for a long time before the rule existed. According to the *Merriam-Webster's Dictionary of English Usage* this rule was first introduced in a rather tentative form in 1770, when the grammarian Robert Baker stated that *less* 'is most commonly used as speaking of a Number; where I should think *Fewer* would be better' (Baker 1770: 55). This formulation explicitly formulates the restriction of *less* in terms of *fewer* in terms of blocking: *fewer* is 'better' and should therefore be used. At the same time the absence of the rule in some varieties of English (see also Kperogi 2015: 104–5) and the absence of the rule before the end of the eighteenth century also shows that blocking does not automatically take place whenever a more specific alternative form exists.

Note also that the expression *a bit* can lose its anti-count behavior when modified by *quite*. Whereas *a bit of books* is odd, *quite a bit of books* is much better, and for many speakers just fine. This type of change is not observed for count quantity expressions: a modifier such as *several* or *few* does not lose its count character due to the presence of a modifier. This asymmetry also suggests that anti-count quantity expressions do not have the same kind of status as count quantity expressions.

A final argument for a blocking analysis of anti-count quantity expressions comes from acquisition. Gathercole (1985) shows that children first use *much* both with count and mass nouns; that is, they use the expression *much* as if it were a non-count rather than an anti-count expression. They start to use it correctly when they have acquired the correct use of *many*. This corresponds to the type of acquisition pattern that is described for blocking phenomena in morphology (cf. Pinker 1995; Ferdinand 1996).

To conclude this section, count and anti-count quantity expressions are not similar categories, one of which is sensitive to count and the other to mass. Rather, anti-count quantity expressions behave as non-count quantity expressions, the distribution of which is restricted by the existence of a more specific count quantity expression.

3.4. Quantity Expressions Across Languages

The types of quantity expressions discussed in the previous section are not limited to English (see Doetjes 2021). It is quite plausible that all languages have quantity expressions that presuppose counting. Even languages that have limited numeral systems – e.g. Mundurucu (Pica et al. 2004) – seem to have quantity expressions that resemble numerals or expressions such as *several* in the sense that they presuppose the availability of units to count. Similarly, all languages seem to have non-count quantity expressions.

The cross-linguistic parallels are obscured by the fact that languages differ from each other in terms of their grammatical properties. In a language such as Mandarin, count quantity expressions typically trigger insertion of a classifier. In English, count quantity expressions are usually restricted to morphologically marked count nouns. In other words, they are not only sensitive to count meaning, but also to count grammar: numerals and other count quantity expressions are not used with nouns such as *furniture* despite their count meaning. This shows that in addition to being sensitive to count meaning, these expressions are also sensitive to the inflectional count–mass system of English.

In Mandarin, count quantity expressions usually require insertion of a classifier, as illustrated in (7) for numerals. Other count quantity expressions, such as *jǐ* 'how many, a few', also trigger insertion of classifiers. Non-count quantity expressions normally combine directly with nouns and do not allow for classifier insertion (e.g. *dàliàng* 'a lot'), while *hěn duō* 'a lot' allows insertion of a classifier depending on the dialect. The expression *yī diǎnr* 'a bit' is typically found with nouns that have a mass interpretation and is incompatible with classifiers (Iljic 1994); in case of a count interpretation, *jǐ* 'a few' is used, suggesting that this restriction may be analyzed in terms of blocking as well.

In many languages the difference between count and non-count quantity expressions is not morphologically marked, but still existent. This can be illustrated by Hungarian examples below (Anikó Lipták, p.c.):

(22) a. Mennyi/Hány könyv áll a polcon?
         how.many book stand.3SG the shelf.on
         'How many books are on the shelf?'
      b. Mennyi/*Hány por áll a polcon?
         how.many dust stand.3SG the shelf.on
         'How much dust is on the shelf?' (Hungarian; Doetjes 2021)

Whereas *hány* is a count quantity expression that triggers a count interpretation of the noun, *mennyi* is indifferent with respect to whether a noun has a count or a mass interpretation. Similar differences have been claimed to exist between quantity expressions in Tagalog; whereas *marami* 'a lot' is compatible with all nouns, *ilan* 'a few' triggers a count interpretation (Schachter and Otanes 1972). As will become clear in the next sub-section, even Yudja, a language in which all nouns can be directly combined with numerals, offers evidence for a difference between count and non-count quantity expressions. As in the case of grammatical markers, quantity expressions offer evidence in favor of the idea that the context in which nouns are used are sensitive to count meaning and/or grammar rather than to mass; cases where sensitivity to mass is found were analyzed in terms of blocking rather than as an inherent selectional property.

The basic types of quantity expressions found across languages may well be related to the ways in which quantities can be mentally represented. Within the literature on magnitude representation, a distinction is made between number representation on the one hand (Dehaene 1997; Feigenson, Dehaene, and Spelke 2004) and global quantity representation on the other (Lourenco and Longo 2011). Lourenco and Longo discuss a number of experiments showing that dimensions such as space, time, and number interact, and take this as evidence for the existence of a general system of magnitude representation with a scalar structure. The two types of magnitude representation may well be at the origin of the distinction between count quantity expressions (corresponding to number representation) and non-count quantity expressions (corresponding to global magnitude representation).

3.5. Count and Mass Meanings and Count and Mass Languages

Next to an opposition between grammatical expressions and quantity expressions that are sensitive to count grammar and/or meaning and ones that are not, one can make a distinction between count and mass meanings for nouns. As shown by the experiments of Barner and Snedeker (2005), nouns such as *furniture*, *silverware*, and *footwear* pattern in certain respects with count nouns such as *tables*, *forks*, and *shoes* rather than with nouns such as *toothpaste*. In a magnitude judgment task, participants were asked to answer the question *Who has more N?* In one of the experiments the participants were confronted with a big object as opposed to three small ones, or in the case of substance nouns, with one big heap of the substance or three small ones. In reaction to this, both children and adults opted almost systematically for an evaluation in terms of number for both count nouns and object denoting mass nouns such as *furniture*. In the context of substance denoting mass nouns, the judgment was based on volume rather than on number. The differences between children and adults were quite small and only a few answers were given that did not correspond to this general pattern (never more than five percent; for the children in all conditions and for the adults only in the object mass condition; Barner and Snedeker 2005: 51). The results of the experiment show that English offers evidence for the linguistic relevance of count and mass meanings for nouns (cf. Hungarian and Dëne Sųłiné).

Mandarin and other obligatory numeral classifier languages are sometimes called 'mass-only' languages. It is clear that this cannot mean that the language lacks nouns that have count meaning. Languages with numeral classifiers offer linguistic evidence for the presence of count meaning, as already indicated in Section 3.1 above (see, among many others, Chao 1968; Doetjes 1997; Cheng and Sybesma 1998; Grinevald 2005; Zhang 2013). Psycholinguistic evidence in favor of the idea that nouns in numeral classifier languages lack count meaning (Lucy 1992; Lucy and Gaskins 2001) has been shown to be due to a language-on-language effect introduced by the experimental task (Li, Dunham, and Carey 2009). Quantity judgment studies similar to the ones of Barner and Snedeker (2005) on Mandarin (Cheung, Barner, and Li 2009; Lin and Schaeffer 2018) and Japanese (Inagaki and Barner 2009) also show evidence for individuated meanings.

A linguistic argument in favor of a distinction between count and mass nouns at a lexical level comes from the distribution of classifiers in Cantonese, which has bare classifier–noun structures that can have a definite interpretation (Cheng and Sybesma 2005):

(23) a. zek^3 gau^2 $soeng^2$ gwo^3 maa^5lou^6
         CL   dog   want   cross   road
         'The dog wants to cross the road.'
      b. Wu^4fei^1 jam^2-$jyun^4$ wun^2 $tong^1$ la^1
         Wufei   drink-finish CL^{bowl} soup   particle
         'Wufei finished eating the soup.' (Cantonese; Cheng and Sybesma 2005)

When the so-called 'plural' classifier di^1 is used instead, a plural reading can be obtained, but only when the noun it combines with has a count meaning (Doetjes 2017b). In the context of the noun gau^2 'dog', replacing the sortal classifier zek^3 by di^1, the result is a definite plural interpretation. In the context of the noun $tong^1$ 'soup', replacing the mensural classifier wun^2 'CL^{bowl}' by di^1 results in a definite mass meaning.

(24) a. di^1 gau^2 $soeng^2$ gwo^3 maa^5lou^6
         CL   dog   want   cross   road
         'The dogs want to cross the road'
      b. Wu^4fei^1 jam^2-$jyun^4$ di^1 $tong^1$ la^1
         Wufei   drink-finish   CL   soup   PRT
         'Wufei finished eating the soup' (Cantonese; cf. Doetjes 2017b)

The only way in which numeral classifier languages could be called 'mass-only' seems to be to use the term mass in the sense of triggering obligatory classifier insertion. Even this is not completely straightforward, as there is evidence that in some cases classifiers are inserted because of properties of numerals rather than because of properties of nouns. Bale and Coon (2014) show that Mi'gmaq (Eastern Algonquian) and Chol (Mayan) have two types of numerals: some numerals are incompatible with classifiers while others require insertion of a numeral classifier. They conclude that classifiers are inserted in order to make the numerals compatible with nouns, rather than to make nouns compatible with numerals (cf. Krifka 1995). For this type of language it is not possible to assume that classifiers are inserted because of some property of nouns that one could call 'mass.'

Whereas mass-only languages do not seem to exist, count-only languages may well exist. In the Tupi language Yudja, numerals and other quantity expressions combine with all nouns, and all nouns naturally get a count interpretation which is not due to coercion (Lima 2014a):[4]

(25) a. Txabïu   ali   wãnã.
          three   child   ran
          'three children ran'   (Yudja; Lima 2014a: 38)
      b. Txabïu   y'a   ipide   pe.
          three   water   on the floor drip
          'three (drops of) water dripped on the floor' (Yudja; Lima 2014a: 112)

Lima (2014a) assumes that all nominal roots in Yudja can be turned into count predicates by a function KO that maps kinds to objects. This function also applies to what Lima calls notional mass nouns: applying KO to the root *apeta* 'blood' 'yields the characteristic function of the set of atoms of blood in the world of evaluation' (Lima 2014a: 110). As a result, all nouns can have a count (contextually) atomic denotation.

According to Deal (2017), this does not mean that Yudja is a count-only language, however, as the fact that all nouns can have a count meaning does not imply that all nouns need to have a count meaning. Her argument is based on a particularly interesting set of data from Nez Perce (Sahaptian). First of all, Nez Perce is similar to Yudja in freely using notional mass nouns with numerals. At first, this suggests that Nez Perce, too, might be a count-only language, but Deal shows that this is not the case. In the context of the quantity expression *'ilex̂ni* 'a lot', plurality is obligatorily marked if possible in case of a count meaning of the noun. Plural is marked on nouns for human nouns, and on adjectives for non-human nouns:

---

[4] See also Whorf (1944: 202), for similar observations on Hopi.

(26) a. 'ileẋni ha-ham/*haama
      a.lot   PL-man/*man.SG
      'a lot of men'
   b. 'ileẋni   ??tiyaaw'ic / ti-tiyaw'ic   wiẋsi'likeecet'es
      a.lot   ??sturdy   / PL-sturdy   Chair
      'a lot of sturdy chairs'   (Nez Perce; Deal 2017: 149, 150)

For nouns such as *samq'ayn* 'fabric, piece(s) of fabric', plural marking is necessary in order to trigger a count interpretation of the noun:

(27) a. 'ileẋni cimuuxcimux   samq'ayn
       a.lot   black   fabric
       'a lot of black fabric'
    b. 'ileẋni cicmuxcicmux   samq'ayn
       a.lot   PL.black   fabric
       'a lot of pieces of black fabric'   (Nez Perce; Deal 2017: 152)

Based on this, Deal concludes that notional mass nouns in Nez Perce also have a mass interpretation. In her view, all languages have a lexical count–mass distinction, which plays an important role in language acquisition, and she claims that results of quantity judgment studies (Lima 2014a) show that Yudja, too, offers evidence for the existence of non-count meanings for notional mass nouns.

Lima carried out quantity judgment experiments using several quantity expressions, including *itxïbï* 'many' and *bitu* 'more.' Whereas questions with *itxïbï* 'many' gave systematically rise to judgments based on number, *bitu* 'more' also permitted evaluations based on volume, suggesting that the former is a count quantity expression while the latter is a non-count quantity expression.

(28) a. Ma de   itxïbï   asa   dju a'u?
        who   many   flour have
        'Who has many portions of flour?'
     b. Ma de   bitu   asa   dju a'u?
        who   more   flour have
        'Who has more flour?'   (Yudja; Lima 2014a: 182, 120)

Both in a condition in which one big heap of flour was compared to three small ones, and in a condition where two big heaps were compared to six small ones, participants gave judgments based on number in a majority of the cases. On the other hand, when they were asked to make a comparison between one big heap and a small heap, eighty-eight percent would opt for a volume reading. This shows, according to Deal, that mass meanings are available.

The interpretation of the data becomes less straightforward when notional count nouns such as *xãã* 'bowl' are taken into account as well:

(29) b. Ma de itxïbï xãã dju a'u?
       who   many   bowl have
       'Who has many bowls?'
    a. Ma de bitu   xãã dju a'u?
       who   more   bowl have
       'Who has more bowls?' (Yudja; Lima 2014a: 183, 121)

Again, the experiment with *itxïbï* 'many' resulted in number-based answers only. In the case of *bitu*, there were again both answers in terms of number and volume. The percentages of number-based answers for notional mass and notional count nouns were almost identical in the experiment with one big heap vs. three small ones (notional count: 85% and notional mass: 83%). In the experiment where the participants had to compare two big heaps and six small ones, there were more volume readings overall, and there were more number-based answers for notional count nouns (76%) than for notional mass nouns (64%). Still, as a whole, the experiments show that number-based answers are strongly preferred in the context of *bitu*, unless the pictures did not allow for an evaluation based on number (that is, comparing one big and one small heap). These results beg the question what is meant by 'mass meaning', as the effects that Deal ascribes to mass meaning of the noun are hardly more readily available for notional mass nouns than for notional count nouns.

An alternative explanation of the data attributes the effects to *bitu* rather than to the meaning of the noun. The results of the experiments show that *bitu* does not force a comparison based on number. It shares this property with non-count quantity expressions such as *more* in English. From a semantic point of view, expressions such as *more* include a measure function, which measures quantities on a context-dependent scale (see for instance Chierchia 1998a), resulting in the availability of different types of interpretations in terms of, e.g., volume, weight, or cardinality, depending on the context. Given that *more* allows both for volume readings and for number readings, it is plausible that this can also be the case for *bitu* in Yudja.

As it turns out, Brazilian Portuguese offers evidence that evaluations in terms of volume do not depend on mass meaning, but rather on the absence of number marking. As shown in the following examples, the noun *farinha* 'flour' is incompatible with count quantity expressions such as the numeral *duas* 'two', but can be combined with the non-count quantity expression *mais* 'more.' The incompatibility of *farinha* and *duas* cannot be attributed to the lack of number marking, as number marking is optional in informal varieties of Brazilan Portuguese (see Ferreira forthcoming):

(30) a. *duas   farinha,   mais   farinha   (Brazilian Portuguese)
        two   flour,   more   flour
     b. duas/mais livro,   duas/mais livros
        two/more book   two/more books
        'two/more books'

The results of quantity judgment tests show that number marking plays a crucial role in the availability of number readings (Beviláqua and Pires de Oliveira 2014 and in this volume, Chapter 8; see also Pires de Oliveira and Rothstein, 2011). The experimental context favored an evaluation based on volume. Substance denoting nouns systematically gave rise to volume readings, and plural object denoting nouns were judged on the basis of number (72%) or as having both options (21%). For singular object denoting nouns most answers were based on volume (61%), even though they were also judged on the basis of number (20%) or as having both options (19%).

These data show that plural marking introduces a strong bias for number-based answers.[5] They also show that all nouns, even when marked for plural, may get a volume-based interpretation in a context that favors an evaluation based on volume. This is clearly different from a count-to-mass shift as in the case of *shelf* or *book* being eaten by termites, where we really seem to talk about the substance shelves or books are made of (see example (1) above).

Given that the Yudja stimuli in (28) and (29) do not contain number markers (number marking is optional and possible for human nouns only), the strong bias for number-based judgments as well as the fact that notional count nouns and notional mass nouns behave similarly shows that the availability of the volume interpretation is not sufficient to conclude that the nouns are interpreted as mass. Rather, the data strongly suggest that the notional mass nouns always have a count meaning, given that count meaning alone does not impose number-based answers in quantity judgment tasks with non-count quantity expressions.

To conclude, there is no clear evidence for treating Yudja as a language which permits both count and mass readings for nouns. Rather, *bitu* 'more' behaves as a non-count quantity expression, and as such is indifferent towards the presence vs. absence of count meaning. As in the case of English *more* and Brazilian Portuguese *mais*, it permits an evaluation of quantity in terms of different scales. The fact that quantity judgment studies show that both nouns with a count meaning and the presence of number marking or a count quantity expression (*itxïbï* 'many') introduce a bias for judgments based on number illustrate the asymmetry between count and mass and the importance of countability, rather than showing that volume readings would require mass meaning.

3.6. To Sum Up: Countability Matters

The data presented in the preceding sub-sections show that there are asymmetries between count and mass at different levels. Grammatical markers typically encode countability rather than the absence thereof, quantity expressions are

---

[5] In Doetjes (2021), I argue that count quantity expressions, number marking, and sortal classifiers can trigger an effect of 'individuation boosting': the fact that these expressions presuppose the presence of count meaning makes individuated, count meaning more salient.

either sensitive to countability or indifferent with respect to count vs. mass properties of the nouns they modify, and whereas a mass-only language seems inconceivable, Yudja may well be a language in which nouns systematically have count meanings. What non-count means depends on the level one is talking about: in the case of quantity expressions, non-count means indifference towards the opposition between mass and count meanings and indifference with respect to count vs. mass grammar. At the level of nouns, a non-count meaning lacks information about countable units. As indicated in Section 2, the lexical effects of a count–mass distinction in languages without inflectional number are sometimes assumed to be due to 'natural atomicity' or ontological properties of referents (Rothstein 2010; Wiltschko 2012). The next section will investigate count meanings and the concept of natural atomicity in more detail based on cross-linguistic comparison.

4. Natural Atomicity and Natural Countability: Count Meanings Across Languages

So far, it has been argued that all languages make use of grammatical expressions (number markers, quantity expressions) that can only be interpreted in relation to nouns that may have a count meaning. In inflectional number marking languages such as English, count quantity expressions are sensitive to grammatical properties of nouns as well, resulting in a grammatical count–mass distinction that does not always reflect the opposition between count vs. non-count meanings of nouns. The discrepancy between count, individuated meaning, and count syntax as realized by inflectional number marking is particularly evident in the results of the quantity judgment experiments of Barner and Snedeker (2005), in which grammatical mass nouns such as *silverware* pattern with count nouns such as *shoes* rather than with substance denoting mass nouns such as *toothpaste*.

In this section I will examine several types of count meanings from a cross-linguistic point of view, focusing on parallels and differences between typologically different languages.

4.1.   The Linguistic Representation of Aggregates: Furniture

The existence of nouns such as *furniture*, which are mass from the point of view of their grammatical properties while being count from the point of view of their meaning, is typical for languages such as English, which present an obligatory singular–plural opposition for count nouns and sensitivity of count quantity expressions to this grammatical marking. These properties make it possible to allow for exceptions that act as mismatches of the system (Chierchia 2010; Doetjes 2021).

It has often been observed that this type of phenomenon typically occurs for certain types of nouns (Bale and Barner 2009; Grimm 2012b). Nouns such as *furniture* are also called collective nouns, and the fact that they are used to refer to collections of items is relevant: the individual pieces of furniture are in a sense put to the background by the absence of a singular–plural contrast. When looking for nouns that, despite their clearly individuated meaning, behave grammatically as mass nouns, nouns that denote collections such as *luggage* and *furniture* are among the usual suspects that one should check. Nouns such as *furniture* illustrate that the opposition between 'there are units that can be counted' and 'there are no units that can be counted' that I argued play a crucial role in the meaning of quantity expressions is too black and white in view of the much more subtle differences in the salience of individuation between types of referents in the real world. These more subtle differences led Grimm (2012b) to postulating the concept of 'degrees of individuation', based on an ordering of types of referents according to their degree of individuation:[6]

(31) individual entities > collections of entities > granular substances > non-granular substances.

I assume that expressions that presuppose the presence of units that can be counted (that is, number markers, sortal classifiers, and count quantity expressions) trigger an effect of 'individuation boosting': their presence 'boosts' an individuated reading of the noun they combine with (Doetjes 2021). Turning back to nouns such as *furniture*, one can observe that a language such as English normally marks nouns that have a count meaning by means of a singular–plural opposition. However, the noun *furniture* is not marked for number, and following Cowper and Hall (2012), I will assume that these nouns have a morphological property that makes them incompatible with number marking, despite their meaning. As number marking in English is highly grammaticized, numerals and other quantity expressions that presuppose counting are not only sensitive to noun meaning but also impose the grammatical requirement of being combined with a noun that bears number. Within a system with systematic number marking, exceptions are possible, which results in making the units of counting less salient. As generally acknowledged (see Section 2 above), one cannot predict which

---

[6] I will only consider nouns whose referents correspond to collective aggregates here. Grimm discusses a much larger number of phenomena, including singulatives (see also Acquaviva 2008) and inverse number marking that reflects salience of individuation (see also Grimm 2012b). For discussion on granular substances, where the presence vs. absence of count meaning is less clear, see Sutton and Filip (2016b).

nouns will be treated as exceptions, which remains to a large extent arbitrary and language specific.

One of the questions is how much obligatory plural marking is necessary for a linguistic system in order to have nouns such as *furniture*. On the one hand, the phenomenon is not restricted to the specific type of number marking found in English. In the Ekoid language Ejagham (Watters 1981), number is marked by means of a noun class system, in which there exist pairs of noun classes that correspond to singular and plural forms of a noun (for number marking in noun class systems, see Marten forthcoming). As Watters shows, Ejagham has a large class of nouns that fall in a single noun class despite their countable meaning, and these nouns behave as *furniture* in the sense that they need insertion of a unit term (which Watters calls a classifier) in order to be combined with numerals. On the other hand, in languages with less contexts in which number marking occurs and/or is obligatory, such as Hungarian and Brazilian Portuguese, the evidence for exceptions is less clear, though perhaps not completely absent. According to Anikó Lipták (p.c.), the nouns *bútor* 'furniture' and *cucc* 'luggage' (informal) have plural forms but sound odd when directly combined with a numeral, while other nouns with similar meanings (e.g. *csomag*, the standard word for 'luggage') do not share this property. As for Brazilian Portuguese, while Pires de Oliveira and Rothstein (2011) treat the noun *mobília* 'furniture' in Brazilian Portuguese as an object denoting mass noun, younger speakers report using the word directly with numerals. More research is needed in order to determine what types of exceptional behavior can be found in inflectional number systems and how this relates to the pervasiveness of plural morphology in the system.

As for languages with numeral classifiers, L. Cheng (2012) observes that the special status of certain types of reference can be encoded by properties of the sortal classifiers that are typically used with these nouns. As shown by Cheng and Sybesma (1998), sortal classifiers in Mandarin differ from mensural classifiers by not allowing adjectival modification of the classifier nor insertion of the predicate marker *de*:

(32) a. sān (*xiǎo) zhī (*de) gǒu
three small CL DE dog
'three dogs'
b. wǔ dà bēi de jiǔ
two big CL^{cup} DE wine
'five big cups of wine' (Mandarin; L. Cheng 2012: 209–10)

The classifier that is used for the noun *jiājiù* 'furniture' is deviant: on the one hand it can be modified by a size adjective, but the obligatory absence of *de* shows that it does not pattern with mensural classifiers such as *xiāng* 'box':

(33) sān   dà   jiàn   (*de) jiājiù
      three big CL^{piece} DE furniture
      'three big suitcases'   (Mandarin; L. Cheng 2012: 211)

In this case the special status of the noun is encoded by particular properties of the sortal classifier with which it is typically combined. A different effect in classifier languages is observed by Erbach et al. (this volume, Chapter 7), who claim that the count quantity expression *nan-byaku-to-iu* 'hundreds of' in Japanese is infelicitous with nouns like *yūbinbutsu* 'mail', *kōtsū* 'traffic', *kaimono* 'shopping goods', despite the fact that they have count meaning.

This brief discussion shows that languages differ in how they can make use of their grammar in order to grammatically mark certain nouns (or classifiers) as being associated with less salient referents. Even though there is a clear tendency as to what types of nouns are affected, it is to a large extent also arbitrary which nouns fall in this category. At the same time, one needs to realize that even in a language such as English, ordinary count nouns with referents that fall in the category of collective aggregates may well have distributional properties as a group that can be attributed to the reduced individuation of their referents. In the psycholinguistic literature, nouns are categorized as plural-dominant if they are more easily associated with a plural form than with a singular form (Baayen et al. 1997). This property can correlate with lower individuation (Grimm 2012a), but it is important to realize that, in English, plural dominant nouns are still count nouns from a morphological perspective. Similarly, Lin and Schaeffer (2018) claim based on corpus-data that nouns that have less clearly individuated referents (which they call aggregate nouns) are much less frequently used with classifiers than nouns that have clearly individuated referents. As in the case of plural dominance, this property is based on frequency of certain combinations of lexemes, which is different from the grammatically encoded reduced individuation of nouns such as *furniture*. The type of number system found in English turns out to be particularly suitable for permitting exceptional cases, and thorough comparison of different types of systems is important to get more insight in the way degrees of individuation are encoded in language.

4.2. Measure Words

Whereas nouns such as *furniture* are clearly atomic, despite the 'reduced individuation' of their referents, measure words constitute a category of expressions that in many languages behave like count nouns, even though they name units that are not necessarily individuated. Cross-linguistically, measure words can be subdivided into two types: some have special syntactic properties and are clearly distinct from ordinary nouns, whereas others behave as ordinary nouns with a count meaning.

English is an example of a language in which measure words are used in a fairly similar way as count nouns in terms of number marking and compatibility with count quantity expressions. This is not only true when they are used on their individuated 'counting' reading but also on their abstract 'measuring reading' (see Rothstein 2009, 2017; Partee and Borschev 2012). As the following examples show, count quantity expressions such as *every* or *several* can be combined with measure words such as *inch* and *yards* on their measuring reading. In these examples the cloth and the fabric are not cut into individuated pieces of one inch/yard (Doetjes 2021):

(34) a. Every inch of cloth is used, nothing is wasted.
b. If you want to make that dress, you will need several yards of fabric.

This is not expected under an analysis that treats measure words as measure functions that map individuals onto numbers, in which case one would expect them to occur with numerals only (cf. Chierchia 1998a: 75; Lasersohn 2011).

Dutch is different, as a subdivision can be made between two types of measure words: one type does not take number marking, and the other type behaves like ordinary nouns (see, among others, Klooster 1972; Doetjes 1997; Vos 1999). Without number marking, only a measuring reading can be obtained. Examples are *twee liter* lit. 'two liter', *twee meter* lit. 'two meter', *twee jaar* lit. 'two year', and *twee uur* lit. 'two hour.' Not all measure words can be used without plural marking, however. Even though some northern varieties of Dutch allow the use of *twee maand* lit. 'two month', the standard variant requires the use of a plural noun (*twee maanden* 'two month-PL'; 'two months'), in which case *maanden* behaves grammatically as a count noun. If a measure word of the first type is used on its 'counting' interpretation, the plural form is used, but this is not the only condition in which the presence of the plural suffix is required (35a). Certain count quantity expressions such as *enkele* 'some, several', which contain the agreement marker *-e*, are incompatible with unmarked measure words irrespectively of the reading they have (35b).

(35) a. twee   meter(??s)   stof
         two   meter   fabric
         'two   meters of fabric'
     b. enkele   meter*(s)   stof
         several.AGR meter.PL   fabric
         'several meters of fabric'

The use of the plural marker in (35a) is only (marginally) possible under a counting reading, that is, there would need to be three separate objects corresponding to one meter of fabric each. This effect is absent in (35b), which is not marginal, and which does not imply that there are several separate objects. To sum up, some measure words in Dutch always behave as nouns, while others show a special grammatical behavior if they have a measuring reading and they are combined with a restricted set of cardinal count quantity expressions (roughly: cardinal numerals and *een paar* 'a few'); if one of these two conditions is not met, they bear number morphology. The subdivision between the two classes is arbitrary, and subject to dialectal variation.

It turns out that numeral classifier languages also offer evidence in favor of two types of measure words. As illustrated in the Mandarin examples below, *tiān* 'day' is incompatible with a classifier, which is usually taken to be an indication that it functions as a mensural classifier itself (cf. *twee jaar* 'two year' in Dutch). Given that *tiān* 'day' is a measure word, this is what we expect under the hypothesis that classifiers are some kind of measure words.

(36) a. sān   tiān
          three   day
          'three days'
      b. *sān   ge   tiān
          three   CL^{general} day   (Mandarin; Li and Thompson 1981: 105)

However, as in Dutch, measure words do not behave as a homogeneous group in this respect: *yuè* 'month' and *zhōngtou* 'hour' need insertion of the general classifier *ge*, and as such behave like ordinary nouns rather than as classifiers:

(37) a. liǎng   ge   yuè   b. *liǎng   yuè
          two   CL^{general} month   two   month
          'two months'
      c. jǐ   ge   zhōngtou   d. *jǐ   zhōngtou
          a.few   CL^{general} hour   a.few   hour
          'a few hours'   (Mandarin; Li and Thompson 1981: 169)

The Austronesian languages Taba (Bowden 2001) and Mokilese (Harrison and Albert 1976) are other examples of obligatory classifier languages in which measure words behave as ordinary nouns in the sense that they require insertion of a numeral classifier (Doetjes 2017c).

To conclude, measure words can have noun-like behavior in typologically distinct languages. Despite their abstract, non-individuated meaning, they typically pattern with nouns that can have a count meaning: they take number marking in English or Dutch, and they combine with the general sortal classifier *ge* in Mandarin. Given that they introduce clear information about how much counts as one unit of counting, a possible way of interpreting this is to assume that we are dealing with an abstract type of non-atomic count meaning (cf. Lasersohn 2011).

4.3. Atomicity and Count Meaning: Fences and Bouquets

A known problem of atomicity as a defining property of count meaning is that some count nouns in English are not atomic (see for instance Feldman 1973; Wiggins 1980; Zucchi and White 2001; Nicolas 2004; Rothstein 2010). Rothstein (2010) focuses on this type of noun in her analysis of the count–mass distinction in languages such as English. Nouns such as *rope, bouquet,* and *fence* are typically not atomic: a rope that is cut into two parts is turned into two ropes; one can put two smaller bouquets together to form one new big bouquet, and fences can be made up of objects that could also be called fences. Rothstein analyzes these nouns as 'semantically atomic' as opposed to 'naturally atomic' (see Section 2 above). According to Filip and Sutton (2017), these nouns become quantized in specific counting contexts, while Grimm (2012b) makes use of a connectedness condition to explain the behavior of this type of nouns, an approach that is also adopted by Lima (2014a) to explain the count properties of notional mass nouns in Yudja.

In this section, I will briefly discuss some cross-linguistic occurrences of this type of noun. It turns out that the type of meaning that we are dealing with is a generally occurring type of meaning for nouns that are compatible with count selecting grammatical expressions (sortal classifiers) or with count quantity expressions.

Consider first the following data from Mandarin. The following example illustrates that the noun *fence* has similar properties as its English counterpart (Yang Yang, p.c.):

(38) zhè-ge dà líba yóu sì-ge líba zǔchéng
 this-CL^{general} big fence by four-CL^{general} fence composed
 'This big fence is composed of four fences.' (Mandarin; Yang Yang, p.c.)

The noun *huā-shù* 'flower bunch, bouquet' is used in a similar context. This noun contains the classifier *shù* 'bunch'. The compound takes the general classifier *ge*:

(39) zhè-ge dà huā-shù yóu sì-ge xiǎo huā-shù zǔchéng
 this-CL^{general} big flower-bunch by four-CL^{general} small flower-bunch composed
 'This big bunch of flowers is composed of four small bunches.' (Mandarin; Jianan Liu, p.c.)

Indonesian, an optional classifier language that has been claimed to easily permit count meanings for notional mass nouns (Dalrymple and Mofu 2012), also permits context-dependent count meanings, as illustrated by the noun *pagar* 'fence' in (40):

(40) Pagar besar ini terdiri dari empat (buah) pagar.
 Fence big this composed of four (CL^{inanimate}) fence
 'This big fence is composed of four fences.' (Indonesian; Nurhayu Santoso, p.c.)

Even though these are just a few examples, it seems that the type of noun exemplified by *fence* and *bouquet* is commonly used in grammatical count contexts across languages, suggesting that this is a natural type of count meaning.

A property that a subclass of these nouns have in common is that they behave as flexible nouns (Filip and Sutton 2017). Again, this correlation is also found for Mandarin and Indonesian, which both also permit measure uses of these nouns, as in Mandarin *liǎng-mǐ líba* 'two CL^{meter} fence' and Indonesian *dua meter pagar* 'two meter fence.'

4.4. Flexible Nouns and Shifts

The phenomenon that one and the same noun can be shown to have both a count and a mass use is very common, as already indicated by Gleason (1965). Whereas in some cases it is hard to say which use is at the basis of the other (see for instance the nouns in Sections 4.1–4.3), other shifts can be described as coercions, as one of the two uses seems to be forced by the grammatical environment in which the noun occurs. At the same time, Lima (2014a) convincingly argues that the types of meanings that are found for nouns such as *apeta* 'blood' and *y'a* 'water' in Yudja do not constitute cases of coercion, unlike #*two waters* in English, which is only permitted in particular contexts.

As coercion is triggered by the grammatical environment of a noun, the possibilities for coercion may vary depending on the grammatical properties of a language. Again, the morphological system of English seems particularly suited for marking exceptions and thus facilitating coercion. The absence of obligatory plural marking on a noun that normally is marked for a singular–plural opposition can force a count-to-mass shift, as illustrated in the example in (1) above. As shown by Cheng, Doetjes, and Sybesma (2008), Mandarin nouns often resist 'grinding', the metaphor generally used for the shift that transforms an object denoting count noun into a mass noun that denotes the substance the original object was made of (Pelletier 1975). The Mandarin example in (41) only has a 'wallpaper reading':

(41) qiáng-shang   dōu   shì   gǒu
      wall-top   all   COP   dog
      'There are dogs all over the wall.'
      NOT: 'There is dog all over the wall.'
      (Mandarin; Cheng, Doetjes, and Sybesma 2008: 50)

Grinding is typically productive in languages that systematically mark the difference between mass and count meanings by morphology. In most cases, a bare singular noun in English can only be interpreted as a mass noun, and therefore the use of a bare count noun that lacks plural marking is interpreted as having a mass meaning. This is why nouns such as *furniture*, which grammatically behave as mass, cannot undergo grinding, as there is no possible trigger for coercion (see Bale and Barner 2009 for a different type of analysis, in which all grammatical count nouns are treated as flexible nouns).

When looking at the types of meanings that are found for nouns that may have both count and mass meanings across languages, one can observe similar patterns on the one hand, and arbitrary differences on the other. When nouns that correspond to the English noun *water* are used in a count context, often a portion reading or a type reading can be obtained, and in many languages this is described as coercion. At the same time, the types of meanings that are obtained cannot be completely explained based on the properties of referents and world knowledge. The Algonquian language Ojibwe is an example of a language which productively allows for pluralization of mass nouns. As observed by Mathieu (2012a), certain types of count meanings, despite their frequent occurrence in other languages, cannot be obtained: liquid-denoting nouns do not permit pluralization and cannot be used in either portion readings or in kind readings; kind readings do not seem to be permitted for other nouns either. When comparing Dutch and English, two typologically similar languages, my impression is that English allows for mass-to-count shifts and pluralization of mass nouns much more easily. The use of *gold* for *gold medal* as in *two Olympic golds* is not possible in (my) Dutch, and *twee bieren* means only *two beers* in the sense of 'two types of beers'; for the serving reading a diminutive form is used (*twee biertjes* 'two beer-DIM-PL').

As for abstract nouns, even more variation seems to occur, both within and across languages (Pelletier and Schubert 1989). Whereas English *advice* and *news* are mass, the corresponding French noun *conseil* and *nouvelle* are count. The difference between the English and French forms could be compared to the difference between English *blush* and French *rougir*. Even though these verbs are near synonyms, the meaning of *rougir* marks the transition between not blushing and blushing (it is a change of state verb), while English *blush* is not: it describes the blushing 'activity' (it is an activity verb). Without assuming that these differences have repercussions on the way French and English speakers perceive the world, it is plausible that there is no one-to-one mapping between phenomena in the real world (particularly abstract ones) and the linguistic representation of these phenomena in the mental lexicon.

As in the previous sections, several observations can be made. In the first place, grammatical systems, and in particular the type of obligatory number marking system of English that requires plural marking in a large number of contexts, makes both coercions and exceptions possible. In the second place, the types of count meanings that are found cross-linguistically are similar, even though some types of count meanings that are easily present in one language may be absent in others (e.g. type of Noun meanings). As far as I can see, there are no systematic differences in the types of meanings that are found between inflectional number marking languages and other languages, and the particular properties of the count–mass distinction seem to be in the first place morphological in nature. Finally, despite the tendencies, one can find a large amount of variation, much of which is rather arbitrary: in many cases nouns seem to have or not have certain count meanings 'par le simple usage'.

5. Conclusions

Count and mass are asymmetrical notions, both when used to describe the properties of grammatical expressions or quantity expressions that interact with countability, and when used to describe the types of meanings nouns may have. In both cases, what seems to be encoded is count: quantity expressions and grammatical markers are sensitive or insensitive to the presence of count meaning, and nouns can have count meanings or meanings that are incompatible with count quantity expressions because they lack information about countable units. Moreover, whereas mass-only languages do not exist, it may well be the case that in some languages, such as Yudja (Lima 2014a), all predicative nouns have count meaning.

The system of English, on which many formal models of count vs. mass are based, is particularly complex, because the systematic requirement to mark singular and plural forms for nouns that have countable meaning offers opportunities to create exceptions that introduce a large amount of extra arbitrariness in the system. Moreover, count quantity expressions are typically limited to nouns that have a singular–plural opposition, and as such they interfere with the morphological complexity introduced by number inflection.

The small cross-linguistic comparison of types of nouns that can be used in the context of grammatical expressions that depend on count meaning suggests that count meanings are rather similar across languages. Something like 'natural atomicity' seems to exist, but 'natural countability' seems a better term, as the different classes of count meanings show that this property is broader than atomicity in a strict sense. In all cases, what seems crucial is that the noun provides information about what counts as a single unit of an N, which comes close to the way Quine defined divided reference, but abstracts away from the morphological complications of the English system. The difference between languages with and without obligatory number marking seems not to be related to fundamental differences in available count meanings, but rather to the presence vs. absence of a grammatical system of number marking and the use languages can make of such a system in order to express a lower degree of individuation or to coerce meaning shifts. It is clear that these claims are at this point rather tentative, and that large-scale cross-linguistic comparison is necessary to gain a deeper understanding of countability in natural language.

5 Divide and Counter

Hagit Borer and Sarah Ouwayda

1. Introduction

The purpose of this paper is to investigate the properties and distribution of the classifier -*ah* in Arabic. The investigation will turn out to shed light on the count–mass distinction in general, and in Arabic in particular, and will result in identifying two distinct types of plural markers, differing in their semantics, in their morphology, and in their syntax, one corresponding roughly to the type of plural marker found in English, at times referred to as *inclusive*, and the other returning solely an *exclusive* plural reading. It will also motivate a structural distinction between quantifiers and cardinals, with the cardinals merging structurally below the quantifiers.

1.1. Theoretical Assumptions

Our starting point is a system in which content lexical items have no syntactic properties as such and specifically the execution of this idea in Borer (2005) (the Exoskeletal Model).[1] In such a system the count–mass distinction must be mediated through syntactic structure. Thus regardless of its epistemological or ontological content, a nominal is count or mass in the context of some functional structure. Following Borer (2005), we assume that such a dedicated structure, effectively a divider, is associated with *count* properties, and that *mass* properties emerge in the absence of a divider, and do not require dedicated functional structure to be available. Illustrations of the relevant structures are in (1)–(2):[2]

---

[1] Specifically, syntactic properties are associated exclusively with (closed class) functors with a rigid designation (in the usual semantic sense but also potentially relative to a fixed syntactic function). See Gajewski (2002, 2009) for some relevant discussion.
[2] Where $\#^{max}$=Quantity^{max}, and where Div^{max} returns a count (non-mass) structure. We abstract away here from some aspects of the execution in Borer (2005, 2013), which are largely irrelevant for our purposes, and specifically, from the view of functional heads as variables bound by functors.

(1) **Count Structure:** 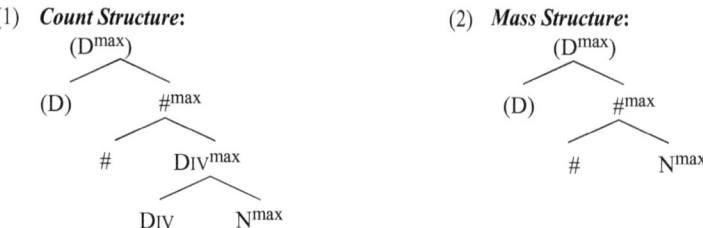 (2) **Mass Structure:**

An immediate advantage of a system that views mass and count as exclusively structural properties is that it provides a direct account for the frequently observed flexibility of the count–mass distinction relative to specific lexical items, without the need to resort to additional mechanisms such as type shifting to map between two readings of the same noun. Some illustrations of such flexibility are in (3)–(5):[3]

(3)   a. I'd like beer, please.
        b. I'd like a beer, please.

(4)   a. There is rabbit all over the floor.
        b. There is a rabbit in the garden.

(5)   a. That's quite a bit of carpet for the money.
        b. That's a nice carpet.

Languages with morphological non-phrasal classifiers provide a direct illustration of the structures in (1), under the assumption that such morphological classifiers are instances of D$_{IV}$. One observes, in particular, the absence of dedicated *mass* inflection vs. the presence of dividing classifiers. Thus consider (6a–b) from Mandarin Chinese, with the proposed structure in (7) (the DP layer set aside here and elsewhere as largely immaterial):

(6)   a. henduo   li   mi   *li*=classifier associated with   *Mandarin*
          a-lot   CL   rice   elongated units   *Chinese*
          'many grains of rice'
       b. san   li   mi
          three   CL   rice
          'three grains of rice'

(7)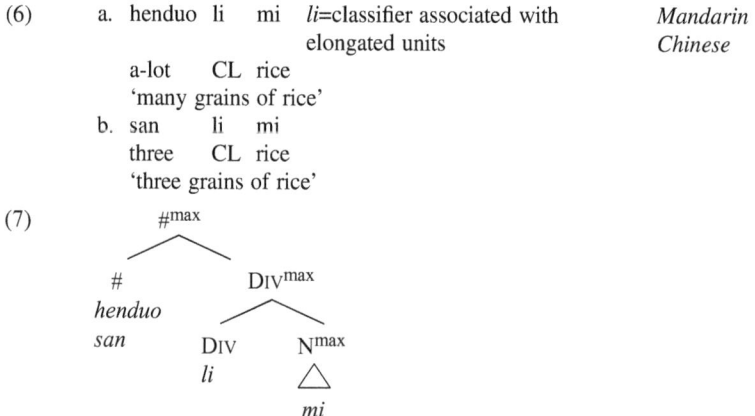

---

[3] And see Chierchia (1998a), i.a. for a fuller review and discussion.

In the absence of DIV, however, mass interpretation emerges and a classifier is impossible. As a consequence, *henduo* is interpreted as 'much' rather than 'many', and cardinals are barred:

(8) a. henduo   mi   *Mandarin Chinese*
       a-lot   rice
       'much rice'
    b. *san   mi
       three   rice
       'three rices/three grains of rice'

(9)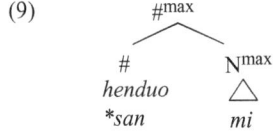

Cross-linguistically, a Chinese-type classifier is not always in evidence. Nonetheless, in English-type languages DIV could be marked by so-called plural marking (cf. Borer 2005). Like morphological classifiers, plural marking may occur with nominals that are otherwise unspecified as mass or count, where it marks the entire projection as divided and hence *count* rather than *mass*. Crucially, from this perspective (so-called) plural marking in itself does not entail the existence of (coherent) atomic singulars or sums, a conclusion amply exemplified by the examples in (10)–(12) (cf. Krifka 1995; Sauerland 2003; Borer 2005; Sauerland, Anderssen, and Yatsushiro 2005, and much subsequent literature):

(10) a. 0.3 apples; 1.0 apples; zero apples
     b. *0.3 apple; *1.0 apple; *zero apple

(11) a. Unfortunately, I noticed bananas in the fruit salad, and so I can't eat it.
     b. #You shouldn't have a problem. I only put one.

(12) a. Do send your children to school!
     b. #Well, I guess I don't have to, as I only have the one.

In Borer (2005), the number-neutral, inclusive reading for *bananas* or *children* in (11)–(12) emerges in the presence of DIV, but the absence of # (cf. 13a). In such structures, plural marking sets the grounds, as would a classifier, for 'counting' by creating a web, or a *reticule*, of an infinite number of cells with an identical restriction, some of which may correspond to fragments of canonical individuals. Actual individuals, and consequently sums (at times referred to as *exclusive* readings), are in turn created by quantity expressions such as *many* or cardinals, which are a function from a given reticule to a specific quantity of cells (and including none, or cells which correspond to a portion of a canonical individual), with the structure in

(13b). Finally, absent D<small>IV</small>, a quantity-of-mass reading is returned in (13c) (copies in angled brackets):[4]

(13) a. (D^{max}) *Inclusive reading*   b. (D^{max}) *Exclusive reading*

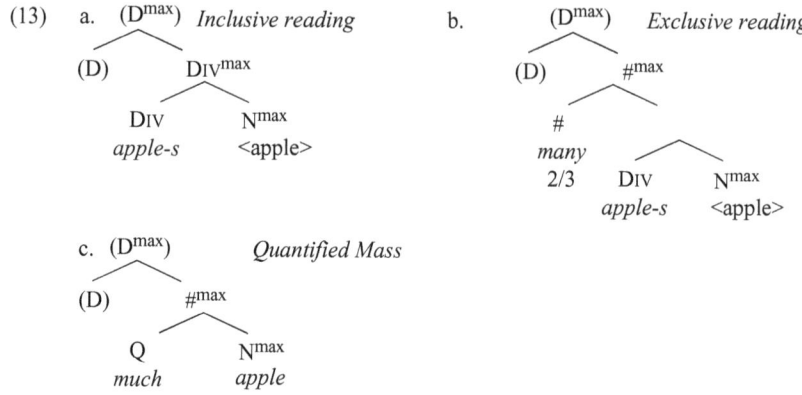

c. (D^{max}) *Quantified Mass*

1.2. Challenging the Analysis

The system, as formulated, directly predicts the complementary distribution of morphological classifiers and plural marking in any given nominal structure. That morphological classifiers do not, in fact, co-occur with plurals has been previously observed, and we quote from T'sou (1976) (and see also Doetjes 1996, 2012; Haspelmath 2001):

(14) [T]he study of nominal classifier systems suggests an important hypothesis that the use of nominal classifiers and the use of plural morpheme [is] in complementary distribution in natural language. More correctly, it suggests that either a) a natural language has either nominal classifiers or plural morphemes, or b) if a natural language has both kinds of morphemes, then their use is in complementary distribution.

(p. 1216) (henceforth *T'sou's Generalization*)

A perusal of nominal structures in a broad range of languages suggests that this proposed universal is extremely robust. While a few cases have been cited as potential counterexamples, such counterexamples are infrequent to begin with, and quite a few of them, upon further scrutiny, turn out not to involve

---

[4] For extensive discussions of *inclusive* vs. *exclusive* readings see Hoeksema (1983); Schwarzschild (1996); Sauerland (2003); Sauerland, Anderssen, and Yatsushiro (2005); Spector (2007); Zweig (2009); Bale, Gagnon, and Khanjian (2011); Grimm (2012a), i.a. See also Dali and Mathieu (2016) for a brief discussion of this issue in Arabic. We return to this matter in Section 6.3. See Borer (2005) for the structural analysis of singulars within this approach, as well as brief comments in footnotes 7 and 21. Note, finally, that, e.g., the inclusive reading in (11) is available without any clear monotone-decreasing licensor, undermining the frequent claim in the literature to the contrary.

'plural' marking in the relevant sense, insofar as it is demonstrably not an instance of DIV.[5] The focus of this paper is to examine yet one more apparent counterexamples to this complementarity, this time in Arabic. As noted by Zabbal (2002, 2005) and Fassi Fehri (2004), the Arabic morpheme -*ah* (at times -*eh* in some vernaculars), frequently just a feminine ending, may be added to a certain class of (otherwise morphologically unmarked) nouns which denote mass or an indeterminate quantity (henceforth referred to as *batch* nouns). In these contexts, -*ah* (henceforth labeled -$\underline{AH}$ in such contexts) functions very much like a divider, or a classifier, as illustrated in (15) for Lebanese Arabic (LA). Identical effects hold for Modern Standard Arabic (SA). In what follows, and unless otherwise noted, all cases in which identical effects hold in Standard and Lebanese are exemplified in Lebanese.

(15)   *'batch/type' reading*   *'unit-of' reading*
      a. ʕaSar-t   laymoun   ʕaSar-t   laymoun-eh
         squeezed-1s   orange   squeezed-1s   orange-$\underline{AH}$
         'I squeezed orange.'   'I squeezed an orange.'
      b. staʕmal-t   waraʔ   staʕmal-t   waraʔ-ah
         used-1s   paper   used-1s   paper-$\underline{AH}$
         'I used paper.'   'I used a piece of paper.'
      c. šreb-t   biirah   šreb-t   biiray-eh
         drank-1s   beer   drank-1s   beer-$\underline{AH}$
         'I drank beer.'   'I drank a beer.'

Under the plausible assumption that -$\underline{AH}$ is a dividing morpheme, and hence an instance of DIV, and continuing to assume that plural marking is, likewise, an instance of DIV, we predict the complementary distribution of -$\underline{AH}$ and plural marking, given that they compete for the same structural (and semantic) slot. As it turns out, however, -$\underline{AH}$ does co-occur with plural marking, as illustrated in (16):

(16)   a. tlat   laymoun-eet
          three   orange-$\underline{AH}$-pl
          'three oranges'
        b. štar-o   sabʕ   djeej-eet
          bought-3pl   seven   chicken-$\underline{AH}$-pl
          'They bought seven chickens.'

In (16), -$\underline{AH}$ is not immediately visible as a discrete morpheme separate from the plural marking -*eet* or at times -*aat*. However, as we will show in Section 3,

---

[5] See, i.a., Park's (2008) analysis of the Korean 'plural' -*tul* as a distributivity marker, rather than a plural marker. See De Belder (2008) for the analysis of Dutch diminutives as instances of a SIZE modifier of DIV, rather than DIV, directly.

it must be structurally present. The resolution of the apparent conflict between the grammaticality of the examples in (16) and the analysis of plural marking as heading DIV is the starting point of this paper. The apparent conflict, once resolved, will turn out in actuality to provide evidence for two distinct types of syntactic and semantic plural markings: one which heads DIV, and which yields a number-neutral, inclusive reading, and another which is inherently linked to cardinals and to #, and which gives rise, perforce, to a reading which excludes singulars (or, for that matter, any cardinality not directly specified). The resulting system, in turn, will lend additional support to a syntactic approach to the count–mass distinction in general, and to the view of (much of) plural marking as linked to DIV, rather than to sums, as such.

1.3. An Outline

Section 2 of this paper is devoted to a brief overview of gender and plural marking in Arabic. In Section 3 we focus on the morphology of plural-marked -AH nouns (PL-AH-Ns), showing that what is transcribed as -eet in (16a–b) must be analyzed as consisting of -AH+eet_{PL}, rather than as a mono-morphemic plural marker which merges directly with the stem.

In Section 4 we turn to a comparison between PL-AH-Ns and other plural-marked forms, focusing on a wide range of syntactic and semantic differences, all pointing toward the conclusion that the plural marking attested with -AH-Ns, although morphologically identical to feminine plural, is nonetheless clearly distinct from plural marking on stems, in particular in requiring the obligatory presence of a cardinal (or a cardinal-like expression such as 'several'). In turn, this very distinction paves the way to motivating different structures for cardinals and quantifiers, a conclusion independently supported, specifically for Arabic, in Section 5. The emerging DP structure is discussed in Section 6. In Section 6 we also revisit the putative Arabic counterexample to T'sou's Generalization, arguing that the plural marking which co-occurs with -AH is not an instance of DIV, but rather an instance of semantically vacuous agreement with a cardinal in [Spec,#]. The interpretation of PL-AH-Ns as exclusive plurals, in turn, follows directly from the obligatory presence of $\#^{max}$. Section 7 concludes.

2. Arabic Nouns – Gender and Number Marking

2.1. The Morpheme -ah and Gender Marking

All Arabic nouns are gender-marked as either masculine or feminine, with gender membership in biologically gendered nominals following obvious lines. While masculine marking is ∅, feminine marking is typically overt and realized as -ah.[6] The relevant cases are exemplified in (17)–(20).

(17) Biologically masculine, *grammatically* masculine
a. Sabi;   bsein   kalb;   mhandes
   boy   cat$_M$ dog$_M$ engineer$_M$
b. rijjaal;   HSaan;   asad;   jamal
   man   horse$_M$ lion$_M$ camel$_M$

(18) Biologically feminine, *grammatically* feminine
a. Sabiy-eh;   bsayn-eh;   kalb-eh;   mhands-eh
   youth-F   cat-F   dog-F   engineer-F
   young woman   cat$_F$ dog$_F$ engineer$_F$
b. mar-ah;   ʕanz-eh;   labw-eh;   neeʔ-ah
   woman   goat   lioness   camel$_F$
   (*mar)   (*ʕanz)   (*labw)   (*neeʔ)

(19) Biologically genderless, *grammatically* masculine
a. kersi;   maktab;   maʕmal;   daraj;   maʔlab
   chair   desk   factory   staircase   prank
b. *kersi-eh   maktab-eh   *maʕmal-eh   daraj-eh   *maʔlab-eh
   *chair-F   library-F   *factory-F   degree-F   *prank-F

(20) Biologically genderless, *grammatically* feminine
a. Taawl-ah;   siyyaar-ah;   ʕelb-eh;   šant-ah
   table   car   box   backpack
   (*Taawl)   (*siyyaar)   (*ʕelb)   (*šant)
b. lawH-ah;   bineey-eh;   ʔalb-eh
   painting   building   flip
   (lawH = board)   (bina = building-activity)   (ʔalb = heart)

In anticipation of the detailed discussion of the divider morpheme -AH, we note that -ah is not a divider or a classifier as such. For one thing, -ah is entirely compatible with mass reading, a point we return to in Section 3.1:

(21) ktiir   serʕ-ah;   ktiir   maHabb-eh
     much   speed-F   much   affection-F
     not 'many speeds'   not 'many affections'

We note further that in all these cases, -ah need not merge specifically with a batch noun, and that frequently there is no discernible (masculine) noun with which -ah merges. Rather, -ah appears to be a pure gender marker (and setting aside the question of how such 'pure gender marking' might be represented.)

The morpheme -ah is grammatically feminine in all its occurrences. However, as already exemplified briefly in (15), and in contrast with the pure

---

[6] Or as -eh in some instances in LA. The morpheme, in both SA and LA, is pronounced as -t-final (-at or -et) in some phonological environments.

gender marking function in (18) and (20)–(21), in some well-defined contexts it functions as a divider of a batch noun (-_AH_), giving rise to a 'unit-of' interpretation. The *batch* nouns with which -_AH_ merges are always grammatically mass, with the range of interpretations typically associated with grammatical mass (an indeterminate quantity, a collective, stuff, etc.). -_AH_ affixation is productive and may affect newly borrowed items:[7]

(22) a. krwasan   → krwason-eh
         croissant   croissant–_AH_
         'croissant' (food type)   'a croissant'
      b. seven?ap   → seven?appey-eh
         Seven-up (food type)   Seven-up–_AH_
         'Seven-up'   'a bottle of Seven-up'

That the batch nouns with which -_AH_ merges are grammatically mass can be demonstrated with the quantifiers *ktiir* 'much/many' and *šway(t)* 'little/a few.' To return a count restriction, *ktiir/šway(t)* must merge with plural-marked nominals. Not so with mass expressions, as illustrated by (23). As expected, batch nouns which may otherwise be -_AH_-divided may occur bare with *ktiir/ šway(t)*, showing them to be grammatically mass, as in (24).[8]

(23) ktiir/šwayt may; ktiir/šwayt Hubb; ktiir/šwayt maʕrifeh;
      much/little water much/little love much/little knowledge

(24) a. ktiir/šwayt teffeeH;   ktiir/šwayt biira; ktiir/šwayt Tabšour;
         much/little apple;   much/little beer; much/little chalk;
      b. ktiir/šwayt hamberger; ktiir/šwayt seven?ap
         much   hamburger much   seven-up

Equally consistent with the grammatical mass property of batch nouns is the fact that in the presence of *weeHed* 'one$_M$' or *waHdeh* 'one$_F$', the batch form receives the interpretation of *kind* (i.e., 'one kind of cow/cattle' in (25c)), and as such is consistent, e.g. with multiple instances of *baʔar*, 'cow.' When divided by -_AH_, on the other hand, a single unit interpretation is the only one available in such contexts, and a kind reading is excluded:

(25) a. biira waHdeh;   biiray-eh waHdeh
         beer one   beer–_AH_ one
         'one type of beer' 'one beer'
         *one beer

---

[7] We adopt the view of the *-ah* morpheme as a classifier first made by Zabbal (2002), who treats it as an instance of a *singulative*. We diverge from his treatment in assuming that -_AH_-Ns are not inherently singular as such, and that a singular reading emerges, for such expressions, in 'singular' structural configurations, which require the identification of D$_{IV}$ and #, a matter set aside in this paper. See Borer (2005) and Ouwayda (2014) for the relevant structural analysis.

[8] PL–_AH_-Ns cannot occur with quantifiers, a matter we return to in Sections 4 and 6. They may, and indeed must, occur with cardinals.

b. Tabšour   weeHed;   Tabšour-ah   waHdeh
   chalk   one   chalk-_AH_   one
   'one type of chalk'   'one chalk'
   one chalk
c. ba?ar   weeHed;   ba?r-ah   waHdeh
   cow   one   cow-_AH_   one
   'one type of cattle' 'one cow'
   one cow

The interpretational contrast between the 'source' mass nominals and their -_AH_-divided counterparts can be nicely illustrated in the context of restrictors such as *bass* 'only' in LA or *laysa – illaa* or *la – illaa* 'not – except' in SA. As illustrated by (26a) and (27a), in the case of undivided stems, what is excluded are all other (relevant) *kinds* or *batches*. With -_AH_-divided stems, on the other hand, it is *units* of the *same type* that are excluded but, crucially, nothing else. This is illustrated in (26b) and (27b):

(26) a. laysa   laday-naa   illaa   tuffaH   SA
         not   at-us   except   apple
         'We only have apple.' (and no other food, and possibly *more than a single apple*)
      b. laysa   laday-naa   illaa   tuffaH-ah
         not   at-us   except   apple-_AH_
         'We only have one apple.' (and specifically no more *apples*, but possibly other food)

(27) a. ken   fi   bass   ?zeez   bi   l-?arD   LA
         was   exist   only   glass   in   the-floor
         'There was only glass on the floor.' (and no other kinds of objects)
      b. ken   fi   bass   ?zeez-eh   bi   l-?arD
         was   exist   only   glass-_AH_ in   the-floor
         'There was only a single piece of glass on the floor.' (no other glass, but possibly other objects)

As is evident from (26)–(27), it is precisely the presence vs. absence of -_AH_ that is crucial for a grammatical distinction to emerge between a count reading and a mass reading. As is further clear, it is the presence of a count interpretation which requires a higher degree of grammatical complexity, regardless of the ontological or epistemological salience of the denotation under consideration. This is by no means a trivial result. We note that, at least arguably, concepts such as 'tree' or 'apple' are considerably more salient as count, and the mass or collective reading associated with them (i.e., 'apple stuff', 'forest') is conceptually derivative. One could easily imagine an inflectional grammatical system that would prioritize conceptual distinctions, with salient mass concepts displaying less grammatical complexity than their units, but salient count concepts displaying less grammatical complexity than the mass that could be formed from them. This, however, is not the case. By and large, we do find, inflectionally, dividing structures including classifiers as well as singulative and plural markers. 'Massifying' grammatical functors, on the other hand, are difficult to come by. There are no classifier-like elements which, when added to count nouns turn them into mass; there are no inflectional mass endings to parallel plural endings, and there are no dedicated mass determiners which distinguish mass from singular, functioning as the mirror image of the indefinite count determiner *a* in English or *uno/una/unos* in Spanish. It therefore emerges that insofar as -*AH* marks division, and at times of nouns which denote concepts that are already salient as count (e.g. *apple*), it provides support for any system in which grammatical properties are divorced from the conceptual properties of open class vocabulary, and in which 'count' grammatical representations are more complex than 'mass' ones.

Our starting point, therefore, is that the structure for -*AH* is as in (28), in line with the structure proposed for count nominals in general in (1):

(28)

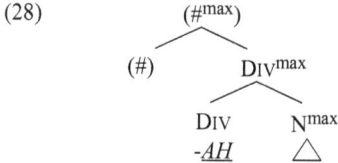

2.2. *Arabic Plurals – Background Notes*

Our null hypothesis is that in Arabic, as in other languages analyzed from the relevant perspective, plural marking resides in DIV. For most instances of plural in Arabic, this assumption is rather straightforward, as we shall see shortly. This is not so, however, for -*AH* marked nouns. As noted already, plural marking does co-occur with -*AH* marked nouns (cf. 16). If such plural marking competes for the DIV node in (28), we do not expect both -*AH* and plural marking to occur in the same noun phrase. Alternatively, as they do co-occur, we must assume that one or the other is not actually in DIV. In the following sections we will embark on showing that this is precisely the case, and that in -*AH*-N-pl, the plural marking is not in actuality an instance of DIV. To show that this is, indeed, the case, we need to embark upon a brief description of Arabic plurals, where considerable morphological complexity is in evidence.

Broadly speaking, plural markings in Arabic belong to three morphophonological classes. The three classes are as follows:

(29)   a. Broken plural (auto-segmental)
       b. Sound masculine plural (affixal)
       c. Sound feminine plural (affixal)

Broken plurals (29a), as in (30)–(31) (abbreviated BR), are morphologically auto-segmental. The consonants of the root are maintained while the vowels differ in the singular (or otherwise unmarked stem) and the plural. A broken plural may occur in both masculine and feminine nouns. There are no lexical-semantic restrictions on its occurrence, and it is productive, insofar as it may be associated with novel words introduced into the language, as illustrated by (32).[9]

(30) *Broken plural, masculine nouns, LA (including biological gender):*
    a. rijjaal → rjeel
        man   man-pl$_{BR}$
        'man'   'men'
    b. fann → funoun
        art   art-pl$_{BR}$
        'art'   'arts'

(31) *Broken plural, feminine nouns, LA:*
    a. šantah → šanat
        bag   bag-pl$_{BR}$
        'bag'   'bags'
    b. madiineh → mudun
        city   city-pl$_{BR}$
        'city' 'cities'

(32) *New coinages/borrowings – broken plurals*
    a. blouzeh → blouwaz   (from the French *blouse*)
        blouse   bouse-pl$_{BR}$
        'blouse' 'blouses'
    b. ʔamiis → ʔemsaan   (from the French *chemise*)
        button-shirt   button-shirt-pl$_{BR}$
        'button shirt' 'button shirts'

Sound masculine plural (29b) (abbreviated SM) occurs only in human masculine nouns. As the term implies, the stem remains 'sound', unchanged, and the plural morpheme *-iin* attaches to it.[10]

(33) *Sound masculine plural, LA:*
    a. serraaʔ → serraaʔ-iin
        thief   thief-pl$_{SM}$
        'thief'   'thieves'
    b. museeʕed → museʕid-iin
        assistant assistant-pl$_{SM}$
        'assistant' 'assistants'

Sound feminine plural (29c) (abbreviated SF), like Sound masculine plural, leaves the stem intact, affixing *-aat/-eet* to it.[11] Sound feminine plural occurs in

---

[9] The choice of particular BR form for a given nominal stem is prosodically driven, and we set it aside here as largely orthogonal to our main point. See in particular Ghalayiini (1912, 2006) for the relevant characteristics.
[10] SA Sound masculine plurals may be marked for case, surfacing as *-oun* (nominative) or *-iin* (accusative/genitive). LA lost case morphology and the Sound masculine plural morpheme is always *-iin*.
[11] In SA, Sound feminine is consistently *-aat*. In LA, the choice between *-aat* or *-eet* is contingent on the phonological properties of the stem.

both biologically feminine nouns and in grammatically feminine nouns. It obeys no discernible lexical restrictions.

(34) *Sound feminine plural, grammatically feminine nouns, LA:*
 a. mxadd-eh → mxadd-eet
    pillow   pillow-pl$_{SF}$
    'pillow'   'pillows'
 b. lamb-ah   → lamb-aat
    lightbulb   lightbulb-pl$_{SF}$
    'lightbulb' 'lightbulbs'

(35) *Sound feminine plural, biologically feminine nouns, LA:*
 a. bsayn-eh → bsayn-eet
    cat   cat-pl$_{SF}$
    'cat'   'cats'
 b. mʕallm-eh → mʕallm-eet
    teacher   teacher-pl$_{SF}$
    'teacher'   'teachers'

In Sound feminine plural forms, note that the presence of the feminine singular morpheme *-ah/-eh* is phonologically masked by the plural marking. As we show in the next section, however, *-ah/-eh* is present syntactically and semantically, excluding a derivation in which *-eet/-aat* merges directly with a masculine or otherwise unmarked stem.

3. Plural Marking and -<u>AH</u>-Divided Nominals

3.1. One Stem, Two Plural Forms, Two Readings

While the plural forms in (16) have been glossed as an affixation of a plural ending to -<u>AH</u>, from a phonological perspective, such an analysis is not self-evident. Another possibility would be to assume that the Sound feminine plural (SF) *-eet/-aat* merges directly with the stem, and no intermediate -<u>AH</u> affixation is involved. The alternative gloss to (16), partially repeated here as (36a), would be as in (36b) and, similarly, the contrast between (36c) and (36d). Ironically enough, the reanalysis in (36) would automatically do away with the puzzle we have set out to solve – if forms such as *laymouneet* 'oranges' or *djeejeet* 'chickens' do not involve the merger of -<u>AH</u>, we would be free to assume that the SF merges as DIV, thus giving rise to a divided reading of the stem directly, with no violation of T'sou's Generalization emerging.

(36) a. štar-o   sabʕ   djeej-eet   b. štar-o   sabʕ   djeej-eet
       bought-3pl seven   chicken-<u>AH</u>-pl   bought-3pl seven   chicken-**pl$_{SF}$**
       'They bought seven chickens.'   'They bought seven chickens.'

c. tlat   laymoun-eet   d. tlat   laymoun-eet
   three   orange-_AH_-pl   three   orange-pl$_{SF}$
   'three oranges'   'three oranges'

Our first task, then, is to show that the glossed parse in (16) *is* the correct one, and that the puzzle set out in Section 1 is likewise real: these *are* cases in which a plural morpheme – specifically Arabic SF – attaches to a divider, and specifically Arabic –_AH_, thereby requiring accommodation if we maintain that plural marking is an instance of DIV. As we shall now show, the parses in (36b,d) give rise to serious independent problems.

For our first argument against the parse in (36b) consider again masculine batch nouns. If it were the case that SF may attach directly to the stem, as in (36b), then it would emerge that such nouns may occur with two distinct plural forms: SF and broken plural. The difficulty, however, would be to account for the fact that each of these plural markers would come with its own distinct interpretation. Thus, when batch nouns occur with broken plural, they denote multiple (distinct) kinds or multiple batches. With this plural marker, they *do not* denote a quantity of units with an identical extension. The very opposite situation holds when SF merges with batch nouns. In those cases, the output could *only* denote a quantity of units with an identical extension. The multiple-type/batch reading is not available:[12]

(37)

	A. Batch noun	B. -_AH_-Ns	C. Broken plural	D. SF Plural
a.	Tabšour$_M$ chalk	Tabšour-ah$_F$ chalk-_AH_ 'piece of chalk'	Tbašiir$_M$ chalk-pl$_{BR}$ 'bunches of chalk' (different) types of chalk *piece of chalk	Tabšour-aat$_F$ chalk-pl$_{SF}$ 'pieces of chalk' *bunches of chalk *(different) kinds of chalk
b.	Hajar$_M$ stone	Hajr-ah$_F$ stone-_AH_ 'a stone'	Hjaar$_M$ stone-pl$_{BR}$ 'heaps/types of stone' *stones	Hajr-aat$_F$ stone-pl$_{SF}$ 'stones' *heaps/kinds of stone
c.	ramel$_M$ sand	raml-eh$_F$ sand-_AH_ 'grain of sand'	rimeel$_M$ sand-pl$_{BR}$ 'heaps/types of sand' *grains of sand	raml-eet$_F$ sand-pl$_{SF}$ 'grains of sand' *heaps/types of sand
d.	samak$_M$ fish-kind	samk-eh fish-_AH_ 'a fish'	ʔasmeek fish-pl$_{BR}$ 'kinds of fish'	samk-eet fish-pl$_{SF}$ 'multiple individual fishes'

---

[12] The forms in column D are given as bare plural forms for expository reasons. In actuality, PL-marked _AH_-Ns must always be accompanied by a cardinal, a matter to which we turn at some length in Section 4. See also fn. 8.

Note that the reading associated with the broken plural forms in (37c) correlates directly with readings which typically emerge when (epistemological) mass terms are pluralized, e.g. *soups, juices,* or *cheeses* (different kinds/batches of *soup/juice/cheese*). In turn, the reading associated with the SF forms in (37d) correlates exactly with what would be expected if that plural attaches to the -*AH*-N in (37b). One could argue that it is the SF marker itself which acts to divide the denotation of the stem in the relevant sense, and that the two plural markers differ precisely insofar as one of them pluralizes kinds or batches, while the other returns 'multiple-units-of-one-kind' readings. But as we have already seen, it is not the case that broken plurals, in general, pluralize only kinds (cf. (30)-(32)), nor is it the case that SF, in and of itself, must give rise to a unit reading. To the contrary, as already noted, SF may attach to (feminine) mass forms, the result of which would be, as predicted, multiple-kind readings, and not units-of-kind readings, casting very serious doubt on the hypothesis that the -*eet/-aat* affix, in and of itself, is responsible for the creation of units-of-kind reading:

(38)   a. ktiir metʕah; b. ktiir maHabbeh; c. ktiir musiiʔah; d. ktiir maʕrifeh;
         much pleasure   much affection   much music   much knowledge

(39)   a. ktiir metʕ-aat;   b. ktiir maHabb-eet;
         many pleasures   many affections
          i. kinds of pleasure   i. kinds of affection
          ii. #instances of pleasure   ii. #instances of love
    c. ktiir musiiʔ-aat;   d. ktiir maʕrif-eet;
       many musics   many knowledges
       i. kinds of music   i. kinds of knowledge
       ii. #instances of music   ii. #instances of knowledge

Our second piece of evidence concerns the fact that a hypothesized direct attachment of SF to the masculine batch stems as in (36b) would give rise to a gender mismatch that cannot be easily resolved. No such mismatch emerges if the parse in (16) is adopted, in which SF merges with the -*AH* affix, and not directly with the stem. Convincing the reader of the existence of such a mismatch, however, is a rather complex matter to which we now turn.

3.2. SF and Gender

Considering again the masculine batch nouns in (37a), we note that the plural-marked output formed with the broken plural, as in (37c), is likewise masculine. The masculinity of the batch nouns under consideration can be demonstrated straightforwardly through the masculine (∅) marking on a modifying adjective, as in (40):

(40)   teffeeH axDar;   Tabšour Txiin;   ramel sexen;   samak azraʔ;
           apple   green-ø   chalk   thick-ø   sand   hot-ø   fish   blue-ø
           'green apple'   'thick chalk'   'hot sand'   'blue fish'

Determining the gender of the plural expressions in (37d) is, however, a trickier matter, because agreement with plural non-human expressions in Arabic shows up in both adjectives and verbs as feminine singular (specifically marked as -*ah*), regardless of the gender of the modified noun.[13] The grammatical gender of plural expressions can nonetheless be determined when we consider the use of gender in singular partitives. In the partitive expressions in (41) and (42), the pronominal 'one' is marked either as masculine (*weeHed*) or as feminine (*waHdeh*), thereby corresponding to the (unambiguous) gender specification of the plural expression:

(41)   a.   weeHed/*waHdeh   men   er-rjeel   LA
            one$_M$/*one$_F$ of/from   the-man-pl$_{BR}$
            'one of the men'   stem: rijjaal (masculine)
       b.   weeHed/*waHdeh   men   el-mhands-iin   LA
            one$_M$/*one$_F$ of/from   the-engineer-pl$_{SM}$
            'one of the engineers'   stem: mhandes (masculine)

(42)   a.   waHdeh/*weeHed   men   el-bsayn-eet   LA
            one$_F$/*one$_M$ of/from   the-cat-pl$_{SF}$
            'one of the cats'   stem: bsayneh (feminine)
       b.   waHdeh/*weeHed   men   el-mhands-eet   LA
            one$_F$/*one$_M$ of/from   the-engineer-pl$_{SF}$
            'one of the (female) engineers'   stem: mhandseh (feminine)

For reasons that we do not understand, a singular pronominal reference to a batch by means of the pronominal 'one' is odd in LA with either gender.[14] There is no such restriction in Standard Arabic, where partitive constructions, furthermore, do not require the preposition *men* and are rather expressed through construct state nominals. In such cases, what we find, as expected, is that the masculine pronominal form of 'one' is required, and the feminine form is ungrammatical:

---

[13] Help in determining gender is not forthcoming from the definite pronominal system either. In LA, plural pronouns are not marked for gender. While in SA they are, feminine plural pronouns are only licit with human antecedents, making their use inapplicable for the key cases under consideration.

[14] And therefore:

i.   a.   ??waHdeh/*weeHed men   el-ʔasmeek   LA
           one$_F$/one$_M$ of/from   the-fish$_{BR}$
    b.   ??waHdeh/*weeHed men   el-Hjaar   LA
           one$_F$/one$_M$ of/from   the-stone$_{BR}$

Note that *waHdeh*/*weeHed* 'one$_{F/M}$' in LA are pronominal here. In their adjectival occurrence, post-nominally, no such restriction is in evidence (cf. 25). For a fuller discussion of these matters, as well as for the argument that these differences do not play a role in the phenomena under discussion here, see Ouwayda (2014).

(43) a. aHadu/*iHdaa l-asmaak   SA
         one_M/*one_F the-fish-pl_BR
         'one kind of fish'
     b. aHadu/*iHdaa r-rimaal
         one_M/*one_F the-sand-pl_BR
         'one kind of sand'

A different result emerges, however, when we apply the 'one-of' test to the SF plural forms in (37d). Here, it is the feminine form of 'one', *waHdeh*, that is required, and the masculine form gives rise to ungrammaticality, in Standard as well as in Lebanese Arabic:

(44) a. iHdaa/*aHadu   s-samk-aat   SA
         one_F/*one_M   the-fish-pl_SF
         'one of the fishes'
     b. iHdaa/*aHadu   r-raml-aat
         one_F/*one_M   the-sand-pl_SF
         'one of the grains of sand'

(45) a. waHdeh/*weeHed men   es-samk-eet   LA
         one_F/*one_M   of/from the-fish-pl_SF
         'one of the fish'
     b. waHdeh/*weeHed men   el-laymoun-eet
         one_F/*one_M   of/from the-orange-pl_SF
         'one of the oranges'

The contrast is of course more striking in Standard Arabic, where the feminine inflection of 'one' in (44) can be directly contrasted with the masculine inflection for 'one' in (43), strongly suggesting that SF merges with a feminine, rather than a masculine, base and specifically *not* with the masculine batch nouns in (37a), but rather with the already feminine *-AH* forms in (37b).

One might be tempted to suggest that SF marking in itself is complicit in bringing about a gender switch, turning what is otherwise a masculine non-plural stem (e.g. *samak* 'fish') into a feminine stem. However, while such cases have been argued to exist in some languages, there is direct evidence to show that this *could not* be the case in Arabic. As is well documented, some nouns, although masculine, are pluralized with the SF exponent, rather than with the SM exponent, as would be expected. Thus SF commonly occurs on derived nominals (46) and borrowed foreign nouns (47) (Ghalayiini 1912/2006), which are at least at times grammatically masculine when singular, as shown by the masculine adjective:

(46) *Derived Nominals*
      a. tanaaquD   waaDeH   →   tanaaquD-aat
         contradiction_M clear-ø   contradiction-pl_SF
      b. xilaaf   jaddi   →   xilaaf-aat
         conflict_M   serious-ø   conflict-pl_SF

(47)   Borrowings
a. computer   mniH   → computer-aat
   computer_M   good-ø   computer-pl_SF
b. talifoon   jdiid   → talifoon-eet
   telephone_M new-ø   telephone-pl_SF

Nonetheless, and although these derived nominals and borrowings are pluralized with an SF exponent, no gender change is attested in singular partitives. To the contrary, and regardless of the presence of the SF exponent, the masculine form of 'one', *weeHed*, is required:

(48)   a. weeHed/*waHdeh   men   el-ittiSaal-eet
          one_M/*one_F   of/from   the-phone call-pl_SF
          'one of the phone calls'
       b. weeHed/*waHdeh   men   el-computer-aat[15]
          one_M/*one_F   of/from   the-computer-pl_SF
          'one of the computers'

The clear conclusion is that the SF exponent, in itself, is not feminine, nor can it accomplish gender switch. Thus the SF forms in (37d) can only emerge from the configuration in (16), involving the merger of SF with the already feminine base created by the merger of a batch noun, itself mostly M, with -$\underline{AH}$ – itself always F, and with the structure [[batch noun+$\underline{AH_F}$] SF]. Our puzzle, then, remains as originally formulated: in a model that assumes that plurals are instances of DIV, how can a dividing morpheme such as -$\underline{AH}$ coexist with plural marking?

In what follows, we shall embark upon showing that the puzzle, nonetheless, can be dissolved once it is shown that although -$\underline{AH}$ and -*aat* can, and do, coexist in the derivations with the parse in (16), they do not in actuality compete for the same slot. While -$\underline{AH}$ is a true divider and merges as DIV, this is not the case for the SF instances in (16), which, we argue, are semantically vacuous cases of agreement with a cardinal in [Spec,#]. In order to show that this is, indeed, the case, we will now proceed to compare, in detail, the behavior of the plural forms in (37d) with the parse in (16) with plural forms which do not contain -$\underline{AH}$, and where a potential conflict does not emerge.

Before moving away from the diversity of plural-marking strategies in Arabic, it is worthwhile noting that in line with Acquaviva (2008), we assume an identical syntactic head for SF and BR (although unlike Acquaviva, we assume that head to be DIV, rather than Num). We depart from the analysis in

---

[15] And similarly in Standard Arabic:

i.   aHadu/*iHdaa   l-ittiSaal-aat
     one-m/one-f   the-phone call-pl_SF

Zabbal (2002), according to which there exist, alongside regular plural marking in Num, a specialized 'group' plural marker with distinct semantics, which is closer to the nominal head, and which may be realized exclusively as BR (although Zabbal specifically assumes both Sound and BR realization are possible in Num). Rather, we assume that a 'group' reading emerges on a par with the multiple kind reading which emerges routinely when conceptually salient mass terms are embedded within count structures such as (13a,b).

Although we subscribe to the view that there are, indeed, two positions in Arabic which correspond to plural marking, we believe that these positions do not correlate with the semantics of BR or SF as such. Rather, one of these 'plural' markers is a divider, semantically, and it is that plural marking which merges as D_{IV}, giving rise to a number-neutral interpretation. The other instantiation of 'plural' marking, on the other hand, is semantically altogether vacuous, and as we shall argue, an instance of agreement with a cardinal in [Spec,#]. In such cases, it is the necessary presence of the cardinal, rather than the 'plural' marking, that gives rise to 'exclusive' reading, and more specifically to a reading that excludes all interpretations not directly tied with that of the explicitly specified cardinality.

4. PL-*AH*-Ns vs. Other Plural Forms

4.1. Bare Plurals

On a par with e.g. Romance languages, Arabic allows bare plurals (with a number-neutral, inclusive reading) exclusively in weak contexts. Gender and the choice of plural exponent have no bearing on the distribution of bare plurals, as shown in (49)–(51):

(49)   *Bare SM plural*
    a. šeft   mhands-iin   bi   lab   el-fonetik
       saw.1s engineer$_{SM}$ in lab the-phonetics
       'I saw engineers in the phonetics lab.'
    b. šeft   šeḤḤaadiin ʕa beeb ej-jeemʕa
       saw.1s beggar$_{SM}$ at door the-university
       'I saw beggars in front of the university.'

(50)   *Bare SF plural*
    a. šeft   šarik-eet   bi   l-madiineh
       saw.1s company-pl$_{SF}$ in the-city
       'I saw companies in the city.'
    b. šeft   mʕallm-eet sabaaya bi l-madraseh
       saw.1s teacher-pl$_{SF}$ young in the-school
       'I saw young teachers in the school.'

(51) Bare BR plural, both F and M
a. šeft   maraaya   bi l-ouda   base: mreyeh (feminine)
   saw.1s mirror-pl$_{BR}$ in the-room
   'I saw mirrors in the room.'
b. šeft   kleeb   bi sheereʕ-na   base: kalb (masculine)
   saw.1s dog-pl$_{BR}$ in street-us
   'I saw dogs in our street'

In what is a rather remarkable contrast, however, PL-<u>AH</u>-Ns may *never* occur as bare plurals. This is illustrated in (52):

(52) a. *šeft   samk-eet   bi l-baHar   base: samk-<u>AH</u>
        saw.1s fish-<u>AH</u>-pl$_{SF}$ in the-sea
        'I saw fish in the sea.'
     b. *šeft   Hajr-aat   ʕa T-Tarii?   base: Hajr-<u>AH</u>
        saw.1s stone-<u>AH</u>-pl$_{SF}$ on the-road
        'I saw stones on the road.'

The restriction, importantly, does not apply to the BR forms formed from the very same stems (cf. 37c), and hence cannot be attributed to properties of either the root or the base noun:

(53) BR of stems that allow -<u>AH</u>, licit as bare indefinites:
a. šeft   ʔasmeek   bi l-baHer   base: samak (masculine)
   saw.1s fish-pl$_{BR}$ in the-sea
   'I saw fishes (many kinds) in the sea.'
b. šeft   Hjaar   honik   base: Hajar (masculine)
   saw.1s stone-pl$_{BR}$ there
   'I saw (various) stone types there.'

Importantly, equally derivationally complex forms (e.g. derived nominals with SF plural exponents) do not display a similar restriction, and the examples in (54) are fully licit:

(54) Bare pluralized derived nominals
a. ʕmelo   ittiSaal-eet   bayneet-kon
   make   connection-pl$_{SF}$ between-you
   'Make connections with each other.'
b. baʕref ʕileej-eet   la   ha-l-marad
   know.1s cure-pl$_{SF}$ to   this-the-disease
   'I know of cures for this disease.'

PL-<u>AH</u>-Ns, recall, are morpho-phonologically indistinguishable from other SF plural nouns. Nonetheless, and unlike all other plural forms, including those occurring with SF, they cannot occur bare. Equally remarkably, they also differ in this respect from their close conceptual relatives, namely the BR plurals formed from the same base batch nouns, but without -<u>AH</u>. The restriction amounts to allowing Arabic to express, as bare, plural expressions corresponding, roughly, to 'heaps of apple stuff', while disallowing reference, through the same grammatical means, just to 'apples', a contrast which is hard to attribute to lexical semantics or, for that matter, to the distinction between mass and count in and of itself.

4.2. Plurals and Pre-Nominal Quantifiers

In LA, all plural exponents may occur with the quantifiers *ktiir* 'many' or *šway(t)* 'a few', as shown in (55)–(56):[16]

(55) a. šeft   ktiir/šwayt   mʕallm-iin   bi   ha-S-Saff   SM
          saw.1s   many/a few   teacher$_{SM}$ in   this-the-class
          'I saw many/a few teachers in this classroom.'
      b. šeft   ktiir/šwayt   šarik-eet   bi ha-l-madiineh   SF
          saw.1s   many/a few   company-pl$_{SF}$ in this-the-city
          'I saw many companies in this city.'

(56) a. šeft   ktiir/šwayt   Hjaar   ʕa   š-šaTT   base: Hjar (masculine)   BR
          saw.1s   many/a few   stone-pl$_{BR}$ on   the-beach
          'I saw many/a few diverse (types of) stones by the beach.'
      b. šeft   ktiir/šwayt   maraaya   bi l-ouda   base: mreyeh (feminine) BR
          saw.1s   many/a few   mirror-pl$_{BR}$ in the-room
          'I saw many/a few diverse (types of) mirrors in the room.'

In a remarkable departure from this picture, PL-$\underline{AH}$-Ns are illicit after the quantifiers 'many' and 'a few.' Particularly striking is the fact that the SF form in (55b) is grammatical, while the PL-$\underline{AH}$-Ns, with a phonologically indistinguishable plural suffix, are ungrammatical, as in (57a). Equally remarkable is the fact that for the very same stem, BR in (56a) may occur with quantifiers while the -$\underline{AH}$-divided nominals with the same stem may not (cf. 57b):

(57) a. *šeft   ktiir/šwayt   samk-eet   bi   l-baHer   base: samk-$\underline{AH}$
          saw.1s   many/a few   fish(-$\underline{AH}$)-pl$_{SF}$ in   the-sea
          'I saw many/a few fish in the sea.'
      b. *šeft   ktiir/šwayt   Hajr-aat   ʕa   T-Tarii?   base: Hajr-$\underline{AH}$
          saw.1s   many/a few   stone(-$\underline{AH}$)-pl$_{SF}$ on   the-road
          'I saw a many/a few stones on the street.'

4.3. Where Are PL-$\underline{AH}$-Ns Licit?

When indefinite, plural-$\underline{AH}$-divided nominals are licit only in the context of cardinals or cardinal-like expressions (e.g. *ʕidda(t)* 'several'). This is illustrated

---

[16] With the exception of *kul+singular*, 'every/each', SA only allows post-nominal (non-complex) quantifiers, making the contrasts under discussion here moot. We briefly return to complex quantifiers in Section 6.2, where some relevant contrasts between PL-marked $\underline{AH}$-N and BR are shown to apply in SA as well. For a brief discussion on non-complex, agreeing post-nominal quantifiers see Section 5.3. For further discussion of all these issues, see Ouwayda (2014).

in (58). Without a cardinal or cardinal-like expression, an indefinite PL-*AH*-N is ungrammatical:

(58) a. šeft   *(tesʕ)   samk-eet   bi   j-jaaT
        saw.1s   nine   fish-*AH*-pl$_{SF}$ in   the-bowl   base: samk -*AH*
        'I saw nine fish in the bowl.'
    b. šeft   *(arbaʕ)   Hajr-aat   ʕa   T-Tarii?
        saw.1s   four   stone-*AH*-pl$_{SF}$ on   the-road   base: Hajr-*AH*
        'I saw four stones on the street.'
    c. šeft   *(ʕiddat)   Tabšour-aat   bi   d-derej
        saw.1s   several   chalk-*AH*-pl in   the-drawer   base: Tabšour-*AH*
        'I saw several pieces of chalk in the drawer.'

We therefore conclude that, in a way that will be further elaborated upon, indefinite -*AH*-divided plural nominals are licensed by the presence of cardinals, turning our attention in the next few sections to the syntactic and semantic ramifications of this conclusion.

Before proceeding, it is worthwhile noting that PL-*AH*-Ns *may* occur without a cardinal when definite, a matter to which we return in Section 6.2.

5. Cardinals Are Not Quantifiers: Towards a Structure

One of the more striking consequences of the discussion in Section 4 is that when it comes to PL-*AH*-Ns, quantifiers and cardinals part company. While the former do not suffice to license the plural marking under consideration, the latter do. In this section we turn to three other important differences between quantifiers and cardinals, specifically in Lebanese Arabic, with the aim of justifying an analysis in which the structure associated with cardinals is different from that associated with quantifiers.

That cardinals are distinct from quantifiers is by no means a novel perspective, although the literature does not necessarily agree on what, exactly, cardinals are. Thus it is frequently claimed that numerals are adjectives (Link 1998: 101–7; Landman 2000, i.a.), or that they are nouns (Hurford 1975, 1987, 2003; Ionin and Matushansky 2004, 2006, 2018, i.a.). A more nuanced perspective is proposed by Stavrou and Terzi (2008), according to which simple numerals are (weak) quantifiers, but complex numerals are nouns, with an expression such as *three hundreds* consisting of a head N (*hundreds*) preceded by a quantifier. Finally, Link (1998) proposes that cardinals are modifiers merging in the Num head, a position which appears closest to the one we will advocate below for Arabic.

An altogether distinct perspective on the matter is proposed by Corbett (2000) (and see also subsequent support in Corver and Zwarts 2004; Zweig 2005) according to which 'cardinal' as such is not a syntactic category, and may be differently realized in distinct languages. In what follows, we will proceed to show that in Arabic, specifically, cardinals cannot be adjectives and cannot be (weak) quantifiers, and that they occupy a position in the nominal spine that is below quantifiers and that, prima facie, is inconsistent with being a noun, thereby suggesting that at least in Arabic, cardinals may constitute a category on their own. We leave open the possibility that in at least some languages cardinals may turn out to have nominal or adjectival properties or, for that matter, quantificational ones.

Importantly, the discussion here concerns quantifiers such as *ktiir* 'many' and *šway(t)* 'a few', which may take a plural restriction in LA, and which occur *pre-nominally* on a par with cardinals. Other pre-nominal quantifiers in LA as well as all pre-nominal quantifiers in SA are complex, head a separate partitive-like construction, and take a PP complement. As such, they are clearly distinct from cardinals.[17]

5.1. Distributivity Effects of Cardinals and Quantifiers

As is frequently the case cross-linguistically, Arabic cardinals distribute *optionally* over the verbal predicate (cf. 59). The quantifiers *ktiir* 'many' and *šway(t)* 'a few', however, do so *obligatorily* (cf. 60):

(59) arbaʕ baneet ʕatoun-i alf
 four girl-pl gave-me thousand
 'Four girls gave me a thousand (Lebanese pounds).'
 i. True in a scenario in which four girls each gave me a thousand pounds.
 ii. True in a scenario in which four girls, together, gave me a thousand pounds, and none gave me a thousand on her own.

(60) ktiir/šwayt wleed akal-ou aaleb gateau
 many/a few child-pl ate-pl pie cake
 'Many/a few kids ate a cake.'
 i. True in a scenario in which many/a few kids each ate a whole cake.
 ii. False in a scenario in which many/a few kids shared a cake and none ate a whole cake on his or her own.

---

[17] As already noted briefly (fn. 16) quantification expressions may occur post-nominally in Arabic. Post-nominal quantifiers, unlike pre-nominal ones, show number, definiteness, and at times gender agreement with the nominal very much on a par with that attested with adjectives, and we will therefore assume, following Shlonsky (2004) i.a., that they are indeed adjectival (and see (70)-(71) for a few examples). As expected, they do not license indefinite PL-*AH*-Ns. While cardinals may occur post-nominally as well, unlike post-nominal quantifiers they are restricted to definite contexts, and do not show number agreement. Whether gender agreement is attested for such post-nominal cardinals in SA (exclusively) is a matter of some debate. The reader is referred to Ouwayda (2014) for further discussion of many of these issues.

Divide and Counter   137

The contrast is even stronger in modal contexts, where the subject receives a *quantity* reading, in the sense of A. Li (1998), as illustrated in the contrast between (61) and (62):

(61) a. tlat   baneet   byeHeml-ou   ha-š-šaxtoura
          three   girl-pl$_{BR}$ carry-ipfv-pl   this-the-boat
          i. Can mean 'This boat is of a weight such that three girls would be able to carry it.'
          ii. Can mean 'There are three girls who can each carry this boat.'
      b. xams   Sebyeen   bixalls-ou   ha-l-keyk
          five   boy-pl$_{BR}$ finish-ipfv-pl   this-the-cake
          i. Can mean 'This cake is of a size such that five boys could finish it.'
          ii. Can mean 'There are five boys who can each finish this cake.'

(62) a. ktiir   baneet   byeHeml-ou   ha-š-šaxtoura
          many   girl-pl$_{BR}$ carry-ipfv-pl   this-the-boat
          i. Cannot mean #'This boat is of a weight such that many girls would be able to carry it.'
          ii. Can only mean 'There are many girls who can each carry this boat.'
      b. šwayt   sebyeen   bixalls-ou   ha-l-keyk
          a few   boy-pl$_{BR}$ finish-ipfv-pl   this-the-cake
          i. Cannot mean #'This cake is of a size such that a few boys could finish it.'
          ii. Can only mean 'There are a few boys who can each finish this cake.'

5.2. Cardinals and Quantifiers: Adjectives and Scope

Cardinals may scope both over and under adjectives (cf. 63), whereas quantifiers always scope over adjectives (cf. 64), suggesting that cardinals may merge lower than some adjectives, but not so quantifiers. By transitivity, it also follows that cardinals and quantifiers do not have identical merging sites, and that quantifiers merge higher than cardinals (and note similar effects in English, reflected more directly in word order and illustrated in (65)–(66)):

(63) a. šeft   tlat   jnoud   bixawfo
          saw.1s   three   soldier-pl   scary
          i. I saw three scary soldiers.
          ii. I saw a scary three soldiers. (scary as a group)
      b. Hmelt   tesʕ   ʕelab   Tʔaal
          carried.1s nine   box-pl   heavy
          i. I carried nine heavy boxes.
          ii. I carried heavy nine boxes. (heavy as a set)

(64) a. Hmelt   šwayt ʕelab   Tʔaal
       carried.1s a few box-pl heavy
       i. I carried a few heavy boxes.
       ii. *I carried a heavy bunch of few boxes. (heavy as a small set)
    b. šeft   ktiir   jnoud   bixawfo
       saw.1s many   soldier-pl scary
       i. I saw many scary soldiers.
       ii. *I saw scary many soldiers. (scary as a group)

(65) a. three heavy bags; five scary soldiers; four competent doctors
    b. heavy three bags; scary five soldiers; competent four doctors

(66) a. many heavy bags; many scary soldiers; a few competent doctors
    b. *heavy many bags; *scary many soldiers; *competent (a) few doctors

Note that both the cardinals and the quantifiers in (64) are pre-nominal, while adjectives are post-nominal, and that as a result the linear ordering of cardinals or quantifiers relative to adjectives is the same regardless of scope. Under the assumption, however, that differences in scope do correspond to structural differences, and taking a page from the word order effects in English in identical contexts, we propose that while the structure in (67a) may correspond to either quantifiers or cardinals, the structure in (67b) is licit for cardinals but not for quantifiers:

(67) a. [cardinal/quantifier   [[N] adjective]]
    b. [[cardinal/*quantifier [N]] adjective]

5.3. Null Pronominals with Cardinals and Quantifiers

A final significant contrast emerges in the context of null pronominals. While a null pronominal restriction is acceptable with cardinals in both definite and indefinite contexts (cf. 68), this is not the case for pre-nominal quantifiers, where null pronominals are never licit:

(68) a. (t-)tleeteh   fallou   (l-)arbʕa   wesl-ou
       (the-)three   left.3pl   (the-)four   arrived-3pl
       '(The) three left.'   '(The) four arrived.'
    b. jebt   (t-)tleeteh   Talabt   (l-)arbʕa
       brought.1s   (the-)three   ordered.1s   (the-)four
       'I brought (the) three.'   'I ordered (the) four.'

(69) a. *(l-)ktiir   fallou;   *(š-)šway   wesl-ou;
       (the-)many   left.3pl   (the-)few   arrived-3pl
       '(The) many left.'   '(The) few arrived.'
    b. *jebt   (l-)ktiir   *Talabt   (š-)šway
       brought.1s   (the)-many   ordered.1s   (the)-few
       'I brought (the-)many.'   'I ordered (the-)few.'

Divide and Counter   139

Note now that the null pronominal restrictions under discussion in this subsection are plural, across the board. It thus emerges that the non-agreeing quantifiers in (69) must be pre-nominal. Post-nominal quantifiers, just like post-nominal adjectives, display full number and definiteness agreement, as well as gender, in SA, thereby lending additional support to analyzing them as adjectives (gender distinctions in plural adjectives are neutralized in LA):

(70) a. tʕarraft   ʕa   (l-)ban-eet   (l-)azkiya   LA
         acquainted on   (the-)girls   (the-)smart-pl$_{BR}$
         'I met (the) smart girls.'
      b. tʕarraft   ʕa   (l-)ban-eet   (l-)ktaar
         acquainted on   (the-)girls   (the-)many-pl$_{BR}$
         'I met (the) many girls.'

(71) a. iltaqaytu   bi-(l-)fatayaat   (að-)ðakiyyaat   SA
         met   with-(the-)girls (the-)smart-pl$_{SF}$
         'I met (the) smart girls.'
      b. iltaqaytu   bi-(l-)fatayaat   (al-)kaθiiraat
         met   with-(the-)girls (the-)many-pl$_{SF}$
         'I met (the) many girls.'

We return to these matters briefly in Section 6.2, where we link the null pronominal distribution directly to the presence of agreement.

6. Cardinal Agreement

6.1. Cardinals and Quantifiers: A Proposal

We established a number of important distinctions between quantifiers and cardinals in Arabic, spanning their syntax as well as their interpretation:

(72) a. Cardinals are optionally distributive; quantifiers *necessarily* are (5.1)
      b. Cardinals may scope under adjectives; quantifiers may not (5.2)
      c. Cardinals may license a null N; quantifiers may not (5.3)
      d. Cardinals license PL-$A\underline{H}$-Ns; quantifiers do not (4.3)

We already noted that (72b) strongly supports the merger of adjective below quantifiers, but possibly above cardinals, a conclusion corroborated by the ungrammaticality, in English, of (66b) and similar. It further supports a higher merge site for quantifiers as compared with cardinals, and hence the schematic structure in (73), with the label # now reserved for cardinals, and the label Q for quantifiers. The two scopal configurations in English (65) now emerge directly from the fact that an adjective may merge either above or below #, but not above Q:[18]

---

[18] The argument here is independent of whether adjectives are specifiers or adjuncts, a matter on which we take no position.

(73)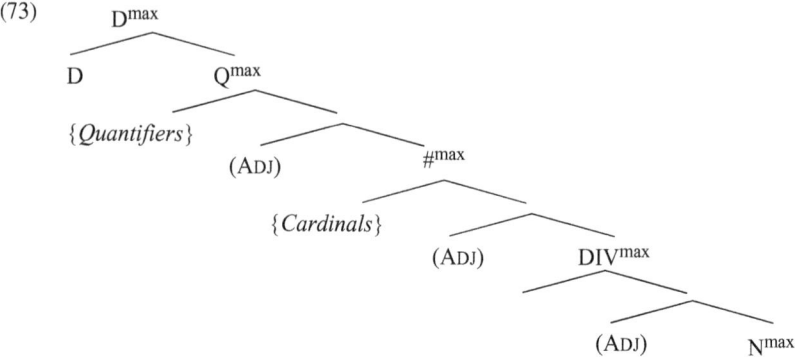

Turning to Arabic, and given the fact that adjectives are always post-nominal, but the quantifiers and cardinals under discussion are always pre-nominal, direct evidence for the structure in (73) is not available from linear order. Evidence for merging Q over # nonetheless is available from the scope contrasts discussed in Section 5.2, and we will therefore proceed to assume that (73) does correspond to the hierarchical relationships within the Arabic nominal spine. In view of that, it is clear that the word order, as attested in Arabic, must be derived by syntactic movement, and we propose, specifically (and in line with Ritter 1991, Siloni 1997, Borer 1999, Fassi Fehri 1999 and Shlonsky 2004, i.a.), that the operation in question involves the movement of (some portion of) the nominal over the adjective. More specifically, suppose N^{min} moves to Q (through Div and #) overtly in Arabic (and possibly covertly in English). Suppose further that cardinals, merging externally as [Spec,#], move to merge as [Spec,Q] (overtly in Arabic, possibly covertly in English). With these assumptions in mind, consider first the derivation in (74a), where, by assumption, the adjective merges above #. With the movement of N to Q and the cardinal to [Spec,Q], the resulting word order is [Cardinal Noun Adjective], as in (74b):

(74) a.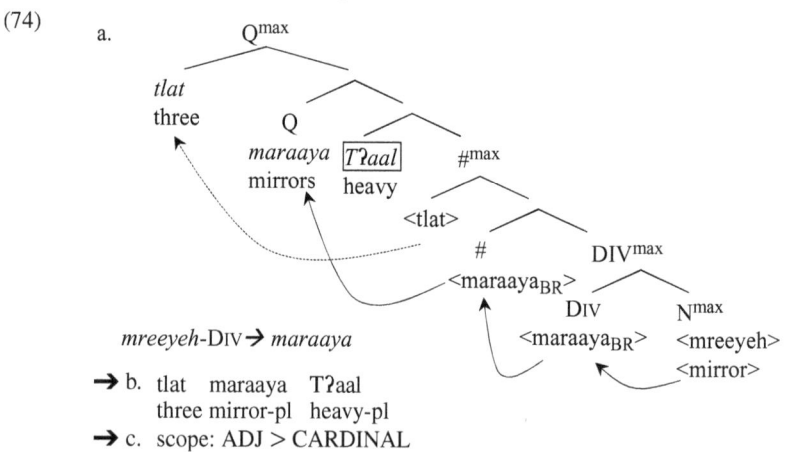

→ b. tlat   maraaya   T?aal
      three mirror-pl heavy-pl
→ c. scope: ADJ > CARDINAL

Assuming now that it is sufficient for an adjective to c-command a copy of the cardinal in order to scope over it, the scope configuration that emerges from (74) is ADJ>CARDINAL, corresponding, as such, to (63a.ii,b.ii).

Consider now a derivation in which the adjective merges below #, as in (75a). Yet again [N+DIV] moves to Q (through #) and the cardinal moves to [Spec,Q]. The resulting word order may be identical to that derived by (74), but the scope that emerges is different, given the fact that the adjective, at no point, c-commands either the cardinal or its copy. The emerging interpretation is as in (63a.i,b.i):

(75)   a.

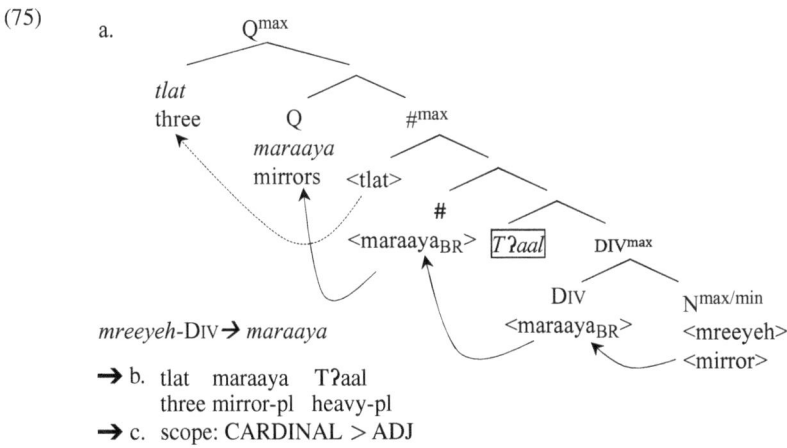

→ b. tlat   maraaya   T?aal
       three mirror-pl heavy-pl
→ c. scope: CARDINAL > ADJ

Turning now to structures containing quantifiers, we assume that such structures do not contain a # projection altogether, and therefore the adjective merges below the quantifier. As before, N moves to Q, and the quantifier itself, by assumption, merges in [Spec,Q]. The result is as in (76), with the quantifier, at all times, scoping over the adjective:

(76)   a.

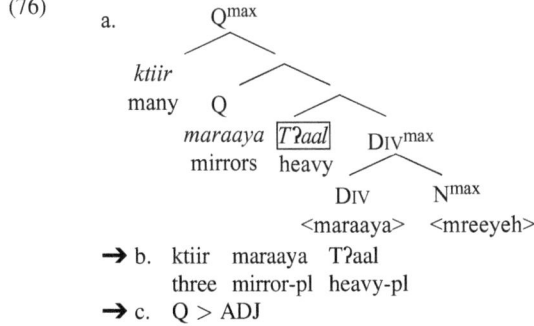

→ b. ktiir maraaya   T?aal
       three mirror-pl heavy-pl
→ c. Q > ADJ

In English, neither the noun nor the cardinal moves overtly, and the two interpretations are associated with two different word orders: a structure such as (74), where the adjective merges above the cardinal, results in (77a), and a structure such as (75), where the adjective merges below the cardinal, results in (77b). There is only one place for adjectives to merge in the context of quantifiers, and that is below the quantifier, as in (76). Without any movements, this gives rise to the word order and interpretation in (77c). Given that adjectives may not merge above quantifiers, we predict that (77d) would be ungrammatical, as is the case.

(77)   a. the heavy three mirrors
          b. the three heavy mirrors
          c. the many heavy mirrors
          d. *the heavy many mirrors

6.2.   Dividing vs. Agreeing Plural Marking

Turning now to (72d), we note that this observation has emerged directly from the investigation of our original puzzle, to which we now return, and which involves the failure of complementarity between the dividing morpheme -$\underline{AH}$ and plural marking. More concretely, the discussion in the previous sections has yielded substantial differences between plural marking in the absence of -$\underline{AH}$ and plural marking as it occurs in conjunction with the divider -$\underline{AH}$. These differences are summarized in (78):

(78)   a. Unlike all other plural forms, indefinite PL-$\underline{AH}$-Ns cannot occur bare (Section 4.1).
          b. Unlike all other plural forms, indefinite PL-$\underline{AH}$-Ns cannot occur following quantifiers that take a plural restriction (Section 4.2).
          c. Indefinite PL-$\underline{AH}$-Ns must occur with cardinals (Section 4.3).

The set of properties in (78) now allows us to reformulate our original puzzle in considerably more informed terms, and specifically as in (79):

(79)   In the context of cardinals, and only in such context, the dividing morpheme -$\underline{AH}$ may co-occur with the SF marking -*eet/aat*. But if both -$\underline{AH}$ and SF are instances of DIV, why is such co-occurrence licit?

An answer to the puzzle would appear to be immediately available, of course, if one were to assume that T'sou's Generalization (14) is simply wrong, and that no complementarity is to be expected between dividing morphemes, or classifiers, and plural marking. But such a move would not in actuality suffice to resolve the puzzle presented by Arabic, as the peculiar restrictions on the co-occurrence of -$\underline{AH}$ and plural marking would remain without any hope of an explanation.

An account for the Arabic facts, on the other hand, is directly available without surrendering T'sou's Generalization, and in fact reinforcing it, if some instances of *-eet/aat* do not spell out DIV, but are, rather, instances of agreement with the cardinals. Specifically, we maintain that *-AH* is a dividing morpheme; we also maintain that plural marking in Arabic in its various morpho-phonological exponents could be a spellout of DIV. However, not all occurrences of plural exponents in Arabic (or elsewhere) realize DIV, nor, for that matter, are they necessarily semantically contentful altogether. Agreement on adjectives is morpho-phonologically identical to semantically contentful plural marking, but by common assumptions need not be semantically contentful on its own.[19] More concretely, we propose that some instances of *-eet/aat*, already attested as agreement markers, e.g., in adjectival contexts, are the realization of *non-singular agreement with a cardinal*. Such cardinal agreement is certainly not an instance of DIV, and hence its occurrence alongside *-AH* does not constitute a violation of T'sou's Generalization. In turn, however, we expect such agreement to occur precisely in the context of cardinals, but to be excluded in their absence.[20]

With this proposal in mind, recall that in definite contexts, *-AH*-Ns can be pluralized with *-eet/aat* even in the absence of a cardinal, as illustrated by (80) (and contrast with examples such as (52a,b) discussed in Section 4.1):

(80) a. s-samk-eet   muš   hon
          the-fish-*AH*-pl_SF not   here   base: samk-*AH*
          'The fish(es) are not here.'
      b. l-Hajr-aat   nramo   base: Hajr-*AH*
          the-stone-*AH*-pl_SF thrown
          'The stones were thrown.'

A natural explanation for this is available now if definite determiners, following Heim (1982) and much subsequent work, are discourse anaphors which inherit their reference from a discourse antecedent (and including deixes, assuming 'pointing' to establish an antecedent in the relevant

---

[19] Which is not to question the fact that distinct agreement may correspond, in some contexts, to syntactic properties that are semantically contentful. A powerful example is discussed in Ouwayda (2014, 2017), where the choice of agreement correlates with the existence of a semantic operator which is responsible for the formation of distributive reading. Importantly, however, that agreement corresponds to distinct properties from those that are semantically associated with Div. It does not reflect *inherent* properties of agreement marking, but rather the properties of the syntactic and semantic environment in which such agreement is realized.
[20] A reviewer points out that agreement should occur with singulars as well. For reasons of space, singulars are not addressed in this paper, but in essence we follow Borer (2005) in assuming that singulars involve the identification of DIV and #, and hence we expect the singular –*AH*, effectively as an instance of the cardinal *one*, to agree. Singular agreement, however, is not overtly marked in Arabic, making the issue moot. Ouwayda (2014) discusses, however, a case of cardinal agreement in Bulgarian, where singular cardinal agreement is overtly attested.

sense). We supplement this with the claim in Borer (2005) that definite determiners inherit not only reference, but also cardinality from their antecedent. Having inherited cardinality from its antecedent, the definite determiner may now value # syntactically and semantically, thereby triggering the occurrence of cardinal agreement in spite of the absence of an actual cardinal.

An interesting confirmation of this conclusion emerges when we consider the properties of pre-nominal partitive quantificational structures. In such configurations, quantifiers always take definite restrictions. Importantly, although the restriction in these cases, in both LA and SA, is always *syntactically* definite, in actuality, the expressions are ambiguous, with the restriction interpreted as either definite or indefinite:

(81)   a. ra'ytu   l-kaθiir/l-qaliil/baʕDan   min   al-ašxaaS   *SA*
         saw.1s the-many/the-few/some of/from the-people
         i.   I saw many/a few/some of the people. (from a mutually recognizable set)
         ii. I saw many/a few/some people.
   b. kell/baʕD/ʔaghlab l-mudun   *LA*
       all/some/most   the-city-pl$_{BR}$
       i.   'all/some/most of the cities (of a mutually recognizable set)'
       ii. 'all/some/most cities'

In attempting to account for the ambiguity of (81a,b), and in particular for the indefinite restriction reading associated with (a.ii) and (b.ii), suppose we assume, following in essence Vergnaud and Zubizarreta (1992), that the definite determiner may at times be an expletive. Such an expletive clearly can inherit neither reference nor cardinality from its antecedent, giving rise to a semantic indefiniteness, in spite of the occurrence of the determiner.

Consider now the occurrence of -$\underline{AH}$-derived nominals in the contexts of partitive quantificational structures. Given the fact that in such structures the restriction always occurs with a definite article, we fully expect their grammaticality, a prediction which is directly verified by the examples in (82a,b). In contrast with (81a,b), however, these cases are *not* ambiguous. Rather, the indefinite construal is systematically excluded:

(82)   a. al-kaθiir/al-qaliil/baʕDan   min   al-baqar-aat/at-dajaaj-aat   *SA*
       the-many/the-few/some of/from the-cow-$\underline{AH}$-pl$_{SF}$/the-chicken-$\underline{AH}$-pl$_{SF}$
       i.   'many of the cows/chickens' (from a mutually recognizable set)
       ii. *'many cows/chickens'
   b. kell/baʕD/ʔaghlab   t-teffeeHaat   *LA*
       all/some/most   the-apple-$\underline{AH}$-pl$_{SF}$
       i.   'all/some/most of the apples' (from a mutually recognizable set)
       ii. *'all/some/most apples'

The contrast between the ambiguous (81a,b) on the one hand, and the non-ambiguous (82a,b) on the other hand, directly establishes the fact that the definiteness required for PL-$_A\underline{H}$-Ns to be licit in the absence of a cardinal must be semantically meaningful, i.e., it requires a true discourse anaphor which inherits from its antecedent both reference and cardinality. When the determiner is an expletive, such inheritance is impossible and as a consequence # may not be valued and hence must be missing. In the absence of #, however, cardinal agreement is excluded, and PL-$_A\underline{H}$-Ns cannot occur. As such, the behavior of partitive constructions gives us direct evidence for the common structural origin of semantically contentful definite PL-$_A\underline{H}$-Ns, and those PL-$_A\underline{H}$-Ns which occur with cardinals: only in these combinations does the structure contain (a valued) #, thereby giving rise to the emergence of licit PL-$_A\underline{H}$-Ns.

Seeking to cast cardinal agreement in terms of Agree, in the sense of Chomsky (2000) and much subsequent work, suppose we assume that # has an interpretable (strong) feature, which following Zabbal we may label [CARD]. [CARD] acts as a probe, with Div optionally endowed with an uninterpretable [uCARD] feature, thereby serving as a goal. Under such an account all cardinals, by assumption necessitating the projection of # (including decimals), would be probing and possibly valuing Div, and -*aat* would be a realization of such probing in the context of -$_A\underline{H}$. By that very same logic, in the definite cases in (80), it is the definite article, having inherited the cardinality of its antecedent, that is associated with a # projection, and hence the feature [CARD], thereby acting as a probe, and with -*eet/aat*, once again, realizing the probe–goal relations in the context of -$_A\underline{H}$.[21]

We note finally that, following Borer (2005), # is absent in bare (weak) DPs, where, therefore, we must assume that Div lacks the uninterpretable optional feature [uCARD]. We further assume (cf. 76) that # is absent in the presence of quantifiers in Q, where, similarly, Div may, and indeed at times must, be realized as plural marking, but where, similarly, the uninterpretable feature [uCARD] must be missing. As a result, we neither expect nor get cardinal agreement on, e.g., *teffeeH*-$_A\underline{H}$ to give rise to bare DPs or with overt quantifiers, yielding in this fashion the ungrammaticality of PL-$_A\underline{H}$-Ns in such contexts.[22]

---

[21] Note that when Div is populated by a divider other than -$_A\underline{H}$ (e.g. 'plural' markers or, for that matter, 'one') cardinal agreement is realized as Ø. See Ouwayda (2014) for discussion. The cardinal *one*, we note, certainly doesn't trigger 'plural' agreement on its restriction, but its status is altogether quite exceptional, in general, and in Semitic languages in particular, where, unlike other cardinals, it never occurs pre-nominally and is always adjectival in nature. See Borer (2005) for the relevant discussion, as well as for an analysis of singulars based on the identification of Div and #.

[22] The optionality of associating Div with [uCARD] has the direct effect of forcing the merger of # exactly when Div is [uCARD] and blocking it otherwise. We note this contingency here, leaving the pursuit of its ramifications to future research.

For reasons of space, we are leaving out a detailed discussion of the distinct properties of quantifiers and cardinals reviewed in Sections 5.1-5.3, and summarized in (72a-d). By way of brief pointers, however, recall, first, that cardinals allow a collective interpretation of the nominal as well as a distributive one (cf. (59, 61)), but that in Arabic, a collective interpretation is barred for quantifiers (cf. 60, 62). Having now put in place a distinct projection for quantifiers (Q) and for cardinals (#), we will follow Ouwayda (2013, 2014, 2017) in assuming that # (and hence cardinals) but not Q (and hence not quantifiers) may participate in the formation of a predicate of plurality, which is necessary for a collective reading to emerge (and see references for relevant motivation and discussion). Turning to (72c) we note that if null pronominals must be licensed by some mode of agreement, as is frequently assumed, and if cardinals trigger agreement, but quantifiers do not, the availability of a null pronominal restriction for the former, but not for the latter, follows. For additional discussion the reader is once again referred to Ouwayda (2014).

6.3. Inclusive vs. Exclusive Plural Marking?

This article serves to establish the fact that plural marking may, and indeed at times must, be associated with two distinct positions in the nominal spine. One of these positions is D<small>IV</small>, by assumption the syntactico-semantic node responsible for the emergence of count (vs. mass) structure through a *Divide* function that establishes an infinite number of cells, which are then potentially countable. The second position is #, the locus not of *count*, as contrasted with *mass*, but of *counters*. In line with Borer (2005), we assume that actual individuals, including those which serve as atoms in sums, emerge not from the division of mass affected by D<small>IV</small>, but rather from the selection of a fixed number of cells (including portions and none) within that division, with an identical extension.

It is worthwhile pausing briefly to consider the role that these two distinct nodes play in the emergence of inclusive vs. exclusive plurals, a topic of much current interest. Within that approach, a bare plural such as *apples* denotes a divided mass, where divisions have an identical extension, but where their counting properties remain entirely undetermined. Following Borer (2005), such D<small>IV</small> constituents may occur without # (or Q) altogether (see (13) and related discussion), where what emerges is a number-neutral denotation, which has an *inclusive* reading, insofar as it fails to exclude singulars (and allows, as noted in Borer 2005, decimals and zero as well). Relative to the cases under discussion in this article, instances of such inclusive reading would be *mxaddeet* 'pillows' or *bsayn-eet* 'cats$_F$' (cf. 34–35 and related discussion), which may occur bare, and which following standard tests allow both plural and singular readings (as well as zero and decimals). In these forms the S<small>F</small> plural marker is that which is associated exclusively with D<small>IV</small>. In Arabic, however (but not in

English), another SF marking is possible, that which appends to -*AH*- forms. These, as we claimed, are divided not through the occurrence of the SF itself, but rather by *AH*-, and the occurrence of SF signals not DIV, but the presence of #. In the presence of #, however, the emerging reading must involve actual counted individuals, and as such could only give rise to an *exclusive* reading (but see fn. 23). That, now, is the interpretation associated with, e.g., *samk-eet* 'fish-pl' with the parse *samak-AH*-pl$_{sf}$. In these cases, a singular reading is excluded, not only in the presence of an overt cardinal (>1), but also in the presence of the definite article, lending further support to its presence in #.

We have, then, a minimal pair here – cases in which plurality appears to be identically marked as *-eet*, but which correspond to the structural availability, or lack thereof, of #. An inclusive plural reading is associated with a bare DIV. An exclusive plural reading is associated with the presence of both DIV and #. That such distinct interpretations emerge not only supports the analysis presented here, but also points the way toward explaining structurally the distinction between inclusive and exclusive readings, across the board.[23]

7. Conclusion

The starting point of this article was an apparent counterexample from Arabic to the generalization that dividing morphemes do not co-occur with 'plural'-marking morphemes, because these compete for the same syntactico-semantic slot, DIV. That such co-occurrence does, indeed, occur in Arabic, pairing the dividing morpheme -*AH* with the plural marker -*aat* was established in some detail in Section 3. However, a closer examination of the facts showed that in the context of the dividing morpheme -*AH*, plural-marked forms behave significantly differently from other plural-marked forms in the language: they are excluded as bare and with quantifiers, and in fact in an indefinite context are only licit with cardinals – all matters discussed in some detail in Section 4. This difference between PL-*AH*-Ns and other plural marked forms in Arabic then served as our starting point for establishing a structural distinction between cardinals and quantifiers, outlined in some detail in Section 5 with evidence from the distribution of adjectives indicating that cardinals (and

---

[23] The notions *inclusion* and *exclusion* fit the picture which emerges here quite imperfectly, insofar as they fail to note that the 'exclusionary' reading, to the extent that it is associated with some cardinality, does not only exclude the singular, but excludes any denotation which is not compatible with that of the cardinality specified. Similarly, the 'inclusion' label focuses on the inclusion of the singular, but sets aside the inclusion of any entities which are neither singular nor plural, e.g., decimals and zero. Nonetheless, we consider it worthwhile to make use of the exclusion/inclusion distinction, all the more so as recent accounts of it often make explicit reference to the necessity of #, or NUM, for the emergence of exclusive plurals. See, most recently, Martí (2020). For a relevant discussion of Arabic plurals in that context see Dali and Mathieu (2016).

cardinal-like expressions such as *several*) must be lower in the nominal spine than quantifiers. A detailed structural proposal was outlined in Section 6.1. More specifically, we proposed that cardinals project under # and quantifiers project under Q, with Q^{max} dominating $\#^{max}$ when the two co-occur. In Section 6.2 we finally turned to the explanation for the puzzle which served as the starting point for this article: the co-occurrence of the dividing singulative morpheme -*AH* with plural marking, proposing that the singulative divider -*AH* is, indeed, an instance of DIV, but that the plural marking that may co-occur with it is an instance of cardinal agreement, instantiated exactly when # projects, but impossible in its absence. PL-*AH*-Ns are therefore barred in all contexts which do not allow for # to project. In particular, this includes structures in which neither # nor Q merge, as well as structures in which Q has merged but not #.

Interesting evidence for the agreement proposal, finally, is summoned from the distribution of PL-*AH*-Ns in definite contexts, where they are allowed without an overt cardinal, and where, demonstrably in Standard Arabic, they are licit *only* where an inheritance of cardinality from some antecedent is clearly in place.

Finally, and making reference to a distinction at times postulated between inclusive and exclusive plurals, we noted that the distinction, however imperfectly stated, falls naturally from the availability of two structurally distinct types of plural marking. One is an instance of DIV, which yields a number-neutral infinite cell division and hence perforce an inclusive reading. The other, which must be assumed to exist alongside Div-marking at the very least in Arabic, is cardinality agreement. This latter marking is associated with specified cardinality, and therefore excludes all cardinalities which are incompatible with it, including, of course, that of the singular.

Implications from Individual Languages

6 Mass-to-Count Shifts in the Galilee Dialect of Palestinian Arabic*

Christine Hnout, Lior Laks, and Susan Rothstein

1. Introduction

This paper explores the mass-to-count shift in the Galilee dialect of Palestinian Arabic (henceforth 'PA$_G$'). We show how in PA$_G$ the contrast between the masculine and feminine marked noun generally marks a contrast between a mass and a count interpretation. (1) gives examples of cases where the unsuffixed, masculine noun has a mass interpretation, while the noun marked with the feminine morpheme -*a*/-*e* has a singular count interpretation.[1] In (1a), the noun *xobez* 'bread' is masculine and has a mass interpretation, while *xobz-e* is feminine and denotes a piece of bread. Similarly, the mass nouns *θalj* 'ice' (1b) and *xaʃab* 'wood' (1c) are converted into count nouns denoting 'ice cube' and 'piece of wood' respectively, with this conversion marked by the feminine suffix. (1d) illustrates what looks like a somewhat different situation: the noun *toffa:ħ* 'apple' which is considered a collective plural (Ryding 2005), called a *sʕenf* form, is suffixed with -*a*/-*e*, and denotes a set of single atomic apples. Once the singular count noun has been derived, it can be pluralized in the standard way.

(1) a. *xobe*   → *xobz-e*   → *xobz-a:t*
        bread.M   bread-F.SG   bread-PL
        'bread'   'piece of bread'   'pieces of bread'
     b. *θalj*   → *θalj-e*   → *θalj-a:t*
        ice.M   ice F.SG I   ice-PL
        'ice'   'ice-cube'   'ice-cubes'
     c. *xaʃab*   → *xaʃab-e*   → *xaʃab-a:t*
        wood.M   wood-F.SG   wood-PL
        'wood'   'piece of wood'   'pieces of wood'

---

* We would like to express our deep gratitude to Fred Landman for his important comments on this paper.
[1] The selection of -*a*/-*e* is subject to variation in the Palestinian dialects, as well as other dialects. The selection of -*a* or -*e* is based mostly on phonological conditions as well as some semantic and syntactic criteria, and it is subject to some degree of variation (see Levin 1994, 2011; Gaash 2010; Shachmon 2011; Al-Wer and Horesh 2017, among others). The distinction between them is irrelevant for the purposes of the current study.

d. toffa:ħ   → toffa:ħ-a   → toffa:ħ-a:t
    apple.SʕENF   apple.F.SG   apple-PL
    'apples'   'apple'   'apples'

The examples suggest that Galilee Palestinian Arabic has a production singulative operation, which derives singular count nouns from apparently mass or collective counterparts. However, in contrast to the mass nouns in (1), there are other nouns that do not undergo this shift. The nouns ʕasal 'honey' (2a) and tˤħi:n 'flour' (2b), for example, could have taken this suffix and denoted some portion of honey and flower respectively. However, such formation does not take place.

(2) a. ʕasal   → *ʕasal -e
         honey.M   honey-F.SG
         'honey'   intended: 'portion of honey'
     b. tˤħi:n   → *tˤħi:n-e
         flour.M   flour-F.SG
         'flour'   intended: 'portion of flour'

The existence of this singulative operation has been discussed in the literature. Fassi Fehri (2004) discusses examples like (1d) in Modern Standard Arabic, arguing that the input to the rule is a kind-denoting term. Ouwayda (2014) discusses the derivation of singular terms from what she calls 'batch nouns' in Lebanese Arabic, arguing that the feminine singular suffix is homonymous with a classifier which allows the derived nouns in (1) to be interpreted as count. However, the phenomenon is more widespread than Fassi Fehri's account suggests (at least in Galilee Palestinian Arabic), while the conditions on the input and the output of the operation are more constrained than Ouwayda's account for Lebanese Arabic.

The contribution of our paper is thus twofold. First, it documents the phenomenon of the singulative operation in the Galilee dialect of Palestinian Arabic. Second, we show that the singulative operator is predictably constrained in what nouns it applies to, and that the output of the operation varies depending on the properties of the denotation of the input noun – whether it denotes liquids, granular substances, solid matter, or a collection of individuals. To the best of our knowledge, while the singulative operation is recognized as part of Modern Standard Arabic grammar as well in at least some dialects, this kind of systematic semantic mapping between denotation of the input and denotation of the output has not been carried out before.

Given that Modern Standard Arabic has a singulative operation, it is not surprising that the grammar of Galilee Palestinian Arabic should also include such an operation. However, it is also not to be taken for granted. Variation among dialects of Arabic is wide, as even a two-way comparison between Galilee Palestinian Arabic and Lebanese Arabic shows.

Mass-to-Count Shifts 153

The results of this study go beyond an account of Arabic grammar and Arabic dialects, and have wider implications for cross-linguistic studies of the count–mass contrast. The constraints on what kind of singular objects the denotation of N+ -*a/-e* will contain can give us insight into what kind of entities can count as atomic individuals in the denotation of a count predicate in Galilee Palestinian Arabic. This is particularly interesting in light of the growing body of data showing cross-linguistic variation in exactly this respect (see Rothstein, this volume, Chapter 3, Lima and Rothstein 2020).

We make the following claims:

(i) -*a/-e* is the morphological reflection of a singulative operation, remarkably similar to the singulative discussed in Mathieu (2012b) for Ojibwe.
(ii) Not all nouns can be the input to this operation.
(iii) The denotation of the count noun, which is the output of the operation, is constrained by the denotation of the input.

This paper is organized as follows. In Section 2, we provide some background on gender and number in PA_G. Section 3 presents the count–mass distinction in PA_G and the distinctions between the two types of nouns. In Section 4, we turn to the mass-to-count operation and the restrictions on its input and output. Section 5 offers a general discussion of the implications of this study for theories of the count–mass distinction.

2. Gender and Number in PA

2.1. Gender

PA is gender sensitive and differentiates between masculine and feminine. Feminine nouns, adjectives and participle forms are marked with the suffix -*a/-e*. This is demonstrated in (3) for animate nouns. In addition, there are some cases of suppletion like *rajol* 'man' and *mara* 'woman'.

(3) Feminine formation of animate nouns

Masculine form	Feminine form	
fanna:n	*fanna:n-e*	'artist'
raqqa:sˤ	*raqqa:sˤ-a*	'dancer'
mʕallem	*mʕallm-e*	'teacher'

In addition, the suffix -*a/-e* can also be part of inanimate feminine nouns with no masculine base (4):

(4) madin-e   'city'
     sayya:ra 'car'
     tˤayya:ra 'airplane'

2.2. Number

Arabic has a four-way grammatical system of number: singular, plural, dual, and collective (see, for example, Holes 1995; Idrissi 1997; Versteegh 1997; Watson 2002; Kihm 2006, among many others). The singular noun in Arabic is the free stem and the basic building block of the inflectional paradigm. Dual formation of nouns is based on the suffix *-e:n*, e.g. *daftar* 'notebook' – *daftar-e:n* 'two notebooks'. There are two main plural formation strategies in Arabic: suffixed-based 'sound plural' (SP) and template-based 'broken plural' (BP). Plurality in Arabic interacts with gender in ways that are beyond the scope of this paper.

2.2.1. Sound Plural

The SP is based on a linear formation in which a suffix is attached to the singular stem. Inanimate nouns with SP take the suffix *-a:t*. This suffix can be attached both to feminine nouns that end with *-a/-e* (5) and to masculine nouns (6):

(5) SP of feminine inanimate nouns[2]

a. Singular	b. Plural	
sayya:ra	sayya:ra:t	'car'
tˤayya:ra	tˤayya:ra:t	'airplane'

(6) SP of masculine inanimate nouns

c. Singular	d. Plural	
matˤa:r	matˤa:ra:t	'airport'
imtifia:n	imtifia:na:t	'exam'

2.3. Broken Plural

The broken plural involves internal modification of the singular base, as in (7). The modification can include a change of vowel, insertion of a consonant, and

---

[2] The feminine suffix *-a/-e* is deleted (Holes 1995). The reasons for this deletion are irrelevant for the current study.

altering of the syllabic structure (Murtonen 1964; Levy and Fidelholtz 1971; Ratcliffe 1998).

(7) BP nouns

Singular	Plural	BP pattern	
maktab	*maka:tib*	CaCa:CiC	'office'
maktu:b	*maka:ti:b*	CaCa:Ci:C	'letter'
qalam	*aqla:m*	aCCa:C	'pen'
madi:ne	*Mudun*	CuCuC	'city'

The selection of a BP pattern, and the selection of either SP or BP, can be partially predicted based on morpho-phonological properties of the singular base (see Hammond 1988, McCarthy and Prince 1990). However, it is a system that is subject to a great deal of irregularity. Examine for example the two feminine nouns *madi:ne* 'city' and *sayya:ra* 'car'. It is unclear why the former takes a BP pattern (*mudun* / * *madi:na:t*), while the latter takes -*a:t* (*sayya:ra:t*). In general, -*a:t* has become the default suffix that is attached to most loanwords that enter the language, e.g. *tilifon* – *tilifona:t* 'telephone' (see Hafez 1996, Lahrouchi and Lampitelli 2014, Laks 2014, Lahrouchi and Ridouane 2016). In addition, Mathieu (2014) shows that the two types of plural behave similarly with respect to their inclusive/exclusive interpretation.

3. The Count–Mass Distinction

Hnout (2017) shows that PA$_G$ distinguishes between count nouns and mass nouns systematically. This can be shown using several diagnostics.

Count nouns can be directly modified by numerals, while mass nouns cannot. The numeral *θala:θ* 'three', for example, can modify count noun *sayya:ra* 'car' in its plural form (8a), while it is impossible with the count noun *ħali:b* 'milk' (8b), similar to the case in English in (9a) and (9b) respectively. Note that this is to do with count, not with plurality. Numerals above ten are followed by nouns in the singular, but mass nouns still cannot be modified by numerals.

(8) a. *θala:θ*   *sayya:ra:t*
       three.F   car-F.PL
       'three cars'
    b. * *θalaθe*   *ħali:b*/   **θalaθe* *ħali:bat*
        three.M   milk-M.SG/   three.M   milk-M.PL
        Intended meaning: 'three milk(s)'

(9) a. eleven cars
     b. *eleven milks

Mass nouns can be counted via classifiers, while count nouns cannot. ḥali:b is modified by the classifier kuba:ye 'cup' (10a), while the count noun sayya:ra cannot be modified by the classifier wiḥda:t 'units' (10b).

(10) a. ʃribet   kuba:yet   ḥali:b
        drink.M.PAST.1ˢᵀ P cup.F.SG.CS   milk
        'I drank one cup of milk'
     b. *θalaθ   wiḥda:t   sayya:ra:t/ sayya:ra
        three.F   unit.F.PL.CS   car.PL/car.SG
        Intended: 'three cars'

Interrogatives also reveal the contrast between count and mass nouns. The interrogative word akam 'how many' is always followed by a noun in the singular. It can be used directly with count nouns as in (11a). In contrast, it cannot precede a mass noun like tˤḥi:n 'flour' (11b), but needs a classifier like ki:s 'pack' (11c).

(11) a. akam   daftar /*dafa:ter   ʔindek?
        How many   notebook.SG/ *notebook.PL you have
        'How many notebooks do you have?'
     b. *akam   tˤḥi:n   ʔindek?
        how much   flour   you have
        Intended: 'How much flour do you have?'
     c. akam   ki:s   tˤḥi:n   ʔindek?
        how much   CLASS.M.SG   flour   you have
        'How many packs of flour do you have?'

In contrast, the interrogative ade:ʃ can occur with both count nouns (which must be in the plural) (12a) and mass nouns (which must be in the singular) (12b):

(12) a. ade:ʃ   ʕindek   wla:d?
        How many   you have   boy.M.BP
        'How many boys do you have?'
     b. ade:ʃ   ʕindek   tḥi:n?
        how many   you have   flour.M.SG
        'How much flour do you have?'

Determiners also show the contrast between mass and count nouns. ʃwaye(t) 'a little' can be used with mass nouns such as ḥali:b 'milk', as in (13a), while it cannot occur with count nouns, as in (13b):

(13) a. ʃwaye(t)   ḥali:b
        little   milk.M.SG
        'a little milk'

b. *ʃwayet   bana:t
   a few   girl.F.PL
   Intended: '(a) few girls'

kθi:r has the same meaning of 'much/many', and it is unrestricted with respect to the count–mass distinction, as in (14). Note, though, that like in the examples in (12), the count noun *bana:t* in (14a) is in the plural while the mass noun *ħali:b* is in the singular:

(14)   a. *fi:*   *kθi:r*   *bana:t*   *ho:n*
          EXIST   many   girl.PL   here
          'There are many girls here'
       b. *insakab*   *kθi:r*   *ħali:b*   *ʕal-*   *ʔaredˤ*
          fall.pst. much   milk   PREP   ground
          'Much milk fell on the ground'

Other tests that can be used to distinguish between count and mass nouns include the use of reciprocals. See Hnout (2017) for details.

4. Mass-to-Count Shift

The singulative operation shows up in Galilee Palestinian Arabic when a mass noun of masculine gender occurs with a feminine singular suffix, as in (15):

(15)   *xobez* + *-a/-e*   →   *xobz-e*   →   *xobz-a:t*
       bread.M   (piece of) bread-F.SG   (piece of) bread-F.PL

While *xobez* is a mass noun meaning 'bread', the suffixed form *xobz-e* denotes a set of pieces or chunks of bread. Crucially, these pieces need not be of any particular size or shape: a loaf of bread or a slice of bread or a chunk broken off a loaf of bread can all be in the denotation of *xobze*.[3] The derived noun has all the properties of a count noun, for example, and while *xobez* cannot be questioned using *akam* (16a), *xobze* can (16b):

(16)   a. * *akam*   *xobez*   *ʔindek*
            what quantity   bread   you have
            Intended meaning: 'How much bread do you have?'
       b. *akam*   *xobze*   *ʔindek*
          what quantity   bread   you have
          'How many pieces of bread do you have?'

The plural of this noun *xobza:t* has a standard plural interpretation, and it denotes pluralities of pieces or chunks of bread. However, these plural forms

---

[3] In some cases, the base undergoes alternations (e.g. vowel deletion) when this morpheme is added. Such alternations are irrelevant for the current study.

have special restrictions: they do not occur as bare plurals or with expressions like 'few' and 'many'. They occur with numerals or in definite NPs.

Ouwayda (2014) shows that the noun that this singulative operation applies to, which she calls a 'batch noun', is indeed mass. However, she does not discuss whether all mass nouns are batch nouns, or what the semantic constraints on the mass-to-count shift are. Following Hnout (2017), we show that there are lexical constraints on the application of the mass-to-count operation and on its output. We now turn to examining these constraints.

4.1. Constraints on the Input Noun

Mass-to-count shift applies to nouns which denote solids like *xobez* (15) or *xaʃab* 'wood' (17a), or which denote granular substances like *rozz* 'rice' (17b):

(17) a. *xaʃab* 'wood' - *xaʃab-e* 'piece of wood'
      b. *rozz* 'rice'   - *rozz-e* 'grain of rice'

In contrast, the operation cannot apply to liquids or powders. The mass noun *ħali:b* 'milk' does not have a count counterpart *ħali:b-e*, which could have denoted a portion or serving of milk. There is therefore no plural form *ħali:ba:t* 'milks', denoting portions or servings of milk, and sentences like (18) are therefore infelicitous:

(18) *ʃribet   xames   ħali:ba:t
      drink.1ˢᵗperson.past five   milk one.M.SG
      *'I drank five milks'

Similarly, *ʕasal* 'honey' (19a) and *tˤħi:n* 'flour' (19b) cannot be the input to the singulative operation:

(19) a. *ʕasal + -a/-e* ➔ **ʕasal -e*
         honey.M   (portion of) honey-F.SG
      b. *tˤħi:n+ -a/-e* ➔ *tˤħi:n-e*
         flour.M   (portion of) flour-F.SG

This is all the more striking because it is possible to count portions of the denotation of nouns like *ħali:b* 'milk' in a restaurant context, but only by using a different construction, as in (20):

(20) *jib-li   θla:θe   ħali:b   sˤoxon*
      2ⁿᵈ person.bring   three.M   milk.M   hot.M
      'Bring me three hot milks'

As (20) shows, the noun *ħali:b* is bare, and has masculine gender, as is clear not only from its morphology, but also from the fact that the numeral that immediately precedes the noun is masculine. This suggests that the noun has remained mass, and that there is a null classifier intervening between the numeral and the noun, as proposed in (21):

(21) θla:θe   [Ø$_{CL}$ ħali:b   s^{ʕ}oxon]
      three.M classifier milk.M   hot
      'three portions of hot milk'

This is clearly a different construction from the mass-to-count operation induced by -a/-e suffixation, since examples like (20) are restricted to restaurant contexts, and make reference to three standardized portions of milk, as in similar English constructions 'We ordered three coffees, three waters, and two milks' (Rothstein this volume, Chapter 3). We return to a discussion of the contrast between these two types of counting constructions in the next sub-section and in Section 5.

4.2. Constraints on the Output Noun

Mass-to-count shift takes as input mass nouns denoting solid substances and maps them onto nouns denoting individual pieces of that substance. Given the ban on applying the operation to nouns denoting liquids and powders, it seems that the constraint is that the individual pieces in the denotation of the count noun must keep their shape independent of any container. However, even within the group of nouns denoting non-liquid/powder substances, there are lexically determined constraints on what the count noun can denote. We distinguish three different lexical groups of nouns to which this singulative process can apply. In the remainder of this sub-section, we argue that the operation deriving count nouns from s^{ʕ}enf nouns is a version of the same singulative operation.

4.2.1. Chunks If the input noun denotes a substance with a 'continuous texture' such as *xobez* 'bread' (22a), the output mass noun denotes a set of disjoint arbitrary chunks. Thus, *xobze wa:ħad-e* 'one (chunk of) bread' (22b) can be a loaf of bread or a slice of bread or a chunk of bread. Crucially, *xames xobza:t* 'five breads' (22c) can denote a collection consisting of pieces of non-uniform shape: two loaves, two slices, and one chunk.

(22) a. *Xobez*   'bread'
      b. *xobze wa:ħad-e*   'one (chunk of) bread'
      c. *xames xobza:t*   'five breads'

These derived count nouns are thus very different from the examples in (21), since the shapes of the five pieces of bread in the denotation of (22c) can be not only non-uniform, but also non-standardized. Other examples which work the same way are given in (23):

(23)   Mass-to-count of nouns with continuous texture

Mass noun		Count noun
xaʃab	'wood'	xaʃab-e
laḥme	'meat'	laḥm-e
jibn	'cheese'	jibn-e
ʔaza:z	'glass'	ʔaza:z-e

4.2.2. Idiosyncratic Interpretations In a restricted set of cases, the derived count noun has a lexically specified interpretation. For example, the mass noun *θalj* 'ice' is the basis for the count noun *θalje*, which means 'ice-cube', while *ʔutˤen* 'cotton' is the basis for deriving *ʔutˤne* 'cotton wool ball'.

(24) a. *θalj*   'ice'   - *θalje* 'ice-cube'
      b. *ʔutˤen* 'cotton'   - *ʔutˤne* 'cotton wool ball'

4.2.3. Granular Substances If the input noun denotes an inherently granular substance, the output count noun denotes a set of individual grains. For example, *rozz* denotes 'rice', and *rozze* denotes a grain of rice (25):

(25) a. *rozz*   'rice'   - *rozz-e*   'grain of rice'
      b. *ʕadas* 'lentil.Mass'   - *ʕadas-e* 'a lentil'

There is an important contrast between these examples and the examples in the previous section. If you take a chunk of bread in the denotation of the singular noun *xobze* and break it in two, then you have two chunks, each of which are in the denotation of *xobze*. However, if you take a grain of rice in the denotation of *rozze* and break it in two, the resulting two pieces are not in the denotation of *rozze* since they are no longer whole grains of rice.

4.2.4. sˤenf nouns Arabic, including PA_G, has a form of noun traditionally referred to as *sˤenf* (see Fassi Fehri 2004; Ryding 2005; among others). Traditionally, these have been considered a form of broken plural with a collective interpretation. The standard paradigm is given in (26)–(28). *toffa:ḥ* (26a) is the *sˤenf* noun denoting 'apples' and is often considered a collective noun, *toffa:ḥ-a* (26b) denotes one single apple and *toffa:ḥ-a:t* (26c) is the plural form. The other examples work similarly.

(26) a. *toffa:ḥ*   b. *toffa:ḥ-a*   c. *toffa:ḥ-a:t*
          apple.SˤENF.M   apple.F.SG   apple.F.PL
          'apples'   'apple'   'apples'

(27) a. *ja:j* b. *ja:j-e* c. *ja:j-a:t*
hen.SˤENF.M hen.F.SG hen.F.PL
'hens' 'hen' 'hens'

(28) a. *bortʔa:n* b. *bortʔa:n-e* c. *bortʔa:n-a:t*
orange. SˤENF orange.F.sg orange.F.PL
'oranges' 'orange' 'oranges'

In some cases, the feminine singular noun (29) may have a broken plural form as well as sound plural:

(29) a. *samak* b. *samake* c. *samaka:t* d. *asma:k*
fish.SˤENF fish.F.SG fish.F.PL fish.BrP
'fish' 'fish' 'fish(es)' 'fish(es)'

As the examples show, nouns traditionally considered *sˤenf* nouns tend to denote natural kinds. As in Standard Arabic (Fassi Fehri 2004), the *sˤenf* form, unlike the sound plurals, allows reference to kinds as well as to individuals. This is shown in (30), where the question 'who has more apples?' can only be answered in terms of cardinality when the word for 'apples' is the sound plural *toffa:ħa:t* (30a) but can be answered in terms of the cardinality, the measure, or the number of kinds when the word used to formulate the question is the *sˤenf* form *toffa:ħ* (30b):

(30) a. *mi:n maʕa:h toffa:ħa:t aktar*[4]
who has apple.F.PL more
'Who has more apples?'
b. *mi:n maʕa:h toffa:ħ aktar*
who has apple. Sˤ*enf* more
'Who has more (kinds of) apples?'

However, the issue of reference to kinds vs. individuals is orthogonal to the topic of this paper (though we will return to it briefly in the final section). Here we focus on the relation between the *sˤenf* form and the feminine singular that it is related to, and show that it is derived via the same mass-to-count operation used to derive the count nouns in the previous three sections. Crucially, the morpheme which distinguishes the singular count noun *toffa:ħ-a* (which is feminine) from the bare *sˤenf* form *toffa:ħ* (which is masculine) is the same morpheme as is used in all these the examples.

A number of pieces of evidence indicate why *sˤenf* nouns are considered a form of plural. The *sˤenf* form is often used in situations in which we might expect a plural, and it can be antecedent for a plural pronoun. As shown in

---

[4] There is some degree of variation with respect to the pronunciation of the interdental consonants. Words like *aktar* can also be pronounced as *akθar*.

(31) the auxiliary verb 'be' is in its plural form (ka:nu), and the adjective 'tasty' (tʕayba:t), which is the complement of the auxiliary, is also in the plural form:

(31) (a) akalet   toffa:ħ   (b) **ka:nu   kti:r   tʕayba:t**
        eat.1ˢᵗperson.pst apple.SʕENF   be.PL   a lot   tasty.PL
        'I ate apples'   'They were very tasty'

As (32) shows, this is not the case with substance mass nouns like *xobez* 'bread'. In (32a), the pronoun dependent on *toffa:ħ* can be either singular or plural, but in (32b), the pronoun dependent on *xobez* must be singular:

(32) a. ʃare:t   kti:r   toffa:ħ   u: ħatʕet-o/ħatʕet-hen   fi-l kya:s
        I bought   a lot of apple.SʕENF and put.M.SG/PL   in the bag
        'I bought a lot of apples and I put it/them in bags.'
     b. ʃare:t   kti:r   xobez   u: ħatʕet-o/*ħatʕet-hen   fi-l kya:s
        I bought   a lot of bread   and   I put.M.SG/*PL   in the bag
        'I bought a lot of bread and I put it/them in bags.'

However, as Ouwayda (2014) showed for Lebanese Arabic and Hnout (2017) showed for Galilee Palestinian Arabic, *sʕenf* forms pattern with mass nouns on all the standard diagnostics, and should be considered grammatically mass. *Sʕenf* nouns cannot be modified by numerals (33a),⁵ but they can be counted using classifiers like *ħaba:t* 'units' (33b). In addition, they cannot occur with the interrogative *akam* (33c), but *akam* can precede a measure phrase like *kilo*, followed by a *sʕenf* noun (33d):

(33) a. *xamse   toffa:ħ
         five   apple.SENF
     b. θala:θ   **ħaba:t**   toffa:ħ
         three.F   unit.F.PL.   apple.SʕENF
         'three apples'
     c. *akam   toffa:ħ   maʕak
         how many   apple. SʕENF   with-you
         Intended reading: 'What quantity of apples do you have?'

---

⁵ Ouwayda (2014) notes that in Lebanese Arabic the *sʕenf* form can be modified by a numeral but can only have a kind interpretation. But using *sʕenf* with numerals does not seem to be allowed in Galilee Palestinian Arabic:

(i) akalet   teffe:ħ-ah   waħdeh   (bi-z-zabet)
     ate.1s   apple.F.SG   one.F   (to-the-exact)
     'ate exactly one apple' (could be two halves of different types)
(ii) akalet   teffeeħ   waħad   (be-z-zabet)
     ate.1s   apple.SʕENF   one.F   (to-the-exact)
     'I ate exactly one type of apple' (regardless of amount)

d. *akam* **ki:lo** *toffa:ħ* *maʕak*
how many kilo.SG apple. SʕENF with-you
'How many kilos of apple do you have?'

Like other mass nouns, the *sʕenf* form can be modified by the quantity word *ʃwaye(t)* (34a), while the regular plural form cannot (34b):

(34) a. *ʃwayet*   *toffa:ħ*
         DET- few   apple.sʕENF
         'a few apples'
      b. *ʃwayet   *toffa:ħa:t*
         DET- few   apple.F.PL
         Intended reading: 'few apples'

Given that *sʕenf* nouns show all the properties of mass nouns, and that the morpheme deriving the feminine singular individual-denoting noun is identical to that marking mass-to-count shift, as shown in (35), it is highly plausible that the same operation is involved here too:

(35) a. *toffa:ħ* → *toffa:ħ-a* 'apple'
      b. *xobez* → *xobz-e* 'bread'

However, as Hnout (2017) shows, there are semantic contrasts in the output of the operation in the two cases. In case the mass noun denotes a natural kind like *toffa:ħ*, instantiated by natural units, in this case whole apples, the related count noun can only denote a set of these natural units. Thus *toffa:ħa* can only denote a set of whole apples and the plural *toffa:ħa:t* must denote the closure of that set under sum. Ouwayda (2014) shows that this is the case in Lebanese Arabic, and the same holds for Palestinian Arabic:

(36) a. *ʕasʕar-t*   *teffe:ħ*
         squeezed.1ps apple
         'I squeezed apple(s)' (could be a whole apple or less than one apple)
      b. *ʕasʕar-t*   *teffe:ħ-ah*
         squeezed.1ps apple-AH
         'I squeezed an apple' (I squeezed at least one whole apple)
                                             (Ouwayda 2014: 48)

However, in the case of *xobez*, the derived count noun *xobze* denotes a set of discrete chunks of bread, not necessarily of uniform size and not corresponding to any 'natural' atoms. As a correlate, a piece of bread in the denotation of the count noun *xobze* can be broken into two (or more) pieces, and, in an updated context, these pieces can both count as instances of *xobze*. In contrast, an object in the denotation of the count noun *toffa:ħa* cannot have apple-parts that will also count as an instance of *toffa:ħa*.

In fact, the count-to-mass shift involving *sʕenf* nouns (i.e. mass nouns denoting natural kinds) looks more like the shift discussed in Section 4.2.3, which applies to mass nouns denoting granulars. We saw that when the count-to-mass shift applies to these nouns, the output of the operation is always a set of 'grains of N', e.g. the shift maps *rozz* 'rice' onto *rozze*, a noun denoting a set of individual rice-grains, and, similarly, it maps *ʕadas* 'lentils' onto *ʕadase*, denoting a set of individual lentils. Crucially, if we break an individual in *ʕadase* or *rozze* into pieces, the resulting pieces do not count as instances of *ʕadase* or *rozze* respectively.

We turn to a discussion of these results in the next section.

5. Discussion

The operation we have seen here is similar to the operation that applies in Ojibwe (Mathieu 2012b), where a unit-of-measure reading is derived from pluralized mass nouns by a gender shift in the singular to express singulativization. The same process is used to derive singular denotations for collective nouns. Pluralized mass nouns are possible because gender shift has been applied in the singular prior to pluralization. As in PA_G, singulativization does not apply to liquids.

Hnout (2017) lists some other highly restricted contexts where mass nouns can be apparently directly modified by a numeral. These include shopping lists, recipes, and restaurant settings, which are portioning contexts. In a shopping list, *θala:θe rozz* (37a), literally three rice, would be interpreted as three bags of rice, but in a recipe it would naturally be interpreted as three cups of rice. However, these are not instances of the singulative operation. In *θala:θe rozz*, the noun has singular morphology, and it denotes three contextually determined portions of rice. In contrast, in *θala:θ rozza:t* 'three rices' (37b), the noun has plural morphology and it denotes three grains of rice.

(37) a. *θala:θe rozz*
       three   rice
    b. *θala:θ rozza:t*
       three   rice-PL

In restaurant contexts, even mass nouns denoting liquids can be modified by a numeral. *θla:θe ħali:b*, literally three milk as in (20), repeated here in (38a), for example, denotes three orders of milk. The singulative form is ungrammatical (*ħali:b-e*) and as a result the plural form is ungrammatical in this context (38b):

(38) a. *jibi:-li   θla:θe   ħali:b   sʕoxon*
       bring.to me. 2nd   three.M   milk.M   hot.M
       'Bring me three hot milks'
    b. * *jibi:-li   θla:θe   ħali:ba:t   sʕoxon*

It appears that in cases like *θala:θe rozz/ħali:b*, the null classifier maps the nouns denoting rice or milk onto NPs denoting contextually relevant portions of rice or milk.

Since the noun is still a mass nouns, it has singular morphology. This is demonstrated in (39). The data suggest that while the lexical operation results in an expression denoting units or pieces of N, the phrasal operation is more appropriate for denoting contextually determined portions.

(39) a. *θala:θe*   [Ø$_{CL}$ *rozz*]
         three.M   classifier   rice.M
         'three (contextually determined) portions of rice'
      b. *θala:θe*   [Ø$_{CL}$ *ħali:b*   *s^{ʕ}oxon*]
         three.M   classifier   milk.M   hot
         'three (contextually determined) portions of hot milk'

If follows that these are two different grammatical mechanisms. The first is a lexical singulative operation involving a count-to-mass operation on noun denotations. It is freely available. The second is a null portion classifier that maps mass nouns denotations onto contextually determined portions. It is contextually restricted and can be used in restaurant contexts, recipes, and shopping lists, for example.

Note that liquid and powder nouns can also be pluralized in specific contexts with no singulative form. In addition to the restaurant contexts the plural form *ħali:b-a:t* can be found in cases like (40):

(40) *baħibb*   *ħali:b-a:t*   *fat^{ʕ}me*
      like.1st.sg.   milks   Fatme
      'I like Fatme's milk'

Such plural forms do not denote kinds or contextually determined portions. Rather, we argue that the plural has a quasi-pluractional interpretation. *ħali:b-a:t*, in such cases, denotes portions of Fatme's milk drunk during different events. However, such examples are relatively less common, and further studies should examine this phenomenon.

Up to this point, we have kept the discussion as theory-neutral as possible, focusing on a description of the -*a*/-*e* suffixation operation. We now turn to implications of this data from Galilee Palestinian Arabic for theories of the count–mass distinction. We note that the mass-to-count operation is a lexical suffixation operation applying at the pre-syntactic level. It applies to nouns that cannot appear with numerals, both 'substance' nouns like *xobez* 'bread' and *xaʃab* 'wood', as well as nouns like *toffa:fi* 'apple', and the output of the operation is a noun that is grammatically countable. This suggests both (i) a lexical distinction between nouns which are countable and those which are not and (ii) a distinction between grammatical countability and natural atomicity in the sense of Rothstein (2010, 2017). The constraints on the interpretation of the mass-to-count operation, and on the denotation of the output noun described in Section 3, indicate that these shifts from mass to count are not coercion operations determined by context.

The contrast between the mass-to-count operation and the portioning operation in restaurant contexts illustrated in (38) suggests that, in addition to the lexical mechanism mass-to-count deriving count nouns from mass nouns, there is an additional syntactic mechanism involving a null classifier, which allows mass nouns denoting liquids to be used in count contexts. This seems to be a shift to a reading that involves conventionalized servings and is derived by a null portion classifier (Khrizman et al. 2015). Both types of shift from mass to count result in an expression (noun or, by hypothesis, noun phrase) that denotes a set of salient or contextually relevant individuals, be they items or portions. Thus, it seems that, contrary to e.g. Chierchia (2010), shifts from mass to count cannot be thought of as involving a contextually determined partition on the set denoted by a mass noun (since the union of a partition is the original set). Thus, while pieces of apple can strictly speaking be in the denotation of *toffa:fi*, as in (41), the count noun only has whole apples in its denotation. Similarly, while the mass noun *xaʃab* 'wood' includes any wood material, the derived count noun *xaʃabe* denotes pieces of wood of a contextually relevant size.

(41)   fi: toffa:fi   bi- l-   salatʕa
       there-is   apple.SENF   in DEF   salad
       'There is apple in the salad'

The data do further support the importance of context in determining what items are in the denotation of the count noun (as argued in Rothstein 2010), and the dynamics of context (in the sense of Stalnaker 2014) may result in shifting the denotation of some count nouns.

7 Object Mass Nouns as an Arbiter for the Count–Mass Category

Kurt Erbach, Peter R. Sutton, Hana Filip, and Kathrin Byrdeck

1. Introduction

Chierchia (2010) argues that object mass nouns constitute a good testing ground for theories of the count–mass distinction, given that these nouns constitute a non-canonical type of mass noun that seems to be restricted to number marking languages (excluding outliers like Greek that admit plural morphology on mass nouns). Taking this idea as a springboard, in this paper we pose the following questions: Are there object mass nouns in classifier languages such as Japanese? What does the answer to this question mean for semantic accounts of the count–mass distinction in classifier languages?

Object mass nouns (e.g. *furniture, jewelry, mail*) are genuine mass nouns insofar as they do not freely admit pluralization, are infelicitous with determiners that select for count predicates (e.g. *many, each,* and *every*), and are felicitous with determiners that select for mass predicates (e.g. *much*). Object mass nouns are non-canonical insofar as they refer to collections of discrete entities (e.g. *jewelry* refers to sets of earrings, necklaces, bracelets, etc.) that are identifiable via semantic tests like the availability of cardinality comparisons in *more than* constructions (Barner and Snedeker 2005), and they are felicitous with stubbornly distributive predicates (Rothstein 2010). In contrast, canonical mass nouns like *water* refer to undifferentiated stuff and behave differently with respect to these semantic tests. Given these characteristics, object mass nouns have been used at least as early as Chierchia (1998a) and B. Gillon (1999) to exemplify the lack of direct alignment between the count–mass distinction and the pre-linguistic substance–object distinction of Soja, Carey, and Spelke (1991) and Spelke (1985). In exemplifying this misalignment,

---

This research is funded as part of DFG Collaborative Research Centre 991: The Structure of Representations in Language, Cognition, and Science, Project C09: A Frame-Based Analysis of Countability. Our thanks to the hosts and attendees of the conference 'The Count–Mass Distinction: A Linguistic Misunderstanding?' at Ruhr-University Bochum for their feedback. We especially thank Genaro Chierchia for his helpful criticisms of the presented version of this work. Thanks, too, to Yasutada Sudo for helpful insights in preparation of this study and to our consultants Kaori Fujita, Natsko Hamasaki, Saki Kudo, Sebastian Steinfelder, Aiko Tendo, and Yuko Wagatsuma.

object mass nouns stand as counterexamples to early analyses of the count–mass distinction that assume count nouns denote individuals and mass nouns do not (e.g. Link 1983).

Analyses of the count–mass distinction in number marking languages such as English account for object mass nouns in various ways. However, when it comes to classifier languages like Japanese and Mandarin, it is sometimes assumed that a parallel, non-canonical class of mass nouns is not similarly attested. Chierchia (2010), for example, argues that classifier languages should have no object mass nouns, which he aligns with their lack of obligatory number marking. Chierchia (2010) and others (e.g. Muromatsu 2003; Nemoto 2005) follow Cheng and Sybesma (1998) in assuming that the count–mass distinction is encoded in classifier languages through the syntax and semantics of classifiers, because shape-based classifiers do not combine with substance denoting mass nouns, at least not without coercing a countable interpretation. In other words, shape-based classifiers only straightforwardly compose with object denoting nouns, and in this sense, classifier languages have count–mass syntax that is sensitive to whether nouns denote substances or objects. These assumptions lead to a picture of classifier languages in which the count–mass distinction aligns with the substance–object distinction.

Some recent studies have proposed that nouns in classifier languages, e.g. Japanese, encode individuation (Inagaki and Barner 2009) and that Japanese has several morphosyntactic reflexes that indicate that determiners are sensitive to the countability of nouns (Sudo to appear). Inagaki and Barner (2009) conclude from quantity comparison tasks that Japanese nouns like *isu* ('chair') encode individuation, because quantities of chairs can be compared in terms of cardinality in the absence of grammatical markers like classifiers. Sudo (to appear) argues that Japanese has nouns (e.g. *hon* 'book') whose denotations are countable. This is based upon, for example, the fact that such nouns can be felicitously modified by counting modifiers like *nan-byaku to iu* ('hundreds of') without an intervening classifier. He coins the term *countable nouns* for such nouns (reserving the term *count nouns* for the class of nouns in English and other languages that stands in opposition with *mass nouns*).

Given that Inagaki and Barner (2009) show that nouns encode individuation and Sudo (to appear) shows that some determiners are sensitive to countability of nouns in Japanese, Inagaki and Barner (2009) and Sudo (to appear) have collectively demonstrated that Japanese contains the necessary characteristics for identifying object mass nouns, which are known to encode individuation and pattern with mass nouns (Barner and Snedeker 2005, i.a.). That said, certain analyses have argued that classifier languages should have no such class of nouns (Chierchia 2010, 2015). This prompts the following question: If nouns in classifier languages encode individuation and the lack of it, and if determiners in classifier languages are sensitive to the countability of nouns, then why should classifier languages like Japanese lack object mass nouns? To address this question, we delimit the class of object mass nouns to those that are grammatically mass and yet are individuated in the sense of Barner and Snedeker (2005). We follow Sudo (to appear) in using determiners as our test for countability in Japanese, and we follow Inagaki and Barner (2009) in using cardinality-based quantity comparison cardinality as our test for individuation.

Using the evidence for individuation from Inagaki and Barner (2009) and countability from Sudo (to appear), we present a means of putting claims like those of Chierchia (2010) to the test: we constructed a felicity judgment task to test the felicity of forty-four nouns from three different conceptual classes (discrete individuals, collections of discrete entities, and undifferentiated stuff) when composed with the determiner *nan-byaku to iu* ('hundreds of'), which selects for *countable nouns* (in the sense of Sudo (to appear)). The results of this study provide some evidence to suggest that at least four Japanese nouns have one of the hallmark properties of object mass nouns, namely exhibiting grammatically mass behavior. We also tested the second hallmark property of object mass nouns, namely that they encode individuation, as argued by Barner and Snedeker (2005) and Inagaki and Barner (2009). Our consultants indicated that they can compare quantities of entities in the extension of these nouns in terms of cardinality. The results of these two tests give us some reason to think that at least four Japanese nouns demonstrate the mass noun behavior of being infelicitous with determiners that select for count nouns, and the object denoting property of being comparable in terms of cardinality. In other words, we have some evidence for the claim that Japanese has a small set of nouns that demonstrate the behavior of object mass nouns.

However, further studies are needed to explore the existence and robustness of a class of object mass nouns in Japanese, including the testing of the same nouns in further grammatical environments that arguably might be considered good diagnostics of the count–mass distinction in Japanese. If Japanese were to have a class of such nouns (admittedly a rather limited one), then the following question arises: What would an analysis of the count–mass distinction in Japanese be like? We outline one proposal that builds upon Sutton and Filip (2016a, 2016b, 2018a, 2020). This proposal is based on the idea that the key property that grounds the grammatical property of countability is quantization relative to a contextually specified *schema of individuation* (details given in Section 4).

2. Background

Since at least Krifka (1995), it has been commonly assumed that all bare nouns in classifier languages denote kinds (Chierchia 2010, 2015; Rothstein 2017;

among others) or are otherwise uniform in their internal structure (Muromatsu 2003).[1] Chierchia (1998a, 1998b) observes that several characteristics of classifier languages naturally follow from the assumption that nouns in classifier languages are kind-denoting arguments: namely, (i) bare arguments freely occur, (ii) there is no obligatory number marking, (iii) there are no definite or indefinite articles, and (iv) there is a generalized classifier system. The generalized classifier system follows from this analysis on the assumption that classifiers provide the necessary semantic criteria to specify a set of individuals to be counted. Chierchia (1998a, 1998b), just like many others (e.g., X.-P. Li 2011; Nemoto 2005; Rothstein 2010, 2017), assumes that all nouns in classifier languages have a macro syntax similar to that of mass nouns in number marking languages. Related to this, it is also observed that the grammars of classifier languages reflect the pre-linguistic distinction between nouns that refer to objects and those that refer to substances in the sense of Soja, Carey, and Spelke (1991).

Recent work on the count–mass distinction has added more refinements. Chierchia (2010, 2015), for example, while maintaining that all nouns in classifier languages denote kinds, also argues that classifier languages should not have object mass nouns, because they lack the prerequisite criteria for the formation of object mass nouns, namely an obligatory number marking system. Bale and Coon (2014), Doetjes (2012), and Inagaki and Barner (2009), on the other hand, propose that a large number of nouns are encoded with individuation criteria, and Sudo (2016; to appear) discusses the properties of what he refers to as *countable* and *non-countable* nouns in Japanese.

2.1. Languages Without Object Mass Nouns

Chierchia (1998a, 1998b, 2010) observes that no noun in classifier languages like Chinese can combine with a numerical without first combining with a classifier which shifts a given noun into a count predicate. Rather than at the lexical level, the count–mass distinction in classifier languages is taken to be reflected in the syntax and semantics of classifiers. For example, while the general classifier in Mandarin *ge* (CL$_{general}$) is typically used with nouns like *ji* ('chicken'), which denote clearly individuated entities, it is infelicitous with nouns like *xue* ('blood') that describe undifferentiated stuff:

(1)   a.   san   ge   ji   Mandarin
                three   CL$_{general}$ chicken
                'three chickens'

---

[1] This is a slight simplification. Krifka (1995) assumes that bare nouns in classifier languages denote *concepts*, which are a proper superset of kinds (concepts can, for example, be the product of combining different kinds).

b. #san   ge   xue
   three CL*general* blood
   'three portions of blood'   (Chierchia, 2010: 106–7)

Such combinatorial properties are typical not only of the general classifier *ge*, but also of shape-based classifiers, which may also enforce a count interpretation on nouns denoting stuff. As Cheng and Sybesma (1998) suggest, shape-based classifiers have a syntactic distribution that differs from that of classifiers that are not restricted to such nouns with countable denotations.

Most importantly, Chierchia (2010, 2015) also argues that classifier languages cannot have object mass nouns, because they lack the prerequisite properties for their existence, namely those that characterize a number marking system defined in terms of (stable) atomicity, as in English, for instance. As defined in (Chierchia, 2015), a predicate (singular or plural) is *stably atomic* if and only if there is a set of stably atomic entities in that predicate's denotation at all worlds in the common ground.

From this analytical assumption, several characteristics of number marking languages follow. By assuming that morphologically singular and plural nouns must refer to atoms, Chierchia's (2010, 2015) analysis explains why it should be the case that mass nouns are singular despite the fact that they can refer to sums of entities. Mass nouns are atomic and can refer to sums of entities, because they are assumed to denote a singleton property, that is, a property which, relative to all worlds for which the property is non-empty, denotes a set with only one member. At a given world, the denotation of a mass noun is the sum or totality of all the instances of the mass noun property. Crucially, the entities in the denotation of mass nouns like *mud* are assumed to be unstable, unlike those in the denotation of count nouns like *chair*, which are stably atomic. Singular count nouns denote individual atoms, and plural count nouns denote these atoms and all of the possible sums thereof. Mass nouns cannot pluralize because their pluralization would be semantically vacuous (given that they denote singleton properties). Furthermore, nouns that refer to stable atoms can be encoded as singleton properties as a matter of lexical choice, giving rise to object mass nouns like *furniture*. Because classifier languages lack obligatory number marking, they lack the semantic requirement that singular nouns must be (stably) atomic. Nouns that refer to unstable individuals are not expected to be encoded as singleton properties, so the encoding of stably atomic predicates as singleton properties via lexical choice is not expected to occur.

The picture of the count–mass distinction in classifier languages that emerges from the work of Cheng and Sybesma (1998) and Chierchia (2010, 2015) is one in which the count–mass distinction falls neatly in line with the substance–object distinction, and in this way they mirror early analyses of the count–mass distinction in English (e.g. Link 1983). More recent research on the count–mass distinction has focused on the ways in which the count–mass distinction deviates from the substance–object distinction (e.g. Barner and Snedeker 2005; Landman 2011; Rothstein 2010; among others); however, outside of some work done by Inagaki and Barner (2009), little work of this kind has been conducted on classifier languages.

2.2. Individuation Without Classifiers: Inagaki and Barner (2009)

Inagaki and Barner (2009) use quantity comparison tasks to explore whether Japanese nouns encode individuation or whether individuation is a prerequisite for counting that is imposed via the semantics of classifiers, as some assume (e.g. Chierchia 1998a; Rothstein 2010, 2017). Inagaki and Barner (2009) compared judgments related to quantities in three languages: English, French, and Japanese. Native speakers of these languages were presented with two sets of items at a time and asked to evaluate their relative quantity. For example, the participant would be directed to look at two portions of spinach, one with a larger cardinality and one with larger volume, as depicted in Figure 7.1. Other examples tested included images of undifferentiated stuff (e.g. mustard), discrete individuals (e.g. shoes), and collections of discrete individuals (e.g. furniture). Japanese participants were asked to compare the quantities of the stuff/entities in the pictures.

For spinach, for example, this was done via the question in (2), which contains no classifier or other grammatical means of specifying that there might be individuals to be counted and compared in terms of cardinality.

(2) Dotira-no hito-ga   yori-ookuno   hoorensoo-o motte-iru desyoo
     which-GEN person-NOM more.than-more spinach-ACC have-PROG COP.QCOP.Q
     'Who has more spinach?'   (Inagaki and Barner (2009): 125)

For *hoorensoo* 'spinach' and other nouns that typically have count and mass counterparts cross-linguistically, Japanese participants were fairly evenly split as to whether or not they compared quantity in terms of

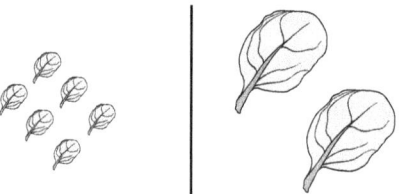

Fig. 7.1: Quantity comparison in the style of Inagaki and Barner (2009)

number or volume. Japanese- and English-speaking participants favored volume-based comparison for nouns that refer to undifferentiated stuff like *karasi* ('mustard'), and they favored cardinality comparisons for nouns like *kutu* ('shoe') that refer to discrete individuals and are count nouns in English. The ability to compare according to cardinality extends to nouns that refer to collections of discrete entities, such as *kagu* ('furniture'), as was also shown to be the case for English nouns in this category by Barner and Snedeker (2005). Based on such observations, Inagaki and Barner (2009) propose that Japanese nouns that refer to discrete individuals can individuate just as they can in English, while those that refer to undifferentiated stuff cannot.

2.3. Arguments for Nominal Individuation: Doetjes (2012)

Doetjes (2012) reviews a number of characteristics of nouns in classifier languages that she argues indicate that classifier languages have 'count meanings and mass meanings at the lexical level' (2577). The first characteristic is that classifier languages do not always require classifiers in counting constructions. Sudo (to appear) also shows this to be the case in Japanese. For example, large round numbers like 1000 can combine directly with nouns that refer to discrete individuals:

(3) sen-(choo)-no bairorin
     1000-CL-GEN violin
     'a thousand violins'   (Sudo (to appear): 4)

Second, general classifiers can be used in the place of sortal classifiers. Doetjes (2012) argues that this indicates that nouns themselves must be individuated, because the general classifier would otherwise have to contribute the individuation criteria for every noun that it can combine with.

Third, some classifier languages have determiners that are sensitive to individuation properties of nouns. The Mandarin determiner *yī diǎnr* ('a little') has been shown by Iljic (1994) to never occur with a classifier, and to typically occur with substance denoting nouns and abstract nouns. Doetjes (2012) argues that these three characteristics of classifier languages indicate that some nouns in classifier language have count meanings.

Although Doetjes (2012) concludes that this evidence supports a view in which nouns in obligatory classifier languages have a lexical count–mass distinction, arguably this is at most evidence for a weaker claim, namely that nouns in such languages encode individuation in the sense of Inagaki and Barner (2009). In other words, a safer conclusion from this evidence would be that a distinction can be drawn between nouns in classifier languages that refer to discrete objects and those that refer to undifferentiated stuff.

2.4. Count–Mass Characteristics in Japanese: Sudo 2016; to appear

Sudo (2016; to appear) shows that there are nouns in Japanese that exhibit syntactic behavior that resembles that which we find with mass and count nouns in languages that have a grammaticized lexical count–mass distinction. As mentioned in the previous sub-section, large round numbers like 100 and 1000 can directly combine with nouns that refer to discrete entities, i.e., his *countable nouns*. Japanese also has five determiners that, as Sudo (to appear) argues, also select for such *countable nouns* and that can be used without classifiers: *tasuu* ('many'), *shoosuu* ('few'), *nan-byaku-toiuu* ('what-100-say'), *dono* ('which'), and *hotondo* ('most'). As shown in (4), the determiner *nan-byaku to iu* ('hundreds of') is felicitous with *komento* ('comment') but not with *ase* ('sweat').

(4) a. sono   tookoo-ni   nan-byaku-toiuu   komento-ga   tsuita.
       that   post-TO   what-100-say   comment-NOM provided.
       'That post got hundreds of comments.'
     b. Taro-wa   nan-byaku-toiuu   ase-o   kaita
        Taro-TOP what-100-say   sweat-ACC   secreted
        (intended) 'Taro sweated a lot.'   (Sudo to appear: 5)

3. Testing for Object Mass Nouns

Recent research on Japanese by Inagaki and Barner (2009), Doetjes (2012), and Sudo (2016; to appear), which we have just summarized, has laid the groundwork for showing that Japanese distinguishes between different kinds of nouns, those that encode individuation versus those that do not (Inagaki and Barner 2009) and those that encode countability versus those that do not (Sudo to appear). We take it that such studies provide relevant observations and tests that allow us to explore the question of whether object mass nouns exist in Japanese. If we can indeed isolate among Japanese nouns those that exhibit notional and distributional properties similar to those of object mass nouns in English, this would serve as evidence for the proposal that Japanese might possess at least some properties of languages with a lexical count–mass distinction among nouns. The putative 'object mass' nouns in Japanese would exhibit a misalignment between individuation properties and the notional substance–object distinction, and so it could then plausibly be claimed that Japanese has at least some reflexes of the grammaticized lexical count–mass distinction.

We set out to test for object mass nouns in Japanese by mainly building upon Sudo's (to appear) observations about Japanese determiners. Specifically, we focused on his observation that the determiner *nan-byaku to iu* ('hundreds of') is felicitous with nouns that denote discrete entities, but not those that

Object Mass Nouns as Arbiter 175

denote undifferentiated stuff, and we formulated a set of test sentences, each containing this determiner and a noun from one of three different conceptual classes: discrete individuals (e.g. *onna no hito* 'woman' in (5)); undifferentiated stuff (e.g. *yuki* 'snow' in (6)); and collections of discrete entities (e.g. *chōrikigu* 'kitchenware' in (7)).

(5) toranpu-shi   ga   daitoryō ni   na-tta   ato,   nan-byaku-to-iu
     Trump-president NOM president ACC become-PST after; what-hundred-to-say
     onna.no.hito ga   washinton de   neriarui-ta
     woman   NOM Washington LOC march-PST
     'After Trump became president, hundreds of women marched in Washington DC.'

(6) # nan-byaku-to-iu   yuki   wa   mō   toke-te   shima-tta
     what-hundred-to-say   snow   NOM   already   melt-TE   finish-PST
     '#Hundreds of snow melted already.'

(7) # Atarashī ryōri   no   gakkō   wa   nan-byaku-to-iu   chōrikigu   o   ka-tta.
     new   cooking GEN   school TOP   what-hundred-to-say   kitchenware ACC   buy-PST
     Dakara   subete   no   seito   ga   benkyōsuru   tame   no   potto to   furaipan
     therefore all   GEN   student NOM study   for   GEN   pot   and   pan
     o   mo-tta.
     ACC   hold-PST
     #'The new culinary school bought hundreds of kitchenware, so every student had pots and pans to work with.'

In languages with a grammaticized lexical count–mass distinction, nouns that refer to undifferentiated stuff (e.g. *mud*) are generally encoded as mass, while nouns that refer to clearly discrete individuals, especially those that are animate (e.g. *woman*), can be encoded as count. Based on such observations, we can immediately make several predictions about what we should expect to find when using our test sentences in an acceptability judgment task. First, sentences containing nouns that refer to discrete individuals composed with *nan-byaku to iu* ('hundreds of') should be judged felicitous, because this determiner selects for countable nouns in Japanese, i.e., nouns that denote discrete individuals, and such nouns are often encoded as count in languages with a grammaticized lexical count–mass distinction.

Second, sentences containing nouns that refer to undifferentiated stuff composed with *nan-byaku to iu* ('hundreds of') should be judged to be infelicitous, because this determiner selects for *countable nouns* (in the sense of Sudo to appear), and nouns that refer to undifferentiated stuff are typically mass in languages with a grammaticized lexical count–mass distinction.

What is less clear is how sentences containing nouns that describe collections of discrete entities composed with *nan-byaku to iu* ('hundreds of') will be judged. Sutton and Filip (2016b) observe that this notional class of nouns is the site of variation in the encoding of nouns as either mass or count, both within and across languages. If sentences containing these nouns are judged to be felicitous, then we have some evidence that these nouns are count. On the other hand, if sentences containing these nouns are judged infelicitous, then we have some evidence that these nouns are mass (i.e. not countable), on the assumption that the infelicity is due to ungrammaticality that results when a determiner that selects for *countable nouns* is composed with such nouns. Any noun that refers to collections of discrete entities and is shown not to be countable is a candidate for being an object mass noun if it can be shown to also encode individuation, for example, in a quantity comparison task like that of Inagaki and Barner (2009).

In addition to these test sentences, we constructed an equal number of filler sentences. Our filler sentences consisted of adjective–noun combinations, a subset of which were infelicitous. The set of survey items had an approximately equal number of felicitous and infelicitous filler constructions and target constructions, as far as such judgments could be predicted based on the chosen data. We tested the felicity of these constructions in an online survey in which participants were asked to judge the naturalness of sentences on a five point Likert scale from 1, *zenzen yokunai* ('not at all good'), to 5, *totemo yoi* ('very good'). Each sentence was judged by fifty native Japanese speakers via the crowd-sourcing platform www.crowdworks.jp.

3.1. Results

As predicted by previous work on Japanese (Sudo to appear), the results of our acceptability judgment task show that sentences with nouns that refer to discrete individuals (e.g. *onna no hito* 'woman') composed with the determiner *nan-byaku to iu* ('hundreds of') are felicitous, while sentences with nouns that refer to undifferentiated stuff (e.g. *yuki* 'snow') composed with the same determiner are infelicitous (see Figure 7.2). More specifically, sentences with nouns referring to discrete individuals have a high average acceptability ($\bar{x} = 4.20$), while sentences with nouns referring to unindividuated stuff have a low average acceptability ($\bar{x} = 2.76$). As a single class, the sentences containing nouns that refer to collections of discrete entities (e.g. *chōrikigu* 'kitchenware') did not pattern as high as those with nouns referring to discrete individuals nor as low as sentences containing nouns that refer to undifferentiated stuff ($\bar{x} = 3.77$).

These results were analyzed using the lme4 package in R (R Core Team 2019) and a generalized linear mixed effects model. The fixed effect was notional class and the random effects were noun and participant. This analysis shows that the judgments of sentences containing nouns that refer to undifferentiated stuff were significantly lower than the judgments of sentences containing nouns that refer to discrete individuals ($p < 0.001$), as were judgments of sentences containing nouns that refer to collections of discrete entities

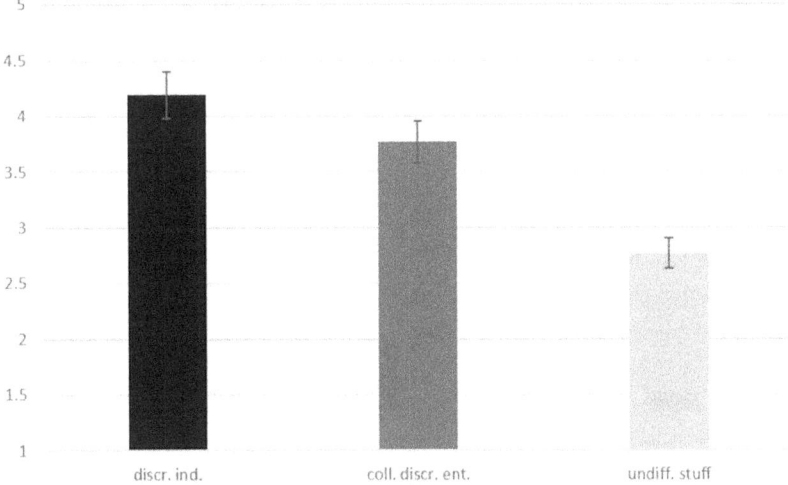

Fig. 7.2: Average judgment by conceptual class

(p < 0.01). Interpreting these results relative to composition with the determiner *nan-byaku to iu* ('hundreds of'), we might say that nouns that refer to undifferentiated stuff are infelicitous with this determiner, as is claimed by Sudo (to appear). Furthermore, the class of nouns that refer to collections of discrete entities does not pattern similarly to nouns that refer to discrete individuals. This result is not predicted by analyses that assume that all nouns that can compose with shape-based classifiers are uniform in their encoding. Instead, what seems to be the case is that the class of nouns that refer to collections of discrete entities shows count–mass variation in Japanese.

To tease apart differences in behavior among nouns that refer to collections of discrete entities, we conducted a post hoc analysis based on how closely the judgments of individual sentences containing these nouns resembled the judgments of sentences containing nouns referring to discrete individuals, and how closely these judgments resembled the judgments of sentences containing nouns referring to undifferentiated stuff. In addition to using the generalized linear mixed effects model to analyze the results of this post hoc analysis, these results were also analyzed with respect to effect size, namely the degree to which a phenomenon exists, which is determined by dividing the difference between two average judgments by the standard deviation of all judgments (Cohen 1988). In acceptability judgment tasks, the measure of grammaticality is the size of the effect (Mahowald et al. 2016). Using the high felicity of sentences containing nouns that refer to discrete entities as our baseline, a trivial effect is an effect size less than 0.2, a small effect is an effect size

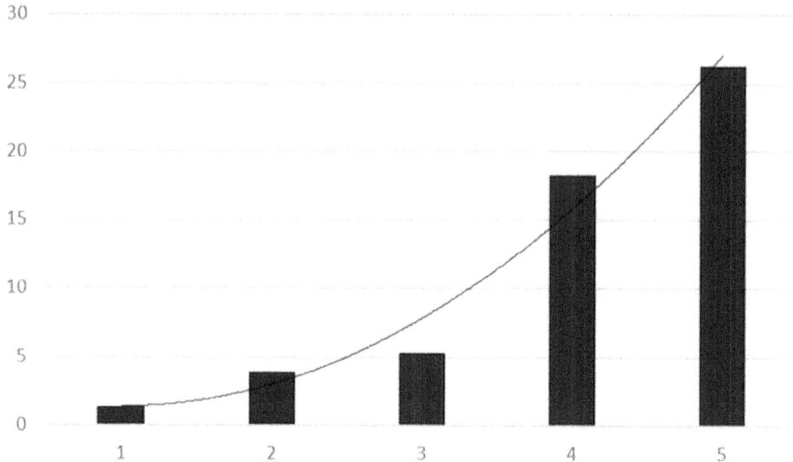

Fig. 7.3: Average judgments: nouns referring to discrete individuals

between 0.2 and 0.5, a medium effect is between 0.5 and 0.8, and a large effect size is anything greater than 0.8.

The graph in Figure 7.3 contains the average number of judgments the sentences containing a noun referring to discrete entities had at each level of the Likert scale. The judgments of sentences containing nouns that refer to discrete individuals had a clear tendency towards the high (felicitous) end of the Likert scale. In this post hoc analysis, we interpret the average judgment of these sentences and this distribution pattern as our baseline of felicity.

The judgments of sentences with nouns that refer to undifferentiated stuff patterned towards the center and only slightly towards the low (infelicitous) end of the Likert scale (Figure 7.4). Notably, this pattern is not the inverse of the felicity pattern seen in judgments of sentences containing nouns that refer to discrete individuals. Despite this distribution of judgments, the difference between this group of sentences and the set of sentences that contain nouns that refer to discrete individuals is statistically significant ($p < 0.001$, effect size > 0.8). We interpret this measure of difference in statistical tests as the criteria for categorization as infelicitous.

The sentences that contain nouns referring to collections of discrete entities were separated in three groups depending on whether the distribution of judgments of these sentences most closely resembled those of sentences containing nouns referring to discrete individuals, those containing nouns referring to undifferentiated stuff, or neither. While having three categories of felicity does not reflect the binary way in which morphosyntactic reflexes of the count–mass distinction are typically discussed, such gradients are common

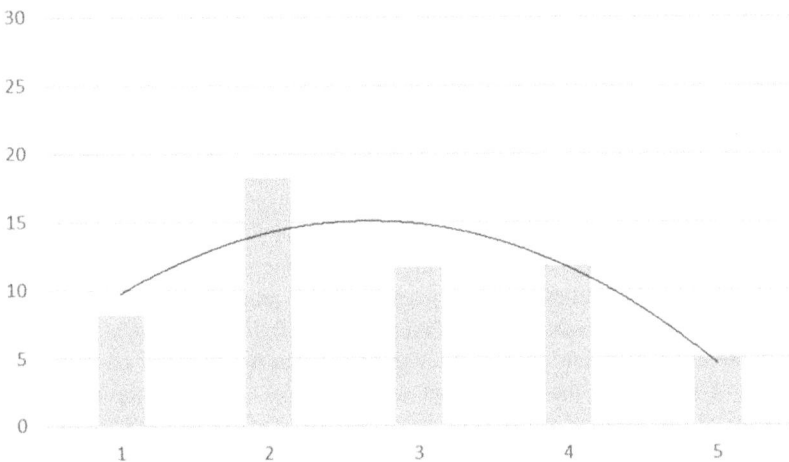

Fig. 7.4: Average judgments: nouns referring to undifferentiated stuff

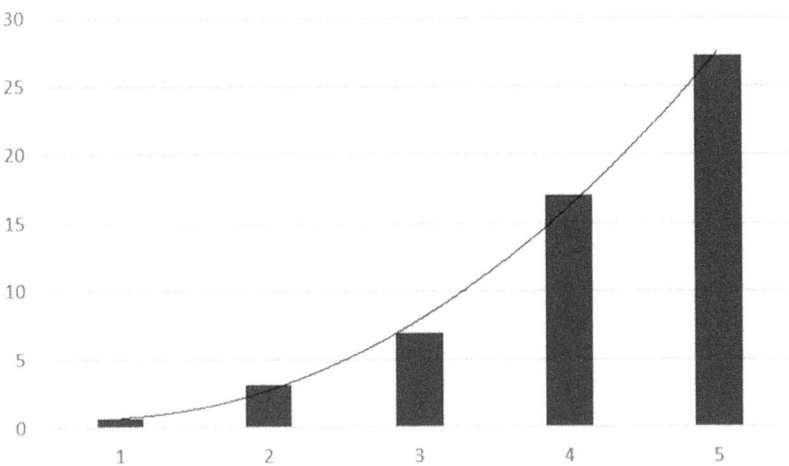

Fig. 7.5: Average judgments: nouns referring to collections of discrete entities, Group 1

in acceptability judgment tasks, (e.g. Bresnan 2007; Bresnan and Ford 2010; Featherston 2005; Keller 2000; Newmeyer 2007; Sorace and Keller 2005; Sprouse 2007), and this more accurately reflects the judgments of the individual sentences in this study.

As depicted in Figure 7.5, one set of sentences containing nouns that refer to collections of discrete entities (Group 1) was judged in a way that is nearly identical to the way that sentences containing nouns that refer to discrete individuals were judged. Furthermore, the average judgment of sentences in this class strongly resembles the average judgment of sentences containing nouns that refer to discrete individuals (n = 7, x̄ = 4.22, p = 0.567, effect size < 0.2). On the assumption that sentences containing nouns that refer to discrete entities are felicitous, the statistical analysis of the judgments of sentences in Group 1, which contain nouns that refer to collections of discrete entities, are such that these sentences are also felicitous.

The judgments of one set of sentences containing nouns referring to collections of discrete entities (Group 3) resemble the judgment of sentences containing nouns that refer to undifferentiated stuff in three ways. First, the judgments of both sets of sentences pattern towards the center of the Likert scale. Additionally, the two sets of sentences meet the same thresholds for statistical significance (p < 0.001) and effect size (>0.8). Despite the fact that the average acceptability judgment of sentences containing collective artifact referring nouns in Group 3 (x̄ = 3.21) is higher than both the middle point of the Likert scale and the average judgment of sentences containing nouns that refer to undifferentiated stuff (x̄ = 2.76), on the assumption that a p-value less than 0.001 and an effect size greater than 0.8 are indicators of infelicity, then the sentences in Group 3 are infelicitous.

Another set of nouns (Group 2) patterned in between Groups 1 and 3, not being judged as straightforwardly felicitous as sentences containing nouns that refer to discrete individuals nor as infelicitous as sentences containing nouns that refer to undifferentiated stuff (n = 7, x̄ = 3.71, p < 0.05, effect size 0.5–0.8). The distribution of judgments across the Likert scale is generally towards the high (felicitous) end of the scale, though not with the same clear pattern as the distribution of judgments of sentences containing nouns that refer to discrete individuals. In other words, the third group of sentences only weakly patterns like those containing nouns that refer to discrete individuals.

The average judgments of each class of nouns in this post-hoc analysis are depicted in Figure 7.8, along with the average judgments of sentences containing nouns that refer to discrete individuals and those referring to undifferentiated stuff. This graph shows three distinct judgment patterns with respect to sentences containing the determiner *nan-byaku to iu* ('hundreds of') and nouns that refer to collections of discrete entities. The nouns in each group are listed in in Table 7.1, where the category *Felicitous* contains the nouns that occurred in sentences that were judged like those containing nouns that refer to discrete entities, *Weakly Felicitous* contains the nouns that occurred in sentences that were judged differently from those containing nouns that refer to discrete entities, albeit weakly so given their p-value and effect size, and *Infelicitous* contains the nouns that occurred in sentences that were judged differently

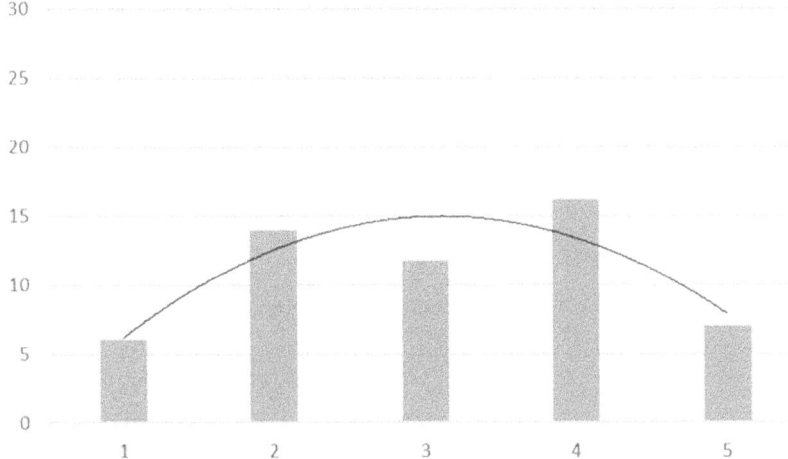

Fig. 7.6: Average judgments: nouns referring to collections of discrete entities, Group 3

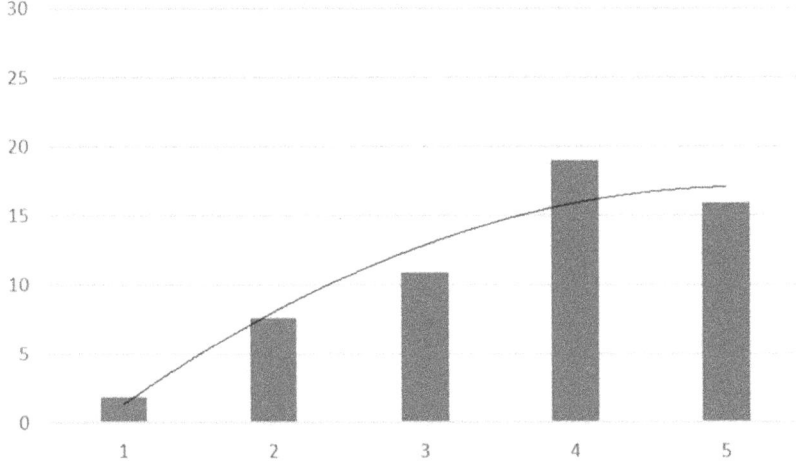

Fig. 7.7: Average judgments: nouns referring to collections of discrete entities, Group 2

Table 7.1. *Felicity with* nan-byaku to iu *('hundreds of')*

Felicitous	Weakly Felicitous	Infelicitous
haikibutsu ('waste')	*shōhin* ('goods/wares')	*hakimono* ('footwear')
kizai ('equipment')	*kagu* ('furniture')	*shinamono* ('wares/articles')
yōfuku ('western clothes')	*shokki* ('dishware')	*kattamono* ('shopped goods')
chōri-ki ('kitchenware')	*sōbi* ('equipment')	*chōri-kigu* ('kitchenware')
yūbin ('mail')	*dōgu* ('tools')	
daidokoro yōhin ('kitchenware')	*yūbinbutsu* ('mail')	
kutsu ('shoes')	*gomi* ('garbage')	

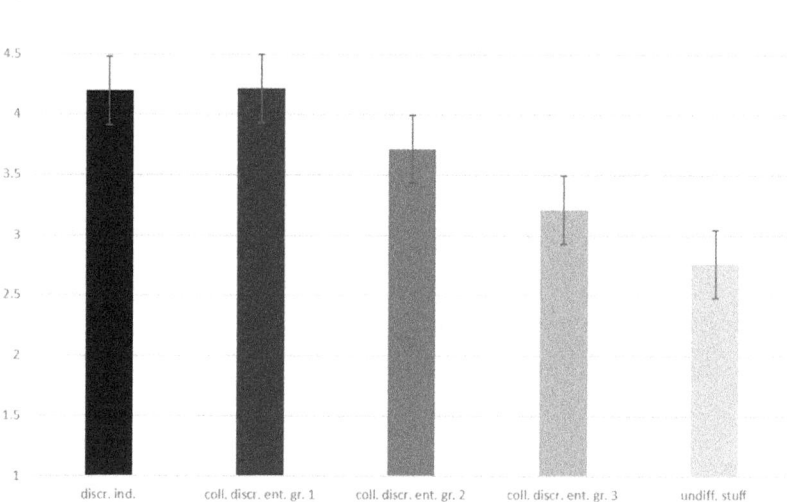

Fig. 7.8: Average judgment: post-hoc classes

from those containing nouns that refer to discrete entities with the same p-value and effect size as those sentences containing nouns that refer to undifferentiated stuff.

3.2. Discussion

Assuming that the results of the study are due solely to the felicity of the composition of the different nouns with the determiner *nan-byaku to iu* ('hundreds of'), these results confirm several predictions and suggest that the lexical encoding of Japanese nouns might not be as uniform with respect to countability as is commonly assumed for classifier languages. First, as proposed by Sudo (to appear), *nan-byaku to iu* ('hundreds of') is felicitous with countable nouns and infelicitous with non-countable nouns. Second, as predicted by Sutton and Filip (2016a), the conceptual class of nouns that refer to discrete *singular* individuals is stably count, the conceptual class of nouns that refer to undifferentiated stuff are stably mass, and the conceptual class of nouns that refer to collections of discrete entities can be encoded as either mass or count, within a particular language and across different languages. These results also suggest that, despite the fact that all nouns require classifiers in order to be counted, they do not behave uniformly with respect to all syntactic environments indicative of the count–mass distinction. Instead, these results suggest that at least four Japanese nouns (22% of those we tested in the relevant class) – *hakimono* ('footwear'), *shinamono* ('wares/articles'), *kattamono* ('shopped goods'), and *chōri-kigu* ('kitchenware') – have the characteristic property of object mass nouns, insofar as they syntactically pattern with non-countable ('mass') nouns.

Rather than relying on whether or not the average judgment of sentences containing one of these four nouns composed with the determiner *nan-byaku to iu* ('hundreds of') is the same as the average judgment of the sentences containing nouns that refer to undifferentiated stuff composed with *nan-byaku to iu* ('hundreds of') in order to determine infelicity, we assess infelicity based on statistically determined differences of the sets of sentences from those that contain nouns that refer to discrete individuals composed with *nan-byaku to iu* ('hundreds of'). Because both the set of sentences containing nouns that refer to undifferentiated stuff and the group of sentences containing *hakimono* ('footwear'), *shinamono* ('wares/articles'), *kattamono* ('shopped goods'), and *chōri-kigu* ('kitchenware') are judged in a way that displays a statistically significant difference ($p < 0.001$, effect size > 0.8) from the group of sentences containing nouns that refer to discrete individuals composed with *nan-byaku to iu* ('hundreds of'), we consider both the set of sentences containing nouns that refer to undifferentiated stuff and the group of sentences containing *hakimono* ('footwear'), *shinamono* ('wares/articles'), *kattamono* ('shopped goods'), and *chōri-kigu* ('kitchenware') to be equally infelicitous in that they are in the same statistically based category when compared to sentences containing nouns that refer to discrete individuals (count nouns).

To confirm that the nouns that refer to collections of discrete entities are individuated in the sense of Barner and Snedeker (2005), and therefore that these nouns have have a hallmark property of object mass nouns, we set up a quantity comparison task for three consultants. Each consultant was given a context in which two people possessed items of the same kind, but in amounts that differed with respect to volume and cardinality. One person's possessions were larger in terms of volume, while the other person's possessions were higher in cardinality.

(8) Mayo no   kago ni   wa ookii mi-ttsu no men   no   fukuro to fatatsu no
    Mayo GEN basket LOC TOP big   3-CL   GEN noodle   GEN bag   and 2-CL GEN
    suika   ga   hai-tte   iru. Ai no   kago ni   wa chiisai yo-ttsu no   men
    watermelon NOM contain-TE IRU Ai GEN basket LOC TOP small   4-CL   GEN noodle
    no   fukuro to mi-ttsu no   satsuma   mikan   ga   hai-tte   iru.
    GEN bag   and 3-CL   GEN satsuma   mandarin NOM contain-TE IRU
    'Mayo's basket has three large packs of noodles and two watermelons in it. Ai's basket has four small packs of noodles and three satsumas in it.'

(9) Dochira no   hito no   kago ga   yori ōku no   kattamono o   motte
    Who   GEN person GEN basket NOM more much GEN goods   DIR carry
    irudeshou?
    stay
    'Whose basket has more goods?'

Our consultants were asked to judge who had more of the item in question. For each of the nouns that refer to collections of discrete entities in our study, the person whose possessions were larger in cardinality was judged to have the larger amount. Following Barner and Snedeker (2005) and Inagaki and Barner (2009), we interpret the results of these cardinality judgment tasks as indicating that the nouns in question denote individuated entities that can be compared according to cardinality. Having this property, combined with the results of our study, suggests that we have at least some evidence for thinking that there are at least some nouns in Japanese that have both of the hallmark properties of object mass nouns.

However, the nature of the differences between average acceptability judgments militates against any strong conclusions regarding whether or not Japanese has a class of object mass nouns. For example, the results were presented with the assumption that the judgments of sentences containing nouns that refer to discrete individuals, like *isu* ('chair'), constituted the baseline for acceptability, and that infelicity is determined by being deviant from this baseline by a statistically significant amount ($p < 0.001$, effect size > 0.8). However, the average judgment of the least acceptable sentences containing nouns that refer to collections of discrete entities like *hakimono* ('footwear') was not as low as the average judgment of the sentences containing nouns that refer to undifferentiated stuff like *yuki* ('snow'). If the average judgment of sentences containing nouns referring to undifferentiated stuff was assumed to be the baseline for infelicity, then the least felicitous sentences containing nouns referring to collections of discrete entities might be classified as *weakly infelicitous* on account of the fact that they might not statistically pattern identically to the sentences containing nouns that refer to undifferentiated stuff.

In addition to the differences between the two least felicitous groups of sentences, the fact that judgments of sentences that contain nouns that refer to collections of discrete individuals were graded suggests that more than just the felicity of nouns and the determiner that selects for countable nouns was at issue in our acceptability judgment task. Differences in the complexity of sentences – for example length, lexical items, topic, syntax, etc. – might have contributed to some sentences being rated higher or lower than others. To investigate the cause of graded judgments and to possibly get a clearer picture of the countability of these nouns, we reviewed the test items with a different consultant than the one who provided the test sentences. This consultant noted several ways in which sentences might be judged to be at least partly unacceptable aside from infelicity of the determiner+noun composition. For example, some sentences were particularly long and could have included commas in order to make them easier to parse. The fact that these sentences were less straightforward to parse could have resulted in lower acceptability judgments. Additionally, certain sentences contained vocabulary of different registers, one which is more formal and one which is more casual, and this mismatch of register might have caused some participants in the study to give lower judgments. Low judgments could also be accounted for, in some cases, due to world knowledge conflicting with the information in the sentence. For example, one sentence described a piano store that sold hundreds of pianos on a single day, which participants might have thought to be very unlikely and therefore less acceptable. This review of test items showed that, across all conceptual classes of nouns, sentences could have been judged to have low acceptability for reasons other than the composition of the target noun and the determiner *nan-byaku to iu* ('hundreds of').

Given the number of reasons why each of the test sentences might have gotten a low judgment, it is less clear whether the results are indicative of genuine object mass nouns or not. When asked to help clarify this picture by reflecting on the felicity of the individual determiner+noun compositions, the consultant reported that both *shinamono* ('wares/articles') and *kattamono* ('shopped goods') seemed particularly strange composed with *nan-byaku to iu*, though the felicity of *hakimono* ('footwear') and *chōri-kigu* ('kitchenware') with this determiner is less clear. We take these results to suggest that, given the current state of research, *shinamono* ('wares/articles') and *kattamono* ('shopped goods') seem to be the most promising candidates for being considered object mass nouns in Japanese. Further investigation is necessary to see if the results for *hakimono* ('footwear') and *chōri-kigu* ('kitchenware') and other nouns that refer to collections of discrete entities can be upheld in this and other syntactic environments that are diagnostic of the count–mass distinction in Japanese. What we can conclude from this study is that there is a set of nouns that refer to collections of discrete entities that straightforwardly pattern with countable nouns (in the sense of Sudo (to appear)) and others that seem like they might not when it comes to being felicitously combined with *nan-byaku to iu* ('hundreds of'). In other words, more investigation is required, both in terms of controlling for potential confounds and testing more grammatical environments.

4. Analysis

In this section, we outline what an analysis of the count–mass distinction in classifier languages would look like on the assumptions that (a) bare nouns are kind-denoting, and (b) the count–mass distinction in classifier languages is not perfectly aligned with the substance–object distinction. Assumption (b) is, however, something that we concede is only weakly supported by the study we have reported. As for assumption (a), an analysis of classifier languages that assumes that nouns are kind-denoting is attractive because, from this assumption, it arguably follows that classifier languages allow bare arguments, require the use of classifiers in counting constructions, and do not have obligatory number marking (Chierchia 2015; see Section 2.1 above). However, given that, standardly, formal theories do not distinguish between kinds for count predicates and kinds for mass predicates even if some do implicitly assume a distinction between kinds of objects and kinds of substances (in order to account for the distribution of shape-based classifiers, for instance), there is a prima facie tension between assumptions (a) and (b).

The prima facie tension between (a) and (b) can be alleviated, however, by adding to a theory a distinction between kinds that are associated with count predicates and mass kinds that are associated with predicates that cannot be grammatically counted. That is to say that we must draw a distinction between kinds that form count predicates under something along the lines of Chierchia's (2010, 2015) 'up' $^\cup$ operator, and kinds that form mass predicates under something along the lines of Chierchia's (2010, 2015) 'down' $^\cap$ operator. This sort of analysis is what we outline below, namely one in which: nouns in Japanese are kind-denoting and so cannot felicitously enter into counting constructions without an intervening classifier; but despite being kind-denoting, nouns come out of the lexicon in some sense 'count' or 'mass', thus accounting for the possibility of being infelicitous with determiners like *nan-byaku to iu* ('hundreds of'). The former point is pretty common in the literature (see Chierchia 1998a, 1998b, 2010, 2015; Krifka 1995; X.-P. Li 2011; Nemoto 2005; Rothstein 2017; and others). The latter point is not exactly novel either insofar as a suggestion for a distinction between count and mass kinds is hinted at in the presented version of Chierchia's Chapter 2 in this volume. What is novel is a theory that formally implements both of these points.

On the (albeit tentative) assumption of (b), above, other accounts of counting constructions in classifier languages do not quite have the right combination of features to capture the kind of grammatical patterns that our studies have suggested may be required, namely that Japanese nouns seem to have a grammaticized lexicalized count–mass distinction, and, of the mass nouns in Japanese, at least some appear to be object mass. A straightforward application of Chierchia's (2010, 2015) theory, for example, is not possible, given that it is custom designed to exclude the possibility of object mass nouns from classifier languages (on this analysis, only number marking languages encode mass nouns as singleton properties, and only this feature licenses a copycat effect in which stably atomic predicates can come to have mass denotations).

On the other hand, analyses in which nouns in classifier languages come out of the lexicon as predicates (Bale and Coon 2014; Erbach et al. 2017; Muromatsu 2003; Sudo 2016)[2] lose the above-stated properties of being able to simply derive, for example, bare arguments, and lack of obligatory number marking in classifier languages (see Chierchia, this volume, Chapter 2).

An analysis along the lines of Krifka (1995) is the closest to what we need. It assumes that nouns in classifier languages denote *concepts* (such that the set of concepts is a superset of the set of kinds), and that counting classifiers, semantically, play the dual role of mapping numerals to numerical modifiers, and shifting concepts 'up' to the set of object units that are realizations of them. Our strategy will be to follow this dual-purpose approach for classifiers in Japanese. However, our approach will also allow for the possibility that, despite the fact that bare nouns in Japanese are interpreted as kinds, some of those that denote physical objects are nonetheless (in a sense to be elaborated upon) mass nouns.

Here we use the same analysis as Sutton and Filip (this volume, Chapter 12), which is based on compositional DRT (Muskens 1996) enriched with mereology along the lines proposed for domain-level plurality by Brasoveanu (2008). Importantly, we allow for discourse referents for properties (this is comparable to the discourse referents for sets of entities employed by Kamp and Reyle (1993) in their analysis of plurals). Specifically, we propose that (count) nouns make available a *counting base* property (see also Khrizman et al. 2015; Landman 2016; Sutton and Filip 2016a; amongst others) that specifies, for any given context, the set of entities that count as one for the relevant noun. (See, Sutton and Filip, this volume, Chapter 12 for the basis for this enrichment to compositional DRT.)

---

[2] Bale and Coon (2014) argue for this analysis for Chol (Mayan) in which classifiers are obligatory with some numericals and ungrammatical with others. It is not presupposed that this analysis applies to languages such as Japanese, Mandarin, etc.

Following Filip and Sutton (2017), Rothstein (2010), and Sutton and Filip (2016a), we assume that count nouns are interpreted relative to a context i. For us, contexts license individuation schemas S_i that are applied to the extensions and counting bases of singular count nouns. Application of an individuation schema yields a quantized (QUA; Krifka 1989) predicate (for a brief discussion of why we opt for 'quantized relative to a context' as opposed to 'disjoint relative to a context', see Sutton and Filip, this volume, Chapter 12):

(10) $QUA(P) \leftrightarrow \forall x, y[P(x) \wedge P(y) \rightarrow \neg x \sqsubset y]$

For a context i and an individuation schema licensed by that context S_i, $S_i(P)$ is a maximally quantized subset of P ($S_i(P) \subseteq_{max.QUA} P$):

(11) $Q \subseteq_{max.QUA} P \leftrightarrow Q \subseteq P \wedge QUA(Q) \wedge \forall R[R \supseteq Q \wedge R \subseteq P \wedge QUA(R) \rightarrow R = Q]$

Mass nouns, we assume, are not sensitive to the particular context of utterance when it comes to determining what counts as one. We model this by saturating the lexical entries of mass nouns with the null individuation schema (S_0), which, semantically, denotes the identity function.

Similarly to Krifka's (1995) OU function, we assume that object denoting nouns include in their lexical semantics a function O such that, $\forall P[O(P) \subseteq P]$ and $O(P)$ is the set of entities that could count as one P on perceptual or functional grounds. Critically, for some predicates, $O(P)$ doesn't denote a set that is a suitable input to the grammatical counting operation, since for some P, $\neg QUA(O(P))$. In such cases, to get a count concept, we would need the application of an individuation schema, i.e., $S_i(O)(P)$.

Finally, we assume the standard, 'down' operator (Chierchia 2010; 2015; amongst others) as it applies at the DRS condition level, but also at the DRS level, here defined only for single condition DRSs. In (13), k is a discourse referent for a kind:

(12) $\cap(P) = \lambda w.\iota P(w)$

(13) $\cap'(\lambda w.\lambda v.[\ |P(w)(v)|]) = \lambda w.[k|k = \cap(P)(w)]$

For the inverse function, 'up', we slightly adapt Chierchia's definition in a way to be made clear below that reflects the fact that we do not make an atomicity assumption. (In brief, we make use of the fact that kinds specify counting bases, the sets of entities that count as one, and 'up' maps kinds to those entities that are part of the upward closure of the counting base under mereological sum.)

Incorporating these ingredients into Compositional DRT, we can distinguish between lexical entries for (object denoting) count nouns such as *kutsu*, 'shoe(s)' (14), and object denoting mass nouns such as *chōri-kigu*, 'kitchenware' (15). Both denote kinds, and both specify a counting base (and make available a discourse referent for the counting base, $cbase_p$). However, the context of

Object Mass Nouns as Arbiter 189

utterance plays a role in determining the counting base of count kinds, but not mass kinds (since mass kinds are saturated with the null individuation schema).

(14) $\llbracket \text{kutsu} \rrbracket^i = \lambda w$

$cbase_s \;\; k_s$
$k_s = {}^\cap({}^*\boldsymbol{S}_i(\boldsymbol{O})(\text{shoe}))(w)$
$cbase_s = \lambda v' \;\; \boxed{{}^*\boldsymbol{S}_i(\boldsymbol{O})(\text{shoe})(w)(v')}$

$\llbracket \text{chōri-kigu} \rrbracket^i$ has two key differences from $\llbracket \text{kutsu} \rrbracket^i$: (i) the counting base (cbase) for $\llbracket \text{chōri-kigu} \rrbracket^i$ is saturated with the null individuation schema, and so (ii) unlike $\llbracket \text{kutsu} \rrbracket^i$, the counting base for $\llbracket \text{chōri-kigu} \rrbracket$ does not specify a quantized set.

(15) $\llbracket \text{chōri-kigu} \rrbracket^i = \llbracket \text{chōri-kigu} \rrbracket = \lambda w$

$cbase_k \;\; k_k$
$k_k = {}^\cap({}^*\boldsymbol{S}_0(\boldsymbol{O})(\text{kitchenware}))(w)$
$cbase_k = \lambda v' \;\; \boxed{{}^*\boldsymbol{S}_0(\boldsymbol{O})(\text{kitchenware})(w)(v')}$

However, we also want to allow for mass noun concepts to be shifted into countable ones (as part of the semantics of counting classifiers, for example). This can be done by applying a maximally quantizing individuation schema to a mass noun concept. We define this via the operation **S** in (16), the output of which is a count concept, namely, when applied to $\llbracket \text{chōri-kigu} \rrbracket)^i$, it returns a kind-denoting term for kitchenware that specifies a quantized set of items of kitchenware, relative to the context.[3]

(16) $\mathbf{S}(\llbracket \text{chōri-kigu} \rrbracket)^i = \lambda w$

$cbase_k \;\; k_k$
$k_k = {}^\cap({}^*\boldsymbol{S}_i(\boldsymbol{O})(\text{kitchenware}))(w)$
$cbase_k = \lambda v' \;\; \boxed{\boldsymbol{S}_i(\boldsymbol{O})(\text{kitchenware})(w)(v')}$

We can now define the 'up' $^\cup$ operation as it applies to DRSs. Importantly, under our analysis, kinds have a standard extension, but *also* specify a counting base set. Hence $^\cup$ applied to a DRS for a kind ($^\cup(\mathbf{k})$) returns a property that denotes all entities and sums of entities in the counting base of the kind ($cbase_\mathbf{k}$).

(17) $^\cup(\mathbf{k}) = \begin{cases} \lambda w.\lambda v. \begin{array}{|c|} \hline cbase_{k'} \\ \hline {}^*cbase_k(w)(v) \\ cbase_{k'} = cbase_\mathbf{k} \\ \hline \end{array} & \text{if } k(w) \text{ is defined} \\ \varnothing, & \text{otherwise} \end{cases}$

---

[3] We provide a simplified version of the operation here. Part of the operation, for example, would more fully be specified as ${}^\cap \boldsymbol{S}_i {}^\cup {}^\cap ({}^*\boldsymbol{S}_0(\boldsymbol{O})(\text{kitchenware}))(w)$, which reduces to the main condition in (16), since for all P, $\boldsymbol{S}_i(\boldsymbol{S}_0(P) \leftrightarrow \boldsymbol{S}_i(P)$.

For example, applied to ⟦kutsu⟧^{i}, we get the following, properties of shoes and sums thereof:

(18) $^∪$⟦kutsu⟧$^i = \lambda w.\lambda v.$

$cbase_s$
*$S_i(\mathcal{O})$(shoe)$(w)(v)$
$cbase_s = \lambda v'$ | $S_i(\mathcal{O})$(shoe)$(w)(v')$

Following Krifka's (1995) proposal for numerical expressions in Mandarin, we assume that numerical expressions in Japanese denote numerals of type n. Sortal classifiers in Japanese, we propose, encode the following three roles: (i) they are functions from numerals and shift numerals (of type n) into numerical modifiers; (ii) they shift kind-denoting terms into predicates using the $^∪$ operator (presupposing that the predicate is object denoting); (iii) they apply **S** to the interpretation of the argument noun, thus shifting any object denoting mass predicate into a count predicate. These three things taken together allow for any object denoting noun in Japanese to be felicitously counted. Put simply, like in the account of Chierchia (2010), classifiers turn kinds into predicates (the right type of argument for numerical modifiers); however, like the analyses of Krifka (1995) and Bale and Coon (2014), sortal classifiers also shift numerals into numerical modifiers. Thirdly, unlike any other account, instead of merely shifting kinds into predicates, they shift object denoting count and mass kinds into object denoting count predicates. The derivation for *chōri-kigu itsu-tsu* ('five pieces of kitchenware') is given in (19)–(21).

(19)   ⟦itsu⟧ = 5

(20)   ⟦tsu⟧$^i = \lambda n.\lambda k.\lambda v.$ | $\mu_\#(v, cbase_k) = 5$
 $\dfrac{u}{cbase_k(u)}$ ⇒ $inanimate(u)$ | ; $^∪S(k)(w)(x)$

(21)   ⟦chōri-kigu itsu-tsu⟧$^i = \lambda w.\lambda v.$

$cbase_k$
*$S_i(\mathcal{O})$(kitchenware)$(w)(v)$
$cbase_k = \lambda v'$ | $S_i(\mathcal{O})$(kitchenware)$(w)(v')$
$\mu_\#(v, cbase_k) = 5$
$\dfrac{u}{cbase_k(u)}$ ⇒ $inanimate(u)$

If it is indeed the case that *nan-byaku to iu* ('hundreds of') selects for count kinds, then this can be modeled as a sensitivity to whether or not the counting base for the relevant noun is quantized. On the assumption that *nan-byaku to iu* ('hundreds of') means *approximately some multiples of hundreds of* and where 100n is a free variable that ranges over multiples of 100, then the semantics for *nan-byaku to iu* ('hundreds of') is that of an approximate number quantifier:

(22a) $[\![\text{nan-byaku-to-iu}]\!]^i = \lambda k.\lambda w.\lambda v.\begin{array}{|c|} \hline \mu_{\#}(v, cbase_k(w)) \approx 100n \\ QUA(cbase_k(w)) \\ \hline \end{array}; \cup(k)$

(22b) $[\![\text{nan-byaku-to-iu isu}]\!]^i = \lambda w.\lambda v.\begin{array}{|c|} \hline cbase_c \\ \hline {}^*S_i(\mathcal{O})(chair)(w)(v) \\ cbase_c = \lambda v' \boxed{S_i(\mathcal{O})(chair)(w)(v')} \\ \mu_{\#}(v, cbase_c(w)) \approx 100n \\ QUA(cbase_c(w)) \\ \hline \end{array}$

Nan-byaku to iu isu ('hundreds of chairs') denotes the set of sums of chairs that have a cardinality of around 100, 200, 300, etc. such that this cardinality is defined in terms of the counting base for individual chairs with the precondition that the counting base set is quantized. If nouns such as *chōri-kigu* ('kitchenware') denote mass kinds, then, since, by hypothesis, $[\![\text{chōri-kigu}]\!]^i$ would specify a non-quantized counting base, it would be infelicitous to compose *chōri-kigu* ('kitchenware') with *nan-byaku to iu* ('hundreds of').

5. Conclusions

Our findings for Japanese raise the possibility that we may not be getting a complete picture from the standard view of classifier languages advocated by Chierchia (2010, 2015; this volume, Chapter 2) and Muromatsu (2003), among others, upon which the count–mass distinction in *all* classifier languages is solely reflected in the syntax and semantics of their classifier systems. We suggest that there is some evidence for the nascent idea that Japanese has a grammaticized lexical count–mass distinction, which is systematically reflected in the syntax and semantics of at least some Japanese nouns. This would mean that Japanese, and perhaps other classifier languages, might be typologically closer than has been previously assumed to number marking languages like English, which have a bona fide grammaticized lexical count–mass distinction. Such a conclusion, if right, would require some alterations to theories of classifier languages in which bare nouns refer to kinds, namely one which can distinguish between kinds that are mapped to count predicates and kinds which are mapped to mass predicates. We outlined what such an analysis might look like. In sum, while our empirical and theoretical results may not be entirely uncontroversial, they at least raise important questions about the nominal systems in classifier languages. Furthermore, we hope to have paved the way for future studies to develop a battery of tests with a wide range of quantifiers to tap into the putative count–mass status of nouns in Japanese, and other classifier languages.

8 Bare Nouns and the Count–Mass Distinction: A Pilot Study Across Languages

Kayron Beviláqua and Roberta Pires de Oliveira

1. Overview

This paper presents the preliminary results of a study comparing the performance of speakers from four different languages. The object of study is bare nouns in comparative sentences (affirmatives and interrogatives). The experiment compares English (Eng), Rioplatense Spanish (RSpan), Brazilian Portuguese (BrP), and Cape-Verdean (CV) in order to have a better understanding of the Bare Singular in Brazilian Portuguese (BrP), a language that has puzzled some of us.[1] The methodology allows an investigation both into a particular language system and also across different languages.

The choice of languages was motivated by Chierchia's (2010, 2015) research agenda. According to his semantic parameters, there are three types of language: number neutral, number marking, and classifier languages. English is our guide language, and Chierchia considers it to be a number marking language, where number morphology is obligatory in the noun. Given that RSpan does not allow Bare Singulars, and has number morphology obligatory in the noun, it is expected to be a number marking language as well. Pires de Oliveira and Martins (2017) argue that Cape Verdean is a number neutral language, because number is not obligatory in the noun, and Bare Singulars are the default nominal phrase. Does BrP pattern with English or with Cape Verdean? The next section reviews the nominal systems of the four languages in this study and presents the hypotheses to be tested.

The third section presents the methodology of the experiment. It consisted of three tests: (i) an acceptability; (ii) a picture matching; and (iii) a quantity-judgment (as in Barner and Snedeker 2005). Noun phrase is the independent variable with five levels: the Bare Singular (BS), the Singular Flexible

---

We would like to thank the reviewers. Any mistakes are our own responsibility.
[1] In this paper, Bare Singulars are noun phrases without a determiner, without plural morphology, and the noun denotes an object, as in *Eu vi gato*, (*I saw cat*), which is ungrammatical in English. Bare Singulars should be distinguished from mass phrases which are singular but where the noun denotes a substance, as in *Eu tomei água* (*I drank water*), which is grammatical in English.

Noun (FLEXSG), the Bare Plural (PL), the plural Flexible Noun (FLEXPL), and Mass Nouns (MASS). In all languages, the bare phrases are in argument position.

The preliminary results, discussed in the fourth section, show that the methodology is reliable, since it gives the expected results for Eng. It also shows that RSpan patterns with Eng, so it too is a number marking language. Moreover, the results for CV support Pires de Oliveira and Martins' (2017) claim that it is a number neutral language. The BS in BrP has a "mixed" behavior, also supporting the experimental literature on bare nouns in BrP (Beviláqua and Pires de Oliveira 2014, 2017; Lima and Gomes 2016). It shows that in BrP there is no difference between BS and FLEXSG; however, we argue that this result should not be analyzed as a case of ambiguity, as proposed by Rothstein and Pires de Oliveira (2020).

The last section provides a theoretical explanation for the results. We argue that Bare Singulars in BrP behave as predicted by Pelletier (2012): they are both mass and count. In the end, however, a number of issues will remain open. There are also some shortcomings in the experimental paradigm that we will be discussing.

2. Nominal Systems Across Languages

This section introduces the nominal systems of the languages that are experimentally investigated in this research. English functions as a guideline since it is the most studied language.[2]

2.1. English (Eng)

English has plural morphology, definite and indefinite articles, Bare Plurals, and Bare Mass nouns, but Bare Singulars are ungrammatical in argument position. Mass and count nouns are grammatically distinguished (Link 1983; Bunt 1985; Chierchia 1998a, 1998b; Rothstein 2010; Doetjes 2017a, 2017b): mass nouns do not accept plural morphology, nor do they combine with numerals: *muds, *three muds. Count nouns, on the other hand, are pluralized and combine directly with numerals: cars, three cars. If the singular count noun is forced in a "mass syntax", it is either shifted into its substance (Pelletier, 1975) – (1a) – or is partitioned (Chierchia, 2010) – (1b):

(1)   a. #There is cat all over the floor.
       b. #John has more house than Mary.

---

[2] For a more detailed description of English, see the Introduction to this volume as well as the contributions of Chierchia, Rothstein, and Doetjes.

Chierchia argues that for (1b) the only interpretation available, due to coercion, is one where a particular house is partitioned and John has the greatest portion. (1a) is an example of the "ground reading", generated by the "universal grinder" (Pelletier 1975), a mechanism that transforms concrete count nouns into a homogeneous mass. (1a) means that there is cat stuff all over the floor.

In this experiment, Bare Singulars, as exemplified in (1b), are compared to Flexible Nouns, exemplified in (2). Flexible Nouns live a "dual life" (Pelletier and Schubert 1989, among others).

(2)   a. This garden has more **stone** than that one. (mass reading)
       b. This garden has more **stones** than that one. (cardinal reading)

They are treated as lexically ambiguous (Bale and Barner 2009; Chierchia 2010, 2015; Rothstein 2010, 2017): *stone* in the sentence (2a) is mass, and *stones* in (2b) is count. (2b) is true only if the number of individual stones in one particular garden is greater than the number of individual stones in another garden; this is the cardinal reading. In (2a), the comparison is about the volume. It seems that only a few nouns in English are flexible in this way (Rothstein 2017: 132 says "In English flexible pairs are unusual, and mass is not the default case ...").

The prediction is that flexible nouns are grammatical in comparatives. They are mass and compared by volume. They thus contrast with the BS in acceptability: (1b) is considered to be ungrammatical or anomalous, but not (2a). In summary, the BS is the only structure that is not acceptable in comparatives; and, when forced in such a structure, it is partitioned, i.e. massified.

2.2. *Rioplatense Spanish (RSpan)*

Rioplatense Spanish is a Romance language spoken mainly in and around Argentina and Uruguay. As with Peninsular Spanish, it distinguishes mass and count nouns: **aguas*, **three aguas*, but *coches* and *three coches*. Oggiani (2011) shows that both the Bare Plural and the Bare Singular are grammatically restricted in argument position. Bare Singulars are ruled out in external position, but some of them may appear, although not productively, in internal position of some verbs, as exemplified below in (3):

(3)   a. *Tigre   caza   por   la   noche.
          Tiger-SG hunt-3P for the night.
          "Tigers hunt at night."

       b. Juan   tiene   auto.
          Juan   has-3P car-SG.
          "Juan has a car."

Dobrovie-Sorin, Bleam, and Espinal (2006) treat (3b) as a case of (pseudo) semantic incorporation, i.e. the Bare Singular *auto* (car) is a predicate that incorporates into the main verb engendering a "conventional" interpretation. Espinal and McNally (2011) suggest that the explanation for the distribution of the BS in Peninsular Spanish is an underlying HAVE-verb. Whatever the explanation, the BS is not productive in comparatives; only plural nouns are acceptable:

(4) a. *Juan tiene más coche que Maria.
        Juan has-3P more car that Maria

    b. Juan tiene más coches que Maria.
        Juan has-3P more cars that Maria.
        "Juan has more cars than Maria."

As far as we know, there is no experimental research on the interpretation of the bare nouns in comparative sentences in RSpan. If RSpan is a number marking language, then the BS is massified in a comparison structure, as happens in English. The prediction, then, is that the BS is ungrammatical in comparatives in RSpan. We also predict that there is a distinction between BSs and FLEXSGs.

2.3. Cape-Verdean (CV)

Cape-Verdean (CV) is a Portuguese-based creole spoken in Cape Verde. The count–mass distinction surfaces with the (im)possibility of combining certain nouns with numerals: *dos leti (*two milk); but dos tomáti (two tomatoes). Cape-Verdean has an indefinite determiner, un(a), which, according to Baptista (2007), is in fact a quantifier. It is optional, though. There is a controversy about the status of kel and kes: some authors argue that they are in the process of grammaticalization as a definite article, others that they are demonstratives. Pires de Oliveira and Martins (2017) argue that neither kel nor kes can be used anaphorically to recover an entity that was already introduced in the discourse; they claim that this is evidence that they do not function as the definite determiner does in languages like Eng and BrP.

The important point is that articles and plural morphemes are not obligatory, and their use is restricted mostly to identifying or characterizing human beings. The default nominal phrase in CV is the Bare Singular:

(5) a. cigáru   ta   máta.
        cigarrette TMA[3]   kill
        "Cigarettes kill."

    b. N   odja   rátu.
        I   see   mouse
        "I saw a/the mouse/mice."   (Pires de Oliveira and Martins (2017))

---

[3] The authors use TMA to indicate that the morpheme expresses Tense, Mood, and Aspect.

In (5a), the BS appears in the external position of a generic predicate, whereas in (5b) it is in the internal position of an episodic predicate.

As far as we know, there are no experiments on CV nominal phrases. Pires de Oliveira and Martins (2017) argue that CV is a number neutral language following Chierchia's characterization: plurality is not obligatorily marked in the noun, and the default structure is the BS. If this is so, then we do not expect any difference between the BS and the PL in CV. Moreover, the BS should be well rated in the grammaticality test. Finally, we predict that the contrast between BS and FLEXSG does not exist in this type of language.

2.4. Brazilian Portuguese (BrP)

BrP is our main focus of investigation. Like English, it also grammatically distinguishes between mass and count: *lamas (muds), carros (cars), *three lamas, three carros. Unlike English and other Romance languages, including European Portuguese, in BrP an argument position may be filled by a BS,[4] as exemplified in (6) below:

(6) a. Cachorro late.
Dog barks.
"Dogs bark."

b. Comprei livro na feira ontem.
buy-Past-1stPS book in+the market yesterday.
"I bought books in the market yesterday."

In (6a), the BS appears in the external position of a generic predicate, whereas in (6b) it is in the internal position of an episodic predicate.

There are two main approaches to the semantics of the BS in BrP: the mass view (Dobrovie-Sorin and Pires de Oliveira 2008; Pires de Oliveira and Rothstein 2011) and the count view (Schmitt and Munn 1999; Müller, 2002). They make different predictions concerning the interpretation of the Bare Singular in comparative sentences such as (7):

(7) João tem mais livro que Maria.
João have3SG more book than Maria
"João has more quantity of books than Maria."[5]

---

[4] The literature on bare nouns in BrP is by now vast, and it is not our aim to review it. See Ferreira (forthcoming) for a survey of Bare Singulars in BrP.
[5] The translation using the Bare Plural misses the volume interpretation. This is the reason why we chose to use "quantity of books", which may be number or volume.

The count view predicts that the BS *livro* (book) is semantically "number neutral", i.e. the noun phrase denotes atoms and pluralities thereof,[6] whereas the PL is an exclusive plurality, i.e. it does not include the atoms. In comparison the BS should behave in exactly the same way as the plural: the comparison has to be about the number of individuals, their cardinality. Thus (7) says that the number of books that João has is greater than the number of books that Maria has. On the other hand, according to the mass view, (7) may have a volume reading. It may be true in a situation where João has four books, and Maria six, but the amount of bookshelf space taken up by João's books is greater than the volume of books that Maria has. The mass reading would only be available for the BS.

Experimental results support the mass view: using different methodologies, Beviláqua and Pires de Oliveira (2014, 2017), Beviláqua, Lima, and Pires de Oliveira (2016), and Lima and Gomes (2016) show that the BS is measured, although it may also be counted. Thus, it does not behave exactly like mass nouns, because BSs can also be counted; but it does not behave as a count noun either, since it may also be compared by volume. Beviláqua and Pires de Oliveira (2017) also found that the volume reading arises even in contexts that are not biased towards a mass interpretation, supporting the idea that it is not the context which is responsible for the mass reading of the Brazilian BS.

In order to explain the idiosyncratic behavior of the BS, Rothstein and Pires de Oliveira (2020) propose that it is a flexible (or "dual life") noun. The proposal has a consequence that all count nouns in BrP are ambiguous between a mass and a count denotation. If this is on the right track, we expect that in BrP there is no difference between the BS in BrP and the FLEXSG in Eng. Summarizing, we can say that in BrP the BS is grammatical in comparison; it is compared both by number of individuals and by volume (i.e. it does not behave as PL); there is no distinction between BSs and FLEXSGs.

3. A Cross-linguistic Experiment

The methodology presented in this paper is, as far as we know, original, though it was inspired by Lima and Rothstein's (2020) questionnaire: the "same" structure is compared in different languages. The experiment investigates the use of Noun Phrases in comparative sentences and questions in our four languages. The first task verifies the acceptability of the sentences. The other two tasks involve the interpretation of the nominal phrases. In all tasks the independent variable is the same: the NP. The NP variable has five levels: BSs, PLs, FLEXSGs, FLEXPLs, and MASS. Substance mass nouns are the control, since the prediction is that

---

[6] Chierchia (2010, 2015) understands number neutrality as a syntactic property of a type of language, i.e. those languages where number is not obligatorily marked.

they are invariably measured by volume across languages. The three tasks were web-based using the "onlinepesquisa.com" platform.

3.1. Task 1: The Acceptability of Nouns in Comparison

3.1.1. Methods and Design Task 1 evaluates the degree of acceptability of the bare noun phrases in comparative sentences across the four languages. For each language, the test had fifteen target sentences and twenty-five distractors. The dependent variable is a seven-point ordinal Likert scale. For the pilot, the target words in English were: *bed*, *house*, and *table* as BS nouns; *soap*, *stone*, and *rope* as FLEXSG nouns; *beds*, *houses*, and *tables* as PL nouns; *soaps*, *stones*, and *ropes* as FLEXPL nouns; and *water*, *mud*, and *sand* as MASS nouns. These lexical items were translated to the other three languages.[7]

Participants read comparative sentences as exemplified in (8) for the BS in all the languages under investigation, and were asked to evaluate its degree of acceptability:

(8) a. John has more bed than Mary.   Eng
    b. Juan tiene más cama que María. RSpan
    c. João tem mais cama que Maria.   BrP
    d. João tem mas kama ki Maria.   CV

Figure 8.1 is an example of the prompt from the English test.

Our hypotheses regarding the acceptability task can be summarized as follows:

(i) BS nouns in Eng and in RSpan will present low rates of acceptability, while being highly rated in both BrP and CV.
(ii) FLEXSG nouns should be highly rated in the four languages.
(iii) PL and FLEXPL nouns are expected to be highly rated in Eng, RSpan, and BrP; however, not in CV.
(iv) Mass nouns should be well rated in all languages.

3.1.2. Participants Forty participants, in total, participated in the experiment: nine native speakers of American English; ten native speakers of Rioplatense Spanish; six native speakers of Cape-Verdean; and fifteen native speakers of Brazilian Portuguese.

3.1.3. Results The results of Task 1 are reported in the graphical output of a cumulative link mixed models test (Figure 8.2). It shows the estimated

---

[7] As indicated by one of the reviewers, more items are needed. We plan to add other items in the revised version of this experiment.

John has more bed than Mary

Bad :(○ ○ ○ ○ ○ ○ ○ Good :)

Fig. 8.1: Example of Stimuli used for BS noun *bed* in English. Target sentence: "John has more bed than Mary."

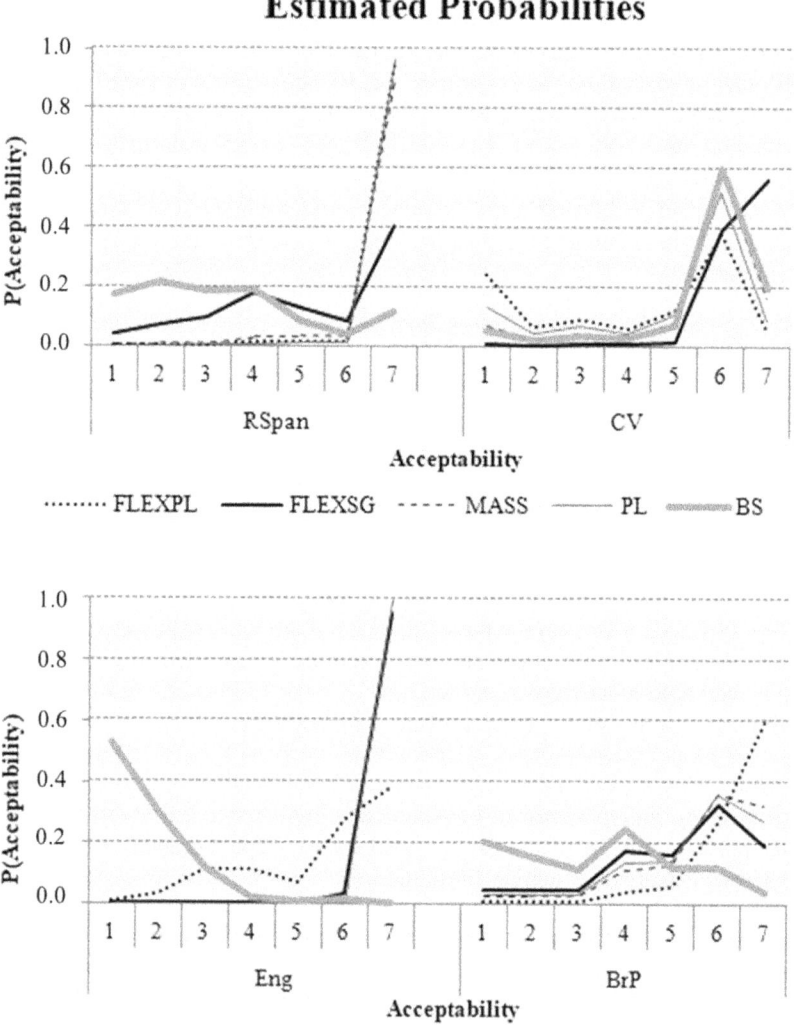

Fig. 8.2: Rating probabilities for NP and language at different experimental conditions

distribution of probabilities for judgments on a seven-point Likert scale for each language and NP. The x-axis is the value of ratings, and the y-axis is the probability of each level of the scale to be used, from 0 (extremely unlikely) to 1 (extremely likely). This means that if two conditions are similar in terms of how participants used the Likert scale to rate the NPs, the lines will appear very close in the graph.

For Eng, we can see that the BS condition and the other NPs are not rated in the same manner: BS is more likely to receive a rating of 1 and less like to receive a rating of 7 than, for instance, the PL condition. This is evidence that BSs in comparative sentences in English are ungrammatical. Our hypothesis for English is then confirmed. We analyzed participants' responses for Eng using a cumulative link mixed model (clmm) test, with fixed effects of NP and random intercepts for participants and items.[8] For English, the model revealed a significant difference between BS, on one side, and PL ($p = 0.0013$) and FLEXSG ($p = 0.02$) on the other. There was no significant difference between BS and FLEXPL ($p = 0.12$).[9]

A very similar result was found for RSpan. A clmm test revealed a significant difference between BSs and the other NPs (PL, MASS, and FLEXPL presenting p-values as $p < 0.0001$; and FLEXSG, $p = 0.04$). The graphic shows that BS nouns are more likely to be low rated compared to FLEXSG, and to plural and mass nouns. Compared to the English BS nouns then, the BS in RSpan had a slightly better acceptability, being more likely to be rated as 2.

For CV, as we expected, singular count nouns (as well as mass nouns) were more likely to receive a rating of 6 or 7. However, one hypothesis was not confirmed: plurals are well rated. A cumulative link mixed model revealed no significant difference, for instance, between the BS and the PL. In CV, the NPs seem all grammatical.

For BrP, PL, MASS, FLEXSG, and FLEXPL nouns are more likely to be rated as 6 (or 7 for FLEXPL) in the scale. According to our hypothesis, we expected that BS would be well rated in BrP. However, it presented major probabilities of being rated as 4 in the Likert scale, which, compared to the maximum of the scale (7 points), is a medium evaluation. Following that, the result of a cumulative link mixed model revealed a significant difference between BS and the other NPs (all presenting p-values as $p < 0.0001$).

In summary, regarding our hypotheses, the test showed that: the BS raises different acceptability judgments in comparison across languages. CV accepts

---

[8] We used the ordinal package (Christensen 2019) for R (R Core Team 2019).
[9] Mass nouns presented ratings of 7 in 100% of instances, blocking the model, since there was no variation. Thus, we removed this level of NP from the analysis.

BSs; while in Eng and RSpan they seem to be deviant. BrP BS nouns received a medium acceptability.[10] Flexible, plural, and mass nouns seem to be grammatical in all languages.

This task aimed at verifying the grammaticality of bare nouns in comparatives across languages. However, it alone cannot give any insight into the semantics of these NPs. The next test might shed light on this issue.

3.2. Task 2: The Interpretation of Nouns in Comparison

Task 2 is a picture-matching activity designed to explore the interpretation of nouns in comparatives. Three interpretations were explored: (i) the number of individuals; (ii) the volume interpretation; and (iii) the partitive reading, where a singular object is partitioned and the comparison is about the fractions of this object. Both the volume and the partitive readings are non-cardinal interpretations, since it is a comparison in which the cardinality of individuals is not the dimension being used.

3.2.1. Methods and Design After reading a comparative sentence, as exemplified in (8), the participant chooses one or more scenarios that she believes are depicted by the sentences (see Figure 8.3). The participant could choose as many answers as she thought were possible scenarios for the sentence. The independent variable is the same as that of Task 1: noun phrases.

In the first scene,[11] three small tables are compared to two bigger ones (with the same perceived total volume), highlighting a comparison about the number of individuals. In the second scene, a big table is compared to two small ones, highlighting a contrast between more volume or more units. Finally, in the last scenario, one object is partitioned, thus John has the biggest portion of the table.

Our hypotheses can be summarized as follows:

(i) In Eng and in RSpan, the BS gives rise only to a partitive reading. In CV, it raises only cardinal answers. In BrP, the interpretation of the BS is free with a tendency towards the cardinal reading.
(ii) FLEXSG in Eng and in RSpan should raise only volume answers. In CV and BrP, they also receive cardinal readings.
(iii) FLEXPL and PL nouns will raise only cardinal reading across languages.
(iv) MASS nouns will raise only volume reading across languages.

---

[10] A number of factors may be influencing the result. In particular, the test used the written form. BS nouns are very common in spoken varieties of BrP.
[11] The images used were downloaded from the website http://clipart-library.com/.

John has more table than Mary.

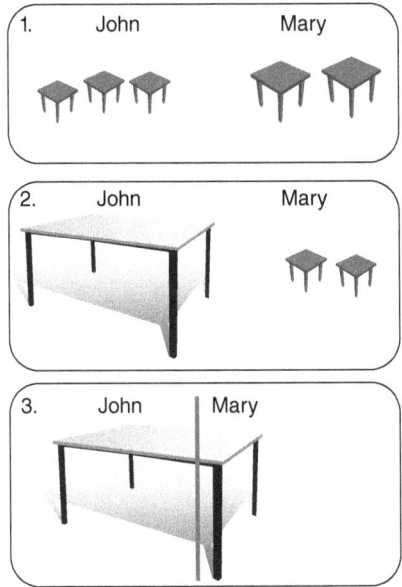

Fig. 8.3: Example of stimuli used for the nouns *table* and *tables* for English. Target sentence: "John has more table than Mary."

3.2.2. Participants The same participants answered Tasks 1 and 2: nine native speakers of English; ten native speakers of Spanish; six native speakers of CV; and fifteen native speakers of BrP.

3.2.3. Results Figure 8.4 shows the results grouped by languages: BrP, Eng, RSpan, and CV, respectively.

The graphic reveals the same pattern for Eng and RSpan. In both languages, Bare Singular nouns are mostly partitioned (77.2% for Eng and 74.3% for RSpan), though they were also interpreted by volume (around 24%). No cardinal interpretation was accessed by the speakers of these two languages. The same pattern emerges for the FLEXSG: participants chose both volume and/or partitive readings with a tendency for partitive; cardinal readings rarely occur (around 7%). For the PL and the FLEXPL, participants chose only the cardinal scenario. Plural forms are interpreted by cardinality. Thus, Eng and RSpan "massify" singular count forms in comparatives: Bare Singulars and Flexible Singulars are partitioned most of the time, though they may be measured by volume. They are never counted.

In CV, all nouns but Mass (BSs, FLEXSGs, PLs, and FLEXPLs) are interpreted by number of individuals. To confirm these visual trends, we

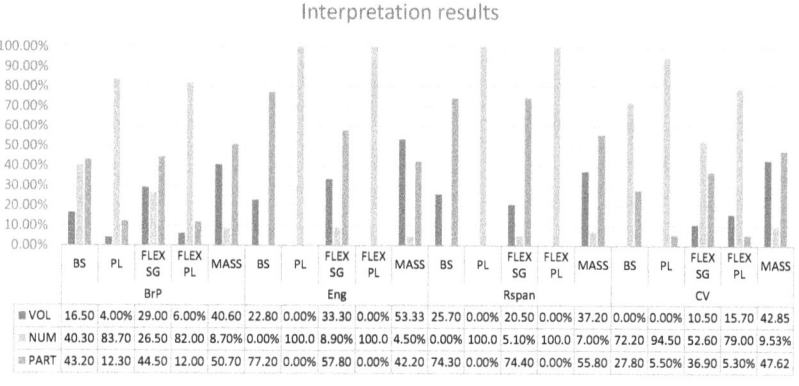

Fig. 8.4: Results of the picture-matching test

analyzed participants' responses using a generalized mixed effects logistic regression model predicting number interpretation with fixed effects of NP and random intercepts for participants and items. The model only revealed a significant difference between BS and MASS (SE = −3.13, Z = 3.287, p = 0.001). Thus, there seems to be no difference between the interpretation of bare nouns in CV – they are interpreted by the number of individuals, except for mass nouns, which are interpreted by volume. The result suggests a strict distinction between count (BS, FLEXSG, FLEXPL, PL) and mass nouns in CV.

BrP was the only language which allowed the three interpretations for BS nouns. It was mainly counted, but it was also often measured by volume and partitioned. The results replicate the findings in the literature on Bare Nouns in BrP: the interpretation of the BS oscillates between the cardinal interpretation (40%) and the measuring interpretations (43% partitioned and 16.5% by volume). If we consider only the cardinal reading, CV and BrP behave alike and in contrast with the Eng/RSpan type of language: in the latter, BSs are counted, in the former, they are measured. We analyzed Brazilians' responses using a generalized mixed effects logistic regression model predicting number interpretation with fixed effects of NP and random intercepts for participants and items. The model revealed significant differences between BS and FLEXPL (p = 0.0001); BS and PL (p = 0.0001); BS and MASS (p < 0.0001); but no difference between BS and FLEXSG (p = 0.07).

FLEXSG nouns in BrP behave like the BS – there is no significant difference between them, as the statistics show. They do not behave as Flexible Nouns in Eng and Rspan, since in those languages they were not evaluated by the cardinality. There is a difference between the BS in Eng/RSpan and in

BrP: in Eng/RSpan, the BS is never counted; most of the time it is partitioned. Finally, the BS in BrP contrasts with the BS in CV, since in BrP it is measured by volume while in CV it is not (0%).

In summary, plural nouns are counted, and mass nouns are measured in all the languages. They differ with respect to the singular forms, the Bare Singular and the Singular Flexible Noun. In languages where the BS is not well evaluated (acceptability task), participants partitioned it or measured it by volume, and it was never counted. In languages where the BS is productive, it was counted. However, CV and BrP contrast precisely with respect to the BS. In CV there is no difference between the BS and the PL: they are always counted. In BrP, the BS contrasts significantly with the PL, although both nouns allow for cardinal interpretation.

3.3. Task 3: Quantity Judgment Across Languages

Task 3 explores the methodology of quantity judgments (Barner and Snedeker 2005). The participants had to choose between two pictures after reading a *Who has more X?* question. The same nouns were used in all the tasks. The independent variable is the same as those of Tasks 1 and 2: the NP. In the quantity judgment, one picture always had three small objects, while the other had one big object of the same kind. The smaller objects not only outnumbered the larger one, but were smaller in volume and in surface area, allowing judgments based on number to be distinguished from those based on volume (the one big object).

3.3.1. Methods and Design The prompts are questions, as exemplified below for all languages:

(9) a. *Who has more table? English
b. *¿Quién tiene más mesa? Spanish
c. Quem tem mais mesa? Brazilian Portuguese
d. Kenha ki tem mas mesa? Cape Verdean

The questions in this task were not subject to an acceptability judgment; however, the prediction is that (9a) and (9b) are not grammatical, whereas (9c) and (9d) are. Thus, the task forces Eng and RSpan participants to choose an interpretation, whereas Brazilians and Cape Verdeans give their natural responses.[12] Figure 8.5 is an example of the stimuli for *stone*.[13]

---

[12] This is an issue that needs to be investigated further.
[13] The images used were downloaded from the website www.clker.com/.

Who has more stone?

Fig. 8.5: Example of Stimuli used for BS noun *stone* for English. Target sentence: "Who has more stone?"

Our hypotheses can be summarized as follows:

(i) In Eng and in RSpan, the BS gives rise only to volume readings. In CV, it is interpreted only by number. In BrP, the BS will be interpreted by volume and by cardinality.
(ii) FLEXSG in Eng and in RSpan should raise only volume answers. In CV and BrP, they are counted.
(iii) FLEXPL and PL nouns will raise only cardinal readings across languages.
(iv) MASS nouns will raise only volume reading across languages.

3.3.2. Participants Five native speakers of English, five native speakers of Rioplatense Spanish, three native speakers of Cape Verdean, and nine native speakers of Brazilian Portuguese participated in the task.

3.3.3. Results The results of the quantity-judgment task are presented in Figure 8.6. They are organized according to the languages: BrP, Eng, RSpan, CV.

The same pattern emerges from that found in Task 2. Eng and RSpan BS nouns were compared exclusively by volume. These noun phrases are never counted. FLEXSG nouns were also only compared by volume. FLEXPL and PL nouns were compared only by cardinality. And MASS nouns were compared only by volume in both languages. Singular forms are measured; plural forms are counted.

For CV, all of BS, FLEXSG, FLEXPL, and PL were compared by cardinality, while mass nouns were judged by volume. We analyzed participants' responses using a generalized mixed effects logistic regression model with fixed effects of NP and random intercepts for participants and items. The model only revealed a marginal difference between BS and MASS ($p = 0.06$).

For BrP, both BS and FLEXSG allowed quantity judgments based on volume and cardinality, without any significant difference. Though FLEXSG

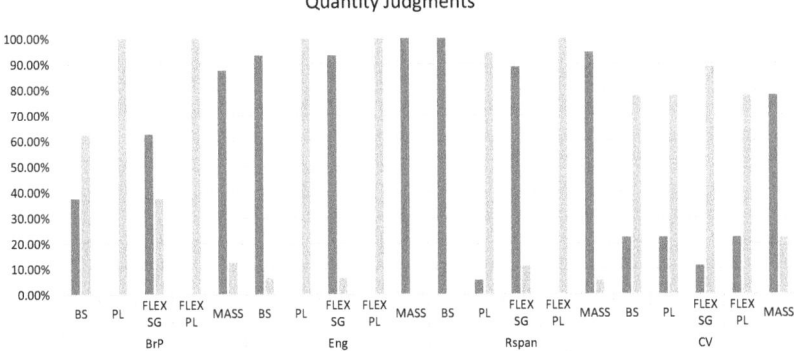

Fig. 8.6: Results of the quantity-judgment test

had slightly more volume interpretations, the difference is not statistically relevant. A generalized mixed effects logistic regression model with fixed effects of NP (and random intercepts for participants and items) revealed no difference between BS and FLEXSG in BrP (p = 0.2). Moreover, in BrP, mass nouns are only interpreted by volume; plural flexible nouns and bare plurals were only evaluated by the number of individuals.

The Bare Singular in BrP and in CV behave alike, because they allow for cardinal readings, in contrast with the Bare Singular in Eng and RSpan, which only allows the volume interpretation. However, there is no contrast between the BS and the PL in CV, whereas in BrP, the contrast is statistically relevant. Finally, the BS in BrP contrasts with mass nouns. In the next section we discuss these preliminary results regarding BS nouns across languages.

4. General Discussion: Bare Singulars Across Languages

In the previous section, we reported the preliminary results of applying the same tasks to different languages in order to compare the impact of the noun phrases in the same construction, comparative sentences (affirmatives and interrogatives). The experiment evaluates a number of predictions concerning bare nouns in comparatives, with the main focus on BrP. In order to understand the results, assuming that they are reliable, one must understand nominal comparatives. Those are cumulative structures, since they give rise to monotonic dimensions for measurement (Schwarzschild 2006; Champollion 2010), i.e. a comparison tracks the part–whole structure of their domains.

A measure function μ is monotonic if and only if for any a, b, if a is a proper part of b, then μ(a) < μ(b). Champollion (2010: 155)

Notice that if a noun denotes an atomic predicate, then it should be ungrammatical in comparatives, because atoms do not have proper parts. Given the semantics for comparison, we consider the results from our tests.

4.1. Bare Singulars in Number Marking Languages

According to Chierchia (2010, 2015), in number marking languages plurality is obligatorily marked in the noun. Thus, the absence of the morpheme indicates that the predicate is singular or atomic, i.e. it denotes an atom (and not a sum). In (10), we present the questions in English, their grammaticality judgments, and interpretations, according to our results, where mass indicates both volume and partitions:

(10)   a. Who has more tables?   cardinal   PL
       b. *Who has more table?   mass   BS
       c. Who has more rope?   mass   FLEXSG
       d. Who has more water?   mass   MASS

Given that comparatives are cumulative, as we saw, the pattern of grammaticality in (10) is expected if *table* is a singular predicate. Both bare plurals, *tables*, and bare mass, *water*, are fine, because they are cumulative: if *water* applies to two portions of water (a, b), then it also applies to the mereological sum of those portions (a + b). Plural nouns are monotonic and cumulative. Flexible singular nouns, *rope* in (10c), are well accepted in comparative constructions because they are cumulative – so they are mass nouns (Bale and Barner 2009). However, a singular count noun like *table* in (10b) is not cumulative: a single table and a single table do not count as a single table.[14] The grammatical mismatch surfaces in the judgment of acceptability of (10b), and in the interpretative tasks. When forced to interpret, participants tend to partition the object, as predicted by Chierchia (2010), because that gives a cumulative interpretation, if a and b are partitions of an object, so is their sum (a+b).

The acceptability of BS nouns in RSpan thus patterns with their acceptability in English, showing estimated probabilities of being low rated (as 2). Flexible singulars in both languages are acceptable. The contrast in acceptability between the BS and the FLEXSG suggests that these two types of noun phrases have different denotations. If singular flexible nouns are mass predicates, whereas BSs are atomic predicates, as in English, then the contrast between these nouns is explained. Moreover, we understand why in

---

[14] As an editor pointed out, this is not true in the case where the two tables are pushed together in an attempt to have a large table.

comparison the BS is never interpreted by number of individuals – it is a singular predicate, so in a cumulative context it must be massified, either by volume or by partition.

Thus, BSs in number marking languages are ruled out in comparatives because they denote sets of atoms. Atomic predicates cannot be in comparatives because they are not monotonic, a requirement of nominal comparatives. When forced in comparatives, the noun is coerced to partitions: *table* is interpreted as the set of partitions of a table. FLEXSG nouns are not atomic predicates, but mass (Chierchia 2010, 2015; Rothstein 2017).

4.2. Bare Singulars in Number Neutral Languages

Chierchia (2010) claims that in number neutral languages plurality is not obligatorily marked on the noun; hence, a predicate that does not carry an overt plural morpheme may be interpreted as a plurality. This is precisely what we see in CV. In this language, the BS is highly accepted, and its interpretation is cardinal. It behaves exactly as the PL. Since the plural morpheme is not obligatory, the BS and the PL are variants in CV. The results support the claim that CV is a number neutral language – bare singulars are plural predicates (corroborating Pires de Oliveira and Martins 2017). Here is the summary for CV bare nouns in interrogative sentences. The sentences in (11) are a word-by-word translation of the sentences in (10):

(11) a. Kenha ki tem mas mesas?   Cardinal   PL
      b. Kenha ki tem mas mesa?   Cardinal   BS
      c. Kenha ki tem mas corda?   Cardinal   FLEXSG
      d. Kenha ki tem mas água?   Mass   MASS

In CV, there is no contrast between the Bare Singular and the Bare Plural. There are no flexible nouns either, since *corda* (rope) behaves as a plurality. The only contrast is between mass and the other nouns, which seem all to be plural. All nouns are acceptable in comparatives because they are cumulative. None of them denotes an atomic predicate.

4.3. Bare Singulars in Brazilian Portuguese

If we compare (10) and (11) to (12) below, where the results for the bare nouns in BrP are presented for the same structures as in Eng and CV, we see that BrP contrasts both with Eng and with CV, and the difference is in the singular forms – the BS and the FLEXSG nouns:

(12) a. Quem tem mais mesas?   Cardinal   PL
      b. Quem tem mais mesa?   Cardinal and mass BS
      c. Quem tem mais corda?   Cardinal and mass FLEXSG
      d. Quem tem mais água?   Mass   MASS

If our results are reliable, then BrP is neither the language type of CV nor that of Eng.

There seem to be FLEXSG nouns in English (10c), i.e. nouns that denote objects in the world, but that in cumulative structures behave in a mass-like manner, whereas this type of noun does not seem to exist in CV or BrP. In CV and BrP, FLEXSG nouns behave exactly as the BS. FLEXSG nouns in English are not compared by cardinality; thus they are mass nouns. In BrP, BSs and FLEXSGs are counted and measured. Thus, there is a distinction between the BS in BrP and FLEXSG in English, against Rothstein and Pires de Oliveira (2020). In CV, FLEXSG and BSs are plural predicates, since they are always counted.

In BrP, the BS contrasts significantly with the BP (against Schmitt & Munn, 1999 and Müller 2002), indicating that it cannot be a sum. As we saw in BrP, the BS marks a contrast with Eng and RSpan, because it is interpreted by number, and it contrasts with CV, because it is interpreted as mass (volume and partitive readings). Thus, it is not mass either (against Pires de Oliveira and Rothstein 2011), since mass nouns are not counted. The conclusion is that the BS in BrP is both mass and count, supporting Pelletier's (2012) proposal for the denotation of all nouns in all languages. We know for sure that plural nouns must be sums, since they only allow for cardinal-based comparison. Mass nouns, on the other hand, only allow non-cardinal comparison. BS nouns present a mixed behavior, allowing both cardinal and non-cardinal comparison.

Lin and Schaeffer (2018) report the results of a quantity judgment task with noun phrases in Mandarin. They show that the bare count noun (without classifiers) allows both number- and volume-based interpretation. In Chierchia's proposal, language variation at the nominal level may be explained by how the lexicon is derived; the choice between predicate, <e, t>, or argument, e, dictates whether we have an English-like or a Mandarin-like language. In English, the lexicon starts as predicates of type <e, t>; while in Mandarin, they start as kinds of type e. However, in Chierchia, nouns are sorted into count and mass kinds. If this is the case, then we expect that when in comparison, even without the classifier, the interpretation of the BS should be cardinal. Lin and Schaeffer's results do not corroborate this prediction since the interpretation of the BSs oscillates between volume and counting. They argue that this provides evidence for Pelletier's (2012) claim that all nouns are semantically both count and mass in the lexicon, and that it is ultimately syntax that decides on the interpretation. If our results and analysis are on the right track, then, perhaps unexpectedly, BrP and Mandarin share this structure.

A full-fledged solution is beyond the scope of this paper; however, our results point towards a better understanding of BSs across languages.

5. Final Remarks

The paper presents the results of a pilot experiment that used a new methodology: by fixing the structure and the tasks, it allows comparison across languages. Four languages were investigated. Participants performed three tasks, where the prompts were comparison sentences (affirmatives and interrogatives). The independent variable is the noun phrase. Five types of nouns were investigated: BS, FLEXSG, PL, FLEXPL, and MASS. Assuming Chierchia's typology of language, the aim was to understand whether BrP patterns with a number marking language, such as Eng, or with a number neutral language, such as CV, or neither.

None of the languages in this study distinguish FLEXPL and PLs. Plurality leads to counting. Mass nouns also show the same pattern across these languages: they are not counted, but measured (volume or partition).

The locus of variation in these languages is the BS and the FLEXSG. The contrast between them seems to exist only in Eng and RSpan. This is an indication that, in these languages, coercion might take place to shift a BS into portions or parts (Chierchia 2010, 2015), a hypothesis to be investigated. In the interpretation tasks, they are interpreted massively, either by volume or by partition, but never by number. Even though the BS denotes an object in the world, grammar dictates the interpretation. The results for the BS, and for FLEXSG, are as predicted in the literature for Eng (Chierchia 2010, 2015; Rothstein 2017). If in these languages number is marked in the noun, as Chierchia (2010, 2015) proposes, then we understand the data: the BS denotes an atomic predicate – and hence cannot figure in comparatives (unless they are partitioned) due to the fact that comparison structure demands monotonic measurements.

In CV, the Bare Singular is accepted in the grammaticality judgment and behaves exactly like the plural noun in all the tasks; there is no statistical difference between them. There is no contrast between BSs and FLEXSGs. Moreover, in this language, both are only counted. Thus, number is not obligatory, because the BS is a plural predicate; so, the BS and the PL are variants. If our results are reliable, CV is a number neutral language, as suggested by Pires de Oliveira and Martins (2017).

In BrP, the interpretation of the Bare Singular oscillates between cardinal and non-cardinal, supporting previous findings in the literature (Beviláqua and Pires de Oliveira 2014, 2017). The Brazilian BS is puzzling because it is a noun that denotes an object in the world, but it may be compared by volume or may be counted. There is no contrast between BSs and FLEXSGs; they both oscillate. However, our results do not endorse Rothstein and Pires de Oliveira's (2020) proposal that flexible nouns in English allow for cardinal interpretation. Thus, the BS in BrP does not behave as flexible nouns in

English do. We brought in the results of Lin and Schaeffer (2018) for Mandarin in order to suggest that in BrP and in Mandarin, the BS behaves as predicted by Pelletier (2012): it denotes all possible denotations.

This paper opens a number of issues. First of all, the results are from a pilot study. Not only are there ameliorations to be implemented, but the number of items tested and the number of participants in each of the languages studied should increase. We also plan to include Mandarin in the new version of this experiment. However, even though preliminary, the results indicate that the methodology is worth pursuing, since it allows a comparison of the same structure across languages, and insights into the semantics of the locus of variation, which in our experiment is on the BS.

9 Counting (on) Bare Nouns: Revelations from American Sign Language

Helen Koulidobrova

1. Introduction

Let us start with Pelletier's (2012) observation that the literature on the count–mass distinction (CMD) tends to diverge in the following way: semantic accounts make reference to universal properties of mass vs. count nouns (as in (1)) while syntactic accounts are technically language-specific and use English as a spring-board (and compare everything else to it), as in (2) from Deal (2017).

(1)   a. Count nouns, but not mass nouns, designate a set of (countable) entities
       b. Mass nouns, but not count nouns, designate stuff   (Pelletier 2012: 10)

(2)   Countability distinctions with examples from English (Deal 2017: 132).

	cat	*footwear*	*water*
(a) pluralization	✓	*	*
(b) direct combination with numerals	✓	*	*
(c) combination with *each, many, fewer*	✓	*	*
(d) combination with *much, less*	*	✓	✓
(e) combination with 'count adjectives'	✓	✓	*
(f) comparison based on number	✓	✓	*
(g) comparison based on mass/volume	*	*	✓

In (2), the leftmost column outlines various properties observed to be true of three different classes of nouns (in italics) – count nouns on the left, mass nouns on the right and aggregates in the middle column. These properties have been further divided into those related to cumulativity/SUMS ((a)–(d)) vs. divisiveness/PARTS ((e)–(f)). Questions relating to (1) and (2), as well as their relationship, have been addressed in various papers on the CMD, but my present goals are much more modest: I explore the divisions provided by (2) in American Sign Language (ASL) – a visuo-gestural language historically related to French Sign Language. While the CMD has not been examined directly in previous work, certain claims have been made and, crucially, the distinction has been utilized in discussions of other phenomena. I aim to show that the diagnostics provided by (2), which have been used in the literature, will not suffice for ASL, which puts ASL on a par with Nez Perce or, arguably, Yudja (Deal 2017). While the application of (2) to ASL yields a language in which mass and count nouns behave identically, it would be wrong to conclude that ASL lacks CDM altogether. So instead of comparing ASL with English (though the comparison is a good starting point), I will rely directly Chierchia (2010, 2015, et seq., and this volume) and examine where ASL fits in the typology in (3).

(3)   Type I: number marking languages of the more extensively studied Indo-European type (English or Russian)
         Type II: *no* noun can combine directly with numerals and, instead, requires a classifier to do this work (Chinese, Japanese, a.k.a. generalized classifier languages)
         Type III: *all* nouns combine freely with numerals (Yudja, Nez Perce) (Chierchia, this volume, Chapter 2)

As Chierchia (2010: 108) proposes, (3) is tightly connected to number marking, as (4) indicates (italics are mine):

(4)   ... (T)hree quite different ways in which the mass count distinction is coded. ... (I)n classifier languages *(Type II)* we detect a different behavior of mass versus count in the classifier system; in number marking languages *(Type I)*, the distinction affects the distributions of plural versus singular morphemes, while in nominal number neutral languages *(Type III)* it shows up in the distribution of numerals.

My goal here then, using the tools in (1)–(4), is to establish where CMD is encoded in ASL and to determine which Type (I–III) ASL belongs to. The paper is structured as follows. In Section 2, I will briefly introduce the basic data; in Sections 3 and 4, I show that ASL is neither a *Type I* nor a *Type II* language by examining its classifiers and number marking and their influence on countability, respectively. Section 5 explores the *Type III* alternative and demonstrates that the CMD is found in a quantity expression; Section 6 concludes and outlines directions for future research. Notation and methodology for data collection are articulated in the Appendix.

2.   Mass Nouns in ASL: Diagnostic (Take 1)

Given the observations in (2), we expect the following generalizations to hold for mass nouns (in general and in ASL):

(5)   Mass nouns:
         a. should not pluralize
         b. should not directly combine with numerals

c. should not combine with *each, many, few(er)*
d. should not combine with 'count adjectives'/stubbornly distributive predicates (Schwarzschild 2005, 2011, i.a.)
e. should not compare based on number but, rather, based on volume (Barner and Snedeker 2005; Bale and Barner 2009).

However, as (6) demonstrates, ASL nouns do not follow the expectations in (5). Below, I also provide our consultants' interpretations with respect to the relevant units of measurement during context manipulations.

(6)   a. WOW {BOOK >+>+ / SHIT$_{arc}$>+>+} HERE   - vs. (5a)
lit. 'Wow, {books / shit-PL} are all over here'
- piles, puddles
b. PLEASE GIVE-1 THREE {BOOK/BLOOD}   - vs. (5b)
lit. 'Please give me three book/blood'
- piles, containers, puddles
c. NEED FEW/MANY
{APPLE/OIL/RAIN/IMAGINATION/LIGHT/FURNITURE}
lit. 'I need a few/many   - vs. (5c)
{apple/oil/rain/imagination/light/furniture}
- piles, containers, puddles, containers, instances of
d. (IX$_a$) {BOOK/GOLD} SMALL   - vs. (5d)
lit. '(That) gold small.'
- a unit (e.g. a book, a golden ring), a pile (e.g. of books, gold pieces), a chunk/puddle (of gold-stuff)
e. *Context: Mary's wine barrel contains more wine (volume) than Peter's fifteen bottles*
PETER HAVE MORE WINE   - vs. (5e)
'Peter has more wine' *(true on the number reading, false on the volume reading)*[1]

So, we might expect BOOK and APPLE in (6) to behave as the English *cats*, and OIL, GOLD, and BLOOD to behave as *water*. But this is not what happens. Specifically, when mass nouns in (6) combine with numerals, 'unconventional situations' are possible (Lima 2014a, 2014b; Chierchia 2015): [THREE BLOOD] can, in fact, be interpreted as a puddle of blood, a container of blood, and a blood-soaked sock; [FEW SHIT] can be interpreted as one puddle and two piles.

At first glance, the question regarding what *Type* of language ASL is has just been answered: all nouns appear to combine with numerals (see (3)). However, two issues remain. First, ASL is a language that robustly employs a classifier

---

[1] Importantly, (6e) is ambiguous: the volume reading remains possible but during different sessions, the consultant showed no consistency in selecting the volume/number answer. The crucial point here is that the number reading is available at all.

system that has been argued to be employed in nominal quantification (Petronio 1995, a.o.), which leads to its framing as a *Type II* language. Additionally, ASL is typically assumed to have a mechanism for number agreement which has been argued to be obligatory (Pfau and Steinbach 2006), which makes it a *Type I* language. Finally, given the data in (6), we might ask whether all nouns in this language are uniform, being all mass or count. It turns out, however, that the aforementioned is unlikely: mass and count nouns cannot be conjoined (7).

(7) a. GIVE-1 BOOK disj-shift PEN
   'Give me a book and a pen'
  b. GIVE-1 BLOOD disj-shift MUD
   'Give me blood and a mud'
  c. * GIVE-1 [BOOK disj-shift BLOOD]
   'Give me a book and blood'

To the degree that coordination is a matter of syntax, and syntax manipulates Logical Form (LF) objects, at least in terms of a syntactic construction something must be said about the difference between the nouns (Pelletier 2012). In the rest of this paper, I explore what the behavior of the nouns in (6) is dependent on. In Sections 3 and 4, marking number, of which pluralization (in the form of '+++') is one example and a numeral classifier is typically another (as in Type I and Type II languages, respectively), will be dismissed as a possibility. In Section 5, I consider the quantity expression itself (as in Type III languages, broadly construed). Section 6 concludes and outlines further directions.

3. ASL is not a *Type I* Language (Not a Typical/Obligatory Number Marking Language)

ASL does not *appear* to mark number the way English does: as may have become evident from (6a–c), ASL nouns can surface in either their bare (a.k.a. singular-looking) or 'repeated' form ('+++' and its phonological variants). On the surface, this marking appears optional: as (8) shows, the same reading can be obtained without this repetition (setting aside recent work by Schlenker and Lamberton 2019 to which we return below).

(8)   ____t____ __t__
  a. 1-POSS FATHER TREE CUT
   'My father has cut a tree / the tree / multiple trees'
       ____t____ __t__
  b. 1-POSS FATHER TREE>>> CUT
   'My father has cut trees'

Much of the descriptive and theoretical literature (Cokely and Baker-Shenk 1980; Fischer 1973; Wilbur 2005; Pfau and Steinbach 2006; Berent, Dupuis, and Brentari 2014) refers to the process in (8b) as 'reduplication', alluding to a similar process found in many spoken languages. However, Petronio (1995) has argued that, just like in Mandarin, Japanese, and Korean – languages without obligatory number marking but with generalized classifiers (*Type II*), the issue to which I will return in Section 5 – the quantificational value of ASL nouns is typically encoded not on the NP but somewhere outside of it, based on context or predicate type. In (9), for example, all of the ASL nouns remain in the non-repeated form even when they are interpreted as plural.

(9)   a.   a-NURSE, 1-IX FINISH INFORM-a$_{\{[singular]/[dual]/[multiple]/[exhaustive]\}}$
           'I informed {the nurse/two nurses/the nurses/all of the nurses}'
     b.   STUDENT FRUSTRATE, TEACHER UPSET
        i.   *Context: The Mastery Test is generally not well liked in the K-12 environment*
           'Students {are/tend to be} frustrated, teachers {are/tend to be} upset'
       ii.   *Context: The argument between a teacher and a student needs to be resolved*
           'The student is frustrated; the teacher is upset'
               _____t
     c.   CAR, TWO STUDENT BUY
        i.   'Two students together bought a car'   = more salient
       ii.   'Two students bought a car each'
               _____t
     d.   BOOK, TWO STUDENT BUY
        i.   'Two students each bought a book'   = more salient
       ii.   'Two students together bought a book'   (adpd. Petronio 1995)

In their analysis of the same phenomenon in German Sign Language (DGS), Pfau and Steinbach (2006, 2016) argue that reduplication is morphological realization of *.PL*, an allomorph of which is zero. Crucially, with a numeral or a reduplicated adjective, the noun must retain its non-plural form; in this, DGS parallels Hungarian, Turkish, and a variety of other languages without the NP-internal number concord, which results in incompatibility with a numeral (see Pfau and Steinbach 2006, 2016 for details). Descriptively, the same can be said for ASL. These properties are shown in (10)–(12).

(10)   'Few / many kids'
       a.   *{FEW / MANY} CHILDREN
       b.   {FEW / MANY} KID

(11)   'Blue/small books'
       a.   *BOOK+++ {BLUE +++/SMALL +++}
       b.   BOOK (+++) {BLUE / SMALL}

(12)   a.   THREE DIFFERENT *{BOWL+>+>+> / *BOOK +++$_{(arc)}$ / *CHILDREN}
           'Three different {bowls/books/children}'
      b.   THREE DIFFERENT {BOWL/BOOK/KID}
           'Three different {bowls/books/children}'

The aforementioned offers a path towards an explanation for some of the data in (6): that is, we now have a potential account of the unacceptability of overt '+++' with count nouns next to a quantity expression (a quantifier in (6b) as well as in (10a), and a numeral in (6c) as well as in (12a)). This also explains why '+++' is expected with count nouns without a quantity expression (as in (6a) and (11b)) but when a plurality reading is intended: after all, according to Pfau and Steinbach, '+++' expones .PL. Two potential problems remain, however. The first one is the optionality of '+++' in (11b), the second the compatibility of '+++' with mass nouns like SHIT in (6a). While plural marking on mass nouns is not as rare as one might think given (2) (Corbett 2000), when it is observed, it tends to result in additional readings (e.g. *abundance*; see an extended discussion in Renans et al. 2018) and has served as an argument for a different syntax of mass vs. count nouns (as in Alexiadou 2011) as well as of the morpho-syntax of number marking itself (Wiltschko 2012).

To quickly sum up the foregoing I offer a quote from Schlenker and Lamberton (2019, p.42):

(13) [Repetition] can be used with mass terms to refer to the plurality of parts of the relevant substance, but what repetition also seems to do is locate the parts in space by denoting their arrangement.

The same can be said for count nouns. This line of research (which incorporates the 'iconic potential' of space denoted by the various articulations of '+++') points towards an analysis of the optionality of '+++' in (11b) and clearly suggests that that '+++' does not behave as a bona fide plurality marker (encoding something like the *-operator). Setting that line of research aside, let us briefly focus on the morpho-syntax of number marking itself.

Rullmann and You (2006) observe that languages like English (number marking) and languages like Mandarin ('general number', Corbett 2000) differ with respect to readings obtained under ellipsis: lexical ambiguity disappears in both, but ambiguity with respect to number only does so in English.

(14) a. John saw a pen and Mary did too
≠ 'John saw a pigpen. Mary saw a writing utensil'
b. John saw pens and Mary did too
≠ 'John saw one pen. Mary saw multiple pens' (adpd. Rullmann and You 2006: 16)

(15) Wo you tie fanwan. Yuehan ye you. (Mandarin Chinese)
I have iron bowl. John also have
a. ≠ 'I have one or more steady jobs. John has one or more iron bowls.'
b. ≠ 'I have one or more iron bowls. John has one or more steady jobs.'

c. = 'I have one or more iron bowls. So does John.'
d. = 'I have one or more steady jobs. So does John.' (Rullmann and You 2006: 18)

Unlike the English (14b), Mandarin (15b) can be uttered if the speaker has one iron bowl/steady job but John has seven, or the speaker has seven iron bowls/ steady jobs and John has one. From diagnostics like this,[2] the authors conclude that Mandarin nouns are not specified for number. What is crucial for us here is the following: on the view that '+++' is a morphological realization of .PL, then if .PL becomes zero (PL→Ø, as has been argued by Pfau and Steinbach 2006), the number value should be preserved. That is, while disappearance of lexical ambiguity is predicted (as in (14a) and (15a–b), we ought not expect 'cross'-readings akin to (15c–d); instead, we should expect something like (14b). Yet, this is not what happens.

ASL behaves on par with Mandarin in (15): when the noun is bare, the same readings obtain (including the crucial (15c–d)); as soon as '+++' is added, the picture changes (as has been shown in other number neutral languages, e.g. Japanese and Malagasy).

(16) a. JOHN SEE {BALL/BOWL/TREE} MARY SAME
'John saw {balls/bowls/trees}, and Mary did too.'
   i. = John saw one {ball/bowl/tree}; Mary saw multiple {balls/bowls/ trees} ≈ (15c)
   ii. = John saw multiple {balls/bowls/trees}; Mary saw one {ball/bowl/ tree} ≈ (15c)
   iii. = John and Mary each saw either a single or multiple {ball/bowl/tree} ≈ (14b)
b. JOHN SEE {BALL+++/BOWL>+>+>/TREE>>>} MARY SAME
'John saw {balls/bowls/trees}; Mary did too'
   i. ≠ John saw one {ball/bowl/tree}; Mary saw multiple {balls/bowls/ trees} ≈ (15c)
   ii. ≠ John saw multiple {balls/bowls/trees}; Mary saw one {ball/bowl/ tree} ≈ (15c)
   iii. = John and Mary each saw multiple {balls/bowls/trees} ≈ (14b)

That is, the 'number value', expected on Pfau and Steinbach's account (15c–d), is not preserved.

Additionally, given the goals of this chapter and the predictions in (4), the question is whether mass nouns behave differently from the count nouns here. The answer is that they do not.

However we wind up packaging *gold* and *shit*, in English, they invite similar ambiguity and are similarly constrained under ellipsis. In (17)–(18), whatever

---

[2] Other diagnostics pointing to number underspecification are subjects of my ongoing research, including discourse anaphora and implicature raising, which I skip for reasons of space.

it is that John saw, Mary also saw – either excrement or a mess, either a set of items or a unit.

(17)   a. John saw shit
            = John saw a pile of random things that must be cleaned up
            = John saw excrement in one or multiple occurrences
       b. John saw shit, and Mary did too.
            = John and Mary saw a pile of gold pieces / = John and Mary saw a piece of gold
            ≠ John saw a pile of gold pieces and Mary saw a piece of gold

(18)   a. Mary saw gold
            = Mary saw a pile of gold pieces / = Mary saw a piece of gold
       b. Mary saw gold, and John did too.
            = John and Mary saw a pile of gold pieces / = John and Mary saw a piece of gold
            ≠ John saw a pile of gold pieces and Mary saw a piece of gold

However, the aforementioned is not true in ASL: mass *SHIT* (19) and *GOLD* (20) are disambiguated under ellipsis only when '+++' is overt.

(19)   a. WOW SEE MANY SHIT 2-IX SAME RIGHT SAME WIGGLE
          'Wow, I see a lot of shit (here). You do too, right?'
          i. = you and I see excrement / = you and I see a mess (e.g. books on the floor)
            ≠ one of us sees excrement and the other sees books on the floor
          ii. = you and I see single or multiple piles of the relevant substance

                                                    y/n
       b. WOW SEE SHIT+>+>+ 2-IX SAME RIGHT SAME WIGGLE
          'Wow, I see a shit.**PL** (here). You do too, right?'
          i. = both you and I see excrement/ = both you and I see a mess (e.g. books on the floor)
            ≠ one of us sees excrement and the other sees a mess (e.g. books on the floor)
          ii. ≠ you and I see single or multiple occurrences of the relevant substance
            = you and I see multiple occurrences of the relevant substance

(20)   a. JOHN SEE GOLD MARY SAME
          i. = John and Mary see melted gold / = John and Mary see jewelry (various metals)
            ≠ John sees melted gold and Mary sees jewelry (various metals)
          ii. = John and Mary see a pile of gold pieces / = John and Mary saw a piece of gold
            = John saw a pile of gold pieces and Mary saw a piece of gold
       b. JOHN SAW GOLD+++ MARY SAME
          i. = John and Mary see melted gold / = John and Mary see jewelry (various metals)
            ≠ John sees melted gold and Mary sees jewelry (various metals)

ii. = John and Mary saw a pile of gold pieces / ≠ John and Mary saw a piece of gold
≠ John saw a pile of gold pieces and Mary saw a piece of gold

That is, without '+++', lexical ambiguity disappears ((19a.i) and (20a.i)), but not number or packaging ((19a.ii) and (20a.ii)); and with that, both (19b) and (20b) are conveyed.

To reinforce the conclusions arising from this section, let us apply the entailment diagnostic. Consider the English example in (21) containing *child-PL* – i.e. *children*. The English sentences remain felicitous even when only one-child families are under discussion; and these facts about felicity have been shown to hold for a number of languages with obligatory plural marking (Borer 2005, Sauerland 2008, and many others). However, the opposite is true in ASL.

(21) a. A: Do you have any children?
          B: Yes, I have one.
          B': #No, only one
      b. Linda has no children

(22)   y/n
    a. A: HAVE TREE>>> / BALL +++ / CHILDREN HERE
       'Do you have {trees / balls}?'
       B: #YES, HAVE ONE {P-I-N-E/BASKETBALL/DAUGHTER}
       'Yes, we have one {pine/basketball/daughter}'
       B': NO, ONLY ONE {P-I-N-E/BASKETBALL/DAUGHTER}
       'No, only one {pine/basketball/daughter}'
    b. TODAY NO HAVE {TREE>>> / BALL +++ / CHILDREN} BUT HAVE ONE {PINE/BASKETBALL/KID}
       'Today there are no {trees/balls/children} here but have one {pine/basketball/kid}'

This is a robust pattern in the language: in (22), TREE is one-handed but produced in the neutral space midsagitally; it is mobile. BALL is two-handed and perseverates ('bounces') in the same location or in an arc. CHILDREN is a two-handed lexical plural (Acquaviva 2008) with hands moving in the opposite directions. The difference between various nouns here is phonological – something that has been argued to be crucial in distinguishing among the various types of pluralization strategies (Wilbur 2005; Pfau and Steinbach 2006, 2016; i.a).[3] Four classes of nouns were tested here, varying in

---

[3] Neither sentence means that there are three books (or trees) here, despite the fact that the relevant noun is repeated three consecutive times (though see Schlenker and Lamberton 2019 on this). With the literature, we conclude that this sign repetition (Cokely and Shenk 1980) does not correspond to the number of repeated events. Note, however, while we observe punctuated

handedness, body-anchoring, path, etc.[4] Those allowing '+++' behaved identically, leading to the following conclusion: ASL does not parallel either English in (21) nor, despite its apparent similarity (Pfau and Steinbach 2006), Turkish in (23).

(23) A: Ormanda ayı-lar-a rastladınız mı? [Turkish]
      'Did you come across bears in the forest?'
      B: Evet, bir tane gördük.
      'Yes, we saw one.'
      B': #Hayır, bir tane gördük.
      'No, we saw one.' (Sağ 2016)

Summarizing this section, we can say that with '+++', ASL behaves on a par with English (14b), and without it with Mandarin (15). That is, the language acts as though it marks exclusively in cases with a plurality (2+) reading and is unspecified for number otherwise.[5] The interaction between clusivity and 'general number' is remains unclear (Harbour 2014), but, crucially, no difference between mass and count nouns was obtained.

4. ASL is not a Type II Language (not a Generalized Classifier Language)

In this section, I offer some arguments to the effect that, despite the apparent similarities, ASL is not a Type II language, like Mandarin.

There are good reasons to draw a parallel between ASL and East Asian languages. For instance, as we have already seen, both Mandarin (also Japanese: Sudo 2016) and ASL are best described as unspecified for number.

---

repetitions of the sort discussed in Schlenker and Lamberton (2019) here (and can evoke iconic semantics), it may be harder to do with CHILDREN – no particular space is allocated to them.

[4] Not all nouns in our sample undergo pluralization via '+++'; some, for instance, are body-anchored and will not bounce/trill (Wilbur 1987). Others resist for different reasons which we leave for future research. Among the latter class, some nouns are 'rescued by' classifiers, such as SAND:

(i) a. JOHN MARY SEE SAND+++
     'John and Mary saw sands'
     b. JOHN MARY SEE SAND CL$^{\text{tall-object}}$ +++
     'John and Mary saw tall sand objects'
     = *Context:* John saw three sand castles, Mary saw five {#sandboxes /^{ok}castles}

[5] We might say that the denotations of KID and TREE vs. CHILDREN and TREE+++ in ASL can be represented as something like (i) (see Bale and Khanjian (2014) for Western Armenian although with a different result). I will explore this possibility in future work.

(i) In a context where *a*, *b*, and *c* are children and trees
     a. [[KID/TREE]] = {*a* , *b* , *c*, *ab* , *ac* , *bc* , *abc* }
     b. [[CHILDREN/TREE+++]] = {*ab* , *ac* , *bc* , *abc*}

The parallelism with the East Asian languages goes further: like other languages of Type II, ASL has classifiers; this is another place where number can be encoded.

(24)   t
    a. a-STORE, MAN CL:/1/-GO-a
    'The man went to a store'
        t
    b. a-STORE, MAN CL:/44/-GO-a
    'The men went to a store' (Petronio 1995)

In Petronio's original notation, *1* stands for a [+human] classifier; she glosses *44* to represent the plurality of such beings. However, one difference between ASL classifiers and what is found in classifier languages is that the aforementioned 'plurality marker' is encoded on the classifier itself, not instead of it (as is typically claimed for classifier languages) or in addition to it.

Cross-linguistic examinations show that classifiers in ASL differ from classifiers in 'numeral classifier' languages, in that the classifier and the numeral are always adjacent (Greenberg-Sanchez generalization of Greenberg 1972), in the latter as in (25). The adjacency cannot be disrupted.

(25)   a. [Noun-Number-Classifier]   b. [Noun-Classifier-Number]
     c. [Number-Classifier-N]   d. [Classifier-Number-Noun]
     e. *[Number-Noun-Classifier] f. [Classifier-Noun-Number]

The adjacency requirement has been observed for Indo-European, Altaic, and Niger-Congo languages and is quite robust (Ikoro 1994; Cheng and Sybesma 1999; Aikhenvald 2000; Doetjes 2012; among others). In ASL, however, an adjacency is not required: As is illustrated in (26), CAR occurs between THREE and CL^{vehicle} (violating (25e)), and adjectives such as YELLOW, HUGE, and DRUNK can show up between the noun and the classifier (see also Pfau and Steinbach 2006 for DGS).

(26)   cha
    a. THREE YELLOW CAR (HUGE) CL^{vehicle} >+>+>+
    'Three huge cars (are standing there)'
    b. WOMAN (DRUNK) CL^{person}1 FALL
    'A drunk woman (standing) fell'

A further argument against equating ASL and Mandarin-style classifiers comes from the 'universal grinder' (Pelletier 1975). Cheng, Doetjes, and Sybesma (2008) demonstrate that Mandarin does not grind its nouns sufficiently, and classifiers are disallowed in such contexts. Yet, the opposite is true in ASL:

(27)   qiáng shang dōu shi gǒu [Mandarin](Cheng, Doetjes, and Sybesma 2008)
     wall top   all be dog
     'There are dogs all over the wall' ≠ 'There is dog (dog-parts) all over the wall'

(28) a. WOW MANY DOG HERE
'Wow, there is a lot of dog here'
= dog-parts splattered, evident that something terrible happened[6]
b. WOW MANY SHIT HERE
'Wow, there is a lot of shit here'

What is more, we also note that Mandarin (representing a generalized classifier language) and ASL behave differently with respect to (3): if ASL is a *Type II* language, it should have different classifiers for mass vs. count nouns, or at least differentiate between them, as is the case in Mandarin (29). Instead, the difference we observe in ASL is sortal: size and shape, and, perhaps, packageability of the noun. In ASL, the combinations in (30) are impossible with a classifier, arguably because there is no classifier for IMAGINATION, LIGHT, or DARK, and not because the nouns are mass.

(29) Classifiers in Type II languages (Doetjes 2012)
a. sān   bên   shū   [Mandarin]
   three CL^{volume} book
b. liǎng jīn   mǐ
   two   CL^{kilo} rice

(30) a. JOHN MARY HAVE (FIVE) TOY CL$^{tall-object}$ +++
'John and Mary have (5) toys that look like tall objects'
b. JOHN MARY SEE (THREE) SAND CL$^{tall-object}$ +++
'John and Mary saw (3) tall sand objects'
b. JOHN MARY SEE (THREE) BLOOD CL$^{circ.area}$+++
'John and Mary saw (3) circular areas of blood/blood puddles'

(31) a. JOHN MARY HAVE (*3) IMAGINATION (*CL)
Lit. 'John and Mary have 3 of imagination'
b. NEED (*TWO) LIGHT (*CL)
Lit. 'We need 2 light'
c. NEED MANY DARK (*CL)
'We need much darkness.'

These data support previous analyses of the classifier (see Abner 2017 and references therein), which differs from what has been proposed for generalized classifier languages.

Let us revisit the main reason for the existence of classifiers at all: according to the theoretical framework we have been assuming, in classifier languages, nouns are kinds (Chierchia 1998b, 2010, 2015) and are lifted into properties by the classifier. This is not what we can say about the CL in ASL, at least not with regards to the CL we have seen thus far. But what this conclusion also points to is that ASL classifiers like CL$^{rounded-pile}$, CL^{person}, etc., cannot be

---

[6] The other reading here is the plural one: *There are a lot of dogs here*. Number marking is explored in the next section.

approached as bona fide substitutions for D^0 or Num^0 in languages without definite articles (as has been argued for sortal classifiers in Chinese by Cheng and Sybesma 1999) – at the moment, there is no evidence that the classifier and the noun form a phrase; in fact, the vast majority of the data suggest the opposite. This leads us to the conclusion that ASL is not a *Type II* language (with a covert classifier).

5. ASL as a Type III Language (a Number Neutral Language where Quantity Expressions Tell Us Something)

Ionin and Matushansky (2006) (see also Landman 2003, 2004, i.a.) argue that numerals have restrictive adjectival semantics (<<et>, <et>>). The adjectival status of numerals in ASL is corroborated by ellipsis data: the number associated with the elided element is simply ignored, as in (32), much in the same way an adjective might in (33) (Koulidobrova 2012, 2017). Something similar can be said about quantifiers (see also Nishiguchi 2009 for Japanese).

(32) A: $_1$IX SEE {THREE/MANY} WHALE TODAY
'I saw {three/many whales today!'
B: $_1$IX {MISS/NOT-SEE} ___
'I {missed/did not see} ___.'
= the same 3, different 3, 5, 10, any number of whales/bits of whale(-meat)

(33) A: TODAY $_1$IX WANT GREEN CAR
'I want a green car today'
B: TEND WANT ___
'(You) usually want___.' = a green car, a red car, any color car.

There is one structure, however, associated with number marking where adjectives and numerals behave differently: the so-called quantifier-split in (34), originally discussed in Boster (1996).

(34) a. 'I want {three/a few} apples'
  i. APPLE $_1$IX WANT {THREE/FEW} ___
  ii. *{THREE/FEW} $_1$IX WANT APPLE ___
 b. 'I want green apples'
  i. *APPLE $_1$IX WANT GREEN
  ii. *GREEN $_1$IX WANT APPLE
 c. 'I want {three/a few} green apples'
  i. GREEN APPLE $_1$IX WANT {THREE/FEW}
  ii. *{THREE/FEW} APPLE $_1$IX WANT GREEN

What (34) immediately illustrates is that numerals, quantifiers, and adjectives should not be treated on par, at least in this construction. In fact, Boster (1996) argues for the expanded QP, the head of which is some type of quantity expression (Chierchia 2010, 2015), with an adnominal adjective being somewhere else. She offers the following structure for the quantified nominal: the quantifier heads a functional projection taking the NP as a complement (she also allows for the possibility of a higher projection – the DP – but presents no evidence for it); see (35).

(35)   [$_{QP}$ [$_Q$ THREE [$_{NP}$ [$_{N'}$ [$_{AP}$ GREEN [$_{N'}$ [$_N$ APPLE]]]]]]] (adpd. Boster 1996, fig. 6.1)

Boster (1996) draws a parallel between the licit cases in (34) and the English partitive in (36a–b) (the aforementioned movement to the left) but also pseudo-partitives (without discussing the issue) in (36c), with the difference between the partitive and the pseudo-partitive cases being definiteness of the NP.

(36)   a. The green apples, I want six of.
        b. (Out) of all of the soldiers (in the parade), I think three had fought in Vietnam but the rest held desk jobs at the Pentagon.
        c. {As for/of} green apples, I want six   (adpd. Boster 1996: 160, 199, 200)

The relevance of the partitive to the discussion at hand here is as follows. Rothstein (2011, et seq.) observes that numerical partitives (like (37a)) take only count nouns as complements while '*some of the*' partitives can take either mass or count nouns (37b); this is not particularly surprising considering the fact that numbers usually combine with count nouns only, and the quantifier *some* with either mass or count nouns.

(37)   a. I want three of the books/*blood
        b. I want some of the books/blood

The asymmetry in (37) offers a prediction: since (i) numerals and quantifiers behave (reasonably uniformly) as adjectives in ASL (see (32)–(33)), and (ii) so do mass and count nouns with various quantificational expressions, including numerals and quantifiers (see (6)), we expect both traditionally mass and traditionally count nouns to be licit in partitive environments – i.e. there should be no contrast of the sort we see in (37a). On the other hand, if there is difference between the two types of noun classes after all, this is precisely where it will show, despite the fact that up till now no difference has been observed. It turns out that this prediction is borne out: despite being able to undergo pluralization and directly combine with numerals and count quantifiers, mass nouns cannot occur in partitive(-like) constructions (38a); only count nouns can (38b).[7]

(38)   a. *BLOOD*i* IX$_1$ WANT {THREE / FEW} BLOOD*i*
        'I want three/a few bloods; *lit:* of blood, I want three/a few'

---

[7] The strikethrough indicates ellipsis.

b. APPLE*i* IX₁ WANT {THREE / FEW} ~~APPLE*i*~~
'I want three/a few apples; *lit:* of apples, I want three/a few'

In other words, (38) finally reveals the countability distinction in ASL. This distinction was brought out by movement. Boster (1996) shows that the movement in question is best described in terms of A-bar movement. Assuming that both such movement and the landing site are blind to CMD, we are left with the conclusion that BLOOD in (38a) and APPLE in (38b) must have originated in different positions: either BLOOD is above APPLE (and is ineligible for movement because it is too close, for example) or BLOOD is below APPLE (and is ineligible for movement to QP because it is too far). (39) below suggests the latter.

Recall the coordination diagnostic we had used in Section 2. It turns out that mass and count nouns cannot be conjoined (39c) unless the mass noun has a quantifier/numeral preceding it (39d).

(39)   a. GIVE-1 BOOK disj-shift PEN
          'Give me a book and a pen'
      b. GIVE-1 MUD disj-shift BLOOD
          'Give me mud and blood' *(says one member of the infantry to another)*
      c. *GIVE-1 [BLOOD disj-shift GUN]   ≈ (7)
          'Give me blood and a gun'
      d. GIVE-1 [BOOK disj-shift FEW / THREE BLOOD][8]
          'Give me a book and a few/three blood'

Here, this diagnostic strongly suggests that in (39), the constituent [BOOK] better resembles [THREE BLOOD] than [BLOOD] – i.e. it takes *a certain amount/quantity of blood* to make the same size constituent as *book* (as is, in fact, argued in Chierchia 2010); this finding yields a view of ASL CMD along the lines of (40).

(40)   a. [$_{NP1}$BOOK] & [$_{NP2}$THREE BLOOD]
      b. [$_{NP1}$N$_{count}$] & [$_{NP2}$ Quantity [N$_{mass}$]]

The pattern is productive and cuts across word classes: OIL, WATER, SAND, FLOUR, WOOD, SNOW, BUTTER, IMAGINATION, CHAIR, HOUSE, DISSERTATION, JACKET, GIRL, ADVICE behave along the same lines.

What is the element that encodes quantity then? It turns out that we have to return to classifiers after all (though not the East Asian variety, as has been shown in Section 3).

---

[8] That the issue is not simply a quantifier scoping over the nouns is evident from (i) below, which remains ungrammatical:
(i)   *GIVE-1 FEW/THREE [BOOK disj-shift BLOOD]
        'Give me few/three books and blood'

Though we have discovered that mass nouns are disallowed in partitive(-like) constructions, this ungrammaticality can be rescued by introducing into the structure an overt classifier, as in (41).[9]

(41) BLOOD$_i$ IX$_1$ WANT {THREE / FEW} CL^{container}+>+>+>
~~BLOOD~~$_i$ 'lit: Of blood, I want three/few CL'

As noted earlier, ASL is a language that allows argument omission, which, in turn, not only elides the argument but also ignores the quantifier/numeral (see (32)). Whatever the ultimate explanation for what happens,[10] the fact that the quantifier is 'ignored' predicts that it also cannot be stranded. However, considering the work that we had observed the CL do throughout and particularly in (41), we might now expect it to be able to rescue the ungrammatical stranded quantifier/numeral in ellipsis contexts, as in (42a). This is indeed what happens (42b) (see Bošković and Şener 2014 for Turkish).

(42) a. *MARY DROP {FEW/THREE}STUDENT, JOHN REGISTER {MANY/FIVE} ___ 'Mary dropped {a few/3} students, John registered {many/5}' (Koulidobrova 2017)
b. MARY DROP {FEW/THREE} STUDENT, JOHN REGISTER {MANY/FIVE} CL^{person}-+++.
'Mary dropped few students, John registered CL-+++'

The question of course is what type of classifier this is with respect to the aforementioned *quantity* (Chierchia 2010, et seq.). Recall a brief discussion of (30), which has illustrated that the nature of this classifier is to be a (size and shape) sortal in nature:

(43) JOHN MARY SEE SAND CL$^{tall-object}$ +++   = (30)
'John and Mary saw tall sand objects'
= John saw 5 sandcastles, Mary saw 5 {#sandboxes / ^{ok}sandcastles}
≠ John saw 1, Mary saw 5 / ≠ John saw 5, Mary saw 1
b. JOHN MARY SEE SAND CL^{box}+++
'John and Mary saw box-shaped sand objects'
= John saw 5 {#sand castles /^{ok}sandboxes}, Mary saw 5 sandboxes
≠ John saw 1, Mary saw 5 / ≠ John saw 5, Mary saw 1

Rothstein (2011) examines two types of classifier phrases the surface string of which is identical (in English): *two glasses of wine*. She illustrates that the phrase has two distinct readings – an individuating one (the number of ___) and

---

[9] This classifier is also optionally available for count nouns.
(i) APPLEi IX-1 WANT {THREE / FEW} CL$^{large-container}$+>+>+> ~~APPLE~~i 'I want three/a few apples; *lit*: of apples, I want three/a few'

[10] Koulidobrova (2017) argues that ellipsis targets an element that is both X^0 and XP simultaneously, which is the reason other phrases outside of bare NP (AP, etc.) are ineligible for it.

a measure one (the amount of __ , irrespective of the number of containers), which result from two distinct structures (Landman 2004; Rothstein 2010). The foregoing discussion has thus far demonstrated that while not an East-Asian style classifier, ASL CL is doing some non-trivial work disambiguating nominal structures; what we would like to know now is whether this work is ultimately individuating or measuring. Whatever we discover here will lead towards a better understanding of the *Quantity* in (40).

Consider (44)–(45), in which, according to the signer giving instructions (A), what matters is the number of containers, not the amount of wine. This is a striking contrast from the original [MANY WINE] or [MORE WINE] in (6d).[11]

(44)   Context: *A shelf with bottles of all sizes is next to the punch bowl*

                  _____y/n   _____y/n
   A: SEE WINE a-IX SEE CL$^{\text{cyllindr-container}}$ +++ PLEASE POUR-IN
      'Do you see the wine over there? See the containers? Please pour the wine in.'

      ___y/n _____ y/n _____ wh
   B: TALL SHORT WHICH
      'The tall ones? The short ones? Which ones?'

      _____neg   _____y/n
   A: NOT-KNOW SAY TWO FINISH MAYBE ONE$_a$ ONE$_b$
      'I don't know. I was told (to put in) two. That's it. Maybe one of each?'

      _____wh
   B: MANY
      'How much (wine)?'

      _____neg
   A: NOT-MATTER
      'Doesn't matter'

Even if '+++' is taken out of (43), the individuating reading is maintained:

(45)   Context: *A shelf with bottles of all sizes is next to the punch bowl*

                  _____y/n
   A: SEE WINE a-IX SEE CL$^{\text{cyllindr-container}}$ PLEASE POUR-IN
      'Do you see the wine over there? See the container? Please pour the wine in.'

      ___y/n _____ y/n _____ wh
   B: TALL SHORT WHICH
      'The big ones? The little ones? Which ones?'

      _____neg   _____y/n
   A: # NOT-KNOW SAY TWO FINISH MAYBE ONE$_a$ ONE$_b$
      'I don't know. I was told (to put in) two. That's it. Maybe one of each?'

---

[11] One thing that is clear in from (44) vis-à-vis (45) is this: while a noun without '+++' has either a singular or plural reading (Section 4), the same cannot be said for a noun with a CL. This offers yet another reason to examine nominal classifiers in conjunction with pluralization more thoroughly.

A': $\overline{\text{NOT-KNOW}}^{\text{neg}}$ CHOOSE ONE FINISH $\overline{\text{MAYBE TALL}}^{\text{y/n}}$
'I don't know. Choose one. Maybe the tall one?'

B: $\overline{\text{MANY}}^{\text{wh}}$
'How much (wine)?

A: $\overline{\text{NOT-MATTER}}^{\text{neg}}$
'Doesn't matter'

What (44)–(45) illustrate is that, in other words, $CL^{\text{cyllindr-container}}$ is not a measuring classifier; it is an individuating/counting one. When the same diagnostic is applied across the classifiers reported in this paper, the same result is obtained. This set of observations squares nicely with the prediction at the end of the last section – in order to rescue the violation resulting from the attempt to conjoin BOOK and BLOOD, what we need is a head that will house a *quantity*, which will surface as one of a quantifier, a cardinal, or a classifier, all of which will be of individuating, not measuring variety.

6. Conclusions and Directions

Let us recall the original set of goals for this exploration. Because simply looking at the list of properties ordinarily associated with the CMD (see (2)) did not yield an answer we had hoped for, we turned to the suggestion in Chierchia (2010) (in (4)), expecting the countability distinction to be found either in the number morpheme (for the obligatory number marking languages, *Type I*), the classifier (for the generalized classifier languages, *Type II*), or in the numeral (for the number neutral languages, *Type III*). It turns out that ASL is best defined as the number neutral language after all, if 'neutral' here ('general number' in Corbett 2000) means something other than 'obligatory' in a language like English, for example. So: in ASL, when the plural PL does not appear in a marked form, then it *really* is not marked. It is not a zero-exponent (as argued for DGS by Pfau and Steinbach 2016) or any other 'invisible' value. Instead, ASL is *really* number neutral. And as expected in such a language, we found the CMD in a (type of) numeral (construction)/quantificational expression. The conclusion we have now arrived at is this: a mass noun (at least) must be preceded by something which is present in the structure either covertly or overtly in order to reach the type of equivalence required for a conjunction. This 'something' is a head that offers information on quantity (40) – the intuition expressed in Deal (2017) and Chierchia (this volume) as [n+_]; movement of a noun past this head creates a violation (unless it is filled with an overt quantity expression, of which a classifier is one).

One issue that has been left untouched and deserves further examination is this: Chierchia (1998b, 2010, 2015, this volume) argues that (3)–(4) is reducible to the richness of the DP layer, within which the role or 'the little *n*' is to decide how each noun starts its life – as a kind or a property. ASL is a language without a definite article with nouns that have kinds and individual readings (Koulidobrova 2012, 2017; Koulidobrova and Lillo-Martin 2016). In such languages, nouns are expected to be able to type-shift (when contextually appropriate) and thus to be able to comfortably exist in anaphoric contexts (Despic 2019). However, while bare NPs are generally fine in anaphoric environments in ASL (as many examples here have indicated), kinds resist such contexts (as in (46)).

(46)   POSS-1 FAMILY GENERATION MAKE WINE. #DRINK AMAZING
'My family has been making wine for generation. (This) drink is amazing.'
#if DRINK refers to WINE = no anaphoric reference to a kind

I take (46) as preliminary evidence against any sort type of unconstrained type-shift from a kind, leading to a suggestion that nouns begin their lives as properties – i.e. ASL is not Yudja after all (Lima 2014b). Many questions remain for which no space could be allocated, including the contribution of partitive- (Rothstein 2010, et seq.) and portion- (Schlenker and Lamberton 2019) readings.

ACKNOWLEDGMENTS:
This work would be impossible without my Deaf and Coda colleagues, especially E. Crawford and J. L. Palmer.

Appendix: Notation and Methodology

Two types of data were used in this paper from two different language consultants. Both consultants are Deaf: one deaf-of-deaf (twenty years of language consulting), the other deaf-of-hearing (ASL acquisition prior to twelve months, two years of language consulting). Data collection occurred in two stages: elicitation and play-back. At neither of the sessions was written English employed (i.e. no written sentences were presented to the consultants).

In line with the general standard in linguistic research, the scale for the grammaticality judgments reported here is as follows: ACCEPT/FINE/ NATIVE ASL (√), AWKWARD/L2 ASL (?/??), and NOT-ASL(*). Recognizing the coarseness of the scale, but also for the sake of simplicity at this stage of the project, '??' and '*' cases were collapsed. In terms of the judgments our consultants accepted, we followed a procedure consistent with Mathewson (2004).

The elicitation stage consisted of three independent steps:

1. The Principal Investigator (PI) recounted the context (in ASL). The consultant was then asked to describe the situation using the target lexical items. The conversation was videotaped.
2. Elicited sentences were checked for a variety of strategies in production.
3. The consultant's decision was followed by a lengthy discussion of potential alternatives.

The play-back (of the signer's own production) part of data collection consisted of two steps as well, with close to a month in between. The first step was the grammaticality/truth-value judgment (sentences and individual signs), resulting in either *discard* [wrong, I made a mistake here] or *keep* [correct]. The second step of the play-back was context matching, done in the form of multiple choice: the consultant chose from the contexts in ##1 and 3 above (Other was always an option, but during the follow-up discussion with the PI, all items in this category were eventually reclassified as belonging to one of the original contexts). The primary consultant is Deaf-of-Hearing, but with the age of exposure to ASL before 1y.o. The final paradigm was additionally checked by four other signers: 2 Deaf-of-Deaf and 2 hearing children of deaf adults (professional interpreters). 90% of agreement was attained. Only items reaching 100% agreement are reported here.

Following conventions in sign-language linguistics, all ASL glosses are in SMALL CAPS. The line above the utterance indicates the spread/duration of the nonmanual marking (such as eyebrow raise) associated with either role-shifted material (RS), topicalization (t), or a question (wh- or y/n-). The letter/number separated with a dash (e.g. a-) indicates the area of signing space dedicated to a particular referent and, thus, the locus of the shift (e.g. '1' indicates the first person, the signer). Subindices $i, j, k, \ldots$ indicate coreference. Addition of '+' indicates repetition/production of the sign multiple times, sometimes in the same area (as in '+++') or along a particular trajectory, with or without punctuated movement ('>+>+' and '>>>') – a convention employed elsewhere in the literature (e.g. Pfau and Steinbach 2006, Schlenker and Lamberton 2019).

Compositional Analyses and Theoretical Issues

10 Ontology, Number Agreement, and the Count–Mass Distinction

Alan Bale

1. Introduction

In this chapter, I discuss how syntactic and semantic theories of number interact with different accounts of the count–mass distinction. Such a discussion is vital to figuring out the relationship between number features and countability (an issue central to the topic discussed by Rothstein, this volume, Chapter 3) as well as theoretical explanations of why *furniture*-like nouns (aka, object mass nouns) cannot combine with numerals (an issue central to the topic discussed by Chierchia, this volume, Chapter 2). I argue that certain accounts of number marking (e.g., Sauerland 2003) "force one's hand" in terms of the semantic representation of mass and count noun phrases (NPs). Such theories – which I label "high number" theories – only work if either (i) the denotations of mass NPs are necessarily disjoint from the denotations of count NPs (see Link 1983; Lønning 1987; Barker 1998) or (ii) mass NPs are assigned a different type than count NPs (see Rothstein 2010). I discuss evidence in support of these "high number" theories and thus, ultimately, evidence that favours certain accounts of the count–mass distinction.[1]

The chapter is organized as follows. In Section 2, I discuss three types of semantic analyses of the count–mass distinction. One maintains two disjoint domains – one mass, the other count. Another maintains a single domain but assigns different semantic types to mass and count NPs respectively. A third maintains a single domain and a single type for all NPs but accounts for distributional differences by appealing to either syntactic features or certain denotational characteristics (join-closure, atomicity, etc.). Having divided

---

I would like to thank September Cowley, Brendan Gillon, and Jeff Pelletier for comments on earlier drafts of this paper, as well as all the participants in the conference "The Count–Mass Distinction: A Linguistic Misunderstanding?" held in Bochum in May 2018. This paper would not be possible without a grant from the Social Sciences and Humanities Research Council of Canada (SSHRC) Insight Grant #435-2016-1376.

[1] The original problem that is central to this chapter was discussed in section 3 of Bale (forthcoming). This paper expands significantly on this problem, not only presenting new data but also advancing new analyses.

theories into these three broad categories, I next turn my attention to number. In Section 3, I discuss two prominent treatments of number marking: "high number" theories and "low number" theories. In "high number" theories (e.g. Sauerland 2003), number features are sister to the DP and do not occur within the NP. In "low number" theories (e.g. Bennett 1974), number features are contained within the NP. The syntactic options (high or low) critically interact with the choice of semantic ontology for the count–mass distinction. "High number" theories are incompatible with an ontology where the denotations of mass nouns and count nouns are taken from the same domain and are of the same type ("single domain, single type" theories). Thus, if we know that "high number" theories are on the right track, then we also know that the denotations of mass and count NPs must be taken from different domains or be of different types. In Section 4, I present evidence in favour of "high number" theories. Such evidence critically hinges on how the choice of number marking influences meaning. In particular, I discuss competition effects as well as variable agreement with coordinated DPs (both conjunctions and disjunctions). "High number" theories can account for these semantic effects. It is not obvious how "low number" theories would be able to handle these facts.

2. Domains and Denotations

Different theoretical accounts of the count–mass distinction hypothesize different types of relationships between NPs and their denotations. Broadly speaking, there are three main approaches. One approach assumes that there are two separate (disjoint) domains, another that there are two different semantic types, while a third assumes that there is a single domain and type for all nominal terms.[2] In this section, I discuss all three approaches. For reasons of time and space, I do not discuss all the weaknesses and advantages of each approach. Rather, I concentrate on the consequences of each theory in terms of how the count–mass distinction at the NP level influences the semantic values at the DP level.

---

[2] For the sake of simplicity, I will not provide a thorough discussion of kind interpretations in this chapter. This is not meant to imply that such interpretations are not important; any adequate theory of the count–mass distinction must account for the fact that both mass nouns and plural count nouns can be used to refer to and talk about kinds. However, both types of terms can also be used to talk about the entities that instantiate these kinds. Any adequate theory of kind readings ends up providing functions that *lift* predicates into a kind interpretation and *lower* kinds to predicate interpretations (see the discussions in Krifka 1995; Chierchia 1998a, 1998b; Rothstein 2010; among others). This section will focus on the nature of these *lowered*, predicate interpretations.

2.1. Disjoint Domains

Theories such as Link's (1983) hypothesize two separate domains of interpretation (see also Lønning 1987; Barker 1998). One domain – the count domain – is a Boolean lattice ordered by the sub-group (or sub-set) relation, while the other – the mass domain – is a semi-lattice ordered by the part-of (or sub-aggregate) relation. The count domain has a set of atoms – the individuals in the domain – and the entire domain can be generated from these atoms via the group formation operator. The mass domain doesn't necessarily have any such atoms. Critically, the two domains are completely disjoint.[3]

The strength of a disjoint–domain theory is that it can explain certain distributional characteristics of mass and count nouns by appealing to semantic ontology – numeral modification and other types of count quantifiers rely on the partial ordering provided in the count domain and are undefined with respect to elements and denotations taken from the mass domain (hence *[those two datapoints]* is a well-defined phrase since the denotation of *datapoints* is taken from the count domain, but *[those two information(s)]* is not since the denotation of *information* is taken from the mass domain). However, as discussed by Bunt (1979, 1985), B. Gillon (1992), Chierchia (1998a), as well as Bale and Barner (2009), the disjoint domain theory is forced to make some unintuitive claims with respect to mass and count NPs when they are used to talk about the same types of entities. For example, in many contexts, the NPs *[clothing in the closet]*, *[shirts and dresses in the closet]*, and *[items of clothing in the closet]* are used to refer to and talk about the same thing, even though one NP is mass and the other two count, as shown in (1).

(1)   a. I don't have much/*many clothing in the closet.
        b. I don't have many/*much shirts and dresses in the closet.
        c. I don't have many/*much items of clothing in the closet.

A disjoint domain theory is forced to hypothesize that ⟦*clothing in the closet*⟧ in (1a) does not overlap with ⟦*shirts and dresses in the closet*⟧ in (1b) and ⟦*items of clothing in the closet*⟧ in (1c). Yet, once one adopts such an assumption, special operations and coercion operators are needed to explain the coherent (almost analytic) sentences in (2).

(2)   a. Those items of clothing in the closet are clothing.
        b. Those shirts and dresses in the closet are clothing.

---

[3] However, there is a homomorphic map from entities in the count domain to the those in the mass domain that preserves their relative ordering (i.e., for any elements x and y in the count domain, if x is a subgroup of y, then $\pi(x)$ is a part-of $\pi(y)$ where π is the map from the elements in the count domain to elements in the mass domain).

The simplest way to analyse the sentences in (2) is to assume that the referent of ⟦*those items of clothing in the closet*⟧ and ⟦*those shirts and dresses in the closet*⟧ are members of the denotation associated with ⟦*clothing*⟧. However, such an analysis would need to assume that ⟦*items of clothing*⟧, ⟦*shirts and dresses*⟧, and ⟦*clothing*⟧ at least overlap in their denotations.[4]

In a similar vein, the disjoint domain theory would need coercion operators to explain the nearly synonymous identity statements in (6).[5]

(6)   a.   The shirts and dresses you found in the closet this morning might be the clothing I forgot to give to Goodwill last week.
           b.   The clothing I forgot to give away to Goodwill last week might be the shirts and dresses you found in the closet this morning.

Once again, the simplest way to analyse the statements in (6) would involve permitting the possibility that the referent of ⟦*the shirts and dresses you found in the closet this morning*⟧ be identical to the referent of ⟦*the clothing I forgot to give to Goodwill last week*⟧ – an identity that would be impossible under the disjoint-domain approach. In summary, a theory like Link's requires us to assume that the connection between ⟦*the clothing ...*⟧ and ⟦*the shirts and dresses ...*⟧ is similar to the connection between ⟦*the gold in the ring*⟧ and ⟦*the (pure-gold) ring*⟧. Although the referents might occupy the same time–space location, they are still not identical ontologically speaking.[6]

---

[4] The reader might be wondering about the lack of grammaticality of the sentences in (3).

(3)   a.   * That clothing in the closet is shirts and dresses.
           b.   * That clothing in the closet are shirts and dresses.

However, this ungrammaticality is most likely due to problems with number agreement. In general, singular subjects cannot be predicated by a plural predicate. For example, the sentences in (4) are ungrammatical. But this cannot be due to the denotation of plurals prohibiting singular referents as the sentence in (5) is perfectly grammatical in a context where pluralia tantum noun *those scissors* refers to a single object.

(4)   a.   * That boy is boys.
           b.   * That boy are boys.

(5)   Those scissors that you are holding are scissors.

[5] Note the use of the modal in the examples in (6). This is done to avoid number-mismatch issues. In present and past tense, "DP be DP" statements require the DPs to match in number but in modal statements this issue can be avoided.

[6] One way of implementing this distinction would be to have the count domain consist of only sets ordered by the subset relation whereas the mass domain would only contain aggregates ordered by the subaggregate relation. In such a system, the denotation of ⟦*the dresses and shirts*⟧ would be a set (e.g., $\{a, b, c, d\}$, where a, b, c, and d are the individual dresses and shirts), while the denotation of ⟦*the clothing*⟧ would be an aggregate (e.g. the entity $abcd$). Count quantifiers would rely on counting set membership and thus would be undefined for members of the mass domain. This is essentially a simplified version of the system implemented by Lønning (1987).

2.2. Type Theory

Rothstein (2010) outlines an interesting alternative to the disjoint-domain approach. She proposes that the referents of certain DPs can indeed be the same despite having different categories of NPs (such as ⟦*those shirts and dresses* ... ⟧ and ⟦*that clothing* ... ⟧); however, to capture the different distributional patterns of mass and count NPs (e.g. *[several shirts and dresses]* vs. **[several clothing(s)]*), she also proposes that these two nouns differ in semantic type. Mass nouns are of type $\langle e, t \rangle$. (Note, for the sake of simplicity, I will not use intensional typing, e.g., $\langle e, \langle s, t \rangle \rangle$ or $\langle s, \langle e, t \rangle \rangle$. The issue of intensions is orthogonal to our present concerns.) As a result, all mass nouns are mapped to sets of entities (or equivalently, functions that are true of certain entities). In contrast, count nouns are associated not just with a set of entities, but also with a counting context.

This type of theory emphasizes that counting can sometimes be context sensitive. As Rothstein notes, it is not always straightforward what counts as *one* vs. *two* in any given situation. For example, what counts as *one quantity of sugar* versus *two quantities of sugar* depends on a contextually salient way to package and distribute the sugar. Similarly, what counts as *one fence* versus *two* can depend on how the fence or fences were built and how they are configured with respect to property lines. Similar considerations hold for *one community* versus *two*, *one project* versus *two*, etc.

To account for this type of context sensitivity, Rothstein (2010) hypothesizes that members of a count-NP denotation are an ordered pair whose first member is an entity of type e and whose second member is a counting context. If we symbolize counting contexts as type c, then we can represent the members of the count domain as type $e \times c$. Thus, count nouns are of type $\langle e \times c, t \rangle$ and are mapped to a set of ordered pairs. The counting context tells us which entities count as being *one* in the context of evaluation, from which it can be derived which entities count as *two*, *three*, etc. If the count domain isn't empty, then it necessarily has minimal parts, namely a set of ordered pairs that consist of a counting context and an entity that counts as *one* in that context.

The advantage of this type of system over one like Link's is that one can still give a similar account of the distributional differences between mass and count NPs without hypothesizing that the referents of DPs derived from mass nouns are necessarily different from those derived from count nouns. For example, let's suppose that ⟦*several*⟧ is a function of type $\langle \langle e \times c, t \rangle, \langle \langle e, t \rangle, t \rangle \rangle$, i.e., a function that takes an NP of type $\langle e \times c, t \rangle$ as an input and yields a generalized quantifier. Since only count NPs are of type $\langle e \times c, t \rangle$, it follows that trying to combine ⟦*several*⟧ with a mass NP like *clothing* would yield a type mismatch. However, despite the type differences, in certain contexts the potential referents of a mass NP like *[clothing]* and a count NP like *[shirts and dresses]* or [items of clothing] could be identical. For example, let's suppose that a and b are shirts whereas d and e are dresses, and that these are the only items of clothing in a given counting context c_1. In such a context, the denotation of ⟦clothing⟧ would be $\{a,b,d,e,ab,ad,ae,bd,be,de,abd,abe,ade,bde,abde\}$ and the referent of ⟦the clothing⟧ would be $abde$. In the same context, the denotation of ⟦shirts and dresses⟧ would be $\{\langle a,c_1\rangle, \langle b,c_1\rangle, \langle d,c_1\rangle, \langle e,c_1\rangle, \langle ab,c_1\rangle, \langle ad,c_1\rangle, \langle ae,c_1\rangle, \langle bd,c_1\rangle, \langle be,c_1\rangle, \langle de,c_1\rangle, \langle abd,c_1\rangle, \langle abe,c_1\rangle, \langle ade,c_1\rangle, \langle bde,c_1\rangle, \langle abde,c_1\rangle\}$ and the referent of ⟦the shirts and dresses⟧ would be $\langle abde,c_1\rangle$. The only contrast between the mass and count NP/DP is the presence of a counting context. Critically, although there is no referential difference between mass and count DPs, there is still a type difference.

2.3. Single Domain, Single Type

Other approaches to the count–mass distinction assume that denotations of all NPs, whether they are mass or count, are taken from the same general domain (for example, see B. Gillon 1992; Krifka 1995; Chierchia 1998a; Bale and Barner 2009; Chierchia 2010; among others). According to these types of theories, all NPs, regardless of their subcategorization, have the same semantic type (e.g., type $\langle e,t\rangle$), the only difference being that count NPs require that their denotations contain atomic minimal parts whereas mass NPs are underspecified in this respect.[7]

An advantage of these types of theories is not only that they permit the denotations of mass NPs and count NPs to overlap, but they also permit DPs that are derived from mass and count nouns to have identical semantic values (e.g., in certain contexts, ⟦the clothing⟧ = ⟦the shirts and dresses⟧). However, since all NPs are of the same type and are subsets of the same general domain, the distributional characteristics of quantifiers cannot be characterized in terms of either type theory or disjoint domains.

Usually, two other explanations are employed to account for quantifier distribution. One explanation hypothesizes that mass and count NPs have different syntactic features. According to this type of explanation, the combination of certain quantifiers with NPs is mediated by the presence or absence of these formal features (rather than semantic types or semantic domains). For example, in such a theory, the quantifier *each* would select for NPs that have a

---

[7] Theories differ in terms of what it means to be an "atomic minimal part". For example, Chierchia (1998a) defines "atoms" as being non-vague, minimal parts (i.e., minimal parts in all possible worlds where such atoms exist), whereas the minimal parts of certain mass nouns are only vaguely determined (i.e., not minimal with respect to all possible worlds). In contrast, Bale and Barner (2009) define "atoms" as being non-overlapping minimal parts relative to a certain NP denotation (i.e., they need not be "minimal parts" in the global domain).

count feature (let's call it + CT). Mass-NPs like *[information]* don't have this feature while count-NPs like *[datapoint]* do. Thus, **[each information]* is not a well-formed DP but *[each datapoint]* is. Hence, the grammatical status of quantifier–NP parings is completely determined by syntax.

Another type of explanation relies on a more semantic approach to subcategorization. For example, Chierchia (1998a) hypothesizes that quantifiers presuppose that the denotations of their NP complements have certain semantic characteristics, such as being closed under join (plural and mass NPs), being a set containing only atoms (singular count NPs), or being a closed set generated by a set containing atoms (plural count NPs). The quantifier *each* selects for a denotation that contains only atoms – ⟦*datapoint*⟧ satisfies this presupposition (in all possible worlds) whereas ⟦*information*⟧ does not. Critically, in either explanation, the distribution of quantifiers is determined by a property that is local to the NP and does not rely on a global distinction such as types or disjoint domains. Furthermore, these local differences do not result in a contrast between mass and count at the DP level.

3. Number Marking

The last section discussed how different theories of count–mass ontologies make different predictions about the nature of NPs and DPs. Two of the theories assign distinct semantic values for mass and count NPs/DPs. The third theory hypothesizes that all NPs and (definite) DPs are of the same type (e.g., type $\langle e, t \rangle$ for NPs and type e for definite DPs). Furthermore, all denotational and referential values are taken from the same domain. Critically, this third theory leaves open the possibility that some mass and count NPs might have overlapping (or identical) values and that some mass and count DPs are semantically identical. These three theories make different predictions in terms of the behaviour of partitive phrases (see Barker 1998; Rothstein 2010, and references therein) as well as patterns of distributivity (see B. Gillon 1992; Schwarzschild 1996, and references therein). I will put these issues aside for now and just concentrate on how these theories interact with various hypotheses concerning number features – in particular singular and plural.

In this section, I group various theories into two categories, using the labels "low number" and "high number" as a crude way of describing what these theories have in common. The two categories differ from each other both in terms of the syntactic position of number features (whether they appear adjoined to the NP or not) and the semantic effect of such features (presuppositions on referents/denotations versus operations that restrict or augment nominal denotations). Although there are important differences within each group, this bipartite grouping roughly characterizes certain consequences number marking has in terms of the ontological characterization of mass and count nouns. In particular, "high number" theories require either an ontological or type-theoretical distinction between mass and count NPs and DPs, whereas "low number" theories do not. Thus, determining the right theory of number marking could potentially help us decide between different ways of representing the count–mass distinction.

3.1. Low Number Theories

One approach to number features is partly motivated by maintaining a close connection between overt plural morphology and the interpretation of number (see the discussions in Bennett 1974; Verkuyl 1981; Link 1983; Chierchia 1998a; Rothstein 2010; among others). For example, consider the representation of the definite DPs *the shirt* and *the shirts* in (7).

(7) **"Low Number" Theories**
 a. Potential singular DP structures

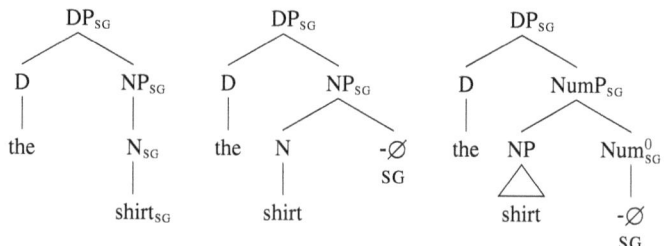

 b. Potential plural DP structures

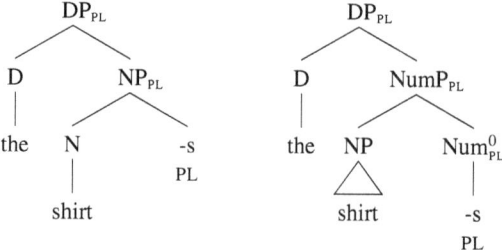

Various possible syntactic representations of singular and plural marking are sketched out in (7a) and (7b) respectively. The syntactic labels of the features or phrases matter little here (i.e., PL might be [+ AUGMENTED], [− MINIMAL], [+ AUGMENTED, − ATOMIC], [− MINIMAL, − ATOMIC], etc. − SG might be [− AUGMENTED], [+ MINIMAL], [− AUGMENTED, + ATOMIC], [+ MINIMAL, + ATOMIC], etc. − see the discussions in Harbour 2003; 2007; 2014). Independent of which features and labels are used, theories are classified as being "low number" if either (i) lexical items are stored as being inherently singular with plural morphology optionally combining with this singular noun/NP or (ii) plural and singular number features (or feature-bundles) are adjoined either within the NP or directly to the NP via some kind of number marking head (Num^0 above). The subscripts in the trees of (7) can either be interpreted as being purely descriptive (i.e. such subscripts do not reflect a difference in terms of a syntactic representation) or as representing the effects of feature percolation (i.e. the singular/plural feature or feature bundle percolates to various XP levels). In these "low number" theories, an auxiliary agrees with the "number" of the DP either by probing within the DP for number features or directly agreeing with the DP itself (given a sufficient theory of feature percolation). The choice between these two approaches matters little in terms of the main concern of this chapter. A more important aspect of this analysis is how number is interpreted and how it affects the denotational value of the NP and the referential value of the DP.

The interpretation of the number features depends on how the bare noun is interpreted. If the bare noun denotes a set of atoms (e.g. $[\![shirt]\!] = \{a, b, c\}$, where a, b, and c are the individual shirts), then the plural morpheme is usually interpreted as a function that maps an atomic set to its closure under the group formation (i.e. $[\![\text{PL}]\!] = * = \lambda P.\{x : x = \cup Q$ for some $Q \subseteq P\}$, where $\cup$ is the generalized join operator; e.g., $\{a, b, c\} \mapsto \{a, b, c, ab, ac, bc, abc\}$).[8] The singular feature in contrast would have no effect (i.e., it would be an identity function). Alternatively, if the bare noun denotes a set that contains all the atoms and the pluralities that can be formed from these atoms (e.g. $[\![shirt]\!] = \{a, b, c, ab, ac, bc, abc\}$ where a, b, and c are the individual shirts), then the singular features would restrict the noun to its atoms (i.e. $[\![\text{SG}]\!] = \lambda P.\{x:$ ATOM(x) & $x \in P\}$; e.g. $\{a, b, c, ab, ac, bc, abc\} \mapsto \{a, b, c\}$), whereas the plural features would not affect the noun.[9]

The interaction between number and mass NPs varies slightly between different versions of the "low number" theories. For example, Chierchia (2010) has the singular feature interpreted as a function that applies to both count and mass NPs. Simplifying somewhat, Chierchia's (2010) function basically presupposes that its complement has "stable units of one", where "stable units of one" are the atoms in count NPs and the supremum in mass NPs (i.e., the element that is equal to the generalized join of all the entities within the denotation of the mass NP). For Chierchia, count NPs like *shirt* denote a set of atoms, whereas mass NPs like

---

[8] Alternatively, the plural feature could augment the singular denotation to a set that only contains pluralities that can be formed from the members of the atomic set (i.e. $[\![\text{PL}]\!] = \oplus = \lambda P.*P - P$; e.g. $\{a, b, c\} \mapsto \{ab, ac, bc, abc\}$).

[9] Alternatively, the plural feature could restrict it to its non-atomic members (i.e. $[\![\text{PL}]\!] = \lambda P.\{x : x \in P$ & $\neg_{\text{ATOM}}(x)\}$; e.g. $\{a, b, c, ab, ac, bc, abc\} \mapsto \{ab, ac, bc, abc\}$). For a discussion of some of the cross-linguistic differences between restriction and augmentation, see the discussions in Bale, Gagnon, and Khanjian (2011); Harbour (2003, 2007, 2014).

246 *Alan Bale*

information denote a set containing only the supremum of all the entities that count as information. In contrast, plural count NPs like *shirts* denote a set that not only contains items of shirts but also all the pluralities that can be formed from these items. Thus, ⟦SG⟧ (⟦*shirt*⟧) is well defined and yields ⟦*shirt*⟧; ⟦SG⟧ (⟦*information*⟧) is also well defined and yields ⟦*information*⟧, but ⟦SG⟧ (⟦*shirts*⟧) is not well defined.

(8)   POTENTIAL MASS DP STRUCTURES

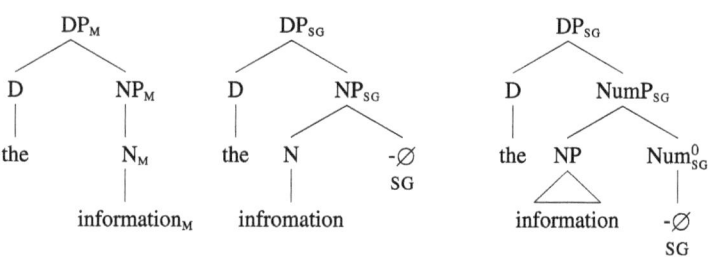

In other "low number" theories (including Chierchia 1998a), the singular feature is either non-existent or doesn't place any restrictions on an NP (i.e., ⟦SG⟧ is the identity function). Rather, what distinguishes mass NPs from singular count NPs is that mass NPs are incompatible with plural morphology (i.e., ⟦PL⟧ (⟦*information*⟧) is undefined either because plural and mass NPs are syntactically incompatible – in other words, plural selects for singular count NPs – or because ⟦PL⟧ is a function that cannot combine with NPs that are already closed under join).[10]

No matter which "low number" theory one prefers, the consequences in terms of semantic ontology are the same. "Low number" theories function well with either a disjoint-domain ontology or an analysis that assigns different types to mass and count NPs. However, "low number" theories are also compatible with ontologies where all NPs are of the same type and have denotations that are subsets of one general domain. In the latter type of ontology, restrictions on what the plural morpheme can apply to, as well as restrictions on the distribution of certain quantifiers, can be locally determined. One could appeal to the syntactic features of the NP – e.g., plural morphemes select for NPs that have the features [+CT, −PL], plural count quantifiers such as *several* select for NPs that have the features [+CT, +PL], etc. Alternatively,

---

[10] Chierchia (1998a) defines the pluralization operator as λP. $*P - P$ and hence application to an NP that is closed under join will necessarily yield an empty denotation. As a result, sentences that have the plural morpheme in combination with a mass NP will either be trivially true or trivially false. An alternative to Chierchia's analysis would be to make the plural function undefined for arguments that are already closed under join in much the same way as Chierchia treats quantifiers that can only combine with singular count NPs.

one could appeal to local denotational properties of the NPs to explain their distribution – e.g., the plural morpheme, as well as certain quantifiers, can only combine with NPs whose denotations contain only disjoint minimal parts, other quantifiers can only combine with denotations that are closed under join, and still others require that the denotations be closed under join but generated from a set of disjoint minimal parts, etc. No matter which strategy is employed, one can divorce the explanation of the distribution of mass and count NPs from ontological or type-theoretical considerations.

3.2. High Number Theories

In contrast to the "low number" theories, Sauerland (2003) proposes that number features are sister to the DP (see also Bale 2014; Sauerland, Anderssen, and Yatsushiro 2005). The so-called plural morpheme is the result of an agreement process, much like the agreement affixes that sometimes appear on verbs and auxiliaries. In this type of theory, the phrases *the shirt*, *the information*, and *the shirts* would have the syntactic representations in (9).

(9) HIGH NUMBER MARKING
    a. POTENTIAL SINGULAR DP STRUCTURES (MASS OR COUNT)

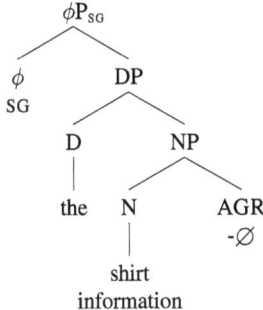

    b. POTENTIAL PLURAL DP STRUCTURES

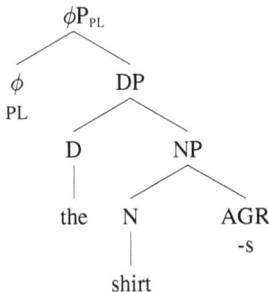

At first blush, it might seem counterintuitive to interpret number marking on the noun as mere agreement. However, it should be kept in mind that number agreement morphemes within the DP are well attested cross-linguistically, especially on adjectives, numeral modifiers, and determiners. In fact, often the only overtly expressed number morphemes are those that appear on the determiners and/or modifiers (e.g. French). Thus, hypothesizing that the so-called plural marker (e.g. -s in English) is just one more agreement affix is not far-fetched.

In Sauerland's (2003) theory, all number features are essentially interpreted as an identity function (i.e. they map any argument onto itself and thus $\llbracket \phi_{SG/PL} \rrbracket$ ($\llbracket DP \rrbracket$) = $\llbracket DP \rrbracket$). However, number features have different effects due to certain preconditions they impose on the DP. For example, $\llbracket \phi_{SG} \rrbracket$ ($\llbracket DP \rrbracket$) is defined if and only if the $\llbracket DP \rrbracket$ is an atomic minimal part or a "mass". For now, I am deliberately leaving the definition of what it means to be "atomic" or "mass" unspecified. I mention it only as a stand-in for the idea that singular morphology can be used with only certain kinds of DPs. In contrast, $\llbracket \phi_{PL} \rrbracket$ ($\llbracket DP \rrbracket$) is always defined. However, due to the principle of maximizing presupposition, MAXIMIZE PRESUPPOSITION (Heim 1991), use of the plural feature often implies that the singular feature could not be used and that the $\llbracket DP \rrbracket$ is hence not an atomic minimal part nor a "mass".

As should be obvious to the reader, a critical part of this theory involves spelling out what it means for a referent to be "mass" or "atomic". This would be easy enough to do given either disjoint domains or an appropriate type-theory. Consider the definitions of $\llbracket \phi_{SG} \rrbracket$ in (10), where D_C is the count domain, $ATOM_{D_C}$ is the set of minimal parts in the count domain, and D_M is the mass domain.

(10) a. DISJOINT DOMAIN THEORY:
$\llbracket \phi_{SG} \rrbracket$ ($\llbracket DP \rrbracket$) is defined if and only if either $\llbracket DP \rrbracket \in ATOM_{DC}$ or $\llbracket DP \rrbracket \in D_M$. When defined, $\llbracket \phi_{SG} \rrbracket$ ($\llbracket DP \rrbracket$) = $\llbracket DP \rrbracket$.
   b. TYPE THEORY:
$\llbracket \phi_{SG} \rrbracket$ ($\llbracket DP \rrbracket$) is defined if and only if either $\llbracket DP \rrbracket = \langle x, c \rangle$ (i.e., is of type $e \times c$) and x counts as 1 in context c, or $\llbracket DP \rrbracket$ is of type e. When defined, $\llbracket \phi_{SG} \rrbracket$ ($\llbracket DP \rrbracket$) = $\llbracket DP \rrbracket$.[11]

In the disjoint domain theory, an "atom" is a minimal part in the count domain whereas a "mass" is any member of the mass domain. In Rothstein's (2010) type theory, an "atom" is an element of type $e \times c$ where the first member of

---

[11] Note, this definition cheats a little if one wants to maintain that each interpretation can only be of one type. Keeping to a strict type-theory, the singular function would have to be associated with two different functions – an identity function of type $\langle e, e \rangle$ and another of type $\langle e \times c, e \times c \rangle$.

the ordered pair counts as being "one" in the context specified by the second member of the ordered pair. In contrast, a "mass" is any entity of type *e*.

With an ontology that only has one domain where definite DPs are all of type *e*, it becomes very difficult to define "mass" and "atomic" in a way that captures the empirical facts. To see why, let's reconsider the DP *[the clothing in the closet]* and the count DP *[the shirts and dresses in the closet]*, discussed in Section 2. When appearing in the subject position, these DPs have opposite agreement patterns. Note that we are using a modifier that generally resists a kind interpretation (i.e., *in the closet*) and a predicate that applies to concrete individuals rather than kinds (i.e., *unexpectedly dirty*) in order to suppress the kind interpretation. We want to assess the DPs when they are being used to refer to specific entities.

(11) a. The clothing in the closet **was** unexpectedly dirty.
b. *The clothing(s) in the closet **were** unexpectedly dirty.

(12) a. The shirts and dresses in the closet **were** unexpectedly dirty.
b. *The shirts and dresses in the closet **was** unexpectedly dirty.

If the two DPs refer to the same entity – namely the collection of shirts and dresses in the closet, then the different patterns of agreement would be completely unexpected. As shown in (13b), in the high-number theory, the two DPs would be sister to the φ-head, and the semantic constraints imposed by the features in that head should affect each DP in the exact same way.

(13) Where the aggregate *abdef* is the group containing all the shirts and dresses in the closet (which happens to be the only clothing in the closet):

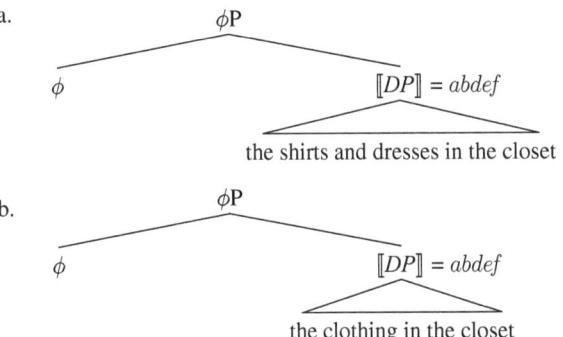

Whatever features are natural for (13a) should also be natural for (13b) and vice versa. The semantic details shouldn't matter since, in terms of their referent, the two DPs are identical.

Within the confines of a "high number" theory, the only way to explain how these two DPs result in completely opposite agreement patterns is to hypothesize that they in fact do not refer to the same thing. Such a hypothesis falls out as a natural consequence of theories that maintain two separate domains. In such an ontology, ⟦*the clothing in the closet*⟧ is necessarily distinct from ⟦*the shirts and dresses in the closet*⟧, even if the two referents are the same in terms of their existence in time and space. (Recall, objects can be distinguished from the substances that make up the objects despite occupying the same time-space coordinates – e.g. *the pure-gold ring* vs. *the gold in the ring*. Also, one could hypothesize a formal difference where ⟦*the shirts and dresses* ... ⟧ = $\{a, b, d, e, f\}$ but ⟦*the clothing* ... ⟧ = $abdef$. One value is a set while the other is an aggregate – see Lønning 1987.) Likewise, in Rothstein's (2010) type theory, the two values of the two DPs are necessarily distinct – ⟦*the clothing* ... ⟧ = $abdef$ whereas ⟦*the shirts and dresses* ... ⟧ = $\langle abdef, c_1 \rangle$, where c_1 is the counting context where each shirt and dress counts as "one".

It is important to note that the same consequences hold for any theory that maintains the basic semantic analysis proposed by Sauerland (2003) – i.e., presuppositions plus competition – regardless of its syntactic position. For example, in a system similar to Sauerland's, the number features could occupy a functional head in the DP that modifies the nominal predicate at some point in the derivation rather than the DP referent (as in Ritter 1991; Deal 2017; among others). In such a theory, one could still maintain the basics of Sauerland's theory by applying the preconditions of the singular function in a point-wise fashion – i.e., ⟦ϕ_{SG}⟧ (X) is defined when either each member of X is an "atom" or each member is a "mass". Once again, this is easy enough to do with the appropriate ontology or type theory, as shown in (14).

(14)   a.   DISJOINT DOMAIN THEORY:
           ⟦ϕ_{SG}⟧ (⟦*NP*⟧) is defined if and only if either ⟦*NP*⟧ $\subseteq$ ATOM$_{D_C}$ or ⟦*NP*⟧ $\subseteq D_M$. When defined, ⟦ϕ_{SG}⟧ (⟦*NP*⟧) = ⟦*NP*⟧.
      b.   TYPE THEORY:
           ⟦ϕ_{SG}⟧ (⟦*NP*⟧) is defined if and only if either (i) ⟦*NP*⟧ is of type $\langle e \times c, t \rangle$ and for each member $\langle x, c \rangle \in$ ⟦*NP*⟧, x counts as 1 in context c, or (ii) ⟦*NP*⟧ is of type $\langle e, t \rangle$. When defined, ⟦ϕ_{SG}⟧ (⟦*NP*⟧) = ⟦*NP*⟧.[12]

However, defining which entities are "atoms" or "mass" becomes complicated in a theory that has a single domain with a single type for NPs, especially when we assume that each member of ⟦*items of clothing in the closet*⟧ is also a member of ⟦*clothing in the closet*⟧ (and vice versa).

---

[12] Once again, this definition cheats a little if one wants to maintain that each interpretation can only be of one type. Keeping to a strict type-theory, the singular function would have to be associated with two different functions – an identity function of type $\langle \langle e, t \rangle, \langle e, t \rangle \rangle$ and another of type $\langle \langle e \times c, t \rangle, \langle e \times c, t \rangle \rangle$.

4. The Argument for "High Number" Theories

Given the ontological and type theoretical consequences of "high number" theories, it is vital to review the evidence for this type of analysis. For time and space reasons, I only highlight some of the main arguments for adopting such a treatment of number. Ideally, a fuller assessment would include counterbalancing these arguments with the cross-linguistic evidence in favour of "low number" theories. I will not do so in this chapter. Rather, the goal of this section is more modest. It discusses the strength of "high number" theories in order to establish that there are empirical facts and generalizations that need to be carefully considered and addressed, especially if one wants to maintain a "single domain, single type" treatment of the count–mass distinction. Below I outline three main sets of facts: (i) evidence that singular and plural are in competition with one another; (ii) evidence for agreement without overt number marking on the associated subject; and (iii) evidence for variable agreement with disjoint subjects.

4.1. Competition

One of the central aspects of Sauerland's (2003) interpretation of plural morphology involves competition – plural number is semantically vacuous and only yields a plural count interpretation when it is in competition with the singular (through MAXIMIZE PRESUPPOSITION).[13] However, in certain contexts, singular NPs and DPs are not viable competitors. Thus, in such contexts, Sauerland predicts plural number will be compatible with both a singular and mass interpretation.

Evidence in support of this prediction comes from the behaviour of pluralia tantum nouns such as *scissors* and *earnings*. In many grammatical environments, such nouns require plural marking. For example, (15a) is a perfectly acceptable sentence whereas (15b) is not. Similarly, (16a) sounds natural (where *earnings* is being used to talk about John's income) whereas (16b) can only have an awkward reading, where *earning* is being used to talk about an event rather than John's income.

(15) a. The scissors in the drawer are broken.
 b. * The scissor in the drawer is broken.

(16) a. John did not report his earnings to the IRS.
 b. ? John did not report his earning to the IRS.

---

[13] One might wonder about the effect of downward entailing contexts on such competition. However, following the observations in Singh 2011 (see also Bale and Khanjian 2014), the inferences derived from MAXIMIZE PRESUPPOSITION are calculated locally rather than globally, and thus are not usually affected by such contexts.

Plausibly, the awkward reading in (16b) stems from the use of *earning* as a VP embedded within a DP, as in *John's earning of my respect was unexpected*. Critically important for our purposes, there is no singular version of *earning* that can be used to refer to income.

If we assume that incompatibility with singular morphology is due to some kind of lexical/morphological constraint, then it would be reasonable to also assume that the singular version of these nouns are not viable competitors in terms of calculating MAXIMIZE PRESUPPOSITION. Given these assumptions, Sauerland's theory predicts that it should be possible for *scissors* and *earnings* to not have the same type of semantic constraints as a plural noun like *shirts* or a mass noun like *mud*. This prediction is borne out. Consider the contrast between the sentences in (17). The sentence in (17a) implies that there are at least two shirts in the closet (i.e., it is incompatible with a context where Mary only bought one shirt and only that one shirt is in the closet). The sentence in (17b) does not have a similar implication.

(17) a. The shirts that Mary bought are in the closet.
      b. The scissors that Mary bought are in the closet.

Unlike (17a), the sentence in (17b) is an acceptable description of a situation where Mary only bought one item – a pair of scissors – and she put that item in the closet. Note, it might be tempting to hypothesize that a pair of scissors counts as being "two"; however this is incompatible with how numerals are used to modify *scissors* in many dialects of English. For example, consider the following sentence taken from a website that advertises sewing products: "Made of gold plated handles and nice quality stainless steel blades, these two small scissors are effective for embroidery, sewing, Artwork, and craft."[14] The website in which this sentence appears clearly shows a picture of two pairs of scissors which are sold in a "two-pack".

A similar observation can be made with respect to the interpretation of the plural marker on pluralia tantum nouns like *earnings* (or more accurately, the lack of interpretation on such nouns). First, note that *earnings* patterns like a prototypical mass noun in that it is compatible with the modifier *much* and is incompatible with numerals like *two*.

(18) a. The plowback ratio is a fundamental analysis ratio that measures how much earnings are retained after dividends are paid out.[15]
      b. * John's two earnings were being investigated by the IRS.[16]

---

[14] www.sewkitkit.com/the-best-embroidery-scissors/.
[15] www.investopedia.com/terms/p/plowbackratio.asp.
[16] It is possible that this sentence could be acceptable under an event/process reading of *earnings*. The star in this sentence represents the unacceptability of the sentence under a reading where *earnings* refers to income.

Ontology, Number Agreement and the CMD 253

With this in mind, consider the following comparatives:

(19) a. John has more mud than Mary.
      b. ?John has more muds than Mary.

As thoroughly discussed by Bale and Barner (2009), the sentences in (19) have very distinct meanings. The use of *mud* without plural morphology in (19a) yields a comparison by some continuous dimension, such as volume or mass (i.e., the sentence is true in situations where John has a greater mass/volume of mud, independent of how that mud is physically divided or how many kinds of mud there are). This contrasts sharply with the truth conditions of (19b). In so far as (19b) is acceptable, it can only be true based on a non-continuous measure. In this particular case, John would have to have a greater number of kinds of mud. Critically, the "mass" interpretation of *mud* is not compatible with plural morphology. In Sauerland's theory, this would follow from competition. The "mass" interpretation is unavailable because the singular noun expresses this meaning.

Given this explanation, Sauerland would predict that plural morphology shouldn't necessarily force a comparison via a non-continuous measure when there is no competition with a singular. With this in mind, consider the contrast in (20):

(20) a. Tencent's smartphone games yielded more earnings than its PC games for the first time in the second quarter of 2017.[17]
      b. *Tencent's smartphone games yielded more earning than its PC games for the first time in the second quarter of 2017.

The sentence in (20b) is not acceptable – *earning* requires a plural marker in this environment. Given the lack of a singular counterpart, it is unsurprising from Sauerland's perspective that the sentence in (20a) involves a comparison by a continuous measure rather than by number. The sentence in (20a) is true in a situation where Tencent's smartphone games made more money than its PC games, where the relevant dimension of measurement has no well-defined unit. Although "earnings" can be expressed in terms of dollars and cents, there is no standard unit – US dollars, euros, pounds, rupees, etc. are all acceptable. Also, expressions that denote one's earnings often contain fractions of the smallest unit – e.g., "When I checked my earnings this morning I was surprised I earned 0.05 cents."[18] Furthermore, like other mass NPs but unlike plural count NPs, *more earnings* does not allow for numerical differentials – e.g.,

---

[17] https://newzoo.com/insights/articles/game-revenues-of-top-25-public-companies-jump-20-to-41-4-billion-in-h1-2017/.
[18] http://davidbkatague.blogspot.com/2014/09/i-am-beginning-to-like-being-hubber.html.

*Tencent's smartphone games yielded **three/many** more earnings than its PC games for the first time in the second quarter of 2017.*

In summary, the fact that pluralia tantum nouns permit both a "singular" and "mass" interpretation falls out as a natural consequence of the "high number" theories. To account for this pattern, "low number" theories would have to incorporate a similar type of competition. However, in order to maintain the "single domain, single type" analysis of the count–mass distinction, "low number" theories would have to implement such an analysis in a way that does not rely on ontological or type-theoretical differences.[19]

4.2. Plural Agreement Without a Plural Affix

According to Sauerland (2003), "high number" theories facilitate a unified analysis of agreement patterns. For example, it is almost a pedestrian fact that common noun DPs like *the shirts* and pronominal plurals like *we* and *they* both trigger plural agreement. However, these two types of DPs do not pattern the same way in terms of plural morphology: common noun DPs can host a plural affix while pronominal DPs cannot. In Sauerland's (2003) theory, the similarities and differences between the two types of DPs can be easily explained. Both DPs trigger plural agreement because they are both sister to a ϕ-head that has a plural feature. However, pronominal DPs differ from common noun DPs in that there is no NP layer and hence no plural affix. (Recall that in "high number" theories, the so-called plural morpheme is just an agreement affix attached to the noun.) A "low number" theory would either have to hypothesize two different number systems (one for pronouns and another for common nouns) or maintain that pronouns are decomposed in some way that permits something akin to an NP layer.

As noted by Sauerland (2003), coordinated DPs such as *texting and driving* are very similar to plural pronouns in that they lack plural morphology but can trigger plural agreement. However, unlike plural pronouns, this agreement seems to be optional. For example, as discussed by Lasersohn (1995), the same coordinated structure can be used with either plural or singular agreement. Critically, the choice of agreement influences the type of interpretation that is given to the coordinated DP. For example, the phrase "texting and driving" in (21a) is understood as a warning about a single event of driving

---

[19] Perhaps the approaches that do not employ MAXIMIZE PRESUPPOSITION – such as Spector (2007) and Zweig (2009) – would be able to maintain a competition analysis without having to define "atom" or "masses" in a global sense. However, this is difficult to say with any certainty. Unlike Sauerland (2003), these theories do not discuss the consequences of competition with respect to mass nouns and it is unclear how they could define "masses" using a "local" strategy.

while texting. In contrast, "texting and driving" in (21b) is understood as a warning about two separate types of events.

(21) a. Texting and driving is dangerous.
b. Texting and driving are dangerous.

Similarly, the phrase "my friend and colleague" in (22a) refers to one person who is both a friend and a colleague, whereas the same phrase in (22b) refers to two different people.

(22) a. My friend and colleague is coming to dinner.
b. My friend and colleague are coming to dinner.

This type of "semantic agreement" falls out naturally from Sauerland's theory where number features combine after the conjoined DP has already been formed. The choice of number feature depends on the nature of the referent that is picked out by the conjoined DP (one event/person versus two) rather than the syntactic composition of the coordinate structure.

A "low number" theory would have to seek an alternative explanation of these facts, either through some kind of optional "feature percolation" that happens to correlate with the differences in interpretation, or by hypothesizing two different syntactic structures for each interpretation that happen to result in the correct agreement pattern.[20] The advantage of Sauerland's theory is that the agreement patterns and the interpretation facts are necessarily connected to one another.

4.3. Disjunction and Agreement

In previous work, I have used Sauerland's (2003) theory to explain agreement patterns with disjunctive subjects in Mi'gmaq, an Eastern Algonquian language (see Pacifique 1939; Bale 2014). I demonstrated how a presuppositional treatment of both number and person features could explain when dual agreement was required and when it was optional for various types of disjunctions. I will not revisit this data here, especially since the nature of the count–mass distinction has not been thoroughly explored in Mi'gmaq. Rather in this section, I concentrate on similar agreement patterns in English, demonstrating how Sauerland's theory can account for certain subtle semantic differences between singular and plural agreement.

---

[20] Perhaps the most promising avenue to pursue for someone who wants to maintain the "single domain, single type" hypothesis would be to assume that conjunction forms a set and that a covert plural morpheme is required when this set doesn't have a maximal element – a requirement that is trivially avoided if the conjunctive set is a singleton.

There are many dialects of English where disjunctive subjects can optionally trigger plural or singular agreement (although critically not all dialects).[21] Consider the examples in (23), taken from a brief Google search.[22]

(23)   a. How much harder will it be to kill this program once Obama or Hillary are in office?[23]
        b. You guys think Trump or Hillary are bad? This guy is currently serving his second term in office![24]
        c. There is little evidence that either Trump or Hillary is deeply devoted to loving and serving God and neighbor.[25]
        d. If, indeed, it turns out that Jean Houston is a congenital liar, there will be the inevitable cynics who will claim that Bill or Hillary is Jean's guru, not the other way around.[26]

For at least a subset of English speakers (see fn. 21), all of the sentences in (23) are acceptable despite the variability in agreement. Furthermore, there are subtle meaning differences.[27] Consider the sentences in (24).[28]

(24)   a. Every person in that room thinks that only Trump or Hillary are the worst.
        b. Every person in that room thinks that only Trump or Hillary is the worst.

The sentence in (24a) is consistent with a context where there are three types of people in the room: (i) one type that thinks that only Trump is the worst (everyone else being "okay", including Hillary); (ii) another that thinks that only Hillary is the worst (everyone else being "okay", including Trump); and (iii) a third that thinks that both Trump and Hillary are the worst (but others are "okay"). This contrasts sharply with (24b) which is inconsistent with there being people of the third type.

Sauerland's theory can explain these subtle differences as long as he makes some fairly standard assumptions about the nature of disjunctions and

---

[21] It is important to emphasize the variation across dialects – some speakers find both types of agreement to be unacceptable, whereas others prefer singular agreement. I have not yet found anyone who prefers plural agreement.
[22] The Google search involved the strings "or Hillary is" and "or Hillary are" and yielded tens of thousands of results.
[23] https://m.dailykos.com/stories/461242.
[24] https://9gag.com/gag/a5rEm3o/you-guys-think-trump-or-hillary-are-bad-this-guy-is-currently-serving-his-second-term-in-office-somehow-he-always-gets-off.
[25] www.catholicvote.org/dear-archbishop-chaput-trump-is-clearly-better-than-hillary/.
[26] http://skepdic.com/houston.html.
[27] One might predict difference in terms of an exclusive vs. inclusive meaning; however such inferences are hard to detect. In fact, some claim that exclusive inferences don't even exist – e.g., see the discussion in Gamut (1991).
[28] Note that I have embedded the disjunction under the universal in order to remove complications involving ignorance implicatures. For example, "John likes Mary or Sue" implies that the speaker is ignorant about who John likes, but "Every boy likes Mary or Sue" does not necessarily imply any ignorance on behalf of the speaker.

cumulativity. First, he would need to analyse the connective *or* as a set-formation operator. The resulting set would then combine with other functions in a pointwise fashion to form a set of alternatives (in the sense of Hamblin 1973). The truth-conditional meaning would then be derived by a separate operator that asserts that one member of the alternative set is true. Over the last two decades, this has become a mainstream analysis of disjunction for a variety of different reasons (see Kratzer and Shimoyama 2002; Aloni 2003; Simons 2005; Alonso-Ovalle 2008; among others).

To give one example of how this analysis would work, consider the sentence *John or Mary swam*. In this type of "alternative-set" analysis, ⟦*John or Mary*⟧ would denote the set $\{j, m\}$ (where j is John and m is Mary). It would combine with ⟦*swam*⟧ point-wise, yielding the alternative set $\{$⟦*swam*⟧ $(j),$ ⟦*swam*⟧ $(m)\}$. A null existential operator would then apply to this set to assert that one of these propositions is true, yielding the proposition ⟦*swam*⟧ $(j) \vee$ ⟦*swam*⟧ (m). Note that in this type of theory, the "existential" operator can apply either locally or globally. For example, the sentence *Everyone likes John or Mary* has one parse where the relevant set that feeds the existential operator contains the quantifier – e.g., $\{$⟦*Everyone*⟧ $(\lambda x.$ ⟦*likes*⟧ $(j)(x)),$ ⟦*Everyone*⟧ $(\lambda x.$ ⟦*likes*⟧ $(m)(x))\}$ – and at least one other where the relevant set does not contain the quantifier but only a variable – e.g., $\{$ ⟦*likes*⟧ $(j)(x),$ ⟦*likes*⟧ $(m)(x)\}$. The first parse yields a meaning that can be paraphrased as "everyone loves John or everyone loves Mary" whereas the latter yields a meaning that can be paraphrased as "everyone loves either John or Mary".

A second assumption that Sauerland would need to adopt is free application of Link's join-closure operator (symbolized as *). Note, such an assumption might be needed anyway to account for cumulativity with verbal and adjectival predicates independent of the disjunctive facts (for details, see Link 1983).

With these two assumptions, we have everything we need to derive the meaning differences in (24). According to Sauerland's analysis of number, the embedded clauses in (24a) and (24b) would both have the following structures, the only difference being the value of the ϕ-head.

(25)   [TP Only [$_{\phi P}$ $\phi_{PL/SG}$ [DP Trump or Hillary]] BE$_{PRES}$ the worst]

For both sentences, ⟦*Trump or Hillary*⟧ would be a set containing Trump and Hillary, $\{t, h\}$. Given our assumptions about the cumulative operator, we could optionally close this set under join, yielding $\{t, h, th\}$. Thus, there are two possible set values that can be derived from the disjoined subject – one closed, the other not. The interpretation of the ϕ-head would apply to either set pointwise – i.e., to each member of the set. With respect to the plural ϕ-head – which is interpreted as an identity function without any presuppositional implications – the result of pointwise application would be identical to the original set (e.g., ⟦ϕ_{PL}⟧ ({t,h}) = { ⟦ϕ_{PL}⟧ (t), ⟦ϕ_{PL}⟧ (h)} = {t,h} and ⟦ϕ_{PL}⟧ ({t,h,th}) = { ⟦ϕ_{PL}⟧ (t), ⟦ϕ_{PL}⟧ (h), ⟦ϕ_{PL}⟧ (th)} = {t,h,th}). However, with respect to the singular ϕ-head – which presupposes that its argument is either an "atom" or a "mass" – the result will only be defined for the set that is not closed under join (e.g., ⟦ϕ_{SG}⟧ ({t,h}) = { ⟦ϕ_{SG}⟧ (t), ⟦ϕ_{SG}⟧ (h)} = {t,h}; however, ⟦ϕ_{SG}⟧ ({t,h,th}) is undefined since ⟦ϕ_{SG}⟧ (th) is undefined). Hence, the ϕP with the plural feature can (optionally) have the alternative set {t,h,th} as its semantic value, whereas the ϕP with the singular feature necessarily has the alternative set {t,h} as its value.

This difference at the ϕP level is inherited throughout the entire structure until the point where the null existential operator yields a truth-conditional meaning. For the sake of argument (and brevity of time and space), let's only consider the parse where this operator applies just before the interpretation of the quantifier phrase. At this point, the alternative set generated from the TP with the singular ϕP has two alternatives, spelled out in (26a) and paraphrased in (26b).

(26) a. {⟦*thinks*⟧ (⟦*only*⟧ (C) ⟦BE *the worst*⟧ (t))(x), ⟦*thinks*⟧ (⟦*only*⟧ (C) ⟦BE *the worst*⟧ (h))(x)}
      b. {x thinks that only Trump is the worst, x thinks that only Hillary is the worst}

Applying the existential operator to this alternative set would be equivalent to the proposition in (27a), paraphrased in (27b). (Note that C is the context set that *only* exhaustifies over. For present purposes, the content of this set does not matter as long as both Trump and Hillary are members.)

(27) a. [⟦*thinks*⟧ (⟦*only*⟧ (C) ⟦BE *the worst*⟧ (t))(x)] ∨ [⟦*thinks*⟧ (⟦*only*⟧ (C) ⟦BE *the worst*⟧ (h))(x)]
      b. x thinks only Trump is the worst or x thinks that only Hillary is the worst.

When the QP universally quantifies over the variable x, the result is a proposition that can be paraphrased as (28).

(28) For all persons x in the room, x thinks only Trump is the worst or x thinks that only Hillary is the worst.

The proposition in (28) is inconsistent with a context where some of the people think Trump and Hillary are both the worst. However, the derivation proceeds differently if ϕP is interpreted as a three-membered set. For example, the alternative set that would result from {t,h,th} is given in (29a) with the paraphrase in (29b).

(29) a. {⟦*thinks*⟧(⟦*only*⟧(C)⟦BE *the worst*⟧(t))(x),⟦*thinks*⟧ (⟦*only*⟧(C)⟦BE *the worst*⟧ (h))(x),⟦*thinks*⟧(⟦*only*⟧(C)⟦BE *the worst*⟧(th))(x)}
      b. {x thinks that only Trump is the worst, x thinks that only Hillary is the worst, x thinks that only Trump and Hillary are the worst}

Applying the existential operator to this three-membered set would be equivalent to the proposition in (30a), paraphrased in (30b). (Once again, C is the context set that *only* exhaustifies over. The content of this set does not matter as long as both Trump and Hillary are members.)

(30) a. [⟦*thinks*⟧(⟦*only*⟧(C)[BE *the worst*⟧(t))(x)] ∨ [⟦*thinks*⟧(⟦*only*⟧(C)[BE *the worst*⟧(h))(x)] ∨ [⟦*thinks*⟧(⟦*only*⟧(C)[BE *the worst*⟧ (th))(x)]
b. *x* thinks only Trump is the worst or *x* thinks only Hillary is the worst or *x* thinks that only Trump and Hillary are the worst.

When the QP universally quantifies over the variable *x*, the result is a proposition that can be paraphrased as (31).

(31) For all persons *x* in the room, *x* thinks only Trump is the worst or *x* thinks that only Hillary is the worst or *x* thinks that only Trump and Hillary are the worst.

Unlike (28), the sentence in (31) can be true when some people in the room think that Trump and Hillary are both the worst.

In summary, Sauerland's presuppositional theory not only predicts the possibility of having variable number agreement with disjunctive phrases, it can also explain fairly subtle differences in meaning that track this variability. A "low number" theory would have to re-imagine the syntactic position of the plurality operator in order to explain the same facts.[29]

5. Conclusion

The goal of this chapter was not to argue for a specific theory of number marking, or a specific semantic treatment of the count–mass distinction, but rather to discuss the interactions between the two. In particular, I argued that "high number" theories require a global definition of what it means for an entity to be an "atom" or a "mass". Such global definitions are easy to outline in theories that either assign different semantic types to mass and count NPs or hypothesize disjoint domains. In the end, I discussed some evidence in favour of "high number" theories – in particular competition patterns, a unified treatment of pronouns and NPs, as well as an account of variable agreement patterns with both conjoined and disjoined DP subjects. I did not have the time

---

[29] Perhaps one could assume that the high application of the join-closure operator to the disjoined DPs is the result of a phonetically null plural morpheme; however this would eliminate the "optionality" of having a conjunctive alternative. The prediction under such an analysis would be that sentences with plural marking are equivalent to sentences with an explicit conjunctive alternative. For example, "Once Hillary or Trump are in office, the political tension should die down" is predicted to be equivalent to "Once Hillary or Trump or both are in office, the political tension should die down." However, these two sentences are clearly not equivalent. The first is consistent with "But if they both get into office, the political tension will be even worse"; the second is not.

nor space to go over alternative analyses of these phenomenon within "low number" theories – nor did I aim to. Rather, my goal was to sketch out a set of grammatical patterns that are predicted by the "high number" theory and thus need to be addressed by researchers who want to maintain a "single domain, single type" analysis of the count–mass phenomenon.

11 The Semantics of Distributed Number

Myriam Dali and Éric Mathieu

1. Introduction

Several articles have recently proposed that morphemes corresponding to the plural can occupy not just one (Borer 2005) but several functional positions depending on their semantics (Alexiadou 2011; Acquaviva 2008; Wiltschko 2008, 2012; Butler 2012; Mathieu 2014; Gillon 2015; Mathieu and Zareikar 2015; Dali and Mathieu 2016; Kramer 2016). The aim of this paper is to provide further evidence for this view, focusing on Tunisian Arabic, Western Armenian (WA), and Turkish.

Like Borer (2005), we adopt the view that complementary distribution is the hallmark of identity, but we argue, following this logic, that the plural is not one but many, appearing in different positions in the nominal spine. We argue for a close mapping between the syntactic structure and the semantics in the DP, since each node corresponds to a different interpretation of the plural, and propose that number projections exist depending on the features they specify (see also Watanabe 2010; Vásquez-Rojas 2012).[1]

We begin the article with a discussion of Tunisian Arabic plurals, based on Dali and Mathieu (forthcoming), which will serve as background theory for our analysis of bare nouns and bare plurals in Western Armenian and Turkish. Then, we turn to the interesting case of indeterminate nouns in these languages: they can express singularity and plurality, depending on the context (often called general or transnumeral number; Corbett 2000). Consider the

---

[1] On the basis of Arabic, and following Abdelkader Fassi Fehri's suggestion, Borer (2005) herself notes in a footnote that it may be the case, after all, that plurality is not a unified notion and may consist of two different grammatical objects with diverse semantic, syntactic, and, at times, morphological properties – one interacting with $<e>_{DIV}$, the other with $<e>_{\#}$, but she does not pursue this idea (neither in the book or in later work; see Borer and Ouwayda 2010). Our research program is one that takes this idea seriously. The underlying analysis and many ideas presented here were first introduced at the count–mass workshop, organized by Diane Massam, University of Toronto, Feb. 7–8, 2009, the published version of which is Mathieu (2012b). The original 2009 material is available at http://www.ericmathieu.ca/uploads/5/6/9/8/56980157/hand out_toronto.pdf. Further results are to be found in Dali and Mathieu (forthcoming). We would like to thank George Balabanian for his precious help on Western Armenian.

example in (1) from Western Armenian and (2) from Turkish (on general number in these languages, see Bliss 2004; Bale, Gagnon, and Khanjian 2010; 2011; Görgülü 2012).

(1) Kirk kənetsi. [Western Armenian]
 book buy.1SG.PERF.PAST
 'I bought a book/books.'

(2) Ali kitap al-dı. [Turkish]
 Ali book buy-PAST.3SG
 'Ali bought a book/books.'

It is customary in the literature to treat such nouns as being equivalent to mass terms (Chierchia 1998b) with a denotation of a kind or alternatively as bare NPs with no number projection (Borer 2005, and many others). For others, such nouns refer to semi-lattices, the denotation being number neutral, thus referring to sums and atoms (Rullmann and You 2006; Bale, Gagnon, and Khanjian 2010, 2011; Bale and Khanjian 2014).

The puzzle with which the present article is concerned is that, as shown in (3) and (4), the nouns in question can be pluralized (Donabédian 1993; Sigler 1996; Bale, Gagnon, and Khanjian 2010, 2011; Görgülü 2012; Bale and Khanjian 2014; Sağ 2016).[2]

(3) Kirker kəetsi. [Western Armenian]
 book.PL buy.1SG.PERF.PAST
 'I bought books.'

(4) Ali kitap-lar al-dı. [Turkish]
 Ali book-PL buy-PAST.3SG
 'Ali bought books.'

This plural is surprising, since the languages in question already have a way to express plurality via general number.[3] Since it is supposed to be referring to sums already, it is impossible for the plural to operate on a semi-lattice directly. It must therefore be the case that such bare nouns are in fact first individuated via the Number head, before they are pluralized (see also Mathieu and Zareikar 2017; Zareikar 2019, for Persian). We thus propose that pluralization of bare nouns in Western Armenian and Turkish is a two-step process.

---

[2] According to Chierchia (1998b), languages with general number are not supposed, typologically, to have plural markers as part of their grammars. But there are, of course, many exceptions, suggesting plurals are not necessarily in complementary distribution with classifiers (it is possible for classifier languages to have optional plurals, as pointed out by Greenberg 1972, 1974; see also Aikhenvald 2000; Gebhardt 2009; Doetjes 2012).
[3] This plural is not a plural of abundance and therefore cannot be claimed to be associated with nP (Acquaviva 2008; Lowenstamm 2008; Tsoulas 2009; Alexiadou 2011; Ghaniabadi 2012).

First, the noun is atomized, giving a singular form (this is achieved via a null exponent of number under Num), and a new noun is created, providing a brand new semi-lattice. This is shown in (5). There are two NumP projections. The lower NumP operates on the semi-lattice and returns a set of atoms.

(5)   [$_{DP}$ [$_{NumP}$ Num [$_{nP}$ n [$_{NumP}$ Num ∅ [$_{nP}$ book]]]]]

Second, the higher NumP operates morphosyntactically on the singular, and returns a set of atoms from the semi-lattice introduced by the higher *n*. This is shown in (6). This is a case of morphological compositionality where one number is built out of another. Each *n* defines a new nominal predicate and semantic interpretation starts afresh with each *n*.

(6)   [$_{DP}$ [$_{NumP}$ Num **PL** [$_{nP}$ n [$_{NumP}$ Num ∅ [$_{nP}$ book]]]]]

Evidence for such a view comes from three main observations. First, it turns out to be possible in some cases for bare nouns in WA-type languages to refer exclusively to singulars. This has been shown by Sağ (2016) for Turkish and Zareikar (2019) for Persian.

(7)   Jerexa-n   ir   kirkə   gartats.   [WA]
       child-DEF.DET   EMPH.3SG.POSS   book.DEF.DET   read-PAST.3SG
       'The child read his book.'
       not 'The children/children read their book.'

(8)   Çocuk   kitab-ı-nı   oku-du.   [Turkish]
       child   book-POSS-ACC   read-PAST
       'The child read his book.'
       not 'The children/children read their book.' (Sağ 2016: 5)

The generalization seems to be that bare nouns in WA-type languages are ambiguous (Sağ 2016): they either refer to general number or are singular. The facts in (7) and (8) show that it is not possible to propose an analysis à la Borer (2005) where, in Div (or Num for us) as input, the plural in (3) and (4) might simply be the bare NP that general number nouns refer to. The morphological plural is acting on a singular, not a bare NP. We have independent evidence of this in Tunisian Arabic where plurals of singulatives operate on nouns that have already been individuated and where the plural is not on Num but generated in a number higher position, as will be made explicit in Section 2. In Tunisian Arabic, we see a renominalization effect, with the added *n* introducing a new semi-lattice.

Second, bare plurals in WA-type languages have a different semantics from bare nouns. English bare plurals, for example, are inclusive in downward entailing environments, i.e. referring to 'one' or 'more than one' (Hoeksema 1983; Krifka 1995; Schwarzschild 1996; Brustad 2000; Sauerland 2003; Sauerland, Anderssen, and Yatsushiro 2005; Spector 2007; Zweig 2009; Farkas and de Swart 2010; Bale, Gagnon, and Khanjian 2011; Grimm, 2012a, 2012b; Martí 2020), but bare plurals in WA-type languages are interpreted exclusively, referring only to 'more than one', thus excluding the singular. Based on our observations from Tunisian Arabic, we propose that the higher plural is always exclusive. Once division – in Borer's (2005) sense – has applied, the plural is exclusive.

That Western Armenian and Turkish plurals are exclusive has been noted before (Bale, Gagnon, and Khanjian 2011, 2010), but these exclusive plurals turn out to be problematic for the generalization these authors put forward, namely that the plural is marked morphologically, but unmarked semantically, always referring to sums as well as atoms. They leave the Western Armenian/Turkish puzzle unresolved, but clearly, in these languages, and incidentally also in Tunisian Arabic, as shall be seen in Section 2, it is possible for the plural to be marked semantically.

Third, our proposal is bolstered by a range of scope facts. We will show that bare nouns in Western Armenian and Turkish have low scope while, under the appropriate controlled environments, nouns with an added plural may receive wide scope.

The rest of the chapter is structured as follows. Section 2 provides the background theory necessary for us to proceed, together with examples of lower and higher plurals in Tunisian Arabic. Section 3 focuses on Western Armenian and Turkish and gives an account of the puzzle presented in this introduction. Section 4 concludes the article.

2. Two Positions for the Plural

According to Borer (2005), the sole function of the plural is to divide. However, in some cases, division is realized by another element (e.g. singulative, a measure word) with possible pluralization of that element, casting doubt on the idea that the notion of plurality is unique and indicating that the plural can have a function other than dividing. To illustrate, let us consider the case of Arabic, which, like other singulative languages (Breton, Welsh, Maltese), allows the atomization of mass and collective nouns via a gender shift operation. Collective nouns are semantically plural but morphosyntactically singular, and number distinctions are marked by a contrast in gender. Our examples are from Tunisian Arabic. (9) shows that a collective noun (masculine) can be turned into a singular by adding a feminine suffix. From this example, we see that gender shift can instantiate division (Ojeda 1992; Zabbal 2002; Fassi Fehri 2004, 2012; Mathieu 2012a, 2012b; Ouwayda, 2014).[4]

---

[4] On Kramer's (2016) view the plural of the singulative is a normal dividing plural, since according to her analysis singulatives are generated under *n*. However, if we adopt this view, we lose the idea that the dividing plural is in complimentary distribution with the singulative.

(9)   bordgen   – bordgen-a   [Tunisian Arabic]
      orange.MASC.COLL – orange-FEM.SING
      'oranges, orange'

Once collective and mass nouns have been portioned out by the singulative operation, the result can be pluralized by the suffixation of the feminine plural marker -*at*, as in (10).

(10) bordgen-a   – bordgen-a-at   [Tunisian Arabic]
      orange.FEM.SING – orange-FEM.SING-PL
      'an orange, oranges'

The collective and the plural of the singulative have different interpretations, and these, we argue, must be translated into different features and levels of representation on the nominal spine. Let us first discuss the notion of the inclusive/exclusive distinction that is crucial in interpreting the different plurals of Arabic. The folk view is that singulars refer to 'one' while plurals refer to 'more than one' (Link 1983). In this view, the plural is *exclusive* in that it excludes reference to the singular. For example, (11) cannot refer to 'one child'.

(11)   I have children.

If a speaker A utters (11), then we understand the speaker has more than one child. The sentence would be false if speaker A had in fact only one child (under Gricean inference, speaker A had the option of saying 'I have a child', but did not).

However, it has been noted that in certain contexts, English bare plurals are interpreted inclusively, i.e. referring to 'one or more' (Hoeksema 1983; Krifka 1989; Schwarzschild 1996; Sauerland 2003; Sauerland, Anderssen, and Yatsushiro 2005; Spector 2007; Zweig 2009; Farkas and de Swart 2010; Bale, Gagnon, and Khanjian 2011; Grimm 2012a; Martí 2020). Consider the interpretation of the plurals in the contexts of a question (12a), a negation (12b), and a conditional (12c).

(12) a. How many children do you have?
      b. I don't have children.
      c. If you have children, raise your hand.

(12a) can be answered by 'three' but also by 'one'. (12b) is false if I have two children or more, but also if I have only one child. (12c) is true if parents with

---

Kramer's *n* is responsible for both idiosyncratic plurals and more productive, atomizing elements such as the singulative. There are many problems with this view. Singulatives are very productive and have all the hallmarks of inflectional morphemes (see Mathieu 2012a, 2014).

two children or more raise their hands, but also if parents with one child raise their hands.

The crucial observation about these examples is that there potentially exist two interpretations for the plural: one that includes reference to the singular, and one that excludes such a reference. We argue that in Arabic the collective and the plural of the singulative each correspond to a different version of this contrast. First, consider the examples of collectives in (13) and plurals of the singulative in (14), in downward entailing contexts.

(13)   a. klit   borgden?   [Tunisian Arabic]
ate.you orange.MASC.COLL
'Did you eat oranges?'

b. ma   klit-ech.   borgden
NEG   ate.I-NEG   orange.MASC.COLL
'I did not eat oranges.'

c. ken ʕandek   borgden mush lezem   temchi l-el   marshi.
If   have.you   orange.   not   necessary go.you to-the   market
                   MASC.COLL
'If you have oranges, you do not need to go to the market.'

(14)   a. klit   borgden-a-at?
ate.you orange-FEM.SING-PL
'Did you eat oranges?'

b. ma   klit-ech   borgden-a-at.
NEG ate.I-NEG orange-FEM.SING-PL
'I did not eat oranges.'

c. ken ʕandek borgden-a-at   mush lezem   temchi l-el   marshi.
if   have.you orange-FEM.SING-PL not   necessary go.you to-the market
'If you have oranges, you do not need to go to the market.'

(13a) can be answered by 'three' but also by 'one'. (13b) is false if I ate one orange or more. According to (13c), you do not need to go to the market if you have one or more oranges. This indicates that the collective forms have an inclusive interpretation in the contexts of (13), just as is the case for English bare plurals in downward entailing environments.

However, when we substitute the collective forms with the plural of the singulative, the interpretation is exclusive. (14a) can be answered by the affirmative only if the speaker ate two or more oranges. (14b) is false only if I eat two oranges or more. In fact, someone can say 'I did not eat oranges, I ate only one' if the plural of the singulative is used in the question. According to (14c), you do not need to go to the market if you have two or more oranges, but you may have to go if you have only one. Whether or not one is convinced of the validity of the inclusive/exclusive distinction in the interpretation of English bare plurals, the data above shows that this distinction is borne out for Tunisian Arabic.

In addition to its exclusive reading, the plural of the singulative is also paucal. While the collective can refer to any amount of entities, the plural of the singulative can only refer to 'a few' entities. Consider the examples in (15).

(15)   a. [When referring to the fish in a fish market]: √ḥut/#ḥut-a-at.
       b. chrit   ḥut/ḥut-a-at
          bought.I fish.MASC.COLL/fish-FEM.SING-PL
       'I bought fish/a few fish'

(15a) shows that, in a context where one is visiting a fish market and wants to refer to all the fish in the market, the appropriate form would be the collective one, and not the plural of the singulative, since a fish market is expected to have more than 'a few fish'. However, in a context where a person bought five fish, both the collective and plural of the singulative forms can be used (15b): the collective form is a general plural that can be used in all contexts, and the plural of the singulative is a paucal form that fits contexts where only a few entities are referred to.[5]

What these observations show is that different plural shapes have different functions in Tunisian Arabic, and this leads us to adopt a structure where the plural is not bound to one specific head, but rather distributed among functional heads along the spine. The task is now to determine which heads host the different plural manifestations.

To account for the number system in Tunisian Arabic and, more specifically, the fact that the plural seems to fill different functions, we adopt our analysis (Dali and Mathieu 2021) of the Arabic facts based on work by Harbour (2011, 2014), who shows that number is reducible to a set of binary features, i.e. [± atomic], [± minimal], and [± additive].

First, we assume, following many previous analyses (Kihm 2005; Acquaviva 2008; Lowenstamm 2008; Kramer 2009; Harbour 2011, 2014; among others) that classificatory features occupy their own projection, namely n and that n takes a root as a complement, as in (16), labelling it as a noun and making it visible to the computational system.

---

[5] Paucity is a well-known concept in grammars of Arabic. Ojeda (1992) defines the plural of the singulative as a 'plural of paucity' that, he notes, citing Wright (1933: 307) 'is used only of persons and things not exceeding ten in number'.

(16)   nP

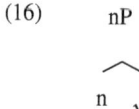

Second, we assume that *n* defines a nominal predicate P and structures the root as a join semi-lattice (Zabbal 2002; Harbour 2011, 2014; Martí 2020) giving us the representation in (17) for the semi-lattice. As pointed out by Harbour (2011), *n* underdetermines whether the noun is count or mass. Like Borer (2005), we assume it is Num (Div for Borer) that actually introduces the distinction. When Num is projected, the noun is count, when Num is not projected, the noun is mass. The semi-lattice introduced by the root is the input to the singular and plural operations.

(17)

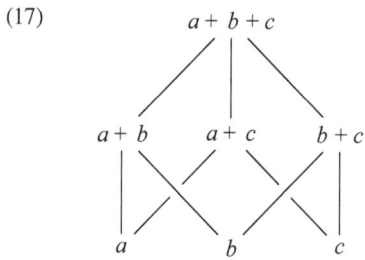

The extended projection of *n* looks like (18) (Borer 2005; Grimshaw 2005). NumP takes *n*P as complement, and DP takes NumP as complement (Borer 2005: Num = Div).

(18)   DP

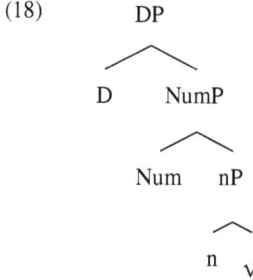

Following Harbour (2011, 2014), we assume that each functional projection in (18) comes with a set of features. Only the features on Num are interpretable. The features on *n* are lexical/syntactic, and the features on D are purely syntactic (uninterpretable), and only encode number agreement. In sum, Num is determined by cardinality (singular, plural), and *n* by lexical properties of the noun. In order to account for a language like Tunisian Arabic, that has singulars, plurals, and paucals, we need the [+/−atomic] and [+/−additive] features.[6] As summarized by Martí (2020: 44), '[±Atomic] is sensitive to atoms/non-pluralities ([+atomic]) vs. non-atoms/pluralities ([−atomic]). [±Minimal] is sensitive to elements with parts ([−minimal]) vs. elements without parts ([+minimal]). [±Additive] is concerned with whether the output set contains, for any two of its members, their join ([+additive]) (a property also known as cumulativity; cf. Krifka 1989) or not ([−additive]).' In addition, we also make use of the [+collective] feature on *n* to distinguish collective nouns from count ones.[7] This feature is purely syntactic and indicates that the noun is part of a system where individual readings are morphologically marked.

First, for the singular, we propose the structure in (19). Num is associated with the features [+atomic; −additive], with matching syntactic features on D. First, the feature [+atomic] acts on the semi-lattice, then the feature [−additive], giving us the interpretation in (19).

(19)

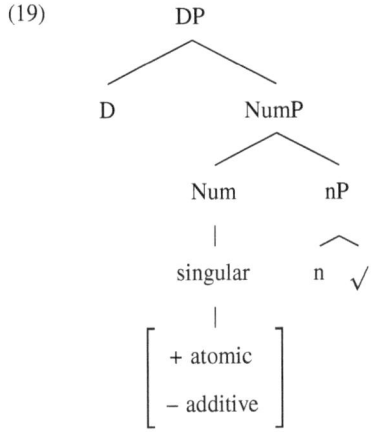

---

[6] The [+/− minimal] feature is necessary to account for the dual. However, Tunisian Arabic only has remnants of dual marking – see Dali and Mathieu (2021) – and paucal marking includes reference to two entities. Therefore, we do not make use of this feature here since it is not necessary for the set of data discussed in this paper.
[7] This class feature is our own innovation to Harbour's (2011, 2014) system to account for the collective class in Arabic.

Plurals with an exclusive interpretation (in regular, upward-entailing contexts) are in complementary distribution with the singular and have the structure in (20), with [−atomic; +additive] features on Num.

(20)

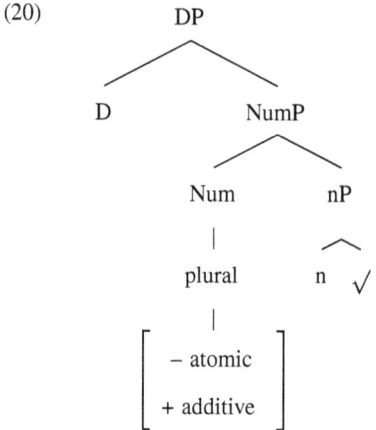

For collectives, we propose the structure in (21), where Num is not projected. This accounts for the fact that collectives syntactically behave like mass nouns in not combining directly with numerals or plural morphology (they need to be divided by the singulative first). Semantically, all we have is a root, i.e. a semi-lattice. This explains why in this case the collective can be interpreted inclusively. Since collective nouns are syntactically singular, they bear a [+atomic] feature on D (features on D are purely syntactic).

(21)

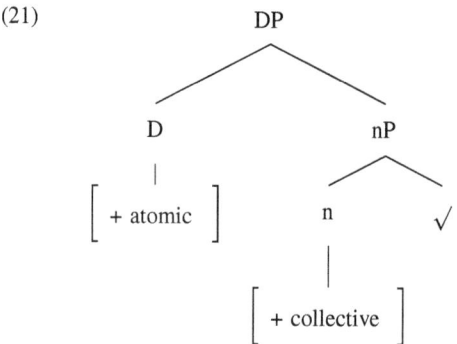

The singulative behaves like a singular in picking out an atom from the semi-lattice. We therefore propose that it is also associated with the feature

[+atomic] in Num, as in (22). The singulative differs from the singular in that it is morphologically marked and operates on a noun of the collective class, as indicated by the [+collective] feature on n.[8]

(22)
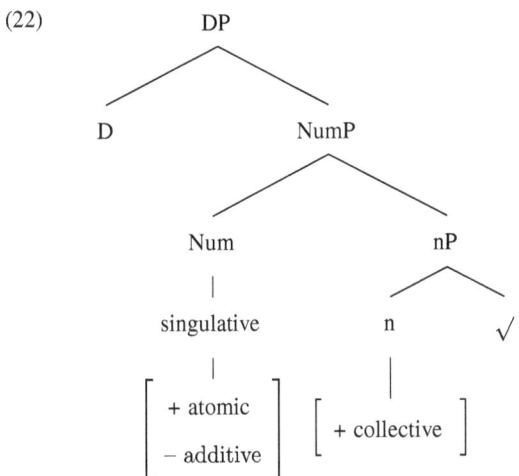

Given its exclusive and paucal interpretation, we propose that the plural of the singulative is a higher plural that belongs to a second NumP projection different from the one discussed so far.[9] Here, we have the plural operating on the singulative, exhibiting a case of morphological compositionality where one number serves as the base of another (see Harbour 2014). The higher Num is associated with the features [−atomic; −additive] to account for the paucal and exclusive interpretation of the plural in question.

---

[8] This is essentially what is proposed by Mathieu (2012a, 2012b, 2014), Borer and Ouwayda (2010), and Ouwayda (2014), except that Num = Div. Other proposals involve different functional heads. Zabbal (2002) proposes that the singulative is associated with ClassP (between nP and NumP). Fassi Fehri (2004) proposes that the singulative is associated with UnitP (between nP and NumP). Note that our [+collective] is a Class feature, not a syntactic or semantic feature.
[9] Without the extra nP layer, the structure would be problematic semantically, since all NumP gives us is a set of atoms. If the higher Num instructs the semantics to look for the nonatomic, nonadditive part of that set of atoms, it will return nothing. We need a new lattice. Since the higher n defines a new nominal predicate, the higher Num is able to operate on a semi-lattice, as expected semantically.

(23)

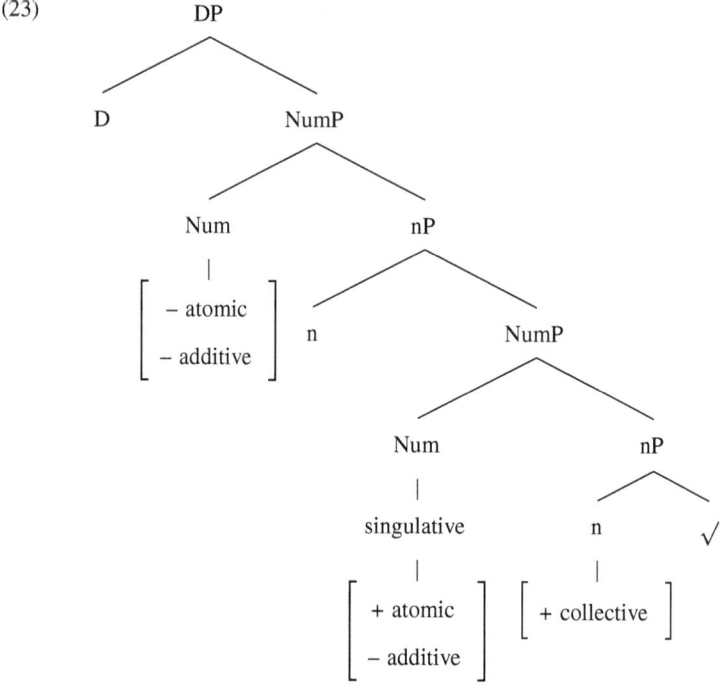

To summarize Section 2, it is possible for plurals to appear in different positions in the syntactic spine (see also Butler 2012, and many others). We see this with plurals of singulatives in Arabic (and plurals of measure words in Persian-type languages; see Mathieu and Zareikar 2015). The lower plural is typically associated with an inclusive reading: it is atomized, but does not refer to number, and this is why it can be referred to as singular or plural in the right environments (roughly, downward-entailing environments). The higher plural, i.e. the counting plural, is typically associated with an exclusive reading: it is atomized and refers to number and this is why it can only refer to 'one or more' and never to 'one'.

In the next section, we provide an analysis of Western Armenian bare plurals and argue that they are associated with the higher NumP.

3. The Analysis

In Section 2, we saw that Tunisian Arabic plurals can be generated either in a lower NumP or in a higher NumP. Plurals of singulatives are generated in the higher NumP: they are interpreted as exclusive and paucal. In this section, we propose that the plural of WA-type bare nouns is systematically associated with the higher NumP. It does not bear paucal features (it is not interpreted as a paucal), but has true plural features. On our account, NumP can apply recursively provided renominalization is involved. Since Western Armenian and Turkish do not have a dual, we will use only two sets of features, namely [+/−atomic] and [+/−additive].

Let us begin with bare nouns in Western Armenian and Turkish. We propose, like Rullmann and You (2006), Bale, Gagnon, and Khanjian (2010; 2011), and Bale and Khanjian (2014) that they refer to semi-lattices, hence their indeterminate number. Our structure in (24) is identical to the one proposed by Borer (2005) (see also Pereltsvaig 2014; Martí 2020).

(24)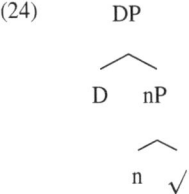

When a plural is added, we propose that this is done in two steps. First, NumP is projected with a null head for singular number, as in (25).

(25)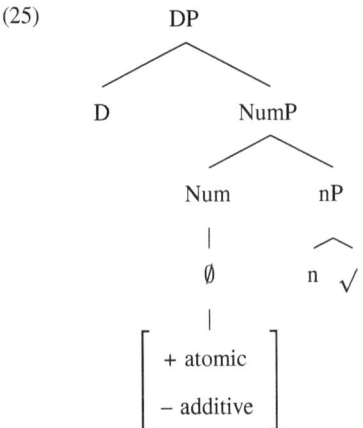

The next step is the introduction of the plural in a higher NumP domain, as in (26). The features associated with the lower Num are [+atomic; −additive], while those associated with the higher Num are [−atomic; +additive].

(26)

```
              DP
             /  \
            D    NumP
                /    \
              Num     nP
               |     /  \
          ⎡ − atomic ⎤  n   NumP
          ⎣ + additive⎦     /   \
                          Num    nP
                           |    /  \
                           ∅   n   √
                           |
                      ⎡ + atomic ⎤
                      ⎣ − additive⎦
```

The question that immediately arises is why not follow a type of analysis à la Borer and propose that the added plural in Western Armenian and Turkish triggers a DivP projection (or Num for us) and that the plural is inserted under Div? There is evidence against this view. As already hinted in the Introduction, it is possible for some cases of bare nouns in Western Armenian and Turkish to denote, not a sum, but an atom. Consider the following examples.[10]

(27) Jerexa-n   ir   kirkə   gartats.   [WA]
      child-DEF.DET   EMPH.3SG.POSS   book.DEF.DET   read-PAST.3SG
      'The child read his book.'
      not 'Children/the children read their book.'

(28) Çocuk   kitab-ı-nı   oku-du.   [Turkish]
      child   book-POSS-ACC   read-PAST
      'The child read his book.'
      not 'Children/the children read their book.' (Sağ 2016: 5)

---

[10] It is also not possible to claim that the plural is just an agreement marker, as done for the Arabic plural of singulatives by Borer and Ouwayda (2010) and Ouwayda (2014), since in Turkish at least, it is not actually possible for numerals to appear with a bare plural. Numerals must merge with a bare noun (Donabédian 1993; Görgülü 2012).

As argued by Sağ (2016) for Turkish, bare nouns appear to be ambiguous: they either refer to general number or are singular. The facts in (27) and (28) show that it must be the case that the morphological plural is acting on a singular, not a bare NP. We have independence of this in Tunisian Arabic where plurals of singulatives operate on a noun that has already been individuated and where the plural is not in the lower Num position, but generated in the higher Num position. In Tunisian Arabic, we see a renominalization effect, with the added *n* introducing a new semi-lattice. We propose that this is exactly what is happening in the case of WA-type bare plurals.

We have independent evidence that the plural is generated not in the lower, but the higher Num. The evidence comes from the inclusive/exclusive contrast and scope. First, we note that bare nouns are felicitous in interrogative contexts (29) and (30). This is expected since such nouns refer to atoms as well as sums, i.e. they are inclusive. The following questions can be answered in the singular, e.g. 'Yes, one', or in the plural, e.g.'Yes, three'. The same judgements are given by Turkish speakers (Sağ 2016).

(29) Bəzdig unis? [Western Armenian]
child have.2.SG
'Do you have (one or more) children?'

(30) Azar çocük bak-r? [Turkish]
Azar child care-IMP.3SG
'Does Azar take care of (one or more) children?'

If we now use a bare plural in the same context, the interpretation is such that the noun is interpreted only as a plural, i.e. exclusively. As Bale, Gagnon, and Khanjian (2011) point out for Western Armenian,

Given a context where it is clearly relevant whether a person has one or more children versus no children and where it is not relevant whether a person has one child versus more than one, Armenian speakers find the question in [(31)] awkward. In fact they often suggest that one should use the singular form of the noun instead. However, when told that (31) is the intended question, speakers will answer no if they only have one child but yes if they have more than one.

(31) Bəzdig-ner unis? [Western Armenian]
child-INDEF.PL have.2.SG
'Do you have (two or more) children?'

(32) Azar çocuk-lar bak-ıyor? [Turkish]
Azar child-PL care-IMP.3SG
'Does Azar take care of (two or more) children?'

Turning now to negative contexts (33) and (34), we see that, as expected, bare nouns are interpreted inclusively – they refer to sums as well as atoms.

(33) Kirk tʃikənetsi. [Western Armenian]
      book NEG.buy.1SG.PERF.PAST
      'I didn't buy (one or more) books.'

(34) Azar çocuk bak-mı-yor. [Turkish]
      Azar child care-NEG-IMP.3SG
      'Azar does not take care of (one or more) children.'

When a bare plural is used as in (35) and (36), the situation is different. The bare plural is interpreted exclusively, referring to more than one systematically.

(35) Kirker tʃikənetsi. [Western Armenian]
      book.PL NEG.buy.1SG.PERF.PAST
      'I didn't buy (two or more) books.'

(36) Azar çocuk-lar-a bak-mı-yor. [Turkish]
      Azar child-PL-DAT care-NEG-IMP.3SG
      'Azar does not take care of (two or more) children.'

Let us now turn to conditionals as shown in (37) and (38). As expected, number-neutral nouns are interpreted inclusively.

(37) Jete kirk məkənes (ne), hajis əse   indzi. [Western Armenian]
      if   book buy.2SG (if), please say.2SG.IMP to-me.
      'If you buy (one or more) books, please let me know.'

(38) Azar çocuk bakır-sa,   bana   haber ver. [Turkish]
      Azar child care-CON.3SG, me.DAT news pass.2SG
      'If Azar is taking care of (one or more) children, let me know.'

On the other hand, a bare plural in the same context yields an exclusive reading: the noun necessarily denotes plurality. The following examples are true if Azar takes care of two children or more but false if she takes care of only one child.

(39) Jete kirk-er məkənes (ne), hajis əse   indzi. [Western Armenian]
      If   book-PL buy.2SG (if), please say.2SG.IMP to-me.
      'If you buy (two or more) books, please let me know.'

(40) Azar çocuk-lar-a bakır-sa,   bana   haber ver. [Turkish]
      Azar child-PL-DAT care-CON.3SG, me.DAT news pass.2SG
      'If Azar is taking care of (two or more) children, let me know.'

As pointed out in the Introduction, these facts have been noticed before by Bale, Gagnon, and Khanjian (2010, 2011) and Bale and Khanjian (2014), but Western Armenian is problematic for them, because it goes against the generalization they put forward, namely that the plural is marked morphologically, but unmarked semantically, always referring to sums as well as atoms. Clearly, in Western Armenian, but also in Turkish, and in fact in Arabic as seen in

Section 2, it is possible for the plural to be marked semantically. This means that in a context where the children are a, b, and c, the English singular 'child', but also the WA-type singular bare noun, denotes as in (41a). The English plural 'children' denotes as in (41b), while the Persian/Azari/Turkish/Western Armenian bare plurals corresponding to 'children' denote as in (41c). Nouns denoting general number correspond to (41b) and have thus the same denotation as English plurals. These facts show that the basic interpretation of the plural is not one that includes sums as well as atoms, as in Sauerland, Anderssen, and Yatsushiro (2005).

(41) a. child = {a, b, c}
      b. children = {a, b, c, ab, ac, bc, abc}
      c. children = {ab, ac, bc, abc}

We now turn to our final piece of evidence. We note that the scope of WA-type bare nouns is obligatorily low. The following sentences cannot be referring to specific books or hats, only to non-specific books or hats.

(42) Kirk gə pəndrem gor.   [Western Armenian]
      book IND find.1SG CONT
      'I am looking for books.'

(43) Şapka arı-yor-muş-dum.   [Turkish]
      hat   search-IMP-PARTP-PAST.3SG
      'He used to look for hats.'

On the other hand, the version of these sentences with a plural marker, as in (44) and (45), allows a wide scope reading.

(44) Kirk-er   gə pndrem gor.   [Western Armenian]
      book-PL IND find.1SG CONT
      'I am looking for books.'

(45) Şapka-lar arı-yor-muş-dum.   [Turkish]
      hat-PL   search-IMP-PARTP-PAST.3SG
      'He used to look for hats.'

Thus, while bare nouns in WA-type languages behave like bare plurals in English (Carlson 1977b; Chierchia 1998b) in receiving narrow scope, their plural counterparts allow a reading where more structure needs projecting than the bare NP structure for bare nouns. We assume that the wide scope is available because the plural is generated high in the structure, allowing it to escape the DP to take scope over the whole sentence à la Borer (2005). The bare noun lower in the structure is not able to escape the DP to take wide scope.

If bare plurals in Western Armenian and Turkish are high plurals, then we begin to understand why they are associated with definiteness (Donabédian 1993). For example, *tun-ə* means 'the house', ə indicating definitiveness, but if we use a definite plural, then not only do we need to add an ə, but we also need to include the plural marker to give *tun-er-ə* 'the houses'. We saw also that when a bare noun in Western Armenian and Turkish is interpreted as singular, rather that as denoting both sums and atoms, the interpretation of the subject noun was definite. That some plurals are linked to specifity or definiteness has been noticed before (Ghomeshi 2003; Hamedani 2011 for Persian and Butler 2012 for Yucatec Maya, among others). These are interesting facts, but must be left for a future paper. We must now conclude.

4. Conclusion

In this chapter, we provided evidence from Tunisian Arabic that the morphosyntactic plural can appear in two positions, a lower Num and a higher Num, and that this contrast is also relevant for languages such as Western Armenian and Turkish when trying to explain differences between bare nouns and bare plurals. Bare nouns refer to sums and atoms and receive low scope while bare plurals refer to sums only and have the possibility of being interpreted as having wide scope. Bare nouns can be interpreted as inclusive, but bare plurals cannot, and we know independently from Arabic that the higher Num position is associated with strict exclusivity. We proposed that the pluralization of bare nouns in Western Armenian and Turkish is a two-step process. First, there is atomization of the noun (via a null head in Num) together with renominalization (the singular form is a word). This is a reflection of the fact that the plural in Western Armenian and Turkish is not in complementary distribution with the singular. Second, the plural operates on the new semi-lattice and refers to sums only. It remains to be seen whether our findings can be generalized to other languages with general number that also have plurals as part of their grammars.

12 Container, Portion, and Measure Interpretations of Pseudo-Partitive Constructions

Peter R. Sutton and Hana Filip

1. Introduction

1.1. Available Readings for Pseudo-Partitive Constructions

A number of recent studies have yielded an increasingly better understanding of the range of possible readings of the pseudo-partitive construction (henceforth PPC), such as *(two) glasses/litres of milk* (Doetjes 1997; Filip and Sutton 2017; Khrizman et al. 2015; Landman 2016; Partee and Borschev 2012; Rothstein 2011, 2016, 2017). Here we focus on PPCs formed with receptacle nouns (*basket*, *bottle*, *box*, *glass*, etc.). We begin by summarising the four readings identified by Khrizman et al. (2015) and adopt most of their terminology (however see Section 1.3 for discussion of some terminological issues). Consider the examples in (1):

(1)   a. There are two glasses of wine standing on the coffee table.
        b. Mary drank two glasses of wine.
        c. Amy poured two glasses of wine into the stew by eye. The second a few minutes after the first.
        d. We stirred half a glass of wine into the stew.

The PPC *two glasses of wine* in (1a) has a *container classifier* (henceforth 'container') reading. It denotes pluralities of two glasses and assumes the existence of some wine in each. In (1b), there is a *contents* reading, enforced by the verb *drink*. On this reading, the PPC denotes sums of two glass-sized portions of wine, and the sentence in (1b) entails the existence of some glass that contains each portion. In (1c), there is a *free portion* reading available.

We are indebted to Susan Rothstein for her constructive criticism on earlier versions of this work. We will miss her deeply. Our thanks go to Fred Landman, Keren Khrizman, Eleni Gregoromichelaki, Kurt Erbach, and the audiences of the following workshops: 'The Count–Mass Distinction: A Linguistic Misunderstanding?' at the Ruhr University, Bochum, 2018; 'Approaches to Coercion and Polysemy (CoPo)' at the University of Oslo, 2017; and 'Ontology as Structured by the Interfaces with Semantics' (OASIS1) at Paris 8, 2018. This research is funded as part of DFG Collaborative Research Centre 991: The Structure of Representations in Language, Cognition, and Science, Project C09: A Frame-Based Analysis of Countability.

This is similar to the contents reading, but the sentence in (1c) does not entail the existence of a glass. In this paper, however, we do not provide an analysis of free portion readings (see below). In (1d), there is an *(ad hoc) measure* reading available, in which only the wine is referred to and it need not have been contained by any glass. The noun *glass* here denotes an ad hoc, or nonstandard, but conventional unit of measurement relative to which the amount of wine is determined. As Partee and Borschev (2012: 459) point out, a good test for the ad hoc measure reading is whether or not fractional units can be used. For example, they point to the oddity of (2) given that *razbili* ('broke', Russian) selects for the container reading.

(2)   # My   razbili   pol-butylki   šampanskogo   [Russian]
      we   broke   half-bottle-ACC.SG champagne-GEN.SG
      '(#)We broke half a bottle of champagne'

Khrizman et al. (2015) compellingly argue that the first three readings are count readings and the ad hoc measure reading is a mass reading. We adopt this position here.

1.2.   Outline

In this paper, we pick up on a number of observations made in the recent literature (most notably in Khrizman et al. 2015; Partee and Borschev 2012; Rothstein 2011, 2016, 2017). We start with Partee and Borschev's (2012) observation that in many contexts the container and contents readings co-occur with the co-predication data they provide (e.g., in English, *Billie picked up and drank a glass of wine*). Such data, as they suggest, might be best analysed along the lines of Asher's (2011) dot types, but given that the required (dot-type) formalism would go beyond a simple type theory, they do not implement it.

First, as an alternative to the suggestion of Partee and Borschev (2012), we argue that we do not need to assume anything beyond mereology and a simple type theory in a dynamic semantics framework to model container+contents readings in a way that also allows us to provide an adequate account that motivates the reference to the container, the contents, and both simultaneously, while still accounting for the fact that containers and contents can be grammatically counted.

Second, we provide an analysis of the *ad hoc measure* interpretation of the PPC that is informed by Khrizman et al. (2015) and Rothstein (2011; 2016; 2017), and especially by Rothstein's (2017) work on the parameters involved in measure functions. In a slight departure from these accounts, we argue that ad hoc measure readings of PPCs formed with receptacle nouns are derived from the interpretation of the receptacle noun on its container+contents reading. The main motivation for this is to follow through on one of Khrizman et al.'s (2015) observations that for container and contents readings, the standard for how much stuff there needs to be as the contents of a container is sensitive to context. For example, a glass of whiskey can be fairly empty compared to a glass of beer. We argue that, since similar contextual restrictions apply to ad hoc measure readings, the semantics of the non-standard measure concept is drawn from the semantics of container+contents concepts.

Finally, we use our analysis of ad hoc measure readings (derived from container+contents readings) to explain why measure interpretations of PPCs in which mass concepts are coerced into count concepts are hard (if at all possible) to obtain. For example, in appropriate contexts, *two white wines* can be interpreted with a container+contents reading *two glasses, each containing (a glass-sized portion of) white wine*, but not *white wine to the measure of two glassfuls*. Our explanation is based on the idea that the locus for coercion must be lexically supplied and not itself the product of a prior coerced interpretation.

1.3. A Note on a Terminological Issue

Partee and Borschev (2012) propose that PPCs have four readings, one of which they dub the *concrete portion* reading. The concrete portion reading presupposes a symmetrically branching syntactic structure, which corresponds to Rothstein's (2011) syntactic structure that correlates with the measure interpretation of the PPC. Responding to this proposal, Khrizman et al. (2015) argue that Partee and Borschev's (2012) *concrete portion* is, in fact, a count reading rather than a measure reading, which, as Khrizman et al. also argue, is mass. They then re-baptise *concrete portion* as *free portion* and provide an account of this reading that is a count and not a measure (mass) reading. Now, we completely agree that Partee and Borschev's (2012) *concrete portion* should not be modelled with symmetrically branching syntactic structure (Rothstein's (2011) measure syntactic structure), and that it should be modelled with a right-branching structure, which corresponds to Rothstein's (2011) count syntactic structure.[1] We thereby think that, in the syntactic sense, Partee and Borschev's (2012) *concrete portion* reading should, indeed, be a count reading with a count syntactic structure to match.

However, we do not think that Khrizman et al.'s (2015) *free portion* reading is a 're-baptism' of Partee and Borschev's (2012) *concrete portion* reading; rather we hold that the *free portion* reading is a new reading that Khrizman et al. (2015) uncovered, and that Partee and Borschev's (2012) *concrete*

---

[1] Where measure syntactic structures are: [$_{NP}$ [$_{MeasP}$ [NUM][$_{N_{meas}}$]] (*of*) [$_N$]] and count syntactic structures are: [$_{NumP}$ [NUM][$_{NP}$ [$_N$](of)[$_{DP}$]]].

portion reading should really be re-baptised (and reformed) to be the *contents* reading. One reason to think this is that Partee and Borschev (2012) say quite categorically that the *concrete portion* reading presupposes the existence of a container. In contrast, a key characteristic of Khrizman et al.'s (2015) *free portion reading* is that it does not presuppose the existence of a container. Second, in discussing whether the concrete portion reading should be subsumed under the measure reading or the container+contents reading (which in their semantics is roughly equivalent to Khrizman et al.'s (2015) *container classifier* reading), Partee and Borschev (2012: 476) conclude that the *concrete portion* reading is 'really not a measure reading'.[2] Partee and Borschev (2012: §3.3.6) further conclude that, on the assumption of an adequate dot-type style analysis for the container+contents reading (that would explain the simultaneous reference to containers and contents) the concrete portion reading would be subsumed by the container+contents reading.

Semantically, it therefore makes more sense to re-baptise Partee and Borschev's (2012) concrete portion reading as the contents reading of Khrizman et al. (2015). (This, of course, necessitates a reform of Partee and Borschev's (2012) proposed semantics, too, not least since, as Rothstein (2017) points out, Partee and Borschev's (2012) concrete portion reading wrongly attributes counting to the counting of containers, not to the counting of portions/contents.)

In summary, we do not think that Partee and Borschev (2012) actually discuss a reading that is conceptually equivalent to Khrizman et al.'s (2015) *free portion* reading, and so in this sense, identifying the free portion reading was one of Khrizman et al.'s (2015) novel contributions. We also think that the syntactic structure of the concrete portion (=contents) reading should be as Khrizman et al. and Rothstein claim. Our terminology, inherited almost exclusively from Khrizman et al., is given in Table 12.1. The one place we differ is that we combine the container and contents reading into one complex container+contents reading.

2. Data

The container+contents interpretation of the PPC. Partee and Borschev (2012) provide co-predication data as evidence that some container+contents uses of PPCs can refer simultaneously to the container and the contents. We propose to bolster this with evidence from pronominal anaphora. In (3), we see a combination of co-predication and pronominal anaphora in which the

---

[2] We suspect that part of the tangle in terminology arises because Partee and Borschev give their concrete portion reading a syntactic structure that Rothstein (2011) argues is a measure and therefore mass structure.

Table 12.1. *A summary of terminologies*

Partee and Borschev (2012)	Khrizman et al. (2015); Rothstein (2017)	Our terminology
container+contents	container (classifier)	container+contents
concrete portion	contents	
-	free portion	free portion
ad hoc measure	ad hoc measure	ad hoc measure
standard measure	standard measure	standard measure

cup and coffee (together) (i) and the coffee (j) can each be picked up by consequent anaphoric pronouns, which suggests that the antecedent *a cup of coffee* makes available both the container and the contents as potential discourse referents.

(3)   Downstairs she made herself a cup of coffee$_{ij}$ and carried it$_j$ out onto the patio and drank it$_i$ at the table ... [BNC]

In (4) and (5), there is no co-predication, but intuitively, the pronouns refer to the containers and contents together. For example, in (4), it is the bottles and the wine they contain which, together, have value, not the bottles or the wine individually. Likewise, in (5), the brewery exports the bottles and beer together, not primarily the bottles or primarily the beer.

(4)   I Have 2 Bottles of vintage wine. Can anyone give me any information on them or how much they are worth. [ukWaC]

(5)   An 18th century brewery here produces up to 60,000 bottles of beer a year, most of them for export. [ukWaC]

Lastly, we note that container+contents PPCs formed with plural receptacle nouns distribute contents to containers and then also containers to (apportioned contents), as indicated by the example in (6), in which for every glass there is a contents of vodka, and for every portion of vodka, there is a glass containing it.

(6)   The waiter brought me two glasses of vodka. I held each one between my thumb and forefinger before drinking it down in one gulp.

The ad hoc measure interpretation of the PPC. Khrizman et al. (2015) and others note that in the ad hoc measure reading, there is no requirement that the measured stuff ever be contained in a relevant container. This claim is further supported by evidence from pronominal anaphora, such as (7) and (8), in which we see that, given a measure PPC antecedent, pronouns can refer to the stuff measured (the wine), but not to the container, be it a whole bottle, half full (i), or some half of a bottle (j).

(7) We then deglazed the pan with a little more than half a $\underline{\text{bottle}}_{ij}$ of red wine$_k$, simmered for half an hour or so and reduced it$_k$ to a few tablespoons worth. [ukWaC]

(8) We then deglazed the pan with a little more than half a $\underline{\text{bottle}}_{ij}$ of red wine$_k$ and stood it$_{\#i,\#j}$ next to the pan.

Partee and Borschev (2012) point out that ad hoc measure readings of PPCs are felicitous with fractions of units, whereas container+contents readings usually are not. Interestingly, in (9), we see what may, superficially, look like a case of a measure NP (*half a bottle of milk*) in which the relative pronoun picks up reference to the container. However, given that what is referred to as being thrown is not a half bottle, but rather a whole bottle, half filled with milk, this suggests that, at least in some contexts, *half a bottle of N* can mean 'a bottle half filled with N' (i.e. a container+contents interpretation, not a measure interpretation).

(9) Shortly later, there I was presenting him with half a bottle of milk from the fridge, and to my surprise he threw it back at me. [ukWaC]

Another important point regarding measure readings of PPCs is made by Khrizman et al. (2015). On the measure reading, the unit of stuff measured is fixed at every context in the sense that, for example, *two and a half glasses of milk* in (10) cannot mean 'milk to the measure of one large glass plus milk to the measure of 1.5 small glasses'.

(10) In the 50s, Swedes drank, on average, nearly two and a half glasses of milk a day.[3]

In contrast, the container+contents reading permits an alternation between the size and the volume of the receptacles that anchor the relevant container+contents reading, as demonstrated by (11).

(11) That all changed one night when Joe Carroll [...] brought 6 odd-shaped and -sized bottles of beer to my house[4]

Finally, we note that when a given PPC is used with the ad hoc measure interpretation, the unit for the ad hoc measure corresponds to the unit of measurement that apportions the volume of stuff that would be expected on the corresponding container+contents interpretation. This is something that, although seemingly obvious, will guide our semantic analysis of ad hoc measure readings of PPCs. For example, the amount of brandy that is referred to on the ad

---

[3] www.readersdigest.ca/food/healthy-food/is-milk-good-for-you (accessed 15 May 2019).
[4] http://scholium.securecheckout.com/product/detail/scho_beer_and_wine.html (accessed 15 May 2019).

hoc measure interpretation of the PPC in (12) and the container+contents interpretation of the PPC in (13) are the same.

(12) 'It was a splendid sauce', said Henry appreciatively. 'Consisting, I understand,' said Milsom heavily, 'of a small glass of brandy, ditto of Madeira . . .' [BNC]

(13) Children leave one or two mince pies on a plate at the foot of the chimney (along with a small glass of brandy, sherry or milk, and a carrot for the reindeer) as a thank you for filling their stockings.[5]

The mass-to-count coercion in NumPs with mass nouns. Assuming a lexicalist theory of the count–mass distinction in which common nouns are lexically specified as either mass or count,[6] when mass nouns are directly combined with numerical expressions in the NumP ($[_{\text{NumP}} [_{\text{Num}}] [_{\text{NP}}]]$), as in *three white wines*, they are coerced into a suitable count denotation depending on context. It is often observed that such coercion is straightforwardly available for mass nouns which denote stuff that is frequently portioned in specific ways.

However, what is less often noticed is that such (coerced) numerical phrases correspond, in their in-context interpretations, to specific readings of PPCs. Specifically, they correspond to container+contents readings (and sometimes subkind readings), while (ad hoc) measure readings are hard to get, if possible at all (see Sutton and Filip 2018b). Consider (14)–(16):

(14) Not that it takes much to get me drunk. Three or four white wines usually do the trick. [ukWaC]

(15) Good Points: The room was very clean and value for money. My only criticsm [*sic*] is that if the room is set for 2 people. Surely more than 2 little milks would be more sensible? [ukWaC]

(16) There were two intervals, so she had three Colas and two ice creams. I had one ice-cream and three waters. Although, she later told my sister that I had two gins. [ukWaC]

In (14), it is, plausibly, three of four glasses of white wine (contents reading) that do the trick. In (15), the hotel room reviewer expresses a wish for more than two of the small plastic containers containing portions of milk to be made available as part of the room's tea and coffee making facilities (container +contents reading). Given the theatre context, in (16), it is plausibly cans of

---

[5] http://projectbritain.com/Xmas/mincepies.htm (accessed 15 May 2019).
[6] This is in contrast to a non-lexicalist position in which, for example, the count–mass status of nouns is only fixed at the level of NPs and DPs. See, e.g., Borer (2005); Pelletier (1975).

cola, small tubs of ice cream, bottles of water, and glasses of gin being referred to (container+contents reading).

In contrast, (17) and (18) are odd, precisely because the NumPs formed with mass nouns are here most naturally understood as having the measure interpretation. The difficulty in accessing the measure interpretation for coerced NumPs with mass Ns is also evident in the confusion expressed by a user in a web forum chat in (19):[7]

(17) #There are two and a half milks left in the fridge/wines left in the bottle.

(18) I'd like a cup of tea with #two and a half milks.

(19) a. The recipe I was using for soup said I needed to use '1 and a half milks'. What does that even mean? [rolling on the floor laughing emoji]
      b. the 1 n half milks probably refers to a pint n half.

There are a few notable exceptions to this. For instance, NumPs formed with *beer* may be acceptable in appropriate contexts: *there are about two and a half beers left in the keg*, where *two and a half beers* can relatively naturally be used to mean 'beer to the measure of 2.5 glassfuls' (p.c. Kurt Erbach). One factor that is plausibly part of the explanation here is world knowledge, namely that beer is served in highly conventionalised portions and in certain routinised contexts, typically in countries with a beer drinking culture. Similarly, in the context of tea making, British English does permit coerced measure interpretations of NumPs with *sugars*. The measure reading of Num *sugars* is highly contextually constrained, however, and means *teaspoons/ lumps of sugar* (such that a standard lump is equal in volume to a teaspoonful): *when I ask for tea with five sugars, I want tea with five sugars. Not four sugars. Not six sugars. Not four and a half sugars. Not five and a half sugars. How many did you put in?*[8]

In summary, the container+contents interpretation of the PPC licenses pronominal anaphoric reference to the container+contents together, or to the container or to the contents separately. The measure interpretation of the PPC, on the other hand, blocks reference to any container. Finally, in NumPs with inherent mass nouns that are coerced into a count interpretation, the accessibility of measure interpretations ('stuff denoted by NP to the amount of the number (Num) of implicit measurement-units') is much lower than that of the container+contents interpretation, even in appropriate contexts.

---

[7] www0.modthesims.info/m/printthread.php?t=463682&page=114&pp=25 (accessed 06 May 2019).
[8] From the novel *Circus of Thieves and the Comeback Caper, or, Mystery of the Spoons* by William Sutcliffe (Simons and Schuster 2016).

3. Analysis

3.1. Main Observations

Container+contents interpretations of PPCs are formed with nouns like *glass* or *bottle* (whose basic meaning is that of concrete physical receptacles). The main data points to be explained are:

(CC1) The container+contents interpretation distributes contents to containers (for each container, there is a contents) and containers to (apportioned) contents (for each contents, there is a container).

(CC2) It can be followed, in discourse, by anaphoric expressions that refer jointly to the container with the contents, or to solely the contents, or to solely the container.

Our compositional analysis will, approximately, follow Rothstein (2011) and Partee and Borschev (2012) in assuming a REL function that applies to the interpretation of sortal receptacle nouns and derives a relational noun concept. We also explicitly incorporate data point (CC1) into our analysis via the inclusion in the REL function of a pair of distribution conditions that crucially rely on the two aspects of our theory of the count–mass distinction: sortal nouns specify a counting base (what counts as one), and grammatical countability requires the application of a context-specific individuation schema (that identifies the objects that can be counted in that context). In relation to (CC2), we propose a mereological dynamic analysis in which container+contents PPCs denote sums of containers and apportioned contents, but also make available reference to the containers and the contents individually (such that these can be counted).

The alternative to a purely mereological analysis is one based on dot types.[9] Dot types are formed with a type constructor • that forms complex types that represent the different facets of an entity. For example, part of the representation for *book* includes the complex type **phys_object** • **informational_object**. Although we cannot exclude this alternative, we would like to note some complications. First, note that simple-minded application of dot types in an analysis for container+contents interpretations is a non-starter. In such an analysis, the container-type and the contents-type could be simple types (like **glass** and like **milk**), yielding the type **glass** • **milk** for *glass of milk*. However, due to the idempotency of • (for all a, $a \bullet a = a$; Asher, 2011: 161), such an analysis cannot work, since we can felicitously talk about *bags of bags* or *boxes of boxes*, the types for which should not be the simple type **bag** or **box**, respectively. What is needed, then, is to draw finer distinctions within a rich

---

[9] For an extensive discussion of dot types, see Asher (2011). A dot type based analysis for PPCs was first suggested in Partee and Borschev (2012).

type theory. For example, Sutton and Filip (2018b) use Type Theory with Records (TTR) (Cooper 2012) to give a semantics for PPCs in which types for containers and contents are highly structured, and so it is possible to account for 'box of boxes' type cases, since one can give distinct types for *box qua container* and *box qua contents*. However, in order to make this work for both singular and plural PPCs, Sutton and Filip (2018b) need not only a rich type system, but also classical mereology. Furthermore, TTR is a formalism that can implement DRT-like discourse referents, and Sutton and Filip's (2018b) analysis makes use of this. Here, we propose that once one has a dynamic formal theory enriched with classical mereology, one already has enough to model container+contents readings of PPCs even when this formal theory is simply typed. Our analysis treats the extension of *boxes of boxes*, for instance, as a set of mereological sums of boxes. What we also do, however, is place constraints on, amongst other things, the mereotopological relationships that hold between some boxes and others. In other words, we capture the PPC data within a simple type theory, and use only mereology and implicitly topological relations such as $contents\_of(a, b)$.

Ad Hoc Measure. The key observations that we seek to explain for the ad hoc measure interpretation of the PPC are:

(M1) The ad hoc measure interpretation blocks anaphoric reference to a container, or the container joint with the contents, but licenses reference to the stuff measured.

(M2) It refers to the same quantities of stuff as the container+contents interpretation of the PPC does in similar contexts.

(M3) It is such that the amount of stuff measured is fixed at every context: e.g., the measure reading of *2.5 glasses of beer* cannot mean 'two and a half volume-wise different measures of beer' (Khrizman et al. 2015).

In relation to (M1), we follow, in large part, Rothstein's (2017) model for ad hoc measures, albeit in our dynamic setting, which will derive (M1) automatically. In relation to (M2), given that, in standard contexts, the relevant unit for the measure interpretation of a *glass of whiskey*, for instance, is identical to the amount of whiskey that counts as a *glass of whiskey* on the container+contents interpretation in the same contexts, we propose that the ad hoc measure interpretation of receptacle nouns in the PPC is derived from the container +contents interpretation of receptacle nouns in the PPC. In a simplified form, and adopting Rothstein's (2011) syntactic framework, the container+contents interpretation of *glass* is of type $\langle et, et \rangle$, a function from a contents predicate (e.g. ⟦milk⟧) to a container+contents predicate (e.g., ⟦glass of milk⟧). We define a measure function, MEAS, of type (simplified) $\langle \langle et, et \rangle, \langle n, \langle et, et \rangle \rangle \rangle$ that applies to things like ⟦glass$_{container+contents}$⟧ and returns a measure function that is sensitive to the stuff measured. This contrasts with other analyses that apply the equivalent of MEAS directly to a sortal receptacle noun concept such as ⟦glass⟧. With this adjustment to previously proposed derivations for measure readings in hand, we can derive (M3) in the same way as Rothstein (2017) insofar as ad hoc measures presuppose that some particular entity is selected from the context as an ad hoc unit calibration for the measurement scale. For us, novelly, this entity is a mereologically complex container +contents entity.

Mass-to-Count Coercion of Mass Nouns in the NumP. Finally, concerning the mass-to-count coercion of mass nouns in the NumP, the main observations to be accounted for are:

(MtC1) The container+contents interpretation is often available in suitable contexts.
(MtC2) The ad hoc measure interpretation is hard to get.

We derive (MtC1) and (MtC2) from our analysis of the ad hoc measure interpretation of the full PPC, and from the hypothesis that the locus of coercion can only be explicit lexical material, and not implicit material which is the output of a (preceding) separate coercion operation. This accounts for why *two white wines* can be interpreted as something equivalent to the container+contents reading of the PPC like *two glasses of white wine* (where ⟦wine⟧ is type shifted by an implicit ⟦REL⟧ (⟦glasses⟧), yielding ⟦REL⟧ (⟦glasses⟧)(⟦wine⟧)). It also explains why *two white wines* cannot be interpreted as something equivalent to the ad hoc measure reading of *two glasses of white wine*, since this would require the implicitly inferred meaning of ⟦REL⟧ (⟦glasses⟧) to be the input to the implicit MEAS function.

3.2. Formal Framework

Given that our analysis, among other things, includes a compositional account of pronominal anaphoric reference, we use Muskens's (1996) compositional DRT, which we enrich with standard extensional mereology (without an atomicity assumption). It is defined in terms of the part ($\sqsubseteq$) and proper part ($\sqsubset$) relations and the mereological sum operation ($\sqcup$). Similarly to Brasoveanu (2008), we introduce plural discourse referents into Muskens's (1996) system.[10] We also allow for discourse referents for properties. Specifically, we propose that (count) nouns make available a *counting base* property (see also Khrizman et al. 2015; Landman 2016; Sutton and Filip 2016a; amongst others) that can be picked up by distributive quantifier expressions. To motivate this assumption, take *Charlie saw two cats. Each had green eyes.* The strongly distributive determiner 'each' requires a singular count noun concept as its antecedent, but the noun in the first sentence is plural. A plausible

---

[10] Brasoveanu's (2008) analysis is more complex than the one we use here, however, since it also allows for discourse-level plurality in order to analyse particular kinds of donkey-sentences.

assumption is that, although *two cats* in the first sentence denotes the set of sums of cats that have a cardinality of two, the semantics of the noun *cats* also licenses the use of the ⟦cat⟧ as a property that can be accessed by distributive determiners. In terms of the formal theory, this is not an enrichment, since Kamp and Reyle (1993), for instance, assume discourse referents that stand for sets of entities in their analysis of plurals. To aid readability, unlike Kamp and Reyle (1993), we do not use capital letters X, Y, etc., as our discourse referents for sets, but instead use, for example, $cbase_{glass}$ as the discourse referent for the counting base of *glass*.

Following Filip and Sutton (2017), Rothstein (2010), and Sutton and Filip (2016a), we assume that count nouns are interpreted relative to a context i. On our approach, contexts make available individuation schemas S_i that are applied to the extensions and counting bases of singular count nouns and yield a quantized (*QUA*; Krifka 1989) predicate:

(20) $QUA(P) \leftrightarrow \forall x, y[P(x) \wedge P(y) \rightarrow \neg x \sqsubset y]$

For a context i and an individuation schema licensed by that context S_i, $S_i(P)$ is a maximal quantized subset of P i.e., $(S_i(P) \subseteq_{max.QUA} P)$:

(21) $Q \subseteq_{max.QUA} P \leftrightarrow Q \subseteq P \wedge QUA(Q) \wedge \forall R[R \supseteq Q \wedge R \subseteq P \wedge QUA(R) \rightarrow R = Q]$

For example, for a set $P={}^*\{a, b, c\}$:

(22) $\{Q | Q \subseteq_{max.QUA} P\} = \begin{Bmatrix} \{a,b,c\}, & \{a, b \sqcup c\}, & \{b, a \sqcup c\}, \\ \{c, a \sqcup b\}, & \{a \sqcup b, a \sqcup c, b \sqcup c\}, & \{a \sqcup b \sqcup c\} \end{Bmatrix}$

Maximally quantized subsets are more permissive than maximally disjoint subsets (Landman 2011) insofar as the former allow overlap at the edges. As argued by Filip and Sutton (2017) and Sutton (2019), this is preferable, since even relative to a context, count nouns have overlapping entities in their extensions, even in specific contexts. For example, fences can overlap at the corners (i.e. share a corner post).[11]

Incorporating these ingredients into compositional DRT, we get lexical entries for singular count nouns (23), plural count nouns (24), and substance mass nouns (25). ⟦*glass*⟧^{i} (⟦*glass*⟧ interpreted at context i) is a function from entities to a DRS that is satisfied if the entity is a glass under individuation schema S_i. It also introduces a discourse referent for the counting base (we return to the importance of this when we model counting and PPC constructions below).

---

[11] Sutton (2019), in fact, argues that even QUA is also too strong and proposes *weakly quantized* (relative to a context) as the condition with the right logical strength for capturing the semantics of count nouns.

(23) ⟦glass⟧^{i} = λv

$cbase_{glass}$
$S_i(glass)(v)$
$cbase_{glass} = \lambda v'$ | $S_i(glass)(v')$

⟦*glasses*⟧^{i} is the same as ⟦*glass*⟧^{i}, except that the predicate S_i(glass) is closed under mereological sum. Notice that the counting base is unchanged between (23) and (24), because what counts as 'one' individuated glass is the same in the denotation of the singular count noun *glass* and its plural counterpart *glasses*.

(24) ⟦glasses⟧^{i} = λv

$cbase_{glass}$
*$S_i(glass)(v)$
$cbase_{glass} = \lambda v'$ | $S_i(glass)(v')$

The mass noun *milk* differs from the count noun *glass* insofar as its interpretation is not sensitive to contexts of individuation (Filip and Sutton 2017; Rothstein 2010; Sutton and Filip 2016a; amongst others). This means that ⟦*milk*⟧^{i} = ⟦*milk*⟧. On our account, in similarity to the work of Landman (2016) and our previous work (Filip and Sutton 2017; Sutton and Filip 2016a; 2018b), mass nouns also introduce a counting base. The difference between mass noun and count noun concepts is that mass noun concepts do not specify a quantized counting base, whereas count noun concepts specify a quantized counting base predicate at every context. (However, not all the count nouns are necessarily interpreted under the same individuation schema, good examples being count nouns like *fence*.)

(25) ⟦milk⟧^{i} = ⟦milk⟧ = λv

$cbase_{milk}$
$milk(v)$
$cbase_{milk} = \lambda v'$ | $milk(v')$

We also want to allow for mass noun concepts to be portioned out, i.e., to be shifted into count interpretations when this shift is sanctioned by the grammar. We propose that such 'apportioning' is at play when mass nouns are used in the PPC in order to get the 'contents' part of the container+contents interpretation. This can be done by applying a maximally quantizing individuation schema to a mass noun concept. We define this via the operation **S** in (26), the output of which is a count concept, namely, some apportioning of milk into a quantized set of portions relative to the context.

(26) $(\mathbf{S}[\![\text{milk}]\!]^i) = \lambda v$

$cbase_{milk}$
$^*\boldsymbol{s}_i(milk)(v)$
$cbase_{milk} = \lambda v' \boxed{\boldsymbol{s}_i(milk)(v')}$

3.3. Counting Constructions

We assume that numerical expressions in English are polysemous between a singular term of type n and a predicate modifier. Without assuming that one meaning is more basic, for simplicity, we define the function that maps the singular term to the modifier in (27). The entry for *two* is given in (28).

(27) $[\![\text{NMOD}]\!] = \lambda n \lambda P_{:[cbase_x]} \lambda v \boxed{\mu_{\#}(cbase_x, v) = n} ; P(v)$

(28) $[\![\text{two}]\!] = \begin{cases} 2 \\ [\![\text{NMOD}]\!](2) \end{cases}$

The NMOD function introduces a cardinality function $\mu_{\#}$ of type $\langle\langle et \rangle, \langle n, \langle et \rangle\rangle\rangle$ that is relative to a counting base property of type et, since the same entity/entities may have different cardinalities depending on the predicate with respect to which we are counting; for example, several volumes can be extensionally equivalent to one dictionary (Link 1983). Similarly to Landman (2011, 2016), we assume that this function is not defined for mass counting base sets (i.e., non-quantized sets for us, non-disjoint sets for Landman). The formalisation of $\mu_{\#}$ is given in set theoretic terms in (29). In words, d counts as n Ps iff the cardinality of the set of P parts of d is n.

(29) For all $d \in \mathcal{D}_e$, for all $P \in \mathcal{D}_t^{\mathcal{P}_e}$, and for all $n \in \mathbb{N}$, if $QUA(P)$, then:

$\mu(P,d) = n$ iff $|\{x : x \in P, x \sqsubseteq d\}| = n$

$\mu_{\#}(P,d)$ is undefined otherwise

The semantics for *two glasses* is given in (30). The extension of (30) is the set of sum entities that are glasses and have a cardinality of two with respect to the counting base for *glass(es)* relative to the individuation schema $\boldsymbol{s}_i$. In this case, since only one counting base set is available, counting is done with the counting base for *glass*. (The case of multiple counting base sets will be discussed momentarily.)

(30) $[\![\text{two glasses}]\!]^i = ([\![\text{NMOD}]\!]([\![\text{two}]\!]))([\![\text{glasses}]\!]^i)$

$= \lambda v$
$cbase_{glass}$
$^*\boldsymbol{s}_i(glass)(v)$
$cbase_{glass} = \lambda v' \boxed{\boldsymbol{s}_i(glass)(v')}$
$\mu_{\#}(cbase_x, v) = 2$
$cbase_x = cbase_{glass}$

In (30), *two glasses* is an NP. However, NumPs and bare plural NPs in English can get the reading of an indefinite DP equivalent to that of *some two glasses* or *some glasses*, respectively. For this, we assume a null determiner DET, which has the semantics of a regular indefinite determiner (see Muskens 1996: 165 for the latter), i.e. a function from an NP denotation to an existential GQ (we abstract away from any differences in selectional restriction here).

(31) $\llbracket \text{DET} \rrbracket = \lambda P \lambda P' \left(\boxed{u_n} ; P'(u_n), P(u_n) \right)$

In (31), the λ-bound variable is saturated with a discourse referent that is introduced at the level at which it is processed (as with other indefinites; Kamp and Reyle 1993: 336). Applied to a predicate P, it returns a function from predicates, Q, to a DRS with the conditions that the discourse referent introduced is a P and a Q.

3.4. The Container+Contents Interpretation of the PPC

The relation REL in (32) maps a sortal receptacle noun concept (e.g., one for *glass*, *bowl*, etc.) to a relational one (a relation between things that are those receptacles and their contents).

In (32), we assume that the P λ-term (the one for the receptacle) is restricted to be a property for a common noun, namely one involving a DRS that introduces a counting base as a discourse referent. The Q λ-term is a variable for the contents predicate and is assumed to be likewise restricted. An innovation of our approach is to allow the entity that saturates the v argument to be a mereologically complex sum of container(s) and contents. The mereological conditions in the main DRS ensure that if something is a sum entity constituting bottles and milk, for instance, both the bottles and the milk are a part of the v argument, and that the sum of the bottles and the milk make up the totality of the v argument (otherwise v could be a sum of bottles and milk and something else).[12] The first conditional sub-DRS (the first duplex condition) in (32) expresses that for every part of the receptacle(s) that counts as one receptacle, there is some Q as its contents. (We use a convention that if u_1 is a discourse referent for a sum entity, then u_{11}, u_{12}, etc. are discourse referents for parts of u_1.) The $Contains_i$ relation is indexed to the context i, given that, as Khrizman et al. (2015) point out, the standards of how full a receptacle needs to be with its contents varies with context and the nature of the container and the contents. (In actuality, therefore, the full version of this should be $Contains_{i,P,Q}$, but we simplify it here.)

---

[12] The **not** $\boxed{u_1 \circ u_2}$ is included to deal with cases such as *boxes (full) of boxes*, in which case, none of the container boxes should also be boxes that are contained by other boxes in the relevant set.

The second conditional sub-DRSs in (32) express that, for every part of the contents (apportioned via the **S** operation; see example 26), there is some receptacle of which it is the contents. REL also introduces a constraint on Q, namely that it is not a quantized predicate (Krifka 1989), thus excluding expressions such as *basket of book* as felicitous (since $[\![book]\!]^i$ is a quantized predicate).

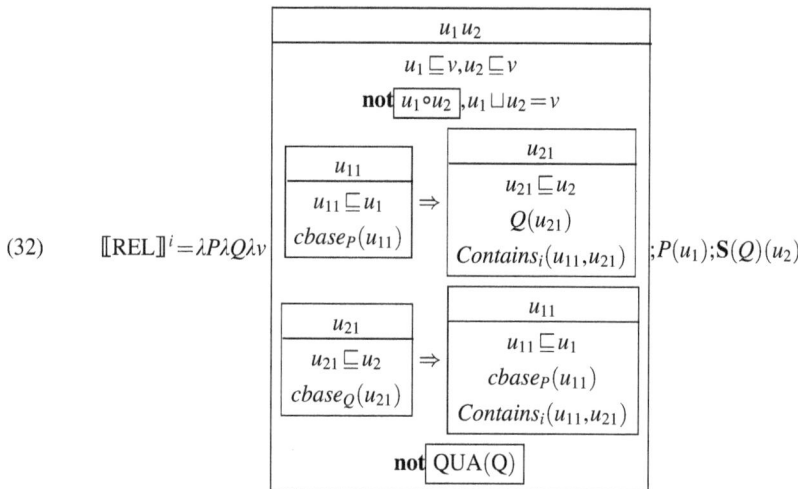

(32) $[\![REL]\!]^i = \lambda P \lambda Q \lambda v$

For brevity, in the following, we abbreviate the conditional DRSs as the following two relations $Contains\_each_i(u_1, u_2)$ and $Each\_contained\_by_i(u_2, u_1)$, which yields an abbreviated version of (32), given below in (33):

(33) $[\![REL]\!]^i = \lambda P \lambda Q \lambda v$

$\begin{array}{|l|}\hline u_1\ u_2 \\ \hline u_1 \sqsubseteq v, u_2 \sqsubseteq v \\ \text{not}\ \boxed{u_1 \circ u_2}, u_1 \sqcup u_2 = v \\ Contains\_each_i(u_1, u_2) \\ Each\_contained\_by_i(u_2, u_1) \\ \text{not}\ \boxed{\text{QUA}(Q)} \\ \hline \end{array}$; $P(u_1); \mathbf{S}(Q)(u_2)$

The container+contents reading for an NP such as *glasses of milk*, on our account refers to both the glasses and their milk contents (i.e. a mereological sum of glass$_1$, glass$_2$, milk$_1$, and milk$_2$). This sets our account apart from others in which only the container is referred to, or in which the contents reading is completely separated from (and in fact derived from) the container reading. However, Partee and Borschev (2012: 476) raise a concern over this kind of strategy, since, in their view, if the PPC applies to mereological sums of containers and contents, 'counting would make no sense'. Yet, given our definitions for $\mu_\#$ and REL and our dynamic framework, we can maintain a simply typed mereological approach in which counting does make sense. Our analysis of *two glasses of milk* is in (34). This gives us the set of sums of glasses and milk portions such that each glass contains a milk portion and each milk portion is contained in a glass. Crucially, as it stands, the representation is underspecified with respect to what is counted. The $cbase_x$ that restricts the cardinality function $\mu_\#$ can be bound to $cbase_{glass}$ or to $cbase_{milk}$. Given the definition of $\mu_\#$, binding to $cbase_{glass}$ restricts the set to sets of two glasses (each containing a portion of milk). Binding to $cbase_{milk}$ restricts the set to sets of two portions of milk (each the contents of a glass).

(34) $[\![\text{two glasses of milk}]\!] = [\![\text{NMOD}]\!] (2) ([\![\text{REL}]\!]^i ([\![\text{glasses}]\!]^i) ([\![\text{milk}]\!]))$

$$= \lambda v \begin{array}{|l|} \hline u_1 \ u_2 \ cbase_{glass} \ cbase_{milk} \\ ^*S_i(glass)(u_1), \ u_1 \sqsubseteq v \\ ^*S_i(milk)(u_2), \ u_2 \sqsubseteq v \\ \textbf{not}\boxed{u_1 \circ u_2}, u_1 \sqcup u_2 = v \\ cbase_{glass} = \lambda v' \ \boxed{S_i(glass)(v')} \\ cbase_{milk} = \lambda v'' \ \boxed{S_i(milk)(v'')} \\ Contains\_each_i(u_1, u_2) \\ Each\_contained\_by_i(u_2, u_1) \\ \textbf{not}(QUA([\![\text{milk}]\!])) \\ \mu_\#(cbase_x, v) = 2 \\ \hline \end{array}$$

Because we analyse the container+contents NumP as introducing discourse referents for both the containers and the contents, we can explain co-predication data and anaphoric reference to containers and contents. For example, by applying DET in (31) to the formula in (34) we would get a discourse reference added to the DRS (call this u_0). This discourse referent can then be picked up as a reference to all of the mereological sums that are glasses containing milk. However, the discourse referents u_1 and u_2 can be used to refer exclusively to the glasses and exclusively to the milk, respectively. For example, if the discourse proceeds with VPs which select for rigid physical objects or potable liquids such as *smashed them* or *drank them*, we get access only to the glasses in the first case, and only to the milk portions in the second. For co-predication constructions, the availability of these three discourse referents (the container+contents sum, the container, and the contents) are all available as arguments to transitive verbs. For example, in *picked up and tasted, but then smashed the glass of milk*, *picked up* is free to apply to the container+contents, *tasted* to the contents, and *smashed* to the container.

We therefore have covered data points (CC1) and (CC2) from above: our compositional analysis which derives the container+contents reading of the PPC from the interpretation of a sortal receptacle noun and a noun denoting the contents is such that the plural PPC distributes contents to containers and containers to contents, and the semantics for the PPC, on this reading, makes available reference to the container+contents, the container, and the contents. Furthermore, we have proposed a way that this can be done using conservative assumptions with respect to the complexity of the formal theory.

3.5. The Ad Hoc Measure Interpretation of the PPC

Our starting point for modelling the ad hoc measure interpretation of the PPC is a point of broad consensus: extensive measure functions are additive functions from entities to the set of real numbers (Krifka 1989). We also assume Rothstein's (2017) analysis of measure functions, which makes them relative to a dimension (such as volume), and a property that specifies the unit for the measurement scale (such as GLASS).

While our analysis is inspired by the analysis of measure functions in the PPC on its ad hoc measure interpretation which is proposed by Rothstein (2017) and Khrizman et al. (2015), it crucially differs from them in one key respect. On our analysis, the ad hoc measure interpretation is derived from the container+contents interpretation, and not from the sortal meanings of the relevant nouns that form a given PPC (such as ⟦glass⟧ and ⟦milk⟧ in the PPC – *a glass of milk* on its ad hoc measure interpretation). This allows us to capture all of points (M1)–(M3) from Section 3.1. We can explain why the amounts of stuff that count as units for ad hoc measures and the amounts of stuff in container+contents readings align in similar contexts (M2). At the same time, we ensure that such containers or contents are not accessible by anaphoric pronouns (M1), and that relative to a single context, the unit for an ad hoc measure is stable (M3).

Rothstein (2011, 2017) argues that the syntax of the ad hoc measure interpretation for a PPC like *two glasses of milk* is symmetrically branching, as in (35), and we adopt this structure as well.

(35) [$_{NP}$ [$_{MeasP}$ [$_{NUM}$ three][$_{N_{meas}}$ glasses]] (*of*) [$_{N}$ milk]]

Implicit in Rothstein's analysis is that the semantics for the N_{meas} *glasses* is derived from the sortal concept ⟦glass⟧ (plural morphology is semantically null for measure readings on her account). Rothstein's analysis of the measure reading of *glass* (=*glassful*) is given in (36).

(36) ⟦glass_{measure head}⟧ $= \lambda n \lambda x.\text{MEASURE}_{\text{VOLUME},\text{GLASS}}(x) = n$
(Rothstein, 2017, p. 58)

In (36), measuring involves 'assigning to a sum an overall value on a dimensional scale calibrated in dimension-appropriate units' (Rothstein 2017: 134). In this scale, VOLUME is a dimension, and GLASS 'is the unit of measurement in the relevant dimension, in terms of which the scale is calibrated' (Rothstein 2017: 135).

Khrizman et al. (2015) propose that the measure head is also related to the predicate that specifies the actual stuff being measured. This is schematised in (37) (Khrizman et al. 2015: 199).[13]

(37) a. [_{measure}glass] $\rightarrow \lambda N \lambda P \lambda x.\left(\mu_{[\text{VOLUME},\text{GLASS},P,c],w,t} \circ N\right)(x) \wedge P(x)$

b. [_{NP}three glasses of wine] $\rightarrow \lambda N \lambda P \lambda x.\mu_{[\text{VOLUME},\text{GLASS},\text{WINE},c],w,t}(x)$
$= 3 \wedge \text{WINE}_{w,t}(x)$

Given that this kind of measure is an ad hoc measure (not an exact, standardised measure), Rothstein (2017: 225) incorporates suggestions from Schvarcz (2014) that, in context, some member of the unit property can be selected such that the ad hoc measure function approximates an exact measure function based on this unit.

In general, we are highly sympathetic to this kind of approach. However, given data point (M2) (repeated below), an implicit assumption is required regarding the way that the unit is selected for the measure function. We propose that, if we make this assumption explicit, it reveals something interesting about how we arrive at the ad hoc measure interpretation of the PPC.

(M2) The ad hoc measure interpretation of the PPC refers to the same quantities of stuff as the container+contents interpretation of the PPC does in similar contexts.

The implicit assumption is that by specifying the context, the dimension (e.g. VOLUME), the unit predicate (e.g. GLASS), and the predicate for the stuff measured (e.g. WHISKEY), the selected unit determines that what is 1 on the measure scale is the same volume as what counts as one on the container +contents reading. In the present example, that would mean that, in most contexts, the ad hoc measure reading of *glass of whiskey* would relate to a volume of whiskey that is small in relation to the interior volume of the glass, just as is the case with the contents part of any container+contents reading in the same contexts. Now, if that is the case, then it makes sense for the same function that determines the relevant size of the glass-sized unit in question and what counts as one portion relative to this glass-unit in the container

---

[13] We make explicit the implicit dimension specifier.

+contents interpretation to also determine what is one portion relative to the same glass-sized unit on the ad hoc measure interpretation.

On our account, this is the pair of distributive relations $Contains\_each_{i,[\![glass]\!],[\![whiskey]\!]}(x,y)$ and $Each\_contained\_by_{i,[\![glass]\!],[\![whiskey]\!]}(y,x)$, the argument structure for which is introduced by REL. On the account of Khrizman et al. (2015), for example, this would be a similar pair of relations introduced by their container and contents readings, respectively (their **contents** and **contents**$^{-1}$). If this is right, then, given that the calibration of an ad hoc measure turns on, in part, the information provided by the relevant container+contents reading, it make sense to derive the former from the latter. It is this strategy that we propose to implement.

Given that we wish to retain the distinction between measure syntax and counting syntax, in a measure NP such as *1.5 glasses of wine*, the semantic structure should be as in (38):

(38)   ($[\![_{Nmeas}$ glasses (of)$]\!]$ ($[\![1.5]\!]$))($[\![milk]\!]$)

This, in turn, suggests that any function MEAS should be a function from concepts such as $[\![_{container+contents}$ glasses (of)$]\!]$ to concepts such as $[\![_{Nmeas}$ glasses (of)$]\!]$. The entry in (39) gives the container+contents reading of *glass (of)* which can provide such an input to the MEAS measure shifting operation. (This is so whether the measure phrase is singular or plural, since we adopt Rothstein's assumption that plural morphology in measure readings of PPCs is semantically vacuous.) In (39), $[\![_{c+c}$ glass of$]\!]$ is shorthand for $[\![_{container+contents}$ glass of$]\!]$.

(39) $[\![_{c+c}$ glass of$]\!] = [\![REL]\!]([\![glass]\!]^i)$

$$= \lambda Q \lambda v \begin{array}{|l|} \hline u_1\ u_2\ cbase_{glass} \\ \hline S_i(glass)(u_1),\quad u_1 \sqsubseteq v,\quad u_2 \sqsubseteq v \\ \text{not}\ \boxed{u_1 \circ u_2},\ u_1 \sqcup u_2 = v \\ cbase_{glass} = \lambda v'\ \boxed{S_i(glass)(v')} \\ Contains\_each_i(u_1, u_2) \\ Each\_contained\_by_i(u_2, u_1) \\ \text{not}\ \boxed{QUA(Q)} \\ \hline \end{array} ; Q(u_2)$$

Where the variable $\Re$ stands for a relational concept such as the one represented in (39), the semantics for our MEAS function is as in (40). One important part of the entry in (40) pertains to the unit of the scale, $\mathfrak{f}_i(\Re(Q))$ in $\mu_{[VOLUME,\mathfrak{f}_i(\Re(Q))]}(v) = n$, which takes a little bit of unpacking to make clear. In this formula, $\Re(Q)$ is the container+contents reading of a PPC

Container, Portion, and Measure Interpretations 299

where $\Re$ is a variable for something like $[\![\text{container+contents glass (of)}]\!]$ and Q is a variable for something like $[\![\text{milk}]\!]$. $\mathfrak{f}_i$ is a choice function (determined by the context variable *i*). Choice functions (Winter 1997) are functions from sets to one member of that set. If the choice function is selected by context, then in $\mathfrak{f}_i(\Re(Q))$, this amounts to a formalisation of Schvarcz's (2014) proposal for the selection of a member of the set denoted by the unit predicate as a calibration for the ad hoc measure. This means that $\mathfrak{f}_i(\Re(Q))$ is an entity, namely some salient container+contents sum in the context (e.g., some specific glass of milk). This yields a final interpretation for the unit specification. Given that, for example, (40) is applied to $[\![\text{glass of}]\!]$ and $[\![\text{milk}]\!]$, the unit is specified in terms of a single container+contents sum of a glass of milk selected from the context.

(40) $[\![\text{MEAS}]\!]^i = \lambda \Re \lambda n \lambda Q \lambda v \boxed{\begin{array}{c} Q(v) \\ \mu_{[VOLUME, \mathfrak{f}_i(\Re(Q))]}(v) = n \end{array}}$

The representation for *1.5 glasses of milk* is in (41). Since the counting base $cbase_{milk}$ is not accessible to the main DRS, potentially countable entities are not accessible either. (This is not relevant for *1.5 glasses of milk* but would be more so for the ad hoc measure reading of, e.g., *two boxes of apples* after which, for example, *each* should not be able to refer to the individual boxes or apples.) The set denoted is a set of milk that measures 1.5 with respect to a volume scale calibrated to a unit based upon a contextually salient container +contents *a glass of milk*.

(41) $[\![1.5 \text{ glasses of milk}]\!] = ([\![\text{MEAS}]\!]^i ([\![\text{REL}]\!]^i ([\![\text{glass}]\!]^i)))(1.5)([\![\text{milk}]\!]^i)$

$$= \lambda v \boxed{\begin{array}{l} \\ \hline cbase_{milk} \\ \hline \text{milk}(v) \\ cbase_{milk} = \lambda v' \boxed{\text{milk}(v')} \\ \hline \mu_{[VOLUME, \mathfrak{f}_i([\![REL]\!]^i([\![glass]\!]^i)([\![milk]\!]^i))]}(v) = 1.5 \end{array}}$$

Importantly, when shifted to a DP (via the application of DET in (31)), the representation in (41) only makes available a discourse referent for the milk (of the relevant measure), and not to the container or contents that is used to define the unit of the measure scale.

Evidence from diminutives. We conclude this section by briefly considering a possible source of further evidence for the view that ad hoc measure readings of PPCs are derived from container+contents readings, namely, those languages that have morphology that encodes a mass-to-count container

+contents shift. (See Hnout, Laks, and Rothstein, this volume, Chapter 6, for a discussion of other mass-to-count shifts in Palestinian Arabic.) Among such languages, two that we will briefly consider here are Dutch and Czech, in which certain uses of the diminutive occur with mass nouns and yield a count noun that has a container+contents interpretation (albeit one where the container is sensitive to conventions, the context, and possibly other socio-cultural world knowledge). The reason such data are relevant is that, if ad hoc measure readings are derived from container+contents readings, then measure readings for numerical expression constructions containing these nouns should be readily available, and, indeed, this is what we find.

In Dutch, *biertje* (beer.DIM) means 'glass/can of beer' and *wijntje* (wine. DIM) means 'glass of wine'. Our theory would predict that *biertje* can be combined directly with numerical expressions and get a measure reading, which is what our preliminary investigation into the evidence suggests, as shown by (42) and (43).

(42) Er   zit   nog   voor twee biertjes   in het vat.   [Dutch]
      there sit.3SG   still for   two   beer.DIM   in the barrel
      'There are still around two glassfuls of beer in the barrel.'

(43) Er   zit   nog   voor twee wijntjes   in de fles.   [Dutch]
      there sit.3SG   still for   two   wine.DIM   in the bottle
      'There are still around two glassfuls of wine in the bottle.'

In Czech, we get the same pattern for *pivečka* ('beer.DIM'), as shown in (44).

(44) V soudku   jsou   ještě nejméně dvě pivečka.   [Czech]
      in barrel.DIM are.3PL   still at.least two beer.DIM
      'There are still around 2 glassfuls of beer in the barrel.'

One issue that we will leave for future consideration is exactly what syntactic and semantic analysis measure readings of such constructions should have. It is tempting to consider them as NumPs, just like other kinds of counting constructions. However, if that is right, then they would differ syntactically and semantically from measure readings of PPCs insofar as they would not have Rothstein's 'measure' syntactic structure. Similar considerations apply on the semantic side with respect to whether we consider the numerical expression to denote a numeral, as in measure readings of PPCs, or to be a numerical modifier, as in NumPs.

3.6. Restrictions on Mass-to-Count Coercion

As observed above (see (MtC1) and (MtC2) in Section 3.1), the main puzzle raised by the counting construction with mass nouns (e.g., *two white wines*) is that the requisite mass-to-count coercion is relatively easy to get under the container+contents reinterpretation, but the ad hoc measure reinterpretation is hard (if not impossible) to get.

What is at stake here is type coercion, which is commonly understood (see, e.g., de Swart 1998) as a process triggered by a type mismatch between a functor and its argument in the composition of a string or utterance, which may trigger a reinterpretation of that string or utterance (by the hearer adding some contextually understood content) to satisfy the input requirement of the functor, and thus restore compositionality. If such a reinterpretation is not possible, that string or utterance will be uninterpretable or even ungrammatical.

In our case, exemplified with *two white wines*, the type mismatch is between a numerical expression in an adjectival use that requires a count NP as an argument, and a mass NP filling its argument slot.[14] This type mismatch triggers the insertion of a hidden coercion operator mapping a mass noun denotation to a count one, or, put differently, the coercion operator reinterprets the mass predicate as a count one. Coercion operators generally allow for a range of possible interpretations, which are constrained by lexical and contextual information. For instance, for *two white wines*, the coercion operator leads to the following enriched interpretations: (a) a set of subkinds of white wines; (b) a set of container+contents entities with white wine as the contents and some contextually specified type of container (e.g. a glass); and, in principle at least, (c) an ad hoc measure function that takes a numerical expression as an argument. In what follows, let us take a closer look at cases (b) and (c), setting aside the subkind coercion (a).

Coerced container+contents interpretations. Consider contexts in which *two white wines* is used in such a way that it can be interpreted as *two* GLASSES OF *white wine*. The coercion process is triggered by a type clash between ⟦two⟧ and ⟦white wine⟧^{i}. To repair the type clash, a contextually salient relational concept is needed. For wine, this may often be something like ⟦REL⟧^{i}(⟦glasses⟧^{i}). Applying ⟦REL⟧^{i}(⟦glasses⟧^{i}) to ⟦white wine⟧^{i} yields something equivalent to a count NP, and compositionality with the numerical is restored.

Coerced ad hoc measure interpretations. Now consider contexts in which it was possible to use *two and a half white wines* in such a way that it could be interpreted as *two and a half* GLASSFULS OF *white wine*. The coercion process would be triggered by a type mismatch between ⟦two and a half⟧ and ⟦white wine⟧^{i}. In this case, the fact that there is a fractional numerical

---

[14] Such clashes could be characterised syntactically or semantically, with the later being dependent on one's semantic theory of countability. For us, this would be between the interpretation of numerical expressions which presuppose an argument that specifies a quantized counting base, and a mass noun concept provided as an argument that does not specify a quantized counting base.

expression militates against a container+contents interpretation. To repair the type mismatch, therefore, a contextually salient measure is needed.

Based on our proposal that the measure interpretation is derived from the container+contents interpretation, the coercion process would have to look as follows. The ad hoc measure interpretation of *two white wines* would have to be derived by retrieving from the context, and then applying the (implicit) ⟦MEAS⟧^{i} function to an implicitly inferred container+contents receptacle concept (such as ⟦REL⟧^{i}(⟦glasses⟧^{i})). But this would mean that the implicitly inferred ⟦MEAS⟧^{i} would have to modify what is an implicitly inferred contextually determined meaning (e.g., ⟦REL⟧^{i}(⟦glasses⟧^{i})), which is the result of reinterpretation triggered by a type mismatch. This type of modification, we propose, is not available via coercion.

There are at least two reasons for ruling this out as coercion, one cognitive, the other theoretical. In relation to cognition, we speculate that it is too cognitively burdensome to perform combinatorial operations on two implicit (non-lexically realised) concepts (namely, applying an implicit MEAS to an implicit ⟦REL⟧^{i}(⟦glasses⟧^{i})). On the theoretical side, we think there is a case to be made that coerced ad hoc measure interpretations, should they be possible at all, are not really what we should solely think of as coercion, but rather as general pragmatic reasoning operating on the output of (i.e. 'on top of') coercion. Whereas coercion has been argued to arise all over the place in natural language communication, processes that tightly combine applying general pragmatic reasoning on top of coercion outputs do not, as far as we are aware, have any precedents in other areas of semantics and pragmatics. Hence, the coerced interpretation of *two and a half white wines* as *two and a half* GLASSFULS OF *white wine* is not possible, since this interpretation requires more than coercion to get it (and so is not, properly speaking, coercion at all).

In summary, we have proposed a reason why ad hoc measure interpretations are not available, via coercion, for many combinations of numerical expressions and mass nouns even though container+contents interpretations often are in rich enough contexts (points (MtC1) and (MtC2) in Section 3.1).

4. Summary

The main novel claims in this paper are threefold. First, we have argued that it is possible to give an adequate analysis of container+contents readings of PPCs in a simply-typed, dynamic, mereological framework. The crucial aspect of this analysis is that PPCs, when used in sentences, make available discourse referents for the container, for the contents, and for the container and contents together. We also accounted for the way in which PPCs make available two counting base sets that can be used as parameters in cardinality functions, one for the containers (each of which has a contents), and one for the contents (each of which is in a container). In this way, we have assuaged the worry of Partee and Borschev (2012) that, on a purely mereological analysis of PPCs, counting would not make sense.

Second, we argued that ad hoc measure readings of PPCs are derived from the container+contents reading insofar as MEAS applies to the container +contents shifted interpretation of *glass*. Our motivating evidence for this was that ad hoc measure readings typically specify the same volumes of stuff relative to container size as container+contents readings (see Sutton and Filip 2018b for other evidence for this based on, inter alia, co-predication data).

Third, we argued that this analysis of ad hoc measure interpretations of PPCs gives us a window on mass-to-count coercion. In NumPs formed with mass nouns, we observed that, in all but a few rarified cases (discussed in Section 2), coerced ad hoc measure interpretations are not available, whereas coerced container+contents interpretations are, modulo a suitable context. We proposed that this restriction is explained by the fact that coerced ad hoc measure interpretations would have to be derived via the application of an implicit (non-lexically provided) MEAS function applying to an implicit (non-lexically provided) container+contents interpretation of a suitable receptacle concept, and that this does not fit the standard pattern of coercion, but would be a combination of general pragmatic reasoning applied on top of coercion, something that may be blocked, we hypothesised, on cognitive and theoretical grounds.

13 Overlap and Countability in Exoskeletal Syntax: A Best-of-Both-Worlds Approach to the Count–Mass Distinction

Hanna de Vries and George Tsoulas

An intuitive approach to the count–mass distinction is to treat it as the grammatical counterpart to the human conceptual categories of substances and objects. These categories are prelinguistic and facilitate word learning in young children (Soja, Carey, and Spelke 1991); conversely, children who have mastered the grammatical count–mass distinction use it in order to decide whether a new word refers to an object or a substance (Gordon 1985; Bloom 1990).

Lexicalist approaches to the count–mass distinction, that treat mass and count as lexical properties of nouns, capture this intuitive link between a noun's grammatical behaviour and human perception and categorisation of stuff and objects in the world. For example, in English, mass nouns cannot appear with numerals or be pluralised without coercing them into a count interpretation. Under a lexicalist approach, this well-known observation may be accounted for by assuming that mass nouns range over a 'stuff' domain that does not provide minimal elements, which means there is nothing to count and nothing to underpin a singular–plural distinction (Link 1983; a related approach is found in Chierchia 1998a, 2010). However, precisely because they have been designed to hardwire certain linguistic regularities into the lexical structure of nouns, such accounts are less well equipped to deal with the large amount of count–mass flexibility that is actually attested both within and between languages. Some languages have been claimed to treat all nouns as mass (Mandarin) or as count (Yudja; Lima 2014a); some allow mass nouns to appear with plurals but not with numerals (Greek; Tsoulas, 2009) or mark (a subclass of) mass nouns plural by default (e.g. Manam (Lichtenberk 1983) and Berber (Mettouchi and Frajzyngier 2013)); many languages have 'object mass nouns' like *furniture* that range over objects but are grammatically mass (Barner and Snedeker 2005); and so on.

We thank audiences at SPiNFest 2017, SPE 9 and the Bochum count–mass workshop for their helpful comments on earlier versions, as well as Agata Renans, Jacopo Romoli, and Raffaella Folli, with whom we collaborated on the project that eventually led to this paper. The research reported in this chapter was funded with Leverhulme Grant #RPG-2016-100.

In contrast, constructionist approaches, that see the count–mass distinction as a purely morphosyntactic one, offer more tools to address both cross-linguistic variation and intra-linguistic count–mass flexibility (Sharvy 1978; Borer 2005). Nothing in a noun's lexical meaning forces or blocks a certain syntax. Instead, meaning – including the distinction between object and stuff reference – is compositionally created by syntactic operations and, as such, subject to all kinds of parametric variation (for example, a plural feature may contribute different semantic or phonological effects depending on its position in the derivation). However, such morphosyntactic determinism leaves little room for conceptual factors, which makes it non-obvious how we could integrate (for example) the aforementioned acquisition data into our theory or account for wider cross-linguistic generalisations (e.g., no language that shows the count–mass distinction expresses the concept CAT as a mass noun and WATER as a count noun). Moreover, the assumption that all meaning is created in syntax faces some of the same conceptual problems as the assumption that all meaning is hardwired into lexical entries: even though it does away with the need for systematic ambiguity or polysemy, it still equates a lack of countability with reference to stuff.

In this chapter, we will offer a new way of analysing the syntax and semantics of the count–mass distinction at the syntax-semantics interface, by synthesising the constructionist framework originating in the work of Borer (2005) with the (lexicalist) 'Iceberg semantics' proposed by Landman (2011, 2016). We believe that this synthesis has several conceptual and empirical advantages over existing frameworks. It combines the flexibility and morphosyntax-driven nature of constructivism with an explicit role for human conceptual categories such as INDIVIDUAL and SUBSTANCE. It allows us to distinguish between different kinds of count–mass shifts and makes explicit why some of them are harder than others. Furthermore, it clarifies the distinction between stuff reference, number neutrality and non-countability, three distinct (although interdependent) nominal properties that are often explicitly or implicitly conflated in existing accounts of the count–mass distinction.

1. Towards a Hybrid Theory of the Count–Mass Distinction

To start off, a few notes on terminology. Even though we will eventually assume that mass and count are syntactic properties, not lexical features, we will rely on some familiar lexicalist terminology. First, we will use 'mass' and 'count' in their grammatical sense; on the meaning side of things, we will use 'stuff reference' and 'object reference'. We will use the terms 'core mass' and 'core count' to refer to nouns that typically occur in respectively mass and count DPs in languages that have a grammatical count–mass distinction. 'Inherently flexible' nouns are nouns that occur naturally in both count and mass DPs, such as *rope, stone, bread* and *hair*. Our use of terms like 'packaging' and 'grinding' is similarly intended to be pretheoretical and does not constitute a claim about the kind of linguistic process involved; one may read 'grinding' as 'stuff interpretation of a core count noun' and 'packaging' as 'object interpretation of a core mass noun'.

1.1. Asymmetries in Flexibility

As is well known, mass and count are rather flexible properties: in the right context and morphosyntactic environment, core mass nouns may be interpreted as count and vice versa (Pelletier 1975; Bunt 1985; and many others). This flexibility is treated as a major argument in favour of constructionism by Borer (2005).

(1)   a. Three coffees, please.   ('packaging')
       b. We offer three white wines.   ('sorting')
       c. After the truck drove into my Halloween display, there
         was pumpkin all over the road.   ('grinding')

Under a lexicalist approach to the count–mass distinction in which mass and count nouns range over different types of entities, the 'core' meaning (whether mass or count) is basic; the shifted meaning needs additional lexical or compositional work.[1] On the other hand, the constructionist approach to the count–mass distinction originating in Borer (2005) acknowledges neither lexical reanalysis nor covert semantic typeshifting; instead, all the count–mass shifts in (1) are treated as morphosyntactic derivations. In addition, the object meanings are always derived from the stuff meanings, regardless of which meaning is typical. *Coffee* in (1a) and *coffee* in 'I like coffee' have the exact same meaning (i.e, the substance coffee); the 'portion of' part is contributed by the plural morpheme *-s* (in a major and influential departure from common semantic assumptions, Borer analyses the plural as a dividing element akin to classifiers, rather than a pluralising operator). Similarly, the meaning of *pumpkin* in (1c) is identical to

---

[1] Concrete proposals differ. One lexicalist approach to count–mass flexibility is based on polysemy or lexical reanalysis; according to such an approach, for instance, the word *coffee* has a default stuff meaning (which behaves like a mass noun) but may be coerced into a count predicate over atomic portions or cups of coffee. Similarly, *pumpkin* in (1c) is reinterpreted as non-countable 'pumpkin stuff'. The second type of lexicalist approach involves systematic covert mappings between object entities and stuff entities; such an approach is taken by, among others, Link (1983) and Chierchia (2010). (In Link's framework, objects and stuff correspond to two separate ontological domains, while Chierchia argues that they share the same domain but are distinguished by the properties of their minimal elements. In both types of ontology, however, mass and count interpretations of the same noun do not share their referents, and the link between the two needs to be established through arbitrary mapping functions that have to be defined as part of the model.)

the meaning of the word in 'I grew an award-winning pumpkin', that is pumpkin stuff; the difference is that the latter sentence involves a dividing element that partitions this pumpkin stuff into individual pumpkins.

The different approaches make different predictions. If count–mass shifts involve reanalysis, they should come with the associated processing cost; for example, processing sentence (1a) should be more costly than processing 'Three muffins, please'. Moreover, grinding, packaging and sorting are all expected to be equally costly. On the other hand, if all count interpretations (whether 'packaged', 'sorted' or core count) involve exactly the same derivation and no lexical reanalysis, they should pattern together both in terms of grammatical behaviour and processing, and the same holds for mass interpretations (whether 'ground' or core mass).

However, the available evidence – though occasionally conflicting – seems to support a hybrid model, in which count/mass shifts differ in their availability and degree of complexity, sometimes involving reanalysis and sometimes syntactic derivation, perhaps varying between languages. Concretely, on the whole, the evidence points towards: (1) an asymmetry between packaging and sorting; (2) an asymmetry between core count/mass nouns and inherently flexible ones; and (3) an asymmetry between packaging and grinding.

Packaging versus sorting. Based on morphosyntactic evidence from different Germanic languages, Wiese and Maling (2005) argue that sorting always involves lexical reanalysis, as does packaging in English; however, other languages may employ different packaging strategies. In particular, they claim that packaging involves a covert classifier structure rather than reanalysis in languages like Icelandic and German (the same applies to Dutch; cf. Khrizman et al. 2015). However, while Wiese and Maling's claim about packaging was confirmed experimentally in an ERP study of Icelandic by Whelpton et al. (2014), the same study also found that sorting was completely effortless (unexpected under a lexical reanalysis hypothesis).

The asymmetry between sorting and packaging is also evident in English, once we look beyond the food-related contexts that are usually invoked. Consider the contrast in (2):

(2) a. I take five sugars in my coffee.
     b. ??I just built a tower out of sugars.

While the use of *sugars* in (2a) is very natural, and interpreted as 'units of sugar' or 'sugar cubes', the same interpretation is much harder to access outside of a food context (e.g. (2b)). Even within food contexts, unit interpretations of mass nouns take on a meaning that seems to be much more specific than the 'standard unit of X' paraphrase that is often suggested; thus, neither (3b) nor (3c) is quite accurate in the given context, even though the paraphrase in (3a) is.

(3) Context: Jess has drunk a beer glass full of wine, which corresponds to two standard units of wine.
   a. Jess has drunk two units of wine.   ✓
   b. Jess has drunk one wine.   ×
   c. Jess has drunk two wines.   ×

Instead, (3b) and (3c) seem to convey that Jess was served a certain number of units of wine in the same number of appropriate (and appropriately sized) containers. In other words, packaging is not just about dividing stuff into portions of a certain size; it also incorporates the packaging 'material' into the meaning of the resulting noun. In English this incorporation of the packaging appears to involve lexical reanalysis while in Icelandic it involves a covert container classifier, but the idea is the same.

Core versus inherently flexible nouns. As previously mentioned, packaging of core mass nouns in the Dutch language manifests the same pattern as Wiese and Maling's analysis of the phenomenon in German, being both very restricted context-wise and involving a dedicated covert classifier construction. Inherently flexible nouns, however, show a very different pattern. While unit interpretations of such nouns behave like ordinary count nouns in every respect (i.e., they accept the full range of count morphosyntax and are not limited to particular contexts), there is some evidence that they are not derived from the mass uses in the same way that sorted interpretations are. Dutch has two grammatical genders, common and neuter. As (4) shows, sorting never changes the gender of a noun; however, it is not unusual for nouns that naturally alternate between mass and count to have a different gender in each incarnation (5):

(4) a. Jo drinkt graag   (een) lekker.∅   bier.
      Jo drinks eagerly   (a) tasty.NEUT   beer
      'Jo likes to drink tasty beer.' / '... a tasty beer.'   (subkind only)
     b. Jan drinkt graag   (een) lekker.e   wijn.
      Jan drinks eagerly   (a) tasty.COMM   wine
      'Jan likes to drink tasty wine.' / '... a tasty wine.'   (subkind only)

(5) a. Het draad   b. De draad
      the-NEUT thread   the-COMM thread
      'the thread' (mass)   'the thread' (count)

     c. Het kiezel   d. De kiezel
      the-NEUT shingle   the-COMM pebble
      'the shingle/gravel'   'the pebble'

Regardless of whether we take a lexicalist or constructionist view of gender, these data again point towards an asymmetry between sorting and packaging that is predicted by neither view. Moreover, it suggests (contra the constructionist view) that there is a derivational difference between count interpretations of inherently flexible nouns and count interpretations of core mass nouns.

Packaging versus grinding. Grinding (i.e., the use of core count nouns in mass DPs), in English as well as Dutch, seems to pattern with sorting rather than with packaging. It is not limited to restaurant contexts or foodstuffs, and is not associated with any special morphosyntax in Dutch.

(6) a. This song needs more cowbell!
  b. Jan and Jo are fighting over three inches of shelf again.
  c. My upstairs neighbour threw a party yesterday, hence the bits of ceiling all over the floor.
  d. Upon opening the door, I was jumped by ninety pounds of excited dog.

Note that, despite the terminology, nothing is actually 'ground' in most of these examples. Measuring dog-stuff or shelf-stuff can be done in many ways, most of which do not require the physical chopping-up of any dogs or shelves. It seems that the 'ground' effect of classic examples like *There was pumpkin all over the road* or *Jimmy the termite loves shelf* is not contributed by the mass-ness of the DP per se, but is an additional inference triggered either by the context (typically, anything food-related) or the particular predicate ('all over the road'). In other words, (6b) – even though it involves a mass DP and a measure construction – is not just about shelf-stuff but about *a particular shelf*, and in (6c) it is clear that what is weighed is not just dog-stuff, but *a dog*. In short, unlike stuff interpretations of inherently flexible nouns, grinding has a derivational flavour; the meaning of the mass DP is determined relative to the noun's object interpretation, which itself continues to be present in the background. In line with this, mass and count uses of core count nouns in Dutch always have the same gender:

(7) a. Al die ruzie om een (paar centimeter) schamel.e boekenplank!
 All that fight over a (few centimeters) measly.COMM book-shelf
 'All that fighting over a measly bookshelf / a few centimeters of measly bookshelf!'
 b. Wat een prachtig.∅ monumentaal.∅ plafond!
 what a gorgeous.NEUT monumental.NEUT ceiling
 'What a gorgeous monumental ceiling!'
 c. Tijdens het feestje van mijn bovenbuurman regende het monumentaal.∅ plafond.
 during the party of my upstairs- rained it monumental. ceiling
 neighbour NEUT
 'During my upstairs neighbour's party, it rained monumental ceiling.'

Taken together, the data in this section suggest that sorting of core mass nouns and grinding of core count nouns are morphosyntactic derivations involving the same lexical items, while packaging of core mass nouns involves either lexical reanalysis or additional (covert) lexical material. In addition, inherently flexible nouns really seem to form a separate class from 'core' count–mass nouns: the Dutch gender data suggest that they either involve distinct lexical entries, or derivations that diverge at a point much closer to the lexical root (before gender is assigned).

1.2. Interpreting the Asymmetries: Towards a Disjointness Semantics . . .

Not all lexicalist approaches to the count–mass distinction rely on an ontological or type distinction between mass and count denotations. An alternative approach, which has gained in popularity over the past few years, is to treat the distinction in terms of overlap versus disjointness (e.g., Rothstein 2011; Landman 2011; Khrizman et al. 2015; Landman 2016; Sutton and Filip 2016b; Rothstein 2017). In Landman's 'Iceberg Semantics', on which we base our models for the remainder of this chapter, both mass and count nouns denote predicates over mereological sums. Perhaps these sums have atomic minimal parts, perhaps they do not; in Iceberg semantics, this does not actually matter, which effectively makes it a single-domain approach in which both mass and count nouns range over 'stuff'. The difference is that count nouns divide that stuff in a way that necessarily excludes any overlap, while mass nouns allow, in principle, for infinite division possibilities. Cats, for instance, are disjoint: the same bit of cat-stuff cannot simultaneously be part of multiple cats. As a consequence, there is only one way to divide a domain of cat-stuff such that it results in a predicate over things that are cats; this means that the cardinality of the predicate **cat** is stable and non-arbitrary, enabling counting. In contrast, there are endless ways in which a domain of water can be divided such that it results in a predicate over things that are water; as a consequence, the predicate **water** does not have a stable cardinality and cannot be counted. Thus, countability is sensitive to disjointness.[2]

If mass and count predicates equally range over sums, turning one into the other can be a simple compositional move, that does not involve any elements that are not already present in the semantics. Deriving a count predicate from a mass one, for example, could be as easy as intersecting it with a disjoint modifier. Similarly, accessing the Boolean parts of a set of disjoint sums can be done compositionally, without lexical reanalysis or typeshifting between ontological domains. In this way, a disjointness-based approach like Iceberg semantics has the potential to account for the asymmetries between different

---

[2] Note that disjointness is a sufficient, but not necessary condition for stable cardinality. Some predicates over non-disjoint sums may still have stable cardinality, and be counted. For example, if two of the cats that make up the extension of CAT are conjoined twins, some of their 'stuff' might not clearly belong to one cat or the other, but no matter how we divide it we will never end up with anything more or less than two cats. See also Rothstein (2010, 2011); Chierchia (2010); Landman (2011); and Sutton and Filip (2016b) for related discussions.

cases of count–mass flexibility. First, it allows for non-costly derivational changes from mass to count and vice versa, as long as the derived predicate does not involve any new 'stuff'. Grinding, for example, involves the same stuff divided in a different way, and is therefore predicted to be non-costly. The same holds for sorting: assuming a Chierchian understanding of kind reference in which kinds can be compositionally derived from their tokens, sorting can also be analysed as a way of reusing the same referential material. On the other hand, we have seen that packaging tends to involve the addition of new lexical material, which would require some form of reanalysis or covert syntax even in an overlap-based semantics; this enables us to account for the exceptional status of packaging with respect to both grinding and sorting. Finally, since Iceberg semantics is a lexicalist framework, it is always possible to rely on lexical ambiguity in order to account for the interpretation of nouns that systematically alternate between mass and count; we do not need to assume that one has to be derived from the other in some way, which means the Dutch gender facts can be straightforwardly dealt with (we will make this more concrete in Section 2.1).

1.3.   ... With a Role for Derivational Processes

On the other hand, Iceberg semantics shares a few shortcomings with its fellow lexicalist accounts. First, a core assumption of Iceberg semantics is that a predicate's overlap properties can only be changed by intersecting it with other lexical material. From this it follows that a change in countability always goes hand in hand with reference to a subset of the original predicate. However, examples like (8) suggest that countability properties may be directly manipulated by functional morphology, without any intersective modification:

(8)   Het ge.dier.te
      the GE.animal.TE
      'the animal(s), the fauna'   (Dutch)

In (8), a perfectly prototypical count noun (*dier* 'animal') is turned into an uncountable number neutral predicate by morphological derivation.[3] The reference itself does not change: *gedierte*, like its stem *dier*, is a predicate over individual animal entities, so there is no reinterpretation or coercion of the meaning of *dier* involved. The only difference between *dier* and *gedierte* is that the former is countable and singular while the latter is uncountable and

---

[3] Object mass nouns of the form *ge.NOUN.te* form a small and no longer productive class in Dutch; other examples are *gebladerte* 'foliage' (from *blad(er)* 'leaf'), *geboomte* 'trees, woods' (from *boom* 'tree'), *gebergte* 'mountain(s), mountain range' (from *berg* 'mountain'), *gevogelte* 'bird(s), avifauna' (from *vogel* 'bird'), *geboefte* 'criminal(s)' (from *boef* 'criminal'), and *ongedierte* 'vermin' (from *dier* 'animal').

number neutral. This means that the mass-like behaviour of *gedierte* must be imposed by the particular morphological derivation; it cannot be lexically inherent in the stem (as in Chierchia's 2010 'lexical accident' approach to object mass nouns) or be due to some conceptual property of its referent (as in the approach to 'neat mass' advocated in Landman 2011 and Sutton and Filip 2016b). This means that the way count–mass flexibility is dealt with in Iceberg semantics is not enough; we need a larger role for derivational morphology.

The second bit of evidence that supports a move towards a more constructionist framework also has to do with the nominal properties of countability and number neutrality. Countability affects the ability of a noun to appear directly with numerals and count quantifiers like *each* or *several*. Number neutrality refers to the inclusion of plural as well as singular individuals or, more generally, closure under sum. Mass nouns like *sand* are uncountable (*each sand) and number neutral: all possible quantities of sand from individual grains to the sum of all the world's sand can be referred to as *sand*. English uninflected count nouns like *cat* are countable but not number neutral: we can say *one cat* or *each cat*, but the sum of my six cats cannot be referred to as *my cat*. Their plural counterparts are also countable (*six cats*); in addition, it is generally agreed in the literature that English plurals like *cats* include singular cats as well as cat-sums in their extension and are therefore number neutral (e.g. Sauerland, Anderssen, and Yatsushiro 2005; Zweig 2009; among others). In many languages, such as Hungarian (Farkas and de Swart 2010), Indonesian (Sneddon 1996; Chung 2000), Turkish (Corbett 2000: 14), and Western Armenian (Bale and Khanjian, 2008; see the example in (9)), uninflected count nouns are arguably number neutral (but may still be pluralised); (British) English itself has a small class of countable number neutral nouns such as *staff, clergy*, and *police* (*three staff, many police*).[4]

(9) a. Bezdig vaze.ts
     child run.PAST(3, SG)
     'One or more children ran.' (Western Armenian; Bale and Khanjian, 2008)

Meanwhile, in pure classifier languages like Mandarin, all nouns are uncountable number neutral. Table 13.1 sums up the cross-linguistic picture.

As Table 13.1 shows, cross-linguistically, uninflected countable predicates may or may not be number neutral. However, the reverse does not hold: there seems to be no language in which uninflected predicates are uncountable but not closed under sum. Thus, no language refers to cats or water with a predicate *tac* or *retaw* such that (10a,b) are ungrammatical and (10c) is true:

---

[4] It should be noted that there is some debate in the literature on the nature of nouns like 'police', with some authors claiming they are not really countable (e.g. Acquaviva 2008). See de Vries (to appear) for an overview of the (sparse) literature.

Table 13.1. *Different classes of uninflected nouns across languages*

	[+number neutral]	[-number neutral]
[+countable]	Count nouns in Hungarian, Western Armenian etc. In English: *police, staff*	Most uninflected count nouns in English and Dutch (*cat, bicycle* etc)
[−countable]	All nouns in Mandarin; (object) mass nouns in English	n/a

(10)   a. *one tac, *each retaw
       b. (Pointing to my six cats) *Look, my tac!
       c. The contents of glass 1 are retaw. The contents of glass 2 are retaw. The contents of glass 1 and 2 put together is not retaw.

This means that out of the four logically possible combinations of [±countable] and [±number neutral], three are attested cross-linguistically while the fourth, [−countable, −number neutral], is not.[5] This means that the two properties can't be reduced to each other, but are not fully independent either. However, in Iceberg semantics, the two properties are independently modelled, which means that the absence of [−countable, −number neutral] nouns needs to be stipulated.

A constructionist account has the benefit of compositionality, which makes missing feature combinations fairly easy to model by assuming a sequence of grammatical operations. In Borer (2005), nouns start out as uncountable and number neutral; a dividing projection DivP optionally turns them countable; then a further NumP projection (which builds on DivP) optionally assigns them a non-neutral number feature (cf. Martí 2020). However, unlike the lexical accounts, the exoskeletal account as put forward in Borer (2005) is unable to distinguish between uncountable number neutral reference to objects and reference to stuff. Both are characterised by a lack of DivP and NumP and should therefore have the same range of meanings. However, as Cheng, Doetjes, and Sybesma (2008) observe, Mandarin bare object-referring nouns lack the 'ground' reading that characterises bare count nouns in English: they may be uncountable and number neutral but they still necessarily refer to objects and not to the stuff the objects are made of. Conversely, English bare count nouns are coerced to a stuff interpretation; they cannot refer to objects in a number neutral way.

---

[5] Chierchia (2010) assumes that mass predicates originate as sets of uncountable atoms, which would make them [−countable, −number neutral], but he then needs to rely on a system of typeshifts in order to explain why mass nouns don't behave in this way (i.e., they always behave as if they range over full mereologies, not just minimal quantities).

Summing up, we need a formal framework in which only [+countable] nouns can be [−number neutral], which does not reduce stuff reference to uncountable number neutrality.

2. 'Exoskeletal Iceberg Semantics'[6]

Our analysis of the count–mass distinction adapts Landman's Iceberg version of disjointness semantics to fit a constructionist 'exoskeletal' syntax based on Borer (2005). In Landman's semantics, nominal predicates do not denote sets but *i-sets* (iceberg sets): a pair ⟨Body, Base⟩ where both Body and Base are sets of mereological sums, and Base *generates* Body: all the elements in Body are (sums of) elements in Base, and Body and Base have the same maximal sum (Body ⊆ *Base and ⊔Body = ⊔Base, where * is inclusive semantic pluralisation, i.e. closure under sum). The body expresses the extension of the noun in the usual way (e.g. BODY(CAT) = the set of individual cats; BODY (*CAT) = the (finite) set of all possible cat-sums; BODY(WATER) = the (possibly infinite) set of all possible water-sums). Since the body is affected by operations such as pluralisation, which turns it into an overlapping set, the mass or count status of a noun or NP is determined by the disjointness properties of its base, which is not affected in the same way. Both *cat* and *cats*, for example, have the same disjoint base **cat** (the set of individual cats). The base can be seen as a representation of the 'building blocks' of a predicate, while the body corresponds to its classical extension.

In our adaptation of Landman's system, rather than being provided lexically, both body and base are derived compositionally. In the first derivational stage, root meanings are converted into a set of predicate building blocks through a series of compositional operations (some of them optional and language-specific). In the second stage, these building blocks are used to construct full predicates – that is, i-sets – with the set of building blocks being preserved as the base. Let's look at each component of the system in a bit more detail.

Root meanings. We assume that lexical items are classless *roots* with very general meanings, which we model as *root concepts*: unions of mereologies (where a 'mereology' is defined as a set of mereological sums that is closed under both sum and parthood). For example, the root √TRUMPET is associated with a 'physical' mereology of trumpet parts and sums, but also with an event mereology of trumpeting events and subevents, a more abstract mereology of trumpet sound, and whatever other ontological domains the word *trumpet* may draw its possible meanings from. We write TRUMPET$^{\sqrt{C}}$ for the root concept.

---

[6] We are currently preparing a more in-depth exposition of this framework, including the general conceptual considerations behind it.

Filtering and predicate formation. Roots are turned into grammatical objects by an intersective filtering operation, which selects from the root concept only those sums that match a criterion imposed by the *filter head*. The available filter heads in the physical domain are INDIVIDUAL and SUBSTANCE:

- INDIVIDUAL: $\lambda C \lambda x$ [C(x) $\wedge$ **individual**(x)].
  For example, INDIVIDUAL(STONE$^{\sqrt{C}}$) is the set of all stone-sums that qualify as individuals.
- SUBSTANCE: $\lambda C \lambda x$ [C(x) $\wedge$ **substance**(x)].
  For example, SUBSTANCE(STONE$^{\sqrt{C}}$) is the set of all stone-sums.

We will call the result of applying a filter to a root concept a *filter set* or *f-set*; the f-set represents a set of predicate building blocks. Note that f-sets derived with INDIVIDUAL are semantically singular while f-sets derived with SUBSTANCE are complete mereologies, i.e. number neutral. In the subsequent derivational step, the actual predicate (an i-set) is constructed from the f-set (F) through a 'predicate formation' operation: PRED_FORM(F) = $\langle$F,F$\rangle$.

Parametric variation. Covert semantic pluralisation with * may obligatorily or optionally apply either immediately after derivation of the f-set (e.g. Mandarin) or after derivation of the i-set (e.g. Hungarian, Indonesian). This is a locus of cross-linguistic variation. We hypothesise that this operation needs to be spelled out phonologically if it is optional, but not if it is obligatory; this rules out hypothetical languages in which individual-denoting predicates are ambiguous between countable and uncountable versions of the same meaning. In Dutch, for instance, the *ge...te* circumfix (see example (8) and surrounding discussion) may be analysed as overt f-set pluralisation, resulting in an uncountable number neutral predicate over individuals, e.g. $\langle$***animal**, ***animal**$\rangle$ (cf. (11b)).

2.1. Back to Our Data

The present framework derives one type of substance predicate and three types of individual predicate: exactly the basic nominal predicates that are cross-linguistically attested. They are all shown in (11), demonstrating how the system is able to distinguish number neutrality and countability while correctly failing to derive the cross-linguistically absent [−countable, −number neutral] nouns. In addition, the system formally distinguishes uncountable number neutral object reference (11b) from stuff reference (11a). In Landman's terminology, the former are *neat mass* (the base is generated by a disjoint set, here **cat**) while the latter are *mess mass* (the base overlaps 'all the way down'). (NB: in (11), trees (c) and (d) have been slightly simplified where they match the one in (b).)

Overlap and Countability in Exoskeletal Syntax 317

(11) a. *Uncountable number neutral stuff reference (universal)*

i-set: ⟨**water, water**⟩

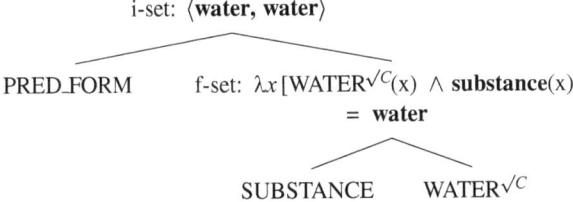

b. *Uncountable number neutral object reference (Mandarin)*

i-set: ⟨*cat, *cat⟩

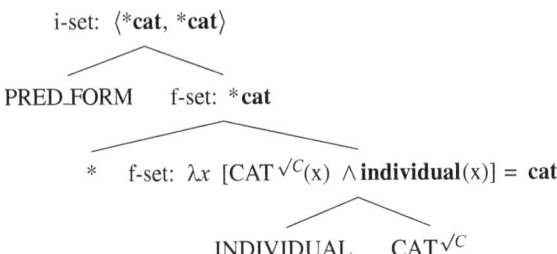

c. *Countable number neutral object reference (Hungarian)*

i-set: ⟨*cat, cat⟩

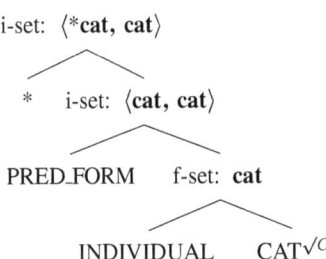

d. *Countable singular object reference (English)*

i-set: ⟨cat, cat⟩

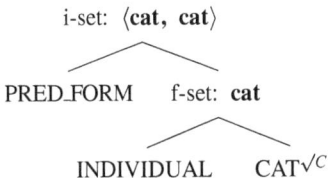

e. *Uncountable singular object reference*
⟨cat, *cat⟩ - underivable

Implementation-wise, our exoskeletal implementation of Iceberg semantics is fully constructional; following Borer, there is no structural difference between 'mass roots' and 'count roots'. However, even though the distinction between objects and stuff is not built into the lexical roots themselves, it plays a large role in the filtering process. We cannot define a filter head such as INDIVIDUAL, which takes a root concept and returns the set of objects embodying that concept, without some kind of notion of what constitutes an object. In this sense, this approach takes psycholinguistic findings on the prelinguistic nature of such notions more seriously than a lexical approach to the count–mass distinction does, since it relies on a truly independent notion of what it means to be individuated.

This does not mean that all filters are equally compatible with all roots, or that a concept like WATER$^{\sqrt{C}}$ can just as easily be embedded in a count DP as it can be embedded in a mass DP. Filtering out the individuals from a root concept is only possible if this root concept is in fact associated with individuals. For example, while it is technically possible to derive an f-set **water** by applying the filter INDIVIDUAL to the root concept WATER$^{\sqrt{C}}$, this f-set will end up empty since water-sums do not correspond to individuated entities as such. As we have seen, even in highly flexible languages like English, a packaged count NP *wine* does not refer just to particular quantities of wine, but to particular quantities of wine along with their appropriately sized containers; it seems reasonable to treat this as a distinct root concept. On the other hand, a root concept like STONE$^{\sqrt{C}}$ can be selected by either an INDIVIDUAL or a SUBSTANCE filter with meaningful (i.e., non-empty) results in both cases, since there are some stone-sums that clearly match our prelinguistic individuation criteria. If we assume, in addition, that nominal gender in Dutch is linked to the choice of filter head (cf. Arsenijevic 2016; Fassi Fehri 2016), the pattern in Section 1.1 neatly falls out: while the mass and count versions of inherently flexible nouns are derived through different filters and may be assigned different genders as a consequence, grinding and sorting are treated as derivational in our system (Section 1.2), which means the underlying filter (and hence the noun's gender) remains the same.

3. Conclusions

At the core of this paper has been a set of observations about count–mass flexibility that we have argued are unexpected from both a Borer-style constructionist view, and a Link/Chierchia-style lexicalist view. We have claimed that a single-domain, overlap-based semantic framework, such as Landman's recent Iceberg semantics, is best equipped to deal with these data. However, we have also noted that a purely lexical implementation of Iceberg semantics has some shortcomings that appear to call for the 'outsourcing' of certain nominal properties to morphosyntax, and have outlined a framework – 'Exoskeletal Iceberg semantics' – that offers precisely this. In further work, we intend to explore some applications of the framework beyond count–mass issues.

New Empirical Approaches to the Semantics of the Count–Mass Distinction

14 The Role of Context and Cognition in Countability: A Psycholinguistic Account of Lexical Distributions

Francesca Franzon, Giorgio Arcara, and Chiara Zanini

1. Introduction

Countability is a semantic feature related to the presence of a boundary (Jackendoff 1991); its opposite, uncountability, refers to the suppression of the reference to a boundary. Now, most (although possibly not all, as some of the papers in this volume argue) languages' lexicon contain words which usually denote entities like bounded objects (*chair*), and others that denote entities whose boundaries are usually not pertinent – like substances (*milk*).[1] As compared to other semantic features, the importance of countability emerges from the fact that it involves the morpho-syntactic level. The close relation with the syntax can be observed by comparing how a same noun (*cake*), presented in a count syntactic context, entails a reference to a boundary and denotes an object (*a cake*), whereas in a mass syntactic context (*some cake*) the reference to a boundary is not encoded.

At the morphological level, it is interesting to note that – in typologically different ways, but consistently across languages – countability constrains morphological Number, a nearly universally represented morphological feature (Corbett 2000; Dryer 2005). In fact, Number inflection is possible only for countable expressions, and uncountability allows only default morphological values to surface; for example, in most Indo-European languages, nouns used in mass references can only occur in the singular.

The phenomenon of countability is pervasive through the structural levels of language, and its near universality uncovers its importance as a core grammar

---

[1] In this regard, one could argue that there are pairs of words such as *garlic* vs. *onions* "where one is mass and the other is count and yet the items in the world that they describe seem to have no obvious difference that would account for this" (Pelletier 2012: 16). As clarified throughout the paper, we argue that boundaries and related concepts like shape are highly salient from a cognitive point of view (Prasada, Ferenz, and Haskell 2002) and likely to be encoded into language. Morpho-syntax, in particular, allows us to refer or not to the boundaries depending on the contextual relevance. Thus, since it is more probable that one cooks one onion, but just one garlic clove, it turns out that the word onion is mainly used in count contexts and so considered a count noun, whereas the word garlic is mainly used in mass contexts and so considered a mass noun.

component. It is thus fundamental to explore the more general question of how language encodes meanings from the referential world. As the issue involves semantics as well as the morphological and the syntactic levels, different types of formalizations of the phenomena related to countability have been proposed so far.

1.1. Formal Linguistics Studies

Approaches based on formal semantics theorize that every noun is originally marked as either mass or count, depending on referential properties and linguistic properties of meaning (Chierchia 1998a, 2010; Jackendoff 1991). An ontological property of an entity would be straightforwardly encoded into language as a binary lexical feature, which would subsequently determine grammatical constraints. Nouns denoting objects should not occur in mass syntactic contexts, and nouns denoting substances should not occur in count contexts. Ad hoc semantic shift operations account for the possibility for nouns to occur in syntactic contexts that should not be admitted, given their original countability feature. Namely, *portioning* operations would turn a mass noun into a count noun, semantically referring to bounded portions of the denoted entity (*a milk*); *grinding* operations would turn a count noun into a mass noun denoting the substance the entity is made of (*some chair*). *Portioning* is reported as intuitively more natural than *grinding*, especially when the latter concerns animate referents; however, in principle both operations are possible, and act on some intrinsic feature that divides the lexicon in two distinct types of nouns.

Other theoretical accounts are less strict in assuming a one-to-one mapping between a property of the entity and a lexical feature, and point to the role of the referential context in determining countability, and to the role of the linguistic context of occurrence in denoting it within nominal expressions (Allan 1980; Pelletier 2012; Rothstein 2010). Among these approaches, the ones that provide syntax-based formalizations describe the steps occurring in the morpho-syntactic computation of nouns, starting from lexical roots whose countability is not specified (Borer 2005; De Belder 2011). Syntax-based descriptions agree on the fact that more syntactic operations are required when encoding a count reference, as compared to a mass reference. At the morphological level, the complexity is related to the possibility to inflect the nouns for Number: nouns used as mass can occur only in the singular, which in that case is used as a default value, needed to perform syntactic operations at the phrase and sentence level. The encoding of countability would be formally more complex than the encoding of uncountability. The different formalizations offered by the linguistic theory can lead to different predictions in the linguistic processing of countability and uncountability.

1.2. Experimental Literature

Studies conducted in experimental psycholinguistics do not provide a clear picture about the representation and processing of mass and count nouns as two distinct categories.

Data collected on experiments based on single word recognition, such as lexical decision tasks, do not consistently point to the same direction: some studies do not report significant time differences in accessing either mass or count nouns (Mondini et al. 2008), whereas others find longer response times in recognizing mass nouns (Gillon, Kehayia, and Taler 1999; Mondini et al. 2009). Longer processing times for mass nouns are also reported in sentence reading, as measured in an eye-tracking study by Frisson and Frazier (2005): when nouns were presented in a context which is unmarked for countability, a disadvantage in terms of fixation times was reported for mass nouns with respect to count nouns.

Studies comparing the brain activity related to the processing of mass and count nouns evidenced differences in some ERP components, both when nouns are presented as single words (Bisiacchi et al. 2005; Chiarelli et al. 2011; El Yagoubi et al. 2006; Mondini et al. 2008) and when nouns are presented in a phrase or sentence context (Chiarelli et al. 2011; Steinhauer et al. 2001). Overall, in the activity attributed to frontal areas, mass nouns seem to elicit a greater processing load with respect to count nouns, which has been related to an increased cognitive effort (Mondini et al. 2008).

Cognitive differences are also suggested by the dissociations reported in aphasia case studies. Patients are more impaired in retrieving mass nouns in naming tasks, and tend to overgeneralize count syntax, with very rare exceptions (Herbert and Best 2010). A preference for count interpretation and count morpho-syntactic contexts is reported in language acquisition as well (Barner and Snedeker 2005; Gathercole 1985). Children tend to assume that a newly presented word refers to a whole object, rather than to a substance (Bloom and Kelemen 1995; Markman 1991), despite the capability to distinguish objects and substances being mastered quite early (Soja, Carey, and Spelke 1991). Even in the presence of an otherwise fully developed grammatical competence, preschool children overextend count syntax to mass nouns (Zanini et al. 2017).

The observed inconsistency in the experimental literature may partly emerge from a suboptimal selection of the stimuli, possibly due to an overreliance upon single native speakers' judgment in assigning nouns to a mass or to a count experimental condition. Only a few recent studies have controlled the frequency of occurrence of experimental nouns as mass or count by means of corpus analysis or rating questionnaires (Vermote, Lauwers, and De Cuypere 2017; Zanini et al. 2017). As a consequence, it is possible that some nouns were categorized as mass for the experimental purposes while they can actually occur frequently with a count interpretation as well.

Although there is some inconsistency in the experimental literature, studies conducted with different research methods suggest that the processing of uncountability requires more cognitive effort than the processing of countability, especially in phrase or sentence context. To our knowledge, no study has ever reported longer response times or inferred a more demanding processing cost for count expressions with respect to mass expressions. Data from psycho- and neurolinguistics, as well as common patterns observed in language development, seem to challenge the theoretical assumption that count references are equally or more complex than mass references, at least for what concerns processing.

Results from studies that consider grammaticality and semantic judgments from a sample of speakers suggest that a great number of nouns can occur frequently in both count and mass contexts.

A rating study by Kulkarni, Rothstein, and Treves (2013) collected a database relative to the mass and count usage of 1434 nouns in six different languages involving sixteen overall informants. A set of metalinguistic questions were asked with respect to specific syntactic contexts and semantic conceptualizations. The authors found that "syntactic classes do not map onto each other, nor do they reflect beyond weak correlations, semantic attributes of the concepts" (Kulkarni, Rothstein, and Treves 2013: 132). Notably, although the metalinguistic questions required a binary (yes–no) answer, the results gave as an output a non-binary distribution of the items, linearly spread along a continuum instead.

Studies on corpora are consistent with such findings. For example, Schiehlen and Spranger (2006) explored a two-hundred-million-token corpus of German assuming a lexically based distinction between mass and count nouns and found that a huge number of noun occurrences remained ambiguous, occurring in both types of syntactic contexts. In fact, nouns spread on an ideal trajectory whose poles are represented by "pure mass" and "pure count" nouns once the syntactic contexts of the occurrences were taken into consideration. Also Katz and Zamparelli (2012) exploited the syntactic context to retrieve the distribution of nouns with respect to their countability in the ukWaC corpus (Baroni and Ueyama 2006) and reported that the nouns mostly found in mass contexts are found also in count contexts, and vice versa.

A binary feature can thus give rise to non-polarized distributions of nouns in the actual use of words. Grammaticality judgments based on a single speaker's intuition do not appear suitable for fully understanding the linear distribution of words in contexts. Other than providing a safer method for experimental stimuli selection, measuring the actual occurrences of words in context offers the possibility to explore unexpected aspects in the complexity of the phenomenon. Therefore, in order to better understand countability, it is desirable to rely on quantitative data that offer positive evidence of what actually happens in the language, and give the opportunity to measure the occurrence of non-random regularities as well as the rarity of marginal events.

2. A Quantitative Approach

We designed a study to measure the occurrence of nouns as mass and as count in Italian. In the first part, we focused on morphological Number. In the second part, we focused on the contexts of occurrence of nouns.

We chose 224 concrete nouns on the base of mass and count theoretical definitions given in traditional grammars. We excluded nouns whose mass/count alternation can correlate with a shift with respect to the reference (e.g., *acqua* "water" – *acque* "waters, oceans" or *erba* "grass" – *erbe* "grasses, herbs").[2] Nouns were inflected both in the singular and in the plural, for a total of 448 stimuli. Absolute frequency of the nouns both in the singular and in the plural was measured in the corpus itWaC (Baroni et al. 2009). Crucially, the list included the plural of 45 nouns for which only singular occurrences would be expected on a normative base ("pure mass" nouns such as *sangue* "blood" – **sangui* "bloods"). The list included only nouns with transparent inflection for Number. The list did not include compound nouns, derived nouns, or loan words.

2.1. Morphological Number: Rating Study

In this first study, we measured the speakers' sensitivity to the constraints of Number. The morphological Number system of Italian entails two values, namely singular and plural. Mass nouns should not occur in the plural, as in most languages.

2.2. Procedure

A questionnaire was designed in order to evaluate the subjective frequency relative to the occurrence of some nouns. The methodology was based on previous rating studies on word frequency (Ferrand et al. 2008). Participants were asked to rate on a seven-point Likert scale the subjective frequency of the nouns. The administered question was: "How frequently have you read or

---

[2] More generally, we tried to control for semantic variables as far as possible, as this is a preliminary study. For this reason, we avoided abstract words, lexical ambiguity, and problematic mass nouns such as *mobilio* 'furniture' (moreover, these latter are not so productive in Italian as in English). We are aware that these issues are central to the count–mass debate and deserve a more in-depth discussion that we leave for subsequent works.

Table 14.1. *Subjective frequency scores for singular and plural*

Score	Singular	Plural
n = 0	0	0
0 < n ≤ 1	0	7
1 ≤ n ≤ 2	3	47
2 ≤ n ≤ 3	45	60
3 ≤ n ≤ 4	88	63
4 ≤ n ≤ 5	70	36
n > 5	14	7

heard these words?" Participants were instructed not to express normative judgments, but to focus on the frequency with which they have encountered the words. The possible answers were: 0 = never heard or seen; 1 = one/few times in my whole life; 2 = once a year; 3 = once a month; 4 = once a week; 5 = once a day; 6 = more than once a day. The task started with fifteen trial nouns that were not included in the experimental list. The questionnaires were administered online by means of the SurveyMonkey platform (surveymonkey.com). The questionnaire was divided into two parts so that a participant never saw both the singular and the plural of the same noun. The nouns in the questionnaires were presented to each participant in a different random order.

2.3. Participants

126 native speakers of Italian took part to this study. Participants varied widely in age (range: 22–76 years; mean = 36.2, SD = 12.46) and education (1% primary school; 35% secondary school; 33% bachelor degree; 36% master degree; 8% PhD/medical specialization).

2.4. Results

Data were analysed using the software R (R Core Team 2019). The distribution of the subjective frequency scores for singular and plural across participants is summarized in Table 14.1 and plotted in Figures 14.1 and 14.2.

To investigate the difference of scoring between singular and plural, we fitted a cumulative link mixed model (ordinal::clmm; Christensen 2019) using Number (singular vs. plural) as predictor and the rating score as dependent variable. A random slope for Number by participants was included in the model. The results from this model indicate that, in general, the participants

The Role of Context and Cognition in Countability 327

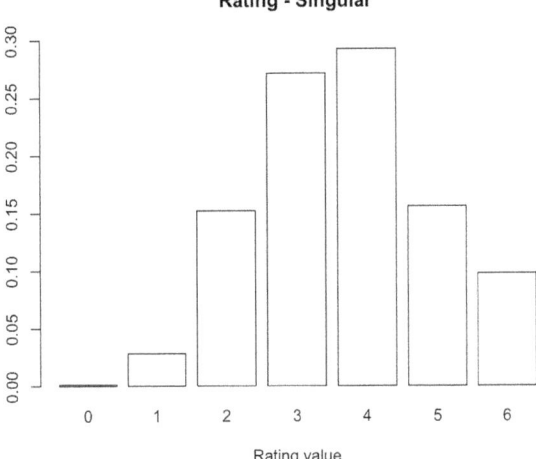

Fig. 14.1: Subjective frequency scores for singular

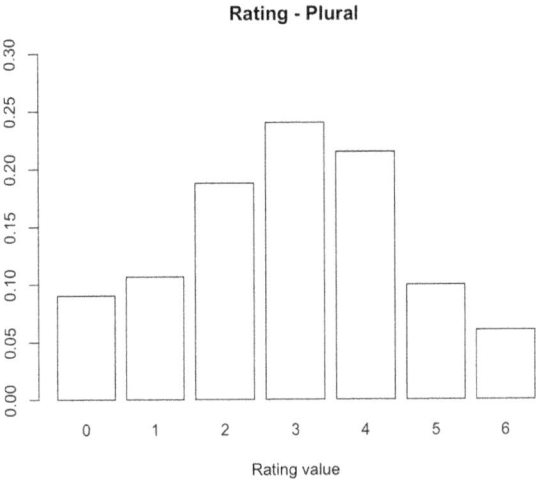

Fig. 14.2: Subjective frequency scores for plural

assigned lower scores to plural nouns [beta(Number = plural) = 0.95, z = 19.22, p < 0.05].[3] However, a detailed inspection of observed results shows that only

---

[3] As the proportional odds assumption was likely not to be met in this model, these general results could be misleading. However, the use of a more detailed approach (like separate logistic mixed regressions, or multinomial mixed regressions) goes outside the goal of this study, whose aim is

7 out of 224 plural items were scored <1: *sangue* "blood", *cacao* "cocoa", *cute* "skin", *pongo* "play dough", *iodio* "iodine", *latte* "milk", *pece* "pitch". Among these, only *sangue* and *latte* stand as outliers displaying a high score for the singular, while the other five nouns received low scores both in the singular and in the plural.

The plural occurrences of nouns considered as mass by normative grammar are well represented in the speakers' experiences. Therefore, every noun in our rating list can be linked to a countable interpretation, even if with a different (subjective) frequency. Plural can be taken as a hallmark of countability; however, nouns presented as single words inflected in the singular may be interpreted either as countable or as uncountable. One possible means of disambiguating these cases is to measure the syntactic contexts of occurrence of nouns by performing queries on corpora.

3. Corpus study

3.1. Procedure

We queried the itWaC corpus (Baroni et al. 2009) in order to check the existence of a correlation between occurrences of a same noun in mass syntax and in count syntax. It is not always possible to unambiguously trace the countability from every syntactic context. Noun phrases like *la pizza* "the pizza" (i.e. definite article + noun) do not provide sufficient information for this purpose. Furthermore, expanding the context up to the sentence level might not provide any additional clues anyway. In the sentence *La pizza che ho mangiato era fatta in casa* "the-SG pizza-SG I ate was home-baked", the noun *pizza* may receive a count or a mass interpretation: one single pizza or the substance the pizza is made from. Given this, we considered only the syntactic contexts unambiguously linked to one interpretation, adapting the methods proposed by Katz and Zamparelli (2012) in a study on English:

(1) Count (singular): Indeterminate article (+Adjective(s)) + Noun-SG
Mass: Verb (+ Adverb(s)) (+Adjective(s)) + bare Noun-SG
Quantification expressions (*molto* "lot of", *poco* "few", *troppo* "too much", ...) + Noun-SG

We performed the queries on the 224 nouns used for the previous rating. The results are plotted in Figure 14.3.

---

not to make detailed conclusions about the difference in occurrence between singular and plural, but to show that plurals could be actually more widespread than expected according to some theoretical perspectives.

The Role of Context and Cognition in Countability 329

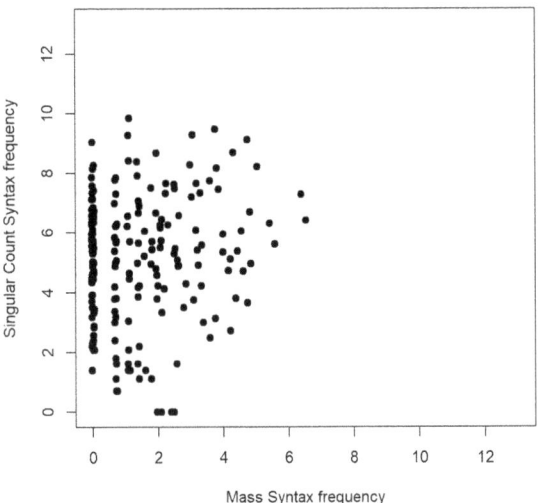

Fig. 14.3: Frequency of occurrence in count and mass syntax of all experimental stimuli

No significant inverse correlation was found on our experimental stimuli r(205) = 0.13 p = 0.07.

By using the same set of queries, we also collected the 100 nouns that occur most frequently in a mass context and the 100 nouns that occur most frequently in a count context. We compared their distribution with respect to both syntactic contexts. The results are plotted in Figures 14.4 and 14.5.

We did not find negative correlations with respect to our stimuli; no significant inverse correlations were found even when considering the nouns most frequently occurring respectively in the mass and in the count context in the whole corpus [100 nouns most frequently used as mass r(98) = 0.26 p = 0.009*; 100 nouns most frequently used as count r(98) = 0.07 p = 0.47]. Indeed, we found null correlations and, in the case of the top 100 nouns most frequently used as mass, a positive correlation. In other words, the fact that a noun is frequently used as count does not imply that it is scarcely used in mass contexts. Even more surprisingly, the positive correlation found for the top 100 nouns most frequently used as mass suggests that the more a noun is used as mass the more the same noun will be used as count, reflecting the bias for countability reported in experimental studies.

The absence of a significance correlation cannot be taken as evidence of equivalence between the two conditions (Lakens, Scheel, and Isager 2018).

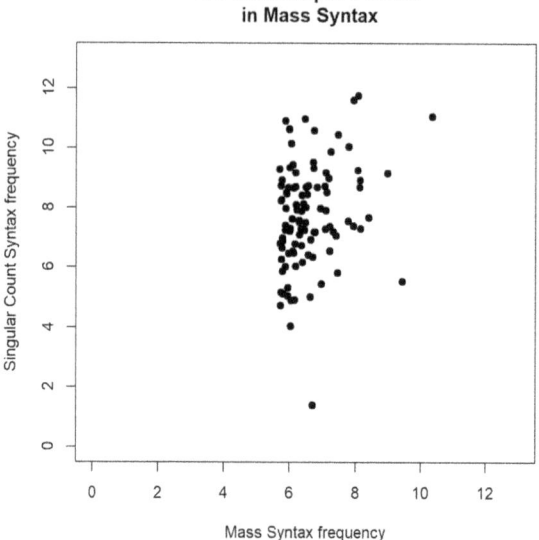

Fig. 14.4: Frequency of occurrence in mass and count syntax of the top 100 nouns that occur most frequently in a mass context

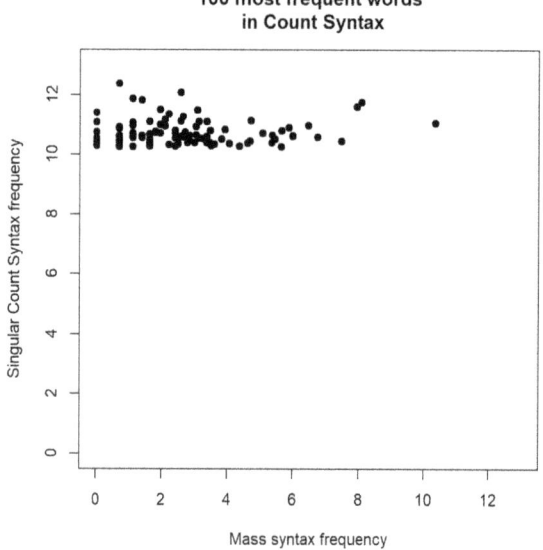

Fig. 14.5: Frequency of occurrence in mass and count syntax of the top 100 nouns that occur most frequently in a count context

Statistically speaking, indeed, a non-significant effect simply indicates that there is no evidence in favor of a difference. There could be many reasons for this lack of the effect, such as a high variability in the data or, in general, low statistical power. An emerging alternative approach to tackle this problem is to use *equivalence* testing. This approach, which returns p-values as in a null hypothesis test, investigates whether the statistical test supports the conclusion of an equivalence rather than a significant difference. In particular, we used the equivalence testing implementation of the TOSTER package. In the equivalence testing it is investigated whether the observed is significantly equivalent to the value within a specified interval. In the case of correlations, equivalence testing requires one to specify an interval of an observed correlation parameter that is thought to indicate the presence of a true correlation. For our analysis, we opted for a very generic interval of correlation values, spanning from 0 to 1, namely spanning from no correlation to the highest positive correlation. This interval would not be expected under a lexical approach to countability, which would rather predict a negative correlation. We observed a significant result of this analysis [p = 0.047], thus supporting evidence against the existence of negative correlation between the frequency of occurrence of a same noun in mass and count contexts.

4. Discussion

4.1. A Context Driven Countability

Consistent with the data reported for other languages, the distribution of Italian nouns in the corpus shows that most nouns can frequently appear both in mass and in count contexts, and do not show two distinct behaviors, since they are not used only as mass or only as count. The lack of observed negative correlations, that is the lack of a polar distribution for the great majority of the nouns, makes it difficult (although not impossible) to defend the idea that the lexicon basically distinguishes between mass and count features, at least in Italian. Indeed, it is less straightforward to decide whether a noun is in origin marked as mass or count if it is equally distributed in both contexts. In other words, it is not possible to disambiguate the starting point for operations of *packaging* and *grinding* intervening at the lexical level. Moreover, even taking on semantic cues, such operations should be assumed to occur most of the time and for most of the nouns: roughly speaking, a noun should undergo category change half of the times it is used. Similarly, on the morphological side, a lexical feature should be argued to frequently occur and block plural Number in nouns (it is unlikely, though, considering the subjective frequency data of this study). Another hypothesis might then suggest that each noun is doubled in the lexicon, once as a count term and once as a mass term.

Although these explanations are sustainable, they seem to be less economic with relation to those theories starting from the idea of a lexicon underspecified for countability. From a theoretical perspective, it is thus more likely that the information about countability is not lexically specified and can be rather contextually encoded by means of morpho-syntax. A nominal expression will be interpreted as mass when the noun occurs in a mass morpho-syntactic context, and as count when the noun occurs in a count morpho-syntactic context. This is coherent even with a more general perspective encompassing languages that express countability with typologically different means (Doetjes 2017b).

However, a hypothesis solely based on a morpho-syntactic context driven countability cannot be maintained in the light of the fact that a few nouns (i.e. the outliers of our study) do occur much more frequently in a mass context, and that there is a bias for a count interpretation (i.e. it is more likely that a noun is mainly used as count and not as mass, but not vice versa). This apparent counter example gives instead the opportunity to examine in-depth the role played by the morpho-syntax in expressing countability contextually and its interplay with cognition in modulating the conceiving of entities with or without boundaries.

4.2. Between Language and Cognition

Although accounts assuming lexical underspecification show greater compatibility with the observed quantitative data, they are not completely predictive of the overall distributions of words. This is not in principle a shortcoming in a linguistic theory, as noticed by De Belder (2011: 201) in stating that linguistics is probably not the appropriate science to account for the salience of the unit for certain concepts and the oddness of the "There is dog on the wall" example which results from it. Therefore, in search of an explanation for the observed data, it could be useful to consider the involvement of extra-linguistic cognitive processing in modulating a phenomenon observed in language.

The patterns observed in the distribution of words are a first step towards walking the path that links linguistic communication to the information present in the referential world, as processed by human cognition. A first, crucial point emerging from the linguistic data is the fact that countability is probably a feature whose value is contextually assigned by morpho-syntax. Namely, it is a morpho-syntactic feature that systematically encodes a semantic feature. Whereas lexical words can potentially encode a wide range of semantic references, only a few semantic features are grammaticalized and handled within the domain of morpho-syntax; among others there are Deixis, Tense and Aspect, Gender, Number. These features are a limited set, and their consistent cross-linguistic diffusion confirms their crucial role among core grammatical structure. Recent perspectives have highlighted the relation between grammaticalized semantic features and the information processed by a fundamental building block of human cognition, namely the core knowledge systems (Franzon, Zanini, and Rugani 2019; Strickland 2017). The core knowledge systems are a toolbox of cognitive abilities, phylogenetically ancient and available early in human infants, that allow individuals to represent salient aspects of the environment in order to behave accordingly (Spelke and Kinzler 2007). Such systems are available independently of the use of language and deal, for example, with proprioception in space and time, recognition of biological movement and animacy, object representation, and an estimation of quantities and numerosity. The information processed by this core knowledge system is closely related to the grammaticalized semantic features that are handled in morphological systems. For example, animacy is a foundation for most gender systems; proprioception is the base for deixis and spatial information; and the numerosity of referents is most likely processed by non-verbal number systems and then grammaticalized in morphological number systems (Franzon, Zanini, and Rugani 2019).

These salient semantic features are among the few that can be encoded in morphological systems. However, the purpose of morpho-syntax in language is mainly functional as it allows for there to be fixed relations between constituents. The assignment of morphological values for agreement is therefore necessary to the sentence building; if there is not a pertinent semantic feature to encode, the value is assigned by default.

Notwithstanding the functional purpose of morphology, cognitive biases are observed when processing morphological features such as interference from the information that is related to the feature usually encoded within that morphological system. Recent studies report that the numerical information is accessed while processing morphological Number, and also animacy is accessed in the processing of fusional morphemes entailing Gender and Number (Arcara et al. 2019; Carreiras et al. 2010; Roettger and Domahs 2015; Zanini et al. 2020).

In particular, the encoding of a Number value, based on the referential numerosity, is constrained by the presence of countability. When the reference to countability is not present, a default value is used to perform operations at the phrase level. In this case, the surfacing value is used to express no information about numerosity; its presence is functionally required, but its semantic interpretation is empty. This interpretation is consistent with the theoretical descriptions assuming a defective Number paradigm when a noun surfaces in the mass syntax: in order to express no reference to a numerosity in a system that is designed for the expression of numerosity, the morphological value needs to keep only the functional information. Therefore, the value used by languages as a default is usually the less informative in a Number paradigm: in case it is the singular, it does not encode a reference to a numerosity of one. In case the language has a general number, the mass reference can surface in the general number; in such cases the numerosity equals one, and becomes a morphological singular (or singulative).

In Number values, interpretability is allowed by countability. From a cognitive point of view, countability is closely related to a core ability, namely object representation. Cues related to perception are important in mastering it and in its development (Hespos, Ferry, and Rips 2009). From a perceptual point of view, each time we visually experience a concrete entity, we see its boundaries. Boundaries are crucial in conceiving an object, because the shape of an object is usually an important cue to recognize the object itself. We recognize a chair because it is shaped as a chair; of course, chairs can have very different shapes; nonetheless each possible shape is an important cue to comprehend that the object is a chair.

Also, substances occur as bounded, when we perceive them visually: milk can assume the boundaries of a glass or of a cup; sand can have the shape of a box or a pile. The boundaries of a substance may or may not vary in different instances of our experience; however, as opposed to what happens with objects like chairs, boundaries cannot be the most important cue to rely on in recognizing that an entity is milk or sand.

Various visual properties suggest a different relevance of shape in conceiving the entity (Prasada, Ferenz, and Haskell 2002). However, the capability to recognize an entity independently of the shape requires some cognitive effort related to the suppression of an often pertinent cue, namely boundaries (Franzon and Zanini 2019; Zanini et al. 2017). Therefore, although some visual properties allow entities to be represented more frequently as objects, and other entities more frequently as substances, it is naïve to assume a straightforward mapping from the physical entities of the world to a grammatical feature in language, without considering the perceptual and cognitive processes that take place in the human brain before linguistic encoding. In other words, it seems easier to conceive an entity within its contingent boundaries and encode as such into a count morpho-syntactic context: this can explain the observed bias for a count interpretation. The fact that some nouns do not show up in count context can be interpreted as a consequence of the (im)probability that mentioning the boundaries of the entity they refer to is somewhat relevant. If it is almost never relevant to refer to the boundaries of an entity, the noun denoting that entity will occur mostly in a mass context. But it does not follow, though, that we are able to conclude that such a noun is lexically marked as mass, since there are very few nouns in our study that behave this way. Rather, it is so improbable that reference to boundaries is pertinent that the frequency with which these nouns are used in a mass context overcomes the bias for a count interpretation.

4.3. Final Remarks: A Multidimensional Approach

This work mainly aims to provide a measure of the distribution of nouns in mass and count contexts; nevertheless, it cannot refrain from comparing the observed preliminary results in the light of the vast literature on this issue. Although results per se cannot lean towards one theory instead of another, they seem to be more easily explainable within frameworks not considering countability as a lexical feature. As already suggested by the theoretical works that treat countability as a context-dependent feature, neither a clear-cut binary division nor the supposed formal simplicity of mass expressions succeeds in fully explaining the observed quantitative data or the experimental results reported in the literature (see, for example, from different perspectives: Allan 1980; Grimm 2018; Kiss et al. 2016; Pelletier 2012).

Our results together with findings reported in the psycholinguistic studies suggest instead that reference to substance is not lexicalized but contextually expressed by means of morpho-syntax and modulated by cognition. The observed distribution is not categorical in nature but seems to reflect the probability with which a noun can (or cannot) denote the boundaries of an entity. Certainly, it emerges from the literature that the mass and count issue is a complex one and cannot be grasped without considering the interplay of different levels of analysis.

5. Conclusions

Observing morpho-syntactically driven patterns in the lexical distribution is an interesting first step in the exploration of how linguistic references encode properties of the physical entities of the world. The pathway from the physical environment to meaningful word combinations encompasses different stages, roughly described as pertaining to processes of perception, cognition, and encoding. We argue that all of the levels can potentially introduce a bias, and warp the space of the lexical distribution observed in language.

For what concerns countability, the observed data can be explained by considering the salience of object representation at the extra-linguistic level. Possibly, also some processes related to the reduction of salient information in morphological encoding play a role in determining the space of occurrence of nouns. All these hypotheses remain open to further investigation.

15 Plurality Without (Full) Countability: On Mass-Like Categories in Lexical Plurals

Peter Lauwers

1. Introduction

In this chapter, I will address some crucial theoretical issues related to the count–mass distinction (CMD) by empirically investigating what have been called *lexical plurals* (Acquaviva 2008). This phenomenon has too often been relegated to a (dismissive) footnote (e.g. Rothstein 2017: 85 n. 1) in formal semantics, as acknowledged by Acquaviva (2008: 86). I therefore particularly welcome the fact that Susan Rothstein brought attention to this issue – albeit with a different terminology and focus – with her talk at the Bochum workshop.

As recalled by Lauwers and Lammert (2016: 207), "*Lexical plurals* are plural forms (*oats*, *remains*) in which plurality constitutes an inherent lexical specification." Since this plurality is morpho-syntactically marked it can be considered a kind of "inherent inflection" (Booij 1996).[1] *Lexical plural* is hence an umbrella term for items that are always plural (cf. *pluralia tantum*), at least for a particular sense. As such, they cannot be accounted for by means of a grammatical rule yielding nouns that mean "many x" as opposed to the meaning of the corresponding singular form "one x" or "one" vs. "one or more" (cf. i.a. Sauerland, Anderssen, and Yatsushiro 2005). Therefore, they have to be learned as part of "what it is to know a word". As a result, despite their plural forms, these items are [−count], or more precisely, they exhibit count deficiency, as shown for instance by their incompatibility with cardinal numbers (*three oats*).

Although lexical plurals might seem a very particular angle to challenge the count–mass distinction, one should not underestimate its importance, both in terms of lexical items and cross-linguistic spread and consistency (Acquaviva 2008).

---

[1] Not to be confused with the semantic interpretation of *lexical plurality* in the discussion of mass roots (Rothstein 2010: 353), as opposed to *grammatically plural*, following Chierchia (1998a).

In this paper I will make the following claims:

(1) Although both properties often go hand in hand, lexical plurals exhibit a neat **dissociation** between countability and plurality: nouns which can pluralize but which cannot be counted (an instance of what Rothstein, this volume, Chapter 3, describes for other types of nouns).

(2) More precisely, (lack of) countability is not a yes-or-no issue; rather, the CMD should be conceived as **a continuum** which can be captured by means of distributional properties, which seem to encode different degrees of conceptual individuation (Langacker 1987: 205; Grimm 2012b).

(3) If it is true that lexical plurals are less count, can they therefore be considered **mass(-like)**? I hope to show that the internal structuring of lexical plurals reflects the typology of singular mass nouns (i.e. compact, dense, granular aggregates, collectives/superordinates). This observation is confirmed by the fact that lexical plural mass nouns also fall within the scope of typical mass > count coercion mechanisms, such as the universal sorter ("kinds of N") and packager ("portions of N").

Admittedly, I am certainly not the first one to tackle issues (1) and (2). As reminded by the organisers of the Bochum workshop in their call for papers, the CMD – regardless of the level(s) on which it is located, whether at the lexical or the syntactic level (NP or DP) – is generally conceived as a binary opposition. As a matter of fact, this binary distinction has survived remarkably well, despite the empirical objections that have been raised against it on many occasions, both on the basis of semantic (e.g. furniture nouns, homogeneity of count nouns such as *line*, etc.) and distributional arguments. As to the latter, the issue of conflicting CMD diagnostics had already been raised as early as 1980 (Allan 1980) and has recently been confirmed by a number of studies based on large-scale annotation tasks and corpus research (Katz and Zamparelli 2012; Kulkarni, Rothstein, and Treves 2013; Kiss, Pelletier, and Stadtfeld 2014). This growing body of work calls for a gradual approach. Interestingly, the gradualness (Gillon 1992: 613 n. 12) of the [count] feature is also in the heart of lexical plurals. Lexical plurals often yield shaky and variable judgements when they are combined with typical [+ count] determiners (Acquaviva 2008: 87–8), suggesting that the "dissociation" between countability and plurality observed by Susan Rothstein and many others (i.a. Ojeda 2005) is gradual.[2]

In this paper I want to elaborate on Susan Rothstein's observations by showing how a typology of French lexical plural nouns emerges from the

---

[2] It should be noted that the CMD is also gradual in another respect, viz. in the count or mass preferences of individual lexical items (Allan 1980; Vermote 2014).

various effects of this *gradual* dissociation and examining the extent to which these plural-only forms resemble [+ mass] nouns. Although the term *plural mass* is quite often found in the literature, the relevance and scope of this label have not yet been questioned (see Section 5).

The structure of the paper is as follows. After having explicated some theoretical assumptions and methodological issues (Section 2), I describe the distributional behaviour of a set of thirty lexical plurals in French. Their gradual loss of countability is compared against a typology of singular mass nouns (Section 3). As a prerequisite to this analysis, it is argued that even the category of (singular) mass is in need of refinement. In the fourth section, it is shown that lexical plurals are subject to count–mass coercion, which in turn confirms their mass status within the French language system. In the final section, I discuss these findings in the light of the mass-status of (some of the) lexical plurals.

2. Theoretical Assumptions and Methodology

2.1. General Assumptions

The research presented here is part of the "empirical turn" that characterises recent research on the CMD, in that it combines big corpora and acceptability surveys to examine a set of lexical items. The level on which the CMD is apprehended is that of word senses (cf. Kiss, Pelletier, and Stadtfeld 2014) within a fundamentally lexicalist approach (cf. Vermote, Lauwers, and De Cuypere 2017), using distributional properties – both naturally occurring in language use and elicited in surveys – as heuristics to detect the "countability degree" of particular lexical items and senses. In addition, the lexical status of count or mass can be contextually overruled by semi-productive coercion mechanisms that generate ephemeral (= low frequency) though generalisable meaning effects. It should be noted that I will stick as much as possible to categories that are backed-up by morpho-syntactic and, more generally, distributional properties, in order to avoid the pitfall of projecting *a priori* real-world features on linguistic (more specifically semantic) representations. This is not to say that, *a posteriori*, one may not look for conceptual (including perceptual) motivations of distributional categories. Since my focus is on the distributional behaviour of lexical items, I will not be interested in modelling the semantics of the count–mass distinction itself in terms of specific semantic features such as atomicity, hetero/homogeneity, boundedness, etc., nor in detecting root and derived semantics. I will only use individuation (Langacker 1987: 205; Grimm 2012b) of individuals/parts/ atoms as an intuitive way to capture the conceptual dimension of count-deficient lexical plurals.

2.2. Methodology: Corpus Study and Acceptability Survey

Crucially, lexical plurals are forms that function outside the regular singular/plural opposition. Such a configuration occurs when the singular form does not exist (the so-called *pluralia tantum*: *les environs/*un environ* "the surroundings/*a surrounding"), when it is very low-frequent (e.g. *un vestige* "a remnant"), or when a (lexical) plural sense is dissociated from the meaning of the singular and its regular plural (e.g. *des épinards* "spinach" vs. *un épinard* "a spinach plant").

For my purpose it is crucial to note that the split between the intrinsically plural form and a corresponding singular entails count deficiency. Not only does the singular/plural alternation disappear – one of the main diagnostic tests for count status – but the use of quantifiers also turns out to be heavily affected (*plusieurs pommes* "several apples" vs. **plusieurs épinards* "several spinach"). As a consequence, the gradual loss of the count status of lexical plurals can be measured by the range of quantifiers they allow for, since each quantifier imposes specific semantic constraints on the noun. Based on the literature on determiners in French (see Lauwers 2014 for an overview), I made the following selection:

- *Les/ces/ses* (definite article, demonstrative, possessive) < *des* (indefinite plural) < *quelques* ("some") < *plusieurs/différents/divers* ("several"/"different"/"various") < cardinal numbers
- *Un peu de* "some"

The quantifiers located toward the right side of the spectrum impose stronger constraints on the grammatical accessibility of the individuated parts or atoms. By contrast, definite determiners do not impose any condition on the internal part/whole structure of the noun, very much like in the singular, which is neutral with regard to the CMD (cf. *le sable* "the sand", *le chapeau* "the hat"). As a consequence, strongly count-deficient lexical plurals only pattern with very few determiners (the less individuating ones), while only weakly count-deficient plurals allow for all of them, albeit with very low frequency. In addition to individuation, *différent/divers* also constrains the noun's capacity to construe qualitatively distinguishable individuals: *different models* vs. **different kilos* (cf. also Acquaviva 2008: 93–7). Note that ambivalent quantifiers such as *beaucoup de* "many", *peu de* "few", *plus de* "more", etc. that combine both with mass (in the singular) and count nouns (in the plural) have not been taken into account. The list of diagnostics has further been completed by *un peu de*, which typically patterns with singular mass, and possibly also with some lexical plurals (Doetjes 2001; Hilgert 2014).

In order to adequately measure this gradual loss of countability, extensive corpus research and sentence ratings tasks have been undertaken on a sample of thirty lexical plurals (based on literature and on the frequency lists for singular and plural provided by *Lexique*). The sample represents a variety of semantic fields (diseases, complex artefacts, food stuff, unbounded spaces, complex events, etc.; cf. Acquaviva 2008). Blatantly polysemous items with a regular singular/plural opposition such as *selles* "faeces" vs. *selle(s)* "saddle(s)" have been discarded from the start. They require a lot of manual disambiguation, which would have made a corpus study impossible. Still, a lot of data cleaning had to be done, since several lexical items appeared to have other (marginal) senses besides their lexical plural sense.

The corpus that has been used is the *frTenTen corpus*, a twelve-billion corpus of the Sketch Engine family. Although web corpora have some important drawbacks, they were the only option available given the lexical nature of the topic. Frequency lists of the items (= determiners) occurring at the left-hand side of the keyword have been generated by the software on the Sketch Engine platform and have been manually cleaned (for irrelevant senses and other false positives), except for the high-frequent determiners (definites and indefinite *des*). For the latter, extrapolations have been made on the basis of random samples of at least fifty corpus instances in order to determine the proportion of relevant instances. This strategy has also been applied to compute the relative frequency of the plural indefinite article (*des*) and the contracted combination preposition *de* + definite article *les*, both surfacing as *des* in the corpus.

In addition to the corpus study, I conducted an online sentence rating task to test count–mass diagnostics that cannot be easily checked by means of corpora, viz. two distributive (= individuating) reciprocal expressions (Wierzbicka 1988; Chierchia 1998a: 86): *l'un après l'autre; les uns après les autres* "the one(s) after the other(s)" and "delimitative" (Zhang 2013) or "stubbornly distributive" adjectives (Schwarzschild 2011), testing the boundedness of individuated subparts (*grand* "big", *long* "long").[3]

The survey has been completed by eleven native speakers; most of them were linguists from Georges Kleiber's *Masscolex* project and speakers of hexagonal French. In order to limit the number of questions to sixty, I allocated the items to two surveys. Informants had to score the sentences on a five-point Likert scale.

3. Quantitative Analysis

Before digging into the analysis of the data, I need to make a number of terminological distinctions with regard to the mass domain. Some of them are

---

[3] Initially, I also included a picture description task (cf. Barner and Snedeker 2005) to test whether lexical plural nouns still accept number-based comparisons. However, this survey caused too many practical difficulties (especially with respect to less concrete nouns) to be taken into account.

not known outside the French linguistic tradition (3.1). These will serve as the background against which the properties of lexical plurals will be projected (3.2).

3.1. Preliminaries: Towards a More Fine-Grained Typology of Mass Nouns

Canonical exemplars of mass nouns include *singularia tantum* items such as *de l'eau* "water", *du sable* "sand", *du sang* "blood". They have denotations that are perceptually homogeneous, without individual parts clearly visible to the naked eye. They combine with the traditional mass quantifiers (*du, un peu de* "some") and ambivalent quantifiers such as *beaucoup de* ("a lot of"), in which case they always remain in the singular. They do not accept delimitative adjectives and pass all the traditional semantic tests (addition, division, no comparison in terms of number, etc.). Following the terminology of Culioli (1973: 84; 1974: 7), I will call them **dense** nouns.

As frequently observed, concrete mass nouns often refer to referents that still contain individual parts, which lack, however, referential salience, such as *du riz* ("rice") (Kleiber 1997: 333–4; Joosten 2006). In fact, mass nouns are characterised by various degrees of individuation (*water > dust > sand*; Langacker 1987: 205). If this individuation makes delimitative adjectives possible, I will call these items **granular aggregate nouns**, following Grimm (2012b). Otherwise, granular aggregate nouns pattern with dense mass nouns.

A third group of nouns has received a lot of attention in the literature: **collective** (e.g., *outillage* "equipment") and **superordinate** (e.g., *mobilier* "furniture") mass nouns. These nouns also allow for delimitative adjectives, but the linguistic (semantic) representation of the parts is even more accessible than in the case of granular aggregates, as shown by the fact that number is still the basis on which their referents are compared (Barner and Snedeker 2005). On the whole, collective and superordinate mass nouns are a little closer to the [+ count] pole. They are second degree mass nouns, referring to heterogeneous objects united by a common function.

Finally, there is an important subclass of mass nouns that, as far as I know, has not been acknowledged outside the French linguistic tradition. As a matter of fact, some mass nouns do not pass the traditional diagnostic test with the partitive article: **de la peste* "plague" (Boone 1989: 111), **de l'environnement* "environment" *??de la blancheur* "whiteness" (Van de Velde 1996). They always appear in the singular and are actually recalcitrant to any form of quantification. They only allow definite determiners, especially the definite article (*le, la, l'*), for these do not interfere with the CMD. Following Culioli (1973: 84; 1974: 7), I call them **compact mass** nouns. Nouns such as *le nord* "the North" which denote unique referents may also be associated with this class. Note that compact nouns can be shifted to the count domain by "qualitative packaging", which is somehow related to both the universal sorter and packager. This mechanism stipulates that if these nouns are modified, they must take the indefinite article (*un/une*), which is [+ count], as has often been observed (Flaux and Van de Velde 2000; Kleiber 2014): *une blancheur éblouissante* "a blinding whiteness", *un environnement merveilleux* "a marvellous environment". The resulting NPs refer to qualitatively distinguishable instances of the concept. Note that the shifted nouns do not yet behave as fully fledged count nouns, for they accept neither pluralisation nor cardinal numbers.

3.2. Results: Mass-Like Lexical Plurals Along the [+/– Count] Continuum

The extended typology of mass nouns will now be mapped onto the results of our inquiry about lexical plurals.

3.2.1. Quantitative Results As a starting point I took the raw data counts of each of the thirty lexical items.[4] For each item, the counts have been transformed into proportions (of 1000‰) in order to allow for between-item comparisons. For instance, *plusieurs petits pois* occurred three times in the corpus, representing 0.47‰ of the total number of occurrences of this lexical item. This is more than the 0.22‰ computed for *plusieurs frais*, which occurred 120 times in the corpus, but whose overall frequency is almost a hundred times higher than that of *petits pois* (550,740 > 6425). As the ranges of the proportions showed considerable variation from one determiner to another (e.g. the permilles of the definite article are considerably higher than those of *plusieurs*), I normalised the data for the sake of comparison.[5] This way, we obtain for each determiner a range from 1 to 0, 1 being the maximum value and 0 the lowest value for the determiner at hand. For instance, with regard to *plusieurs*, the item *oreillons* "mumps" has the lowest value (0‰, hence 0), while *commodités* "facilities" has the highest (8.17‰, hence 1). I added a black-and-white colour scale in Excel to visualise the differences. By choosing a scale between 1 and 0 (rather than on the basis of z-score, around the mean), one can easily visualise count (black) and non-count (white)

---

[4] Note that the (marginal) instances of count–mass coercion have been kept in the dataset. While they could easily be identified for the most critical quantifiers through manual inspection (cf. description in Section 4), they were so infrequent that I was unable to estimate their weight within the thousands of tokens of high-frequency determiners.
[5] This was carried out in R (R Core Team 2019) with the function *standardize* from the library *psycho*.

344 Peter Lauwers

Table 15.1. *Distributional behaviour of thirty lexical items (normalised between 0 and 1)*

item	les	ces	poss	des	quelques	plusieurs	differents	divers	num	les_uns	l'un	stubs	les_uns	l'un	stubs
oreillons	1,000	0,000	0,001	0,000	0,000	0,000	0,000	0,000	0,000	0,000	0,275	0,083	1	1	1
alentours	0,751	0,099	0,269	0,008	0,001	0,004	0,000	0,000	0,000	0,348	0,058	0,200	2,5	1	1
arrhes	0,541	0,289	0,077	0,546	0,006	0,000	0,000	0,000	0,000	0,217	0,000	0,000	1	1 NA	
aigreurs	0,112	0,202	0,183	1,000	0,455	0,000	0,000	0,000	0,000	0,113	0,087	0,000	1	1 NA	
balayures	0,554	0,651	0,036	0,471	0,698	0,000	0,000	0,000	0,000	0,322	0,087	0,100	2	1	1
b_manieres	0,755	0,181	0,192	0,084	0,083	0,000	0,000	0,022	0,002	0,426	0,609	0,000	3	2 NA	
neiges	0,942	0,076	0,021	0,049	0,015	0,010	0,004	0,000	0,004	0,113	0,087	0,050	2	1	1
intemperies	0,897	0,549	0,000	0,093	0,032	0,022	0,004	0,056	0,002	0,374	0,087	0,000	2	1 NA	
urines	0,804	0,052	0,093	0,161	0,001	0,009	0,006	0,013	0,009	0,217	0,000	0,000	1	1	1
rillettes	0,380	0,527	0,105	0,093	0,714	0,042	0,000	0,000	0,018	0,165	0,174	0,100	1	1	1
epinards	0,663	0,029	0,145	0,068	0,403	0,025	0,000	0,000	0,000	0,522	0,130	0,333	3,5	1,5	2
moeurs	0,708	0,176	0,274	0,055	0,006	0,000	0,007	0,014	0,001	0,635	0,087	0,000	4	1 NA	
losiris	0,597	0,153	0,397	0,057	0,051	0,000	0,000	0,000	0,000	0,270	0,348	0,600	2	2	3
decombres	0,902	0,331	0,030	0,068	0,039	0,007	0,005	0,019	0,001	0,609	0,348	0,750	2	2	4,5
vivres	0,320	0,177	0,073	0,124	0,095	0,563	0,024	0,013	0,043	0,826	0,420	0,417	5	2	1,5
fonts_baptism	0,854	0,332	0,022	0,152	0,006	0,040	0,000	0,000	0,002	0,957	0,855	0,700	5	3,5	4
represailles	0,505	0,205	0,028	0,662	0,078	0,037	0,000	0,076	0,001	0,322	0,174	0,300	2	1	2
excrements	0,363	0,231	0,145	0,345	0,459	0,037	0,000	0,008	0,034	0,739	0,638	0,917	4,5	3	5
ebats	0,000	0,538		0,096	0,122	0,070	0,007	0,015	0,012	0,957	0,420	0,917	5	2	5
petits_pois	0,486	0,145	0,624	0,205	0,057	0,000	0,000	0,000	0,102	0,530	0,783	0,500	3	3	3
pourparlers	0,602	0,960	0,031	0,442	0,050	0,078	0,022	0,070	0,002	0,565	0,420	0,875	3	2	5
dechets	0,777	0,647	0,124	0,095	0,028	0,016	0,012	0,116	0,005	1,000	0,855	0,708	5	2,5	4
frais	0,704	0,419	0,151	0,192	0,028	0,027	0,041	0,117	0,001	0,565	0,493	0,000	3	1,5 NA	
donnees	0,598	1,000	0,125	0,311	0,073	0,114	0,030	0,087	0,022	0,896	0,696	0,200	5	3 NA	
visceres	0,793	0,193	0,145	0,066	0,099	0,228	0,083	0,083	0,048	0,652	0,420	0,375	4	2	2
mauv_herbes	0,859	0,292	0,014	0,134	0,165	0,226	0,007	0,257	0,007	0,948	0,783	0,650	4	3	4
commodites	0,763	0,415	0,070	0,157	0,227	1,000	0,242	1,000	0,010	0,530	0,174	0,400	4	2	2
vestiges	0,612	0,823	0,056	0,289	1,000	0,477	0,058	0,263	0,030	0,870	0,783	0,792	4	2,5	5
ossements	0,413	0,931	0,128	0,517	0,546	0,519	0,047	0,361	0,051	0,957	0,203	1,000	5	1,5	5
agres	0,432	0,391	0,219	0,156	0,141	0,971	1,000	0,705	1,000	0,913	1,000	0,750	5	3	4,5

behaviour for each of the thirty lexical items with regard to each of the criteria. As one can see in Table 15.1, on the whole, the behaviour of the thirty lexical items is remarkably consistent for the critical contexts (except for the definites), the dark cells being found in the second half of the table, while the light ones are located in the upper half.

Note that we did not apply a similar normalisation to the results of the acceptability judgements (three last columns), which are scores on a five-point Likert scale. To summarise the results we took the medians of the participant scores for each lexical item and added a similar colour scale. The same continuum appears (with considerably lower scores for the most severe test, viz. *l'un ... l'autre*). Once again, dark and white cells are clearly separated.

Table 15.1 mirrors the fact that count deficiency is a continuum. Moreover, the critical distributional features are highly correlated. Some of them (e.g., *plusieurs* and cardinal numbers) exhibit a Pearson Correlation higher than 0.9 ($p < 0.01$). This means that if a lexical plural has a relatively high proportion of *plusieurs*, it also has a high proportion of cardinal numbers. However, in this gradual landscape different levels can be distinguished on the basis of clusters of distributional properties. We know from the literature that determiners can be ordered with respect to the constraints on individuation they impose (cf. Section 3.1 above). The relevance of this ordering for lexical plurals is now confirmed. The (quantitative) results posit the lexical items on this implicational scale: if a noun allows for Quantifier 1 (e.g. *plusieurs*), then it also allows for Quantifier 2 (e.g. *des*) if the latter is located on the left side of the continuum:

definite determiner
< *des* < *quelques*
< *plusieurs*, numerals, (*différents/divers*)

3.2.2. Mass-Like Types We can now try to cluster the lexical items on the basis of their combined distributional properties along the countability continuum.[6] It appears that the typology of lexical plurals exhibits striking analogies with the typology of mass nouns presented in Section 2.2.

Since the delicate issue of taxonomic and meronymic relations that underpin the collective/superordinate distinction is somehow orthogonal to the CMD, I will leave this discussion aside. It suffices to mention that some lexical items realise both relations (e.g. *viscères*; cf. Lammert 2016) and that superordinate plurals often require conjunction of co-hyponyms to comply with the usual taxonomic test (Lauwers 2014: 126):

(1)   Les pommes de terre, le lait et le sucre sont des vivres.
       "Potatoes, milk and sugar are food supplies"

(1')   ?Les pommes de terre sont des vivres.
       "Potatoes are food supplies"

This particular behaviour of at least some of the superordinate lexical plurals might be a trace of their originally collective meaning (Mihatsch 2016). Collective nouns do indeed presuppose (spatial) contiguity within a set.

On the whole, the main dimension that shapes the field of mass and count in French seems to be degree of (conceptual) individuation (cf. McCawley 1975: 314; cf. also Grimm 2012b, which shows that this parameter also structures cross-linguistic choices; cf. also "unity" in Acquaviva 2008)[7].

However, there is one category of nouns that falls outside this mass-like typology: internal plurals. These do not have a singular mass counterpart. They refer to bounded objects that can be counted[8] if one has more of them (n > 2), but the constitutive parts each object is made of are not countable, linguistically speaking. Note that boundedness can be inferred from the fact that internal plurals pattern with delimitative adjectives:

---

[6] See Lauwers (2014) for quantitative thresholds.
[7] Additional parameters include identity (cf. *different/divers*), boundedness, and cohesion, the latter two being intrinsically related to [+/- individuation] (Acquaviva 2008: 101).
[8] This is why they are considered count nouns by McCawley (1975: 320).

Table 15.2. Typology of lexical plurals

Category	Mass_example	Plural_example[a]	Criteria_lex_plural	Additional criteria_lex_plural[b]
Compact	*peste* "plague"	*oreillons* "mumps", *alentours* "surroundings"	[-des], [-quelques], [-plusieurs], [-différents/divers], [-cardinal numbers], [- les uns … les autres]	[-delim.], [-comp. number][c]
Dense	*eau* "water"	*épinards* "spinach", *rillettes* (a kind of *pâté*), *urines* "urine", *neiges* "snow", *balayures* "sweepings", *bonnes manières* "good manners", *décombres* "rubble", *loisirs* "leisure time", *aigreurs d'estomac* "sour stomach", *mœurs* "customs", *arrhes* "deposit"	[**+des**], [**+quelques**], [-plusieurs], [-différents/divers],	[-delim.], [-comp. number]
Granular aggregate	*riz* "rice"	*petits pois* "peas", [*pâtes* "pasta"]	[-cardinal numbers], [-les uns … les autres]	[+delim.], [-comp. number]
Collective[d]	*outillage* "equipment"	*ossements* "bones", *vestiges* "remnants", *, frais* "costs", *données* "data"	[+des], [+quelques], [**+?plusieurs**],	[+delim.], [+comp. number], [-hyperon.]
Superordinate	*mobilier* "furniture"	*excréments* "excrements", *mauvaises herbes* "weeds", *viscères* "entrails", *vivres* "foodstuff", *commodités* "facilities", *déchets* "waste", *agrès* "gym apparatus", *intempéries* "bad weather"	[**+?différents/divers**], [**+?cardinal numbers**], [**+les uns… les autres**]	[+delim.], [+comp. number], [+hyperon.]

Note that the last column presents additional criteria that allow one to distinguish subtypes within each category.
[a] Nouns between brackets were not represented in my initial sample of thirty lexical plurals.
[b] If applicable (e.g. not for abstract nouns).
[c] Comparison on the basis of number has been added here. This feature is not applicable to abstract nouns. That is why it had not been included in the statistics mentioned above.
[d] At this point, the analysis here departs from the typology proposed in Lauwers (2014).

Table 15.3. *Internal plurals*

Category	Mass_examples	Criteria_lex_plural	Additional criteria_lex_plural[9]	Plural_example
Internal (plural)	NONE	[+des$^{1/n}$], [+quelques^n], [+plusieurs^n], [+différents^n/divers^n], [+cardinal numbers^n], [+les uns ... les autres^n]	[+delim.$^{1/n}$]	**Concrete:** *fonts baptismaux* "baptismal font"
			[delim. = NA] (-> abstract nouns !)	**Events:** [*félicitations* "congratulations"], *pourparlers* "negotiations", *ébats* "frolics", *représailles* "retaliation »*

(2) à l'entrée se trouvaient les fonts baptismaux **ronds** à double piscine[10]
"the round baptismal font with double bath was located at the entrance"

So the picture is as given in Table 15.3.
Internal plurals easily accept definite determiners and plural indefinite quantifiers (*{des/les} fonts baptismaux*). In that case they are ambiguous: they may refer to one single bounded object (index "1" in Table 15.3) or to several bounded objects (index "n") like *scissors* does. The other determiners, however, inevitably trigger a (external) plural reading (hence "n"). For instance, *quelques fonts baptismaux* ("some baptismal fonts") refers to multiple objects, as do cardinal numbers:

(3) Les églises du Trégor finistérien possèdent **six fonts baptismaux sculptés**.
[...] du mobilier caché dans l'obscurité des églises. (Google Books, Bulletin de la Société archéologique du Finistère, 2004)
"The churches of Finisterian Tregor possess six sculpted baptismal fonts [...] furniture hidden in the obscurity of the churches."

What is counted here are not the individual parts (whatever they may be) a baptismal font is made of, but distinct fonts that are placed in six different churches. In other words, numeration does not relate to the internal subparts of the complex object but only to the wholes. One might term this "external multiplication of the referent denoted by the internal plural". The constitutive subparts of the object denoted by the internal plural are not accessible (any more) to the counting operation. In cases such as *fonts baptismaux* "baptismal

---

[9] When applicable, e.g. not for abstract nouns.
[10] https://archive.org/stream/LaProvinceDuMaine1903/La_Province_du_Maine_1903_djvu.txt.

fonts", an expression borrowed from Church Latin *fontes* (with the same meaning), *fontes* being the plural of *fons* "source, fountain" (TLFi, s.v. *fonts*), it is even difficult to come up with individual entities/parts in the real word – even historically speaking – which might have motivated the internal plural marking. This internal opacity makes them at some point similar to compact mass nouns such as *alentours* "surroundings" and *règles* "menses", which, however, are clearly unbounded, as shown by their behaviour with regard to delimitative adjectives (compare with (2) above):

(4)   *des alentours ronds "round surroundings"

Abstract nouns referring to complex events such as *félicitations* "congratulations", *pourparlers* "negotiations", or *ébats* "frolics" share more or less the same properties. Their subparts – in this case subevents – are not accessible either. If one combines these nouns with determiners that require a strongly individualised part/whole structure, only external multiplication turns out to be possible: a plurality of "acts of congratulation" (with their sub-events), uttered at various times, at different places, or which succeed each other in time:

(5)   Londres reçoit **plusieurs félicitations** "London receives several congratulations"

On the basis of the coercion effect in cases such as (5), in a previous publication (Lauwers 2016) I considered external multiplication to be the result of a shifting mechanism transposing the count operation to the level of the complex whole. However, since the external count reading is almost the default one in the case of internal plurals referring to bounded objects such as *fonts baptismaux*, and since the complex whole is already bounded even when the speaker is referring to one object:

(6)   Les fonts baptismaux dans cette église sont **ronds**.
        "The baptismal font in this church is round."

I prefer henceforth to qualify them as regular count nouns, albeit with a formal plural constraint, which forces them to refer to one single object despite their plural form. As a consequence, they fall outside the count deficiency continuum.

4.   Mass > Count Coercion in Mass Plurals

The parallelism between the structuring of the field of lexical plurality and the mass spectrum is confirmed by the fact that at least some (categories of) lexical plurals pattern with singular mass when it comes to coercion mechanisms. For this section, I also looked at some other lexical plural items, which had not been incorporated in the quantitative corpus study.

As a matter of fact, lexical plurals may constitute the input for mass > count shifting operations that enhance their [+ count] status. The resulting count status can be inferred from their being compatible with strongly individuating quantifiers. The coercion mechanisms reported in the lexical plural domain appear to line up with two canonical mass > count transfers, viz. the universal sorter and the universal packager. Parallel to the taxonomic shift from *de la neige* (mass) "snow" to *deux neiges* (count) "two kinds of snow", one also finds, for instance (*French Ten Ten Corpus*):

(7)   **12 mauvaises herbes** "12 kinds of weeds"

(8)   **110 déchets** "110 kinds of rubbish"

As is known, the Universal Pack(ag)er (Bunt 1985; Jackendoff 1991) transforms mass nouns denoting food substances or beverages (*pizza, beer,* ...) into nouns denoting conventional portions of that substance or beverage (*a pizza, a beer,* ...). It also shifts materials to objects made of these materials (*du papier* "paper" > *un papier* "sheet of paper"). Applied to the lexical plural domain, the Universal Packager comes in various subtypes, according to the nature of the input-noun:

- packaging in three-dimensional space: *4 rillettes* "4 plates consisting of rillettes"
- temporal bounding: *2 vacances* "2 holiday periods"
- "qualitative" packaging: *des règles douleureuses* "painful menses".

First, the meaning of lexical plurals denoting edible substances (*rillettes, frites* "French fries", *épinards* "spinach") can be bounded in three-dimensional space, transforming them into conventional portions, like in the case of *a pizza*:

(9)   Coffret découverte de **7 rillettes**, Lot de **4 rillettes** aux noix de Saint-Jacque[s]
"discovery box of 7 rillettes, a batch of 4 rillettes with scallops"

This portioning mechanism also applies to lexical plurals denoting residual corporal substances. Admittedly, we are not really interested in counting this kind of stuff, but there may be situations in which it really is relevant to count samples of urine (*urines*) or faeces (*fèces*), for instance:

(10)   Dans une étude portant sur **460 urines**, 27 avaient un VCGcys > 3000 mm3 / mm3. **Ces 27 urines** provenaient de 24 patients différents.
"In a study on 460 samples of urine, 27 had a [...]. These 27 samples came from 24 patients"

The second Universal Packager effect consists of temporal bounding when applied to nouns referring to unbounded quantities of time, such as *vacances* "leisure time":

(11)   Ils passent même **plusieurs vacances** ensemble.[11]
"They even spent several holidays together"

The resulting NP refers to discrete periods which can be counted, i.e. "official holiday periods" or even "holiday stays" (Acquaviva 2008: 44).

Finally, the third kind of packaging only applies to compact plurals, the less countable ones. As we have seen, these nouns do not accept any indefinite determiner (not even *des*), but if one adds a qualitative modifier, they can be used with *des* and *quelques*, that is, the lesser constraint quantifiers (cf. "qualitative packaging", Section 3.1):

(12)   Découverte **des alentours verdoyants et escarpés** de Belo Horizonte (*Brésil, Petit Fûté*, 2019, Google Books)
"discovery of the green and steep surroundings of Belo Horizonte"

(13)   **des règles abondantes, difficiles, douloureuses, irrégulières** (TLFi)
"abundant, difficult, painful, irregular menses"

However, these shifted nouns do not reach full count status; they remain deficient, since the most individuating determiners are still impossible:

(14)   *Elle a eu {**trois/plusieurs**} règles douloureuses
"She has had {three/several} painful menses"

So, here packaging only enhances the count status of the lexical plural. This does not come as a surprise, since the same deficiency is observed with shifted compact nouns in the singular such as *environnement* "environment" (cf. Section 3.1). When modified by a qualitative expression, they can be combined with the singular indefinite, but they still cannot be counted, nor even pluralised:

(15)   *{**des/trois**} environnements paisibles[12]
"{Ø/three} peaceful environments"

This mechanism has been called the "qualitative packager" (Kleiber 2014); the qualitative modifier extrinsically bounds the compact noun within its situation of occurrence. Once again, one notes the striking parallelism between (compact) lexical plurals and (compact) singular mass.

In some cases, mass > count coercion may trigger back-formation of the singular count form, restoring the grammatical number opposition:

(16)   *Une* rillette, *une!* "one plate of rillettes, just one" (example cited in Wilmet 2010: 393).

---

[11] www.edarling.fr/conseils-rencontres/psychologie/saga-de-l-ete (accessed 18 April 2019).
[12] Of course, we do not consider here the technical use of "ICT environment", which is, of course, a full [+ count] sense.

These operations *beyond* plural mass in turn confirm both the genuine mass status ("mass" being conceived both as "dense" and "compact") of these lexical plurals and the lexical – rather than contextual – nature of the form/meaning pairings that constitute them. Were they not lexical mass but only contextual mass[13] uses instead, they could not have been shifted towards the count domain, according to what has been observed in the literature (Kerleroux 1996: 154; Kleiber 1999: 113). Only lexically stable items (hence polysemous ones) can be shifted further. Thus, these transfers suggest that lexical plurals are not a "dead end"; they still may be picked up in productive mechanisms.

5. Discussion and Conclusions: Does Gradual Count Deficiency Reach Mass?

Let us summarise the main findings of this paper. We started out from plural nouns that normally should have been [+ count]. However, in the end, did we finally reach [+ mass]? As a matter of fact, the heuristic strategy I developed here illustrates at some point the count–mass asymmetry pointed at by Jenny Doetjes in her paper in this volume (Chapter 4). By comparing lexical items to the gold standard of prototypical countability – taking countability as the default – we came across different kinds of plural nouns in which countability gradually fades away. As a corollary, the plural nouns progressively seem to tap into the mass domain. But are these plural nouns really mass or do we need something "more" to qualify them as fully fledged plural mass nouns?

First and foremost, several observations point to the conclusion that lexical plurals are really *mass-* or *uncount-like*: structurally, like mass nouns, they do not allow for the regular singular/plural opposition as in the case of grammatical plurals. Both *singularia tantum* and *pluralia tantum* do not (any longer) operate within the canonical number opposition. As a consequence, lexical plurals exhibit count deficiency, which appears to be gradual. This finding confirms the gradualness of countability (or, in other words, the count–mass distinction), as already argued by Allan (1980), Katz and Zamparelli (2012), Kulkarni, Rothstein, and Treves (2013), and Kiss, Pelletier, and Stadtfeld (2014), although my starting point here was not a random set of nouns but a representative set of plural-only nouns. On the conceptual level, the distributional continuum reflects a decrease of conceptual individuation of the individual parts, which goes beyond the canonical "massification" effect inherent to the multiplication of individuals in default grammatical plural readings (cf. Mufwene 1981; Link 1983; Langacker 1987: 302: "replicate mass"; Bosveld-de Smet 2001).

---

[13] This is also why collectives and superordinates seem to resist shifting mechanisms between count and mass (cf. Doetjes, this volume, Chapter 4).

The main finding of this paper concerns the shape of the lexical plural domain: it reflects the internal structure of the singular mass domain, which contains similar types and similar orthogonal distinctions such as meronymic and taxonomic semantic structures. The intrinsic – that is *lexical* – mass-status of lexical plurals is further confirmed by their ability to serve as an input to various kinds of canonical count–mass coercion, like singular mass items do. Therefore, it seems fair to state that at least some of the lexical plurals are linguistically speaking mass items. Hence, the designation "plural mass nouns" that is often used (e.g., McCawley 1975: 320; Wierzbicka 1988; Corbett 2000: 173; Acquaviva 2008: 86–9; Rothstein 2017: 85), though without much reflection, appears to be fully justified. However, in my analysis, the mass-status of plural forms has a considerably broader scope than, for instance, in Susan Rothstein's work. Unlike authors such as McCawley (1975: 320), who assign "plural mass" status to *clothes*, *brains*, *guts*, *intestines*, and *hemorrhoids*, Susan Rothstein (2017: 85) seems to restrict the notion of mass plural to nouns that are intrinsically *mass*, such as *water/eau* or *rain/pluie*. What makes them special is that they also might appear in the plural: although they are mass items, they have both a singular and a plural form. Admittedly, in cases such as *pluies* "rains" and *waters*, one may derive the plural mass meaning from the singular mass meaning (which persists after pluralisation). However, this way of explaining mass plurals runs into problems, since the plural items may also have marginal count usages, which, theoretically, can be a potential source of the lexical–plural readings:

(17)   une (forte) pluie "a (heavy) rain"

The case of *eaux* is slightly different: admittedly, its obsolete singular count use ("watercourse") may have given rise to the lexical–plural meaning "network of watercourses":

(18)   le torrent est **une eau** qui ne coule en quantité, que pendant les orages (Fabre, *Essai sur la théorie des torrens et des rivières*, 1797; Google books)
"the water torrent is a water that only flows in quantity during storms"

Still, this sense seems to be quite different from the "abundant" plural mass meaning, viz. *les eaux* "water mass",[14] which sticks to the singular mass reading and therefore perfectly fits within Susan Rothstein's vision. In addition to cases such as *pluies*, other intrinsic mass nouns may have derived their lexical plural sense from a lesser-known count use. Names for substances and

---

[14] In the same vein, *neige* has also two lexical plural usages: a fuzzy plurality of successive weather phenomena (similar to *pluies*) and a landscape abundantly covered with snow (Lauwers 2016: 284).

materials, which are intrinsically mass nouns, such as *coton*, etc., also refer to fuzzy, uncountable sets of objects made of the same material in the plural (Vermote 2014: 61). Even in this case, the fuzzy plural mass use might be explained by massification of a (marginal) count use, since *un coton* denotes an individual object made of that material. So, in all these cases mass plural use appears to be supported also by singular count usage. What is even more compelling though for a broader definition of mass plural beyond intrinsic singular mass-items is that some of the lexical items examined here do *not* have a singular mass use at all. They are regular count nouns that have been massified by virtue of the conceptual mechanism inherent to lexical plurals described above. Thus, lexical plural forms may behave like mass items, as independent of the existence of a singular mass counterpart.

Although the previous observations point to (a broader conception of) plural mass, some nuances should be considered. First, not all lexical plurals can be shifted back to the count domain with a novel count meaning. Collectives and superordinates, which are very important subcategories, seem to resist. This might have something to do with the fact that they still profile their individual parts, as evidenced by the fact they are still marginally found in the singular. Counting only reactivates in a forceful way this original count use (e.g. *three excrements*, i.e. objects), rather than shifting the interpretation to event-related samples. In these cases, the lexical plural is not yet completely lexicalised; they are not yet fully fledged *lexical* plurals. On the other hand, for *internal plurals* – to which we may add *internal duals*, such as *scissors*, etc. – the count reading is almost the default one, to the extent that it is counter-intuitive to conceive the count use (see exampl (3)) as the result of a shifting operation. Internal lexical plurals are hence [+ count] but exhibit some peculiarities when they denote one single object.

Besides the fact that *not all* lexical plurals are open to mass-like coercion mechanisms, one can also come up with other counter-arguments suggesting that even those lexical plurals that might be taken into account for mass status are not yet fully fledged mass nouns. First, lexical plurals do not pattern with the partitive article (*du, de la, de l'*). Actually, the partitive article is ruled out by agreement rules, which might be independent of any possible features of count or mass:

(19)   du beurre   "Ø butter$_{sg}$"

(19')   *de l'épinards   "Ø spinach$_{pl}$"

As a matter of fact, the same kind of number agreement restriction holds for quantifiers at the opposite of the count–mass spectrum, such as *chaque* "each" or *aucun* "none of". Though truly [+ count], they are not compatible with plural forms. Therefore, I think the blocking of the singular partitive article does not make the case for challenging the mass status of lexical plurals. Moreover, if one qualifies the plural indefinite *des* as a "partitive" expression, like its singular counterpart *du* (Zribi-Hertz 2006: 141), then the agreement issue with *du* essentially becomes a false problem. The second possible objection must be handled more delicately. As is known, [+ mass] quantifiers are much rarer than [+ count] quantifiers (Doetjes, this volume, Chapter 4), but there does exist a second [+ mass] quantifier, viz. *un peu de* "some" (Doetjes 2001; Hilgert 2014), which patterns with some lexical plurals, but not with all of them. Here are the results of the *French Ten Ten Corpus*, limiting myself to those items with more than two occurrences:

un peu de ... rillettes (7.3‰; 17 instances), épinards (0.76‰; 9), loisirs (1.06‰; 48), vivres (2.38‰; 49), bonnes manières (0.50‰; 4), petits pois (0.62‰; 4), déchets (0.19‰; 45), frais (0.12‰; 64,7), mauvaises herbes (0.72‰; 9), données (0.02‰; 20)

Now, the question is why? At first sight, it seems fair to say that *un peu de* confirms the mass status of about one-third of our items. However, it also seems to impose additional constraints on the noun, more than the partitive article does. This does not come as a surprise, since *un peu de* goes back to a grammaticalised nominal expression which still has richer semantics than the partitive article. Yet, there is an additional problem with *un peu de*: it is also found with some grammatical plurals. This incoherent behaviour casts serious doubts on its status as a genuine mass diagnostic:

(20) un peu de {carottes/briques/...} "some carrots/bricks/..." (Nicolas 2002a: 85; Hilgert 2014)

I cannot explore this issue further here, but it is clear that we need a thorough contrastive analysis of *un peu de* and *du* to see what is going on here, and especially to determine whether these marginal uses are cases of mass coercion.

A third and final problem for the mass account of – at least some sorts of – lexical plurals lies in the small semantic differences that have been detected between singular mass nouns and mass plurals (Wierzbicka 1988: 535, 544; Acquaviva 2008: 272). For instance, with regard to *oats*, Wierzbicka (1988: 535) states the following:

quantitatively and spatially limited stuffs clearly composed of small particles [...] which are nonetheless too conspicuous for the "stuff" in question to be thought as homogeneous.

These nuances might be the semantic counterpart of plural marking, which cannot be simply dismissed as a semantically empty affix since "plurality does affect the interpretation, no matter how elusive its function may be", according to Acquaviva.[15] The question remains whether such tiny conceptual distinctions can be proven to be linguistically relevant, for instance by means of additional distributional evidence, including word embeddings. One may also argue that such nuances should first be backed-up with psycholinguistic evidence, showing, for example, that speakers experience a difference between, let's say, *spinach* and *épinards*. These questions call for additional research.

---

[15] Acquaviva (2008: 89). He mentions "manifoldness" or "complexity", "concreteness", elimination of "boundedness" (e.g. *woods* = "wooded landscape form") as important semantic effects (Acquaviva 2008: 89).

.

16 Determining Countability Classes

Scott Grimm and Aeshaan Wahlang

1. Introduction

Most works on countability quite sensibly begin with a set of grammatical and/or semantic diagnostics which isolate different classes of nouns, named mass or count, or given other labels. Despite the uniformity among works in the literature that they possess a discussions of how to determine countability classes, there is a large variability in what results from such discussions. A range of classification schemes have been proposed for countability, based on many different criteria, and, as such, many questions immediately arise: How comparable are the different criteria? How much do they overlap? Are the different countability schemes picking up on distinct aspects of the problem?

To give a sense of the variation, we single out three approaches. The first, the paradigm example of which is Allan (1980), is strictly based on grammatical and/or syntactic contrasts, such as that numeral modifiers are often incompatible with substance nouns like *gold*. A set of these syntactic criteria then determine a number of countability classes. A second approach recognizes syntactic diagnostics, but adds semantic diagnostics, such as cumulative reference (Quine 1960) or quantificational behavior with comparatives (Barner and Snedeker 2005), which in turn may partially correlate with the nouns' syntactic behavior or differentiate into different semantically motivated classes of nouns that appear, from their syntactic behavior, to be similar. A third approach, exemplified in Wierzbicka (1988), is based in groupings of intuitively similar lexical items, which manifest a cluster of syntactic and semantic correlates.

The varying applications of different diagnostics lead to very different answers to how many distinct classes of nouns are recognizable in their countability behavior. In fact, the researchers just cited come to quite different conclusions as to the number of countability classes: Quine (1960) establishing

---

The authors would like to thank the current and former members of the Quantitative Semantics Lab at the University of Rochester, especially Yufei Du, Rebecca Friedman, Elizabeth Lee, Caleb New, Isabelle Schmit, and Xuan Tang. We also would like to thank the organizers and audience of "The Count–Mass Distinction: A Linguistic Misunderstanding?" for their stimulating feedback.

two classes, Barner and Snedeker (2005) three, Allan (1980) eight, and Wierzbicka (1988) fourteen.

In addition to each study using its own set of diagnostics, the set of nouns used differs across studies and in all cases is very limited – normally to several dozen in the more data-intensive studies – in comparison to the many thousands of common nouns in the English vocabulary. This limitation to a small set of nouns is an unfortunate necessity of traditional methodologies, and in each study it is a reasonable limitation to make. Collectively, however, it is challenging to compare in detail different studies' conclusions in the face of varying diagnostics and data sets.

This paper argues that common techniques from the fields of data science and machine learning can assist to increase the scale of countability studies and provide techniques to compare different diagnostics and classifications. In this, it joins other large-scale studies, such as Kulkarni, Rothstein, and Treves (2013), Kiss, Pelletier, and Stadtfeld (2014), and Kiss et al. (2016), which contribute studies of semantic and syntactic diagnositics across a large portion of the vocabulary. The focus in this paper, however, is on the common grammatical diagnostics for countability and does not invoke semantic diagnostics at all.

We take as our starting point the study of Allan (1980), who through using a battery of diagnostics argues that nouns do not divide cleanly into countable and non-countable; instead, many sub-classes arise, which can in fact be ordered in terms of their "degree of countability" with respect to the grammatical diagnostics employed. We discuss Allan's (1980) approach in Section 2 and critically examine the environments for diagnosing countability across a large corpus in Section 3. We then assess the importance of different countability environments in predicting whether a noun is (non-) countable using machine learning methods in Section 4, observing, among other things, that bare occurrences of nouns are the strongest predictor of countability status. Section 5 performs clustering on the data to automatically induce a countability classification based on the countability environments. Section 6 concludes, highlighting the implications for the semantic contrasts of countability.

2. Background: Countability Preferences (Allan 1980)

The wide-ranging and pioneering study of Allan (1980) argued that a binary, or even ternary, countability classification understates the variation of the nominal domain. Using a set of syntactic tests, he argues for (at least) eight degrees of countability "preferences" nouns may have. We first provide a discussion of the diagnostics that Allan (1980) argues for before discussing his eventual classification. Like most diagnostics, a fair amount of care needs to be taken when applying them, and the reader is directed to Allan (1980) for discussion of a variety of nuances that arise in applying these diagnostics.

Allan first distinguishes a class of elements in the nominal phrase that he terms "denumerators". Denumerators include cardinal numbers, but also quantifiers such as *every* or *both*, and their defining characteristic is that they presuppose that the noun refers to a number of discrete entities. Thus, *each* is a denumerator, since it presupposes discrete entities that in turn can be counted (*each boy/*each sand*), while *some* is not a denumerator, since it does not presuppose discrete individuals (*some boy/some sand*). Allan argues for the following generalization: If the head constituent of an NP falls within the scope of a denumerator, it is countable. Thus, a noun's countability status follows from its co-occurrence with denumerators.

Allan distinguishes three subtypes of denumerators, UNIT (A+N), FUZZY (F+N), and OTHER (O-DEN). The unit denumerators consist of only the indefinite determiner *a(n)* and *one*. Allan argues that while some nouns, such as *admiration*, reject combining with most denumerators, they have licit uses with unit denumerators, as in (1):

(1)   Penelope's is an admiration that I treasure.   (Allan 1980: example 27)

Fuzzy denumerators include quantifiers and other terms that specify an imprecise number of entities. Allan exemplifies this group of denumerators with *(a) few*, *several*, *many*, *a dozen or so*, *about fifty*, and high round numbers such as *five hundred cattle*, *70,000 cattle*.

Allan argues that this class of denumerators distinguishes pluralia tantum nouns such as *cattle*, which reject precise cardinals, such as *two* or *four*, yet accept fuzzy denumerators, such as *many* or *about fifty*, as shown in (2).[1]

(2)   a. *Two cattle were severely injured   (Allan 1980: example 28)
         by the falling wall.
      b. Many cattle died in the cyclone.   (Allan 1980: example 28)

The class of "other denumerators", abbreviated as O-DEN, is defined as all the denumerators that are neither unit nor fuzzy denumerators. This, as Allan notes, is a heterogeneous collection, including cardinal numerals and quantifiers such as *each* or *both*.

Allan isolates two other environments which determine a noun's countability preference. First, certain nouns (and noun phrases) are morphologically undifferentiated from a singular form, but have plural reference, as with *sheep*

---

[1] Although fuzzy denumerators and approximative numbers have been less at issue in the literature on countability in general, certain members of this class, such as *hundreds of*, have turned out to be very important testing grounds for classifier languages such as Japanese. See Sudo (2016) for discussion.

Table 16.1. *Countability preferences of select nouns across the five environments (from Allan 1980: 562)*

Environment	Noun							
	car	oak	cattle	Himalayas	scissors	mankind	admiration	equipment
EX-PL	+	+	+	+	+	+		
A+N	+	+		+			+	+
All+N	+		+	+		+		
F+Ns	+	+	+			?		
O-DEN	+	+						

or *the poor*, which is detectable as they license plural agreement elsewhere in the clause. Allan (1980: 551) states that this diagnostic identifies "an NP as countable if it governs plural external number registration", and abbreviates it as EX-PL. This is shown in (3).

(3) Three sheep *were* nibbling the carrot tops when farmer Giles noticed *them*. (Allan 1980: example 38)

Second, Allan observes that a distinguishing environment for uncountable nouns is the co-occurence in the singular with the universal quantifier *all*, as shown in (4a), while countable nouns do not permit this, as shown in (4b):

(4)   a. All lightning is caused by the discharge   (Allan 1980: example 52)
         of electricity from the clouds.
      b. *All car is 20th century man's horse.   (Allan 1980: example 53)

Together, these five environments provide a classification over nouns that is potentially very fine-grained. Although the number of potential combinations is rather large ($2^5 = 32$), not all are completely independent from one another, nor are they all of the same discriminatory power. Allan argues that there is an ordering among three of the diagnostics, namely that nouns that may occur in O-DEN environments may also occur in F+N environments, and those that occur in F+N environments may also occur in EX-PL environments. The converse relation among these environments does not hold. Through analyzing the behavior of several dozen nouns in the various environments, Allan (1980) adduces eight sets of nouns that represent countability classes, or classes of countability preferences, shown in Table 16.1. The nouns are cross-classified by each environment in which they are able to occur, here marked by a +, or in the case of *All*+N, fail to occur (since *not* occurring in the All+N environment is diagnostic of countable nouns).

From the table, one can distinguish highly countable nouns, such as *car*, and highly uncountable nouns, such as *equipment*, and between those two poles spans a range of nouns with mixed countability properties. This result is notable for several reasons. First, this indicates that there may be a range of distinctions in play for countability, not all of which lead to a simple bifurcation of nominal meaning into countable and non-countable. Second, and not unrelated, the range of nominal data included is wider than most studies, as it includes pluralia tantum, proper nouns, and abstract nouns, all of which are rarely seen in the countability literature. Thus, Allan (1980) argues that the challenge of determining countability contrasts is not simply limited to understanding the contrast between, e.g., objects (*dogs*) and substances (*water*) but is far broader and more nuanced. Finally, this result, as Allan (1980) remarks, is purely syntactic, and except for the initial definition of denumerators, hardly any relation to nominal meaning is asserted.

While the work of Allan (1980) is clearly a pioneering effort, there are several avenues left open for investigation. The study reports on a larger set of data than typically used, yet the amount of data is still quite restricted. Similarly for the different countability environments isolated, these are exemplified by a handful of lexical elements rather than exhaustively tested, nor is much claimed about elements that are not denumerators, namely if they are able to aid in discerning countability preferences. We take these issues up in the next section.

3. Quantifying Countability Environments

In this section, we provide a corpus-driven investigation of the differing preferences among nouns for different grammatical environments that bear on countability. We first discuss the details of the corpus, its processing, and the automatic coding of the various countability environments, then analyze the findings, and in turn examine a more fine-grained classification of countability environments.

3.1. Methodology: Data Processing and Annotation

We constructed a database of grammatical behavior of nouns to assess the varying countability behaviors of nouns. All data comes from the Corpus of Contemporary American English (COCA) (Davies 2009). COCA is a useful resource since it presents a collection of well-balanced texts that are controlled for quality, and does not inject the sort of uncertainty into studies that, say, raw internet data or Twitter data might. This study focuses on using four of the five genre types in the corpus: *Fiction, Popular Magazines, Newspaper,* and *Academic.* (We set aside the *Spoken* genre as it results in too many parsing errors.) In total, the study spans over a roughly 350-million word portion of the 450-million word corpus. This size of a corpus evades many issues related to data sparsity. While some extremely rare words do not occur in the corpus, in practice it is uncommon not to find a noun of interest.

We developed a natural language processing (NLP) pipeline to process the data and populate a database containing all relevant information. First, it is parsed with the CoreNLP suite (Manning et al. 2014), which includes dependency parsing (De Marneffe, MacCartney, and Manning 2006) that proves critical for efficiently identifying grammatical patterns. Subsequent processing with a Python script extracts from the parsed output all relevant grammatical relations and represents them as features in the database. More concretely, if the output from the dependency parser contains the dependency DET(DOG, THE), then the script will extract the determiner *the* and, then, in the relevant row of the database representing this occurrence of *dog* in the corpus, mark that the determiner was *the*.[2]

Various post-processing steps were taken to ensure the quality of data. For instance, an enormous number of words get tagged as a "noun" by the part-of-speech tagger, which may have been abbreviations, brand names, or even unusual punctuation. We filtered the nouns that populated the database so as to consist of only the nouns that occur in the CELEX database (Baayen, Piepenbrock, and Gulikers 1996), which is a large and representative sample of standard English vocabulary. (One drawback of this technique is it will exclude more recent innovations like *bling*.) Of the sentences that contained a noun recognized by this criteria, further exclusion criteria were applied, the most important being the exclusion of instances of the noun where it serves as a modifier in a compound, e.g. compounds such as *school bus* were excluded from the analysis of *school*.[3]

It is worth noting that such a method, while applied to nouns and to the COCA corpus, is very general and could be applied to investigate any part of speech on any corpus. Further, since we employ "Universal Dependencies" (De Marneffe et al. 2014), that is, dependency annotations that are designed to be cross-linguistically comparable, this general strategy can be applied to a large number of languages in a comparable way.

In order to quantitatively assess Allan's (1980) countability classification, we transposed his countability environments to a set of search patterns over the corpus. There were several challenges in carrying this out. First, only a handful of denumerators are discussed in the text of Allan (1980); thus a major task was simply extending the classification to all naturally occurring elements of the

---

[2] More information was extracted than is at issue in this paper, such as position in the clause, modifiers, and all other aspects of the grammatical distribution detectable through the dependencies. This information is not used in this study, however.
[3] Further, sentences in the corpus were not included in the final database due to limitations of the NLP tools, such as sentences that were too long for the parser or contain html code that make the parser fail.

nominal phrase. While the A+N and *All*+N environments were straightforward to detect, the *Fuzzy* and *Other* denumerators are essentially unlimited in number. Additionally, it was necessary to delimit the class of non-denumerators.[4] Finally, while almost all of the countability environments could be detected in the corpus, recognizing the EX-PL environment was not possible to do in a quantitatively reliable way, due to the fact a very large number of occurrences simply show ambiguous agreement, and thus it is not discernible if it is external singular or plural agreement.

3.2. Assessing Allan (1980)

We are now in a position to assess if Allan's (1980) claims hold up across a much larger set of data. First, we examine the distribution of just the eight nouns from Table 16.1. A straightforward comparison with Table 16.1 is given in Table 16.2, which shows the divergence between Allan's claims and what was found in the corpus. Occurrences of nouns in environments other than those claimed by Allan (1980) are marked with a √.

The nouns were observed to occur in nearly all the environments, just as discussed by Allan (1980), the only exception being that no instances of *scissors* with fuzzy denumerators were found. At the same time, several nouns passed diagnostics in the corpora that were asserted not to pass in Allan (1980). In particular, *cattle* and *scissors* were able to be used in more countable environments than expected. *Cattle* appeared (not infrequently) with numerals, and as such is licit in O-DEN environments, as shown in (5):[5]

(5) "My father had **27 cattle**, which I looked after."

Scissors appeared with both numerals and with indefinite articles, and thus was observed in both O-DEN and A+N environments, as shown in (6) and (7), respectively:

(6) "He belted on the leather shoulder-holster he had custom-made for **his three silver-plated styling scissors**.

(7) "First, careful cutting of young leaves, with **a scissors**, will encourage the plant to continue producing more leaves well into the summer."

Although the occurrence of these nouns in these environments was unexpected given what was reported by Allan (1980), the general classificatory result remains: As Table 16.2 shows, eight distinct noun classes remain of differing compatibility with the countability environments.

---

[4] A full listing of the mapping from elements of the noun phrase to the Allan categories, as well as all code, models, and dataframes, is available at https://quantitativesemanticslab.github.io/.
[5] All examples are from the COCA corpus.

Table 16.2. *Countability preferences of select nouns across the five environments as recognized in the database*

	Noun							
Environment	car	oak	cattle	Himalayas	scissors	mankind	admiration	equipment
EX-PL	+	+	+	+	+	+		
A+N	+	+		+	√	+	+	
All+N	+		+	+	+			
F+Ns	+	+	+					
O-DEN	+	+	√		√			

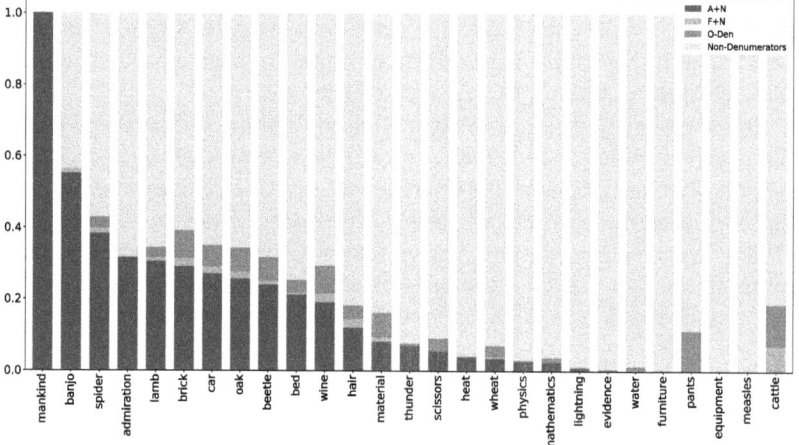

Fig. 16.1: Distribution of nouns across Allan environments

A different perspective on the data can be gained by examining the frequency with which these nouns occur in the different environments. Figure 16.1 shows the quantitative distribution of the different denumerator environments (A+N, F+N, O-DEN) as well as occurrences in "non-denumerator" environments over a larger set of nouns. This set of nouns contains most of the nouns discussed in Allan (1980), although it excludes proper names. Looking at this distribution permits examining if the categories asserted in Tables 16.1 and 16.2 are representative across larger groups of nouns. Non-denumerator environments include determiners, quantifiers, and all other material that may occur in a noun phrase, e.g. comparatives, but that do not qualify as denumerators (since they do not presuppose discrete individuals).

(The class of non-denumerators does not include bare plural or singular occurrences, to which we will turn shortly.)

Several trends are visible in Figure 16.1. First, there is a split between nouns that permit denumerators and those that do not, which corresponds to the traditional intuition of the count/non-count distinction. Thus, *equipment*, *measles*, *furniture*, and *evidence* do not show the presence of any denumerators, and for *water* and *lightning* their presence is exceedingly rare. To this latter group should be added *mankind*, for which there were only four occurrences of an indefinite determiner and all other occurrences were in the bare singular. (Since no other (non-)denumerators co-occur with *mankind*, it has a peculiar position in Figure 16.1.)

Second, of the different types of denumerators, the A+N is the most frequently found, clearly due to its role as an indefinite determiner and not just as a signal of quantity. Allan (1980) argues for the presence of an asymmetry amongst the possible combinations between denumerators and nouns. One of these asymmetries clearly holds: nouns that permit A+N do not necessarily permit the other denumerator types to occur in its environment. On the other hand, the proposed generalization that if a noun occurs in an O-DEN environment then it will also occur in an F+N environment appears less clear. Nouns may occur in the O-DEN environment, but show no evidence of occurring in the F+N environment, as is the case for *physics* and *thunder*, exemplified in (8a) and (8b), respectively. Both examples show non-typical uses of the noun at issue. In (8a), the interpretation is a type-level interpretation, as it is discussing types of physics, while in (8b), it is a metaphorical extension, that is, *thunder* does not refer to the natural event but a sound event that can be described as "thunder". It seems prudent not to assume that fuzzy denumerator uses come for free simply because a nouns has O-DEN uses.

(8) a. With the Multi-field solver, **each physics** can have totally independent meshes and solution settings.
b. As he cleared the last embattled pair of behemoths he heard **another thunder** of flesh headed into the battle.

We now turn to decomposing the Allan environments to detect more fine-grained generalizations.

3.3.   Decomposing the Allan (1980) Environments

While examining nominal countability through the environments argued for by Allan (1980) provides a more nuanced view on the distribution of nouns with respect to syntactic properties of countability, there is much internal variation in each of the environments. For instance, O-DEN includes both numerals and quantifiers while F+N includes even more types of elements, such as modified

Table 16.3. *Correspondence between Allan environments and subtypes thereof*

Allan Environment	Subtype
Unit	*a/an*
	one
Fuzzy	imprecise quantifier (*few, many*)
	plural numeral (*hundreds*)
	approximative (*about 50*)
	round numbers (*100, 1000*)
	comparative values (*more than 10*)
O-DEN	numbers (*seven*, ...)
	digits (*27*, ...)
	precise quantifiers (*both, every*, ...)
Non-Denumerators	*the*
	measures *half of, quarts of*
	non-denumerating quantifiers *most, all*, ...
	non-quantificational *enough, more than, just*, ...

numerals (*about 50*). As such, the original classification scheme in Allan (1980) might be obscuring further patterns in the data. Yet another type of information that we aim to keep track of is other elements of the nominal phrase that do not strictly qualify as denumerators, including the definite determiner, quantifiers that do not presuppose individuals (*some, any*), measure terms (*kilo of, half of*), or special terms like *pair of*. Table 16.3 shows the correspondence between the Allan environments and the subtypes of those environments.

Figure 16.2 shows the distribution of the different subtypes of the same nouns from Figure 16.1. As expected, the distribution of the different subtypes yields a yet more nuanced view than visible with the more coarse-grained Allan environments. First, there are some additional outliers that are now visible. *Measles* is similar to other non-countable nouns by rejecting all denumerators, but is dissimilar to, say, *equipment* or *furniture*, since it also rejects all non-denumerators save the definite determiner *the*. *Cattle*, still an outlier, is an outlier in a different way: it manifests the most diversity of different types of quantificational and non-quantificational elements, excepting, of course, the indefinite determiner.

Further contrasts can be seen that are not present in the Allan classification. For instance, tracking not only whether a noun accepts cardinal modification, but also whether it is represented textually as a word or as a digit shows a further distinction between nouns that are tracked in large quantities, such as *cattle* and *wine*, which have a substantial number of uses with digits. Additionally, as would be expected, tracking nouns' co-occurrence with *pair of*

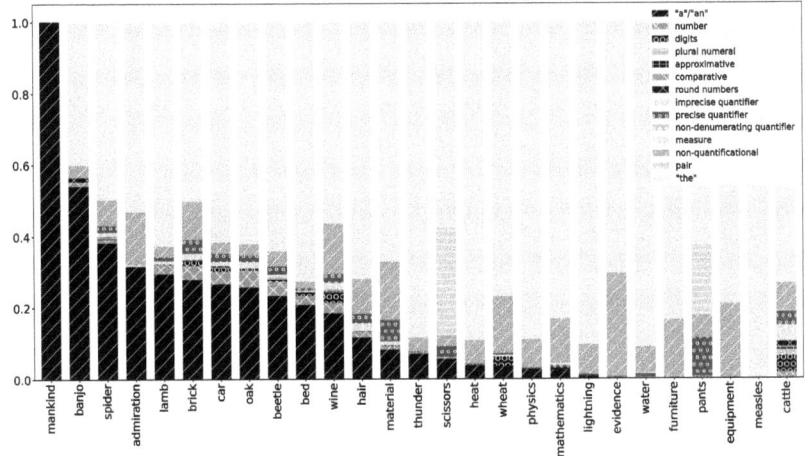

Fig. 16.2: Distribution of nouns across subtypes of Allan environments

isolates certain pluralia tantum nouns (*pants, scissors*) far more clearly than the other environments.

From one perspective, there is not a radical contrast between the distribution in Figures 16.1 and 16.2: there are highly countable nouns (*banjo, car*) and highly non-countable nouns (*equipment, furniture*) and a range of behaviors between, some of which are distinctive, in the case of pluralia tantum nouns, and some of which are simply quantitatively different, in the case of *beetle* and *spider*, which do not differ in any categorical way although do so quantitatively. On the other hand, a clearer contrast emerges between nouns that occur in a high diversity of environments, most obviously *cattle* and *wine*, and those that occur in a much more restricted set of environments, such as *admiration* or *lightning*. This is revealing in that while, e.g., *furniture* and *cattle* may have been thought of as semantically similar in that they are both non-countable nouns which have individuals in their denotations, in fact their grammatical behavior is quite divergent, with *cattle* hosting a range of quantifiers and other elements while *furniture* is limited to non-quantificational elements and the definite determiner.

Having performed a rather detailed assessment of these environments, both the original countability environments from Allan (1980) and more fine-grained subtypes, we now turn to a broad-scale assessment of these environments. Section 4 assesses how predictive the different environments are of countability status using a supervised machine learning method, namely using a form of random forest classification. Section 5 examines if these environments can be used to automatically induce countability classes through unsupervised clustering.

4. Assessing the Predictive Strength of Countability Environments

This section examines the influence of the individual environments on determining whether a noun is countable or non-countable. Using the environments described in the last section, both the original environments from Allan (1980), and the subtypes of those environments elaborated in Section 3.3, we assess through machine learning methods which environments are most predictive.

We use a gradient boosted ensemble learning algorithm similar to random forest classification, XGBoost or "extreme gradient boosting" (Chen and Guestrin 2016). The core method is random forest classification, which yields a classification by means of constructing a multitude of decision trees (see Hastie, Tibshirani, and Friedman 2009 for discussion and references). An advantage of using random forest classification is that it reduces the effect of overfitting on training data, which is common for decision tree algorithms. Gradient boosting is a technique to build a strong predictor model from an ensemble of weak predictors, in our case an ensemble of decision trees, wherein it attempts to minimize a loss function as it adds each tree to the ensemble. The XGBoost model trains a random forest with gradient boosting. For our purposes, this technique allows us to robustly measure the importance of each environment in a classification task.

We use this method in a supervised fashion, that is, we assume to know whether a noun is countable or not, and then assess what features influence its countability status. We make use of the countability classification performed in the CELEX database (Baayen, Piepenbrock, and Gulikers 1996), which labels each noun as countable, uncountable, or both countable and uncountable. Thus, we analyze two cases: (i) what is predictive of nouns that are labeled as countable and (ii) what is predictive of nouns that are labeled as uncountable. In addition, we construct one set of models using the Allan environments and one set using the subtypes of those environments. We also assess how these environments compare with information that can be gleaned from two other syntactic environments that are diagnostic of countable or non-countable status, namely occurrence as a bare plural or bare singular, respectively. The bare plural and bare singular occurrences have a much higher rate of occurrence than any given Allan or Subtype environment, risking obscuring any effect of the latter. To adjust for this, we weight the Allan and Subtype environments by using the calculated proportion of occurrence with respect to all (non-)denumerators, whereas we use the proportion of bare singular and bare plural uses of the noun with respect to all occurrences of the noun.

Table 16.4 shows the models' results classifing whether a noun was labeled countable or uncountable in CELEX from the different environments and their combinations. Regardless of which set of environments were used as features in the classifier, it is much more difficult to predict whether a noun is

Table 16.4. *Model accuracy results predicting countable and uncountable nouns*

Environment	Class	Accuracy
Allan	Countable	73.26%
Allan	Uncountable	66.11%
Allan + Bare	Countable	81.17%
Allan + Bare	Uncountable	73.45%
Subtypes	Countable	73.24%
Subtypes	Uncountable	68.72%
Subtypes + Bare	Countable	81.24%
Subtype + Bare	Uncountable	73.91%

uncountable than it is to predict if it is countable, by a 5%–8% difference. Table 16.4 also shows that there is little difference in the classification accuracy whether the Allan environments are used or the Subtype environments are used; however, there is a significant increase in accuracy in both cases if information from bare plurals and singulars is added.

Figure 16.3 shows the overall information gained relative to each feature (the gain) for each of the eight models. Examining the Allan environments (upper left panel of Figure 16.3), it is notable that they perform reasonably close to what could be expected based on the discussion of Allan (1980). The A+N, F+N, and O+DEN environments all contribute to classifying a noun as countable, and in an ordering of importance reminiscent of Allan's (1980) claims. Additionally, the high performance of the *All*+N environment indicates that it is indeed a robust diagnostic for uncountability.

Comparing the models without and with the bare plural and bare singular included, the left and right panels of the figure, respectively, show the overwhelming importance of bare plural and bare singular for predicting countability. While it is not surprising that the bare singular is highly significant for predicting uncountable nouns, it is more surprising that the bare plural outperforms, many times over, all other environments that have been observed to signal countable nouns, a point to which we will return in Section 6.

5. Clusters of Countability

We now turn to assessing the relevance of these environments to developing countability classes. We use unsupervised clustering to examine which nouns cluster together in terms of the relevant countability properties. Unlike the last experiment where we assumed a gold standard annotation for countability provided by Baayen, Piepenbrock, and Gulikers (1996), in this experiment we provide no information about countability external to the occurrence of the

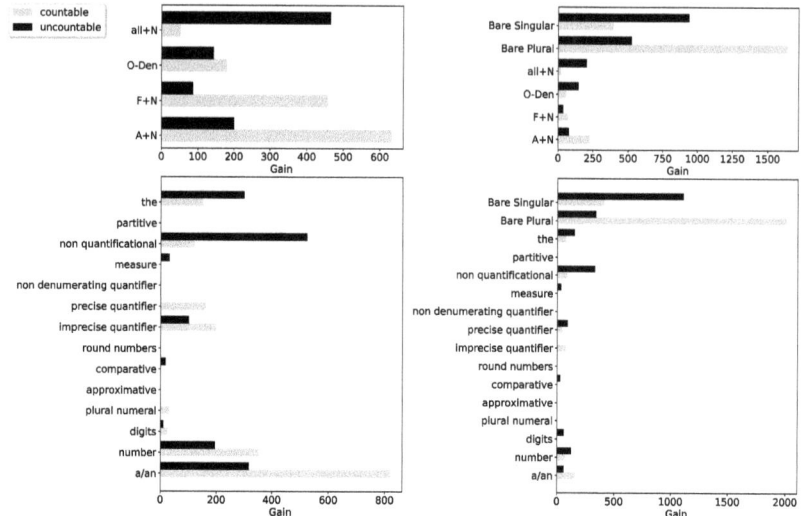

Fig. 16.3: Variable importance in classifying nouns as countable or uncountable across Allan (top) and subtype (bottom) environments with (right) and without (left) bare plural and bare singular included

nouns in the different environments and attempt to induce countability classes directly from that information. Essentially, this is an update on Allan's (1980) original approach using machine learning techniques.

We applied the *Density-based spatial clustering of applications with noise (DBSCAN)* algorithm (Ester et al. 1996) to explore latent countability classes in our data. This algorithm is particularly suited to exploratory work with this sort of data. Operating over a given a set of points in some space – here each noun is a point in the space determined by the values of occurrence in each environment – the algorithm groups together points that are close together.[6] Intuitively, if two nouns behave similarly in terms of the different environments, they will fall under the same cluster.

We explored multiple ways of clustering the data (and also multiple algorithms) but discuss here two of those clusterings that are most directly related to the claims being tested in this paper. For these clustering models, we clustered a total of 6,872 nouns. In one experiment, we clustered solely on the environments isolated in Allan (1980): A+N, F+N, O-Den, and *All*+N. This returned a model with a relatively small number (12) of clusters, each of

---

[6] This method is non-parametric, so there are no assumptions of a particular distribution, e.g. normal, underlying the data.

relatively large size (average 485 words per cluster).[7] Only a small percentage were classified as noise (561 nouns, 8.2%), that is, were not identified with a particular cluster. This clustering was able to identify some of the countability contrasts one would expect to see. For instance, the resulting clustering identified *cattle*, *oak*, and *wine* as belonging to one cluster, intuitively representing nouns with primarily a non-countable use yet which also have substantial occurrence with indefinites and numerals, in contrast to a separate cluster for more uniformly non-countable nouns such as *equipment*, *thunder*, *evidence*, and *furniture*. We performed a qualitative assessment of this clustering result, however, which indicates that it is both too coarse-grained and consistently conflates nouns that would seemingly be distinct in terms of countability. For instance, a third cluster contains *beetle*, *lightning*, and *scissors*, which intuitively, and according to Allan (1980), should be separated into different countability classes. Given the findings of Section 4, this is not altogether surprising as two important environments are not taken into account, the bare singular and the bare plural.

A second clustering was performed with all the Allan environments previously used in conjunction with the bare singular and bare plural environments. This returned a larger number (23) of clusters of smaller size than the preceding model (average 180 words per cluster). This model classified a higher number of nouns as noise (2,545 nouns, 37.0%).

While the coverage of this model is not as high as the previous model, a qualitative assessment of the clustering indicated that it was identifying a large number of the countability contrasts, and also classes, that appear in the literature. This clustering again groups together *equipment, thunder, evidence,* and *furniture*, but correctly separates *lightning* (which occurs in a cluster together with *heat, physics,* and *water*) from *scissors* (which occurs in a cluster together with certain other pluralia tantum terms which are potentially denumerable, such as *binoculars* and *handcuffs*).

We list below the major clusters identified and provide labels for them. While 23 clusters were identified, we list 15, having excluded clusters that were uninformative, being either very small (6 clusters) or not coherent (2 clusters). The list below also presents for each cluster a small number of nouns to indicate the trends in each cluster. (The full results can be viewed at https://quantitativesemanticslab.github.io/).

---

[7] The parameters for this model were set at EPS = 0.9 (a parameter for the maximum distance between two samples in the clustering), minimum samples = 8 (that is, clusters must contain at least eight members), where the Canberra distance metric was used. The parameters for the subsequent model are identical save for a lower EPS value (.8) to promote conservative clustering in the face of a higher number of features.

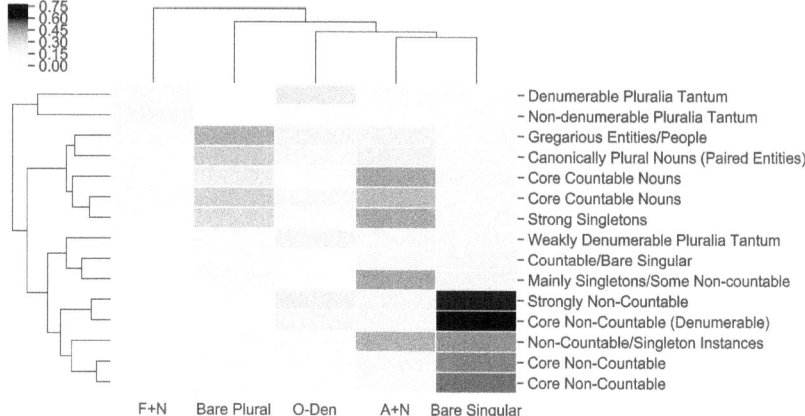

Fig. 16.4: Heatmap representing the clusters' distributional tendencies across countability environments

Figure 16.4 displays a heatmap which represents the distribution of the clusters across each environment. The greater the percentage of occurrences in a given environment, the higher the hue, as shown in the legend. In the following, both in the text and the labels of the clusters, we use the terms SINGLETON and GREGARIOUS to indicate the tendency of a noun to refer to single or multiple entities, respectively.

- **Denumerable Pluralia Tantum**: Nearly all pluralia tantum nouns, which occur frequently with numerals and other O-DEN denumerators (*briefs, cattle, clothes, fries, singles, species, spectacles, supplies, troops*)
- **Non-Denumerable Pluralia Tantum**: Nearly all pluralia tantum nouns or similar, which do not generally occur with denumerators (*belongings, brethren, clergy, dealings, furnishings*)
- **Gregarious Entities/People**: Entities or person types, which frequently occur in large numbers or groups (*freckle, noodle, petal, photon, tentacle, customer, delegate, fundamentalist, recruit, refugee, spectator*)
- **Canonically Plural Nouns (Paired Entities)**: Nouns that have very high rates of plurals, including paired entities and some vegetables (*artichoke, beet, boot, cheekbone, datum, goal, leek, pea, shoe, slipper, standard, yolk*)
- **Core Countable Nouns**: Two clusters of fully countable nouns which have differing preferences in frequency of occurrence in denumerator environments. One cluster trends towards singleton:

basket, bouquet, contest, ditch, dream, kite, paradigm, return, splash, sum, tornado. Another cluster trends towards gregariousness: *bead, bullet, cookie, follower, hue, impediment, parasite, skyscraper, undergraduate, weapon*.

Strong Singletons: Countable nouns which preferentially occur in A+N environments, primarily professional titles (*anthropologist, banker*) and clearly delimited physical objects or events (*asteroid, handbag, mistake, puddle, reward, tattoo*)

Weakly Denumerable Pluralia Tantum: Nearly all pluralia tantum nouns, which may occur with numerals and other O-DEN denumerators (*cheek, goggles, gymnastics, jeans, pants, proceedings, savings*)

Countable/Bare Singular: Nouns which have a significant use both in bare singular and countable environments; significant subgroups include locations, which often have a bare singular use with prepositions (*bed, deck*), group nouns (*committee, commission, crew*), and some pluralia tantum nouns (*handcuffs, proceeds, scissors*)

Mainly Singletons/Some Non-Countable: Nouns which occur primarily with A+N and some bare singular uses; highly varied semantic domains (*axe, belly, briefcase, cello, convent, necklace, reputation, rope, rhythm, skirt, spatula*), but body parts and artifacts are frequent

Strongly Non-Countable: Nouns which nearly only have a bare singular use (*aviation, fennel, ginger, homelessness, modernism, parenthood, profanity, urbanization*) along with various proper names (*Gregory, Havana*)

Core Non-Countable (Denumerable): Comprised primarily of substances, which have dominant use in the bare singular; yet some may be counted or quantified in certain contexts, e.g., financial contexts (*gold, oil, barley*), along with various proper names (*Frank, Holland*)

Non-Countable/Singleton Instances: Nouns with a primary bare singular use but also a significant use of singulars, often designating an instance of a quality or material (*addiction, awareness, breakfast, calm, guitar, ham, shame, straw*)

Core Non-Countable: Two clusters of primarily standard non-countable nouns, often substances and abstract entities (*awe, bacon, candlelight, colonization, despair, foliage, freedom, nutmeg*)

The organization of the clusters, as displayed in Figure 16.4, serves as a validation of one of Allan's (1980) insights, namely that there are degrees of countability that can be detected through different grammatical environments. Further, as indicated by the dendograms along the x- and y-axes of Figure 16.4, there is a structure to the different clusters and countability environments. The dendogram on the y-axis of Figure 16.4 shows three coarse-grained groups among the clusters: (i) pluralia tantum (denumerable and non-denumerable), (ii) countable (plural, core countable, and strong singleton nouns), and (iii) non-countable (weakly denumerable pluralia tantum, bare singular, and non-countable nouns). On the other hand, the dendogram on the x-axis of Figure 16.4 is based on the similarity of the various environment distributions across the clusters. We see no distinct groups formed in the hierarchy, which implies that these environments are distinct from one another and make independent contributions to the classifications, as can be verified by looking at the distributional patterns in the heatmap. On examining the heatmap we can see that F+N is useful for determining pluralia tantum nouns, as argued by Allan (1980), although not in all cases, as there are three classes of pluralia tantum nouns identified: Denumerable and Weakly Denumerable, which have a relatively high proportion of F+N occurrences, but also Non-Denumerable Pluralia Tantum nouns, which do not appear proportionately more in F+N environments.

6. Outlook: Implications for the Semantics of Countability

In this section, we redirect our focus from the syntactic distribution of nouns to the semantic implications of this study's results, and the implications for the countability literature more broadly. In particular, we consider three issues: (i) current semantic models' underfitting the space of variation; (ii) varieties of non-countable nouns; and (iii) the importance of bare plurals as a diagnostic.

The most general point arising from this study is that there is much greater variation in nominal behavior than generally acknowledged in theoretical models. Many popular approaches, e.g., Bale and Barner (2009) or Deal (2017), advocate a primarily three-way division between nouns (countable, substance, and *furniture*-type nouns), while others note other semantic classes, such as countable nouns like *fence* (Rothstein 2010). Even more flexible approaches, such as Grimm (2018), do not provide specific analyses of substantially more classes. Yet, reviewing the data and the classes induced in Section 5 indicates a much higher degree of variability in nominal behavior and many unexplored semantic contrasts. As such, our semantic models are likely severely underfitting the true variation in nominal meaning as regards countability. One possible response is that this variation is innocent and merely fluctuates in ways that are uninteresting for theoretical linguistics; however, usage frequencies and variation in one language, in this study English, have long been know to correspond to grammatical distinctions in other languages

(Bresnan, Dingare, and Manning 2001). Thus, these quantitative distinctions observed in English may be crucial to unraveling cross-linguistic variation in countability classification, both in related languages, such as French or German, but also in languages which have a much more elaborate and overt nominal classification system, such as Niger-Congo languages.

More pointedly, a contrast that came clearly to light in Section 5 is the different types of non-countable nouns. The contrast between substances (*water*) and non-countable nouns with individuals (*furniture*) is well-known. Thus far not discussed in the literature, however, are nouns such as *parenthood* or *urbanization*, those which are strongly non-countable and whose grounds for being non-countable elude the current state of the art of nominal semantics. Even the contrast between *cattle* and *furniture*, two nouns which have garnered a fair amount of discussion, remains obscure, as noted in Section 3.3. In sum, the semantic work needed to understand the contrasts present in a realistically large swath of English vocabulary is substantial. Importantly, both lexical and formal semantic work are critical for this enterprise.

Finally, one of the more surprising results from the study in Section 4 was that the bare plural served as a more informative environment to determine if a noun was countable or not than any other diagnostic. Although, to our knowledge, this has not been discussed, there is a clear intuitive basis for this, as bare plural usage would appear to be even more discriminative than combinations with the indefinite article or numerals. In particular, some weakly countable nouns, such as *admiration* or *thunder*, may take an indefinite article or occasionally numbers, in contexts, such as packaging or sorting, where individual entities or instances must be identified; however, the bare plural form, whose most well-known use is for generic reference, is less likely to be licensed due to particular contextual needs. In addition, there is likely competition from the use of the bare singular for any required generic uses.[8] Thus, another clear avenue for future research is to examine more closely countability phenomena in generic contexts.

---

[8] See Grimm (2016) for discussion of how this competition plays out for the noun *crime*, which possesses both a non-countable and countable usage, and interestingly appears to only permit kind-level reference with the bare singular, while the bare plural preferably refers to specific crime events or subkinds of crime.

17 Polysemy and the Count–Mass Distinction: What Can We Derive from a Lexicon of Count and Mass Senses?

Tibor Kiss, Francis Jeffry Pelletier, and Halima Husić

1. Introduction

While there is some controversy in the literature on the count–mass distinction concerning its lexical base (with some proponents assuming that the count–mass distinction is not a lexical distinction at all), it is undisputed that lexical items in one way or another are affected by the count–mass distinction. From this perspective, it is remarkable that current research on the count–mass distinction does not elaborate on two aspects that might provide new insights: *lexical variation* and *lexical ambiguity*. We borrow the term *lexical variation* from experimental linguistics, where it is stated that experiments should make use of a certain number of lexical items, of which the linguist implicitly assumes that they belong to the same class. With the exception of Allan (1980), lexical variation does not figure prominently in dealing with the count–mass distinction, and hence the count–mass distinction as a binary one is mostly maintained without question. Most analyses, including influential works such as Pelletier (1975), Link (1983), Bunt (1985), Krifka (1989), Landman (1989, 2011, 2016), Pelletier and Schubert (1989/2003), Chierchia (1998a; 2010; this volume, Chapter 2), and Rothstein (2010, 2017; this volume, Chapter 3), among others, rest on a small set of so-called celebrity nouns (the term comes from an unpublished talk by Scott Grimm at the 2012 LSA meetings) such as *table, horse, cat, child, ring, cow, children, water, sand, mud, wine, footwear, gold, furniture* being representative for the whole class of nominals to which the count–mass distinction applies, to which recently (cf. Zucchi and White 2001; Rothstein 2010) *twig, rope,* and *bouquet* have been added (or rediscovered, since the properties of these nouns had already been discussed in Krifka 1989). These analyses tacitly assume that what is said about the respective celebrities carries over to the other members of the respective countability class (which includes the assumption that there are only two classes with a few notorious exceptions, such as *furniture* or *twig*). In the following, we will show that a deeper look into the data will reveal variation that remains unaccounted for, and that in addition, ambiguity with regard to countability differences raises further questions.

Lexical ambiguity does not actually need an introduction, as every linguist knows about the pitfalls and problems of homonymy and polysemy (not the least being the question of how to disentangle the aforementioned terms). While the early discussion of the count–mass distinction within formal semantics acknowledged the role of ambiguity (cf. Pelletier 1975), lexical ambiguity was only slowly taken for granted and even considered as irrelevant, as the discussion of the count–mass distinction progressed. A famous example of a problematic treatment of ambiguity in the count–mass distinction can be found in Payne and Huddleston (2002: 334–5), where the authors show "polysemy" between count and mass senses. Some of the examples they provide, however, make use of a form that should be categorized as a noun in one sense, but as a part of a support verb construction (1a,b) or even as a participle (1c,d) in the other.

(1)   a. This proposal has three *advantages*. [count]
       b. They took *advantage* of us. [mass according to Payne and Huddleston]
       c. It is certainly a fine *building*. [count]
       d. There's plenty of *building* going on. [mass according to Payne and Huddleston]

It is highly questionable that we are dealing with a case of ambiguity here that has any bearing on the count–mass distinction (and particularly so in (1c,d)). But there are other, quite common cases of dealing with ambiguity in a somewhat agnostic way. Two typical cases are so-called *dual-life* nouns (Pelletier and Schubert 1989) and a set of countability shifts including cases of *grinding* (Pelletier 1975), *packaging* (Bach 1986), and *sorting* (Bunt 1985).

As for the former case, Pelletier (2012) assumes that the noun *chocolate* has the same meaning (modulo individuation vs. stuff) in (2a) and (2b). In the first case, *chocolate* is shown in a mass context, while in the second case, it appears in a count context:

(2)   a. a lot of chocolate
       b. many more chocolates

The question regarding the nouns in (2) is: what should remain as the common semantic core of *chocolate* in (2a) and (2b) that actually justifies the claim that the noun and its semantics remain constant while undergoing a shift in countability? Pelletier remarks that *chocolates* have to be in a confection to be used as in (2b), but no such constraint applies to *chocolate* in (2a). In addition, one might argue that *chocolates* do not necessarily have to contain *chocolate*, which again raises the question of the identity of the two nouns in (2).[1] The

---

[1] It is interesting to observe how different languages lexically realize the concepts in question. While German draws a clear distinction between *Schokolade* and *Pralinen*, French uses *chocolat* vs. *bouchée au chocolat* or even *offrir de chocolats* (with a plural, meaning: *to give away chocolates*).

Polysemy and the Count–Mass Distinction   379

original grinder explanation in Pelletier (1975) was restricted to objects designated by concrete nouns, and it generated "undifferentiated stuff" that contained all the materials that comprised the starting object. So, if one supplied an octopus to the grinder, one would end up with a gooey mess that contained the total remnants of the octopus – eyeballs, beak, suction cups, and all. Clearly this is different from (for example) the edible portions of an octopus. And (3b) and (3c) are different, only the former being an application of a grinder-like operation envisaged by Pelletier (1975) on the meaning given by the WordNet sense in (3a) (Miller 1995; Fellbaum 1998).

(3)   a. armadillo#1: burrowing, chiefly nocturnal mammal with body covered with strong horny plates.
      b. There is armadillo all over the road
      c. We're having armadillo for dinner this evening.

Some authors use the notion of "grinding" for both of these meanings, and even more generally for any way of generating a mass meaning from a count meaning.[2] The following discussion of grinding in Rothstein (2010: 390–4) further illustrates the point. Referring to Pelletier and Schubert (1989), Rothstein starts by considering examples like (4), and proposes the rule SHIFT$_{mass}$ to turn count nouns into "ground" mass nouns:

(4)   a. After he had finished the job, there was bicycle all over the floor.
      b. After the accident, there was boy all over the ground.

(5) $\lambda P \lambda x. \exists y [y \in \pi_1(P) \wedge x \leq y \wedge \neg x = y]$

What (5) says is that one can take the first projection of a count predicate (i.e. the set of atoms that are contextually determined as such, since Rothstein (2010) assumes that count predicates are of type $<<e \times k>, t>)$[3] and turn this predicate into a predicate denoting a set of proper parts of the atoms. It is already unclear why the set of parts must be proper, i.e. not consisting of everything the atom was made of, but even leaving this aside, this would again only account for the contrast between (3a) and (3b).

Clearly, in the (3c) case we are employing a different sense of *armadillo* from the one used in (3a) – indeed, even the denotation of the two occurrences of *armadillo* are different. The case is not quite so clear in contrasting (3b)

---

[2] For example, Chierchia (2010: 106) uses "universal grinder" to massify a count noun N. Chierchia (this volume, Chapter 2) takes grinding to be the main count to mass application, and thus assumes: "For any count property P$_C$, G(P$_C$), if defined, is the mass property corresponding to P$_C$" (p. 31).
[3] Rothstein (2010) actually uses type $<d \times k, t>$ following Landman (1996) who uses type d for entities and type e for events. We have converted this to the more usual convention: e for entities and v for events. Cf. also the discussion below in Section 5.

with (3a), since at least all the parts of the relevant armadillo are the same, even if the structural integrity differs. Here, one needs to take into consideration that the outcome of the Universal Grinder is indeed a difference in structural integrity, whereas shifts from mass to count, as for instance (3c) and (1b), are different. As for Rothstein's approach (which remains one of the very few to actually provide a formal account of grinding), we note that it makes a wrong prediction with regard to (3a) and (3c), for even in the case that we would like to have *armadillo* for dinner tonight, we might not expect all arbitrary parts of the armadillo to be served (which, counter our intuitions, would be sufficient if Rothstein's grinder would apply to (3a,c)). By means of many more examples that we will discuss in this paper, we will clarify that it is not possible to narrow down all marked mass uses of nouns (either accounted for as specific senses or coerced meanings) to an operation of grinding, no matter how widely understood, since the core function underlying grinding, viz. transforming an object to ground stuff of all the ingredients of that object, is not what is happening with the denotation of nouns used in mass contexts, such as (3c) and (1b).

As an illustration of various mass uses of nouns that do not result from grinding, consider the following more realistic scenario. A visitor of the swamps of Florida appears to be hungry to the person he visits, so that person remarks that *there is alligator in the fridge*. Of course, the visitor will not expect to be attacked by an alligator after opening the fridge (because $alligator_{mass}$ refers to meat, not to the animal). Nor would the visitor expect a ground up totality of alligator – the scales, claws, teeth. In sum, the aforementioned examples show a difference between count and mass, but also a difference between two related senses. Landman (2011) has argued that *grinding* should not be used as an argument for or against possible analyses of the count–mass distinction, because there will always be a change in a sense that has nothing to do with the distinction between count and mass proper. By the same line of reasoning, Quirk et al. (1985: 1564) dismiss grinding in favor of characterizing examples like *an inch of pencil* or *a few square feet of floor* as instances of a polysemy that they call "N viewed in terms of measurable extent."

This paper follows the same lead but tries to systematize different cases of polysemy in the area of the count–mass distinction. We will argue below that the majority of cases called grinding are actually realizations of a regular polysemy (cf. Falkum 2010).

Lexical ambiguity within the count–mass distinction also has an inhibiting effect on empirical research such as corpus studies. Unless a corpus is fully annotated for different meanings of the same noun form, a quantitative study may come to the conclusion that count occurrences and mass occurrences of the very same noun occur in equal numbers. As an illustration, consider the case of *alarm*, which receives the following four definitions in WordNet (Fellbaum 1998):

(6) *alarm*:
   a. fear resulting from the awareness of danger
   b. a clock that wakes a sleeper at some preset time
   c. a device that signals the occurrence of some undesirable event
   d. an automatic signal (usually a sound) warning of danger

We do not want to engage in a discussion of whether the definitions provided in (6) are the result of polysemy or homonymy, but crucially, *alarm* in (6a) is taken to be a *mass* noun, while the other three definitions refer to *count* uses. With a purely structural analysis, i.e. without further *semantic* annotations in the corpus, it is likely that the count and mass senses of *alarm* cannot be discerned, and hence wrong conclusions are drawn with respect to the count and mass occurrences of *alarm*, even up to the point where *alarm* is assigned the status of a *dual-life noun*. In order to add some structure to discussions of the term *dual-life noun*, we will speak of *proper dual life nouns* when we refer to nouns that show (at least) two discernible senses, where the difference between the senses only pertains to the count–mass distinction. It should be obvious from the definitions provided in (6) that *alarm* is not a *proper dual-life noun*:[4] while the different senses listed in (6) may fall on either side of a count–mass distinction, they also exhibit different senses irrespective of the count–mass distinction.

This paper addresses the aforementioned methodological problem by introducing the *Bochum English Countability Lexicon (BECL)* (Kiss, Pelletier, and Stadtfeld 2014; Kiss et al. 2016). BECL is a database of approximately 11,000 count and mass nouns, based on syntactic and semantic annotations of pairs of a noun form with a specific sense derived from WordNet (Fellbaum 1998). BECL addresses *lexical variation* and *lexical ambiguity* at the same time. Of course, BECL – as a lexicon – does not free the researcher from the task of annotating occurrences of count and mass nouns in a corpus, but it guides the researcher in various ways. So, BECL, which is based on the sense definitions of WordNet (for instance containing information about count and mass types related to senses), can thus be used to systematically extract contexts for individual words, which despite other ambiguities would only occur as count or mass nouns respectively. If deviations from this pattern are found, this may imply that the set of definitions was not complete or may lead to further characterization of systematic polysemy in the count–mass distinction. BECL also provides indications for further research that are not easily accessible if the empirical base is formed only by the aforementioned celebrity

---

[4] And perhaps should not even be considered a *dual-life noun*.

nouns. As an example, in BECL, e.g., we find about 3.5 times more count than mass noun sense types.[5]

In Section 2, we will briefly introduce BECL. Section 2 will also address the distribution of count and mass types within BECL and its implications. Section 3 presents four different kinds of ambiguity found in BECL, the last type of which is called T4 ambiguity, which, we believe, presents a particularly interesting case in light of the count–mass distinction, because according to the annotations, it looks as if these nouns show a unique semantics that differs only with regard to the count–mass distinction – hence the relevant nouns are *proper dual life nouns*. Importantly, this is not the case with common count–mass variations such as *lamb* or *rabbit*. T4 ambiguity will be dealt with in Section 4. Section 5 will address implications derived from BECL. We conclude by assuming that our findings are generally compatible with theories of the count–mass distinction that place this distinction in the semantics of nouns (such as Chierchia (1998a; 2010; this volume, Chapter 2) and Rothstein (2010; this volume, Chapter 3)), although these theories need to disentangle lexical ambiguity and not lump all cases together: dual-life, proper dual-life, and coercion in one pot. Furthermore, our findings provide clear challenges for theories that assume that lexical nouns are neutral with respect to the count–mass distinction, and that syntactic contexts mainly determine whether nouns are count or mass (such as Borer (2005) and Pelletier (1975, 2012)).

2. The Bochum English Countability Lexicon

The Bochum English Countability Lexicon (BECL) is a lexicon of English noun–sense pairs enriched with countability information. Four native speakers of Canadian English have annotated a set of pairs consisting of a noun form and a sense with regard to their behavior in four syntactic and two semantic patterns. The nouns have been derived in an arbitrary fashion from frequently occurring nouns in the Open American National Corpus (www.anc.org), for which sense definitions are provided in WordNet (Fellbaum 1998).[6]

The annotators had to determine whether (a) the noun–sense pair may occur in the syntactic contexts provided by four syntactic tests, and (b) depending on

---

[5] Here and in the following we define a *noun sense type* as a type of noun with a specific sense. Since BECL is a lexicon, it does not contain noun sense tokens, but only noun sense types. The observation is thus that the lexicon contains about 3.5 times more pairs of a noun and a sense that are classified as count than pairs that are classified as mass. We do not make any claim about the frequency of occurrence in natural language data but would like to point out that the noun forms chosen to derive BECL were drawn from high frequency noun forms in the Open American National Corpus.

[6] It should be noted that our pragmatic reliance on WordNet does not necessarily entail that we think that all senses come neatly cut and packaged. Indeed, we are aware of the various shortcomings that are part of the art and science of lexicography.

Table 17.1. *Major classes in BECL*

major class	example	sum
count	academy#3 (a school for special training)	8,390
mass	pride#1 (a feeling of self-respect and personal worth)	2,405
count and mass	ambition#2 (a strong drive for success)	698
neither mass nor count	commons#4 (the common people)	141
		11,634

the outcome of the first two syntactic tests, had to answer two questions about the interpretation of the resulting constructions.[7] A combination of a noun and a sense was included in the classification if it received identical annotations from independent annotators. A total number of over 18,000 noun–sense pairs have been annotated by up to four annotators.[8] From these, we derived the approximately 11,000 noun–sense pairs that form BECL (the current version being 2.1). We have collected the independent annotations and classified them so that four major and eighteen sub-classes could be identified. The four major classes are described in Table 17.1: (a) regular count, (b) regular mass, (c) count and mass, and (d) noun–sense pairs that are neither count nor mass.[9]

The general structure of BECL thus indicates that the concepts *count noun* and *mass noun* are discernible, even if their basic characteristics are unclear. If the sample of nouns we have annotated is approximately representative,[10] then it follows that the majority of English noun–sense pairs are uniquely count; another large group (which, however, is much smaller than the count noun group) is mass; and we find two further, significantly smaller groups that can be classified as either being *both* mass and count or *neither* mass *nor* count. We will refer to these four groups (and also to subgroups of these four groups) as *countability classes*. Each countability class contains further sub-classes,

---

[7] For more details on the annotation process we refer to Kiss, Pelletier, and Stadtfeld (2014) and Kiss et al. (2016), which include a documentation of syntactic and semantic tests used in the annotation process. The tests are also discussed briefly in Section 4.

[8] The majority of the data was annotated by two independent speakers of Canadian English. One part of the data (approx. 1000 noun senses) was given to all four annotators as a trial test of inter-annotator agreement. The noun senses that ended up in BECL were annotated unanimously by all annotators, either two or four.

[9] We named the classes according to the outputs of the annotation process. A noun–sense pair which is both mass and count means that the annotations indicate count and mass features (as will become clear in Section 4, when T4 is discussed). Importantly, a noun-sense from the final major class, neither mass nor count, is not meant to be a noun without countability, but rather a noun-sense that does not show any particular tendencies towards a classification as count or as mass.

[10] We are aware, of course, that no corpus is representative, so what we can claim here is basically that the nouns derived from the corpus have been derived in a sufficiently arbitrary way.

which emerge from different options in the answers the annotators have chosen. In total, BECL contains eighteen different sub-classes for count and mass noun–sense pairs. The distribution of count and mass noun–sense pairs, however, is highly remarkable.

Most linguistic theories of the count–mass distinction follow the assumption – clearly stated in Chierchia (1998a: 56) and subsequent work – that the count–mass distinction is independent of matter. But this assumption raises the issue as to what the linguistic impact of the count–mass distinction actually is. Perhaps one can assume that count expressions are conceptualized as having boundaries, or of coming in "basic" units, and mass expressions as having no boundaries, and not coming in units. The question then is why we find many more nouns that can be classified as count than those being classified as mass. This observation is particularly striking if we further consider that *packaging/sorting* is a productive process, and hence that starting with mass nouns and using packaging/sorting will yield the required count conceptualizations without much ado. There is also a trace of packaging in Chierchia's (this volume, Chapter 2) Type III languages (Yudja, Nez Perce, Indonesian). These languages allow free combination of count *and* mass nouns with numerals but yield container readings when realized in count syntax.[11] In fact, we will show in Section 4 that T4 ambiguity shows the very same effect in English.

There is, however, a further interpretation, to which we will return in Section 5, viz. that count expressions exhibit more structure than mass expressions. To this end, we will assume that at least one way to arrive at a count expression is that it is derived from a mass expression undergoing a process of unit building. This process leads to the imposition of a unit structure on the denotation of the expression, which means in general that structure is added. The present proposal is thus generally in line with approaches like Chierchia (1998a, 2010; this volume, Chapter 2) and Rothstein (2010; this volume, Chapter 3) in assuming that the count–mass distinction reflects a difference in denotational structure of the model to the extent that count senses show more denotational structure than mass senses. In many areas of linguistics, we move from less structure to more structure, but almost never in the other direction. (For example, in discourse, expressions become more specified by context, not less). The very same reason accounts for the pervasiveness of

---

[11] One could argue that this is a matter of perspective, and that one could similarly argue that Type III languages make no distinction between count and mass. If one takes countability as a feature that distinguishes count from mass nouns, then Type II and III languages will have countability distinctions, but their manifestations are not as in English. However, if one assumes that grammatical features that divide "count" and "mass" nouns for English (such as the plural, numerals, or indefinite articles) are universal, then Type II and Type III languages do not show a count–mass distinction because the grammatical features (which is being assumed to be universal) are not restricted in these languages, as they are in English.

sorting and portioning, and the somewhat obscure status of grinding. The former add structure, the latter, if conceived properly, removes structure. Lexical ambiguity can be used as a probe into the aforementioned process of structure building, which is why it is necessary to consider lexical ambiguity in BECL more closely.

3. Four types of ambiguity in BECL

The core of BECL consists of noun–sense pairs, which by themselves do not make the relation between the count–mass distinction and possible ambiguities apparent. We have thus provided an addition to BECL (to be included in future releases) where all nouns are combined with all annotated senses, and their corresponding countability classes. On the basis of the reorganization of the noun–sense pairs based on noun forms and corresponding senses as well as countability classes, four different types of lexical ambiguity can be identified, as provided in (7).

(7) Types of lexical ambiguity in BECL:
     T1: Homonymy
     T2: Polysemy without countability shifts
     T3: Polysemy with countability shifts
     T4: Ambiguity imposed on a single sense by a countability shift

Of the four types listed in (7), the last one, T4 is of particular interest and bears some implications for the analysis of the count–mass distinction as a whole, which we will elaborate on in Section 4. Although the first two types are of no relevance for the count–mass distinction in itself, they are nevertheless relevant insofar as ignoring these types yields awkward results when the pertinent ambiguities – which we assume are T3 and T4 – are discussed (as was observed in our brief discussion of Payne and Huddleston (2002)). Hence, we will briefly discuss all types.

The first type of lexical ambiguity is homonymy (called T1 here), where two or more senses do not bear a discernible semantic relation. The different senses accidentally share one form, and there can be an assignment to different countability classes, as in (8), but this is not mandatory, as illustrated in (9), and in fact is orthogonal to countability.

(8) a. capital#4 (one of the large alphabetic characters used as the first COUNT
        letter in writing or printing proper names and sometimes for
        emphasis)
     b. capital#2 (wealth in the form of money or property owned by a MASS
        person or business and human resources of economic value)

(9) a. pen#1 (a writing implement with a point from which ink flows) COUNT
     b. pen#2 (an enclosure for confining livestock) COUNT

Homonymy will not shed direct light on the count–mass distinction because it is a defining feature of homonymy that we find a coupling of unrelated meanings to the same form, as can be witnessed in (8) and (9). The detection of homonymy, however, is important from the perspective of methodology, since homonymy forms pitfalls for theoretical and empirical approaches, as has already been mentioned in the introduction, and again can be stressed with (6). A further extension of BECL 2.1 is a homonymy index, which is particularly appropriate if nouns occurring frequently as count nouns also appear frequently as mass nouns. In fact, no generalization concerning the count–mass distinction can or should be drawn from frequent occurrences of the *nouns* in (6), for the simple reason that we could always be dealing with two different *nouns*. Without further time-consuming scrutiny, the differences cannot be detected. BECL thus provides checks and balances against unwarranted conclusions concerning the count–mass distinction drawn from empirical work where a specific semantic annotation of the nouns in question is not available.

T2 and T3 differ from T1 in that a relationship between the senses can be established, a relationship that can be expressed at different levels of generality, and also at different levels of productivity. The example in (10) provides a T2 ambiguity, i.e. polysemy without a countability shift.

(10) a. hypothesis#1 (a proposal intended to explain certain facts or observations) COUNT
b. hypothesis#2 (a tentative insight into the natural world; a concept that is not yet verified but that if true would explain certain facts or phenomena) COUNT
c. hypothesis#3 (a message expressing an opinion based on incomplete evidence) COUNT

Of course, T2 ambiguity is of little interest if the count–mass distinction is at stake, since all senses of one noun with T2 ambiguity belong to the same countability class – as is witnessed in (8). Contrary to that is the case of T3 ambiguity, where polysemy also leads to an assignment to different countability classes, as is illustrated in (11).

(11) a. chicken#1 (the flesh of a chicken used for food) MASS
b. chicken#2 (a domestic fowl bred for flesh or eggs; believed to have been developed from the red jungle fowl) COUNT

When cases like (11) are considered, they are quite often either presented as *dual-life* nouns or as cases of grinding. But the polysemy observed in (9) is not the result of an application of the *Universal Grinder*, which is characterized in (Pelletier 1975) as a thought machine that is aimed at functioning on the cognitive level. The input of the grinder is, however, not a noun, but the denotation of that noun, which is then being ground. The result should be ground stuff of the input. Hence, the grinder turns an entity that is an object to stuff, and presuming that stuff is generally denoted by mass nouns, the output, the ground stuff, should be expressed with a mass term. This does not apply to (11) for the simple reason that beyond the distinction between count and mass, we find a further semantic distinction in that (11a) denotes meat, while (11b) denotes an animal (or a kind of an animal). It is somewhat surprising that the Universal Grinder is actually made responsible for the polysemy in (11), as e.g. in Chierchia (2010). It should be clear that the two senses in (11) are distinct not only in terms of countability but also in their basic characteristics: chickens are not bred for themselves, but for the flesh they provide, and meat does not provide eggs, of course. If the count noun *chicken* would undergo an operation of the Universal Grinder then the outcome would not be chicken meat – which is the actual mass meaning of *chicken* – but ground chicken stuff, which includes chicken bones, plumes, eyes and everything else. This is particularly evident if a formal definition of grinding is provided, as in Rothstein (2010: 392) and discussed above. There is no way to apply Rothstein's definition to arrive at (11a) from (11b). Hence the denotation of the ground term differs both from its input – the countable *chicken#2* in (11b) – and from the denotation of the mass expression in (11a). Grinding in this sense would form an additional sense of *chicken* that (almost) does not exist but is often invoked for the purpose of a funny description of a roadkill.

Recently, Landman (2011) has argued in the same line, suggesting that grinding is not an operation yielding a difference in count and mass, and nothing else, but instead that grinding in most cases is used as a cover term for an unclear semantic relationship between two senses that happen to belong to two different countability classes. The same considerations apply to the Universal Packager (Bach 1986) or the Universal Sorter (Bunt 1985). We argue that countability shifts are much more complex than what can be expressed with grinding or sorting.

As long as the term *dual-life noun* is not properly defined, it is always dangerous to classify a noun like *chicken* with the presented polysemy (which, we have seen, carries over to other animal/meat pairs depending on what is considered edible) as a dual-life noun. The term is also problematic since it seems to describe a lexical property, but it should be clear that the relevant property is actually one of semantic features (cf. (10) above). In Section 4, we will use the term *proper dual-life noun* to delineate nouns showing T4 ambiguity (which is one of countability, and not of other semantic features) from cases of polysemy as discussed here.[12]

Falkum (2010), Husić (2020), and Zamparelli (2020) have proposed generalizations regarding count-to-mass shifts (or vice versa) motivated by the

---

[12] We make explicit use of the overly specific term *proper* dual-life noun to make clear that many nouns that are usually called *dual-life nouns* are not addressed by this term

regularity of certain cases of polysemy, so-called regular polysemy in the sense of Apresjan (1974).

(12) Regular polysemy (Apresjan 1974, p.16)
Polysemy of the word α with the meanings a_i and a_j is called regular if, in the given language, there exists at least one other word β with the meanings b_i and b_j, which are semantically distinguished from each other in exactly the same way as a_i and a_j, and if a_i and b_i, a_j and b_j are nonsynonymous.

Falkum (2010) thus directly employs such rules of regular polysemy to account for cases like (11). We consider the rules that she proposes to be more appropriate then invoking grinding to cover these cases. The pertinent rules are provided in (13):

(13) a. If an expression has an "animal" use, it also has a "meat"/"fur"/"animal stuff" use.
b. If an expression has a "tree" use, it also has a "wood" use.
c. If an expression has a "fruit" use, it also has a "fruit stuff"/"tree" use.
(Falkum 2010: 17)

It should also be noted that such transformations are not restricted to concrete objects; abstract nouns are affected by polysemy, which often results in a shift of countability, too. Husić (2020) argues that abstract nouns are even more sensitive to polysemy and countability shifts and argues that some count senses can regularly be derived from mass expressions which refer to qualities, processes, or states:

(14) if a noun X has a mass sense α which denotes a quality, a process or a state, then it will have a count sense β with one of the possible interpretations:

1. bounded process
2. instances thereof
3. (itemized) placeholders (Husić 2020: 366)

Examples for the three shifts from BECL are provided in (15), (16), and (17).

(15) bounded processes
a. respiration#3 (the bodily process of inhalation and exhalation) MASS
b. respiration#2 (a single complete act of breathing in and out) COUNT

(16) instances thereof
a. inquiry#1 (a search for knowledge) MASS
b. inquiry#2 (an instance of questioning) COUNT

(17) (itemized) placeholders
a. necessity#1 (the condition of being essential or indispensable) MASS
b. necessity#2 (anything indispensable) COUNT

The countability shifts discussed in Falkum (2010) and Husić (2020) cannot be explained in terms of either *grinding* or *packaging*. At this point, we want to emphasize the diversity of countability shifts that have tacitly been assumed as the result of universal thought machines. In addition, formal theories of the semantics of count and mass nouns typically focus on the mere shift between count and mass and tend to ignore the changes in interpretation that occur with them (cf. Chierchia 2010: 128–30; Rothstein 2010: 390), which again proves that a fine-grained distinction of different types of ambiguity is necessary for a proper assessment of the count–mass distinction. Let us now turn to T4 ambiguities.

4. T4 Ambiguities: (Almost the) Same Meaning, Different Countability

T4 ambiguity is characterized by a single sense of a noun that allows *both* count and mass interpretations, where the count interpretation differs only in a single aspect from the mass interpretation, which can be characterized by individualizing the mass interpretation. (We tacitly assume that the mass interpretation is logically prior to the count interpretation, an assumption that will be discussed in more detail below.)

Since this will play a role in Section 5, we would like to explicitly point out the reactions of the annotators towards nouns showing T4 ambiguities. Annotators were asked to embed the pertinent noun in four syntactic contexts, and to further provide semantic estimates if certain of the embeddings were possible. The four syntactic contexts are as follows:

- Syntax 1: [more N_{sg}] Can the noun appear with *more* when realized in singular number?
- Syntax 2: [more N_{pl}] Can the noun appear with *more* when realized in plural number?
- Syntax 3: [[$_{Det}$ indef] N_{sg}] Can the noun appear with an indefinite determiner?[13]
- Syntax 4: [ø N_{sg}] Can the singular noun appear without a determiner?

We would expect that mass nouns may appear in Syntax 1, while count nouns may appear in Syntax 2. Similarly, count nouns should appear in Syntax 3, while mass nouns should appear in Syntax 4. The first two and the second two syntactic contexts can thus be viewed as quasi-opposites. An affirmative answer to either Syntax 1 or Syntax 2, however, may be due to a meaning shift, which we must detect, in order to not conflate different senses. With regard to Syntax 1, an affirmative answer may have been provided with a comparison in mind that does not address individual items. With regard to

---

[13] Since English does not show indefinite plural determiners, the context is tantamount to assuming that the noun appears in singular number.

Syntax 2, an affirmative answer could have come about because the annotator had a hidden container reading in mind. Thus, affirmative answers to Syntax 1 and Syntax 2 will lead to further asking Semantics 1 or Semantics 2, respectively:

- Semantics 1: If Syntax 1 is answered affirmatively: Is the comparison based on counting individual items or on some other mode of measurement?
- Semantics 2: If Syntax 2 is answered affirmatively: Is the plural equivalent to a hidden classifier reading (*kinds of, containers of, types of*)?

T4 ambiguities are remarkable in that all four syntactic contexts are answered affirmatively, and the two semantic clarifications are answered negatively, i.e. the noun appears in Syntax 1, but the comparison is not based on individual items (as opposed to typical fake mass nouns such as *furniture* or *lingerie*; cf. Kiss, Pelletier, and Stadtfeld (2014)); and the noun also appears in Syntax 2 but there is no hidden classifier reading. The general position in discussions of the count–mass distinction is to expect opposite reactions to Syntax 1 and 2, and if the reactions are not opposite, we expect that either Semantics 1 or 2 is answered affirmatively. In these cases, the nouns are classified as either mass or count nouns. But in the present case (and also with affirmative answers to Syntax 3 and 4), the nouns are classified as being *both* count and mass nouns.

The definitions of some of the nouns falling in this class given in WordNet are provided in (18).

(18)   a. brunch#1: combination breakfast and lunch; usually served in late morning
        b. candy#1: a rich sweet made of flavored sugar and often combined with fruit or nuts
        c. rainfall#1: water falling in drops from vapor condensed in the atmosphere
        d. cake#3: baked goods made from or based on a mixture of flour, sugar, eggs, and fat
        e. casserole#1: food cooked and served in a casserole
        f. salad#1: food mixtures either arranged on a plate or tossed and served with a moist dressing; usually consisting of or including greens
        g. swamp#1: low land that is seasonally flooded; has more woody plants than a marsh and better drainage than a bog
        h. confirmation#1: additional proof that something that was believed (some fact or hypothesis or theory) is correct
        i. contradiction#3: the speech act of contradicting someone

In order to reproduce the count and mass uses of the nouns in (18) we provide examples from the Contemporary Corpus of American English (COCA; Davies 2009), in which we present the mass interpretation in the a)-sentences, singular count interpretations in the b)-sentences, and plural count interpretations in the c)-sentences.

(19) a. He would hire me for brunch shifts because most cooks hated doing *brunch*.
b. We sleep till noon, have the maid cook *a brunch* and a snack before each meal.
c. But only on Sundays does it serve *its superb brunches*.

(20) a. The EU response includes *deployment of naval vessels and surveillance planes* to the area.
b. The captain was midway through *a deployment in the Mediterranean*.
c. In the last decade, there have been *twenty-seven army deployments*.

(21) a. In 1935, it became clear why *emigration* was halted.
b. During 2007, there was *a massive emigration* of Arabs from the Palestine territories.[14]
c. I survived *two emigrations*.

(22) a. There was *major looting*, no ifs, ands, or buts about it.
b. The fracas turned into *a mob looting* that lasted till 1 a.m.
c. In all, county police are investigating *40 lootings*.

(23) a. The international development community wanted Amazonians to cut down *rainforest*, plant pasture, and raise cattle.
b. REDD could protect one rainforest from clear-cutting merely by sending the logging trucks to *a different rainforest*.
c. The Asian tree frog lives in *the moist rainforests* of India.

(24) a. There is *swamp* where Florida should be.
b. We emerged from *one swamp* and landed in another.
c. The river was obscured by *two great swamps*.

It should be clear now that cases of T4 are pure (in fact: the only) instances of what is called *dual-life nouns*. As T3 cases come together with a shift and/or addition of meaning, there is only a single meaning change affecting T4 cases, which leads to an individuation of the mass meaning, as can be initially characterized by the definition in (25):

(25) T4 ambiguity: If *X* is the mass interpretation, when used as a count noun, the interpretation becomes *an individual X*.

Given the different semantic types of nouns involving T4 ambiguity, it becomes necessary, however, to further specify what is meant and allowed by (25). The first case to be considered can be illustrated with *brunch*. This noun is already ambiguous, in that it can mean the aggregate food that can be eaten, or the event during which the food is eaten.[15] We will call this a stuff/event ambiguity. Note that the ambiguity is not affected when *brunch* undergoes T4 realizations, i.e. the event and the stuff sense show up on both sides of the count–mass distinction, and the count sense can be characterized as an

---

[14] This can be a closed aggregate of individual instances but can also be an individual instance.
[15] WordNet does not draw this distinction, but it becomes obvious once a sufficient number of examples is considered.

individuation. In (19), we see the stuff sense; hence (26) provides event senses showing the same T4 ambiguity:

(26) a. *Brunch* can take a while so start slowly with a fresh fruit platter.
 b. On Sunday, the Renaissance Waverly Hotel hosts *a brunch* with Mr. and Mrs. Claus.
 c. Weekend dances and *Sunday brunches* became fixtures in the postwar era.

The second aspect to note is that *individuation* does not necessarily mean that we are talking about single individuals. This has already been illustrated with *brunch*, which – in the pertinent sense – can be characterized as an aggregate of food, which can be individualized *as an aggregate* (the same point can be illustrated with *rainforest* and *emigration*). This holds for event interpretations as well, with the addition that the nouns allow genuine ambiguity with regard to an aggregation of individual events, an ambiguity that is not necessarily resolved, as can be witnessed by (21b), where *emigration* may refer to an aggregate of emigrations, or to a single event.

Of course, these examples also show that nouns expressing T4 ambiguity do not have to refer to concrete entities, but allow *event-like* structures, and may also denote abstract entities, as is witnessed by *friendship* in (27).

(27) a. He has been tapped to compose a speech promoting *friendship* between Washington and the "Muslim world."
 b. He did have *a close friendship* with the warden.
 c. My brother had *very long friendships*.

A possible further property of these nouns will be noted with some caution: the corpus data revealed that the count instances more often than not are realized in the plural, but that numerals occur rarely (as, e.g., illustrated in the c)-examples of (20), (21), (22), and (24)). After initially realizing that the extracted samples showed numerals only rarely, we explicitly searched for numerals but found no further occurrences with these nouns. The average proportion of numerals occurring with these nouns is extremely low, a mere three percent. We will return to this issue in Section 5.

To sum up, nouns showing a T4 ambiguity are both count and mass, with the only difference in meaning stemming from an individuation. The nouns in question can have concrete and abstract interpretations. Individuations may yield single individuals, but also single aggregates. In the following section, we will discuss the implications of T4 ambiguities for theories of the count–mass distinction.

5. Implications for Count–Mass Theories

BECL shows an interesting distribution of count and mass noun senses: the majority of noun sense types show unique count syntax, i.e. annotators have uniquely classified the pertinent noun–sense pairs to occur in syntactic count contexts. A smaller group uniquely occurs in mass syntax. If we compare these findings with the major strands of current research on the count–mass distinction, they seem to suggest that *not all nouns are count and mass at the same time*. This contradicts the account found in Borer (2005) and Pelletier (2012), where semantically neutral nouns are realized in given syntactic contexts and become count or mass at a phrasal level.

T4 ambiguities have further shown that the class of nouns that are count and mass at the same time is rather small. These nouns can appear in both count and mass syntax, and apart from the introduction of an individuation, the senses used in count and mass syntax cannot be discerned. We assume that nouns showing T4 ambiguities are the only nouns that can be classified as proper *dual life nouns*.[16]

Pelletier (1975; 2012) has argued that grinding can be used to propose that nouns are count and mass at the same time. The findings of BECL do not support this claim: To begin with, it remains rather unclear which phenomena should be encompassed by grinding. Following Falkum (2010) and Landman (2011), we have pointed out that putative cases of grinding show differences in meaning and can be captured by rules of polysemy as well – thus putting these cases in the class of T3 ambiguities, where a discernible but related semantic difference is associated with a given noun form if it is realized either in count or in mass syntax. T4 nouns, on the other hand, show no trace of *grinding* effects. With regard to *grinding* in general, we note that mass-to-count conversions (Universal Sorter, Universal Packager) appear to be much more productive than count-to-mass conversions (Universal Grinder), most illustrations of which are either freely constructed, or drawn from puns or advertisements. Katz and Zamparelli (2012: 374) seem to contradict our claim. They state that the frequent mass use of "'obvious' count nouns such as *car*, *ski*, and *piano* seem surprising."

(28)   a.   How much car can you afford?
        b.   Phantom 87s were too much ski for me.
        c.   I always practice too much piano.

Yet, they also conclude that "the meaning shifts which seem to take place when a count form is used as a mass are a lot more diverse than [the simple version of universal grinding of the material]."[17] They also admit that other syntactic and semantic factors may play a role, that e.g. *practice too much*

---

[16] We note that this BECL class contains at least one celebrity noun, which is typically used to illustrate dual life nouns, viz. *cake*.

[17] Of course, we would not speak of count *forms*, since we assume that the count–mass distinction applies at the level of the sense (but see footnote 18 below).

piano in (28c) could be a reduction from *practice too much piano playing*, where mass syntax does not appear to be surprising since *playing* is the actual (reduced) head of the construction, and of course *mass*. Cases like (28a) are found quite often in advertisements, particularly advertisements referring to possible affective reactions, which also plays a role in (28b). All this shows that the interpretations of the nouns are affected in more than one way, basically yielding different interpretations, which are independent of the count–mass distinction, but of course may interact with it.

With regard to T4, we note that the parallel appearance of *more* with a singular and plural occurrence of pertinent nouns does not lead to meaning shifts. For a noun like *swamp*, the mode of measurement is not based on number when it shows up as part of the phrase [$_{NP}$ more swamp], and it does not induce a hidden type or packaging reading when used as part of the phrase [$_{NP}$ more swamps].

Given these observations, an analysis of the count–mass distinction that relies on a semantic difference between count and mass nouns seems to us more plausible. Such a proposal would clearly account for the clear-cut classifications for the majority of nouns in BECL (which holds for 93% of the annotated noun types, with count nouns amounting to 72%, and mass nouns to 21%).

A large group of the remaining 7% consists of noun senses that are classified as being neither mass nor count, because they generate negative answers to all four syntactic context questions. Some thirty-eight of these senses were proper nouns or what we have called "quasi-proper nouns" (where other senses of these lemmas fall into other, more ordinary groups of senses), as illustrated in (29).

(29)   a. milk#3 (a river that rises in the Rockies in northwestern Montana and flows eastward to become a tributary of the Missouri River)
           b. devil#1 ((Judeo-Christian and Islamic religions) chief spirit of evil and adversary of God; tempter of mankind; master of Hell)

Leaving these cases aside, we are left with a number of rather common noun senses that do not show what we have taken to be the characteristic properties of count or mass meanings. A few examples are provided in (30).

(30)   a. midair#1: some point in the air; above ground level; "the planes collided in midair"
           b. nature#3: the natural physical world including plants and animals and landscapes, etc.; "they tried to preserve nature as they found it"
           c. unison#1: corresponding exactly; "marching in unison"
           d. open#2: where the air is unconfined; "he wanted to get outdoors a little"
           e. open#4: information that has become public; "all the reports were out in the open"

f. limelight#1: a focus of public attention; "he enjoyed being in the limelight"
g. dollar#4: a symbol of commercialism or greed; "he worships the almighty dollar"
h. midst#1: the location of something surrounded by other things; "in the midst of the crowd"
i. heyday#1: the period of greatest prosperity or productivity
j. bitch#1: an unpleasant difficulty; "this problem is a real bitch"

It is not so clear to us how these noun senses will fit into a fully unified account of the count–mass distinction. We hence have to leave this issue to future research.

Coming back to the bulk of the count and mass senses, a proposal should also answer why there are many more count than mass noun types (count noun types outnumber mass noun types by a factor of 3.5 in BECL), in addition to providing a place for T4 ambiguities. Both Chierchia (1998a; 2010; this volume, Chapter 2) and Rothstein (2010; this volume, Chapter 3) have argued that there is a denotational distinction between count and mass nouns that is reflected in their syntax. Rothstein (2010; this volume, Chapter 3) explicitly assumes that count and mass nouns are of different types ($<e \times k, t>$ and $<e, t>$, respectively, where k provides a context in which individuals count as atoms). Rothstein further assumes that count and mass denotations are not independent of each other but instead that count denotations are derived from mass denotations by providing a context in which semantic atoms are present. Similarly, Chierchia (1998a, 2010; this volume, Chapter 2) shows that various denotational constraints (as, e.g., whether something is a property or a kind) interact to distinguish count and mass nouns, which at the same time have common roots.

Chierchia (this volume, Chapter 2) suggests a distinction in three types of languages when it comes to the count–mass distinction:

- Type I languages allow count nouns to appear in count syntax.
- Type II languages require additional means to allow nouns to occur in count syntax.
- Type III languages allow all nouns in count and in mass syntax.

Let us combine our findings with Chierchia's typology. With regard to English, we note that the majority of noun senses have been classified as count senses, and hence the nouns bearing the senses are classified as count nouns.[18]

---

[18] In fact, it is even correct to claim that BECL mostly contains count *nouns*. For the currently unreleased version 3.0, we have transformed the entries into a lexicon of nouns, where each noun is assigned *a set of meanings and the corresponding set of countability classes*. This information is used to compile classes across senses and countability assignments. The most frequent classes according to this classification are unique count nouns (4,493 entries) and unique mass nouns (1,257 entries). It is remarkable that the ratio between count and mass nouns equals the ratio between count and mass senses.

A minority, however, behave as if it belonged to a Type III language, and hence allow appearances in count and mass syntax equally well. Here we assume that Chierchia's meaning shift from mass denotations to containers is equivalent to what we call individuation.

Now, there are many more count noun types than mass noun types in BECL. So, there are many nouns that either exclusively occur in count syntax or in mass syntax. What is more, we note that mass-to-count shifts occur more often than count-to-mass shifts. And finally, we observe T4 ambiguities with a small class of nouns in English. If one takes Rothstein's (2010; this volume, Chapter 3) denotational system as a starting point, one notes that mass expressions are simpler than count expressions typewise. It would, however, be a somewhat bold proposal to conclude from this denotational difference that mass expressions are logically prior to count expressions.[19] Instead, let us assume that expressions are more or less likely to start their existence as showing up in count or mass contexts. With regard to count and mass shifts, Rothstein (2010: 391) considers count-to-mass shifts more problematic than mass-to-count shifts. Her analysis, however, invokes a reference to *natural atomic predicates* in addition to being *semantically atomic predicates*. Following Chierchia (1998a), she further assumes "that type shifting will be blocked unless the resulting interpretation is sufficiently different from interpretations that are otherwise available" (Rothstein 2010: 391). In light of these suggestions, we may conclude that T4 ambiguity ensues because an individuation leads to count syntax, and to an enriched denotational structure (in other words: individuals become available, once again, possibly through providing semantic atoms, but this could also be achieved by employing the system provided by Chierchia (this volume, Chapter 2)). Consequently, the nouns can actually be counted.

In any case, we assume that structure is added to the interpretation of a noun. This is the basic difference that we can observe in T4 ambiguities: nouns like *swamp* start out as mass expressions but then become individualized units (which in itself, as the discussion of *brunch* has shown, do not have to be atomic individuals). The additional structure may eventually lead to a petrification of the count sense, which in terms of Rothstein's (2010) analysis might amount to the assumption that semantically atomic predicates are taken to become natural atomic predicates. For this reason, there are many more count than mass nouns: there is nothing that forces a noun to add denotational structure, but once this has happened, there is no way back.

---

[19] We take it, for instance, as highly unlikely that *tables* was ever used as a mass expression. Although we obviously do not endorse an ontological analysis of the count–mass distinction, we cannot but acknowledge that certain aspects of the count–mass distinction remain unaccounted for in all approaches unless one either accepts hidden circular explanations or an ontological base.

This conclusion will also shed light on the distribution of grinding and packaging (or sorting). As we have pointed out already (just as Rothstein (2010) did), grinding is less productive than packaging and sorting and also comes with strings attached insofar as they show pun-like qualities and other forms of metaphor and metonymy. Grinding, of course, was always considered to *remove* structure, to turn some individual into a bunch of goo (to quote George Patton here). What we have argued is that such a removal of structure goes against the grain of language. Expressions can be (comparatively) unstructured – as is shown by proper mass nouns – but once they have shown a count sense (either as an additional sense without further changes in meaning, such as T4 ambiguities, or after petrification and addition of meaning, so that the mass sense is gradually lost), their denotational domain provides more structure, and moving from more to less information is generally not favored by language.

References

Abner, N. (2017). What you see is what you get: Surface transparency and ambiguity of nominalizing reduplication in American Sign Language. *Syntax*, 20: 352–71.
Acquaviva, P. (2008). *Lexical Plurals: A Morphosemantic Approach*. Oxford: Oxford University Press.
Aikhenvald, A. (2000). *Classifiers: A Typology of Noun Categorization Devices*. Oxford: Oxford University Press.
Al-Wer, E. and U. Horesh. (2017). Dialect contact and change in an Arabic morpheme: Examining Jordanian and Palestinian dialects. A paper presented at the North American Research Network in Historical Sociolinguistics (NARNiHS).
Alexiadou, A. (2011). Plural mass nouns and the morpho-syntax of number. In M. Washburn et al. (eds.), *Proceedings of the 28th West Coast Conference on Formal Linguistics*. Somerville, MA: Cascadilla Proceedings Project, pp. 33–41.
Allan, K. (1980). Nouns and countability. *Language*, 56: 541–67.
Aloni, M. (2003). Free choice in modal contexts. In M. Weisgerber (ed.), *Proceedings of Sinn und Bedeutung (SuB 7)*. Konstanz: Sprachwissenschaft, Universität Konstanz, pp. 25–37.
Alonso-Ovalle, L. (2008). Innocent exclusion in an alternative semantics. *Natural Language Semantics*, 16: 115–28.
Apresjan, J. D. (1974). Regular polysemy. *Linguistics*, 14: 5–32.
Arcara, G., F. Franzon, S. Gastaldon, S. Brotto, C. Semenza, F. Peressotti, and C. Zanini (2019). One can be some but some cannot be one: ERP correlates of numerosity incongruence are different for singular and plural. *Cortex*, 116: 104–21.
Arnauld, A. and C. Lancelot. (1660). *Grammaire générale et raisonnée*. Paris: Pierre le Petit.
Arsenijevic, B. (2016). Gender as a grammaticalized classifier system: The case of the Serbo-Croatian neuter. Available at https://ling.auf.net/lingbuzz/002848.
Asher, N. (2011). *Lexical Meaning in Context: A Web of Words*. Cambridge: Cambridge University Press.
Baayen, H., R. Harald, T. Dijkstra, and R. Schreuder. (1997). Singulars and plurals in Dutch: Evidence for a parallel dual-route model. *Journal of Memory and Language*, 37: 94–117.
Baayen, R., R. Piepenbrock, and L. Gulikers. (1996). *Celex2*. Philadelphia, PA: Linguistic Data Consortium.
Bach, E. (1986). The algebra of events. *Linguistics and Philosophy*, 9: 5–16.

References

Baker, R. (1770). *Remarks on the English Language, in the Manner of Those of Vaugelas on the French: Being a Detection of Many Improper Expressions Used in Conversation, and of Many Others to Be Found in Authors*. London: J. Bell.

Bale, A. (2014). To agree without AGREE: The case for semantic agreement. In H-L. Huang et al. (eds.), *Proceedings of NELS 43, Vol. 1*. Amherst, MA: GLSA, pp. 13–24.

(forthcoming). Number and the mass–count distinction. In P. Cabredo Hofherr and J. Doetjes (eds.), *Oxford Handbook of Grammatical Number*. Oxford: Oxford University Press.

Bale, A. and D. Barner. (2009). The interpretation of functional heads: Using comparatives to explore the mass/count distinction. *Journal of Semantics*, 26: 217–52.

Bale, A. and J. Coon. (2014). Classifiers are for numerals, not for nouns: Consequences for the mass/count distinction. *Linguistic Inquiry*, 45: 695–707.

Bale, A. and H. Khanjian. (2008). Classifiers and number marking. In T. Friedman and S. Ito (eds.) *Proceedings of Semantics and Linguistic Theory (SALT 18)*. Ithaca, NY: LSA and CLC Publications, pp. 74–88.

(2014). Syntactic complexity and competition: The singular/plural distinction in Western Armenian. *Linguistic Inquiry*, 45: 1–26.

Bale, A., M. Gagnon, and H. Khanjian. (2010). Cross-linguistic representations of numerals and number marking. In N. Li and D. Lutz (eds.), *Proceedings of Semantics and Linguistic Theory (SALT 20)*. Ithaca, NY: LSA and CLC Publications, pp. 582–98.

(2011). On the relationship between morphological and semantic markedness: The case of plural morphology. *Morphology*, 21: 197–221.

Baptista, M. (2007). On the syntax and semantics of DP in Cape Verdean creole. In M. Baptista and J. Guéron (eds.), *Noun Phrases in Creole Languages: A Multifaceted Approach*. Amsterdam: John Benjamins, pp. 61–106.

Bardagil-Mas, B. (2020). Number morphology in Panará. *Linguistic Variation*, 20: 312–23.

Barker, C. (1998). Partitives, double genitives and anti-uniqueness. *Natural Language and Linguistic Theory*, 16: 679–717.

Barner, D. and J. Snedeker. (2005). Quantity judgments and individuation: Evidence that mass nouns count. *Cognition*, 97: 41–66.

Baroni, M., S. Bernardini, A. Ferraresi, A., and E. Zanchetta. (2009). The WaCky Wide Web: A collection of very large linguistically processed web-crawled corpora. *Language Resources and Evaluation*, 43: 209–26.

Baroni, M. and M. Ueyama. (2006). Building general- and special-purpose corpora by web crawling. In *Proceedings of the 13th NIJL International Symposium; Language Corpora: Their Compilation and Application*. Tokyo: PUBLISHER, pp. 31–40.

Bates, D., M. Maechler, B. Bolker, and S. Walker. (2014). lme4: Linear Mixd-Effects Models Using Eigen and S4. In R Package, version 1.1-7. http://CRAN.R-project.org/package=lme4.

Bennett, M. (1974). Some extensions of a Montague fragment of English. PhD dissertation, UCLA.

Berent, I., A. Dupuis, and D. Brentari. (2014). Phonological reduplication in sign language: Rules rule. *Frontiers in Psychology*, 10. https://doi.org/10.3389/fpsyg.2014.00560

Beviláqua, K., S. Lima, and R. Pires de Oliveira. (2016). Coercion and bare nouns in Brazilian Portuguese: An experimental study on grinding. *Baltic International Yearbook of Cognition, Logic and Communication*, 11.
Beviláqua, K. and R. Pires de Oliveira. (2014). Brazilian bare nouns and referentiality: Evidence from an experiment. *Revista Letras*, 90: 235–75.
  (2017). Brazilian bare nouns in comparatives: Experimental evidence for non-contextual dependency. *Revista Letras*, 96: 354–76.
Bisiacchi, P., S. Mondini, A. Angrilli, K. Marinelli, and C. Semenza. (2005). Mass and count nouns show distinct EEG cortical processes during an explicit semantic task. *Brain and Language*, 95: 98–9.
Bliss, H. (2004). The semantics of the bare noun in Turkish. Master's thesis, University of Calgary.
Bloom, P. (1990). *Semantic Structure and Language Dvelopment*. Cambridge, MA: MIT Press.
Bloom, P. and D. Kelemen. (1995). Syntactic cues in the acquisition of collective nouns. *Cognition*, 56: 1–30.
Booij, G. (1996). Inherent versus contextual inflection and the split morphology hypothesis. In G. Booij and J. Van Marle (eds.), *Yearbook of Morphology 1995*. Dordrecht: Kluwer, pp. 1–16.
Boone, A. (1989). La distinction massif/comptable et les noms de maladies. In J. David and G. Kleiber (eds.), *Termes massifs et termes comptables*. Metz/Paris: Université de Metz/Klincksieck, pp. 109–23.
Borer, H. (1999). Deconstructing the construct. In K. Johnson and I. Roberts (eds.), *Beyond Principles and Parameters*. Dordrecht: Springer, pp. 43–89.
  (2005). *Structuring Sense I. In Name Only*. Oxford: Oxford University Press.
  (2013). *Structuring Sense III. Taking Form*. Oxford: Oxford University Press.
Borer, H. and S. Ouwayda. (2010). Men and their apples: Dividing plural and agreement plural. Paper presented at "GLOW in Asia VIII", Beijing Language and Culture University. Available at: http://webspace.qmul.ac.uk/hborer/Downloads/2010-AGLOW.pdf.
Bošković, Ž. and S. Şener. (2013). The Turkish NP. In P. Cabredo Hofherr (ed.), *Crosslinguistic Studies on Noun Phrase Structure and Reference*. Leiden: Brill, pp. 102–42.
Boster, C.T. (1996). On the quantifier-noun phrase split in American Sign Language and the structure of quantified noun phrases. In W. Edmondson and R. Wilbur (eds.), *International Review of Sign Linguistics Vol. 1*. Mahwah, NJ: Lawrence Erlbaum Psychology Press, pp. 159–208.
Bosveld-de Smet, L. (2001). Le pluriel et le massif: une paire unique. In D. Amiot, W. De Mulder, and N. Flaux (eds.), *Le syntagme nominal: syntaxe et sémantique*. Arras: Artois Presses Université, pp. 27–45.
Bowden, J. (2001). *Taba: Description of a South Halmahera Language*. Canberra: Pacific Linguistics.
Brasoveanu, A. (2008). Donkey pluralities: Plural information states versus non-atomic individuals. *Linguistics and Philosophy*, 31: 129–209.
Bresnan, J. (2007). Is syntactic knowledge probabilistic? Experiments with the English dative alternation. In S. Featherston and W. Sternefeld (eds.), *Roots: Linguistics in Search of its Evidential Base*. Berlin: de Gruyter, pp. 75–96.

Bresnan, J., S. Dingare, and C. Manning. (2001). Soft constraints mirror hard constraints: Voice and person in English and Lummi. In *Proceedings of the LFG01 Conference*. Stanford, CA: CSLI Publications, pp. 13–32.
Bresnan, J. and M. Ford. (2010). Predicting syntax: Processing dative constructions in American and Australian varieties of English. *Language*, 86: 168–213.
Brooks, N., A. Pogue, and D. Barner. (2011). Piecing together numerical language: Children's use of default units in early counting and quantification. *Developmental Science*, 14: 44–57.
Brustad, K. (2000). *The Syntax of Spoken Arabic*. Washington, DC: Georgetown University Press.
Bunt, H. (1979). Ensembles and the formal semantics properties of mass terms. In F.J. Pelletier (ed.), *Mass Terms: Some Philosophical Problems*. Dordrecht: Reidel, pp. 249–77.
  (1985). *Mass Terms and Model-Theoretic Semantics*. New York: Cambridge University Press.
Butler, L. (2012). Crosslinguistic and experimental evidence for non-number plural. *Linguistic Variation*, 12: 27–56.
Cabredo Hofherr, P. (forthcoming). Nominal number morphology. In P. Cabredo Hofherr and Jenny Doetjes (eds.), *Oxford Handbook of Grammatical Number*. Oxford: Oxford University Press.
Carey, S. (1978). The child as word learner. In M. Halle and G. Miller (eds.), *Linguistic Theory and Psychological Reality*. Cambridge, MA: MIT Press, pp. 264–93.
  (1985). *Conceptual Change in Childhood*. Cambridge, MA: MIT Press.
Carey, S. and E. Spelke. (1996). Science and core knowledge. *Philosophy of Science*, 63: 515–33.
Carlson, G. (1977a). Reference to Kinds in English. PhD dissertation, University of Massachusetts. (Published 1980 by Garland Press, New York.)
  (1977b). A unified analysis of the English bare plural. *Linguistics and Philosophy*, 1: 413–56.
Carreiras, M., L. Carr, H. Barber, and A. Hernandez. (2010). Where syntax meets math: Right intraparietal sulcus activation in response to grammatical number agreement violations. *NeuroImage*, 49: 1741–9.
Cartwright, H. (1979). Amounts and measures of amount. In Pelletier (1979), pp. 179–98.
Champollion, L. (2010). Parts of a whole: Distributivity as a bridge between aspect and measurement. PhD dissertation, University of Pennsylvania. Available at https://repository.upenn.edu/cgi/viewcontent.cgi?article=2117&context=edissertations.
Chao, Y. (1968). *A Grammar of Spoken Chinese*. Berkeley, CA: University of California Press.
Chen, T. and C. Guestrin. (2016). Xgboost: A scalable tree boosting system. In *Proceedings of the 22nd ACM SIGKDD International Conference on Knowledge Discovery and Data Mining*. New York: ACM, pp. 785–94.
Cheng, C-Y. (1973). Comments on Moravcsik's paper. In J. Hintikka, J. Moravcsik, and P. Suppes (eds.), *Approaches to Natural Language*. Dordrecht: Reidel, pp. 286–8.
Cheng, L. (2012). Counting and classifiers. In Massam 2012, pp. 199–219.

Cheng, L., J. Doetjes, and R. Sybesma. (2008). How universal is the universal grinder? In M. van Koppen and B. Botma (eds.), *Linguistics in the Netherlands 2008*. Amsterdam: John Benjamins, pp. 50–62.
Cheng, L. and R. Sybesma. (1998). *Yi-wan tang, yi-ge tang*: Classifiers and massifiers. *Tsing Hua Journal of Chinese Studies*, 28: 385–412.
  (1999). Bare and not-so-bare nouns and the structure of NP. *Linguistic Inquiry*, 30: 509–42.
  (2005). Classifiers in four varieties of Chinese. In G. Cinque and R. Kayne (eds.), *The Oxford Handbook of Comparative Syntax*. Oxford: Oxford University Press, pp. 259–92.
Cheung, P., D. Barner, and P. Li. (2009). Syntactic cues to individuation in Mandarin Chinese. *Journal of Cognitive Science*, 10: 135.
Chiarelli, V., R. El Yagoubi, S. Mondini, P. Bisiacchi, and C. Semenza. (2011). The syntactic and semantic processing of mass and count nouns: An ERP study. *PLoS One*, 6: e25885.
Chierchia, G. (1998a). Plurality of mass nouns and the notion of "semantic parameter". In S. Rothstein (ed.), *Events and Grammar*. Dordrecht: Kluwer Academic Publishers, pp. 53–104.
  (1998b). Reference to kinds across languages. *Natural Language Semantics*, 6: 339–405.
  (2010). Mass nouns, vagueness and semantic variation. *Synthèse*, 174: 99–149.
  (2013). *Logic in Grammar*. Oxford: Oxford University Press.
  (2015). How universal is the mass/count distinction? Three grammars of counting. In Y. Li and W. Tsai (eds.), *Chinese Syntax: A Cross-Linguistic Perspective*. Oxford: Oxford University Press, pp. 147–77.
  (2017). Clouds and blood: More on the mass/count distinction. *Synthèse*, 194: 2523–38.
Chomsky, N. (2000). Minimalist inquiries: The framework. In R. Martin, D. Michaels, and J. Uriagereka (eds.), *Step by Step: Essays on Minimalist Syntax in Honor of Howard Lasnik*. Cambridge, MA: MIT Press, pp. 89–156.
Christensen, R.H.B. (2019). ordinal – Regression Models for Ordinal Data. R package version 10 December 2019. https://CRAN.R-project.org/package=ordinal.
Chung, S. (2000). On reference to kinds in Indonesian. *Natural Language Semantics*, 8: 157–71.
Cohen, J. (1988). *Statistical Power Analysis for the Behavioral Sciences*, 2nd edition. Hillsdale, NJ: Lawrence Erlbaum Associates.
Cokely, D. and C. Baker-Shenk. (1980). *American Sign Language: The Original Green Books*. Washington, DC: Gallaudet University Press.
Cooper, R. (2012). Type theory and semantics in flux. In R. Kempson, T. Fernando, and N. Asher (eds.), *Philosophy of Linguistics*. Berlin: Elsevier, pp. 271–323.
Corbett, G. (2000). *Number*. Cambridge: Cambridge University Press.
Corver, N. (1997). *Much*-support as a last resort. *Linguistic Inquiry*, 28: 119–64.
Corver, N. and J. Zwarts. (2004). Prepositional numerals. *Lingua*, 116: 811–35.
Coutinho, I. (2020a). The count/mass distinction in Taurepang (Karib). *Linguistic Variation*, 20: 352–65.
  (2020b). The count/mass distinction in Ye'kwana (Karib). *Linguistic Variation*, 20: 409–19.

Cowell, M. (1964). *A Reference Grammar of Syrian Arabic*. Washington, DC: Georgetown University Press.
Cowper, E. and D. Hall. (2012). Aspects of individuation. In Massam 2012, pp. 27–53.
Culioli, A. (1973). Sur quelques contradictions en linguistique. *Communications*, 20: 83–91.
  (1974). A propos des énoncés exclamatifs. *Langue française*, 22: 6–15.
Dali, M. and É. Mathieu. (2016). Les pluriels internes féminins de l'arabe tunisien. *Lingvisticæ Investigationes*, 39: 253–71.
  (forthcoming). *A Theory of Distributed Number*. Amsterdam: John Benjamins.
Dalrymple, M. and S. Mofu. (2012). Plural semantics, reduplication, and numeral modification in Indonesian. *Journal of Semantics*, 29: 229–60.
Davies, M. (2009). The 385+ million word corpus of contemporary American English (1990–2008+): Design, architecture, and linguistic insights. *International Journal of Corpus Linguistics*, 14: 159–90.
Dayal, V. (2004). Number marking and (in)definiteness in kind terms. *Linguistics and Philosophy*, 27: 393–450.
  (2011). Bare noun phrases. In C. Maienborn, K. von Heusinger, and P. Portner (eds.), *Semantics: An International Handbook of Natural Language Meaning, Vol. 2*. Berlin: de Gruyter Mouton, pp. 1088–109.
  (2012). Bangla classifiers: Mediating between kinds and objects. *Italian Journal of Linguistics*, 24: 195–226.
  (2013). On the existential force of bare plurals across languages. In I. Caponigro and C. Cecchetto (eds.), *From Grammar to Meaning: The Spontaneous Logicality of Language*. Cambridge: Cambridge University Press, pp. 49–80.
De Belder, M. (2008). Size matters: Towards a syntactic decomposition of countability. In N. Abner, and J. Bishop (eds.), *Proceedings of the 27th West Coast Conference on Formal Linguistics*. Somerville, MA: Cascadilla Proceedings Project, pp. 116–22.
  (2011). A morphosyntactic decomposition of countability in Germanic. *Journal of Comparative Germanic Linguistics*, 14: 173–202.
De Marneffe, M-C., T. Dozat, N. Silveira, K. Haverinen, F. Ginter, J. Nivre, and C. Manning. (2014). Universal Stanford dependencies: A cross-linguistic typology. In N. Calzolari et al. (eds.), *Proceedings of the Ninth International Conference on Language Resources and Evaluation (LREC-14)*. Paris: European Language Resources Association (ELRA), pp. 4585–92.
De Marneffe, M-C., B. MacCartney, and C. Manning. (2006). Generating typed dependency parses from phrase structure parses. In N. Calzolari et al. (eds.), *Proceedings of the Fifth International Conference on Language Resources and Evaluation (LREC-06)*. Paris: European Language Resources Association (ELRA), pp. 449–54.
Deal, A. (2017). Countability distinctions and semantic variation. *Natural Language Semantics*, 25: 125–71.
Dehaene, S. (1997). *The Number Sense*. Oxford: Oxford University Press.
Despic, M. (2019). On kinds and anaphoricity in languages without definite articles. In A. Aguilar-Guevara et al. (eds.), *Definiteness across Languages*. Berlin: Language Sciences Press, pp. 259–91.
Di Sciullo, A.-M. and E. Williams. (1987). *On the Definition of Word*. Cambridge, MA: MIT Press.

Dobrovie-Sorin, C., T. Bleam, and M. Espinal. (2006). Bare nouns, number and types of incorporation. In L. Tasmowski and S. Vogeleer (eds.), *Non-Definiteness and Plurality*. Amsterdam: John Benjamins, pp. 51–79.

Dobrovie-Sorin, C. and R. Pires de Oliveira. (2008). Reference to kinds in Brazilian Portuguese: Definite singulars vs. bare singulars. In A. Grønn (ed.), *Proceedings of Sinn und Bedeutung 12*. Oslo: Ilos, pp. 107–21.

Doetjes, J. (1996). Mass and count: Syntax or semantics. In A. Arregui and C. Cremers (eds.), *Proceedings of Meaning on the HIL 1*. Leiden: Leiden University, pp. 34–52.

(1997). Quantifiers and selection: On the distribution of quantifying expressions in French, Dutch and English. PhD dissertation, Leiden University. The Hague: Holland Academic Graphics.

(2001). La distribution des expressions quantificatrices et le statut des noms non-comptables. In G. Kleiber, B. Laca, and L. Tasmowski (eds.), *La typologie des groupes nominaux*. Rennes: Presses Universitaires de Rennes, pp. 119–42.

(2012). Count/mass distinctions across languages. In C. Maienborn, K. von Heusinger, and P. Portner (eds.), *Semantics: An International Handbook of Natural Language Meaning, Vol. 3*. Berlin: de Gruyter, pp. 2559–80.

(2017a). The count/mass distinction in grammar and cognition. *Annual Review of Linguistics*, 3: 199–217.

(2017b). Noun phrase. In R. Sybesma (ed.), *Encyclopedia of Chinese Language and Linguistics, Vol. 3*. Leiden: Brill, pp. 247–54. Available also at http://dx.doi.org/10.1163/2210-7363_ecll_COM_00000299.

(2017c). Measure words and classifiers. *Revista Letras*, 96: 291–308.

(2021). Quantity systems and the count/mass distinction. In Filip 2021, pp. 54–84.

Donabédian, A. (1993). Le pluriel en arménien moderne. *Faits de langues*, 2: 179–88.

Doron, E. and A. Müller. (2014). The cognitive basis of the mass–count distinction: Evidence from bare nouns. In P. Cabredo Hofherr and A. Zribi-Hertz (eds.), *Crosslinguistic Studies on Noun Phrase Structure and Reference*. Leiden: Brill, pp. 172–211.

Dryer, M. (2005). Coding of nominal plurality. In M. Haspelmath et al. (eds.), *The World Atlas of Language Structures*. Oxford: Oxford University Press, pp. 138–41.

El Yagoubi, R., S. Mondini, P. Bisiacchi, V. Chiarelli, A. Angrilli, and C. Semenza. (2006). The electrophysiological basis of mass and count nouns. *Brain and Language*, 99: 187–8.

Epstein-Naveh, N. (2015). Pluralisation of mass nouns in Modern Hebrew. Master's thesis, Bar-Ilan University.

Erbach, K., P. Sutton, H. Filip, and K. Byrdeck. (2017). Object mass nouns in Japanese. In A. Cremers et al. (eds.), *Proceedings of the 21st Amsterdam Colloquium*. Amsterdam: Institute for Logic, Language, and Computation at the University of Amsterdam, pp. 235–44.

Espinal, M. and L. McNally. (2011). Bare nominals and incorporating verbs in Spanish and Catalan. *Journal of Linguistics*, 47: 87–128.

Ester, M., H. Kriegel, J. Sander, and X. Xu. (1996). A density-based algorithm for discovering clusters in large spatial databases with noise. In E. Simoudis et al. (eds.), *Proceedings of the Second International Conference on Knowledge Discovery and Data Mining (KDD-96)*. Menlo Park, CA: AAAI Press, pp. 226–31.

Falkum, I. (2010). Systematic polysemy and the count–mass distinction. *University College, London, Working Papers*, 22: 16–40.
Farkas, D. and H. de Swart. (2010). The semantics and pragmatics of plurals. *Semantics and Pragmatics*, 3: 1–54.
Fassi Fehri, A. (1999). Arabic modifying adjectives and DP structures. *Studia Linguistica*, 53: 105–54.
  (2004). Nominal classes, and functional parameters, with particular reference to Arabic. *Linguistic Variation Yearbook*, 4: 41–108.
  (2012). *Key Features and Parameters in Arabic Grammar*. Amsterdam: John Benjamins.
  (2016). Semantic gender diversity and its architecture in the grammar of Arabic. *Journal of Afroasiatic Languages and Linguistics*, 8: 154–99.
Featherston, S. (2005). The Decathlon model of empirical syntax. In A. Kertész, E. Moravcsik, and C. Rákosi (eds.), *Current Approaches to Syntax: A Comparative Handbook*. Berlin: de Gruyter, pp. 187–208.
Feigenson, L., S. Dehaene, and E. Spelke. (2004). Core systems of number. *Trends in Cognitive Sciences*, 8: 307–14.
Feldman, F. (1973). Sortal predicates. *Noûs*, 7: 268–82.
Fellbaum, C. (1998). *WordNet: An Electronic Lexical Database*. Cambridge, MA: MIT Press.
Ferdinand, A. (1996). The development of functional categories. PhD dissertation, Leiden University.
Ferrand, L., P. Bonin, A. Méot, M. Augustinova, B. New, C. Pallier, and M. Brysbaert. (2008). Age-of-acquisition and subjective frequency estimates for all generally known monosyllabic French words and their relation with other psycholinguistic variables. *Behavior Research Methods*, 40: 1049–54.
Ferreira, M. (forthcoming). Bare nominals in Brazilian Portuguese. In P. Cabredo Hofherr and J. Doetjes (eds.), *Oxford Handbook of Grammatical Number*. Oxford: Oxford University Press.
Filip, H. (ed.) (2021). *Countability in Natural Language*. Cambridge: Cambridge University Press.
Filip, H. and P. Sutton. (2017). Singular count NPs in measure constructions. In D. Burgdorf et al. (eds.), *Proceedings of Semantics and Linguistic Theory (SALT 27)*. Ithaca, NY: LSA and CLC Publications, pp. 340–57.
Fine, K. (1975). Vagueness, truth, and logic. *Synthèse*, 30: 275–300.
Fischer, S. (1973). Two processes of reduplication in American Sign Language. *Foundations of Language*, 9: 469–80.
Flaux, N. and D. Van de Velde (2000). *Les noms en français: esquisse de classement*. Gap: Ophrys.
Frantz, D. and N. Russell. (1995). *Blackfoot Dictionary of Stems, Roots and Affixes*, 2nd ed. Toronto: University of Toronto Press.
Franzon, F. and C. Zanini. (2019). Different degrees of abstraction from visual cues in processing concrete nouns. In M. Bolognesi and G. Steen (eds.), *Perspectives on Abstract Concepts: From Cognitive Processing to Semantic Representation*. Amsterdam: John Benjamins, pp. 167–84.
Franzon, F., C. Zanini, and R. Rugani. (2019). Do non-verbal number systems shape grammar? Numerical cognition and number morphology compared. *Mind and Language*, 34: 37–58.

Frisson, S. and L. Frazier. (2005). Carving up word meaning: Portioning and grinding. *Journal of Memory and Language*, 53: 277–91.
Gaash, A. (2010). The development of the proto-semitic feminine ending -at in the noun and verb in contemporary Neo-Arabic dialects. Doctoral dissertation, Hebrew University of Jerusalem.
Gaatone, D. (1981). Observations sur l'opposition *très/beaucoup*. *Revue de linguistique romane*, 45: 74–95.
Galucio, A. and C. Costa. (2020). Count–mass distinction in Sakurabiat. *Linguistic Variation*, 20: 324–35.
Gajewski, J. (2002). On analyticity in natural language. Available at https://jon-gajewski.uconn.edu/wp-content/uploads/sites/1784/2016/08/analytic.pdf.
  (2009). L-triviality and grammar. Available at https://jon-gajewski.uconn.edu/wp-content/uploads/sites/1784/2016/08/Logic.pdf.
Gamut, L.T.F. (1991). *Logic, Language, and Meaning, Volume 1: Introduction to Logic*. Chicago, IL: University of Chicago Press.
Gathercole, V. (1985). He has too much hard questions. The acquisition of the linguistic mass–count distinction in *much* and *many*. *Journal of Child Language*, 12: 395–415.
  (1986). Evaluating competing linguistic theories with child language data: The case of the mass–count distinction. *Linguistics and Philosophy*, 9: 151–90.
Gebhardt, L. (2009). Numeral classifiers and the structure of DP. PhD dissertation, Northwestern University.
Ghalayiini, M. (1912/2006). Jaamiʕ ad-duruus al-ʕarabiyyah. [A Compilation of Arabic Lessons]. Beirut: al-maktabah al-ʕaSriyyah. (2006 revision by Salem Shams Ed-diin).
Ghaniabadi, S. (2012). Plural marking beyond count nouns. In Massam 2012, pp. 112–28.
Ghomeshi, J. (2003). Plural marking, indefiniteness, and the noun phrase. *Studia Linguistica*, 57: 47–74.
Gillon, B. (1992). Towards a common semantics for English count and mass nouns. *Linguistics and Philosophy*, 15: 597–640.
  (1999). The lexical semantics of English count and mass nouns. In E. Viegas (ed.), *Breadth and Depth of Semantic Lexicons*. Dordrecht: Springer, pp. 19–37.
Gillon, B., E. Kehayia, and V. Taler. (1999). The mass/count distinction: Evidence from on-line psycholinguistic performance. *Brain and Language*, 68: 205–11.
Gillon, C. (2015). Innu-aimun plurality. *Lingua*, 162: 128–48.
Gleason, H. (1955). *An Introduction to Descriptive Linguistics*. New York: Holt.
  (1965). *Linguistics and English Grammar*. Toronto: Holt, Rinehard, Winston.
Gordon, P. (1985). Evaluating the semantic categories hypothesis: The case of the mass/count distinction. *Cognition*, 20: 209–42.
Görgülü, E. (2012). Semantics of nouns and the specification of number in Turkish. PhD dissertation, Simon Fraser University.
Greenberg, J. (1972). Numeral classifiers and substantive number problems in the genesis of a linguistic type. *Working Papers on Language Universals*, 9: 2–39.
  (1974). Studies in numeral systems, I: Double numeral systems. *Working Papers on Language Universals*, 14: 75–89.
Grimm, S. (2012a). Individuation and inverse number marking in Dagaare. In Massam 2012, pp. 75–98.

References

(2012b). Number and individuation. PhD dissertation, Stanford University. Available at http://www.sas.rochester.edu/lin/sgrimm/publications/grimm_dissertation.pdf.
(2016). Crime investigations: The countability profile of a delinquent noun. *Baltic International Yearbook of Cognition, Logic, and Communication*, 11.
(2018). Grammatical number and the scale of individuation. *Language*, 94: 527–74.
Grimshaw, J. (2005). Extended projection. In J. Grimshaw (ed.), *Words and Structure*. Stanford, CA: CSLI Publications, pp. 1–74.
Grinevald, C. (2005). Classifiers. In C. Lehmann et al. (eds.), *Morphology: A Handbook on Inflection and Word Formation*. Berlin: Walter de Gruyter, pp. 1016–31.
Hafez, O. (1996). Morphological integration of loanwords in Egyptian Arabic. *Egype/Monde Arabe*, 27–8: 383–410.
Hamblin, C. (1973). Questions in Montague grammar. *Foundations of Language*, 10: 41–53.
Hamedani, L. (2011). The function of number in Persian. PhD dissertation, University of Ottawa.
Hammond, M. (1988). Templatic transfer in Arabic broken plurals. *Natural Language and Linguistic Theory*, 6: 247–70.
Harbour, D. (2003). The Kiowa case for feature insertion. *Natural Language and Linguistic Theory*, 21: 543–78.
(2007). *Morphosemantic Number: From Kiowa Noun Classes to UG Number Features*. Dordrecht: Springer.
(2011). Valence and atomic number. *Linguistic Inquiry*, 42: 561–94.
(2014). Paucity, abundance, and the theory of number. *Language*, 90: 185–229.
Harrison, S. and S. Albert. (1976). *Mokilese Reference Grammar*. Honolulu: University Press of Hawaii.
Haspelmath, M. (2001). Non-canonical marking of core arguments in European languages. In A. Aikhenvald, R. Dixon, and M. Onishi (eds.), *Non-Canonical Marking of Subjects and Objects*. Amsterdam: Benjamins, 53–83.
Hastie, T., R. Tibshirani, and J. Friedman. (2009). *The Elements of Statistical Learning: Data Mining, Inference, and Prediction*, 2nd edition. New York: Springer-Verlag.
Hauser, M. and S. Carey. (2003). Spontaneous representation of small numbers of objects by rhesus macaque: Examination of content and format. *Cognitive Psychology*, 47: 367–401.
Heim, I. (1982). The semantics of definite and indefinite noun phrases. PhD dissertation, University of Massachusetts.
(1991). Artikel und Definitheit. In A. von Stechow and D. Wunderlich (eds.), *Semantik: Ein internationales Handbuch der zeitgenössischen Forschung*. Berlin: de Gruyter, pp. 487–534.
Herbert, P. and W. Best. (2010). The role of noun syntax in spoken word production: Evidence from aphasia. *Cortex*, 46: 329–342.
Hespos, S., A. Ferry, and L. Rips. (2009). Five-month-old infants have different expectations for solids and liquids. *Psychological Science*, 20: 603–11.
Hilgert, E. (2014). Un révélateur de massivité: l'énigmatique *un peu de*. *Langue française*, 183: 101–16.
Hnout, C. (2017). Counting and measuring in Arabic: Plurality and S$^\text{c}$enf. Master's thesis, Bar-Ilan University.

Hoeksema, J. (1983). Plurality and conjunction. In A. ter Meulen (ed.), *Studies in Model-Theoretic Semantics*. Dordrecht: Foris, pp. 63–83.

Hoepelman, J. and D. Rohrer. (1981). On the mass–count distinction and the French *imparfait* and *passé simple*. In C. Rohrer (ed.), *Time, Tense and Quantifiers*. Tübingen: Niemeyer, pp. 85–112.

Holes, C. (1995). *Modern Arabic: Structures, Functions and Varieties*. London: Longman.

Hurford, J. (1975). *The Linguistic Theory of Numerals*. Cambridge: Cambridge University Press.

(1987). *Language and Number: The Emergence of a Cognitive System*. Oxford: Blackwell.

(2003). The interaction between numerals and nouns. In F. Plank (ed.), *Noun Phrase Structure in the Languages of Europe*. The Hague: de Gruyter, pp. 561–620.

Husić, H. (2020). A vagueness based analysis of abstract mass nouns. In M. Franke et al. (eds.), *Proceedings of Sinn und Bedeutung (SuB 24), Vol. 1*. Konstanz: Sprachwissenschaft, Universität Konstanz, pp. 359–76.

Idrissi, A. (1997). Plural formation in Arabic. In M. Eid and R. Ratcliffe (eds.), *Perspectives on Arabic Linguistics: Papers from the Annual Symposium on Arabic Linguistics X*. Amsterdam: John Benjamins, pp. 123–45.

Ikoro, S. (1994). Numeral classifiers in Kana. *Journal of African Languages and Linguistics*, 15: 7–28.

Iljic, R. (1994). Quantification in Mandarin Chinese: Two markers of plurality. *Linguistics*, 32: 91–116.

Inagaki, S. and D. Barner. (2009). Countability in absence of count nouns: Evidence from Japanese quantity judgments. *Studies in Language Sciences*, 8: 111–25.

Ionin, T. and O. Matushansky. (2004). A singular plural. In B. Schmeiser et al. (eds.), *Proceedings of the 23rd West Coast Conference on Formal Linguistics*. Somerville, MA: Cascadilla Press, pp. 399–412.

(2006). The composition of complex cardinals. *Journal of Semantics*, 23: 315–60.

(2018). *Cardinals: The Syntax and Semantics of Cardinal-Containing Expressions*. Cambridge, MA: MIT Press.

Jackendoff, R. (1991). Parts and boundaries. *Cognition*, 41: 9–45.

Jespersen, O. (1914). *A Modern English Grammar on Historical Principles, Part 2*. Heidelberg: Carl Winter Universitätsbuchhandlung. Reprinted with alterations and additions: N. Haislund (ed.). London: Allen & Urwin, 1948.

(1924). *The Philosophy of Grammar*. London: Allen & Urwin.

Jiang, J. (2017). Mandarin associative plural *-men* and NPs with *-men*. *International Journal of Chinese Linguistics*, 4: 191–256.

(2018). Definiteness in Nuosu Yi and the theory of argument formation. *Linguistics and Philosophy*, 41: 1–39.

(2020). *Nominal Arguments and Language Variation*, Oxford: Oxford University Press.

Joosten, F. (2006). Why *club* and *lingerie* do not belong together. A plea for redefining collective nouns. In G. Kleiber, C. Schnedecker, and A. Theissen (eds.), *La relation partie-tout*. Paris and Leuven: Peeters, pp. 73–88.

Kamp, H. and U. Reyle. (1993). *From Discourse to Logic: Introduction to Model-Theoretic Semantics of Natural Language, Formal Logic and Discourse Representation Theory*. Dordrecht: Kluwer.

Katz, G. and R. Zamparelli. (2012). Quantifying count/mass elasticity. In J. Choi et al. (eds.), *Proceedings of the 29th West Coast Conference on Formal Linguistics*. Somerville, MA: Cascadilla Proceedings Project, pp. 371–9.

Keller, F. (2000). Gradience in grammar: Experimental and computational aspects of degrees of grammaticality. PhD dissertation, University of Edinburgh. Available at https://rucore.libraries.rutgers.edu/rutgers-lib/38303/.

Kerleroux, F. (1996). *La coupure invisible*. Lille: Septentrion.

Khrizman, K., F. Landman, S. Lima, S. Rothstein, and B.R. Schvarcz. (2015). Portion readings are count readings, not measure readings. In T. Brochhagen et al. (eds.), *Proceedings of the 20th Amsterdam Colloquium*. Amsterdam: Institute for Logic, Language, and Computation at the University of Amsterdam, pp. 197–206.

Kihm, A. (2005). Noun class, gender, and the lexicon-syntax-morphology interfaces: A comparative study of Niger-Congo and Romance languages. In G. Cinque and R. Kayne (eds.), *The Oxford Handbook of Comparative Syntax*. Oxford: Oxford University Press, pp. 459–512.

(2006). Nonsegmental concatenation: A study of Classical Arabic broken plurals and verbal nouns. *Morphology*, 16: 69–105.

Kiss, T., F.J. Pelletier, H. Husić, J. Poppek, and N. Simunic. (2016). A sense-based lexicon of count and mass expressions: The Bochum countability lexicon. In N. Calzolari et al. (eds.), *Proceedings of the Tenth International Conference on Language Resources and Evaluation (LREC-16)*. Paris: European Language Resources Association (ELRA), pp. 2810–14.

Kiss, T., F.J. Pelletier, and T. Stadtfeld. (2014). Building a reference lexicon for countability in English. In N. Calzolari et al. (eds.), *Proceedings of the Ninth International Conference on Language Resources and Evaluation (LREC-14)*. Paris: European Language Resources Association (ELRA), pp. 995–1000.

Kleiber, G. (1997). Massif/comptable et partie/tout. *Verbum*, 19: 321–37.

(1999). *Problèmes de sémantique. La polysémie en questions*. Villeneuve d'Ascq: Presses universitaires du Septentrion.

(2014). Massif/comptable et noms de propriétés. *Langue française*, 183: 71–86.

Klooster, W. (1972). *The Structure Underlying Measure Phrase Sentences*. Dordrecht: Reidel.

Koulidobrova, E. (2012). *When the quiet surfaces: "Transfer" of argument omission in the speech of ASL-English bilinguals*. PhD dissertation, University of Connecticut.

Koulidobrova, E. and D. Lillo-Martin. (2016). Point of inquiry: The case of the (non-) pronominal *IX* in ASL. In P. Grodzs and P. Patel-Grodz (eds.), *The Impact of Pronominal Form on Interpretation*. Boston, MA: de Gruyter, pp. 221–50.

(2017). Elide me bare: Argument omission in ASL. *Natural Language and Linguistic Theory*, 35: 397–446.

Kperogi, F. (2015). *Global English: The Changing Face and Forms of Nigerian English in a Global World*. New York: Peter Lang.

Kramer, R. (2009). Definite markers, phi-features, and agreement: A morphosyntactic investigation of the Amharic DP. PhD dissertation, University of California, Santa Cruz.

(2016). A split analysis of plurality: Number in Amharic. *Linguistic Inquiry*, 47: 527–59.

Kratzer, A. and J. Shimoyama. (2002). Indeterminate pronouns: The view from Japanese. In Y. Otsu (ed.), *Proceedings of the Third Tokyo Conference on Psycholinguistics (TCP)*. Tokyo: Hituzi Syobo, pp. 1–25.

Krifka, M. (1989). Nominal reference, temporal constitution and quantification. In R. Bartsch, J. van Benthem, and P. van Emde Boas (eds.), *Semantics and Contextual Expression*. Dordrecht: Foris, pp. 75–111.

(1994). Mass expressions. In R. Asher and J. Simpson (eds.), *The Encyclopedia of Language and Linguistics, Vol. 5*. Oxford: Pergamon Press, pp. 2612–14.

(1995). Common nouns: A contrastive analysis of English and Chinese. In G. Carlson and F.J. Pelletier (eds.), *The Generic Book*. Chicago, IL: University of Chicago Press, 398–411.

Kulkarni, R., S. Rothstein, and A. Treves. (2013). A statistical investigation into the cross-linguistic distribution of mass and count nouns: Morphosyntactic and semantic perspectives. *Biolinguistics*, 7: 132–68.

Lahrouchi, M. and N. Lampitelli. (2014). On plurals, noun phrase and num(ber) in Moroccan Arabic and Djibouti Somali. In S. Bendjaballah, N. Faust, M. Lahrouchi, and N. Lampitelli (eds.), *The Form of Structure, the Structure of Form: Essays in Honor of Jean Lowenstamm*. Amsterdam: John Benjamins, pp. 303–14.

Lahrouchi, M. and R. Ridouane. (2016). On diminutives and plurals in Moroccan Arabic. *Morphology*, 26: 453–75.

Lakens, D., A. Scheel, and P. Isager. (2018). Equivalence testing for psychological research: A tutorial. *Advances in Methods and Practices in Psychological Science*, 1: 259–69.

Laks, L. (2014). Plural word formation of loan words in Palestinian and Jordanian Arabic. *Journal of Arabic Linguistics*, 60: 5–34.

Lammert, M. (2016). Lexical plurals through meronymy and hyperonymy. *Lingvisticæ Investigationes*, 39: 335–54.

Landman, F. (1989). Groups I. *Linguistics and Philosophy*, 12: 559–605.

(1991). *Structures for Semantics*. Dordrecht: Kluwer.

(1996). Plurality. In S. Lappin (ed.), *Handbook of Contemporary Semantic Theory*. Oxford: Blackwell.

(2000). *Events and Plurality: The Jerusalem Lectures*. Dordrecht: Kluwer Academic Publishers.

(2003). Predicate–argument mismatches and the adjectival theory of indefinites. In M. Coene and Y. d'Hulst (eds.), *From NP to DP: The Syntax and Semantics of Noun Phrases*. Amsterdam: John Benjamins, pp. 211–37.

(2004). *Indefinites and the Type of Sets*. Oxford: Blackwell.

(2010). Boolean pragmatics. Available at https://www.tau.ac.il/~landman/. Originally appeared on a Festschrift page in honour of Martin Stokhof's 60th birthday.

(2011). Count nouns – mass nouns, neat nouns – mess nouns. *Baltic International Yearbook of Cognition, Logic and Communication*, 6.

(2016). Iceberg semantics for count nouns and mass nouns: The evidence from portions. *The Baltic International Yearbook of Cognition Logic and Communication*, 11.

(2020). *Iceberg Semantics for Mass Nouns and Count Nouns: A New Framework for Boolean Semantics*. Springer: Cham.

Langacker, R. (1987). *Foundations of Cognitive Grammar. Vol. 1: Theoretical Prerequisites*. Stanford, CA: Stanford University Press.
Lasersohn, P. (1995). *Plurality, Conjunction and Events*. Dordrecht: Kluwer.
 (2011). Mass nouns and plurals. In C. Maienborn et al. (eds.), *Semantics: An International Handbook of Natural Language Meaning, Vol. 2*. Berlin: de Gruyter, pp. 1131–53.
Lauwers, P. (2014). Les pluriels "lexicaux": typologie quantifiée des déficits de dénombrabilité. *Langue française*, 183: 117–32.
 (2016). Les pluriels lexicaux dits "massifs" face au conditionneur universel. *Lingvisticæ Investigationes*, 39: 272–88.
Lauwers, P. and M. Lammert. (2016). Introduction: New perspectives on lexical plurals. *Lingvisticæ Investigationes*, 39 (special issue: P. Lauwers and M. Lammert (eds.), *Lexical Plurals and Beyond*): 207–16.
Levin, A. (1994). *A Grammar of the Arabic Dialect of Jerusalem*. Jerusalem: The Hebrew University Magnes Press. (in Hebrew).
 (2011). 'Imala. In K. Versteegh, M. Eid, A. Elgibali, M. Woidich, and A. Zabroski (eds.), *Encyclopedia of Arabic Language and Linguistics, Vol. 2*. Leiden: Brill, pp. 311–15.
Levy, M. and J. Fidelholtz. (1971). Arabic broken plurals, rule features and lexical features. *Glossa*, 5: 57–70.
Li, A. (1998). Argument determiner phrases and number phrases. *Linguistic Inquiry*, 29: 693–702.
Li, C. and S. Thompson. (1981). *Mandarin Chinese: A Functional Reference Grammar*. Berkeley, CA: University of California Press.
Li, P., Y. Dunham, and S. Carey (2009). Of substance: The nature of language effects on entity construal. *Cognitive Psychology*, 58: 487–524.
Li, X.-P. (2011). On the semantics of classifiers in Chinese. PhD dissertation, Bar-Ilan University. www.semanticsarchive.net/Archive/mY3YWYzO/semantics%20of%20classifier.pdf.
Lichtenberk, F. (1983). *A Grammar of Manam*. Honolulu, HI: University of Hawai'i Press.
Lima, S. (2014a). The grammar of individuation and counting. PhD dissertation, University of Massachusetts.
 (2014b). All notional mass nouns are count nouns in Yudja. In T. Snider et al. (eds.), *Proceedings of Semantics and Linguistic Theory (SALT 24)*. Ithaca, NY: LSA and CLC Publications, pp. 534–54.
 (2016). Container constructions in Yudja: Locatives, individuation and measure. *Baltic International Yearbook of Cognition, Logic and Communication*, 11.
Lima, S. and A.P.Q. Gomes. (2016). The interpretation of Brazilian Portuguese bare singulars in neutral contexts. *Revista Letras*, 93: 193–209.
Lima, S. and S. Rothstein. (2020). A typology of the count/mass distinction in Brazil and its relevance for count/mass theories. *Linguistic Variation*, 20: 174–218.
Lin, J. and J. Schaeffer. (2018). Nouns are both mass and count: Evidence from unclassified nouns in adult and child Mandarin Chinese. *Glossa: A Journal of General Linguistics*, 3: 54.
Link, G. (1983). The logical analysis of plurals and mass terms: A lattice-theoretical approach. In R. Bäuerle, C. Schwarze, and A. von Stechow (eds.), *Meaning, Use and Interpretation of Language*. Berlin: de Gruyter, pp. 302–23.

Link G. (1998). *Algebraic Semantics in Language and Philosophy*. Cambridge, MA: CSLI Publications.
Lønning, J. (1987). Mass terms and quantification. *Linguistics and Philosophy*, 10: 1–52.
Lourenco, S. and M. Longo. (2011). Origins and development of generalized magnitude representation. In S. Dehaene and E. Brannon (eds.), *Space, Time, and Number in the Brain: Searching for the Foundations of Mathematical Thought*. Amsterdam: Elsevier-Academic Press, pp. 225–44.
Lowenstamm, J. (2008). On little n, √, and types of nouns. In J. Hartmann, V. Hegedus, and H. van Riemsijk (eds.), *Sounds of Silence: Empty Elements in Syntax and Phonology*. Amsterdam: Elsevier, pp. 105–44.
Lucy, J. (1992). *Grammatical Categories and Cognition*. Cambridge: Cambridge University Press.
Lucy, J. and S. Gaskins. (2001). Grammatical categories and the development of classificational preferences. In M. Bowerman and S. Levinson (eds.), *Language Acquisition and Conceptual Development*. Cambridge: Cambridge University Press, pp. 257–83.
McCarthy, J. and A. Prince. 1990. Foot and word in prosodic morphology: The Arabic broken plural. *Natural Language and Linguistic Theory*, 8: 209–83.
McCawley, J. (1975). Lexicography and the count–mass distinction. In C. Cogen et al. (eds.), *Proceedings of the First Berkeley Linguistic Society Conference, Vol. 1*. Berkeley, CA: Linguistics Department at the University of California, pp. 314–21. Reprinted in J. McCawley (ed.), *Adverbs, Vowels, and Other Objects of Wonder*. Chicago, IL: University of Chicago Press, 1979, pp. 165–73.
Macnamara, J. (1972). Cognitive basis of language learning in infants. *Psychological Review*, 79: 1–13.
Mahowald, K., P. Graff, J. Hartman, and E. Gibson. (2016). SNAP judgments: A small N acceptability paradigm (SNAP) for linguistic acceptability judgments. *Language*, 92: 619–35.
Manning, C., M. Surdeanu, J. Bauer, J. Finkel, S. Bethard, and D. McClosky. (2014). The Stanford CoreNLP natural language processing toolkit. In K. Bontcheva and J. Zhu (eds.), *Association for Computational Linguistics: System Demonstrations*. Baltimore, MD: Association for Computational Linguistics, pp. 55–60.
Markman, E. (1991). *Categorization and Naming in Children: Problems of Induction*. Cambridge, MA: MIT Press.
Marten, L. (forthcoming). Noun classes and plurality in Bantu languages. In P. Cabredo Hofherr and J. Doetjes (eds.), *Oxford Handbook of Grammatical Number*. Oxford: Oxford University Press.
Martí, L. (2020). Inclusive plurals and the theory of number. *Linguistic Inquiry*, 51: 37–73.
Massam, D. (ed.) (2012). *Count and Mass across Languages*. Oxford: Oxford Univerity Press.
Mathieu, É. (2012a). Flavors of division. *Linguistic Inquiry*, 43: 650–79.
  (2012b). On the mass/count distinction in Ojibwe. In Massam 2012, pp. 172–98.
  (2014). Many a plural. In A. Aguilar-Guevara, B. Le Bruyn, and J. Zwarts (eds.), *Weak Referentiality*. Amsterdam: John Benjamins, pp. 157–81.
Mathieu, É. and G. Zareikar. (2015). Measure words, plurality, and cross-linguistic variation. *Linguistic Variation*, 2: 169–200.

Matthewson, L. (2004). On the methodology of semantic fieldwork. *International Journal of American Linguistics*, 70: 369–415.
Mettouchi, A. and Z. Frajzyngier. (2013). A previously unrecognized typological category: The state distinction in Kabyle (Berber). *Linguistic Typology*, 17: 1–20.
Mihatsch, W. (2016). Collectives, object mass nouns and individual count nouns: Nouns between lexical and inflectional plural marking. *Lingvisticæ Investigationes*, 39: 289–308.
Moltmann, F. (1997). *Parts and Wholes in Semantics*. Oxford: Oxford University Press.
 (ed.) (2020). *Mass and Count in Linguistics, Philosophy, and Cognitive Science*. Amsterdam: Benjamins.
Mondini, S., A. Angrilli, P. Bisiacchi, C. Spironelli, K. Marinelli, and C. Semenza. (2008). Mass and count nouns activate different brain regions: An ERP study on early components. *Neuroscience Letters*, 430: 48–53.
Mondini, S., E. Kehaya, B. Gillon, G. Arcara, and G. Jarema. (2009). Lexical access of mass and count nouns. How word recognition reaction times correlate with lexical and morphosyntactic processing. *The Mental Lexicon*, 4: 354–79.
Mufwene, S. (1981). Non-individuation and the count–mass distinction. In R. Hendrick et al. (eds.), *Papers from the 17th Regional Meeting of the Chicago Linguistic Society*. Chicago, IL: Chicago Linguistic Society, pp. 221–38.
Müller, A. (2002). The semantics of generic quantification in Brazilian Portuguese. *Probus*, 14: 279–98.
Muromatsu, K. (2003). Classifiers and the count/mass distinction. In Y-H. Li and A. Simpson (eds.), *Functional Structure(s), Form and Interpretation*. London: Routledge, pp. 65–128.
Murtonen, A. (1964). *Broken Plurals: The Origin and Development of the System*. Leiden: E. J. Brill.
Muskens, R. (1996). Combining Montague semantics and discourse representations. *Linguistics and Philosophy*, 19: 143–86.
Nemoto, N. (2005). On mass denotations of bare nouns in Japanese and Korean. *Linguistics*, 43: 383–413.
Newmeyer, F. (2007). Commentary on Sam Featherston, *Data in generative grammar: The stick and the carrot*. *Theoretical Linguistics*, 33: 395–9.
Nicolas, D. (2002a). *La distinction entre noms massifs et noms comptables: aspects linguistiques et conceptuels*. Leuven: Peeters.
 (2002b). Do mass nouns constitute a semantically uniform class? *Kansas Working Papers in Linguistics*, 26: 113–21.
 (2004). Is there anything characteristic about the meaning of a count noun? *Revue de la lexicologie*, 18–19: 125–38.
Nishiguchi, S. (2009) Quantifiers in Japanese. In P. Bosch et al. (eds.), *Logic, Language and Computation: TbiLLC 2007*. Berlin: Springer, pp. 153–64.
Oggiani, C. (2011). On discourse referential properties of bare singulars in Spanish. PhD dissertation, Utrecht University.
Ojeda, A. (1992). The semantics of number in Arabic. In C. Barker and D. Dowty (eds.), *Proceedings of Semantics and Linguistic Theory (SALT 2)*. Ithaca, NY: LSA and CLC Publications, pp. 303–26.

(2005). The paradox of mass plurals. In S. Mufwene, E. Francis, and R. Wheeler (eds.), *Polymorphous Linguistics. Jim McCawley's Legacy*. Cambridge, MA: MIT Press, pp. 389–410.
Ouwayda, S. (2013). Where plurality is: Agreement and DP structure. In S. Keine and S. Sloggett (eds.), *Proceedings of NELS 42*. Amherst, MA: GLSA Publications, pp. 81–94.
(2014). Where number lies: Plural marking, numerals, and the collective–distributive distinction. PhD dissertation, University of Southern California. Available at http://digitallibrary.usc.edu/cdm/ref/collection/p15799coll3/id/411905.
(2017). On the DP dependence of collective interpretation with numerals. *Natural Language Semantics*, 25: 263–314.
Pacifique, P. (1939). *Leçons grammaticales théoriques et pratiques de la langue micmaque*. Toronto: Global Language Press (Reprinted 2007).
Park, S.Y. (2008). Plural marking in classifier languages: A case study of the so-called plural marking *-tul* in Korean. *Toronto Working Papers in Linguistics*, 28: 281–95.
Partee, B. and V. Borschev. (2012). Sortal, relational, and functional interpretations of nouns and Russian container constructions. *Journal of Semantics*, 29: 445–86.
Payne, J. and R. Huddleston. (2002). Nouns and noun phrases. In R. Huddleston and G. Pullum (eds.), *The Cambridge Grammar of the English Language*. Cambridge: Cambridge University Press, pp. 323–523.
Pelletier, F.J. (1975). Non-singular reference: Some preliminaries. *Philosophia*, 5: 451–65. Reprinted in Pelletier 1979, pp. 1–14).
(1979). *Mass Terms: Some Philosophical Problems*. Dordrecht: Reidel.
(2012). Lexical nouns are both +mass and +count, but they are neither +mass nor +count. In Massam 2012, pp. 9–26.
Pelletier, F.J. and L. Schubert. (1989/2003). Mass expressions. In F. Guenthner and D. Gabbay (eds.), *Handbook of Philosophical Logic, Vol. 4*, 1st edition. Dordrecht: Kluwer, pp. 327–407. See also the updated version of this entry in Vol. 10, pp. 249–336 of the 2nd edition (2003).
Pereltsvaig, A. (2014). On number and numberlessness in languages with and without articles. In P. Cabredo Hofherr and A. Zribi-Hertz (eds.), *Crosslinguistic Studies on Noun Phrase Structure and Reference*. Leiden and Boston, MA: Brill, pp. 52–73.
Petronio, K. (1995). Bare noun phrases, verbs, and quantification in ASL. In E. Bach et al (eds.), *Quantification in Natural Language*. Dordrecht: Kluwer, pp. 603–18.
Pfau, R. and M. Steinbach. (2006). Pluralization in sign and in speech: A cross-modal typological study. *Linguistic Typology*, 10: 135–82.
(2016). Complex sentences in sign languages: Modality – typology – discourse. In R. Pfau et al. (eds.) *A Matter of Complexity: Subordination in Sign Languages*. Berlin: de Gruyter Mouton, pp. 1–35.
Pica, P., C. Lemer, V. Izard, and S. Dehaene. (2004). Exact and approximate arithmetic in an Amazonian indigene group. *Science*, 306: 499–503.
Pinker, S. (1995). *The Language Instinct: How the Mind Creates Language*. New York: Harper Collins.
Pires de Oliveira, R. and J. Martins. (2017). Preliminary remarks on the nominal phrase in Cape Verdean: The semantics of bare nouns cross-linguistically. *Glossa: A Journal of General Linguistics*, 2: 100.

Pires de Oliveira, R. and S. Rothstein. (2011). Bare singular noun phrases are mass in Brazilian Portuguese. *Lingua*, 121: 2153–75.
Prasada, S., K. Ferenz, and T. Haskell (2002). Conceiving of entities as objects and as stuff. *Cognition*, 83: 141–65.
Quine, W.V. (1960). *Word and Object*. Cambridge, MA: MIT Press.
Quirk, R., S. Greenbaum, G. Leech, and J. Svartvik. (1985). *A Comprehensive Grammar of the English Language*. Burnt Hill: Longman.
R Core Team (2019). *R: A language and environment for statistical computing*. Vienna: R Foundation for Statistical Computing, url: https://www.R-project.org/
Ratcliffe, R. (1998). *The "Broken" Plural Problem in Arabic and Comparative Semitic: Allomorphy and Analogy in Non-Concatenative Morphology*. Amsterdam: John Benjamins.
Renans, A., J. Romoli, M. Makri, L. Thieu, H. de Vries, R. Folli, and G. Tsoulas. (2018). The abundance inference of pluralized mass nouns is an implicature: Evidence from Greek. *Glossa: A Journal of General Linguistics*, 3. Available at www.glossa-journal.org/articles/10.5334/gjgl.531.
Rieux, J. and B. Rollin. (1975). *The Port-Royal Grammar*. The Hague: Mouton.
Ritter, E. (1991). Two functional categories in noun phrases: Evidence from Modern Hebrew. In S. Rothstein (ed.), *Syntax and Semantics 25: Perspectives on Phrase Structure: Heads and Licensing*. San Diego, CA and London: Academic Press, pp. 37–62.
Roettger, T. and F. Domahs. (2015). Grammatical number elicits SNARC and MARC effects as a function of task demands. *The Quarterly Journal of Experimental Psychology*, 68: 1231–48.
Rothstein, S. (2009). Individuating and measure readings of classifier constructions: Evidence from Modern Hebrew. *Brill's Annual of Afroasiatic Languages and Linguistics*, 1: 106–45.
  (2010). Counting and the mass/count distinction. *Journal of Semantics*, 27: 343–97.
  (2011). Counting, measuring and the semantics of classifiers. *The Baltic International Yearbook of Cognition, Logic and Communication*, 6.
  (2016). Counting and measuring: A theoretical and crosslinguistic account. *The Baltic International Yearbook of Cognition Logic and Communication*, 11.
  (2017). *Semantics for Counting and Measuring*. Cambridge: Cambridge University Press.
Rothstein, S. and S. Lima. (2018). Quantity evaluations in Yudja: The relation between judgements, language and cultural practice. *Synthèse*, 197: 3851–73.
Rothstein, S. and R. Pires de Oliveira. (2020). Comparatives in Brazilian Portuguese: Counting and measuring. In Moltmann 2020, pp. 141–57.
Rullmann, H. and A. You. (2006). General number and the semantics and pragmatics of indefinite bare nouns in Mandarin Chinese. In K. von Heusinger and K. Turner (eds.), *Where Semantics Meets Pragmatics*. Amsterdam: Elsevier, pp. 175–96.
Ryding, K. (2005). *A Reference Grammar for Modern Standard Arabic*. Cambridge: Cambridge University Press.
Sağ, Y. (2016). On the semantics of classifiers: A new perspective from an optional classifier language, Turkish. Available at https://ling.auf.net/lingbuzz/002999.

Sauerland, U. (2003). A new semantics for number. In R. Youn and Y. Zhou (eds.), *Proceedings of Semantics and Linguistic Theory (SALT 13)*. Ithaca, NY: LSA and CLC Publications, pp. 258–75.
  (2008). On the semantic markedness of phi-features. In D. Harbour (ed.), *Phi Theory*. Oxford: Oxford University Press, pp. 57–83.
Sauerland, U., J. Anderssen, and K. Yatsushiro. (2005). The plural is semantically unmarked. In S. Kepser and M. Reis (eds.), *Linguistic Evidence: Empirical, Theoretical and Computational Perspectives*. Berlin/New York: Mouton de Gruyter, pp. 413–34.
Schachter, P. and F. Otanes. (1972). *A Tagalog Reference Grammar*. Los Angeles, CA: University of California Press.
Schiehlen, M. and K. Spranger. (2006). The mass–count distinction: Acquisition and disambiguation. In N. Calzolari et al. (eds.), *Proceedings of the Fifth International Conference on Language Resources and Evaluation (LREC-5)*. Paris: European Language Resources Association (ELRA), pp. 265–70.
Schlenker, P. and J. Lamberton. (2019). Iconic plurality. *Linguistics and Philosophy*, 42: 45–108.
Schmitt, C. and A. Munn. (1999). Against the Nominal Mapping Parameter: Bare nouns in Brazilian Portuguese. In P. Tamanji et al. (eds.), *Proceedings of NELS 29*. Amherst, MA: GLSA, pp. 339–54.
Schvarcz, B. (2014). The Hungarians who say -nyi: Issues in counting and measuring in Hungarian. Master's thesis, Bar-Ilan University.
Schwarzschild, R. (1996). *Pluralities*. Dordrecht: Kluwer.
  (2005). Measure phrases as modifiers of adjectives. *Recherches linguistiques de Vincennes*, 35: 207–28.
  (2006). The role of dimensions in the syntax of noun phrases. *Syntax*, 9: 67–110.
  (2011). Stubborn distributivity, multiparticipant nouns and the count/mass distinction. In S. Lima, K. Mullin, and B. Smith (eds.) *Proceedings of NELS 39*. Amherst, MA: GLSA, pp. 661–78.
Scontras, G. (2017). A new kind of degree. *Linguistics and Philosophy*, 40: 165–205.
Scontras, G., K. Davidson, A. Deal, and S. Murray. (2017). Who has more? The influence of linguistic form on quantity judgments. *Proceedings of the Linguistic Society of America*, v. 2, 41: 1–15.
Shachmon, O. (2011). Pausal final *imāla* in central Palestinian dialects. *Jerusalem Studies in Arabic and Islam (JSAI)*, 38: 145–61.
Sharvy, R. (1978). Maybe English has no count nouns: Notes on Chinese semantics. *Studies in Language*, 2: 345–65.
Shipley, E. and B. Shepperson. (1990). Countable entities: Developmental changes. *Cognition*, 34: 109–36.
Shlonsky, U. (2004). The form of Semitic nominals. *Lingua*, 114: 1465–526.
Sigler, M. (1996). Specificity and agreement in standard Western Armenian. PhD dissertation, MIT.
Siloni, T. (1997). Event nominals and the construct state. In L. Haegeman (ed.), *New Comparative Syntax*. London: Longman, pp. 165–88.
Simons, M. (2005). Semantics and pragmatics in the interpretation of "or". In E. Georgala and J. Howell (eds.), *Proceedings of Semantics and Linguistic Theory (SALT 15)*. Ithaca, NY: LSA and CLC Publications, pp. 205–22.

Singh, R. (2011). "Maximize Presupposition!" and local contexts. *Natural Language Semantics*, 19: 149–68.
Sneddon, J. (1996). *Indonesian: A Comprehensive Grammar*. London: Routledge.
Soja, N., S. Carey, and E. Spelke. (1991). Ontological categories guide young children's inductions of word meaning: Object terms and substance terms. *Cognition*, 38: 179–211.
Sorace, A. and F. Keller (2005). Gradience in linguistic data. *Lingua*, 115: 1497–524.
Spector, B. (2007). Aspects of the pragmatics of plural morphology: On higher order implicature. In U. Sauerland and P. Stateva (eds.), *Presupposition and Implicature in Compositional Semantics*. Basingstoke: Macmillan, pp. 243–81.
Spelke, E. (1985). Perception of unity, persistence, and identity: Thoughts on infants' conceptions of objects. In J. Mehler and R. Fox (eds.), *Neonate Cognition: Beyond the Blooming Buzzing Confusion*. Hillsdale, NJ: Erlbaum, pp. 89–113.
Spelke, E. and K. Kinzler. (2007). Core knowledge. *Developmental Science*, 10: 89–96.
Sprouse, J. (2007). Continuous acceptability, categorical grammaticality, and experimental syntax. *Biolinguistics*, 1: 123–34.
Stalnaker, R. (2014). *Context*. Oxford: Oxford University Press.
Stavrou, M. and A. Terzi. (2008). Types of numerical nouns. In C.B. Chang and H.J. Haynie (eds.), *Proceedings of WCCFL 26*. Somerville, MA: Cascadilla Press, pp. 429–37.
Steinhauer, K., R. Pancheva, A. Newman, S. Gennari, and M. Ullman. (2001). How the mass counts: An electrophysiological approach to the processing of lexical features. *Cognitive Neuroscience and Neuropsychology*, 12: 999–1005.
Strickland, B. (2017). Language reflects "core" cognition: A new theory about the origin of cross-linguistic regularities. *Cognitive Science*, 41: 70–101.
Sudo, Y. (2014). Dependent plural pronouns with Skolemized choice functions. *Natural Language Semantics*, 22: 265–97.
  (2016). The semantic role of classifiers in Japanese. *Baltic International Yearbook of Cognition, Logic and Communication*, 11.
  (to appear). Countable nouns in Japanese. In *Proceedings of WAFL 11*. Available at www.ucl.ac.uk/~ucjtudo/pdf/wafl11.pdf.
Sutton, P. (2019). Individuation, countability, and the problem of the many. Presented at the Research Colloquium for Logic and Epistemology, Ruhr-Universität, Bochum, 7 November 2019. Available at: http://peter-sutton.co.uk/wp-content/uploads/2020//03/3tests.pdf.
Sutton, P. and H. Filip. (2016a). Counting in context: Count/mass variation and restrictions on coercion in collective artifact nouns. In M. Moroney et al. (eds.), *Proceedings of Semantics and Linguistic Theory (SALT 26)*. Ithaca, NY: LSA and CLC Publications, pp. 350–70.
  (2016b). Mass/count variation: A mereological, two-dimensional semantics. *Baltic International Yearbook of Cognition, Logic and Communication*, 11.
  (2018a). Restrictions on subkind coercion in object mass nouns. In R. Truswell et al. (eds.), *Proceedings of Sinn und Bedeutung 21*. Konstanz: Sprachwissenschaft, Universität Konstanz, pp. 1195–213.

(2018b). Counting constructions and coercion: Container, portion and measure interpretations. *Oslo Studies in Language*, 10: 97–119.

(2021). The count/mass distinction for "granular" nouns. In Filip 2021, pp. 375–415.

De Swart, H. (1998). Aspect shift and coercion. *Natural Language and Linguistic Theory*, 16: 347–85.

Sweet, H. (1898). *A New English Grammar, Vol. II*. Oxford: Oxford University Press.

T'sou, B. (1976). The structure of nominal classifier systems. In P. Jenner, S Starosta, and L. Thompson (eds.), *Austroasiatic Studies, Vol 2*. Honolulu: University Press of Hawaii, pp. 1215–48.

Tsoulas, G. (2009). On the grammar of number and mass terms in Greek. In C. Halpert, J. Hartman, and D. Hill (eds.), *Proceedings of the 2007 Workshop in Greek Syntax and Semantics at MIT*. Cambridge, MA: MIT Press, pp. 333–48.

Van de Velde, D. (1996) *Le spectre nominal. Des noms de matière aux noms d'abstraction*. Paris and Leuven: Peeters.

Vásquez-Rojas, V. (2012). The syntax and semantics of Purépecha noun phrases and the mass/count distinction. PhD dissertation, New York University.

Veltman, F. (1985). Logics for conditionals. PhD dissertation, University of Amsterdam.

Vergnaud, J. and M. Zubizarreta. (1992). The definite determiner and the inalienable constructions in French and in English. *Linguistic Inquiry*, 23: 595–652.

Verkuyl, H. (1981). Numerals and quantifiers in X-bar syntax and their semantic interpretation. In J. Groenendijk et al. (eds.), *Formal Methods in the Study of Language, Part 2*. Amsterdam: Mathematisch Centrum, pp. 567–99.

Vermote, T. (2014). *L'opposition massif-comptable: flexibilité et modélisation. Études de corpus, enquêtes d'acceptabilité et expérience d'amorçage en français et en néerlandais*. PhD dissertation, Ghent University.

Vermote T., P. Lauwers, and L. De Cuypere. (2017). Transcending the lexical vs. grammatical divide regarding the mass/count distinction. Lessons from corpus studies and acceptability surveys in French and Dutch. *Language Sciences*, 62: 37–51.

Versteegh, K. (1997). *The Arabic Language*. Edinburgh: Edinburgh University Press.

Vos, R. (1999). A grammar of partitive constructions. PhD dissertation, Tilburg University.

de Vries, H. (to appear). Collective nouns. In P. Cabredo Hofherr and J. Doetjes (eds.), *Oxford Handbook of Grammatical Number*. Oxford: Oxford University Press.

Watanabe, A. (2010). Vague quantity, numerals, and natural numbers. *Syntax*, 13: 37–77.

Watson, J. (2002). *The Phonology and Morphology of Arabic*. Oxford: Oxford University Press.

Watters, J. (1981). A phonology and morphology of Ejagham, with notes on dialect variation. PhD dissertation, UCLA.

Whelpton, M., D. Trotter, Th. Gudmundsdottir-Beck, C. Anderson, J. Maling, K. Durvasula, and A. Beretta. (2014). Portions and sorts in Icelandic: An ERP study. *Brain and Language*, 136: 44–57.

Whorf, B. (1944). The relation of habitual thought and behavior to language. *Etc: A Review of General Semantics*, 1: 197–215. Also republished in J. Carroll (ed.), *Language, Thought and Reality: Selected Writings of Benjamin Lee Whorf* (MIT Press: Cambridge, MA, 1956), pp. 143–59.
Wierzbicka, A. (1988). Oats and wheat: Mass nouns, iconicity, and human categorization. In idem, *The Semantics of Grammar*. Amsterdam: John Benjamins, pp. 499–560.
Wiese, H. and J. Maling. (2005). *Beers, Kaffi*, and *Schnaps*: Different grammatical options for restaurant talk coercions in three Germanic languages. *Journal of Germanic Linguistics*, 17: 1–38.
Wiggins, D. (1980). *Sameness and Substance*. Oxford: Blackwell.
Wilbur, R. (1987). *American Sign Language: Linguistic and Applied Dimensions*. New York: Little & Brown.
  (2005). A reanalysis of reduplication in American Sign Language. In B. Hurch (ed.), *Studies on Reduplication*. Berlin: de Gruyter, pp. 595–623.
Wilhelm, A. (2008). Bare nouns and number in Dëne Sųłiné. *Natural Language Semantics*, 16: 39–68.
Wilmet, M. (2010). *Grammaire critique du français*, 5th edition. Louvain-la-Neuve: De Boeck Supérieur.
Wiltschko, M. (2005). A part of wood is not a tree. On the absence of the mass/count distinction in Halkomelem. In J. Brown et al. (eds.), Papers for the Fortieth Conference on Salish and Neighbouring Languages. Vancouver: University of British Columbia Working Papers in Linguistics, Volume 16: 264–88. Available at https://lingpapers.sites.olt.ubc.ca/files/2018/02/Wiltschko_2005.pdf.
  (2008). The syntax of non-inflectional plural marking. *Natural Language and Linguistic Theory*, 26: 639–94.
  (2012). Decomposing the mass/count distinction. Evidence from languages that lack it. In Massam 2012, pp. 146–71.
Winter, Y. (1997). Choice functions and the scopal semantics of indefinites. *Linguistics and Philosophy*, 20: 399–467.
Wright, W. (1933). *A Grammar of the Arabic Language, Vol. 1*. Cambridge: Cambridge University Press.
Zabbal, Y. (2002). The semantics of number in the Arabic noun phrase. Master's thesis, University of Calgary.
  (2005). *The Syntax of Numeral Expressions*. Available at LingBuzz: https://ling.auf.net/lingbuzz/005104.
Zamparelli, R. (2020). Countability shifts and abstract nouns. In Moltmann 2020, pp. 191–224.
Zanini, C., S. Benavides-Varela, R. Lorusso, and F. Franzon. (2017). Mass is more: The conceiving of (un) countability and its encoding into language in 5-year-old children. *Psychonomic Bulletin and Review*, 24: 1330–49.
Zanini, C., R. Rugani, D. Giomo, F. Erssotti, and F. Franzon. (2020). Effects of animacy on the processing of morphological number: A cognitive inheritance? *Word Structure*, 13: 22–44.
Zareikar, G. (2019). The distribution and function of number in Azeri. PhD dissertation, University of Ottawa.
Zhang, N. (2013). *Classifier Structures in Mandarin Chinese*. Berlin: de Gruyter.

Zribi-Hertz, A. (2006) Pour une analyse unitaire de DE partitif. In F. Corblin, S. Ferrando, and L. Kupferman (eds.), *Indéfini et prédication* (Paris: PU Paris-Sorbonne) pp. 141–54.

Zucchi, S. and M. White. (2001). Twigs, sequences and the temporal constitution of predicates. *Linguistics and Philosophy*, 24: 223–70.

Zweig, E. (2005). Nouns and adjectives in numeral NPs. In L. Bateman et al. (eds.), *Proceedings of NELS 35, Vol. 2*. Amherst, MA: GLSA, pp. 663–78.

(2009). Number-neutral bare plurals and the multiplicity implicature. *Linguistics and Philosophy*, 32: 353–407.

Language Index

American Sign Language, 13, 213–33
Arabic (Lebanese), 11, 119, 123, 125, 129–30, 134–5, 152, 162–3
Arabic (Modern Standard), 10, 115, 119–26, 129–31, 135–6, 139–40, 142, 146–8, 152, 160–1
Arabic (Palestinian), 11, 151–66, 300
Arabic (Tunisian), 14, 261, 263–9, 272, 275, 278
Armenian (Western). *See* Western Armenian
Azari, 277

Bangla, 22, 39
Berber, 305
Blackfoot, 10, 89
Breton, 264

Cantonese, 10, 23, 99
Cape-Verdean, 12, 193–212
Chinese, 22, 117, 170, 214, 225
Chol, 100
Czech, 300

Danish, 5
Dëne Sųłiné, 10, 60, 76, 86, 88, 99
Dutch, 61, 63, 93, 108–9, 112, 119, 300, 308–10, 312, 316

Ejagham, 106
English (British), 313
English (Canadian), 382

French, 10, 16, 40, 94–5, 112, 248, 337–55, 375, 378
French Sign Language, 213

German, 2, 308–9, 324, 375, 378
German Sign Language, 217
Germanic Languages, 308
Greek (Modern), 9, 23, 33, 42, 44–5, 52, 63, 89, 167, 305

Halkomelem, 10, 89
Hebrew (Modern), 10, 58–60, 62–4, 68, 72, 77, 79
Hindi, 41, 50
Hungarian, 10, 97, 99, 106, 217, 313, 316

Icelandic, 308
Indonesian, 10, 22, 110, 313, 316, 384
Italian, 15, 23–4, 32, 44–5, 325–6, 331

Japanese, 12, 22, 99, 107, 167–92, 214, 217, 219, 222, 225, 359

Korean, 119, 217

Latin, 63
Latin (Church), 348

Malagasy, 219
Maltese, 264
Manam, 305
Mandarin, 10, 12, 23, 38, 46, 48, 53–4, 58, 86, 90–1, 97, 99, 106, 109–11, 116, 168, 170, 173, 190, 210, 212, 217–19, 222–3, 305, 313–14, 316
Mi'gmaq, 100, 255
Mokilese, 109
Mundurucu, 97

Nez Perce, 10, 22, 41, 48–52, 89, 100, 214, 384
Nuosu Yi, 22, 39

Objiwbe, 68, 112, 153, 164

Panará, 10, 59, 71–2, 79
Persian, 63, 262–3, 272, 277–8
Portuguese (Brazilian), 10, 12, 102, 106, 193, 199, 205
Portuguese (European), 197

422   Language Index

Russian, 41, 50, 214, 280

Sakurabiat, 10, 59, 73–4, 78–9
Spanish (Peninsular), 124, 195
Spanish (Rioplatense), 12, 193–212

Taba, 109
Tagalog, 89, 98
Taurepang, 10, 59, 74–5, 79
Turkish, 14, 170, 173–92, 217, 222, 228, 261–4, 273–8, 313

Ugro-Finnish, 27, 30

Wayaro, 10
Welsh, 264
Western Armenian, 14, 59, 67, 168, 222, 261–4, 273–8, 313

Ye'kwana, 10, 59, 74–5, 78–9
Yudja, 10, 13, 22, 25, 32–49, 52, 58–9, 69–72, 79, 82, 98, 100–4, 110–11, 113, 214, 231, 305, 384

Subject Index

Abundance reading of plurals. *See* Plurality: Abundance reading of
Acceptability judgment task, 175–7, 179, 184–5, 193, 198–207
Aggregate nouns. *See* Object mass nouns
Allan, Keith, 16, 322, 338, 357–61, 365–8
American National Corpus, 382
American Sign Language
 as a number neutral language, 225
 mass nouns in, 214–16
 not a classifier language, 222
 not a number marking language, 216–22
Anaphora/Anaphoric reference, 14, 143, 145, 196, 231, 282–3, 286–9, 295–6
Anti-count expression, 10, 93–4, 96–7
Asymmetries in Count-Mass, 10, 14, 81–114
Atomic. *See* Atomicity
Atomic predicate. *See* Atomicity
Atomicity, 6, 21, 26, 28, 30–1, 36–7, 41–3, 45, 47, 51, 54, 85, 104–13, 171, 188, 198, 208–9, 211, 237, 239, 242–3, 245, 248–50, 259, 264, 272, 289, 339–40
 natural vs. semantic, 11, 36, 49, 82, 87, 104, 113, 165
 semantic, 87
Atomization, 38, 278
Atoms. *See* Atomicity

Bare argument, 210
Bare noun. *See* Noun:Bare
Bare plural, 132–4, 261, 265–6, 275–8, 368–9, 371–5, *See also* Plural:bare
Bare singular, 207, 368–9, 371–5
Bochum English Countability Lexicon (BECL), 381–2, 385–6, 388, 392, 394
 numbers of count vs. mass senses in, 395–6
Boundaries
 and count vs. mass, 334
 and visual shape, 333–4
Bouquet noun. *See* Homogeneous object noun

Cardinal modification, 359, 366
Cardinal(-ity), 11, 16, 43, 59, 77, 92, 109, 115, 117, 120, 131–2, 134–40, 143–8, 161, 167, 172–3, 184, 191, 195, 206–7, 209–11, 230, 269, 292, 295, 302, 311, 337, 340, 343–4, 347, 359, 366
Celebrity Nouns, 377, 382
Chierchia's typology of languages, 9, 12–13, 21, 76, 187, 193, 211, 395
Classifier, 2, 5–6, 9–10, 12–14, 21, 23, 26, 90–1, 97, 99–100, 106, 109, 115–18, 124, 156, 159, 165–6, 186–7, 228, 230, 279, 282, 308–9, 368
 general, 90, 109, 173
 hidden, 390
 in ASL, 215, 222
 mensural, 81, 90–1, 99, 106, 109
 number marking, 91
 numeral, 86, 109, 216
 shape-based, 168, 171, 177, 186, 228
 sortal, 81, 90–1, 99, 105–7, 109–10, 173, 190, 225, 228
Coercion (Count-Mass), 4, 7, 9, 11, 13–14, 57, 61, 65, 72, 77–9, 100, 111–12, 114, 166, 168, 195, 209, 211, 239–40, 281, 285–6, 289, 300–3, 305, 312, 338–9, 348, 350, 352–4, 382, *See also* Countability Shift, Grinding, Packaging, Sorting, Portion reading
Collective, 265, 270
comparison of noun denotations
 number vs. volume, 202–5
Concrete portion reading, 281
Continuum, Count-Mass as, 16, 324, 338, 343–8, 351
Core knowledge systems, 82, 91, 333
 magnitude representation in, 98
Corpus of Contemporary American English, 16, 361–2, 390
Corpus studies of Count-Mass, 15–16, 107, 324–5, 328, 338, 341, 361, 382

423

Count quantity expression, 96–8, 101, 103, 108–10, 113
Countability, 104–13, 321–3, 335
 and context, 331–2
 and lexical underspecification, 332
Countability diagnostics, 357–8
Countability Shift, 7, 11, 17, 57, 60, 62, 64–6, 76, 88, 91, 103, 114, 116, 151, 157–9, 163, 166, 189–90, 194, 216, 227, 291, 298, 300, 303, 306–8, 322, 378, 380, 385, 387–8
Counting base, 187–91, 287, 289–93, 299, 302
Counting constructions, 159, 173, 186, 292–3, 300
Cumulative reference, 83–4, 357

Denumerator, 364–5
Denumerators, 359
Diminutives, 299
Discourse referent, 188
Discourse referents, 187–8, 289, 299, 302
Discourse Representation Theory, 187–8, 288–99
Discrete individuals, 169, 172–6, 178–80, 183, 359
 collections of, 167, 172, 175, 180
Discreteness/Disjointness, 55, 57, 64, 68, 72–6
Disjoint domains for count and mass, 239
Distributive reference, 84–5
Divided reference, 84, 113
Dot types, 280, 287

Exclusive plurals, 9, 11, 115, 146–7, 155

Fake mass nouns. *See* Object mass nouns
Fence noun. *See* Homogeneous object noun
Fraction, 202, 253, 280, 284, 301
Furniture nouns. *See* Object mass nouns
Fuzzy denumerator, 365
Fuzzy denumerators, 359

Grammars
 count, 98
 count vs. non-count, 88, 91, 97
Grinding, 7, 14, 17, 31–2, 34, 111, 195, 223, 307–8, 310, 312, 318, 322, 331, 378–80, 385–8, 393, 397

History of Count-Mass description, 3–5
Homogeneous object noun, 2, 6, 87–8, 110–11, 241, 290, 374
Homonymy, 378, 381, 385–6

Inclusive plurals, 145–7, 155
Individuation, 2, 8, 72, 82, 92, 104–5, 107, 114, 168, 170, 172–4, 176, 189, 290, 318, 338–40, 342, 344–5, 351, 378, 391–2, 396
 degrees of, 105, 107, 342
 schema of, 14, 169, 188–9, 287, 290

Jespersen, Otto (1860-1943), 4–5, 83

Kind reference, 312
Kind-oriented language, 48
Kinds
 count vs. mass, 32–4
 denotation in classifier languages, 169

Language
 classifier, 2, 9, 12, 21, 23–4, 36–9, 52, 86, 99, 109–10, 116, 167–71, 173, 183, 186, 191, 193, 214, 217, 230, 313
 count only, 100
 count vs. mass, 98–103
 generalized classifier, 13, 38–40, 51, 170, 214, 224
 generalized number, 9, 13, 21, 23–4, 46–52, 218, 230
 number marking, 9, 12–13, 21, 23–4, 39–46, 52, 76, 104, 112–13, 167, 187, 191, 193, 208–9, 211, 214, 230, 321
 number neutral, 193, 211, 384
 numeral classifier, 86, 90, 99, 223
 singulative, 264, *See also* Singulative
Lexical ambiguity, 218–19, 221, 312, 377–8, 380–2, 385
Lexical Plural, 15, 337–55, *See also* Pluralia tantum
Lexical variation, 91, 377, 381

Masscolex project, 341
Meanings
 count, 98
 count vs. mass, 81, 98–103
Measure function, 38, 102, 108, 207, 280, 288, 296–7, 301
Measure words, 86, 91, 107–10, 272
Mereology, 8, 187, 280, 288–9, 315
Minimal part, 68

Non-atomic count meaning, 109
Non-count quantity expression, 7, 93, 97–8
Noun
 abstract, 1, 9, 64, 112, 173, 348, 361, 373
 abstract vs. Concrete, 3–4, 388, 392
 bare, 7, 12, 14, 16, 39, 169, 210–12, 261–78
 classifier, 296

Subject Index

collective, 105, 338, 342, 345, 353
dual life, 7, 17, 195, 198, 378, 381–2, 386–7, 391, 393
flexible, 7, 12, 14, 60–1, 66, 111–13, 193–212, 306, 308–10, 318
homogeneous count noun, 209, *See also* Homogeneous object noun
indeterminate, 261, 273
relational, 38, 287, 293, 298, 301
sortal, 287–8, 293, 296
stably atomic, 41–2, 51, 171, 183, 187
Number
  general, 218, 222, 230, 262–3, 275, 277–8, 334
  referential and relation to countability, 333
Number marking, 102–3, 105–6, 108–9
Number neutrality, 14, 67, 86, 117, 120, 132, 306, 312–17

Object mass nouns, 2, 6, 12, 21, 23–4, 32, 43–4, 58, 84–5, 87–8, 97–9, 104–7, 111, 167–92, 237, 305, 313, 338, 342, 345, 353, 374–5, 377, 390

Packaging, 7, 14, 31–2, 34, 50, 219, 221, 307–8, 310, 312, 331, 343, 349–50, 375, 378, 384, 387–8, 394, 397
Philosophy/Philosophers, 7, 83
Pluralia Tantum, 361, 367, 371–4, *See also* Lexical plural
Plurality, 9, 26, 45, 56–7, 68, 83, 100, 146, 155, 187, 197–8, 211, 218, 222–3, 261–78
  abundance reading of, 9, 33, 42, 52, 63, 67, 74, 77, 89, 218
  classical (Link) theory of, 58–60
  lexical. *See* Lexical plural
  of mass nouns, 62
  relation to countability, 10, 16, 26, 55, 57, 70, 72–6, 79
Pluralization, 9, 68
  relation to countability, 64
Plurals
  abundance reading of, 63
  bare, 193–212, *See also* Bare Plural
  exclusive. *See* Exclusive plurals
  inclusive. *See* Inclusive plurals
  lexical. *See* Lexical plural
Polysemy, 306, 378, 380–1, 385–7, 393
Portion reading, 57, 64, 72–8, 112, 281–2
Portioning, 164, 291, 322, 349, 384

Pseudopartitive construction, 279–303
  container+contents reading, 280–9, 291, 293–302
  free portion reading, 279, 281
  measure reading (ad hoc), 280–9, 296–302
  measure reading (standard), 281, 297
  types of readings, 281–2
Psychology (cognitive), 4, 7–8, 15, 22, 335
Psychology (experimental), 15, 323–4

Quantifier-split
  in ASL, 13
Quantifier-split in ASL, 225
Quantity comparison task, 99, 101, 104, 168, 172, 176, 183, 205–6, 210
Quantity judgment task, 103
Quantization, 14, 27, 32–4, 48, 169, 188–9, 191, 290–2, 301

Renominalization, 14, 263, 273, 275, 278
Ring paradox, 85
Rope noun. *See* Homogeneous object noun

Single domain for both count and mass, 242
Singulative, 263–6, 270–2, 275, 334
Sorting, 7, 14, 307–10, 312, 318, 375, 378, 384, 387, 397
Spelke objects/substances, 9, 22, 36, 44, 92, 167, 323, 333
Substance-Object distinction, 186, 306, 321–2, 384
Superordinate nouns. *See* Object mass nouns
Sweet, Henry (1845-1912), 3–4

Type I language. *See* Language: number marking
Type II language. *See* Language: Classifier
Type III languages. *See* Language: generalized number
Type mismatch, 301
Type theory with records, 288

Undifferentiated stuff, 167, 169–70, 172–3, 175–84, 379

Vague minimal parts, 85
Variation in Count-Mass, 6, 9–10, 14, 16, 21, 23–5, 28, 34, 52, 54, 58, 68–9, 91, 112, 153, 175, 210, 306, 358, 374, 377, 382
  as function of language-type, 25–6
Variation in number marking, 52

WordNet, 379, 381–2, 390

Milton Keynes UK
Ingram Content Group UK Ltd.
UKHW022259060324
439010UK00017BA/105